D0585783

The Bodley Head

# G. K. CHESTERTON

# The Bodley Head
# G. K. CHESTERTON

*Selected and*
*with an Introduction by*
## P. J. KAVANAGH

THE BODLEY HEAD

LONDON

British Library Cataloguing
in Publication Data
Chesterton, G. K.
The Bodley Head G. K. Chesterton.
I. Title   II. Kavanagh, P. J.
828'.91209   PR4453.C4
ISBN 0-370-30579-5

© Miss D. E. Collins 1985
This selection and Introduction
©The Bodley Head 1985
Printed in Finland for
The Bodley Head Ltd
9 Bow Street, London WC2E 7AL
by Werner Söderström Oy
Set in 10pt Ehrhardt
by J & L Composition Ltd
Filey, N. Yorkshire
*First published 1985*

# Contents

# CONTENTS

# CONTENTS

# Sources and Acknowledgements

Grateful thanks to Miss D. E. Collins, and to her agents, Messrs. A. P. Watt, for permission to reproduce the material in this anthology. We also wish to acknowledge the original publishers in each case, as mentioned in the following list of sources:

All Things Considered, Methuen, 1908
  (Woman. Oxford From Without.)

The Apostle and the Wild Ducks, Elek, 1975
  (The Need of Personalities in Politics. The Voice of Shelley. A Theory of Tyrants. What is Right with the World.)

Charles Dickens, Methuen, 1906
  (Chapters 6 and 7.)

Collected Poems, Methuen, 1915, 1932

The Common Man, Sheed and Ward, 1950
  (A Midsummer Night's Dream. Two Stubborn Pieces of Iron. The Erastian on the Establishment.)

The Everlasting Man, Hodder & Stoughton, 1925
  (Chapter 2, Part 2.)

A Handful of Authors, Sheed and Ward, 1953
  (Oscar Wilde. Romantic Love.)

Heretics, The Bodley Head, 1905
  (From Chapters 3, 6, 13, 14 and 16.)

The Innocence of Father Brown, Cassell, 1910
  (The Queer Feet.)

Lunacy and Letters, Sheed and Ward, 1958
  (The Perpetuation of Punishment. Tommy and the Traditions.)

The Man Who Was Thursday, Dent, 1908

A Miscellany of Men, Methuen, 1912
(The Mad Official.)

Orthodoxy, The Bodley Head, 1908
(Chapters 4, 5, 6, 8 and 9.)

Robert Browning, Macmillan, 1903
(Chapters 3, 6 and 8.)

St Thomas Aquinas, Hodder and Stoughton, 1933
(Chapters 2, 4, 7 and 8.)

A Short History of England, Chatto & Windus, 1917
(New Introduction, Chapters 2, 6, 7, 8, 11 and 12.)

Tremendous Trifles, Methuen, 1909
(Some Policemen and a Moral.)

Twelve Types, Hatchards, 1902
(Thomas Carlyle.)

The Wild Knight and Other Poems, Dent, 1900
(Three poems.)

William Cobbett, Hodder and Stoughton, 1925
(Chapter 2.)

In the United States these works were nearly all originally published by Dodd Mead. *St Thomas Aquinas* was published by Sheed and Ward, as were the more recent collections of writings—*The Common Man*, *A Handful of Authors* and *Lunacy and Letters*. *The Apostle and the Wild Ducks* was published by Elek.

# Introduction

## by P.J. Kavanagh

G. K. Chesterton began as a Party Liberal. In fact he began as an art student, at the Slade, but as soon as he started to write as a journalist it was in Liberal newspapers and in what he considered to be the Liberal interest. He early became disillusioned with the Party, and then with the Party system, because he did not believe it represented people's real needs. To him it was more like a share-out of jobs and privileges between several, often related, families on both sides of the House, with newcomers like Lloyd George heartily joining in.

For a man of his views, who wanted radical reform, the obvious course was to become a Socialist, like Bernard Shaw (who revered Chesterton) or, in some degree, like H. G. Wells. But Chesterton could not do this because, detesting the abuse of privilege, he also feared too great an increase in the power of the State and, even more important, he was haunted from the beginning by a sense of a broken historical continuity, which he wanted to help mend. This remained one of his central themes. Programmes of Socialist reform concerned themselves with social needs: Chesterton wanted something that satisfied the whole of a man, his spiritual needs as well as his material ones, and came to believe this balance had once been achieved in the past, and then was destroyed by the greed of a rising middle class. This led him eventually to be considered the advocate of a return to a senti-mentalised 'Merrie England', which in a sense he was, but Chesterton was more intelligent than that and can be allowed to explain himself. (A chapter of *A Short History of England* is called 'The Meaning of Merry England'. He always delighted in meeting his critics head-on.)

This standing apart from his time, both from received opinion and from progressive ideas, had the advantage of keeping him clear of movements that were merely fashionable—which he called 'fads'—but it also kept him out of the general intellectual drift of his generation, which is something more powerful and significant than fashion, though of course it can be wrong. He became the odd man out among his peers (Belloc hardly counts in this respect because he was a professional odd man out, which Chesterton was not). This was dangerous for Chesterton, and still is, because he wanted his ideas listened to by the unconverted. There are two things to note about this isolation: one is that it never made him sound strident or angry, the other is that he was so popular and widely read it is extraordinary, looking back, to see how intellectually alone he was.

You would never guess it from his tone, which is confident and genially magisterial. He seems always to be addressing a large and friendly audience, past the heads of the 'moderns', the 'professors', the 'scientists' (or, worst of all, the 'modern scientific professors') and telling a receptive gathering what it half-knew already and would now, after his explanation, agree to be obviously true. Possibly these are 'the people of England, that never have spoken yet' and he is speaking for them, as well as to them. Very possibly: 'modernist' Ezra Pound was heard to sigh, despairingly, 'Chesterton *is* the mob!'

He is as much a political writer as George Orwell. Politics, in the narrow, as well as the widest, sense, informs and inspires his writing, which is why he remained all his life a journalist, to the despair of those who recognised the enormous scale of his gifts. But that is what Chesterton wanted to be, a 'jolly journalist' (as he unfortunately described himself, the phrase has affected his reputation) because he thought his message important and from Fleet Street it could reach the people who needed it most, and who perhaps had the best chance of understanding it.

He would have appreciated Pound's remark about the mob because for him the mob—unintellectual, fundamentally decent, duped—was not a mindless thing, if it was given a chance. He uses the word in his peroration to a chapter ('The Return of the Barbarian') in *A Short History of England*, published in 1917; he is referring to the Great War: 'The English poor, broken in every revolt, bullied by every fashion, long despoiled of property, entered history with a noise of trumpets, and turned themselves in two years into one of the iron armies of the world. And when the critic of politics and literature, feeling that this war is after all heroic, looks around him to find the hero, he can point to nothing but a mob.'

It is possible that even now Chesterton's use of the word 'mob' could be misunderstood. He was frequently and astonishingly misunderstood by his opponents in his own day. He meant of course that the 'mob', the ordinary people, was the best thing about the nation. This was a belief he could not always find among Socialists.

He was involved as a writer in almost every day-to-day controversy of his time and, among his contemporaries, though sometimes they privately cheered him on, was usually in a minority of one. There is insufficient space in a collection such as this to give many examples, though the subjects remain topical: birth control, genetic engineering, the position of women, the secularisation of Christianity, and so on. But it is odd that so dedicated a battler should be remembered by many as the author of the 'Father Brown' stories and of charming trifles with titles like 'A Piece of Chalk' or 'What I Found in my Pockets'. There are reasons for this—you don't poke intelligent fun at your generation and then expect it to praise your judgement—and his own refusal to be pompous is one of them; but, as he is one of the great intellects England has produced, it is a pity.

His biographer, Maisie Ward, quotes from one of the many lengthy political exchanges in which Chesterton exulted, and it is worth reproducing here because, apart from the continual pleasure to be derived from Chesterton's *tone*, it gives proof of the extraordinary difficulty some minds experienced, despite his patient clarity, in grasping what he was driving at.

He had written to the editor of the Liberal *Nation* pointing out, among other things, the illiberality of the new licensing laws. The editor, publishing the letter, had been unwise enough to add a brief comment of his own. Here is Chesterton's reply:

'Jan 26 1911,

Sir,

In a note to my last week's letter you remark, "We must be stupid; but we have no idea what Mr Chesterton means." As an old friend I can assure you that you are by no means stupid; some other explanation of this unnatural darkness must be found; and I find it in the effect of that official party phraseology which I attack, and which I am by no means alone in attacking. If I had talked about "true Imperialism", or "our loyalty to our gallant leader", you might have thought you knew what I meant: because I meant nothing. But I do mean something; and I do want you to understand what I mean. I will, therefore, state it with total dullness, in separate paragraphs; and I will number them.

(1) I say a democracy means a State where the citizens first desire something and then get it. That is surely simple.

(2) I say that where this is deflected by the disadvantage of representation, it means that the citizens desire a thing and tell the representatives to get it. I trust I make myself clear.

(3) The representatives, in order to get it at all, must have some control over detail; but the design must come from the popular desire. Have we got that down?

(4) You, I understand, hold that English M.P.s today do thus obey the public in design, varying only in detail. That is a quite clear contention.

(5) I say they don't. Tell me if I am being too abstruse.

(6) I say our representatives accept designs and desires almost

entirely from the Cabinet class above them; and practically not at all from the constituents below them. I say the people does not wield a Parliament which wields a Cabinet. I say the Cabinet bullies a timid Parliament which bullies a bewildered people. Is that plain?

(7) If you ask why the people endure and play this game, I say they play it as they would play the official games of any despotism or aristocracy. The average Englishman puts his cross on a ballot-paper as he takes off his hat to the King—and would take it off if there were no ballot papers. There is no democracy in the business. Is that definite?

(8) If you ask why we have thus lost democracy, I say from two causes; (a) The omnipotence of an unelected body, the Cabinet; (b) the Party system, which turns all politics into a game like the Boat Race. Is that all right?

(9) If you want examples I could give you scores. I say the people did not cry out that all children whose parents lunch on cheese and beer in an inn should be left out in the rain . . .' etc.

It is hard to see that much of what Chesterton complained of in our method of government has changed. This is perhaps unsurprising if the opacity of the editor is anything to go by. He still could not see what was worrying Chesterton. He now complained that Chesterton's criticisms only concerned 'small' things. Considering this was a large part of his meaning Chesterton is remarkably patient in his reply: 'What,' he asks with deceptive mildness, 'can be more fundamental than food and drink and children?'

On the particular point, anyone who has travelled about Britain with small children has had cause to curse the Children's Act of 1910. Only now is some small compromise being attempted, with gloomy 'Children's Rooms' in some public houses and hotels. The larger point, that it is precisely the 'small' and everyday that matters and to this our rulers pay too little attention, is Chesterton's constant theme. Indeed, again and again, with a thousand illustrations, he points out that we non-rulers cannot see the infinite significance of small things either, that we can barely see at all. This could be described, fundamentally, as the religious point of view; it is certainly that of a poet. Chesterton's poems are usually thoughts expressed in verse, or emotion expressed thoughtfully. He is as much a poet in his prose as in his verse, and this can be a useful way of approaching his work. It is certainly as a poet that he dislikes the way we prefer the general to the particular, because it is easier. He puts the point in verse (albeit light verse, but effectively) in a book—*New Poems*, 1932—published twenty years after the letter just quoted:

## THE WORLD STATE

'Oh, how I love Humanity,
    With love so pure and pringlish,
And how I hate the horrid French,
    Who never will be English!

The International Idea,
    The largest and the clearest,
Is welding all the nations now,
    Except the one that's nearest.

This compromise has long been known,
    This scheme of partial pardons,
In ethical societies
    And small surburban gardens—

The villas and the chapels where
    I learned with little labour
The way to love my fellow-man
    And hate my next-door neighbour.'

It is a simple criticism that Chesterton never tires of making but, if we look around fifty years later, there is little sign that it is too simple to be worth repeating.

Thus, among other things, it was the generalised nature of Socialist plans for amelioration that Chesterton did not like, though he was eager for change and, if necessary, revolution; although it is never quite clear how he envisaged such a thing. It seldom is, even in more practically-minded reformers. His political thinking took the form, roughly, of somehow giving back to the people what had been taken from them and this later came to be called 'Distributism', with *G.K.'s Weekly* as its mouthpiece. The idea attracted a following and, having established the idea, the way Chesterton interpreted his political rôle—apart from being badly out of pocket and dangerously overburdened with work because of it—is somewhere between the lines of this gentle, rather sad, rebuke to the more zealous of his followers, in 1929. There had been quarrelling among them:

'... I could only manage to keep this paper in existence at all, by earning money in the open market; and more especially in that busy and happy market where corpses are sold in batches: I mean the mart of Murder and Mystery, the booth of the Detective Story. Many a squire has died in a dank garden arbour, transfixed by a mysterious dagger, many a millionaire has perished silently though surrounded by a ring of private secretaries, in order that Mr Belloc may have a paper ... Many an imperial jewel has vanished from its golden setting, many a detective crawled about on the carpet for clues, before some of those little printers' bills could be settled which enabled the most distinguished and intelligent of Distributists to denounce each other as Capitalists and Communists, in the columns of the "Cockpit" and elsewhere. This being my humble and even highly irrelevant contribution to the common team-work, it is obvious it could not be done at the same time as a close following of the various shades of thought in the Distributist debates. And, this ignorance of mine, though naturally very irritating to people better informed, has at least the advantage of giving some genuineness to my impartiality. I have never belonged distinctively to any of the different Distributist groups. I have never had time.' (*Gilbert Keith Chesterton*, Maisie Ward)

Nevertheless, to have an alternative programme to hand which you consider practical is a great assistance towards the clarification of ideas and the identification of what is wrong. Even more important, his overwork and lack of political quietism—so deplored by friends who wanted him to give up journalism, in order to write his 'great' book—his journalistic and editorial immersion in affairs and his attempts at the proffering of a solution, led him to a detestation of the group-soul and a veneration of the individual one; led him, in other words, to the religious, more specifically, Christian and, latterly, Roman Catholic position. This of course separated him even further from his time; something he bore with his accustomed cheerfulness.

It is important to recognise that it was his practical political concerns that led him to Roman Catholicism; it was not his increasingly dogmatic (in the true sense) Christianity that originally inspired his politics. In a way he *discovered* Christianity, found that for him it contained the solutions he sought, and he makes sure we can track him in this slow process from *Orthodoxy* in 1908, when he was hardly a Christian at all, but an enquirer, to *The Everlasting Man* in 1925, by which time he had become a Christian apologist. He was not received into the Roman Catholic Church until 1922, when he was nearly fifty.

He is always clear about the stages in his thought and then clear about his position; too clear for some. But the clarity is undeniable, though many still refused to believe that he meant what he said. In 1922 in *What I Saw in America* he puts it in a sentence: 'There is no basis for democracy except in a dogma about the divine origin of man.'

It is a challenge thrown down. It contains two words guaranteed to raise nearly every British hackle, 'divine' and 'dogma'. If the first doesn't do it the second certainly will. But Chesterton believed that dogma, willingly assented to, was the basis of intellectual and political liberty, because it was a shared premise. Perhaps he knew too little of what it was like to live in a Church-dominated country. Shaw tried to warn him, citing the example of Ireland. But that is perhaps not so relevant after all: he was writing in England. He would have had different targets in Ireland, or Spain—or for that matter in the Soviet Union. For him dogma was the frame within which man could move freely, with tolerance. Also, of course, he came to believe in the divine.

But he does not just leave it there, for the reader to agree or disagree. Even when apparently talking about something else, Chesterton is concerned to explain why he believes as he does, step by step, inviting the reader to argue with him. Any reader would have to be more in love with the secularised corporate state than he is likely to be, for him to turn away in disgust at the invitation, even if the writing itself were not so entertaining. However, it is possible that the entertainment Chesterton so prodigally provides can prevent an unwary reader (like the editor of the *Nation*) from hearing what he says. Chesterton disliked the way the world was going and tried to divert that progress: that he failed has caused him to be neglected, sometimes derided, but that does not prove him wrong.

He is, for example, frequently accused of being wilfully paradoxical, of standing ideas on their heads for fun. In fact he rarely does so. His gift is for brilliant analogies, often absurd ones. Belloc called it 'his genius for illustration by parallel ... I can speak here with experience, for in these conversations with him or listening to his conversation with others I was always astonished at an ability in illustration which I not only have never seen equalled but cannot remember to have seen attempted. He never sought such things; they poured from him as easily as though they were not the hard forged products of intense vision, but spontaneous remarks.' (Maisie Ward, *op.cit.*) Belloc also says it is the way Chesterton '*taught*' (he italicises the word) and Chesterton certainly was a teacher, wanting to help us see, with our eyes as well as, figuratively, with our minds. For so speculative a man he is surprisingly visual. One remembers that he began as an art student, and drew all his life (frequently demons: behind his geniality, or rather at the root of it and of all his work, is a lively sense of the power of evil). But, although his mind was illustrative, he was myopic, and this may have affected his method; he preferred the broad sweep, both pictorially and intellectually, to the focused detail. Not that this led to any vagueness or evasiveness in argument, or blurring of outline; on the contrary, it added vigour to the forward march of his prose, as though it refused to be distracted by brief roadside glimpses. Nevertheless, though he seldom numbers the petals on a rose, his description of landscape (and townscape) and climatic *effects* in the Father Brown stories, for example, are often the best things in them; and they came from a man who was not only short-sighted but who could seldom bring himself even to go for a walk.

His work is filled with pictures, usually absurd ones; here are a couple (from *A Short History of England*): 'It is almost necessary to say nowadays that a saint means a very good man. The notion of eminence merely moral, consistent with complete stupidity or unsuccess, is a revolutionary image grown unfamiliar by its very familiarity, and needing, as do so many things of this older society, some almost preposterous modern parallel to give its original freshness and point. If we entered a foreign town and found a pillar like the Nelson Column, we should be surprised to learn that the hero on top of it had been famous for his politeness and hilarity during a chronic toothache. If a procession came down the street with a brass band and a hero on a white horse, we should think it odd to be told that he had been very patient with a half-witted maiden aunt. Yet some such pantomime impossibility is the only measure of the Christian idea of a popular and recognised saint. It must especially be realised that while this kind of glory was the highest, it was also in a sense the lowest. The materials of it were almost the same as those of labour and domesticity: it did not need the sword or sceptre, but rather the staff or spade. It was the ambition of poverty.'

It is the 'preposterous' nature of these analogies that reinforce our surprise at being reminded of something we already knew: that great saints were sometimes spectacularly unsuccessful men, and yet were revered. It is in fact a paradox. But the analogies are also right in another way; it is of course the 'small' things which all of us know, which are without attendant drama—toothache, elderly relatives—that test our heroism. These are the same small things the importance of which was beyond the comprehension of the unfortunate editor of the *Nation*. Chesterton's work is all of a piece throughout. And the 'preposterous' can lead without strain to a noble and subtle sentence: 'It was the ambition of poverty.' This is only an apparent, not a genuine, paradox. The ambition to be poor we can understand, but now we understand afresh the spiritual poverty of our usual definition of ambition.

Chesterton's paradoxes are therefore not a form of play, they are literary devices, analogues to the paradoxical nature of history and truth. Even the Gospels are paradoxical—'the meek shall inherit the earth,' and so on. The meek, in the form of monks (with the ambition of poverty) did indeed inherit the earth because by working it and putting it in good order their monasteries became rich. (One of the best chapters of *Orthodoxy* is called 'The Paradoxes of Christianity.')

Chesterton's use of analogy and visual illustration is demonstrated in the opening pages of the early novel *The Napoleon of Notting Hill* (1904), a book so important to Chesterton (not for its quality—he never thought of his work in that way—but for what hc hoped it contained) that he said if he had not written it he could not have gone on writing. Auberon Quin, a Government official, is walking behind two colleagues, dressed in the style of their class in 1904, which is to say in frock-coats.

'So the short Government official looked at the coat-tails of the tall Government officials, and through street after street, and round corner after corner, saw only coat-tails, coat-tails, and again coat-tails—when, he did not in the least know why, something happened to his eyes.

'Two black dragons were walking backwards in front of him. Two black dragons were looking at him with evil eyes. The dragons were walking backwards, it is true, but they kept their eyes fixed on him none the less. The eyes which he saw were, in truth, only the two buttons at the back of a frock-coat; perhaps some traditional memory of their meaningless character gave this half-witted prominence to their gaze. The slit between the tails was the noseline of the monster: whenever the tails flapped in the winter wind the dragons licked their lips. It was only a momentary fancy, but the small clerk found it embedded in his soul ever afterwards.'

It is a commonplace experience sometimes to see in this way but here it has a purpose: Quin is not seeing dragons; he is seeing frock-coats, as though for the first time, and seeing their absurdity. He sees that they represent all that is pompous and solemn and self-satisfied in the official, middle-class world—and they have evil eyes.

Born in 1874, Chesterton was for roughly half his life a Victorian, a period during which the gulf between the official and middle classes and the working class was probably wider than it has ever been, before or since. He was born into the comfortable middle-class himself (the estate agents, Chesterton, still exist in Kensington), fortunate in his settled and interesting (and agnostic) parents, but for him the unhealthiness of the class division was self-evident. He remarked that people laughed at medieval barons who put their vassals below the salt who themselves put their servants below the stairs. He therefore detested the uniform—the frock-coats—that was used to emphasise this separation and, although never self-consciously a bohemian, would not, or could not, wear it. After he was married in 1901, his wife, despairing of keeping him tidy, invented with a stroke of genius the Chesterton style: a cloak, which he did not have to try to keep buttoned, a slouch hat, which he did not have to keep brushed. But Chesterton is not only satirising, in some sense illustrating, the cruel pretension of his class, he is saying in the novel that the dragon exists and St George can slay it, that pageantry and chivalry and local loyalty can reveal below the unpromising appearance of Notting Hill a place that is, or could be, magical, fantastical, alive with romance and with romantics. He is talking of the wonder-filled landscape of his childhood, he was born near Notting Hill, and is saying, '*Look*! Can't you see?'

It is not surprising, with this perception of the drama of the ordinary and gift for truth-bearing exaggeration, that he should feel kinship with Robert Browning and Charles Dickens. About each of them he wrote a book at the outset of his career, and on his chosen subjects he became, at once, an outstanding literary critic before there was such a thing as 'literary studies' and before Dickens, certainly, was fashionable.

In 1903, *Robert Browning* marked his commencement as a writer of books, as opposed to short pieces and poems. He was twenty-nine, and the book bursts with pent-up energy and ideas. He said of it later that it was really filled with themes of his own, 'a book in which the name of Browning was introduced from time to time, I might almost say with considerable art ... ' There ought to have been a law to prevent Chesterton saying things like that about his work because there were too many prepared to take him at his word. It is a brilliant book, illuminating about Chesterton (as it ought to be) and illuminating about Browning because Chesterton understood him.

But Chesterton always refused to speak seriously of himself and therefore there are those, bewilderingly, who cannot regard the work as serious. Because his touch is light they think his head is, whereas it would not be difficult to make a case that there is no more serious writer. Hardly a line of the enormous number he piled together is not concerned with the sort of questions liable to empty a room, such as 'the meaning of life', how we can best understand it, and live it. His touch was light because he was more interested in winning an audience than in status. He continued to work through Fleet Street because, doubtless, he enjoyed the fray and the companionship, but also because he cared more for his message than he cared for himself. Few men of genius have been so little interested in posthumous fame.

He probably did not care for himself enough. The size of his output was certainly bad for his health. Apart from commissioned books he wrote a long column in the *Illustrated London News* every week for thirty years (refusing to ask for an increased fee when he could have asked for anything he liked, because they had helped him with regular work when he needed it most). There was also, for years, the column in the *Daily News*, a multitude of regular or semi-regular contributions elsewhere, lectures all over the country, 'Father Brown' stories and novels and poems and long public controversies like the one quoted from the *Nation*; there were also public debates with people like Shaw. It was too much. In 1909 his wife managed to move them from London to Beaconsfield (which, contrary to the murmurs of disgruntled friends, who missed him, Chesterton makes clear he enjoyed) but the output continued as great. Between 1909 and 1915, apart from a quantity of journalism that would break any normal man, twenty-one books were published. Some of these were collections of newspaper pieces and stories, but the list includes three novels (*The Ball and the Cross, Manalive, The Flying Inn*), studies of Bernard Shaw and William Blake, *The Victorian Age in Literature*, a full-length epic poem *The Ballad of the White Horse* and a play,

*Magic*. His absence of mind became legendary, but it was inevitable; he must have been composing sentences in his head, when he was not actually writing them, most of his waking hours. The jolly, bibulous journalist that Chesterton was happy to be considered had become almost pure mind.

But of course he kept that a secret, until in 1915 he collapsed and lay in a coma, or near-coma, for several months, his life despaired of.

After his recovery (when he immediately asked for newspapers; back numbers so that he could trace in detail the course of the War), Shaw wrote to tell him, 'You have carried out a theory of mine that every man of genius has a critical illness at 40, Nature's object being to make him go to bed for several months. Sometimes Nature overdoes it: Schiller and Mozart died.'

There is a lessening of élan after the recovery. There were many reasons for this: the war, of course; the misery of the Marconi Affair (in which his brother Cecil more or less took on the Government, accusing people connected with it of corruption). The malign atmosphere of this episode, in which he supported his brother, deeply distressed Chesterton; it seems he lost the last of his trust in public men. Then in 1918 Cecil died and, out of love for him, Chesterton continued his brother's political crusades; these involved him in burdensome editorships, culminating in *G.K.'s Weekly*, which were not only a drain on his pocket but also on his health.

But apart from these griefs and burdens that weighed down the wonderful springiness of his early style, there was also the natural disappointment, bound to come as the years pass, of a champion who sees that his causes will not triumph in his day, that for all his efforts the world goes on as before, or goes on worse. But Chesterton never became exasperated, as most men do. Although it is true that after the death of his brother he was guilty for the first and last time of violent language in public, it was to do with one of his dead brother's bitter battles, the Marconi affair.

Yet, if one suspects a final diminution of energy, there comes *St Thomas Aquinas* (1933), a brilliant book on so tricky a subject that the Thomist philosopher Etienne Gilson threw up his hands in admiration and despair: 'The few readers who have spent twenty or thirty years studying St Thomas Aquinas and who, perhaps, have themselves published two or three volumes on the subject, cannot fail to perceive that the so-called "wit" of Chesterton has put their scholarship to shame.' Before that, in 1925, there had been *The Everlasting Man*, a massively ambitious work in which Chesterton attempts to pull together and in some sense systematise his whole view of the world. Its aim is to adjust an anti-Christendom imbalance in H. G. Wells's enormously successful *Outline of History* (which Chesterton admired) and so, despite its length, it can be considered yet another salvo in the continuous battle Chesterton conducted, more or less single-handed, with his time. Some have considered it his most important book. And there is the posthumously published *Autobiography* (1936) which is among his best books.

When he was received into the Church, thirteen years before he died, it was natural that the Church should use, and over-use, so notable a convert. His explicitly Roman Catholic work often suffers both from a too great sense of responsibility towards his subject, which is a form of humility, and a new sense of exclusiveness; for the first time he can sound too aggressively flippant to his opponents. The faltering in tone is only occasional but in a man whose tone is normally so exceptionally agreeable, it is audible. Also, his explicit Christianity, his view of 'Christendom' as a continuing imaginative and spiritual entity, could lead him not so much into mistakes as into mistaken emphases. He undervalued Oriental mysticisms, for example. He was much less than fair to the influence of Islam and, notoriously, was led to make some (but not many) regrettable remarks about the Jews.

The violent language mentioned earlier, after the death of his brother, was addressed to Jewish politicians and financiers such as Godfrey Isaacs, whom his brother had attacked. In an Open Letter to Sir Rufus Isaacs (by this time Lord Reading) he talks of the Isaacs 'tribe' and says: 'You are far more unhappy than I; for your brother is still alive.' Grief had unbalanced him, but he detested Imperialism and Capitalism anyway, and suspected some highly-placed Jews (it is important to remember that his criticisms were aimed at men of great power) of manipulating both of these to their own, supra-national ends. He did not believe they could be loyal to his concept of Christendom because they did not belong to that tradition. He was not a racialist, he disbelieved in the existence of continuing racial characteristics in the displaced and frequently says so, scornful of the 'Teutonism' that was becoming fashionable in pre-War England. He did not object to these men on grounds of race but because of what he suspected about their personal behaviour, which he thought derived from their religion, whether they were religious or not. He was a Zionist because he believed a man could only be loyal to his own tradition. That Jews could become loyal Englishmen he appears not to have believed. If he did not do so he was wrong, but so would we be wrong, with our special and terrible hindsight, if we condemn him too much. Such views were a distasteful component of the atmosphere of his time and are perhaps the only example of Chesterton, consciously or unconsciously, breathing that atmosphere without caution. There are those who blame this on loyalty to his brother, and on the influence of his friend Belloc. But Chesterton can bear the responsibility himself. He early detected the threat of Hitler, and warned against him when hardly anyone else had noticed. He continued to do so when the Government began to parley with the Nazis. To say that some of Chesterton's best friends were Jews will only raise a sad smile, but it was true; however, financiers, and above all non-Christian financiers, clearly worried him to distraction.

But what is most remarkable about Chesterton, considering what a battler he was, is not his enmity but his lack of it. It is astonishing how few enemies he made, if he made any. It was always to be seen that it was the idea he hated, not the man. The man he enjoyed; and, if he could, liked. The more one reads Chesterton, and thinks about him, the more it becomes clear, quite apart from his views, how extraordinarily 'Christian' he was, in the everyday use of that word. He approaches most people's idea of a good man. His brother made many enemies, so did Belloc, who gloried in doing so: 'There is something sundering about Hilary's quarrels,' Chesterton was heard to murmur, sadly. His were not like that. Indeed, Belloc regarded this as a weakness in him, and was wrong, because Chesterton's lack of interest in drawing an individual's blood on particular issues keeps the issues clearer, makes them remain of interest to us.

Those he argued with remained his friends. H. G. Wells, hearing after his death of some secret kindness Chesterton had done him, said he was not surprised: 'I have never known a man so steadily true to form as GKC.' People who worked for him loved him, and stayed. His final secretary, Dorothy Collins, became almost an adopted daughter (the Chestertons, who loved children, were able to have none of their own) and she has devoted the rest of her life to making well-chosen collections of his scattered pieces, which have been of great use to this selection.

There remains the popular notion that Chesterton was never quite as good as he could have been, 'a genius who wrote no masterpiece'. It is impossible to argue with such a view, whether true or not. If it is indeed a 'popular notion', Chesterton would say its popularity guaranteed that it contained a truth, as it might, for all he cared. 'I have no feeling for immortality,' he said, as a young man. 'I don't care for anything except to be in the present stress of life as it is. I would rather live now and die, from an artistic point of view, than keep aloof and write things that will remain in the world hundreds of years after my death. What I say is subject to some modification. It so happens that I couldn't be immortal: but if I could, I shouldn't want to be. What I value in my own work is what I may succed in striking out of others.'

It is true he never wrote an unflawed novel, if such a thing exists. *The Man Who Was Thursday* comes nearest to being a conventional story, a sequence of events leading to a predetermined end. But the sustained extravagance of *The Napoleon of Notting Hill*, the exuberance (tinged with sadness) of *The Flying Inn*, the clowning of *Manalive*, the ingenuity of *The Ball and the Cross* all seem parts of a larger whole. They are not masterpieces but pieces of a master.

Likewise, it is true that great books like *Orthodoxy*, *A Short History of England*, *St Thomas Aquinas*, can give the impression of being collections of essays attached to a theme; closely attached, but not an obviously developing sequence. Yet it has been found, when trying to separate one chapter from another for this selection, that it is difficult to do so without loss; there is an inner connection.

This sense of the indivisibility of Chesterton grows. Thus, though it might be argued that the emphasis here is on Chesterton the essayist and controversialist, rather than the inventor of fictions, it can also be suggested that his novels were as much a part of the continuing discussion he conducted with the world as his more explicitly argued pieces. It is remembered that he said if he had not written *The Napoleon of Notting Hill* he could not have gone on writing. He had something to say in it, a point to make; he dressed this up in a fabulous narrative but the narrative was not the reason for the writing. In fact it is the narrative of his novels which usually lets them down. The end of that novel, which is a battle with real swords in which nobody gets really hurt, is the only silly thing in it, and dates it badly. Such an account of a battle could not have been written after 1918.

But always, in poems and novels and everywhere else, it is Chesterton the teacher, the helper, at work. His attitude to writing was the same as Dr Johnson's, and as serious: he wrote in order to be useful, and did so from the beginning. In this he never changed.

This selection is arranged more or less chronologically, for convenience, but almost any other arrangement could have been adopted. For Chesterton did not 'develop', in the ordinary sense. He sprang into the arena with enough in his head to last a lifetime, and all he saw confirmed his early insight. In fact he was always saying the same thing, or things. Most writers do this, but in Chesterton the surprise is in the continually fresh way he manages to say them, and this has to do with his sense of the inexhaustible importance of what he has to say.

As a young man he exploded into the literary life like a display of fireworks, and if there is a 'development' (though he could often erupt again) it is in the direction of self-limitation, as though tired of pyrotechnics, aware they have dazzled too much and too many, aware now that everything must be spelled out again, without impatience but more slowly, more plainly, as though to the lazy ones at the back of the class—for they too must be helped to pass their Final Examination. He dims his lamp to stop it shining in their eyes. Evelyn Waugh is said to have wished he could re-write *The Everlasting Man*, because its content was so good, in order to take out the exasperating Chesterton mannerisms. But it is clear in that comparatively stately book that Chesterton was trying to do so himself. This is perhaps why many like it best of all, it is so obviously serious. But, though now attempting to bring everything together, he is saying in it few things he has not said elsewhere quicker and more brilliantly.

As examples of this flattening and slowing-up of the style (which must have been conscious because, as has been said, he continued to be able to speed up and dazzle when he wanted to) it might be instructive to put two passages, chosen more or less at random, side by side; one from an early book, *Orthodoxy* (1908), and one from *The Everlasting Man* (1925).

'Imagination does not breed insanity. Exactly what does breed insanity is reason. Poets do not go mad; but chess-players do. Mathematicians go mad, and cashiers; but creative artists very seldom. I am not, as will be seen, in any sense attacking logic: I only say that this danger does lie in logic, not in imagination. Artistic paternity is as wholesome as physical paternity. Moreover it is worthy of remark that when a poet really was morbid it was commonly because he had some weak spot of rationality on his brain. Poe, for instance, really was morbid: not because he was poetical, but because he was specially analytical. Even chess was too poetical for him; he disliked chess because it was full of knights and castles, like a poem. He avowedly preferred the black discs of draughts, because they were more like the black dots on a diagram. Perhaps the strongest case of all is this: that only one great English poet went mad, Cowper. And he was definitely driven mad by logic, by the ugly and alien logic of predestination. Poetry was not the disease, but the medicine; poetry partly kept him in health. He could sometimes forget the red and thirsty hell to which his hideous necessitarianism dragged him, among the wide waters and the white flat lilies of the Ouse. He was damned by John Calvin; he was almost saved by John Gilpin.'

That is the earlier passage. Here is the later one:

'In considering the elements of pagan humanity, we must begin by an attempt to describe the indescribable. Many get over the difficulty of describing it by the expedient of denying it, or at least ignoring it; but the whole point of it is that it was something that was never quite eliminated even when it was ignored. They are obsessed by their evolutionary monomania that every great thing grows from a seed, or something smaller than itself. They seem to forget that every seed comes from a tree, or from something larger than itself. Now there is very good ground for guessing that religion did not originally come from some detail that was forgotten, because it was too small to be traced. Much more probably it was an idea that was abandoned because it was too large to be managed.'

Both passages are recognisably by the same writer. The second is more obviously reflective, whereas the first grabs hold of the reader as he hurries past. The later passage is grave with responsibility, the subject is of consequence and the reader is presumed ready to listen. In the earlier, Chesterton is aware he has to startle in order to be heard at all. As a result the antitheses come fast on each other, and there is clear delight in the play of his own mind, which leaps from juxtaposition to juxtaposition, with dabs of colour on the way ('the white flat lilies of the Ouse'), until arriving, with apparent delight, at the brilliant and wholly successful pairing of John Calvin and John Gilpin, an insight of such appositeness it would keep most men aglow with self-satisfaction for a lifetime. The slow, pondering, abstract movement of the later passage makes impossible such sudden leaps of the imagination. Chesterton, as has been said, holds himself in check.

Of course this is unfair, the passages are from different books with somewhat different intentions. But enough will have been said to explain why the present editor is more excited (though there are exceptions) by the earlier Chesterton.

Nevertheless, the life's work seems more of a whole than is the case with most writers. If Chesterton was 'a genius who never wrote a masterpiece' a sense of masterpiece persists, though it is difficult to point at a book and confidently say, 'There, throughout, he is at his best.' Early in his career he was accused by outraged publishers of villainously misquoting Browning. He replied, rather grandly, 'I quote from memory both by temper and on principle. That is what literature is for; it ought to be a part of the man.' Perhaps that is where the impression of a masterpiece lies, in the part of the man that is his work. As his 'critic of politics and literature', looking for a hero of the Great War, could only point to the mob, so perhaps, looking for a masterpiece, we could point to the mob Ezra Pound called Chesterton.

\*     \*     \*     \*     \*

He was fond, some thought over-fond, of making jokes about his great size (which must have been an affliction to him). So it is perhaps a too predictable levity to say there is only room for a small portion of him here; especially as it has been decided, where possible, to give substantial extracts from books, rather than short ones (collections of these already exist), in order to allow him scope to develop his arguments, and to save him from the reputation of a man who occasionally said good things. But it soon became clear, even in a selection of a quarter of a million words, that the problem was going to be what to leave out, the standard was so high.

Therefore an attempt has been made to be representative: Chesterton the poet, the essayist, the historian, the literary critic, the humorist, the novelist and story-teller, the religious enquirer, the Christian apologist. Examples from all these categories cried out so loudly to be included, and made such a large pile, that soon there was seen to be no room for more. The criterion for selection from the pile has been Chesterton at his most serious (though not necessarily at his most grave, which he seldom was) on topics that seemed of most utility to the present day; a standard of which he would surely have approved. The final judgement lay, as it must, in the editor's enjoyment. To read a writer *in extenso* is a severe test of reader as well as writer. But if there come moments when the reader's attention is caught and held so firmly that he hears himself muttering 'this *must* go in, whatever else is left out', the matter is made simpler. Of such moments is this book composed.

There were many more. There will be Chestertonians who will regret, possibly resent, the omission of this or that and, though we might not always agree (each man has his own, preferred Chesterton), there is certainly much that should be here that cannot be. It would have been good to include long passages from *The Flying Inn*, a wilder book than *The Man Who Was Thursday*, but out of context they would have seemed even too wild. It would have been good to include the whole of *Orthodoxy* and *A Short History of England*, because making extractions from these was painful and led to the discovery of how close-knit Chesterton's arguments are, though not always obviously sequential; there were many other reluctant omissions, such as the extraordinary epic *The Ballad of the White Horse*. Nevertheless (to return to the original figure) the hope is to have presented a rounded part of a large whole.

P.J. Kavanagh, 1984

# Poems

### THE DONKEY

When fishes flew and forests walked
   And figs grew upon thorn,
Some moment when the moon was blood
   Then surely I was born.

With monstrous head and sickening cry
   And ears like errant wings,
The devil's walking parody
   On all four-footed things.

The tattered outlaw of the earth,
   Of ancient crooked will;
Starve, scourge, deride me: I am dumb,
   I keep my secret still.

Fools! For I also had my hour;
   One far fierce hour and sweet:
There was a shout about my ears,
   And palms before my feet.

### FEMINA CONTRA MUNDUM

The sun was black with judgment, and the moon
   Blood: but between
I saw a man stand, saying, 'To me at least
   The grass is green.

The Wild Knight and Other Poems, 1900

'There was no star that I forgot to fear
  With love and wonder.
The birds have loved me'; but no answer came—
  Only the thunder.

Once more the man stood saying, 'A cottage door,
  Wherethrough I gazed
That instant as I turned—yea, I am vile;
  Yet my eyes blazed

'For I had weighed the mountains in a balance,
  And the skies in a scale,
I come to sell the stars—old lamps for new—
  Old stars for sale.'

Then a calm voice fell all the thunder through,
  A tone less rough:
'Thou hast begun to love one of my works
  Almost enough.'


## THOU SHALT NOT KILL

I had grown weary of him; of his breath
And hands and features I was sick to death.
Each day I heard the same dull voice and tread;
I did not hate him: but I wished him dead.
And he must with his blank face fill my life—
Then my brain blackened, and I snatched a knife.

But ere I struck, my soul's grey deserts through
A voice cried, 'Know at least what thing you do.
This is a common man: knowest thou, O soul,
What this thing is? somewhere where seasons roll
There is some living thing for whom this man
Is as seven heavens girt into a span,
For some one soul you take the world away—
Now know you well your deed and purpose. Slay!'
Then I cast down the knife upon the ground
And saw that mean man for one moment crowned.
I turned and laughed: for there was no one by—
The man that I had sought to slay was I.

# Thomas Carlyle

There are two main moral necessities for the work of a great man: the first is that he should believe in the truth of his message; the second is that he should believe in the acceptability of his message. It was the whole tragedy of Carlyle that he had the first and not the second.

The ordinary capital, however, which is made out of Carlyle's alleged gloom is a very paltry matter. Carlyle had his faults, both as a man and as a writer, but the attempt to explain his gospel in terms of his 'liver' is merely pitiful. If indigestion invariably resulted in a *Sartor Resartus*, it would be a vastly more tolerable thing than it is. Diseases do not turn into poems; even the decadent really writes with the healthy part of his organism. If Carlyle's private faults and literary virtues ran somewhat in the same line, he is only in the situation of every man; for every one of us it is surely very difficult to say precisely where our honest opinions end and our personal predilections begin. But to attempt to denounce Carlyle as a mere savage egotist cannot arise from anything but a pure inability to grasp Carlyle's gospel. 'Ruskin', says a critic, 'did, all the same, verily believe in God; Carlyle believed only in himself.' This is certainly a distinction between the author he has understood and the author he has not understood. Carlyle believed in himself, but he could not have believed in himself more than Ruskin did; they both believed in God, because they felt that if everything else fell into wrack and ruin, themselves were permanent witnesses to God. Where they both failed was not in belief in God or in belief in themselves; they failed in belief in other people. It is not enough for a prophet to believe in his message; he must believe in its acceptability. Christ, St Francis, Bunyan, Wesley, Mr Gladstone, Walt Whitman, men of indescribable variety, were all alike in a certain faculty of treating the average man as their equal, of trusting to his reason and good feeling without fear and without condescension. It was this simplicity of confidence not only in God, but in the image of God, that was lacking in Carlyle.

Twelve Types, 1902

But the attempts to discredit Carlyle's religious sentiment must absolutely fall to the ground. The profound security of Carlyle's sense of the unity of the Cosmos is like that of a Hebrew prophet; and it has the same expression that it had in the Hebrew prophets—humour. A man must be very full of faith to jest about his divinity. No Neo-Pagan delicately suggesting a revival of Dionysius, no vague, half-converted Theosophist groping towards a recognition of Buddha, would ever think of cracking jokes on the matter. But to the Hebrew prophets their religion was so solid a thing, like a mountain or a mammoth, that the irony of its contact with trivial and fleeting matters struck them like a blow. So it was with Carlyle. His supreme contribution, both to philosophy and literature, was his sense of the sarcasm of eternity. Other writers have seen the hope or the terror of the heavens, he alone saw the humour of them. Other writers had seen that there could be something elemental and eternal in a song or statue, he alone saw that there could be something elemental and eternal in a joke. No one who ever read it will forget the passage, full of dark and agnostic gratification, in which he narrates that some Court chronicler described Louis XV as 'falling asleep in the Lord'. 'Enough for us that he did fall asleep; that, curtained in thick night, under what keeping we ask not, he at least will never, through unending ages, insult the face of the sun any more ... and we go on, if not to better forms of beastliness, at least to fresher ones.'

The supreme value of Carlyle to English literature was that he was the founder of modern irrationalism; a movement fully as important as modern rationalism. A great deal is said in these days about the value or valuelessness of logic. In the main, indeed, logic is not a productive tool so much as a weapon of defence. A man building up an intellectual system has to build like Nehemiah, with a sword in one hand and the trowel in the other. The imagination, the constructive quality, is the trowel, and argument is the sword. A wide experience of actual intellectual affairs will lead most people to the conclusion that logic is mainly valuable as a weapon wherewith to exterminate logicians.

But though this may be true enough in practice, it scarcely clears up the position of logic in human affairs. Logic is a machine of the mind, and if it is used honesly it ought to bring out an honest conclusion. When people say that you can prove anything by logic, they are not using words in a fair sense. What they mean is that you can prove anything by bad logic. Deep in the mystic ingratitude of the soul of man there is an extraordinary tendency to use the name for an organ, when what is meant is the abuse or decay of that organ. Thus we speak of a man suffering from 'nerves', which is about as sensible as talking about a man suffering from ten fingers. We speak of 'liver' and 'digestion' when we mean the failure of liver and the absence of digestion. And in the same manner we speak of the dangers of logic, when what we really mean is the danger of fallacy.

But the real point about the limitation of logic and the partial overthrow of logic by writers like Carlyle is deeper and somewhat different. The fault of the great mass of logicians is not that they bring out a false result, or, in other words, are not logicians at all. Their fault is that by an inevitable psychological habit they tend to forget that there are two parts of a logical process— the first the choosing of an assumption, and the second the arguing upon it; and humanity, if it devotes itself too persistently to the study of sound reasoning, has a certain tendency to lose the faculty of sound assumption. It is astonishing how constantly one may hear from rational and even rationalistic persons such a phrase as 'He did not prove the very thing with which he started', or 'The whole of his case rested upon a pure assumption', two peculiarities which may be found by the curious in the works of Euclid. It is astonishing, again, how constantly one hears rationalists arguing upon some deep topic, apparently without troubling about the deep assumption involved, having lost their sense, as it were, of the real colour and character of a man's assumption. For instance, two men will argue about whether patriotism is a good thing and never discover until the end, if at all, that the cosmopolitan is basing his whole case upon the idea that man should, if he can, become as God with equal sympathies and no prejudices, while the rationalist denies any such duty at the very start, and regards man as an animal who has preferences, as a bird has feathers.

Thus it was with Carlyle: he startled men by attacking not arguments but assumptions. He simply brushed aside all the matter which the men of the nineteenth century held to be incontrovertible, and appealed directly to the very different class of matters which they knew to be true. He induced men to study less the truth of their reasoning and more the truth of the assumptions upon which they reasoned. Even where his view was not the highest truth, it was always a refreshing and beneficent heresy. He denied every one of the postulates upon which the age of reason based itself. He denied the theory of progress which assumed that we must be better off than the people of the twelfth century. Whether we were better than the people of the twelfth century according to him depended entirely upon whether we chose or deserved to be.

He denied every type and species of prop or association or support which threw the responsibility upon civilization or society, or anything but the individual conscience. He has often been called a prophet. The real ground of the truth of this phrase is often neglected. Since the last era of purely religious literature, the era of English Puritanism, there has been no writer in whose eyes the soul stood so much alone.

Carlyle was, as we have suggested, a mystic, and mysticism was with him, as with all its genuine professors, only a transcendent form of common sense. Mysticism and common sense alike consist in a sense of the dominance of certain truths and tendencies which cannot be formally demonstrated or even formally named. Mysticism and common sense are alike appeals to realities that we all know to be real, but which have no place in argument except as postulates. Carlyle's work did consist in breaking through formulae, old and new, to these old and silent and ironical sanities. Philosophers might abolish kings a hundred times over, he maintained, they could not alter the fact that every man and woman does choose a king and repudiate all the pride of citizenship for the exultation of humility. If inequality of this kind was a weakness, it was a weakness bound up with the very strength of the universe. About hero worship, indeed, few critics have done the smallest justice to Carlyle. Misled by those hasty and choleric passages in which he sometimes expressed a preference for mere violence, passages which were a great deal more connected with his temperament than with his philosophy, they have finally imbibed the notion that Carlyle's theory of hero worship was a theory of terrified submission to stern and arrogant men. As a matter of fact, Carlyle is really inhumane about some questions, but he is never inhumane about hero worship. His view is not that human nature is so vulgar and silly a thing that it must be guided and driven; it is, on the contrary, that human nature is so chivalrous and fundamentally magnanimous a thing that even the meanest have it in them to love a leader more than themselves, and to prefer loyalty to rebellion. When he speaks of this trait in human nature Carlyle's tone invariably softens. We feel that for the moment he is kindled with admiration of mankind, and almost reaches the verge of Christianity. Whatever else was acid and captious about Carlyle's utterances, his hero worship was not only humane, it was almost optimistic. He admired great men primarily, and perhaps correctly, because he thought that they were more human than other men. The evil side of the influence of Carlyle and his religion of hero worship did not consist in the emotional worship of valour and success; that was a part of him, as, indeed, it is a part of all healthy children. Where Carlyle really did harm was in the fact that he, more than any modern man, is responsible for the increase of that modern habit of what is vulgarly called 'Going the whole hog'. Often in matters of passion and conquest it is a singularly hoggish hog. This remarkable modern craze for making one's philosophy, religion, politics, and temper all of a piece, to seeking in all incidents for opportunities to assert and reassert some favourite mental attitude, is a thing which existed comparatively little in other centuries. Solomon and Horace, Petrarch and Shakespeare were pessimists when they were melancholy, and optimists when they were happy. But the optimist of today seems obliged to prove that gout and unrequited love make him dance with joy, and the pessimist of today to prove that sunshine and a good supper convulse him with inconsolable anguish. Carlyle was strongly possessed with this mania for spiritual consistency. He wished to take the same view of the wars of the angels and of the paltriest riot at Donnybrook Fair. It was this species of insane logic which led him into his chief errors, never his natural enthusiasms. Let us take an example. Carlyle's defence of slavery is a thoroughly ridiculous thing, weak alike in argument and in moral instinct. The truth is, that he only took it up from the passion for applying everywhere his paradoxical defence of aristocracy. He blundered, of course, because he did not see that slavery has nothing in the world to do with aristocracy, that it is, indeed, almost its opposite. The defence which Carlyle and all its thoughtful defenders have made for aristocracy was that a few persons could more rapidly and firmly decide public affairs in the interests of the people. But slavery is not even supposed to be a government for the good of the governed. It is a possession of the governed avowedly for the good of the governors. Aristocracy uses the strong for the service of the weak; slavery uses the weak for the service of the strong. It is no derogation to man as a spiritual being, as Carlyle firmly believed he was, that he should be ruled and guided for his own good like a child—for a child who is always ruled and guided we regard as the very type of spiritual existence. But it is a derogation and an absolute contradiction to that human spirituality in which Carlyle believed that a man should be owned like a tool for someone else's good, as if he has no personal destiny in the Cosmos. We draw attention to this particular error of Carlyle's because we think that it is a curious example of the waste and unclean places into which that remarkable animal 'the whole hog' more than once led him.

In this respect Carlyle has had an unquestionably long and an unquestionably bad influence. The whole of that recent political ethic which conceives that if we only go far enough we may finish a thing for once and all, that being strong consists chiefly in being deliberately deaf and blind, owes a great deal of its complete sway to his example. Out of him flows most of the philosophy of Nietzsche, who is in modern times the supreme maniac of this moonstruck consistency. Though Nietzsche and Carlyle were in reality profoundly different, Carlyle being a stiff-necked peasant and Nietzsche a very fragile aristocrat, they were alike in this one quality of which we speak, the strange and pitiful audacity with which they applied their single ethical test to everything in heaven and earth. The disciple of Nietzsche, indeed, embraces immorality like an austere and difficult faith. He urges himself to lust and cruelty with the same tremendous enthusiasm with which a Christian urges himself to purity and patience; he struggles as a monk struggles with bestial visions and temptations with the ancient necessities of honour and justice and compassion. To this madhouse, it can hardly be denied, has Carlyle's intellectual courage brought many at last.

# Browning and His Marriage

Robert Browning had his faults, and the general direction of those faults has been previously suggested. The chief of his faults, a certain uncontrollable brutality of speech and gesture when he was strongly roused, was destined to cling to him all through his life, and to startle with the blaze of a volcano even the last quiet years before his death. But any one who wishes to understand how deep was the elemental honesty and reality of his character, how profoundly worthy he was of any love that was bestowed upon him, need only study one most striking and determining element in the question—Browning's simple, heartfelt, and unlimited admiration for other people. He was one of a generation of great men, of great men who had a certain peculiar type, certain peculiar merits and defects. Carlyle, Tennyson, Ruskin, Matthew Arnold, were alike in being children of a very strenuous and conscientious age, alike in possessing its earnestness and air of deciding great matters, alike also in showing a certain almost noble jealousy, a certain restlessness, a certain fear of other influences. Browning alone had no fear; he welcomed, evidently without the least affectation, all the influences of his day. A very interesting letter of his remains in which he describes his pleasure in a university dinner. 'Praise,' he says in effect, 'was given very deservedly to Matthew Arnold and Swinburne, and to that pride of Oxford men, Clough.' The really striking thing about these three names is the fact that they are united in Browning's praise in a way in which they are by no means united in each other's. Matthew Arnold, in one of his extant letters, calls Swinburne 'a young pseudo-Shelley,' who, according to Arnold, thinks he can make Greek plays good by making them modern. Mr Swinburne, on the other hand, has summarised Clough in a contemptuous rhyme:—

> 'There was a bad poet named Clough,
> Whom his friends all united to puff.
> But the public, though dull,
> Has not quite such a skull
> As belongs to believers in Clough.'

Robert Browning, 1903

8

The same general fact will be found through the whole of Browning's life and critical attitude. He adored Shelley, and also Carlyle who sneered at him. He delighted in Mill, and also in Ruskin who rebelled against Mill. He excused Napoleon III and Landor who hurled interminable curses against Napoleon. He admired all the cycle of great men who all condemned each other. To say that he had no streak of envy in his nature would be true, but unfair; for there is no justification for attributing any of these great men's opinions to envy. But Browning was really unique, in that he had a certain spontaneous and unthinking tendency to the admiration of others. He admired another poet as he admired a fading sunset or a chance spring leaf. He no more thought whether he could be as good as that man in that department than whether he could be redder than the sunset or greener than the leaf of spring. He was naturally magnanimous in the literal sense of that sublime word; his mind was so great that it rejoiced in the triumphs of strangers. In this spirit Browning had already cast his eyes round in the literary world of his time, and had been greatly and justifiably struck with the work of a young lady poet, Miss Barrett.

That impression was indeed amply justified. In a time when it was thought necessary for a lady to dilute the wine of poetry to its very weakest tint, Miss Barrett had contrived to produce poetry which was open to literary objection as too heady and too high-coloured. When she erred it was through an Elizabethan audacity and luxuriance, a straining after violent metaphors. With her reappeared in poetry a certain element which had not been present in it since the last days of Elizabethan literature, the fusion of the most elementary human passion with something which can only be described as wit, a certain love of quaint and sustained similes, of parallels wildly logical, and of brazen paradox and antithesis. We find this hot wit, as distinct from the cold wit of the school of Pope, in the puns and buffooneries of Shakespeare. We find it lingering in *Hudibras*, and we do not find it again until we come to such strange and strong lines as these of Elizabeth Barrett in her poem on Napoleon:—

> 'Blood fell like dew beneath his sunrise—sooth,
> But glittered dew-like in the covenanted
> And high-rayed light. He was a despot—granted,
> But the *avrós* of his autocratic mouth
> Said 'Yea' i' the people's French! He magnified
> The image of the freedom he denied.'

Her poems are full of quaint things, of such things as the eyes in the peacock fans of the Vatican, which she describes as winking at the Italian tricolor. She often took the step from the sublime to the ridiculous: but to take this step one must reach the sublime. Elizabeth Barrett contrived to assert, what still needs but then urgently needed assertion, the fact that womanliness, whether in life or poetry, was a positive thing, and not the negative of manliness. Her verse at its best was quite as strong as Browning's own, and very nearly as clever. The difference between their natures was a difference between two primary colours, not between dark and light shades of the same colour.

Browning had often heard not only of the public, but of the private life of this lady from his father's friend Kenyon. The old man, who was one of those rare and valuable people who have a talent for establishing definite relationships with people after a comparatively short intercourse, had been appointed by Miss Barrett as her 'fairy godfather.' He spoke much about her to Browning, and of Browning to her, with a certain courtly garrulity which was one of his talents. And there could be little doubt that the two poets would have met long before had it not been for certain peculiarities in the position of Miss Barrett. She was an invalid, and an invalid of a somewhat unique kind, and living beyond all question under very unique circumstances.

Her father, Edward Moulton Barrett, had been a landowner in the West Indies, and thus, by a somewhat curious coincidence, had borne a part in the same social system which stung Browning's father into revolt and renunciation. The part played by Edward Barrett, however, though little or nothing is known of it, was probably very different. He was a man Conservative by nature, a believer in authority in the nation and the family, and endowed with some faculties for making his conceptions prevail. He was an able man, capable in his language of a certain bitter felicity of phrase. He was rigidly upright and responsible, and he had a capacity for profound affection. But selfishness of the most perilous sort, an unconscious selfishness, was eating away his moral foundations, as it tends to eat away those of all despots. His most fugitive moods changed and controlled the whole atmosphere of the house, and the state of things was fully as oppressive in the case of his good moods as in the case of his bad ones. He had, what is perhaps the subtlest and worst spirit of egotism, not that spirit merely which thinks that nothing should stand in the way of its ill-temper, but that spirit which thinks that nothing should stand in the way of its amiability. His daughters must be absolutely at his beck and call, whether it was to be brow-beaten or caressed. During the early years of Elizabeth Barrett's life, the family had lived in the country, and for that brief period she had known a more wholesome life than she was destined ever to know again until her marriage long afterwards. She was not, as is the general popular idea, absolutely a congenital invalid, weak, and almost moribund from the cradle. In early girlhood she was slight and sensitive indeed, but perfectly active and courageous. She was a good horsewoman, and the accident which handicapped her for so many years afterwards happened to her when she was riding. The injury to her spine, however, will be found, the more we study her history, to be only one of the influences which were to darken those bedridden years, and to have among them a far less important place than has hitherto been attached to it. Her father moved to a melancholy house in Wimpole Street; and his own character growing gloomier and stranger as time went on, he mounted guard over his daughter's sickbed in a manner compounded of the pessimist and the disciplinarian. She was not permitted to stir from the sofa, often not even to cross two rooms to her bed. Her father came and prayed over her with a kind of melancholy glee, and with the avowed solemnity of a watcher by a deathbed. She was surrounded by that most poisonous and degrading of all atmospheres—a medical atmosphere. The existence of this atmosphere has nothing to do with the actual nature or prolongation of disease. A man may pass three hours out of every five in a state of bad health, and yet regard, as Stevenson regarded, the three hours as exceptional and the two as normal. But the curse that lay on the Barrett household was the curse of considering ill-health the natural condition of a human being. The truth was that Edward Barrett was living emotionally and aesthetically, like some detestable decadent poet, upon his daughter's decline. He did not know this, but it was so. Scenes, explanations, prayers, fury, and forgiveness had become bread and meat for which he hungered; and when the cloud was upon his spirit, he would lash out at all things and every one with the insatiable cruelty of the sentimentalist.

It is wonderful that Elizabeth Barrett was not made thoroughly morbid and impotent by this intolerable violence and more intolerable tenderness. In her estimate of her own health she did, of course, suffer. It is evident that she practically believed herself to be dying. But she was a high-spirited woman, full of that silent and quite unfathomable kind of courage which is only found in women, and she took a much more cheerful view of death than her father did of life. Silent rooms, low voices, lowered blinds, long days of loneliness, and of the sickliest kind of sympathy, had not tamed a spirit which was swift and headlong to a fault. She could still own with truth the magnificent fact that her chief vice was impatience, 'tearing open parcels instead of untying them;' looking at the end of books before she had read them was, she said, incurable with her. It is difficult to imagine anything more genuinely stirring than the achievement of this woman, who thus contrived, while possessing all the excuses of an invalid, to retain some of the faults of a tomboy.

Impetuosity, vividness, a certain absoluteness and urgency in her demands, marked her in the eyes of all who came in contact with her. In after years, when Browning had experimentally shaved his beard off, she told him with emphatic gestures that it must be grown again 'that minute.' There we have very graphically the spirit which tears open parcels. Not in vain, or as a mere phrase, did her husband after her death describe her as 'all a wonder and a wild desire.'

She had, of course, lived her second and real life in literature and the things of the mind, and this in a very genuine and strenuous sense. Her mental occupations were not mere mechanical accomplishments almost as colourless as the monotony they relieved, nor were they coloured in any visible manner by the unwholesome atmosphere in which she breathed. She used her brains seriously; she was a good Greek scholar, and read Æschylus and Euripides unceasingly with her blind friend, Mr Boyd; and she had, and retained even to the hour of her death, a passionate and quite practical interest in great public questions. Naturally she was not uninterested in Robert Browning, but it does not appear that she felt at this time the same kind of fiery artistic curiosity that he felt about her. He does appear to have felt an attraction, which may almost be called mystical, for the personality which was shrouded from the world by such sombre curtains. In 1845 he addressed a letter to her in which he spoke of a former occasion on which they had nearly met, and compared it to the sensation of having once been outside the chapel of some marvellous illumination and found the door barred against him. In that phrase it is easy to see how much of the romantic boyhood of Browning remained inside the resolute man of the world into which he was to all external appearance solidifying. Miss Barrett replied to his letters with charming sincerity and humour, and with much of that leisurely self-revelation which is possible for an invalid who has nothing else to do. She herself, with her love of quiet and intellectual companionship, would probably have been quite happy for the rest of her life if their relations had always remained a learned and delightful correspondence. But she must have known very little of Robert Browning if she imagined he would be contented with this airy and bloodless tie. At all times of his life he was sufficiently fond of his own way; at this time he was especially prompt and impulsive, and he had always a great love for seeing and hearing and feeling people, a love of the physical presence of friends, which made him slap men on the back and hit them in the chest when he was very fond of them. The correspondence between the two poets had not long begun when Browning suggested something which was almost a blasphemy in the Barrett household, that he should come and call on her as he would on any one else. This seems to have thrown her into a flutter of fear and doubt. She alleges all kinds of obstacles, the chief of which were her health and the season of the year and the east winds. 'If my truest heart's wishes avail,' replied Browning obstinately, 'you shall laugh at east winds yet as I do.'

Then began the chief part of that celebrated correspondence which has within comparatively recent years been placed before the world. It is a correspondence which has very peculiar qualities and raises many profound questions.

It is impossible to deal at any length with the picture given in these remarkable letters of the gradual progress and amalgamation of two spirits of great natural potency and independence, without saying at least a word about the moral question raised by their publication and the many expressions of disapproval which it entails. To the mind of the present writer the whole of such a question should be tested by one perfectly clear intellectual distinction and comparison. I am not prepared to admit that there is or can be, properly speaking, in the world anything that is too sacred to be known. That spiritual beauty and spiritual truth are in their nature communicable, and that they should be communicated, is a principle which lies at the root of every conceivable religion. Christ was crucified upon a hill, and not in a cavern, and the word Gospel itself involves the same idea as the ordinary name of a daily paper. Whenever, therefore, a poet or any similar type of man can, or conceives that he can, make all men partakers in some splendid secret of his own heart, I can imagine nothing saner and nothing manlier than his course in doing so. Thus it was that Dante made a new heaven and a new hell out of a girl's nod in the streets of Florence. Thus it was that Paul founded a civilisation by keeping an ethical diary. But the one essential which exists in all such cases as these is that the man in question believes that he can make the story as stately to the whole world as it is to him, and he chooses his words to that end. Yet when a work contains expressions which have one value and significance when read by the people to whom they were addressed, and an entirely different value and significance when read by any one else, then the element of the violation of sanctity does arise. It is not because there is anything in this world too sacred to tell. It is rather because there are a great many things in this world too sacred to parody. If Browning could really convey to the world the inmost core of his affection for his wife, I see no reason why he should not. But the objection to letters which begin 'My dear Ba,' is that they do not convey anything of the sort. As far as any third person is concerned, Browning might as well have been expressing the most noble and universal sentiment in the dialect of the Cherokees. Objection to the publication of such passages as that, in short, is not the fact that they tell us about the love of the Brownings, but that they do not tell us about it.

Upon this principle it is obvious that there should have been a selection among the Letters, but not a selection which should exclude anything merely because it was ardent and noble. If Browning or Mrs Browning had not desired any people to know that they were fond of each other, they would not have written and published 'One Word More' or 'The Sonnets from the Portuguese.' Nay, they would not have been married in a public church, for every one who is married in a church does make a confession of love of absolutely national publicity, and tacitly, therefore, repudiates any idea that such confessions are too sacred for the world to know. The ridiculous theory that men should have no noble passions or sentiments in public may have been designed to make private life holy and undefiled, but it has had very little actual effect except to make public life cynical and preposterously unmeaning. But the words of a poem or the words of the English Marriage Service, which are as fine as many poems, is a language dignified and deliberately intended to be understood by all. If the bride and bridegroom in church, instead of uttering those words, were to utter a poem compounded of private allusions to the foibles of Aunt Matilda, or of childish secrets which they would tell each other in a lane, it would be a parallel case to the publication of some of the Browning Letters. Why the serious and universal portions of those Letters could not be published without those which are to us idle and unmeaning it is difficult to understand. Our wisdom, whether expressed in private or public, belongs to the world, but our folly belongs to those we love.

There is at least one peculiarity in the Browning Letters which tends to make their publication far less open to objection than almost any other collection of love letters which can be imagined. The ordinary sentimentalist who delights in the most emotional of magazine interviews, will not be able to get much satisfaction out of them, because he and many persons more acute will be quite unable to make head or tail of three consecutive sentences. In this respect it is the most extraordinary correspondence in the world. There seem to be only two main rules for this form of letter-writing: the first is, that if a sentence can begin with a parenthesis it always should; and the second is, that if you have written from a third to half of a sentence you need never in any case write any more. It would be amusing to watch any one who felt an idle curiosity as to the language and secrets of lovers opening the Browning Letters. He would probably come upon some such simple and lucid passage as the following: 'I ought to wait, say a week at least, having killed all your mules for you, before I shot down your dogs. ... But not being Phoibos Apollon, you are to know further that when I *did* think I might go modestly on ... ὤμοι, let me get out of this slough of a simile, never mind with what dislocated ankles.'

What our imaginary sentimentalist would make of this tender passage it is difficult indeed to imagine. The only plain conclusion which appears to emerge from the words is the somewhat curious one—that Browning was in the habit of taking a gun down to Wimpole Street and of demolishing the live stock on those somewhat unpromising premises. Nor will he be any better enlightened if he turns to the reply of Miss Barrett, which seems equally dominated with the great central idea of the Browning correspondence that the most enlightening passages in a letter consist of dots. She replies in a letter following the above: 'But if it could be possible that you should mean to say you would show me. ... Can it be? or am I reading this "Attic contraction" quite the wrong way. You see I am afraid of the difference between flattering myself and being flattered ... the fatal difference. And now will you understand that I should be too overjoyed to have revelations from the Portfolio ... however incarnated with blots and pen scratches ... to be able to ask impudently of them now? Is that plain?' Most probably she thought it was.

With regard to Browning himself this characteristic is comparatively natural and appropriate. Browning's prose was in any case the most round-about affair in the world. Those who knew him say that he would often send an urgent telegram from which it was absolutely impossible to gather where the appointment was, or when it was, or what was its object. The fact is one of the best of all arguments against the theory of Browning's intellectual conceit. A man would have to be somewhat abnormally conceited in order to spend sixpence for the pleasure of sending an unintelligible communication to the dislocation of his own plans. The fact was, that it was part of the machinery of his brain that things came out of it, as it were, backwards. The words 'tail foremost' express Browning's style with something more than a conventional accuracy. The tail, the most insignificant part of an animal, is also often the most animated and fantastic. An utterance of Browning is often like a strange animal walking backwards, who flourishes his tail with such energy that every one takes it for his head. He was in other words, at least in his prose and practical utterances, more or less incapable of telling a story without telling the least important thing first. If a man who belonged to an Italian secret society, one local branch of which bore as a badge an olive-green ribbon, had entered his house, and in some sensational interview tried to bribe or blackmail him, he would have told the story with great energy and indignation, but he would have been incapable of beginning with anything except the question of the colour of olives. His whole method was founded both in literature and life upon the principle of the 'ex pede Herculem,' and at the beginning of his description of Hercules the foot appears some sizes larger than the hero. It is, in short, natural enough that Browning should have written his love letters obscurely, since he wrote his letters to his publisher and his solicitor obscurely. In the case of Mrs Browning it is somewhat more difficult to understand. For she at least had, beyond all question, a quite simple and lucent vein of humour, which does not easily reconcile itself with this subtlety. But she was partly under the influence of her own quality of passionate ingenuity or emotional wit of which we have already taken notice in dealing with her poems, and she was partly also no doubt under the influence of Browning. Whatever was the reason, their correspondence was not of the sort which can be pursued very much by the outside public. Their letters may be published a hundred times over, they still remain private. They write to each other in a language of their own, an almost exasperatingly impressionist language, a language chiefly consisting of dots and dashes and asterisks and italics, and brackets and notes of interrogation. Wordsworth when he heard afterwards of their eventual elopement said with that slight touch of bitterness he always used in speaking of Browning, 'So Robert Browning and Miss Barrett have gone off together. I hope they understand each other—nobody else would.' It would be difficult to pay a higher compliment to a marriage. Their common affection for Kenyon was a great element in their lives and in their correspondence. 'I have a convenient theory to account for Mr Kenyon,' writes Browning mysteriously, 'and his otherwise unaccountable kindness to me.' 'For Mr Kenyon's kindness,' retorts Elizabeth Barrett, 'no theory will account. I class it with mesmerism for that reason.' There is something very dignified and beautiful about the simplicity of these two poets vying with each other in giving adequate praise to the old dilettante, of whom the world would never have heard but for them. Browning's feeling for him was indeed especially strong and typical. 'There,' he said, pointing after the old man as he left the room, 'there goes one of the most splendid men living—a man so noble in his friendship, so lavish in his hospitality, so large-hearted and benevolent, that he deserves to be known all over the world as "Kenyon the Magnificent."' There is something thoroughly worthy of Browning at his best in this feeling, not merely of the use of sociability, or of the charm of sociability, but of the magnificence, the heroic largeness of real sociability. Being himself a warm champion of the pleasures of society, he saw in Kenyon a kind of poetic genius for the thing, a mission of superficial philanthropy. He is thoroughly to be congratulated on the fact that he had grasped the great but now neglected truth, that a man may actually be great, yet not in the least able.

Browning's desire to meet Miss Barrett was received on her side, as has been stated, with a variety of objections. The chief of these was the strangely feminine and irrational reason that she was not worth seeing, a point on which the seeker for an interview might be permitted to form his own opinion. 'There is nothing to see in me; nor to hear in me.—I never learned to talk as you do in London; although I can admire that brightness of carved speech in Mr Kenyon and others. If my poetry is worth anything to any eye, it is the flower of me. I have lived most and been most happy in it, and so it has all my colours; the rest of me is nothing but a root, fit for the ground and dark.' The substance of Browning's reply was to the effect, 'I will call at two on Tuesday.'

They met on May 20, 1845. A short time afterwards he had fallen in love with her and made her an offer of marriage. To a person in the domestic atmosphere of the Barretts, the incident would appear to have been paralys-ing. 'I will tell you what I once said in jest ...' she writes, 'If a prince of El Dorado should come with a pedigree of lineal descent from some signory in the moon in one hand and a ticket of good behaviour from the nearest Independent chapel in the other!—"Why, even *then*," said my sister Arabel, "it would not *do*." And she was right; we all agreed that she was right.'

This may be taken as a fairly accurate description of the real state of Mr Barrett's mind on one subject. It is illustrative of the very best and breeziest side of Elizabeth Barrett's character that she could be so genuinely humor-ous over so tragic a condition of the human mind.

Browning's proposals were, of course, as matters stood, of a character to dismay and repel all those who surrounded Elizabeth Barrett. It was not wholly a matter of the fancies of her father. The whole of her family, and most probably the majority of her medical advisers, did seriously believe at this time that she was unfit to be moved, to say nothing of being married, and that a life passed between a bed and a sofa, and avoiding too frequent and abrupt transitions even from one to the other, was the only life she could expect on this earth. Almost alone in holding another opinion and in urging her to a more vigorous view of her condition, stood Browning himself. 'But you are better,' he would say; 'you look so and speak so.' Which of the two opinions was right is of course a complex medical matter into which a book like this has neither the right nor the need to enter. But this much may be stated as a mere question of fact. In the summer of 1846 Elizabeth Barrett was still living under the great family convention which provided her with nothing but an elegant deathbed, forbidden to move, forbidden to see proper daylight, forbidden to receive a friend lest the shock should destroy her suddenly. A year or two later, in Italy, as Mrs Browning, she was being dragged up hill in a wine hamper, toiling up to the crests of mountains at four o'clock in the morning, riding for five miles on a donkey to what she calls 'an inaccessible volcanic ground not far from the stars.' It is perfectly incredible that any one so ill as her family believed her to be should have lived this life for twenty-four hours. Something must be allowed for the intoxication of a new tie and a new interest in life. But such exaltations can in their nature hardly last a month, and Mrs Browning lived for fifteen years afterwards in infinitely better health than she had ever known before. In the light of modern knowledge it is not very difficult or very presumptuous of us to guess that she had been in her father's house to some extent inoculated with hysteria, that strange affliction which some people speak of as if it meant the absence of disease, but which is in truth the most terrible of all diseases. It must be remembered that in 1846 little or nothing was known of spine complaints such as that from which Elizabeth Barrett suffered, less still of the nervous conditions they create, and least of all of hysterical phenomena.

In our day she would have been ordered air and sunlight and activity, and all the things the mere idea of which chilled the Barretts with terror. In our day, in short, it would have been recognised that she was in the clutch of a form of neurosis which exhibits every fact of a disease except its origin, that strange possession which makes the body itself a hypocrite. Those who surrounded Miss Barrett knew nothing of this, and Browning knew nothing of it; and probably if he knew anything, knew less than they did. Mrs Orr says, probably with a great deal of truth, that of ill-health and its sensations he remained 'pathetically ignorant' to his dying day. But devoid as he was alike of expert knowledge and personal experience, without a shadow of medical authority, almost without anything that can be formally called a right to his opinion, he was, and remained, right. He at least saw, he indeed alone saw, to the practical centre of the situation. He did not know anything about hysteria or neurosis, or the influence of surroundings, but he knew that the atmosphere of Mr Barrett's house was not a fit thing for any human being, alive, dying, or dead. His stand upon this matter has really a certain human interest, since it is an example of a thing which will from time to time occur, the interposition of the average man to the confounding of the experts. Experts are undoubtedly right nine times out of ten, but the tenth time comes, and we find in military matters an Oliver Cromwell who will make every mistake known to strategy and yet win all his battles, and in medical matters a Robert Browning whose views have not a technical leg to stand on and are entirely correct.

But while Browning was thus standing alone in his view of the matter, while Edward Barrett had to all appearance on his side a phalanx of all the sanities and respectabilities, there came suddenly a new development, destined to bring matters to a crisis indeed, and to weigh at least three souls in the balance. Upon further examination of Miss Barrett's condition, the physicians had declared that it was absolutely necessary that she should be taken to Italy. This may, without any exaggeration, be called the turning-point and the last great earthly opportunity of Barrett's character. He had not originally been an evil man, only a man who, being stoical in practical things, permitted himself, to his great detriment, a self-indulgence in moral things. He had grown to regard his pious and dying daughter as part of the furniture of the house and of the universe. And as long as the great mass of authorities were on his side, his illusion was quite pardonable. His crisis came when the authorities changed their front, and with one accord asked his permission to send his daughter abroad. It was his crisis, and he refused.

He had, if we may judge from what we know of him, his own peculiar and somewhat detestable way of refusing. Once when his daughter had asked a perfectly simple favour in a matter of expediency, permission, that is, to keep her favourite brother with her during an illness, her singular parent remarked that 'she might keep him if she liked, but that he had looked for greater self-sacrifice.' These were the weapons with which he ruled his people. For the worst tyrant is not the man who rules by fear; the worst tyrant is he who rules by love and plays on it as on a harp. Barrett was one of the oppressors who have discovered that last secret of oppression, that which is told in the fine verse of Swinburne:—

> 'The racks of the earth and the rods
> Are weak as the foam on the sands;
> The heart is the prey for the gods,
> Who crucify hearts, not hands.'

He, with his terrible appeal to the vibrating consciences of women, was, with regard to one of them, very near to the end of his reign. When Browning heard that the Italian journey was forbidden, he proposed definitely that they should marry and go on the journey together.

Many other persons had taken cognisance of the fact, and were active in the matter. Kenyon, the gentlest and most universally complimentary of mortals, had marched into the house and given Arabella Barrett, the sister of the sick woman, his opinion of her father's conduct with a degree of fire and frankness which must have been perfectly amazing in a man of his almost antiquated social delicacy. Mrs Jameson, an old and generous friend of the family, had immediately stepped in and offered to take Elizabeth to Italy herself, thus removing all questions of expense or arrangement. She would appear to have stood to her guns in the matter with splendid persistence and magnanimity. She called day after day seeking for a change of mind, and delayed her own journey to the continent more than once. At length, when it became evident that the extraction of Mr Barrett's consent was hopeless, she reluctantly began her own tour in Europe alone. She went to Paris, and had not been there many days, when she received a formal call from Robert Browning and Elizabeth Barrett Browning, who had been married for some days. Her astonishment is rather a picturesque thing to think about.

The manner in which this sensational elopement, which was, of course, the talk of the whole literary world, had been effected, is narrated, as every one knows in the Browning Letters. Browning had decided that an immediate marriage was the only solution; and having put his hand to the plough, did not decline even when it became obviously necessary that it should be a secret marriage. To a man of his somewhat stormily candid and casual disposition this necessity of secrecy was really exasperating; but every one with any imagination or chivalry will rejoice that he accepted the evil conditions. He had always had the courage to tell the truth; and now it was demanded of him to have the greater courage to tell a lie, and he told it with perfect cheerfulness and lucidity. In thus disappearing surreptitiously with an invalid woman he was doing something against which there were undoubtedly a hundred things to be said, only it happened that the most cogent and important thing of all was to be said for it.

It is very amusing, and very significant in the matter of Browning's character, to read the accounts which he writes to Elizabeth Barrett of his attitude towards the approaching *coup de théâtre*. In one place he says, suggestively enough, that he does not in the least trouble about the disapproval of her father; the man whom he fears as a frustrating influence is Kenyon. Mr Barrett could only walk into the room and fly into a passion; and this Browning could have received with perfect equanimity. 'But,' he says, 'if Kenyon knows of the matter, I shall have the kindest and friendliest of explanations (with his arm on my shoulder) of how I am ruining your social position, destroying your health, etc., etc.' This touch is very suggestive of the power of the old worldling, who could manœuvre with young people as well as Major Pendennis. Kenyon had indeed long been perfectly aware of the way in which things were going; and the method he adopted in order to comment on it is rather entertaining. In a conversation with Elizabeth Barrett, he asked carelessly whether there was anything between her sister and a certain Captain Cooke. On receiving a surprised reply in the negative, he remarked apologetically that he had been misled into the idea by the gentleman calling so often at the house. Elizabeth Barrett knew perfectly well what he meant; but the logical allusiveness of the attack reminds one of a fragment of some Meredithian comedy.

The manner in which Browning bore himself in this acute and necessarily dubious position is, perhaps, more thoroughly to his credit than anything else in his career. He never came out so well in his long years of sincerity and publicity as he does in this one act of deception. Having made up his mind to that act, he is not ashamed to name it; neither, on the other hand, does he rant about it, and talk about Philistine prejudices and higher laws and brides in the sight of God, after the manner of the cockney decadent. He was breaking a social law, but he was not declaring a crusade against social laws. We all feel, whatever may be our opinions on the matter, that the great danger of this kind of social opportunism, this pitting of a private necessity against a public custom, is that men are somewhat too weak and self-deceptive to be trusted with such a power of giving dispensations to themselves. We feel that men without meaning to do so might easily begin by breaking a social by-law and end by being thoroughly anti-social. One of the best and most striking things to notice about Robert Browning is the fact that he did this thing considering it as an exception, and that he contrived to leave it really exceptional. It did not in the least degree break the rounded clearness of his loyalty to social custom. It did not in the least degree weaken the sanctity of the general rule. At a supreme crisis of his life he did an unconventional thing, and he lived and died conventional. It would be hard to say whether he appears the more thoroughly sane in having performed the act, or in not having allowed it to affect him.

Elizabeth Barrett gradually gave way under the obstinate and almost monotonous assertion of Browning that this elopement was the only possible course of action. Before she finally agreed, however, she did something, which in its curious and impulsive symbolism, belongs almost to a more primitive age. The sullen system of medical seclusion to which she had long been subjected has already been described. The most urgent and hygienic changes were opposed by many on the ground that it was not safe for her to leave her sofa and her sombre room. On the day on which it was necessary for her finally to accept or reject Browning's proposal, she called her sister to her, and to the amazement and mystification of that lady asked for a carriage. In this she drove into Regent's Park, alighted, walked on to the grass, and stood leaning against a tree for some moments, looking round her at the leaves and the sky. She then entered the cab again, drove home, and agreed to the elopement. This was possibly the best poem that she ever produced.

Browning arranged the eccentric adventure with a great deal of prudence and knowledge of human nature. Early one morning in September 1846 Miss Barrett walked quietly out of her father's house, became Mrs Robert Browning in a church in Marylebone, and returned home again as if nothing had happened. In this arrangement Browning showed some of that real insight into the human spirit which ought to make a poet the most practical of all men. The incident was, in the nature of things, almost overpoweringly exciting to his wife, in spite of the truly miraculous courage with which she supported it; and he desired, therefore, to call in the aid of the mysteriously tranquillising effect of familiar scenes and faces. One trifling incident is worth mentioning which is almost unfathomably characteristic of Browning. It has already been remarked in these pages that he was pre-eminently one of those men whose expanding opinions never alter by a hairsbreadth the actual ground-plan of their moral sense. Browning would have felt the same things right and the same things wrong, whatever views he had held. During the brief and most trying period between his actual marriage and his actual elopement, it is most significant that he would not call at the house in Wimpole Street, because he would have been obliged to ask if Miss Barrett was disengaged. He was acting a lie; he was deceiving a father; he was putting a sick woman to a terrible risk; and these things he did not disguise from himself for a moment, but he could not bring himself to say two words to a maidservant. Here there may be partly the feeling of the literary man for the sacredness of the uttered word, but there is far more of a certain rooted traditional morality which it is impossible either to describe or to justify. Browning's respectability was an older and more primeval thing than the oldest and most primeval passions of other men. If we wish to understand him, we must always remember that in dealing with any of his actions we have not to ask whether the action contains the highest morality, but whether we should have felt inclined to do it ourselves.

At length the equivocal and exhausting interregnum was over. Mrs Browning went for the second time almost on tiptoe out of her father's house, accompanied only by her maid and her dog, which was only just successfully prevented from barking. Before the end of the day in all probability Barrett had discovered that his dying daughter had fled with Browning to Italy.

They never saw him again, and hardly more than a faint echo came to them of the domestic earthquake which they left behind them. They do not appear to have had many hopes, or to have made many attempts at a reconciliation. Elizabeth Barrett had discovered at last that her father was in truth not a man to be treated with; hardly, perhaps, even a man to be blamed. She knew to all intents and purposes that she had grown up in the house of a madman.

# Browning as a Literary Artist

Mr William Sharp, in his *Life* of Browning, quotes the remarks of another critic to the following effect: 'The poet's processes of thought are scientific in their precision and analysis; the sudden conclusion that he imposes upon them is transcendental and inept.'

This is a very fair but a very curious example of the way in which Browning is treated. For what is the state of affairs? A man publishes a series of poems, vigorous, perplexing, and unique. The critics read them, and they decide that he has failed as a poet, but that he is a remarkable philosopher and logician. They then proceed to examine his philosophy, and show with great triumph that it is unphilosophical, and to examine his logic and show with great triumph that it is not logical, but 'transcendental and inept.' In other words, Browning is first denounced for being a logician and not a poet, and then denounced for insisting on being a poet when they have decided that he is to be a logician. It is just as if a man were to say first that a garden was so neglected that it was only fit for a boys' playground, and then complain of the unsuitability in a boys' playground of rockeries and flower-beds.

As we find, after this manner, that Browning does not act satisfactorily as that which we have decided that he shall be—a logician—it might possibly be worth while to make another attempt to see whether he may not, after all, be more valid than we thought as to what he himself professed to be—a poet. And if we study this seriously and sympathetically, we shall soon come to a conclusion. It is a gross and complete slander upon Browning to say that his processes of thought are scientific in their precision and analysis. They are nothing of the sort; if they were, Browning could not be a good poet. The critic speaks of the conclusions of a poem as 'transcendental and inept'; but the conclusions of a poem, if they are not transcendental, must be inept. Do the people who call one of Browning's poems scientific in its analysis realise the meaning of what they say? One is tempted to think that they know a scientific analysis when they see it as little as they know a good poem. The one supreme difference between the scientific method and the artistic method is, roughly speaking, simply this—that a scientific statement means the same thing wherever and whenever it is uttered, and that an artistic statement means something entirely different, according to the relation in which it stands to its surroundings. The remark, let us say, that the whale is a mammal, or the remark that sixteen ounces go to a pound, is equally true, and means exactly the same thing, whether we state it at the beginning of a conversation or at the end, whether we print it in a dictionary or chalk it up on a wall. But if we take some phrase commonly used in the art of literature—such a sentence, for the sake of example, as 'the dawn was breaking'—the matter is quite different. If the sentence came at the beginning of a short story, it might be a mere descriptive prelude. If it were the last sentence in a short story, it might be poignant with some peculiar irony or triumph. Can any one read Browning's great monologues and not feel that they are built up like a good short story, entirely on this principle of the value of language arising from its arrangement? Take such an example as 'Caliban upon Setebos,' a wonderful poem designed to describe the way in which a primitive nature may at once be afraid of its gods and yet familiar with them. Caliban in describing his deity starts with a more or less natural and obvious parallel between the deity and himself, carries out the comparison with consistency and an almost revolting simplicity, and ends in a kind of blasphemous extravaganza of anthropomorphism, basing his conduct not merely on the greatness and wisdom, but also on the manifest weaknesses and stupidities, of the Creator of all things. Then suddenly a thunderstorm breaks over Caliban's island, and the profane speculator falls flat upon his face—

> 'Lo! 'Lieth flat and loveth Setebos!
> 'Maketh his teeth meet through his upper lip,
> Will let those quails fly, will not eat this month
> One little mess of whelks, so he may 'scape!'

Surely it would be very difficult to persuade oneself that this thunderstorm would have meant exactly the same thing if it had occurred at the beginning of 'Caliban upon Setebos.' It does not mean the same thing, but something very different; and the deduction from this is the curious fact that Browning is an artist, and that consequently his processes of thought are not 'scientific in their precision and analysis.'

No criticism of Browning's poems can be vital, none in the face of the poems themselves can be even intelligible, which is not based upon the fact that he was successfully or otherwise a conscious and deliberate artist. He may have failed as an artist, though I do not think so; that is quite a different matter. But it is one thing to say that a man through vanity or ignorance has built an ugly cathedral, and quite another to say that he built it in a fit of absence of mind, and did not know whether he was building a lighthouse or a first-class hotel. Browning knew perfectly well what he was doing; and if the reader does not like his art, at least the author did. The general sentiment expressed in the statement that he did not care about form is simply the most ridiculous criticism that could be conceived. It would be far nearer the truth to say that he cared more for form than any other English poet who ever lived. He was always weaving and modelling and inventing new forms. Among all his two hundred to three hundred poems it would scarcely be an exaggeration to say that there are half as many different metres as there are different poems.

The great English poets who are supposed to have cared more for form than Browning did, cared less at least in this sense—that they were content to use old forms so long as they were certain that they had new ideas. Browning, on the other hand, no sooner had a new idea than he tried to make a new form to express it. Wordsworth and Shelley were really original poets; their attitude of thought and feeling marked without doubt certain great changes in literature and philosophy. Nevertheless, the 'Ode on the Intimations of Immortality' is a perfectly normal and traditional ode, and 'Prometheus Unbound' is a perfectly genuine and traditional Greek lyrical drama. But if we study Browning honestly, nothing will strike us more than that he really created a large number of quite novel and quite admirable artistic forms. It is too often forgotten what and how excellent these were. *The Ring and the Book*, for example, is an illuminating departure in literary method—the method of telling the same story several times and trusting to the variety of human character to turn it into several different and equally interesting stories. *Pippa Passes*, to take another example, is a new and most fruitful form, a series of detached dramas connected only by the presence of one fugitive and isolated figure. The invention of these things is not merely like the writing of a good poem—it is something like the invention of the sonnet or the Gothic arch. The poet who makes them does not merely create himself—he creates other poets. It is so in a degree long past enumeration with regard to Browning's smaller poems. Such a pious and horrible lyric as 'The Heretic's Tragedy,' for instance, is absolutely original, with its weird and almost blood-curdling echo verses, mocking echoes indeed—

> 'And clipt of his wings in Paris square,
>  They bring him now to be burned alive.
>
> *[And wanteth there grace of lute or clavicithern,*
>  *ye shall say to confirm him who singeth—*
>
> We bring John now to be burned alive.'

A hundred instances might, of course, be given. Milton's 'Sonnet on his Blindness,' or Keats's 'Ode on a Grecian Urn,' are both thoroughly original, but still we can point to other such sonnets and other such odes. But can any one mention any poem of exactly the same structural and literary type as 'Fears and Scruples,' as 'The Householder,' as 'House' or 'Shop,' as 'Nationality in Drinks,' as 'Sibrandus Schafnaburgensis,' as 'My Star,' as 'A Portrait,' as any of 'Ferishtah's Fancies,' as any of the 'Bad Dreams'?

The thing which ought to be said about Browning by those who do not enjoy him is simply that they do not like his form; that they have studied the form, and think it a bad form. If more people said things of this sort, the world of criticism would gain almost unspeakably in clarity and common honesty. Browning put himself before the world as a good poet. Let those who think he failed call him a bad poet, and there will be an end of the matter. There are many styles in art which perfectly competent æsthetic judges cannot endure. For instance, it would be perfectly legitimate for a strict lover of Gothic to say that one of the monstrous rococo altar-pieces in the Belgian churches with bulbous clouds and oaken sun-rays seven feet long, was, in his opinion, ugly. But surely it would be perfectly ridiculous for any one to say that it had no form. A man's actual feelings about it might be better expressed by saying that it had too much. To say that Browning was merely a thinker because you think 'Caliban upon Setebos' ugly, is precisely as absurd as it would be to call the author of the old Belgian altar-piece a man devoted only to the abstractions of religion. The truth about Browning is not that he was indifferent to technical beauty, but that he invented a particular kind of technical beauty to which any one else is free to be as indifferent as he chooses.

There is in this matter an extraordinary tendency to vague and unmeaning criticism. The usual way of criticising an author, particularly an author who has added something to the literary forms of the world, is to complain that his work does not contain something which is obviously the speciality of somebody else. The correct thing to say about Maeterlinck is that some play of his in which, let us say, a princess dies in a deserted tower by the sea, has a certain beauty, but that we look in vain in it for that robust geniality, that really boisterous will to live which may be found in *Martin Chuzzlewit*. The right thing to say about *Cyrano de Bergerac* is that it may have a certain kind of wit and spirit, but that it really throws no light on the duty of middle-aged married couples in Norway. It cannot be too much insisted upon that at least three-quarters of the blame and criticism commonly directed against artists and authors falls under this general objection, and is essentially valueless. Authors both great and small are, like everything else in existence, upon the whole greatly under-rated. They are blamed for not doing, not only what they have failed to do to reach their own ideal, but what they have never tried to do to reach every other writer's ideal. If we can show that Browning had a definite ideal of beauty and loyally pursued it, it is not necessary to prove that he could have written *In Memoriam* if he had tried.

Browning has suffered far more injustice from his admirers than from his opponents, for his admirers have for the most part got hold of the matter, so to speak, by the wrong end. They believe that what is ordinarily called the grotesque style of Browning was a kind of necessity boldly adopted by a great genius in order to express novel and profound ideas. But this is an entire mistake. What is called ugliness was to Browning not in the least a necessary evil, but a quite unnecessary luxury, which he enjoyed for its own sake. For reasons that we shall see presently in discussing the philosophical use of the grotesque, it did so happen that Browning's grotesque style was very suitable for the expression of his peculiar moral and metaphysical view. But the whole mass of poems will be misunderstood if we do not realise first of all that he had a love of the grotesque of the nature of art for art's sake. Here, for example, is a short distinct poem merely descriptive of one of those elfish German jugs in which it is to be presumed Tokay had been served to him. This is the whole poem, and a very good poem too—

'Up jumped Tokay on our table,
Like a pigmy castle-warder,
Dwarfish to see, but stout and able,
Arms and accoutrements all in order;
And fierce he looked North, then, wheeling South
Blew with his bugle a challenge to Drouth,
Cocked his flap-hat with the tosspot-feather,
Twisted his thumb in his red moustache,
Jingled his huge brass spurs together,
Tightened his waist with its Buda sash,
And then, with an impudence nought could abash,
Shrugged his hump-shoulder, to tell the beholder,
For twenty such knaves he would laugh but the bolder:
And so, with his sword-hilt gallantly jutting,
And dexter-hand on his haunch abutting,
Went the little man, Sir Ausbruch, strutting!'

I suppose there are Browning students in existence who would think that this poem contained something pregnant about the Temperance question, or was a marvellously subtle analysis of the romantic movement in Germany. But surely to most of us it is sufficiently apparent that Browning was simply fashioning a ridiculous knick-knack, exactly as if he were actually moulding one of these preposterous German jugs. Now before studying the real character of this Browningesque style, there is one general truth to be recognised about Browning's work. It is this—that it is absolutely necessary to remember that Browning had, like every other poet, his simple and indisputable failures, and that it is one thing to speak of the badness of his artistic failures, and quite another thing to speak of the badness of his artistic aim. Browning's style may be a good style, and yet exhibit many examples of a thoroughly bad use of it. On this point there is indeed a singularly unfair system of judgment used by the public towards the poets. It is very little realised that the vast majority of great poets have written an enormous amount of very bad poetry. The unfortunate Wordsworth is generally supposed to be almost alone in this; but any one who thinks so can scarcely have read a certain number of the minor poems of Byron and Shelley and Tennyson.

Now it is only just to Browning that his more uncouth effusions should not be treated as masterpieces by which he must stand or fall, but treated simply as his failures. It is really true that such a line as

'Irks fear the crop-full bird, frets doubt the maw-crammed beast?'

is a very ugly and a very bad line. But it is quite equally true that Tennyson's

'And that good man, the clergyman, has told me words of peace,'

is a very ugly and a very bad line. But people do not say that this proves that Tennyson was a mere crabbed controversialist and metaphysician. They say that it is a bad example of Tennyson's form; they do not say that it is a good example of Tennyson's indifference to form. Upon the whole, Browning exhibits far fewer instances of this failure in his own style than any other of the great poets, with the exception of one or two like Spenser and Keats, who seem to have a mysterious incapacity for writing bad poetry. But almost all original poets, particularly poets who have invented an artistic style, are subject to one most disastrous habit—the habit of writing imitations of themselves. Every now and then in the works of the noblest classical poets you will come upon passages which read like extracts from an American book of parodies. Swinburne, for example, when he wrote the couplet—

'From the lilies and languors of virtue
To the raptures and roses of vice,'

wrote what is nothing but a bad imitation of himself, an imitation which seems indeed to have the wholly unjust and uncritical object of proving that the Swinburnian melody is a mechanical scheme of initial letters. Or again, Mr Rudyard Kipling when he wrote the line—

'Or ride with the reckless seraphim on the rim of a red-maned star,'

was caricaturing himself in the harshest and least sympathetic spirit of American humour. This tendency is, of course, the result of the self-consciousness and theatricality of modern life in which each of us is forced to conceive ourselves as part of a *dramatis personæ* and act perpetually in character. Browning sometimes yielded to this temptation to be a great deal too like himself.

> 'Will I widen thee out till thou turnest
> From Margaret Minnikin mou' by God's grace,
> To Muckle-mouth Meg in good earnest.'

This sort of thing is not to be defended in Browning any more than in Swinburne. But, on the other hand, it is not to be attributed in Swinburne to a momentary exaggeration, and in Browning to a vital æsthetic deficiency. In the case of Swinburne, we all feel that the question is not whether that particular preposterous couplet about lilies and roses redounds to the credit of the Swinburnian style, but whether it would be possible in any other style than the Swinburnian to have written the Hymn to Proserpine. In the same way, the essential issue about Browning as an artist is not whether he, in common with Byron, Wordsworth, Shelley, Tennyson, and Swinburne, sometimes wrote bad poetry, but whether in any other style except Browning's you could have achieved the precise artistic effect which is achieved by such incomparable lyrics as 'The Patriot' or 'The Laboratory.' The answer must be in the negative, and in that answer lies the whole justification of Browning as an artist.

The question now arises, therefore, what was his conception of his functions as an artist? We have already agreed that his artistic originality concerned itself chiefly with the serious use of the grotesque. It becomes necessary, therefore, to ask what is the serious use of the grotesque, and what relation does the grotesque bear to the eternal and fundamental elements in life?

One of the most curious things to notice about popular æsthetic criticism is the number of phrases it will be found to use which are intended to express an æsthetic failure, and which express merely an æsthetic variety. Thus, for instance, the traveller will often hear the advice from local lovers of the picturesque, 'The scenery round such and such a place has no interest; it is quite flat.' To disparage scenery as quite flat is, of course, like disparaging a swan as quite white, or an Italian sky as quite blue. Flatness is a sublime quality in certain landscapes, just as rockiness is a sublime quality in others. In the same way there are a great number of phrases commonly used in order to disparage such writers as Browning which do not in fact disparage, but merely describe them. One of the most distinguished of Browning's biographers and critics says of him, for example, 'He has never meant to be rugged, but has become so in striving after strength.' To say that Browning never tried to be rugged is to say that Edgar Allan Poe never tried to be gloomy, or that Mr W. S. Gilbert never tried to be extravagant. The whole issue depends upon whether we realise the simple and essential fact that ruggedness is a mode of art like gloominess or extravagance. Some poems ought to be rugged, just as some poems ought to be smooth. When we see a drift of stormy and fantastic clouds at sunset, we do not say that the cloud is beautiful although it is ragged at the edges. When we see a gnarled and sprawling oak, we do not say that it is fine although it is twisted. When we see a mountain, we do not say that it is impressive although it is rugged, nor do we say apologetically that it never meant to be rugged, but became so in its striving after strength. Now, to say that Browning's poems, artistically considered, are fine although they are rugged, is quite as absurd as to say that a rock, artistically considered, is fine although it is rugged. Ruggedness being an essential quality in the universe, there is that in man which responds to it as to the striking of any other chord of the eternal harmonies. As the children of nature, we are akin not only to the stars and flowers, but also to the toad-stools and the monstrous tropical birds. And it is to be repeated as the essential of the question that on this side of our nature we do emphatically love the form of the toad-stools, and not merely some complicated botanical and moral lessons which the philosopher may draw from them. For example, just as there is such a thing as a poetical metre being beautifully light or beautifully grave and haunting, so there is such a thing as a poetical metre being beautifully rugged. In the old ballads, for instance, every person of literary taste will be struck by a certain attractiveness in the bold, varying, irregular verse—

> 'He is either himsell a devil frae hell,
>  Or else his mother a witch maun be;
>  I wadna have ridden that wan water
>  For a' the gowd in Christentie,'

is quite as pleasing to the ear in its own way as

> 'There's a bower of roses by Bendemeer stream,
>  And the nightingale sings in it all the night long,'

is in another way. Browning had an unrivalled ear for this particular kind of staccato music. The absurd notion that he had no sense of melody in verse is only possible to people who think that there is no melody in verse which is not an imitation of Swinburne. To give a satisfactory idea of Browning's rhythmic originality would be impossible without quotations more copious than entertaining. But the essential point has been suggested.

> 'They were purple of raiment and golden,
> Filled full of thee, fiery with wine,
> Thy lovers in haunts unbeholden,
> In marvellous chambers of thine,'

is beautiful language, but not the only sort of beautiful language. This, for instance, has also a tune in it—

> 'I—"next poet." No, my hearties,
> I nor am, nor fain would be!
> Choose your chiefs and pick your parties,
> Not one soul revolt to me!
> \*    \*    \*    \*    \*
> Which of you did I enable
> Once to slip inside my breast,
> There to catalogue and label
> What I like least, what love best,
> Hope and fear, believe and doubt of,
> Seek and shun, respect, deride,
> Who has right to make a rout of
> Rarities he found inside?'

This quick, gallantly stepping measure also has its own kind of music, and the man who cannot feel it can never have enjoyed the sound of soldiers marching by. This, then, roughly is the main fact to remember about Browning's poetical method, or about any one's poetical method—that the question is not whether that method is the best in the world, but the question whether there are not certain things which can only be conveyed by that method. It is perfectly true, for instance, that a really lofty and lucid line of Tennyson, such as—

> 'Thou art the highest, and most human too'

and

> 'We needs must love the highest when we see it'

would really be made the worse for being translated into Browning. It would probably become

'High's human; man loves best, best visible,'

and would lose its peculiar clarity and dignity and courtly plainness. But it is quite equally true that any really characteristic fragment of Browning, if it were only the tempestuous scolding of the organist in 'Master Hugues of Saxe-Gotha'—

> 'Hallo, you sacristan, show us a light there!
>    Down it dips, gone like a rocket.
> What, you want, do you, to come unawares,
> Sweeping the church up for first morning-prayers,
> And find a poor devil has ended his cares
> At the foot of your rotten-runged rat-riddled stairs?
>    Do I carry the moon in my pocket?'

—it is quite equally true that this outrageous gallop of rhymes ending with a frantic astronomical image would lose in energy and spirit if it were written in a conventional and classical style, and ran—

> 'What must I deem then that thou dreamest to find
> Disjected bones adrift upon the stair
> Thou sweepest clean, or that thou deemest that I
> Pouch in my wallet the vice-regal sun?'

Is it not obvious that this statelier version might be excellent poetry of its kind, and yet would be bad exactly in so far as it was good; that it would lose all the swing, the rush, the energy of the preposterous and grotesque original? In fact, we may see how unmanageable is this classical treatment of the essentially absurd in Tennyson himself. The humorous passages in *The Princess*, though often really humorous in themselves, always appear forced and feeble because they have to be restrained by a certain metrical dignity, and the mere idea of such restraint is incompatible with humour. If Browning had written the passage which opens *The Princess*, descriptive of the 'larking' of the villagers in the magnate's park, he would have spared us nothing; he would not have spared us the shrill uneducated voices and the unburied bottles of ginger beer. He would have crammed the poem with uncouth similes; he would have changed the metre a hundred times; he would have broken into doggerel and into rhapsody; but he would have left, when all is said and done, as he leaves in that paltry fragment of the grumbling organist, the impression of a certain eternal human energy. Energy and joy, the father and the mother of the grotesque, would have ruled the poem. We should have felt of that rowdy gathering little but the sensation of which Mr Henley writes—

'Praise the generous gods for giving,
    In this world of sin and strife,
With some little time for living,
    Unto each the joy of life,'

the thought that every wise man has when looking at a Bank Holiday crowd at Margate.

To ask why Browning enjoyed this perverse and fantastic style most would be to go very deep into his spirit indeed, probably a great deal deeper than it is possible to go. But it is worth while to suggest tentatively the general function of the grotesque in art generally and in his art in particular. There is one very curious idea into which we have been hypnotised by the more eloquent poets, and that is that nature in the sense of what is ordinarily called the country is a thing entirely stately and beautiful as those terms are commonly understood. The whole world of the fantastic, all things top-heavy, lop-sided, and non-sensical are conceived as the work of man, gargoyles, German jugs, Chinese pots, political caricatures, burlesque epics, the pictures of Mr Aubrey Beardsley and the puns of Robert Browning. But in truth a part, and a very large part, of the sanity and power of nature lies in the fact that out of her comes all this instinct of caricature. Nature may present itself to the poet too often as consisting of stars and lilies; but these are not poets who live in the country; they are men who go to the country for inspiration and could no more live in the country than they could go to bed in Westminster Abbey. Men who live in the heart of nature, farmers and peasants, know that nature means cows and pigs, and creatures more humorous than can be found in a whole sketch-book of Callot. And the element of the grotesque in art, like the element of the grotesque in nature, means, in the main, energy, the energy which takes its own forms and goes its own way. Browning's verse, in so far as it is grotesque, is not complex or artificial; it is natural and in the legitimate tradition of nature. The verse sprawls like the trees, dances like the dust; it is ragged like the thundercloud, it is top-heavy like the toad-stool. Energy which disregards the standard of classical art is in nature as it is in Browning. The same sense of the uproarious force in things which makes Browning dwell on the oddity of a fungus or a jellyfish makes him dwell on the oddity of a philosophical idea. Here, for example, we have a random instance from 'The Englishman in Italy' of the way in which Browning, when he was most Browning, regarded physical nature.

'And pitch down his basket before us,
   All trembling alive
With pink and grey jellies, your sea-fruit;
   You touch the strange lumps,
And mouths gape there, eyes open, all manner
   Of horns and of humps,
Which only the fisher looks grave at.'

Nature might mean flowers to Wordsworth and grass to Walt Whitman, but to Browning it really meant such things as these, the monstrosities and living mysteries of the sea. And just as these strange things meant to Browning energy in the physical world, so strange thoughts and strange images meant to him energy in the mental world. When, in one of his later poems, the professional mystic is seeking in a supreme moment of sincerity to explain that small things may be filled with God as well as great, he uses the very same kind of image, the image of a shapeless sea-beast, to embody that noble conception.

'The Name comes close behind a stomach-cyst,
   The simplest of creations, just a sac
That's mouth, heart, legs, and belly at once, yet lives
   And feels, and could do neither, we conclude,
If simplified still further one degree.'

                                           (Sludge.)

These bulbous, indescribable sea-goblins are the first thing on which the eye of the poet lights in looking on a landscape, and the last in the significance of which he trusts in demonstrating the mercy of the Everlasting.

There is another and but slightly different use of the grotesque, but which is definitely valuable in Browning's poetry, and indeed in all poetry. To present a matter in a grotesque manner does certainly tend to touch the nerve of surprise and thus to draw attention to the intrinsically miraculous character of the object itself. It is difficult to give examples of the proper use of grotesqueness without becoming too grotesque. But we should all agree that if St Paul's Cathedral were suddenly presented to us upside down we should, for the moment, be more surprised at it, and look at it more than we have done all the centuries during which it has rested on its foundations. Now it is the supreme function of the philosopher of the grotesque to make the world stand on its head that people may look at it. If we say 'a man is a man' we awaken no sense of the fantastic, however much we ought to, but if we say, in the language of the old satirist, 'that man is a two-legged bird, without feathers,' the phrase does, for a moment, make us look at man from the outside and gives us a thrill in his presence. When the author of the Book of Job insists upon the huge, half-witted, apparently unmeaning magnificence and might of Behemoth, the hippopotamus, he is appealing precisely to this sense of wonder provoked by the grotesque. 'Canst thou play with him as with a bird, canst thou bind him for thy maidens?' he says in an admirable passage. The notion of the hippopotamus as a household pet is curiously in the spirit of the humour of Browning.

But when it is clearly understood that Browning's love of the fantastic in style was a perfectly serious artistic love, when we understand that he enjoyed working in that style, as a Chinese potter might enjoy making dragons, or a mediæval mason making devils, there yet remains something definite which must be laid to his account as a fault. He certainly had a capacity for becoming perfectly childish in his indulgence in ingenuities that have nothing to do with poetry at all, such as puns, and rhymes, and grammatical structures that only just fit into each other like a Chinese puzzle. Probably it was only one of the marks of his singular vitality, curiosity, and interest in details. He was certainly one of those somewhat rare men who are fierily ambitious both in large things and in small. He prided himself on having written *The Ring and the Book*, and he also prided himself on knowing good wine when he tasted it. He prided himself on re-establishing optimism on a new foundation, and it is to be presumed, though it is somewhat difficult to imagine, that he prided himself on such rhymes as the following in *Pacchiarotto*: —

> 'The wolf, fox, bear, and monkey,
> By piping advice in one key—
> That his pipe should play a prelude
> To something heaven-tinged not hell-hued,
> Something not harsh but docile,
> Man-liquid, not man-fossil.'

This writing, considered as writing, can only be regarded as a kind of joke, and most probably Browning considered it so himself. It has nothing at all to do with that powerful and symbolic use of the grotesque which may be found in such admirable passages as this from 'Holy Cross Day': —

> 'Give your first groan—compunction's at work;
> And soft! from a Jew you mount to a Turk.
> Lo, Micah—the self-same beard on chin
> He was four times already converted in!'

This is the serious use of the grotesque. Through it passion and philosophy are as well expressed as through any other medium. But the rhyming frenzy of

Browning has no particular relation even to the poems in which it occurs. It is not a dance to any measure; it can only be called the horse-play of literature. It may be noted, for example, as a rather curious fact, that the ingenious rhymes are generally only mathematical triumphs, not triumphs of any kind of assonance. 'The Pied Piper of Hamelin,' a poem written for children, and bound in general to be lucid and readable, ends with a rhyme which it is physically impossible for any one to say:—

> 'And, whether they pipe us free, fróm rats or fróm mice,
> If we've promised them aught, let us keep our promise!'

This queer trait in Browning, his inability to keep a kind of demented ingenuity even out of poems in which it was quite inappropriate, is a thing which must be recognised, and recognised all the more because as a whole he was a very perfect artist, and a particularly perfect artist in the use of the grotesque. But everywhere when we go a little below the surface in Browning we find that there was something in him perverse and unusual despite all his working normality and simplicity. His mind was perfectly wholesome, but it was not made exactly like the ordinary mind. It was like a piece of strong wood with a knot in it.

The quality of what can only be called buffoonery which is under discussion is indeed one of the many things in which Browning was more of an Elizabethan than a Victorian. He was like the Elizabethans in their belief in the normal man, in their gorgeous and over-loaded language, above all in their feeling for learning as an enjoyment and almost a frivolity. But there was nothing in which he was so thoroughly Elizabethan, and even Shakespearian, as in this fact, that when he felt inclined to write a page of quite uninteresting nonsense, he immediately did so. Many great writers have contrived to be tedious, and apparently aimless, while expounding some thought which they believed to be grave and profitable; but this frivolous stupidity had not been found in any great writer since the time of Rabelais and the time of the Elizabethans. In many of the comic scenes of Shakespeare we have precisely this elephantine ingenuity, this hunting of a pun to death through three pages. In the Elizabethan dramatists and in Browning it is no doubt to a certain extent the mark of a real hilarity. People must be very happy to be so easily amused.

In the case of what is called Browning's obscurity, the question is somewhat more difficult to handle. Many people have supposed Browning to be profound because he was obscure, and many other people, hardly less mistaken, have supposed him to be obscure because he was profound. He was frequently profound, he was occasionally obscure, but as a matter of fact the two have little or nothing to do with each other. Browning's dark and elliptical mode of speech, like his love of the grotesque, was simply a characteristic of his, a trick of his temperament, and had little or nothing to do with whether what he was expressing was profound or superficial. Suppose, for example, that a person well read in English poetry but unacquainted with Browning's style were earnestly invited to consider the following verse:—

> 'Hobbs hints blue—straight he turtle eats.
> Nobbs prints blue—claret crowns his cup.
> Nokes outdares Stokes in azure feats—
> Both gorge. Who fished the murex up?
> What porridge had John Keats?'

The individual so confronted would say without hesitation that it must indeed be an abstruse and indescribable thought which could only be conveyed by remarks so completely disconnected. But the point of the matter is that the thought contained in this amazing verse is not abstruse or philosophical at all, but is a perfectly ordinary and straightforward comment, which any one might have made upon an obvious fact of life. The whole verse of course begins to explain itself, if we know the meaning of the word 'murex,' which is the name of a sea-shell, out of which was made the celebrated blue dye of Tyre. The poet takes this blue dye as a simile for a new fashion in literature, and points out that Hobbs, Nobbs, etc., obtain fame and comfort by merely using the dye from the shell; and adds the perfectly natural comment:—

> '... Who fished the murex up?
> What porridge had John Keats?'

So that the verse is not subtle, and was not meant to be subtle, but is a perfectly casual piece of sentiment at the end of a light poem. Browning is not obscure because he has such deep things to say, any more than he is grotesque because he has such new things to say. He is both of these things primarily, because he likes to express himself in a particular manner. The manner is as natural to him as a man's physical voice, and it is abrupt, sketchy, allusive, and full of gaps. Here comes in the fundamental difference between Browning and such a writer as George Meredith, with whom the Philistine satirist would so often in the matter of complexity class him. The works of George Meredith are, as it were, obscure even when we know what they mean. They deal with nameless emotions, fugitive sensations, sub-conscious certainties and uncertainties, and it really requires a somewhat curious and unfamiliar mode of speech to indicate the presence of these. But the great part of Browning's actual sentiments, and almost all the finest and most literary of them, are perfectly plain and popular and eternal sentiments. Meredith is really a singer producing strange notes and cadences difficult to follow because of the delicate rhythm of the song he sings. Browning is simply a great demagogue, with an impediment in his speech. Or rather, to speak more strictly, Browning is a man whose excitement for the glory of the obvious is so great that his speech becomes disjointed and precipitate: he becomes eccentric through his advocacy of the ordinary, and goes mad for the love of sanity.

If Browning and George Meredith were each describing the same act, they might both be obscure, but their obscurities would be entirely different. Suppose, for instance, they were describing even so prosaic and material an act as a man being knocked downstairs by another man to whom he had given the lie, Meredith's description would refer to something which an ordinary observer would not see, or at least could not describe. It might be a sudden sense of anarchy in the brain of the assaulter, or a stupefaction and stunned serenity in that of the object of the assault. He might write, 'Wainwood's "Men vary in veracity," brought the baronet's arm up. He felt the doors of his brain burst, and Wainwood a swift rushing of himself through air accompanied with a clarity as of the annihilated.' Meredith, in other words, would speak queerly because he was describing queer mental experiences. But Browning might simply be describing the material incident of the man being knocked downstairs, and his description would run:—

> 'What then? "You lie" and doormat below stairs
> Takes bump from back.'

This is not subtlety, but merely a kind of insane swiftness. Browning is not like Meredith, anxious to pause and examine the sensations of the combatants, nor does he become obscure through this anxiety. He is only so anxious to get his man to the bottom of the stairs quickly that he leaves out about half the story.

Many who could understand that ruggedness might be an artistic quality, would decisively, and in most cases rightly, deny that obscurity could under any conceivable circumstances be an artistic quality. But here again Browning's work requires a somewhat more cautious and sympathetic analysis. There is a certain kind of fascination, a strictly artistic fascination, which arises from a matter being hinted at in such a way as to leave a certain tormenting uncertainty even at the end. It is well sometimes to half understand a poem in the same manner that we half understand the world. One of the deepest and strangest of all human moods is the mood which will suddenly strike us perhaps in a garden at night, or deep in sloping meadows, the feeling that every flower and leaf has just uttered something stupendously direct and important, and that we have by a prodigy of imbecility not heard or understood it. There is a certain poetic value, and that a genuine one, in this sense of having missed the full meaning of things. There is beauty, not only in wisdom, but in this dazed and dramatic ignorance.

But in truth it is very difficult to keep pace with all the strange and unclassified artistic merits of Browning. He was always trying experiments; sometimes he failed, producing clumsy and irritating metres, top-heavy and over-concentrated thought. Far more often he triumphed, producing a crowd of boldy designed poems, every one of which taken separately might have founded an artistic school. But whether successful or unsuccessful, he never ceased from his fierce hunt after poetic novelty. He never became a conservative. The last book he published in his life-time, *Parleyings with Certain People of Importance in their Day*, was a new poem, and more revolutionary than *Paracelsus*. This is the true light in which to regard Browning as an artist. He had determined to leave no spot of the cosmos unadorned by his poetry which he could find it possible to adorn. An admirable example can be found in that splendid poem 'Childe Roland to the Dark Tower came.' It is the hint of an entirely new and curious type of poetry, the poetry of the shabby and hungry aspect of the earth itself. Daring poets who wished to escape from conventional gardens and orchards had long been in the habit of celebrating the poetry of rugged and gloomy landscapes, but Browning is not content with this. He insists upon celebrating the poetry of mean landscapes. That sense of scrubbiness in nature as of a man unshaved, had never been conveyed with this enthusiasm and primeval gusto before.

> 'If there pushed any ragged thistle-stalk
>   Above its mates, the head was chopped; the bents
>   Were jealous else. What made those holes and rents
> In the dock's harsh swarth leaves, bruised as to baulk
> All hope of greenness? 'tis a brute must walk
>   Pashing their life out, with a brute's intents.'

This is a perfect realisation of that eerie sentiment which comes upon us, not so often among mountains and water-falls, as it does on some half-starved common at twilight, or in walking down some grey mean street. It is the song of the beauty of refuse; and Browning was the first to sing it. Oddly enough it has been one of the poems about which most of those pedantic and trivial questions have been asked, which are asked invariably by those who treat Browning as a science instead of a poet, 'What does the poem of "Childe Roland" mean?' The only genuine answer to this is, 'What does anything mean?' Does the earth mean nothing? Do grey skies and wastes covered with thistles mean nothing? Does an old horse turned out to graze mean nothing? If it does, there is but one further truth to be added—that everything means nothing.

# The Philosophy of Browning

The great fault of most of the appreciation of Browning lies in the fact that it conceives the moral and artistic value of his work to lie in what is called 'the message of Browning,' or 'the teaching of Browning,' or, in other words, in the mere opinions of Browning. Now Browning had opinions, just as he had a dress-suit or a vote for Parliament. He did not hesitate to express these opinions any more than he would have hesitated to fire off a gun, or open an umbrella, if he had possessed those articles, and realised their value. For example, he had, as his students and eulogists have constantly stated, certain definite opinions about the spiritual function of love, or the intellectual basis of Christianity. Those opinions were very striking and very solid, as everything was which came out of Browning's mind. His two great theories of the universe may be expressed in two comparatively parallel phrases. The first was what may be called the hope which lies in the imperfection of man. The characteristic poem of 'Old Pictures in Florence' expresses very quaintly and beautifully the idea that some hope may always be based on deficiency itself; in other words, that in so far as man is a one-legged or a one-eyed creature, there is something about his appearance which indicates that he should have another leg and another eye. The poem suggests admirably that such a sense of incompleteness may easily be a great advance upon a sense of completeness, that the part may easily and obviously be greater than the whole. And from this Browning draws, as he is fully justified in drawing, a definite hope for immortality and the larger scale of life. For nothing is more certain than that though this world is the only world that we have known, or of which we could even dream, the fact does remain that we have named it 'a strange world.' In other words, we have certainly felt that this world did not explain itself, that something in its complete and patent picture has been omitted. And Browning was right in saying that in a cosmos where incompleteness implies completeness, life implies immortality. This then was the first of the doctrines or opinions of Browning: the hope that lies in the imperfection of man. The second of the great Browning doctrines requires some audacity to express. It can only be properly stated as the hope that lies in the imperfection of God.

That is to say, that Browning held that sorrow and self-denial, if they were the burdens of man, were also his privileges. He held that these stubborn sorrows and obscure valours might, to use a yet more strange expression, have provoked the envy of the Almighty. If man has self-sacrifice and God has none, then man has in the Universe a secret and blasphemous superiority. And this tremendous story of a Divine jealousy Browning reads into the story of the Crucifixion. If the Creator had not been crucified He would not have been as great as thousands of wretched fanatics among His own creatures. It is needless to insist upon this point; any one who wishes to read it splendidly expressed need only be referred to 'Saul.' But these are emphatically the two main doctrines or opinions of Browning which I have ventured to characterise roughly as the hope in the imperfection of man, and more boldly as the hope in the imperfection of God. They are great thoughts, thoughts written by a great man, and they raise noble and beautiful doubts on behalf of faith which the human spirit will never answer or exhaust. But about them in connection with Browning there nevertheless remains something to be added.

Browning was, as most of his upholders and all his opponents say, an optimist. His theory, that man's sense of his own imperfection implies a design of perfection, is a very good argument for optimism. His theory that man's knowledge of and desire for self-sacrifice implies God's knowledge of and desire for self-sacrifice is another very good argument for optimism. But any one will make the deepest and blackest and most incurable mistake about Browning who imagines that his optimism was founded on any arguments for optimism. Because he had a strong intellect, because he had a strong power of conviction, he conceived and developed and asserted these doctrines of the incompleteness of Man and the sacrifice of Omnipotence. But these doctrines were the symptoms of his optimism, they were not its origin. It is surely obvious that no one can be argued into optimism since no one can be argued into happiness. Browning's optimism was not founded on opinions which were the work of Browning, but on life which was the work of God. One of Browning's most celebrated biographers has said that something of Browning's theology must be put down to his possession of a good digestion. The remark was of course, like all remarks touching the tragic subject of digestion, intended to be funny and to convey some kind of doubt or diminution touching the value of Browning's faith. But if we examine the matter with somewhat greater care we shall see that it is indeed a thorough compliment to that faith. Nobody, strictly speaking, is happier on account of his digestion. He is happy because he is so constituted as to forget all about it. Nobody really is convulsed with delight at the thought of the ingenious machinery which he possesses inside him; the thing which delights him is simply the full possession of his own human body. I cannot in the least understand why a good digestion—that is, a good body—should not be held to be as mystic a benefit as a sunset or the first flower of spring. But there is about digestion this peculiarity throwing a great light on human pessimism, that it is one of the many things which we never speak of as existing until they go wrong. We should think it ridiculous to speak of a man as suffering from his boots if we meant that he had really no boots. But we do speak of a man suffering from digestion when we mean that he suffers from a lack of digestion. In the same way we speak of a man suffering from nerves when we mean that his nerves are more inefficient than any one else's nerves. If any one wishes to see how grossly language can degenerate, he need only compare the old optimistic use of the word nervous, which we employ in speaking of a nervous grip, with the new pessimistic use of the word, which we employ in speaking of a nervous manner. And as digestion is a good thing which sometimes goes wrong, as nerves are good things which sometimes go wrong, so existence itself in the eyes of Browning and all the great optimists is a good thing which sometimes goes wrong. He held himself as free to draw his inspiration from the gift of good health as from the gift of learning or the gift of fellowship. But he held that such gifts were in life innumerable and varied, and that every man, or at least almost every man, possessed some window looking out on this essential excellence of things.

Browning's optimism then, since we must continue to use this somewhat inadequate word, was a result of experience—experience which is for some mysterious reason generally understood in the sense of sad or disillusioning experience. An old gentleman rebuking a little boy for eating apples in a tree is in the common conception the type of experience. If he really wished to be a type of experience he would climb up the tree himself and proceed to experience the apples. Browning's faith was founded upon joyful experience, not in the sense that he selected his joyful experiences and ignored his painful ones, but in the sense that his joyful experiences selected themselves and stood out in his memory by virtue of their own extraordinary intensity of colour. He did not use experience in that mean and pompous sense in which it is used by the worldling advanced in years. He rather used it in that healthier and more joyful sense in which it is used at revivalist meetings. In the Salvation Army a man's experiences mean his experiences of the mercy of God, and to Browning the meaning was much the same. But the revivalists' confessions deal mostly with experiences of prayer and praise; Browning's dealt pre-eminently with what may be called his own subject, the experiences of love.

And this quality of Browning's optimism, the quality of detail, is also a very typical quality. Browning's optimism is of that ultimate and unshakeable order that is founded upon the absolute sight, and sound, and smell, and handling of things. If a man had gone up to Browning and asked him with all the solemnity of the eccentric, 'Do you think life is worth living?' it is interesting to conjecture what his answer might have been. If he had been for the moment under the influence of the orthodox rationalistic deism of the theologian he would have said, 'Existence is justified by its manifest design, its manifest adaptation of means to ends,' or, in other words, 'Existence is justified by its completeness.' If, on the other hand, he had been influenced by his own serious intellectual theories he would have said, 'Existence is justified by its air of growth and doubtfulness,' or, in other words, 'Existence is justified by its incompleteness.' But if he had not been influenced in his answer either by the accepted opinions, or by his own opinions, but had simply answered the question 'Is life worth living?' with the real, vital answer that awaited it in his own soul, he would have said as likely as not, 'Crimson toadstools in Hampshire.' Some plain, glowing picture of this sort left on his mind would be his real verdict on what the universe had meant to him. To his traditions hope was traced to order, to his speculations hope was traced to disorder. But to Browning himself hope was traced to something like red toadstools. His mysticism was not of that idle and wordy type which believes that a flower is symbolical of life; it was rather of that deep and eternal type which believes that life, a mere abstraction, is symbolical of a flower. With him the great concrete experiences which God made always come first; his own deductions and speculations about them always second. And in this point we find the real peculiar inspiration of his very original poems.

One of the very few critics who seem to have got near to the actual secret of Browning's optimism is Mr Santayana in his most interesting book *Interpretations of Poetry and Religion*. He, in contradistinction to the vast mass of Browning's admirers, had discovered what was the real root virtue of Browning's poetry; and the curious thing is, that having discovered that root virtue, he thinks it is a vice. He describes the poetry of Browning most truly as the poetry of barbarism, by which he means the poetry which utters the primeval and indivisible emotions. 'For the barbarian is the man who regards his passions as their own excuse for being, who does not domesticate them either by understanding their cause, or by conceiving their ideal goal.' Whether this be or be not a good definition of the barbarian, it is an excellent and perfect definition of the poet. It might, perhaps, be suggested that barbarians, as a matter of fact, are generally highly traditional and respectable persons who would not put a feather wrong in their head-gear, and who generally have very few feelings and think very little about those they have. It is when we have grown to a greater and more civilised stature that we begin to realise and put to ourselves intellectually the great feelings that sleep in the depths of us. Thus it is that the literature of our day has steadily advanced towards a passionate simplicity, and we become more primeval as the world grows older, until Whitman writes huge and chaotic psalms to express the sensations of a schoolboy out fishing, and Maeterlinck embodies in symbolic dramas the feelings of a child in the dark.

Thus, Mr Santayana is, perhaps, the most valuable of all the Browning critics. He has gone out of his way to endeavour to realise what it is that repels him in Browning, and he has discovered the fault which none of Browning's opponents have discovered. And in this he has discovered the merit which none of Browning's admirers have discovered. Whether the quality be a good or a bad quality, Mr Santayana is perfectly right. The whole of Browning's poetry does rest upon primitive feeling; and the only comment to be added is that so does the whole of every one else's poetry. Poetry deals entirely with those great eternal and mainly forgotten wishes which are the ultimate despots of existence. Poetry presents things as they are to our emotions, not as they are to any theory, however plausible, or any argument, however conclusive. If love is in truth a glorious vision, poetry will say that it is a glorious vision, and no philosophers will persuade poetry to say that it is the exaggeration of the instinct of sex. If bereavement is a bitter and continually aching thing, poetry will say that it is so, and no philosophers will persuade poetry to say that it is an evolutionary stage of great biological value. And here comes in the whole value and object of poetry, that it is perpetually challenging all systems with the test of a terrible sincerity. The practical value of poetry is that it is realistic upon a point upon which nothing else can be realistic, the point of the actual desires of man. Ethics is the science of actions, but poetry is the science of motives. Some actions are ugly, and therefore some parts of ethics are ugly. But all motives are beautiful, or present themselves for the moment as beautiful, and therefore all poetry is beautiful. If poetry deals with the basest matter, with the shedding of blood for gold, it ought to suggest the gold as well as the blood. Only poetry can realise motives, because motives are all pictures of happiness. And the supreme and most practical value of poetry is this, that in poetry, as in music, a note is struck which expresses beyond the power of rational statement a condition of mind, and all actions arise from a condition of mind. Prose can only use a large and clumsy notation; it can only say that a man is miserable, or that a man is happy; it is forced to ignore that there are a million diverse kinds of misery and a million diverse kinds of happiness. Poetry alone, with the first throb of its metre, can tell us whether the depression is the kind of depression that drives a man to suicide, or the kind of depression that drives him to the Tivoli. Poetry can tell us whether the happiness is the happiness that sends a man to a restaurant, or the much richer and fuller happiness that sends him to church.

Now the supreme value of Browning as an optimist lies in this that we have been examining, that beyond all his conclusions, and deeper than all his arguments, he was passionately interested in and in love with existence. If the heavens had fallen, and all the waters of the earth run with blood, he would still have been interested in existence, if possible a little more so. He is a great poet of human joy for precisely the reason of which Mr Santayana complains: that his happiness is primal, and beyond the reach of philosophy. He is something far more convincing, far more comforting, far more religiously significant than an optimist: he is a happy man.

This happiness he finds, as every man must find happiness, in his own way. He does not find the great part of his joy in those matters in which most poets find felicity. He finds much of it in those matters in which most poets find ugliness and vulgarity. He is to a considerable extent the poet of towns. 'Do you care for nature much?' a friend of his asked him. 'Yes, a great deal,' he said, 'but for human beings a great deal more.' Nature, with its splendid and soothing sanity, has the power of convincing most poets of the essential worthiness of things. There are few poets who, if they escaped from the rowdiest waggonette of trippers, could not be quieted again and exalted by dropping into a small wayside field. The speciality of Browning is rather that he would have been quieted and exalted by the waggonette.

To Browning, probably the beginning and end of all optimism was to be found in the faces in the street. To him they were all the masks of a deity, the heads of a hundred-headed Indian god of nature. Each one of them looked towards some quarter of the heavens, not looked upon by any other eyes. Each one of them wore some expression, some blend of eternal joy and eternal sorrow, not to be found in any other countenance. The sense of the absolute sanctity of human difference was the deepest of all his senses. He was hungrily interested in all human things, but it would have been quite impossible to have said of him that he loved humanity. He did not love humanity but men. His sense of the difference between one man and another would have made the thought of melting them into a lump called humanity simply loathsome and prosaic. It would have been to him like playing four hundred beautiful airs at once. The mixture would not combine all, it would lose all. Browning believed that to every man that ever lived upon this earth had been given a definite and peculiar confidence of God. Each one of us was engaged on secret service; each one of us had a peculiar message; each one of us was the founder of a religion. Of that religion our thoughts, our faces, our bodies, our hats, our boots, our tastes, our virtues, and even our vices, were more or less fragmentary and inadequate expressions.

In the delightful memoirs of that very remarkable man Sir Charles Gavan Duffy, there is an extremely significant and interesting anecdote about Browning, the point of which appears to have attracted very little attention. Duffy was dining with Browning and John Forster and happened to make some chance allusion to his own adherence to the Roman Catholic faith, when Forster remarked, half jestingly, that he did not suppose that Browning would like him any the better for that. Browning would seem to have opened his eyes with some astonishment. He immediately asked why Forster should suppose him hostile to the Roman Church. Forster and Duffy replied almost simultaneously, by referring to 'Bishop Blougram's Apology,' which had just appeared, and asking whether the portrait of the sophistical and self-indulgent priest had not been intended for a satire on Cardinal Wiseman. 'Certainly,' replied Browning cheerfully, 'I intended it for Cardinal Wiseman, but I don't consider it a satire, there is nothing hostile about it.' This is the real truth which lies at the heart of what may be called the great sophistical monologues which Browning wrote in later years. They are not satires or attacks upon their subjects, they are not even harsh and unfeeling exposures of them. They are defences; they say or are intended to say the best that can be said for the persons with whom they deal. But very few people in this world would care to listen to the real defence of their own characters. The real defence, the defence which belongs to the Day of Judgment, would make such damaging admissions, would clear away so many artificial virtues, would tell such tragedies of weakness and failure, that a man would sooner be misunderstood and censured by the world than exposed to that awful and merciless eulogy. One of the most practically difficult matters which arise from the code of manners and the conventions of life, is that we cannot properly justify a human being, because that justification would involve the admission of things which may not conventionally be admitted. We might explain and make human and respectable, for example, the conduct of some old fighting politician, who, for the good of his party and his country, acceded to measures of which he disapproved; but we cannot, because we are not allowed to admit that he ever acceded to measures of which he disapproved. We might touch the life of many dissolute public men with pathos, and a kind of defeated courage, by telling the truth about the history of their sins. But we should throw the world into an uproar if we hinted that they had any. Thus the decencies of civilisation do not merely make it impossible to revile a man, they make it impossible to praise him.

Browning, in such poems as 'Bishop Blougram's Apology,' breaks this first mask of goodness in order to break the second mask of evil, and gets to the real goodness at last; he dethrones a saint in order to humanise a scoundrel. This is one typical side of the real optimism of Browning. And there is indeed little danger that such optimism will become weak and sentimental and popular, the refuge of every idler, the excuse of every ne'er-do-weel. There is little danger that men will desire to excuse their souls before God by presenting themselves before men as such snobs as Bishop Blougram, or such dastards as Sludge the Medium. There is no pessimism, however stern, that is so stern as this optimism, it is as merciless as the mercy of God.

It is true that in this, as in almost everything else connected with Browning's character, the matter cannot be altogether exhausted by such a generalisation as the above. Browning's was a simple character, and therefore very difficult to understand, since it was impulsive, unconscious, and kept no reckoning of its moods. Probably in a great many cases, the original impulse which led Browning to plan a soliloquy was a kind of anger mixed with curiosity; possibly the first charcoal sketch of Blougram was a caricature of a priest. Browning, as we have said, had prejudices, and had a capacity for anger, and two of his angriest prejudices were against a certain kind of worldly clericalism, and against almost every kind of spiritualism. But as he worked upon the portraits at least, a new spirit began to possess him, and he enjoyed every spirited and just defence the men could make of themselves, like triumphant blows in a battle and towards the end would come the full revelation, and Browning would stand up in the man's skin and testify to the man's ideals. However this may be, it is worth while to notice one very curious error that has arisen in connection with one of the most famous of these monologues.

When Robert Browning was engaged in that somewhat obscure quarrel with the spiritualist Home, it is generally and correctly stated that he gained a great number of the impressions which he afterwards embodied in 'Mr Sludge the Medium.' The statement so often made, particularly in the spiritualist accounts of the matter, that Browning himself is the original of the interlocutor and exposer of Sludge, is of course merely an example of that reckless reading from which no one has suffered more than Browning despite his students and societies. The man to whom Sludge addresses his confession is a Mr Hiram H. Horsfall, an American, a patron of spiritualists, and, as it is more than once suggested, something of a fool. Nor is there the smallest reason to suppose that Sludge considered as an individual bears any particular resemblance to Home considered as an individual. But without doubt 'Mr Sludge the Medium' is a general statement of the view of spiritualism at which Browning had arrived from his acquaintance with Home and Home's circle. And about that view of spiritualism there is someting rather peculiar to notice. The poem, appearing as it did at the time when the intellectual public had just become conscious of the existence of spiritualism, attracted a great deal of attention, and aroused a great deal of controversy. The spiritualists called down thunder upon the head of the poet, whom they depicted as a vulgar and ribald lampooner who had not only committed the profanity of sneering at the mysteries of a higher state of life, but the more unpardonable profanity of sneering at the convictions of his own wife. The sceptics, on the other hand, hailed the poem with delight as a blasting exposure of spiritualism, and congratulated the poet on making himself the champion of the sane and scientific view of magic. Which of these two parties was right about the question of attacking the reality of spiritualism it is neither easy nor necessary to discuss. For the simple truth, which neither of the two parties and none of the students of Browning seem to have noticed, is that 'Mr Sludge the Medium' is not an attack upon spiritualism. It would be a great deal nearer the truth, though not entirely the truth, to call it a justification of spiritualism. The whole essence of Browning's method is involved in this matter, and the whole essence of Browning's method is so vitally misunderstood that to say that 'Mr Sludge the Medium' is something like a defence of spiritualism will bear on the face of it the appearance of the most empty and perverse of paradoxes. But so, when we have comprehended Browning's spirit, the fact will be found to be.

The general idea is that Browning must have intended 'Sludge' for an attack on spiritual phenomena, because the medium in that poem is made a vulgar and contemptible mountebank, because his cheats are quite openly confessed, and he himself put into every ignominious situation, detected, exposed, throttled, horsewhipped, and forgiven. To regard this deduction as sound is to misunderstand Browning at the very start of every poem that he ever wrote. There is nothing that the man loved more, nothing that deserves more emphatically to be called a speciality of Browning, than the utterance of large and noble truths by the lips of mean and grotesque human beings. In his poetry praise and wisdom were perfected not only out of the mouths of babes and sucklings, but out of the mouths of swindlers and snobs. Now what, as a matter of fact, is the outline and development of the poem of 'Sludge'? The climax of the poem, considered as a work of art, is so fine that it is quite extraordinary that any one should have missed the point of it, since it is the whole point of the monologue. Sludge the Medium has been caught out in a piece of unquestionable trickery, a piece of trickery for which there is no conceivable explanation or palliation which will leave his moral character intact. He is therefore seized with a sudden resolution, partly angry, partly frightened, and partly humorous, to become absolutely frank, and to tell the whole truth about himself. He excuses himself for the first time not only to his dupe, but to himself for the earlier stages of the trickster's life by a survey of the border-land between truth and fiction, not by any means a piece of sophistry or cynicism, but a perfectly fair statement of an ethical difficulty which does exist. There are some people who think that it must be immoral to admit that there are any doubtful cases of morality, as if a man should refrain from discussing the precise boundary at the upper end of the Isthmus of Panama, for fear the inquiry should shake his belief in the existence of North America. People of this kind quite consistently think Sludge to be merely a scoundrel talking nonsense. It may be remembered that they thought the same thing of Newman. It is actually supposed, apparently in the current use of words, that casuistry is the name of a crime; it does not appear to occur to people that casuistry is a science, and about as much a crime as botany. This tendency to casuistry in Browning's monologues has done much towards establishing for him that reputation for pure intellectualism which has done him so much harm. But casuistry in this sense is not a cold and analytical thing, but a very warm and sympathetic thing. To know what combinations of excuse might justify a man in manslaughter or bigamy, is not to have a callous indifference to virtue; it is rather to have so ardent an admiration for virtue as to seek it in the remotest desert and the darkest incognito.

This is emphatically the case with the question of truth and falsehood raised in 'Sludge the Medium.' To say that it is sometimes difficult to tell at what point the romancer turns into the liar is not to state a cynicism, but a perfectly honest piece of human observation. To think that such a view involves the negation of honesty is like thinking that red is green because the two fade into each other in the colours of the rainbow. It is really difficult to decide when we come to the extreme edge of veracity, when and when not it is permissible to create an illusion. A standing example, for instance, is the case of the fairy-tales. We think a father entirely pure and benevolent when he tells his children that a beanstalk grew up into heaven, and a pumpkin turned into a coach. We should consider that he lapsed from purity and benevolence if he told his children that in walking home that evening he had seen a beanstalk grow halfway up the church, or a pumpkin grow as large as a wheelbarrow. Again, few people would object to that general privilege whereby it is permitted to a person in narrating even a true anecdote to work up the climax by any exaggerative touches which really tend to bring it out. The reason of this is that the telling of the anecdote has become, like the telling of the fairy-tale, almost a distinct artistic creation; to offer to tell a story is in ordinary society like offering to recite or play the violin. No one denies that a fixed and genuine moral rule could be drawn up for these cases, but no one surely need be ashamed to admit that such a rule is not entirely easy to draw up. And when a man like Sludge traces much of his moral downfall to the indistinctness of the boundary and the possibility of beginning with a natural extravagance and ending with a gross abuse, it certainly is not possible to deny his right to be heard.

We must recur, however, to the question of the main development of the Sludge self-analysis. He begins, as we have said, by urging a general excuse by the fact that in the heat of social life, in the course of telling tales in the intoxicating presence of sympathisers and believers, he has slid into falsehood almost before he is aware of it. So far as this goes, there is truth in his plea. Sludge might indeed find himself unexpectedly justified if we had only an exact record of how true were the tales told about Conservatives in an exclusive circle of Radicals, or the stories told about Radicals in a circle of indignant

Conservatives. But after this general excuse, Sludge goes on to a perfectly cheerful and unfeeling admission of fraud: this principal feeling towards his victims is by his own confession a certain unfathomable contempt for people who are so easily taken in. He professes to know how to lay the foundations for every species of personal acquaintanceship, and how to remedy the slight and trivial slips of making Plato write Greek in naughts and crosses.

> 'As I fear, sir, he sometimes used to do
> Before I found the useful book that knows.'

It would be difficult to imagine any figure more indecently confessional, more entirely devoid of not only any of the restraints of conscience, but of any of the restraints even of a wholesome personal conceit, than Sludge the Medium. He confesses not only fraud, but things which are to the natural man more difficult to confess even than fraud—effeminacy, futility, physical cowardice. And then, when the last of his loathsome secrets has been told, when he has nothing left either to gain or to conceal, then he rises up into a perfect bankrupt sublimity and makes the great avowal which is the whole pivot and meaning of the poem. He says in effect: 'Now that my interest in deceit is utterly gone, now that I have admitted, to my own final infamy, the frauds that I have practised, now that I stand before you in a patent and open villainy which has something of the disinterestedness and independence of the innocent, now I tell you with the full and impartial authority of a lost soul that I believe that there is something in spiritualism. In the course of a thousand conspiracies, by the labour of a thousand lies, I have discovered that there is really something in this matter that neither I nor any other man understands. I am a thief, an adventurer, a deceiver of mankind, but I am not a disbeliever in spiritualism. I have seen too much for that.' This is the confession of faith of Mr Sludge the Medium. It would be difficult to imagine a confession of faith framed and presented in a more impressive manner. Sludge is a witness to his faith as the old martyrs were witnesses to their faith, but even more impressively. They testified to their religion even after they had lost their liberty, and their eyesight, and their right hands. Sludge testifies to his religion even after he has lost his dignity and his honour.

It may be repeated that it is truly extraordinary that any one should have failed to notice that this avowal on behalf of spiritualism is the pivot of the poem. The avowal itself is not only expressed clearly, but prepared and delivered with admirable rhetorical force:—

> 'Now for it, then! Will you believe me though?
> You've heard what I confess: I don't unsay
> A single word: I cheated when I could,

Rapped with my toe-joints, set sham hands at work,
Wrote down names weak in sympathetic ink.
Rubbed odic lights with ends of phosphor-match,
And all the rest; believe that: believe this,
By the same token, though it seem to set
The crooked straight again, unsay the said,
Stick up what I've knocked down; I can't help that,
It's truth! I somehow vomit truth to-day.
This trade of mine—I don't know, can't be sure
But there was something in it, tricks and all!'

It is strange to call a poem with so clear and fine a climax an attack on spiritualism. To miss that climax is like missing the last sentence in a good anecdote, or putting the last act of *Othello* into the middle of the play. Either the whole poem of 'Sludge the Medium' means nothing at all, and is only a lampoon upon a cad, of which the matter is almost as contemptible as the subject, or it means this—that some real experiences of the unseen lie even at the heart of hypocrisy, and that even the spiritualist is at root spiritual.

One curious theory which is common to most Browning critics is that Sludge must be intended for a pure and conscious impostor, because after his confession, and on the personal withdrawal of Mr Horsfall, he bursts out into horrible curses against that gentleman and cynical boasts of his future triumphs in a similar line of business. Surely this is to have a very feeble notion either of nature or art. A man driven absolutely into a corner might humiliate himself, and gain a certain sensation almost of luxury in that humiliation, in pouring out all his imprisoned thoughts and obscure victories. For let it never be forgotten that a hypocrite is a very unhappy man; he is a man who has devoted himself to a most delicate and arduous intellectual art in which he may achieve masterpieces which he must keep secret, fight thrilling battles, and win hair's-breadth victories for which he cannot have a whisper of praise. A really accomplished impostor is the most wretched of geniuses; he is a Napoleon on a desert island. A man might surely, therefore, when he was certain that his credit was gone, take a certain pleasure in revealing the tricks of his unique trade, and gaining not indeed credit, but at least a kind of glory. And in the course of his self-revelation he would come at last upon that part of himself which exists in every man—that part which does believe in, and value, and worship something. This he would fling in his hearer's face with even greater pride, and take a delight in giving a kind of testimony to his religion which no man had ever given before—the testimony of a martyr who could not hope to be a saint. But surely all this sudden tempest of candour in the man would not mean that he would burst into tears and become an exemplary ratepayer, like a villain in the worst parts of

Dickens. The moment the danger was withdrawn, the sense of having given himself away, of having betrayed the secret of his infamous freemasonry, would add an indescribable violence and foulness to his reaction of rage. A man in such a case would do exactly as Sludge does. He would declare his own shame, declare the truth of his creed, and then, when he realised what he had done, say something like this:—

> 'R-r-r, you brute-beast and blackguard! Cowardly scamp!
> I only wish I dared burn down the house
> And spoil your sniggering!'

and so on, and so on.

He would react like this; it is one of the most artistic strokes in Browning. But it does not prove that he was a hypocrite about spiritualism, or that he was speaking more truthfully in the second outburst than in the first. Whence came this extraordinary theory that a man is always speaking most truly when he is speaking most coarsely? The truth about oneself is a very difficult thing to express, and coarse speaking will seldom do it.

When we have grasped this point about 'Sludge the Medium', we have grasped the key to the whole series of Browning's casuistical monologues— *Bishop Blougram's Apology, Prince Hohenstiel-Schwangau, Fra Lippo Lippi, Fifine at the Fair, Aristophanes' Apology*, and several of the monologues in *The Ring and the Book*. They are all, without exception, dominated by this one conception of a certain reality tangled almost inextricably with unrealities in a man's mind, and the peculiar fascination which resides in the thought that the greatest lies about a man, and the greatest truths about him, may be found side by side in the same eloquent and sustained utterance.

> 'For Blougram, he believed, say, half he spoke.'

Or, to put the matter in another way, the general idea of these poems is, that a man cannot help telling some truth even when he sets out to tell lies. If a man comes to tell us that he has discovered perpetual motion, or been swallowed by the sea-serpent, there will yet be some point in the story where he will tell us about himself almost all that we require to know.

If any one wishes to test the truth, or to see the best examples of this general idea in Browning's monologues, he may be recommended to notice one peculiarity of these poems which is rather striking. As a whole, these apologies are written in a particularly burly and even brutal English. Browning's love of what is called the ugly is nowhere else so fully and extravagantly indulged. This, like a great many others things for which Browning as an artist is blamed, is perfectly appropriate to the theme. A vain, ill-mannered, and untrustworthy egotist, defending his own sordid doings with his own cheap and weather-beaten philosophy, is very likely to express himself best in a language flexible and pungent, but indelicate and without dignity. But the peculiarity of these loose and almost slangy soliloquies is that every now and then in them there occur bursts of pure poetry which are like a burst of birds singing. Browning does not hesitate to put some of the most perfect lines that he or anyone else have ever written in the English language into the mouths of such slaves as Sludge and Guido Franceschini. Take, for the sake of example, 'Bishop Blougram's Apology.' The poem is one of the most grotesque in the poet's works. It is intentionally redolent of the solemn materialism and patrician grossness of a grand dinner-party *à deux*. It has many touches of an almost wild bathos, such as the young man who bears the impossible name of Gigadibs. The Bishop, in pursuing his worldly argument for conformity, points out with truth that a condition of doubt is a condition that cuts both ways, and that if we cannot be sure of the religious theory of life, neither can we be sure of the material theory of life, and that in turn is capable of becoming an uncertainty continually shaken by a tormenting suggestion. We cannot establish ourselves on rationalism, and make it bear fruit to us. Faith itself is capable of becoming the darkest and most revolutionary of doubts. Then comes the passage:—

> 'Just when we are safest, there's a sunset-touch,
> A fancy from a flower-bell, some one's death,
> A chorus ending from Euripides,—
> And that's enough for fifty hopes and fears
> As old and new at once as Nature's self,
> To rap and knock and enter in our soul,
> Take hands and dance there, a fantastic ring,
> Round the ancient idol, on his base again,—
> The grand Perhaps!'

Nobler diction and a nobler meaning could not have been put into the mouth of Pompilia, or Rabbi Ben Ezra. It is in reality put into the mouth of a vulgar fashionable priest, justifying his own cowardice over the comfortable wine and the cigars.

Along with this tendency to poetry among Browning's knaves, must be reckoned another characteristic, their uniform tendency to theism. These loose and mean characters speak of many things feverishly and vaguely; of one thing they always speak with confidence and composure, their relation to God. It may seem strange at first sight that those who have outlived the indulgence, and not only of every law, but of every reasonable anarchy, should still rely so simply upon the indulgence of divine perfection. Thus

Sludge is certain that his life of lies and conjuring tricks has been conducted in a deep and subtle obedience to the message really conveyed by the conditions created by God. Thus Bishop Blougram is certain that his life of panic-stricken and tottering compromise has been really justified as the only method that could unite him with God. Thus Prince Hohenstiel-Schwangau is certain that every dodge in his thin string of political dodges has been the true means of realising what he believes to be the will of God. Every one of these meagre swindlers, while admitting a failure in all things relative, claims an awful alliance with the Absolute. To many it will at first sight appear a dangerous doctrine indeed. But, in truth, it is a most solid and noble and salutary doctrine, far less dangerous than its opposite. Every one on this earth should believe, amid whatever madness or moral failure, that his life and temperament have some object on the earth. Every one on the earth should believe that he has something to give to the world which cannot otherwise be given. Every one should, for the good of men and the saving of his own soul, believe that it is possible, even if we are the enemies of the human race, to be the friends of God. The evil wrought by this mystical pride, great as it often is, is like a straw to the evil wrought by a materialistic self-abandonment. The crimes of the devil who thinks himself of immeasurable value are as nothing to the crimes of the devil who thinks himself of no value. With Browning's knaves we have always this eternal interest, that they are real somewhere, and may at any moment begin to speak poetry. We are talking to a peevish and garrulous sneak; we are watching the play of his paltry features, his evasive eyes, and babbling lips. And suddenly the face begins to change and harden, the eyes glare like the eyes of a mask, the whole face of clay becomes a common mouthpiece, and the voice that comes forth is the voice of God, uttering His everlasting soliloquy.

# *From* Some Policemen and a Moral

The other day I was nearly arrested by two excited policemen in a wood in Yorkshire. I was on a holiday, and was engaged in that rich and intricate mass of pleasures, duties, and discoveries which for the keeping off of the profane we disguise by the exoteric name of Nothing. At the moment in question I was throwing a big Swedish knife at a tree, practising (alas, without success) that useful trick of knife-throwing by which men murder each other in Stevenson's romances.

Suddenly the forest was full of two policemen; there was something about their appearance in and relation to the greenwood that reminded me, I know not how, of some happy Elizabethan comedy. They asked what the knife was, who I was, why I was throwing it, what my address was, trade, religion, opinions on the Japanese war, name of favourite cat, and so on. They also said I was damaging the tree; which was, I am sorry to say, not true, because I could not hit it. The peculiar philosophical importance, however, of the incident was this. After some half-hour's animated conversation, the exhibition of an envelope, an unfinished poem, which was read with great care, and, I trust, with some profit, and one or two other subtle detective strokes, the elder of the two knights became convinced that I really was what I professed to be, that I was a journalist, that I was on the *Daily News* (this was the real stroke; they were shaken with a terror common to all tyrants), that I lived in a particular place as stated, and that I was stopping with particular people in Yorkshire, who happened to be wealthy and well-known in the neighbourhood.

In fact the leading constable became so genial and complimentary at last that he ended up by representing himself as a reader of my work. And when that was said, everything was settled. They acquitted me and let me pass.

'But,' I said, 'what of this mangled tree? It was to the rescue of that Dryad, tethered to the earth, that you rushed like knight-errants. You, the higher humanitarians, are not deceived by the seeming stillness of the green things

*Daily News*, 16 April, 1904. Collected in Tremendous Trifles, 1909

a stillness like the stillness of the cataract, a headlong and crashing silence. You know that a tree is but a creature tied to the ground by one leg. You will not let assassins with their Swedish daggers shed the green blood of such a being. But if so, why am I not in custody; where are my gyves? Produce, from some portion of your persons, my mouldy straw and my grated window. The facts of which I have just convinced you, that my name is Chesterton, that I am a journalist, that I am living with the well-known and philanthropic Mr Blank of Ilkley, cannot have anything to do with the question of whether I have been guilty of cruelty to vegetables. The tree is none the less damaged, even though it may reflect with a dark pride that it was wounded by a gentleman connected with the Liberal press. Wounds in the bark do not more rapidly close up because they are inflicted by people who are stopping with Mr Blank of Ilkley. That tree, the ruin of its former self, the wreck of what was once a giant of the forest, now splintered and laid low by the brute superiority of a Swedish knife, that tragedy, constable, cannot be wiped out even by stopping for several months more with some wealthy person. It is incredible that you have no legal claim to arrest even the most august and fashionable persons on this charge. For if so, why did you interfere with me at all?'

I made the later and larger part of this speech to the silent wood, for the two policemen had vanished almost as quickly as they came. It is very possible, of course, that they were fairies. In that case the somewhat illogical character of their view of crime, law, and personal responsibility would find a bright and elfish explanation; perhaps if I had lingered in the glade till moonrise I might have seen rings of tiny policemen dancing on the sward; or running about with glow-worm belts, arresting grasshoppers for damaging blades of grass. But taking the bolder hypothesis, that they really were policemen, I find myself in a certain difficulty. I was certainly accused of something which was either an offence or was not. I was let off because I proved I was a guest at a big house. The inference seems painfully clear; either it is not a proof of infamy to throw a knife about in a lonely wood, or else it is a proof of innocence to know a rich man. Suppose a very poor person, poorer even than a journalist, a navvy or unskilled labourer, tramping in search of work, often changing his lodgings, often, perhaps, failing in his rent. Suppose he had read Stevenson's novels. Suppose he had been intoxicated with the green gaiety of the ancient wood. Suppose he had thrown knives at trees and could give no description of a dwelling-place except that he had been fired out of the last. As I walked home through a cloudy and purple twilight I wondered how he would have got on.

# A Midsummer Night's Dream

The greatest of Shakespeare's comedies is also, from a certain point of view, the greatest of his plays. No one would maintain that it occupied this position in the matter of psychological study if by psychological study we mean the study of individual characters in a play. No one would maintain that Puck was a character in the sense that Falstaff is a character, or that the critic stood awed before the psychology of Peaseblossom. But there is a sense in which the play is perhaps a greater triumph of psychology than *Hamlet* itself. It may well be questioned whether in any other literary work in the world is so vividly rendered a social and spiritual atmosphere. There is an atmosphere in *Hamlet*, for instance, a somewhat murky and even melodramatic one, but it is subordinate to the great character, and morally inferior to him; the darkness is only a background for the isolated star of intellect. But *A Midsummer Night's Dream* is a psychological study not of a solitary man, but of a spirit that unites mankind. The six men may sit talking in an inn; they may not know each other's names or see each other's faces before or after, but night or wine or great stories, or some rich and branching discussion may make them all at one, if not absolutely with each other, at least with that invisible seventh man who is the harmony of all of them. That seventh man is the hero of *A Midsummer Night's Dream.*

A study of the play from a literary or philosophical point of view must therefore be founded upon some serious realisation of what this atmosphere is. In a lecture upon *As You Like it*, Mr Bernard Shaw made a suggestion which is an admirable example of his amazing ingenuity and of his one most interesting limitation. In maintaining that the light sentiment and optimism of the comedy were regarded by Shakespeare merely as the characteristics of a more or less cynical pot-boiler, he actually suggested that the title 'As You Like It' was a taunting address to the public in disparagement of their taste and the dramatist's own work. If Mr Bernard Shaw had conceived of Shakespeare as insisting that Ben Jonson should wear Jaeger underclothing

*Good Words*, 1904. Collected in The Common Man, 1950

or join the Blue Ribbon Army, or distribute little pamphlets for the non-payment of rates, he could scarcely have conceived anything more violently opposed to the whole spirit of Elizabethan comedy than the spiteful and priggish modernism of such a taunt. Shakespeare might make the fastidious and cultivated Hamlet, moving in his own melancholy and purely mental world, warn players against an over-indulgence towards the rabble. But the very soul and meaning of the great comedies is that of an uproarious communion between the public and the play, a communion so chaotic that whole scenes of silliness and violence lead us almost to think that some of the 'rowdies' from the pit have climbed over the footlights. The title 'As You Like It' is, of course, an expression of utter carelessness, but it is not the bitter carelessness which Mr Bernard Shaw fantastically reads into it; it is the god-like and inexhaustible carelessness of a happy man. And the simple proof of this is that there are scores of these genially taunting titles scattered through the whole of Elizabethan comedy. Is 'As You Like It' a title demanding a dark and ironic explanation in a school of comedy which called its plays 'What you Will', 'A Mad World, My Masters', 'If It Be Not Good, the Devil Is In It', 'The Devil is an Ass', 'An Humorous Day's Mirth', and 'A Midsummer Night's Dream'? Every one of these titles is flung at the head of the public as a drunken lord might fling a purse at his footman. Would Mr Shaw maintain that 'If It Be Not Good, the Devil Is In It', was the opposite of 'As You Like It', and was a solemn invocation of the supernatural powers to testify to the care and perfection of the literary workmanship? The one explanation is as Elizabethan as the other.

Now in the reason for this modern and pedantic error lies the whole secret and difficulty of such plays as *A Midsummer Night's Dream*. The sentiment of such a play, so far as it can be summed up at all, can be summed up in one sentence. It is the mysticism of happiness. That is to say, it is the conception that as man lives upon a borderland he may find himself in the spiritual or supernatural atmosphere, not only through being profoundly sad or meditative, but by being extravagantly happy. The soul might be rapt out of the body in an agony of sorrow, or a trance of ecstasy; but it might also be rapt out of the body in a paroxysm of laughter. Sorrow we know can go beyond itself; so, according to Shakespeare, can pleasure go beyond itself and become something dangerous and unknown. And the reason that the logical and destructive modern school, of which Mr Bernard Shaw is an example, does not grasp this purely exuberant nature of the comedies is simply that their logical and destructive attitude have rendered impossible the very experience of this preternatural exuberance. We cannot realise *As You Like It* if we are always considering it as we understand it. We cannot have *A Midsummer's Night Dream* if our one object in life is to keep ourselves awake with the black coffee of criticism. The whole question which is balanced, and balanced nobly and fairly, in *A Midsummer Night's Dream*, is whether the life of waking, or the life of the vision, is the real life, the *sine quâ non* of man. But it is difficult to see what superiority for the purpose of judging is possessed by people whose pride it is not to live the life of vision at all. At least it is questionable whether the Elizabethan did not know more about both worlds than the modern intellectual; it is not altogether improbable that Shakespeare would not only have had a clearer vision of the fairies, but would have shot very much straighter at a deer and netted much more money for his performances than a member of the Stage Society.

In pure poetry and the intoxication of words, Shakespeare never rose higher than he rises in this play. But in spite of this fact, the supreme literary merit of *A Midsummer Night's Dream* is a merit of design. The amazing symmetry, the amazing artistic and moral beauty of that design, can be stated very briefly. The story opens in the sane and common world with the pleasant seriousness of very young lovers and very young friends. Then, as the figures advance into the tangled wood of young troubles and stolen happiness, a change and bewilderment begins to fall on them. They lose their way and their wits for they are in the heart of fairyland. Their words, their hungers, their very figures grow more and more dim and fantastic, like dreams within dreams, in the supernatural mist of Puck. Then the dream-fumes begin to clear, and characters and spectators begin to awaken together to the noise of horns and dogs and the clean and bracing morning. Theseus, the incarnation of a happy and generous rationalism, expounds in hackneyed and superb lines the sane view of such psychic experiences, pointing out with a reverent and sympathetic scepticism that all these fairies and spells are themselves but the emanations, the unconscious masterpieces, of man himself. The whole company falls back into a splendid human laughter. There is a rush for banqueting and private theatricals, and over all these things ripples one of those frivolous and inspired conversations in which every good saying seems to die in giving birth to another. If ever the son of a man in his wanderings was at home and drinking by the fireside, he is at home in the house of Theseus. All the dreams have been forgotten, as a melancholy dream remembered throughout the morning might be forgotten in the human certainty of any other triumphant evening party; and so the play seems naturally ended. It began on the earth and it ends on the earth. Thus to round off the whole midsummer night's dream in an eclipse of daylight is an effect of genius. But of this comedy, as I have said, the mark is that genius goes beyond itself; and one touch is added which makes the play colossal. Theseus and his train retire with a crashing finale, full of humour and wisdom and things set right, and silence falls on the house. Then there comes a faint sound of little feet, and for a moment, as it were, the elves look into the house, asking which is the reality. 'Suppose we are the realities and they the shadows.' If that ending were acted properly any modern man would feel shaken to his marrow if he had to walk home from the theatre through a country lane.

It is a trite matter, of course, though in a general criticism a more or less indispensable one to comment upon another point of artistic perfection, the extraordinarily human and accurate manner in which the play catches the atmosphere of a dream. The chase and tangle and frustration of the incidents and personalities are well known to every one who has dreamt of perpetually falling over precipices or perpetually missing trains. While following out clearly and legally the necessary narrative of the drama, the author contrives to include every one of the main peculiarities of the exasperating dream. Here is the pursuit of the man we cannot catch, the flight from the man we cannot see; here is the perpetual returning to the same place, here is the crazy alteration in the very objects of our desire, the substitution of one face for another face, the putting of the wrong souls in the wrong bodies, the fantastic disloyalties of the night, all this is as obvious as it is important. It is perhaps somewhat more worth remarking that there is about this confusion of comedy yet another essential characteristic of dreams. A dream can commonly be described as possessing an utter discordance of incident combined with a curious unity of mood; everything changes but the dreamer. It may begin with anything and end with anything, but if the dreamer is sad at the end he will be sad as if by prescience at the beginning; if he is cheerful at the beginning he will be cheerful if the stars fall. *A Midsummer Night's Dream* has in a most singular degree effected this difficult, this almost desperate subtlety. The events in the wandering wood are in themselves, and regarded as in broad daylight, not merely melancholy but bitterly cruel and ignominious. But yet by the spreading of an atmosphere as magic as the fog of Puck, Shakespeare contrives to make the whole matter mysteriously hilarious while it is palpably tragic, and mysteriously charitable, while it is in itself cynical. He contrives somehow to rob tragedy and treachery of their full sharpness, just as a toothache or a deadly danger from a tiger, or a precipice, is robbed of its sharpness in a pleasant dream. The creation of brooding sentiment like this, a sentiment not merely independent of but actually opposed to the events, is a much greater triumph of art than the creation of the character of Othello.

It is difficult to approach critically so great a figure as that of Bottom the Weaver. He is greater and more mysterious than Hamlet, because the interest of such men as Bottom consists of a rich subconsciousness, and that of Hamlet in the comparatively superficial matter of a rich consciousness. And it is especially difficult in the present age which has become hag-ridden with the mere intellect. We are the victims of a curious confusion whereby being great is supposed to have something to do with being clever, as if there were the smallest reason to suppose that Achilles was clever, as if there were not on the contrary a great deal of internal evidence to indicate that he was next door to a fool. Greatness is a certain indescribable but perfectly familiar and palpable quality of size in the personality, of steadfastness, of strong flavour, of easy and natural self-expression. Such a man is as firm as a tree and as unique as a rhinoceros, and he might quite easily be as stupid as either of them. Fully as much as the great poet towers above the small poet the great fool towers above the small fool. We have all of us known rustics like Bottom the Weaver, men whose faces would be blank with idiocy if we tried for ten days to explain the meaning of the National Debt, but who are yet great men, akin to Sigurd and Hercules, heroes of the morning of the earth, because their words were their own words, their memories their own memories, and their vanity as large and simple as a great hill. We have all of us known friends in our own circle, men whom the intellectuals might justly describe as brainless, but whose presence in a room was like a fire roaring in the grate changing everything, lights and shadows and the air, whose entrances and exits were in some strange fashion events, whose point of view once expressed haunts and persuades the mind and almost intimidates it, whose manifest absurdity clings to the fancy like the beauty of first-love, and whose follies are recounted like the legends of a paladin. These are great men, there are millions of them in the world, though very few perhaps in the House of Commons. It is not in the cold halls of cleverness where celebrities seem to be important that we should look for the great. An intellectual salon is merely a training-ground for one faculty, and is akin to a fencing class or a rifle corps. It is in our own homes and environments, from Croydon to St John's Wood, in old nurses, and gentlemen with hobbies, and talkative spinsters and vast incomparable butlers, that we may feel the presence of that blood of the gods. And this creature so hard to describe, so easy to remember, the august and memorable fool, has never been so sumptuously painted as in the Bottom of *A Midsummer Night's Dream.*

Bottom has the supreme mark of this real greatness in that like the true saint or the true hero he only differs from humanity in being as it were more human than humanity. It is not true, as the idle materialists of today suggest, that compared to the majority of men the hero appears cold and dehumanised; it is the majority who appear cold and dehumanised in the presence of greatness. Bottom, like Don Quixote and Uncle Toby and Mr Richard Swiveller and the rest of the Titans, has a huge and unfathomable weakness, his silliness is on a great scale, and when he blows his own trumpet it is like the trumpet of the Resurrection. The other rustics in the play accept his leadership not merely naturally but exuberantly; they have to the full that primary and savage unselfishness, that uproarious abnegation which makes simple men take pleasure in falling short of a hero, that unquestionable element of basic human nature which has never been expressed, outside this play, so perfectly as in the incomparable chapter at the beginning of *Evan Harrington* in which the praises of The Great Mel are sung with a lyric energy by the tradesmen whom he has cheated. Twopenny sceptics write of the egoism of primal human nature; it is reserved for great men like Shakespeare and Meredith to detect and make vivid this rude and subconscious unselfishness which is older than self. They alone with their insatiable tolerance can perceive all the spiritual devotion in the sound of a snob. And it is this natural play between the rich simplicity of Bottom and the simple simplicity of his comrades which constitutes the unapproachable excellence of the farcical scenes in the play. Bottom's sensibility to literature is perfectly fiery and genuine, a great deal more genuine than that of a great many cultivated critics of literature—'the raging rocks, and shivering shocks shall break the locks of prison gates, and Phibbus' car shall shine from far, and make and mar the foolish fates', is exceedingly good poetical diction with a real throb and swell in it, and if it is slightly and almost imperceptibly deficient in the matter of sense, it is certainly every bit as sensible as a good many other rhetorical speeches in Shakespeare put into the mouths of kings and lovers and even the spirits of the dead. If Bottom liked cant for its own sake the fact only constitutes another point of sympathy between him and his literary creator. But the style of the thing, though deliberately bombastic and ludicrous, is quite literary, the alliteration falls like wave upon wave, and the whole verse, like a billow mounts higher and higher before it crashes. There is nothing mean about this folly; nor is there in the whole realm of literature a figure so free from vulgarity. The man vitally base and foolish sings 'The Honeysuckle and the Bee'; he does not rant about 'raging rocks' and 'the car of Phibbus'. Dickens, who more perhaps than any modern man had the mental hospitality and the thoughtless wisdom of Shakespeare, perceived and expressed admirably the same truth. He perceived, that is to say, that quite indefensible idiots have very often a real sense of, and enthusiasm for letters. Mr Micawber loved eloquence and poetry with his whole immortal soul; words and visionary pictures kept him alive in the absence of food and money, as they might have kept a saint fasting in a desert. Dick Swiveller did not make his inimitable quotations from Moore and Byron merely as flippant digressions. He made them because he loved a great school of poetry. The sincere love of books has nothing to do with cleverness or stupidity any more than any other sincere love. It is a quality of character, a freshness, a power of pleasure, a power of faith. A silly person may delight in reading masterpieces just as a silly person may delight in picking flowers. A fool may be in love with a poet as he may be in love with a woman. And the triumph of Bottom is that he loves rhetoric and his own taste in the arts, and this is all that can be achieved by Theseus, or for the matter of that by Cosimo di

Medici. It is worth remarking as an extremely fine touch in the picture of Bottom that his literary taste is almost everywhere concerned with sound rather than sense. He begins the rehearsal with a boisterous readiness, 'Thisby, the flowers of odious savours sweete.' 'Odours, odours,' says Quince, in remonstrance, and the word is accepted in accordance with the cold and heavy rules which require an element of meaning in a poetical passage. But 'Thisby, the flowers of odious savours sweete', Bottom's version, is an immeasurably finer and more resonant line. The 'i' which he inserts is an inspiration of metricism.

There is another aspect of this great play which ought to be kept familiarly in the mind. Extravagant as is the masquerade of the story, it is a very perfect aesthetic harmony down to such *coup-de-maître* as the name of Bottom, or the flower called Love in Idleness. In the whole matter it may be said that there is one accidental discord; that is in the name of Theseus, and the whole city of Athens in which the events take place. Shakespeare's description of Athens in *A Midsummer Night's Dream* is the best description of England that he or any one else ever wrote. Theseus is quite obviously only an English squire, fond of hunting, kindly to his tenants, hospitable with a certain flamboyant vanity. The mechanics are English mechanics, talking to each other with the queer formality of the poor. Above all, the fairies are English; to compare them with the beautiful patrician spirits of Irish legend, for instance, is suddenly to discover that we have, after all, a folk-lore and a mythology, or had it at least in Shakespeare's day. Robin Goodfellow, upsetting the old women's ale, or pulling the stool from under them, has nothing of the poignant Celtic beauty; his is the horse-play of the invisible world. Perhaps it is some debased inheritance of English life which makes American ghosts so fond of quite undignified practical jokes. But this union of mystery with farce is a note of the medieval English. The play is the last glimpse of Merrie England, that distant but shining and quite indubitable country. It would be difficult indeed to define wherein lay the peculiar truth of the phrase 'merrie England', though some conception of it is quite necessary to the comprehension of *A Midsummer Night's Dream*. In some cases at least, it may be said to lie in this, that the English of the Middle Ages and the Renaissance, unlike the England of today, could conceive of the idea of a merry supernaturalism. Amid all the great work of Puritanism the damning indictment of it consists in one fact, that there was one only of the fables of Christendom that it retained and renewed, and that was the belief in witchcraft. It cast away the generous and wholesome superstition, it approved only of the morbid and the dangerous. In their treatment of the great national fairy-tale of good and evil, the Puritans killed St George but carefully preserved the Dragon. And this seventeenth-century tradition of dealing with the psychic life still lies like a great shadow over England and

America, so that if we glance at a novel about occultism we may be perfectly certain that it deals with sad or evil destiny. Whatever else we expect we certainly should never expect to find in it spirits such as those in *Aylwin* as inspirers of a tale of tomfoolery like the *Wrong Box* or *The Londoners*. That impossibility is the disappearance of 'merrie England' and Robin Good-fellow. It was a land to us incredible, the land of a jolly occultism where the peasant cracked jokes with his patron saint, and only cursed the fairies good-humouredly, as he might curse a lazy servant. Shakespeare is English in everything, above all in his weaknesses. Just as London, one of the greatest cities in the world, shows more slums and hides more beauties than any other, so Shakespeare alone among the four giants of poetry is a careless writer, and lets us come upon his splendours by accident, as we come upon an old City church in the twist of a city street. He is English in nothing so much as in that noble cosmopolitan unconsciousness which makes him look eastward with the eyes of a child towards Athens or Verona. He loved to talk of the glory of foreign lands, but he talked of them with the tongue and unquenchable spirit of England. It is too much the custom of a later patriotism to reverse this method and talk of England from morning till night, but to talk of her in a manner totally un-English. Casualness, incon-gruities, and a certain fine absence of mind are in the temper of England; the unconscious man with the ass's head is no bad type of the people. Materialistic philosophers and mechanical politicians have certainly suc-ceeded in some cases in giving him a greater unity. The only question is, to which animal has he been thus successfully conformed?

# The Need of Personalities in Politics

The village I now inhabit (as a locum tenens in the temporary absence of the Village Beauty) was in a great stir last night, owing to the arrival of the Liberal Van, which was regarded with more gravity than I should have thought possible. It drew up on the village green; its speakers opened a meeting, and everything would have gone smoothly and respectably if it had not happened that among the promoters of the meeting, standing beside the van, was a man with that air of strained intellectuality which marks a reader of *The Daily News*. He heard my name by some social accident; and remembered seeing it in the paper. 'I have read your articles,' said this excellent Liberal, with a friendly smile, while I faintly condoled with him. Then he said, after a pause of some length, 'I think I know what some of them mean'. I implored him to share with me this secret and painful knowledge, but he refused, and I shall go to my grave without it. But my encounter with the man had drawn me into the dangerous circle. And when the Chairman, a local Liberal magnate, was obliged to leave half-way through the meeting, they hoisted me into the chair instead of him. The chair was a kind of wooden ledge a little way above the shafts; and I took the chair with so dignified a decisiveness as almost to wreck the van. Then, I regret to say, the proceedings took on a more turbulent character. My rising to say anything was greeted (I cannot explain this phenomenon) with loud shouts coming exclusively from little boys. I think I somehow stirred in them a sickening hope that after all it was going to be a circus.

Then there was a sombre Conservative on the outskirts of the crowd, who interrupted so consistently and continuously that it came to be a rather delicate logical question whether he was interrupting our speeches or we were interrupting his. But it was not so much the quantity as the quality of his interruptions that pleased and at the same time perplexed me. One thing was firmly embedded in his mind, the fruitful seed of continuously flowering satire. This was the conviction that all of us in the van were persons of

*Daily News*, July 1905. Collected in The Apostle and the Wild Ducks, 1975

enormous wealth. He even professed to know the sources of that wealth. When I was making some remarks about poverty, he hurled at my head, with a deadly aim, this mysterious sarcasm: 'Ha! We ain't *all* on the Civil List.' I made, of course, the somewhat obvious retort, that some of us seemed to be on the Uncivil List; but to this moment I cannot imagine what was the meaning of that unfathomable sneer. Is there something in my air and manner, something of official dignity and decorum, touched with a servile prosperity that suggests that I am in receipt of a bloated pension? Or has somebody really given or left me some money (poignant and improbable thought) since I have been away from town?

Let us leave this merely personal enigma and pass on to the final development, which from a deeper point of view, at any rate, was the most interesting. The temperature of the meeting, I am proud to say, rose higher and higher: a perfect rattle of repartees, the sympathisers on each side rocked and roared, a large fat farmer of Conservative opinions was beginning with a dreadful and dangerous slowness to think of something to say; and when I wound up the meeting and thanked everybody for their patience, politeness, and good temper, they were ready to kick each other round the green.

And then an interesting thing happened. Ten minutes after the end of the meeting the large, deliberate farmer of Conservative opinions was delivered of the thing that he wanted to say; and eclipse and thunder accompanied that portentous birth. The thing he wanted to say was—Could anybody there say he'd ever cut down any man's wages? This seemed to me a very essential, a very serious, and a very manly challenge, immeasurably more important not only than anything said at our meeting, but than anything that is ever said in the House of Commons.

It was followed by a kind of restless silence, such as occurs in such mobs at such moments, and in the next instant there was drama. A pale, coarse-looking lad, his arm half out of his coat with eagerness and anger, thrust his face forward. His wages had been cut down, he said; he had been underpaid, and underpaid by this man. The farmer, staring at him through the darkness, at first denied all knowledge of his face. Then a voice broke out of him, a loud and wrathful and decisive voice, crying, 'Why, I know yer now. I know yer now, I sacked yer for—'. Then the sense of English respectability awoke suddenly in everybody, and the men were torn apart and soothed wildly by their friends. Whatever happened, we must not be asked to decide on a matter of real and diurnal right and wrong. Whatever happened we must not have a plain personal challenge answered by a plain personal reply. The farmer went away, shaking with his furious secret; the lad went away shaking with his. Yet here was present on that dark green, in that dim group, what is often the eternal substance and whole meaning of society and government. Two men were calling upon their neighbours to give judgement on their wrongs. This is politics. We had fixed the frontiers of India; we had examined the imports of Canada; we had meditated on the quarrels between Dutchmen and German Jews; we had criticised kindly but firmly the condition of the Prussian working classes; we had thought imperially and also in continents; we had seen the kingdoms of the earth and the glory of them.

But this doing of justice between one angry man and another never crossed our minds as a public duty. This was the last business that could be expected of us—this which would be the first business of a primitive community, this which would be the first business of a tribe of Zulus. Our politics for the night had ended. Our politics had ended exactly at the point where all politics ought to begin.

It seemed to me that on this little green, as on a green baize stage, was acted an allegory of the whole situation of our contemporary statesmanship. Everything goes on daily as long as we are dealing with things. Everything stops abruptly the moment we come to men. We are allowed to say: 'The supporters of the Blue-nosed Monkeys Modification and Improvement Act are corrupt scoundrels.' We are allowed to say, 'Sir William Guppy is a supporter of the Blue-nosed Monkeys Modification and Improvement Act.'

We are not allowed to complete the syllogism. Everybody says with one accord in our English Parliament: 'Let us have no personalities in politics.' Every Briton says at his breakfast-table: 'At least, we are not like the French and the Irish; we have no personalities in our politics.' And because we have no personalities we have no responsibilities.

# GKC

# *From* On Mr Rudyard Kipling

Now, the first and fairest thing to say about Rudyard Kipling is that he has borne a brilliant part in thus recovering the lost provinces of poetry. He has not been frightened by that brutal materialistic air which clings only to words; he has pierced through to the romantic, imaginative matter of the things themselves. He has perceived the significance and philosophy of steam and of slang. Steam may be, if you like, a dirty by-product of science. Slang may be, if you like, a dirty by-product of language. But at least he has been among the few who saw the divine parentage of these things, and knew that where there is smoke there is fire—that is, that wherever there is the foulest of things, there also is the purest. Above all, he has had something to say, a definite view of things to utter, and that always means that a man is fearless and faces everything. For the moment we have a view of the universe, we possess it.

Now, the message of Rudyard Kipling, that upon which he has really concentrated, is the only thing worth worrying about in him or in any other man. He has often written bad poetry, like Wordsworth. He has often said silly things, like Plato. He has often given way to mere political hysteria, like Gladstone. But no one can reasonably doubt that he means steadily and sincerely to say something, and the only serious question is, What is that which he has tried to say? Perhaps the best way of stating this fairly will be to begin with that element which has been most insisted by himself and by his opponents—I mean his interest in militarism. But when we are seeking for the real merits of a man it is unwise to go to his enemies, and much more foolish to go to himself.

Now, Mr Kipling is certainly wrong in his worship of militarism, but his opponents are, generally speaking, quite as wrong as he. The evil of militarism is not that it shows certain men to be fierce and haughty and excessively warlike. The evil of militarism is that it shows most men to be tame and timid and excessively peaceable. The professional soldier gains

Heretics, 1905

69

more and more power as the general courage of a community declines. Thus the Pretorian guard became more and more important in Rome as Rome became more and more luxurious and feeble. The military man gains the civil power in proportion as the civilian loses the military virtues. And as it was in ancient Rome so it is in contemporary Europe. There never was a time when nations were more militarist. There never was a time when men were less brave. All ages and all epics have sung of arms and the man; but we have effected simultaneously the deterioration of the man and the fantastic perfection of the arms. Militarism demonstrated the decadence of Rome, and it demonstrates the decadence of Prussia.

And unconsciously Mr Kipling has proved this, and proved it admirably. For in so far as his work is earnestly understood, the military trade does not by any means emerge as the most important or attractive. He has not written so well about soldiers as he has about railway men or bridge builders, or even journalists. The fact is that what attracts Mr Kipling to militarism is not the idea of courage, but the idea of discipline. There was far more courage to the square mile in the Middle Ages, when no king had a standing army, but every man had a bow or sword. But the fascination of the standing army upon Mr Kipling is not courage, which scarcely interests him, but discipline, which is, when all is said and done, his primary theme. The modern army is not a miracle of courage; it has not enough opportunities, owing to the cowardice of everybody else. But it is really a miracle of organization, and that is the truly Kiplingite ideal. Kipling's subject is not that valour which properly belongs to war, but that interdependence and efficiency which belongs quite as much to engineers, or sailors, or mules, or railway engines. And thus it is that when he writes of engineers, or sailors, or mules, or steam-engines, he writes at his best. The real poetry, the 'true romance' which Mr Kipling has taught, is the romance of the division of labour and the discipline of all the trades. He sings the arts of peace much more accurately than the arts of war. And his main contention is vital and valuable. Everything is military in the sense that everything depends upon obedience. There is no perfectly epicurean corner; there is no perfectly irresponsible place. Everywhere men have made the way for us with sweat and submission. We may fling ourselves into a hammock in a fit of divine carelessness. But we are glad that the net-maker did not make the hammock in a fit of divine carelessness. We may jump upon a child's rocking-horse for a joke. But we are glad that the carpenter did not leave the legs of it unglued for a joke. So far from having merely preached that a soldier cleaning his side-arm is to be adored because he is military, Kipling at his best and clearest has preached that the baker baking loaves and the tailor cutting coats is as military as anybody.

Being devoted to this multitudinous vision of duty, Mr Kipling is naturally a cosmopolitan. He happens to find his examples in the British Empire, but almost any other empire would do as well, or, indeed, any other highly civilized country. That which he admires in the British army he would find even more apparent in the German army; that which he desires in the British police he would find flourishing in the French police. The ideal of discipline is not the whole of life, but it is spread over the whole of the world. And the worship of it tends to confirm in Mr Kipling a certain note of worldly wisdom, of the experience of the wanderer, which is one of the genuine charms of his best work.

The great gap in his mind is what may be roughly called the lack of patriotism—that is to say, he lacks altogether the faculty of attaching himself to any cause or community finally and tragically; for all finality must be tragic. He admires England, but he does not love her; for we admire things with reasons, but love them without reasons. He admires England because she is strong, not because she is English. There is no harshness in saying this, for, to do him justice, he avows it with his usual picturesque candour. In a very interesting poem, he says that—

*'If England was what England seems'*

—that is weak and inefficient; if England were not what (as he believes) she is—that is, powerful and practical—

*'How quick we'd chuck 'er! But she ain't!'*

He admits, that is, that his devotion is the result of a criticism, and this is quite enough to put it in another category altogether from the patriotism of the Boers, whom he hounded down in South Africa. In speaking of the really patriotic peoples, such as the Irish, he has some difficulty in keeping a shrill irritation out of his language. The frame of mind which he really describes with beauty and nobility is the frame of mind of the cosmopolitan man who has seen men and cities.

'For to admire and for to see,
For to be'old this world so wide.'

He is a perfect master of that light melancholy with which a man looks back on having been the citizen of many communities, of that light melancholy with which a man looks back on having been the lover of many women. He is the philanderer of the nations. But a man may have learnt much about women in flirtations, and still be ignorant of first love; a man may have known as many lands as Ulysses, and still be ignorant of patriotism.

71

Mr Rudyard Kipling has asked in a celebrated epigram what they can know of England who know England only. It is a far deeper and sharper question to ask, 'What can they know of England who know only the world?' for the world does not include England any more than it includes the Church. The moment we care for anything deeply, the world—that is, all the other miscellaneous interests—becomes our enemy. Christians showed it when they talked of keeping one's self 'unspotted from the world'; but lovers talk of it just as much when they talk of the 'world well lost.' Astronomically speaking, I understand that England is situated on the world; similarly, I suppose that the Church was a part of the world, and even the lovers inhabitants of that orb. But they all felt a certain truth—the truth that the moment you love anything the world becomes your foe. Thus Mr Kipling does certainly know the world; he is a man of the world, with all the narrowness that belongs to those imprisoned in that planet. He knows England as an intelligent English gentleman knows Venice. He has been to England a great many times; he has stopped there for long visits. But he does not belong to it, or to any place; and the proof of it is this, that he thinks of England as a place. The moment we are rooted in a place, the place vanishes. We live like a tree with the whole strength of the universe.

The globe-trotter lives in a smaller world than the peasant. He is always breathing an air of locality. London is a place, to be compared to Chicago; Chicago is a place, to be compared to Timbuctoo. But Timbuctoo is not a place, since there, at least, live men who regard it as the universe, and breathe, not an air of locality, but the winds of the world. The man in the saloon steamer has seen all the races of men, and he is thinking of the things that divide men—diet, dress, decorum, rings in the nose as in Africa, or in the ears as in Europe, blue paint among the ancients, or red paint among the modern Britons. The man in the cabbage field has seen nothing at all; but he is thinking of the things that unite men—hunger and babies, and the beauty of women, and the promise or menace of the sky. Mr Kipling, with all his merits, is the globe-trotter; he has not the patience to become part of anything. So great and genuine a man is not to be accused of a merely cynical cosmopolitanism; still, his cosmopolitanism is his weakness. That weakness is splendidly expressed in one of his finest poems, *The Sestina of the Tramp Royal*, in which a man declares that he can endure anything in the way of hunger or horror, but not permanent presence in one place. In this there is certainly danger. The more dead and dry and dusty a thing is the more it travels about; dust is like this and the thistle-down and the High Commissioner in South Africa. Fertile things are somewhat heavier, like the heavy fruit trees on the pregnant mud of the Nile. In the heated idleness of youth we were all rather inclined to quarrel with the implication of that proverb which says that a rolling stone gathers no moss. We were inclined to ask,

'Who wants to gather moss, except silly old ladies?' But for all that we begin to perceive that the proverb is right. The rolling stone rolls echoing from rock to rock; but the rolling stone is dead. The moss is silent because the moss is alive.

# *From* Christmas and the Æsthetes

And now I have to touch upon a very sad matter. There are in the modern .world an admirable class of persons who really make protest on behalf of that *antiqua pulchritudo* of which Augustine spoke, who do long for the old feasts and formalities of the childhood of the world. William Morris and his followers showed how much brighter were the dark ages than the age of Manchester. Mr W. B. Yeats frames his steps in prehistoric dances, but no man knows and joins his voice to forgotten choruses that no one but he can hear. Mr George Moore collects every fragment of Irish paganism that the forgetfulness of the Catholic Church has left or possibly her wisdom preserved. There are innumerable persons with eye-glasses and green garments who pray for the return of the maypole or the Olympian games. But there is about these people a haunting and alarming something which suggests that it is just possible that they do not keep Christmas. It is painful to regard human nature in such a light, but it seems somehow possible that Mr George Moore does not wave his spoon and shout when the pudding is set alight. It is even possible that Mr W. B. Yeats never pulls crackers. If so, where is the sense of all their dreams of festive traditions? Here is a solid and ancient festive tradition still plying a roaring trade in the streets, and they think it vulgar. If this is so, let them be very certain of this, that they are the kind of people who in the time of the maypole would have thought the maypole vulgar; who in the time of the Canterbury pilgrimage would have thought the Canterbury pilgrimage vulgar; who in the time of the Olympian games would have thought the Olympian games vulgar. Nor can there be any reasonable doubt that they were vulgar. Let no man deceive himself; if by vulgarity we mean coarseness of speech, rowdiness of behaviour, gossip, horseplay, and some heavy drinking, vulgarity there always was whenever there was joy, wherever there was faith in the gods. Wherever you have belief you will have hilarity, wherever you have hilarity you will have some dangers. And as creed and mythology produce this gross and vigorous life, so in its turn this gross and

Heretics, 1905

vigorous life will always produce creed and mythology. If we ever get the English back on to the English land they will become again a religious people, if all goes well, a superstitious people. The absence from modern life of both the higher and lower forms of faith is largely due to a divorce from nature and the trees and clouds. If we have no more turnip ghosts it is chiefly from the lack of turnips.

# *From* On Certain Modern Writers and the Institution of the Family

The family may fairly be considered, one would think, an ultimate human institution. Every one would admit that it has been the main cell and central unit of almost all societies hitherto, except, indeed, such societies as that of Lacedæmon, which went in for 'efficiency', and has, therefore, perished, and left not a trace behind. Christianity, even enormous as was its revolution, did not alter this ancient and savage sanctity; it merely reversed it. It did not deny the trinity of father, mother, and child. It merely read it backwards, making it run child, mother, father. This it called, not the family, but the Holy Family, for many things are made holy by being turned upside down. But some sages of our own decadence have made a serious attack on the family. They have impugned it, as I think wrongly; and its defenders have defended it, and defended it wrongly. The common defence of the family is that, amid the stress and fickleness of life, it is peaceful, pleasant, and at one. But there is another defence of the family which is possible, and to me evident; this defence is that the family is not peaceful and not pleasant and not at one.

It is not fashionable to say much nowadays of the advantages of the small community. We are told that we must go in for large empires and large ideas. There is one advantage, however, in the small state, the city, or the village, which only the wilfully blind can overlook. The man who lives in a small community lives in a much larger world. He knows much more of the fierce varieties and uncompromising divergences of men. The reason is obvious. In a large community we can choose our companions. In a small community our companions are chosen for us. Thus in all extensive and highly civilized societies groups come into existence founded upon what is called sympathy, and shut out the real world more sharply than the gates of a monastery. There is nothing really narrow about the clan; the thing which is really narrow is the clique. The men of the clan live together because they all wear the same tartan or are all descended from the same sacred cow; but in their

Heretics, 1905

76

souls, by the divine luck of things, there will always be more colours than in any tartan. But the men of the clique live together because they have the same kind of soul, and their narrowness is a narrowness of spiritual coherence and contentment, like that which exists in hell. A big society exists in order to form cliques. A big society is a society for the promotion of narrowness. It is a machinery for the purpose of guarding the solitary and sensitive individual from all experience of the bitter and bracing human compromises. It is, in the most literal sense of the words, a society for the prevention of Christian knowledge.

We can see this change, for instance, in the modern transformation of the thing called a club. When London was smaller, and the parts of London more self-contained and parochial, the club was what it still is in villages, the opposite of what it is now in great cities. Then the club was valued as a place where a man could be sociable. Now the club is valued as a place where a man can be unsociable. The more the enlargement and elaboration of our civilization goes on, the more the club ceases to be a place where a man can have a noisy argument, and becomes more and more a place where a man can have what is somewhat fantastically called a quiet chop. Its aim is to make a man comfortable, and to make a man comfortable is to make him the opposite of sociable. Sociability, like all good things, is full of discomforts, dangers, and renunciations. The club tends to produce the most degraded of all combinations—the luxurious anchorite, the man who combines the self-indulgence of Lucullus with the insane loneliness of St Simeon Stylites.

If we were to-morrow morning snowed up in the street in which we live, we should step suddenly into a much larger and much wilder world than we have ever known. And it is the whole effort of the typically modern person to escape from the street in which he lives. First he invents modern hygiene and goes to Margate. Then he invents modern culture and goes to Florence. Then he invents modern imperialism and goes to Timbuctoo. He goes to the fantastic borders of the earth. He pretends to shoot tigers. He almost rides on a camel. And in all this he is still essentially fleeing from the street in which he was born; and of this flight he is always ready with his own explanation. He says he is fleeing from his street because it is dull; he is lying. He is really fleeing from his street because it is a great deal too exciting. It is exciting because it is exacting; it is exacting because it is alive. He can visit Venice because to him the Venetians are only Venetians; the people in his own street are men. He can stare at the Chinese because for him the Chinese are a passive thing to be stared at; if he stares at the old lady in the next garden, she becomes active. He is forced to flee, in short, from the too stimulating society of his equals—of free men, perverse, personal, deliberately different from himself. The street in Brixton is too glowing and overpowering. He has to soothe and quiet himself among tigers and vultures, camels and crocodiles. These creatures are indeed very different from himself. But they do not put their shape or colour or custom into a decisive intellectual competition with his own. They do not seek to destroy his principles and assert their own; the stranger monsters of the suburban street do seek to do this. The camel does not contort his features into a fine sneer because Mr Robinson has not got a hump; the cultured gentleman at No 5 does exhibit a sneer because Robinson has not got a dado. The vulture will not roar with laughter because a man does not fly; but the major at No 9 will roar with laughter because a man does not smoke. The complaint we commonly have to make of our neighbours is that they will not, as we express it, mind their own business. We do not really mean that they will not mind their own business. If our neighbours did not mind their own business they would be asked abruptly for their rent, and would rapidly cease to be our neighbours. What we really mean when we say that they cannot mind their own business is something much deeper. We do not dislike them because they have so little force and fire that they cannot be interested in themselves. We dislike them because they have so much force and fire that they can be interested in us as well. What we dread about our neighbours, in short, is not the narrowness of their horizon, but their superb tendency to broaden it. And all aversions to ordinary humanity have this general character. They are not aversions to its feebleness (as is pretended), but to its energy. The misanthropes pretend that they despise humanity for its weakness. As a matter of fact, they hate it for its strength.

Of course, this shrinking from the brutal vivacity and brutal variety of common men is a perfectly reasonable and excusable thing as long as it does not pretend to any point of superiority. It is when it calls itself aristocracy or æstheticism or a superiority to the bourgeoisie that its inherent weakness has in justice to be pointed out. Fastidiousness is the most pardonable of vices; but it is the most unpardonable of virtues. Nietzsche, who represents most prominently this pretentious claim of the fastidious, has a description somewhere—a very powerful description in the purely literary sense—of the disgust and disdain which consume him at the sight of the common people with their common faces, their common voices, and their common minds. As I have said, this attitude is almost beautiful if we may regard it as pathetic. Nietzsche's aristocracy has about it all the sacredness that belongs to the weak. When he makes us feel that he cannot endure the innumerable faces, the incessant voices, the overpowering omnipresence which belongs to the mob, he will have the sympathy of anybody who has ever been sick on a steamer or tired in a crowded omnibus. Every man has hated mankind when he was less than a man. Every man has had humanity in his eyes like a blinding fog, humanity in his nostrils like a suffocating smell. But when Nietzsche has the incredible lack of humour and lack of imagination to ask us to believe that his aristocracy is an aristocracy of strong muscles or an aristocracy of strong wills, it is necessary to point out the truth. It is an aristocracy of weak nerves.

We make our friends; we make our enemies; but God makes our next-door neighbour. Hence he comes to us clad in all the careless terrors of nature; he is as strange as the stars, as reckless and indifferent as the rain. He is Man, the most terrible of the beasts. That is why the old religions and the old scriptural language showed so sharp a wisdom when they spoke, not of one's duty towards humanity, but one's duty towards one's neighbour. The duty towards humanity may often take the form of some choice which is personal or even pleasurable. That duty may be a hobby; it may even be a dissipation. We may work in the East End because we are peculiarly fitted to work in the East End, or because we think we are; we may fight for the cause of international peace because we are very fond of fighting. The most monstrous martyrdom, the most repulsive experience, may be the result of choice or a kind of taste. We may be so made as to be particularly fond of lunatics or specially interested in leprosy. We may love negroes because they are black, or German Socialists because they are pedantic. But we have to love our neighbour because he is *there*—a much more alarming reason for a much more serious operation. He is the sample of humanity which is actually given us. Precisely because he may be anybody he is everybody. He is a symbol because he is an accident.

Doubtless men flee from small environments into lands that are very deadly. But this is natural enough; for they are not fleeing from death. They are fleeing from life. And this principle applies to ring within ring of the social system of humanity. It is perfectly reasonable that men should seek for some particular variety of the human type so long as they are seeking for that variety of the human type, and not for mere human variety. It is quite proper that a British diplomatist should seek the society of Japanese generals, if what he wants is Japanese generals. But if what he wants is people different from himself, he had much better stop at home and discuss religion with the housemaid. It is quite reasonable that the village genius should come up to conquer London if what he wants is to conquer London. But if he wants to conquer something fundamentally and symbolically hostile and also very strong, he had much better remain where he is and have a row with the rector. The man in the suburban street is quite right if he goes to Ramsgate for the sake of Ramsgate—a difficult thing to imagine. But if, as he expresses it, he goes to Ramsgate 'for a change,' then he would have a much more romantic and even melodramatic change if he jumped over the wall into his neighbour's garden. The consequences would be bracing in a sense far beyond the possibilities of Ramsgate hygiene.

Now, exactly as this principle applies to the empire, to the nation within the empire, to the city within the nation, to the street within the city, so it applies to the home within the street. The institution of the family is to be commended for precisely the same reasons that the institution of the nation, or the institution of the city, are in this matter to be commended. It is a good thing for a man to live in a family for the same reason that it is a good thing for a man to be besieged in a city. It is a good thing for a man to live in a family in the same sense that it is a beautiful and delightful thing for a man to be snowed up in a street. They all force him to realize that life is not a thing from outside, but a thing from inside. Above all, they all insist upon the fact that life, if it be a truly stimulating and fascinating life, is a thing which, of its nature, exists in spite of ourselves. The modern writers who have suggested, in a more or less open manner, that the family is a bad institution, have generally confined themselves to suggesting, with much sharpness, bitterness, or pathos, that perhaps the family is not always very congenial. Of course the family is a good institution because it is uncongenial. It is wholesome precisely because it contains so many divergencies and varieties. It is, as the sentimentalists say, like a little kingdom, and, like most other little kingdoms, is generally in a state of something resembling anarchy. It is exactly because our brother George is not interested in our religious difficulties, but is interested in the Trocadero Restaurant, that the family has some of the bracing qualities of the commonwealth. It is precisely because our uncle Henry does not approve of the theatrical ambitions of our sister Sarah that the family is like humanity. The men and women who, for good reasons and bad, revolt against the family, are, for good reasons and bad, simply revolting against mankind. Aunt Elizabeth is unreasonable, like mankind. Papa is excitable, like mankind. Our youngest brother is mischievous, like mankind. Grandpapa is stupid like the world; he is old, like the world.

Those who wish, rightly or wrongly, to step out of all this, do definitely wish to step into a narrower world. They are dismayed and terrified by the largeness and variety of the family. Sarah wishes to find a world wholly consisting of private theatricals; George wishes to think the Trocadero a cosmos. I do not say, for a moment, that the flight to this narrower life may not be the right thing for the individual, any more than I say the same thing about flight into a monastery. But I do say that anything is bad and artificial which tends to make these people succumb to the strange delusion that they are stepping into a world which is actually larger and more varied than their own. The best way that a man could test his readiness to encounter the common variety of mankind would be to climb down a chimney into any house at random, and get on as well as possible with the people inside. And that is essentially what each one of us did on the day that he was born.

This is, indeed, the sublime and special romance of the family. It is romantic because it is a toss-up. It is romantic because it is everything that its enemies call it. It is romantic because it is arbitrary. It is romantic because it is there. So long as you have groups of men chosen rationally, you have some special or sectarian atmosphere. It is when you have groups of men chosen irrationally that you have men. The element of adventure begins to exist; for an adventure is, by its nature, a thing that comes to us. It is a thing that chooses us, not a thing that we choose. Falling in love has been often regarded as the supreme adventure, the supreme romantic accident. In so much as there is in it something outside ourselves, something of a sort of merry fatalism, this is very true. Love does take us and transfigure and torture us. It does break our hearts with an unbearable beauty, like the unbearable beauty of music. But in so far as we have certainly something to do with the matter; in so far as we are in some sense prepared to fall in love and in some sense jump into it; in so far as we do to some extent choose and to some extent even judge—in all this falling in love is not truly romantic, is not truly adventurous at all. In this degree the supreme adventure is not falling in love. The supreme adventure is being born. There we do walk suddenly into a splendid and startling trap. There we do see something of which we have not dreamed before. Our father and mother do lie in wait for us and leap out on us, like brigands from a bush. Our uncle is a surprise. Our aunt is, in the beautiful common expression, a bolt from the blue. When we step into the family, by the act of being born, we do step into a world which is incalculable, into a world which has its own strange laws, into a world which could do without us, into a world that we have not made. In other words, when we step into the family we step into a fairy-tale.

# Celts and Celtophiles

Science in the modern world has many uses; its chief use, however, is to provide long words to cover the errors of the rich. The word 'kleptomania' is a vulgar example of what I mean. It is on a par with that strange theory, always advanced when a wealthy or prominent person is in the dock, that exposure is more of a punishment for the rich than for the poor. Of course, the very reverse is the truth. Exposure is more of a punishment for the poor than for the rich. The richer a man is the easier it is for him to be a tramp. The richer a man is the easier it is for him to be popular and generally respected in the Cannibal Islands. But the poorer a man is the more likely it is that he will have to use his past life whenever he wants to get a bed for the night. Honour is a luxury for aristocrats, but it is a necessity for hall-porters. This is a secondary matter, but it is an example of the general proposition I offer—the proposition that an enormous amount of modern ingenuity is expended on finding defences for the indefensible conduct of the powerful. As I have said above, these defences generally exhibit themselves most emphatically in the form of appeals to physical science. And of all the forms in which science, or pseudoscience, has come to the rescue of the rich and stupid, there is none so singular as the singular invention of the theory of races.

When a wealthy nation like the English discovers the perfectly patent fact that it is making a ludicrous mess of the government of a poorer nation like the Irish, it pauses for a moment in consternation, and then begins to talk about Celts and Teutons. As far as I can understand the theory, the Irish are Celts and the English are Teutons. Of course, the Irish are not Celts any more than the English are Teutons. I have not followed the ethnological discussion with much energy, but the last scientific conclusion which I read inclined on the whole to the summary that the English were mainly Celtic and Irish mainly Teutonic. But no man alive, with even the glimmering of a real scientific sense, would ever dream of applying the terms 'Celtic' or 'Teutonic' to either of them in any positive or useful sense.

Heretics, 1905

That sort of thing must be left to people who talk about the Anglo-Saxon race, and extend the expression to America. How much of the blood of the Angles and Saxons (whoever they were) there remains in our mixed British, Roman, German, Dane, Norman, and Picard stock is a matter only interesting to wild antiquaries. And how much of that diluted blood can possibly remain in that roaring whirlpool of America into which a cataract of Swedes, Jews, Germans, Irishmen, and Italians is perpetually pouring, is a matter only interesting to lunatics. It would have been wiser for the English governing class to have called upon some other god. All other gods, however weak and warring, at least boast of being constant. But science boasts of being in a flux for ever; boasts of being unstable as water.

And England and the English governing class never did call on this absurd deity of race until it seemed, for an instant, that they had no other god to call on. All the most genuine Englishmen in history would have yawned or laughed in your face if you had begun to talk about Anglo-Saxons. If you had attempted to substitute the ideal of race for the ideal of nationality, I really do not like to think what they would have said. I certainly should not like to have been the officer of Nelson who suddenly discovered his French blood on the eve of Trafalgar. I should not like to have been the Norfolk or Suffolk gentleman who had to expound to Admiral Blake by what demonstrable ties of genealogy he was irrevocably bound to the Dutch. The truth of the whole matter is very simple. Nationality exists, and has nothing in the world to do with race. Nationality is a thing like a church or a secret society; it is a product of the human soul and will; it is a spiritual product. And there are men in the modern world who would think anything and do anything rather than admit that anything could be a spiritual product.

A nation, however, as it confronts the modern world, is a purely spiritual product. Sometimes it has been born in independence, like Scotland. Sometimes it has been born in dependence, in subjugation, like Ireland. Sometimes it is a large thing cohering out of many smaller things, like Italy. Sometimes it is a small thing breaking away from larger things, like Poland. But in each and every case its quality is purely spiritual, or, if you will, purely psychological. It is a moment when five men become a sixth man. Every one knows it who has ever founded a club. It is a moment when five places become one place. Every one must know it who has ever had to repel an invasion. Mr Timothy Healy, the most serious intellect in the present House of Commons, summed up nationality to perfection when he simply called it something for which people will die. As he excellently said in reply to Lord Hugh Cecil, 'No one, not even the noble lord, would die for the meridian of Greenwich.' And that is the great tribute to its purely psychological character. It is idle to ask why Greenwich should not cohere in this spiritual manner while Athens or Sparta did. It is like asking why a man falls in love with one woman and not with another.

Now, of this great spiritual coherence, independent of external circumstances, or of race, or of any obvious physical thing, Ireland is the most remarkable example. Rome conquered nations, but Ireland has conquered races. The Norman has gone there and become Irish, the Scotchman has gone there and become Irish, the Spaniard has gone there and become Irish, even the bitter soldier of Cromwell has gone there and become Irish. Ireland, which did not exist even politically, has been stronger than all the races that existed scientifically. The purest Germanic blood, the purest Norman blood, the purest blood of the passionate Scotch patriot, has not been so attractive as a nation without a flag. Ireland, unrecognized and oppressed, has easily absorbed races, as such trifles are easily absorbed. She has easily disposed of physical science, as such superstitions are easily disposed of. Nationality in its weakness has been stronger than ethnology in its strength. Five triumphant races have been absorbed, have been defeated by a defeated nationality.

This being the true and strange glory of Ireland, it is impossible to hear without impatience of the attempt so constantly made among her modern sympathizers to talk about Celts and Celticism. Who were the Celts? I defy anybody to say. Who are the Irish? I defy anyone to be indifferent, or to pretend not to know. Mr W. B. Yeats, the great Irish genius who has appeared in our time, shows his own admirable penetration in discarding altogether the argument from a Celtic race. But he does not wholly escape, and his followers hardly ever escape, the general objection to the Celtic argument. The tendency of that argument is to represent the Irish or the Celts as a strange and separate race, as a tribe of eccentrics in the modern world immersed in dim legends and fruitless dreams. Its tendency is to exhibit the Irish as odd, because they see the fairies. Its trend is to make the Irish seem weird and wild because they sing old songs and join in strange dances. But this is quite an error; indeed, it is the opposite of the truth. It is the English who are odd because they do not see the fairies. It is the inhabitants of Kensington who are weird and wild because they do not sing old songs and join in strange dances. In all this the Irish are not in the least strange and separate, are not in the least Celtic, as the word is commonly and popularly used. In all this the Irish are simply an ordinary sensible nation, living the life of any other ordinary and sensible nation which has not been either sodden with smoke or oppressed by moneylenders, or otherwise corrupted with wealth and science. There is nothing Celtic about having legends. It is merely human. The Germans who are (I suppose) Teutonic, have hundreds of legends, wherever it happens that the Germans are human. There is nothing Celtic about loving poetry; the English loved poetry more, perhaps, than any other people before they came under the shadow of the chimney-pot and the shadow of the chimney-pot hat. It is not Ireland which is mad and mystic; it is Manchester which is mad and mystic, which is incredible, which is a wild exception among human things. Ireland has no need to play the silly game of the science of races; Ireland has no need to pretend to be a tribe of visionaries apart. In the matter of visions, Ireland is more than a nation, it is a model nation.

# *From* Mr McCabe and a Divine Frivolity

Mr McCabe thinks that I am not serious but only funny, because Mr McCabe thinks that funny is the opposite of serious. Funny is the opposite of not funny, and of nothing else. The question of whether a man expresses himself in a grotesque or laughable phraseology, or in a stately and re-strained phraseology, is not a question of motive or of moral state, it is a question of instinctive language and self-expression. Whether a man chooses to tell the truth in long sentences or short jokes is a problem analogous to whether he chooses to tell the truth in French or German. Whether a man preaches his gospel grotesquely or gravely is merely like the question of whether he preaches it in prose or verse. The question of whether Swift was funny in his irony is quite another sort of question to the question of whether Swift was serious in his pessimism. Surely even Mr McCabe would not maintain that the more funny *Gulliver* is in its method the less it can be sincere in its object. The truth is, as I have said, that in this sense the two qualities of fun and seriousness have nothing whatever to do with each other, they are no more comparable than black and triangular. Mr Bernard Shaw is funny and sincere. Mr George Robey is funny and not sincere. Mr McCabe is sincere and not funny. The average Cabinet Minister is not sincere and not funny.

In short, Mr McCabe is under the influence of a primary fallacy which I have found very common in men of the clerical type. Numbers of clergymen have from time to time reproached me for making jokes about religion; and they have almost always invoked the authority of that very sensible com-mandment which says, 'Thou shalt not take the name of the Lord thy God in vain.' Of course, I pointed out that I was not in any conceivable sense taking the name in vain. To take a thing and make a joke out of it is not to take it in vain. It is, on the contrary, to take it and use it for an uncommonly good object. To use a thing in vain means to use it without use. But a joke may be exceedingly useful; it may contain the whole earthly sense, not to mention

Heretics, 1905

86

the whole heavenly sense, of a situation. And those who find in the Bible the commandment can find in the Bible any number of the jokes. In the same book in which God's name is fenced from being taken in vain, God himself overwhelms Job with a torrent of terrible levities. The same book which says that God's name must not be taken vainly, talks easily and carelessly about God laughing and God winking. Evidently it is not here that we have to look for genuine examples of what is meant by a vain use of the name. And it is not very difficult to see where we have really to look for it. The people (as I tactfully pointed out to them) who really take the name of the Lord in vain are the clergymen themselves. The thing which is fundamentally and really frivolous is not a careless joke. The thing which is fundamentally and really frivolous is a careless solemnity. If Mr McCabe really wishes to know what sort of guarantee of reality and solidity is afforded by the mere act of what is called talking seriously, let him spend a happy Sunday in going the round of the pulpits. Or, better still, let him drop in at the House of Commons or the House of Lords. Even Mr McCabe would admit that these men are solemn —more solemn that I am. And even Mr McCabe, I think, would admit that these men are frivolous —more frivolous than I am. Why should Mr McCabe be so eloquent about the danger arising from fantastic and paradoxical writers? Why should he be so ardent in desiring grave and verbose writers? There are not so very many fantastic and paradoxical writers. But there are a gigantic number of grave and verbose writers; and it is by the efforts of the grave and verbose writers that everything that Mr McCabe detests (and everything that I detest, for that matter) is kept in existence and energy. How can it have come about that a man as intelligent as Mr McCabe can think that paradox and jesting stop the way? It is solemnity that is stopping the way in every department of modern effort. It is his own favourite 'serious methods'; it is his own favourite 'momentousness'; it is his own favourite 'judgment' which stops the way everywhere. Every man who has ever headed a deputation to a minister knows this. Every man who has ever written a letter to *The Times* knows it. Every rich man who wishes to stop the mouths of the poor talks about 'momentousness.' Every Cabinet minister who has not got an answer suddenly develops a 'judgment.' Every sweater who uses vile methods recommends 'serious methods.' I said a moment ago that sincerity had nothing to do with solemnity, but I confess that I am not so certain that I was right. In the modern world, at any rate, I am not so sure that I was right. In the modern world solemnity is the direct enemy of sincerity. In the modern world sincerity is almost always on one side, and solemnity almost always on the other. The only answer possible to the fierce and glad attack of sincerity is the miserable answer of solemnity. Let Mr McCabe, or anyone else who is much concerned that we should be grave in order to be sincere, simply imagine the scene in some Government office in which Mr Bernard Shaw should head a Socialist deputation to Mr Austen Chamberlain. On which side would be the solemnity? And on which the sincerity?

# Dickens and America

The essential of Dickens's character was the conjunction of common sense with uncommon sensibility. The two things are not, indeed, in such an antithesis as is commonly imagined. Great English literary authorities such as Jane Austen and Mr Chamberlain, have put the word 'sense' and the word 'sensibility' in a kind of opposition to each other. But not only are they not opposite words: they are actually the same word. They both mean receptiveness or approachability by the facts outside us. To have a sense of colour is the same as to have a sensibility to colour. A person who realizes that beefsteaks are appetizing shows his sensibility. A person who realizes that moonrise is romantic shows his sense. But it is not difficult to see the meaning and need of the popular distinction between sensibility and sense, particularly in the form called common sense. Common sense is a sensibility duly distributed in all normal directions; sensibility has come to mean a specialized sensibility in one. This is unfortunate, for it is not the sensibility that is bad, but the specializing; that is, the lack of sensibility to everything else. A young lady who stays out all night to look at the stars should not be blamed for her sensibility to starlight, but for her insensibility to other people. A poet who recites his own verses from ten to five with the tears rolling down his face should decidedly be rebuked for his lack of sensibility —his lack of sensibility to those grand rhythms of the social harmony, crudely called manners. For all politeness is a long poem, since it is full of recurrences. This balance of all the sensibilities we call sense; and it is in this capacity that it becomes of great importance as an attribute of the character of Dickens.

Dickens, I repeat, had common sense and uncommon sensibility. That is to say, the proportion of interests in him was about the same as that of an ordinary man, but he felt all of them more excitedly. This is a distinction not easy for us to keep in mind, because we hear to-day chiefly of two types, the dull man who likes ordinary things mildly, and the extraordinary man who

Charles Dickens, 1906

likes extraordinary things wildly. But Dickens liked quite ordinary things; he merely made an extraordinary fuss about them. His excitement was sometimes like an epileptic fit; but it must not be confused with the fury of the man of one idea or one line of ideas. He had the excess of the eccentric, but not the defects, the narrowness. Even when he raved like a maniac he did not rave like a monomaniac. He had no particular spot of sensibility or spot of insensibility: he was merely a normal man minus a normal self-command. He had no special point of mental pain or repugnance, like Ruskin's horror of steam and iron, or Mr Bernard Shaw's permanent irritation against romantic love. He was annoyed at the ordinary annoyances: only he was more annoyed than was necessary. He did not desire strange delights, blue wine or black women with Baudelaire or cruel sights east of Suez with Mr Kipling. He wanted what a healthy man wants, only he was ill with wanting it. To understand him, in a word, we must keep well in mind the medical distinction between delicacy and disease. Perhaps we shall comprehend it and him more clearly if we think of a woman rather than a man. There was much that was feminine about Dickens, and nothing more so than this abnormal normality. A woman is often, in comparison with a man, at once more sensitive and more sane.

This distinction must be especially remembered in all his quarrels. And it must be most especially remembered in what may be called his great quarrel with America, which we have now to approach. The whole incident is so typical of Dickens's attitude to everything and anything, and especially of Dickens's attitude to anything political, that I may ask permission to approach the matter by another, a somewhat long and curving avenue.

Common sense is a fairy thread, thin and faint, and as easily lost as gossamer. Dickens (in large matters) never lost it. Take, as an example, his political tone, or drift throughout his life. His views, of course, may have been right or wrong; the reforms he supported may have been successful or otherwise: that is not a matter for this book. But if we compare him with the other men that wanted the same things (or the other men that wanted the other things) we feel a startling absence of cant, a startling sense of humanity as it is and of the eternal weakness. He was a fierce democrat, but in his best vein he laughed at the cocksure Radical of common life, the red-faced man who said, 'Prove it!' when anybody said anything. He fought for the right to elect: but he would not whitewash elections. He believed in Parliamentary government; but he did not, like our contemporary newspapers, pretend that Parliament is something much more heroic and imposing than it is. He fought for the rights of the grossly oppressed Nonconformists, but he spat out of his mouth the unction of that too easy seriousness with which they oiled everything, and held up to them like a horrible mirror the foul fat face of Chadband. He saw that Mr Podsnap thought too little of places outside

England. But he saw that Mrs Jellaby thought too much of them. In the last book he wrote he gives us, in Mr Honeythunder, a hateful and wholesome picture of all the Liberal catchwords pouring out of one illiberal man. But perhaps the best evidence of this steadiness and sanity is the fact that, dogmatic as he was, he never tied himself to any passing dogma: he never got into any *cul de sac* of civic or economic fanaticism: he went down the broad road of the Revolution. He never admitted that economically, we must make hells of workhouses, any more than Rousseau would have admitted it. He never said the State had no right to teach children or save their bones, any more than Danton would have said it. He was a fierce Radical; but he was never a Manchester Radical. He used the test of Utility, but he was never a Utilitarian. While economists were writing soft words he wrote 'Hard Times,' which Macaulay called 'sullen Socialism,' because it was not complacent Whiggism. But Dickens was never a Socialist any more than he was an Individualist; and, whatever else he was, he certainly was not sullen. He was not even a politician of any kind. He was simply a man of very clear, airy judgment on things that did not inflame his private temper, and he perceived that any theory that tried to run the living State entirely on one force and motive was probably nonsense. Whenever the Liberal philosophy had embedded in it something hard and heavy and lifeless, by an instinct he dropped it out. He was too romantic, perhaps, but he would have to do only with real things. He may have cared too much about Liberty. But he cared nothing about '*Laissez Faire.*'

Now, among many interests of his contact with America this interest emerges as infinitely the largest and most striking, that it gave a final example of this queer, unexpected coolness and candour of his, this abrupt and sensational rationality. Apart altogether from any question of the accuracy of his picture of America, the American indignation was particularly natural and inevitable. For the large circumstances of the age must be taken into account. At the end of the previous epoch the whole of our Christian civilization had been startled from its sleep by trumpets to take sides in a bewildering Armageddon, often with eyes still misty. Germany and Austria found themselves on the side of the old order, France and America on the side of the new. England, as at the Reformation, took up eventually a dark middle position, maddeningly difficult to define. She created a democracy, but she kept an aristocracy: she reformed the House of Commons, but left the magistracy (as it is still) a mere league of gentlemen against the world. But underneath all this doubt and compromise there was in England a great and perhaps growing mass of dogmatic democracy; certainly thousands, probably millions expected a Republic in fifty years. And for these the first instinct was obvious. The first instinct was to look across the Atlantic to where lay a part of ourselves already Republican, the van of the advancing

English on the road to liberty. Nearly all the great Liberals of the nineteenth century enormously idealized America. On the other hand, to the Americans, fresh from their first epic of arms, the defeated mother country, with its coronets and county magistrates, was only a broken feudal keep.

So much is self-evident. But nearly half-way through the nineteenth century there came out of England the voice of a violent satirist. In its political quality it seemed like the half-choked cry of the frustrated republic. It had no patience with the pretence that England was already free, that we had gained all that was valuable from the Revolution. It poured a cataract of contempt on the so-called working compromises of England, on the oligarchic cabinets, on the two artificial parties, on the government offices, on the J P's, on the vestries, on the voluntary charities. This satirist was Dickens, and it must be remembered that he was not only fierce, but uproariously readable. He really damaged the things he struck at, a very rare thing. He stepped up to the grave official of the vestry, really trusted by the rulers, really feared like a god by the poor, and he tied round his neck a name that choked him; never again now can he be anything but Bumble. He confronted the fine old English gentleman who gives his patriotic services for nothing as a local magistrate, and he nailed him up as Nupkins, an owl in open day. For to this satire there is literally no answer; it cannot be denied that a man like Nupkins can be and is a magistrate, so long as we adopt the amazing method of letting the rich man of a district actually be the judge in it. We can only avoid the vision of the fact by shutting our eyes, and imagining the nicest rich man we can think of; and that, of course, is what we do. But Dickens, in this matter, was merely realistic; he merely asked us to look on Nupkins, on the wild, strange thing that we had made. Thus Dickens seemed to see England not at all as the country where freedom slowly broadened down from precedent to precedent, but as a rubbish heap of seventeenth-century bad habits abandoned by everybody else. That is, he looked at England almost with the eyes of an American democrat.

And so, when the voice, swelling in volume, reached America and the Americans, the Americans said, 'Here is a man who will hurry the old country along, and tip her kings and beadles into the sea. Let him come here, and we will show him a race of free men such as he dreams of, alive upon the ancient earth. Let him come here and tell the English of the divine democracy towards which he drives them. There he has a monarchy and an oligarchy to make game of. Here is a republic for him to praise.' It seemed, indeed, a very natural sequel, that having denounced undemocratic England as the wilderness, he should announce democratic America as the promised land. Any ordinary person would have prophesied that as he had pushed his rage at the old order almost to the edge of rant, he would push his encomium of the new order almost to the edge of cant. Amid a roar of republican idealism, compliments, hope, and anticipatory gratitude, the great democrat entered the great democracy. He looked about him; he saw a complete America, unquestionably progressive, unquestionably self-governing. Then, with a more than American coolness, and a more than American impudence, he sat down and wrote 'Martin Chuzzlewit.' That tricky and perverse sanity of his had mutinied again. Common sense is a wild thing, savage, and beyond rules; and it had turned on them and rent them.

The main course of action was as follows; and it is right to record it before we speak of the justice of it. When I speak of his sitting down and writing 'Martin Chuzzlewit,' I use, of course, an elliptical expression. He wrote the notes of the American part of 'Martin Chuzzlewit' while he was still in America; but it was a later decision presumably that such impressions should go into a book, and it was little better than an afterthought that they should go into 'Martin Chuzzlewit.' Dickens had an uncommonly bad habit (artistically speaking) of altering a story in the middle as he did in the case of 'Our Mutual Friend.' And it is on record that he only sent young Martin to America because he did not know what else to do with him, and because (to say truth) the sales were falling off. But the first action, which Americans regarded as an equally hostile one, was the publication of 'American Notes,' the history of which should first be given. His notion of visiting America had come to him as a very vague notion, even before the appearance of 'The Old Curiosity Shop.' But it had grown in him through the whole ensuing period in the plaguing and persistent way that ideas did grow in him and live with him. He contended against the idea in a certain manner. He had much to induce him to contend against it. Dickens was by this time not only a husband, but a father, the father of several children, and their existence made a difficulty in itself. His wife, he said, cried whenever the project was mentioned. But it was a point in him that he could never, with any satisfaction, part with a project. He had that restless optimism, that kind of nervous optimism, which would always tend to say 'Yes;' which is stricken with an immortal repentance, if ever it says 'No.' The idea of seeing America might be doubtful, but the idea of not seeing America was dreadful. 'To miss this opportunity would be a sad thing,' he says. '... God willing, I think it *must* be managed somehow!' It was managed somehow. First of all he wanted to take his children as well as his wife. Final obstacles to this fell upon him, but they did not frustrate him. A serious illness fell on him; but that did not frustrate him. He sailed for America in 1842.

He landed in America, and he liked it. As John Forster very truly says, it is due to him, as well as to the great country that welcomed him, that his first good impression should be recorded, and that it should be 'considered independently of any modification it afterwards underwent.' But the modification it afterwards underwent was, as I have said above, simply a sudden kicking against cant, that is, against repetition. He was quite ready to believe that all Americans were free men. He would have believed it if they had not all told him so. He was quite prepared to be pleased with America. He would have been pleased with it if it had not been so much pleased with itself. The 'modification' his views underwent did not arise from any modification of America as he first saw it. His admiration did not change because America changed. It changed because America did not change. The Yankees enraged him at last, not by saying different things, but by saying the same things. They were a republic; they were a new and vigorous nation; it seemed natural that they should say so to a famous foreigner first stepping on to their shore. But it seemed maddening that they should say so to each other in every car and drinking saloon from morning till night. It was not that the Americans in any way ceased from praising him. It was rather that they went on praising him. It was not merely that their praises of him sounded beautiful when he first heard them. Their praises of themselves sounded beautiful when he first heard them. That democracy was grand, and that Charles Dickens was a remarkable person, were two truths that he certainly never doubted to his dying day. But, as I say, it was a soulless repetition that stung his sense of humour out of sleep; it woke like a wild beast for hunting, the lion of his laughter. He had heard the truth once too often. He had heard the truth for the nine hundred and ninety-ninth time, and he suddenly saw that it was falsehood.

It is true that a particular circumstance sharpened and defined his disappointment. He felt very hotly, as he felt everything, whether selfish or unselfish, the injustice of the American piracies of English literature, resulting from the American copyright laws. He did not go to America with any idea of discussing this; when, some time afterwards, somebody said that he did, he violently rejected the view as only describable 'in one of the shortest words in the English language.' But his entry into America was almost triumphal; the rostrum or pulpit was ready for him; he felt strong enough to say anything. He had been most warmly entertained by many American men of letters, especially by Washington Irving, and in his consequent glow of confidence he stepped up to the dangerous question of American copyright. He made many speeches attacking the American law and theory of the matter as unjust to English writers and to American readers. The effect appears to have astounded him. 'I believe there is no country,' he writes, 'on the face of the earth where there is less freedom of opinion on any subject in reference to which there is a broad difference of opinion than in this. There! I write the words with reluctance, disappointment, and sorrow; but I believe it from the bottom of my soul. ... The notion that I, a man alone by myself in America, should venture to suggest to the Americans that there was one point on which they were neither just to their own countrymen nor to us, actually struck the boldest dumb! Washington Irving, Prescott, Hoffman, Bryant, Halleck, Dana, Washington Allston—every man who writes in this country is devoted to the question, and not one of them *dares* to raise his voice and complain of the atrocious state of the law. ... The wonder is that a breathing man can be found with temerity enough to suggest to the Americans the possibility of their having done wrong. I wish you could have seen the faces that I saw down both sides of the table at Hartford when I began to talk about Scott. I wish you could have heard how I gave it out. My blood so boiled when I thought of the monstrous injustice that I felt as if I were twelve feet high when I thrust it down their throats.'

That is almost a portrait of Dickens. We can almost see the erect little figure, its face and hair like a flame.

For such reasons, among others, Dickens was angry with America. But if America was angry with Dickens, there were also reasons for it. I do not think that the rage against his copyright speeches was, as he supposed, merely national insolence and self-satisfaction. America is a mystery to any good Englishman; but I think Dickens managed somehow to touch it on a queer nerve. There is one thing, at any rate, that must strike all Englishmen who have the good fortune to have American friends; that is, that while there is no materialism so crude or so material as American materialism, there is also no idealism so crude or so ideal as American idealism. America will always affect an Englishman as being soft in the wrong place and hard in the wrong place; coarse exactly where all civilized men are delicate, delicate exactly where all grown-up men are coarse. Some beautiful ideal runs through this people, but it runs aslant. The only existing picture in which the thing I mean has been embodied is in Stevenson's 'Wrecker,' in the blundering delicacy of Jim Pinkerton. America has a new delicacy, a coarse, rank refinement. But there is another way of embodying the idea, and that is to say this—that nothing is more likely than that the Americans thought it very shocking in Dickens, the divine author, to talk about being done out of money. Nothing would be more American than to expect a genius to be too high-toned for trade. It is certain that they deplored his selfishness in the matter; it is probable that they deplored his indelicacy. A beautiful young dreamer, with flowing brown hair, ought not to be even conscious of his copyrights. For it is quite unjust to say that the Americans worship the dollar. They really do worship intellect—another of the passing superstitions of our time.

If America had then this Pinkertonian propriety, this new, raw sensibility, Dickens was the man to rasp it. He was its precise opposite in every way. The decencies he did respect were old-fashioned and fundamental. On top of these he had that lounging liberty and comfort which can only be had on the basis of very old conventions, like the carelessness of gentlemen and the deliberation of rustics. He had no fancy for being strung up to that taut and quivering ideality demanded by American patriots and public speakers. And there was something else also, connected especially with the question of copyright and his own pecuniary claims. Dickens was not in the least desirous of being thought too 'high-souled' to want his wages, nor was he in the least ashamed of asking for them. Deep in him (whether the modern reader likes the quality or no) was a sense very strong in the old Radicals— very strong especially in the old English Radicals—a sense of personal *rights*, one's own rights included, as something not merely useful but sacred. He did not think a claim any less just and solemn because it happened to be selfish; he did not divide claims into selfish and unselfish, but into right and wrong. It is significant that when he asked for his money, he never asked for it with that shamefaced cynicism, that sort of embarrassed brutality, with which the modern man of the world mutters something about business being business or looking after number one. He asked for his money in a valiant and ringing voice, like a man asking for his honour. While his American critics were moaning and sneering at his interested motives as a disqualification, he brandished his interested motives like a banner. 'It is nothing to them,' he cries in astonishment, 'that, of all men living, I am the greatest loser by it' (the Copyright Law). 'It is nothing that I have a claim to speak and be heard.' The thing they set up as a barrier he actually presents as a passport. They think that he, of all men, ought not to speak because he is interested. He thinks that he, of all men, ought to speak because he is wronged.

But this particular disappointment with America in the matter of the tyranny of its public opinion was not merely the expression of the fact that Dickens was a typical Englishman; that is a man with a very sharp insistence upon individual freedom. It also worked back ultimately to that larger and vaguer disgust of which I have spoken—the disgust at the perpetual posturing of the people before a mirror. The tyranny was irritating, not so much because of the suffering it inflicted on the minority, but because of the awful glimpses that it gave of the huge and imbecile happiness of the majority. The very vastness of the vain race enraged him, its immensity, its unity, its peace. He was annoyed more with its contentment than with any of its discontents. The thought of that unthinkable mass of millions, every one of them saying that Washington was the greatest man on earth, and that the Queen lived in the Tower of London, rode his riotous fancy like a nightmare. But to the end he retained the outlines of his original republican ideal and lamented over America not as being too Liberal, but as not being Liberal enough. Among others, he used these somewhat remarkable words: 'I tremble for a Radical coming here, unless he is a Radical on principle, by reason and reflection, and from the sense of right. I fear that if he were anything else he would return home a Tory. .... I say no more on that head for two months from this time, save that I do fear that the heaviest blow ever dealt at liberty will be dealt by this country, in the failure of its example on the earth.'

We are still waiting to see if that prediction has been fulfilled; but nobody can say that it has been falsified.

He went west on the great canals; he went south and touched the region of slavery; he saw America superficially indeed, but as a whole. And the great mass of his experience was certainly pleasant, though he vibrated with anticipatory passion against slave-holders, though he swore he would accept no public tribute in the slave country (a resolve which he broke under the pressure of the politeness of the South), yet his actual collisions with slavery and its upholders were few and brief. In these he bore himself with his accustomed vivacity and fire, but it would be a great mistake to convey the impression that his mental reaction against America was chiefly, or even largely, due to his horror at the negro problem. Over and above the cant of which we have spoken, the weary rush of words, the chief complaint he made was a complaint against bad manners; and on a large view his anti-Americanism would seem to be more founded on spitting than on slavery. When, however, it did happen that the primary morality of man-owning came up for discussion, Dickens displayed an honourable impatience. One man, full of anti-abolitionist ardour, button-holed him and bombarded him with the well-known argument in defence of slavery, that it was not to the financial interest of a slave-owner to damage or weaken his own slaves. Dickens, in telling the story of this interview, writes as follows: 'I told him quietly that it was not a man's interest to get drunk, or to steal, or to game, or to indulge in any other vice; but he *did* indulge in it for all that. That cruelty and the abuse of irresponsible power were two of the bad passions of human nature, with the gratification of which considerations of interest or of ruin had nothing whatever to do. ....' It is hardly possible to doubt that Dickens, in telling the man this, told him something sane and logical and unanswerable. But it is perhaps permissible to doubt whether he told it to him quietly.

He returned home in the spring of 1842, and in the later part of the year his 'American Notes' appeared, and the cry against him that had begun over copyright swelled into a roar in his rear. Yet when we read the 'Notes' we can find little offence in them, and, to say truth, less interest than usual. They are no true picture of America, or even of his vision of America, and this for two reasons. First, that he deliberately excluded from them all mention of that copyright question which had really given him his glimpse of how tyrannical a democracy can be. Second, that here he chiefly criticizes America for faults which are not, after all, especially American. For example, he is indignant with the inadequate character of the prisons, and compares them unfavourably with those in England, controlled by Lieutenant Tracey, and by Captain

Chesterton at Coldbath Fields, two reformers of prison discipline for whom he had a high regard. But it was a mere accident that American gaols were inferior to English. There was and is nothing in the American spirit to prevent their effecting all the reforms of Tracey and Chesterton, nothing to prevent their doing anything that money and energy and organization can do. America might have (for all I know, does have) a prison system cleaner and more humane and more efficient than any other in the world. And the evil genius of America might still remain—everything might remain that makes Pogram or Chollop irritating or absurd. And against the evil genius of America Dickens was now to strike a second and a very different blow.

In January, 1843, appeared the first number of the novel called 'Martin Chuzzlewit.' The earlier part of the book and the end, which have no connection with America or the American problem, in any case require a passing word. But except for the two gigantic grotesques on each side of the gateway of the tale, Pecksniff and Mrs Gamp, 'Martin Chuzzlewit' will be chiefly admired for its American excursion. It is a good satire embedded in an indifferent novel. Mrs Gamp is, indeed, a sumptuous study, laid on in those rich, oily, almost greasy colours that go to make the English comic characters, that make the very diction of Falstaff fat, and quaking with jolly degradation. Pecksniff also is almost perfect and much too good to be true. The only other thing to be noticed about him is that here, as almost everywhere else in the novels, the best figures are at their best when they have least to do. Dickens's characters are perfect as long as he can keep them out of his stories. Bumble is divine until a dark and practical secret is entrusted to him—as if anybody but a lunatic would entrust a secret to Bumble. Micawber is noble when he is doing nothing; but he is quite unconvincing when he is spying on Uriah Heep, for obviously neither Micawber nor anyone else would employ Micawber as a private detective. Similarly, while Pecksniff is the best thing in the story, the story is the worst thing in Pecksniff. His plot against old Martin can only be described by saying that it is as silly as old Martin's plot against him. His fall at the end is one of the rare falls of Dickens. Surely it was not necessary to take Pecksniff so seriously. Pecksniff is a merely laughable character; he is so laughable that he is lovable. Why take such trouble to unmask a man whose mask you have made transparent? Why collect all the characters to witness the exposure of a man in whom none of the characters believe? Why toil and triumph to have the laugh of a man who was only made to be laughed at?

But it is the American part of 'Martin Chuzzlewit' which is our concern, and which is memorable. It has the air of a great satire; but if it is only a great slander it is still great. His serious book on America was merely a squib, perhaps a damp squib. In any case, we all know that America will survive such serious books. But his fantastic book may survive America. It may survive America as 'The Knights' has survived Athens. 'Martin Chuzzlewit' has this quality of great satire that the critic forgets to ask whether the portrait is true to the original, because the portrait is so much more important than the original. Who cares whether Aristophanes correctly described Kleon, who is dead, when he so perfectly describes the demagogue, who cannot die? Just as little it may be, will some future age care whether the ancient civilization of the west, the lost cities of New York and St Louis, were fairly depicted in the colossal monument of Elijah Pogram. For there is much more in the American episodes than their intoxicating absurdity; there is more than humour in the young man who made the speech about the British Lion, and said, 'I taunt that lion. Alone I dare him;' or in the other man who told Martin that when he said that Queen Victoria did not live in the Tower of London he 'fell into an error not uncommon among his countrymen.' He has his finger on the nerve of an evil which was not only in his enemies, but in himself. The great democrat has hold of one of the dangers of democracy. The great optimist confronts a horrible nightmare of optimism. Above all, the genuine Englishman attacks a sin that is not merely American, but English also. The eternal, complacent iteration of patriotic half-truths; the perpetual buttering of one's self all over with the same stale butter; above all, the big defiances of small enemies, or the very urgent challenges to very distant enemies; the cowardice so habitual and unconscious that it wears the plumes of courage--all this is an English temptation as well as an American one. 'Martin Chuzzlewit' may be a caricature of America. America may be a caricature of England. But in the gravest college, in the quietest country house of England, there is the seed of the same essential madness that fills Dickens's book, like an asylum, with brawling Chollops and raving Jefferson Bricks. That essential madness is the idea that the good patriot is the man who feels at ease about his country. This notion of patriotism was unknown in the little pagan republics where our European patriotism began. It was unknown in the Middle Ages. In the eighteenth century, in the making of modern politics, a 'patriot' meant a discontented man. It was opposed to the word 'courtier,' which meant an upholder of present conditions. In all other modern countries, especially in countries like France and Ireland, where real difficulties have been faced, the word 'patriot' means something like a political pessimist. This view and these countries have exaggerations and dangers of their own; but the exaggeration and dangers of England is the same as the exaggeration and danger of *The Watertoast Gazette*. The thing which is rather foolishly called the Anglo-Saxon civilization is at present soaked through with a weak pride. It uses great masses of men not to procure discussion but to procure the pleasure of unanimity; it uses masses like bolsters. It uses its organs of public opinion not to warn the public, but to soothe it. It really succeeds not only in ignoring the rest of the world, but actually in forgetting it. And when a civilization really forgets the rest of the world—lets it fall as something obviously dim and barbaric— then there is only one adjective for the ultimate fate of the civilization, and that adjective is 'Chinese.'

Martin Chuzzlewit's America is a mad-house: but it is a mad-house we are all on the road to. For completeness and even comfort are almost the definitions of insanity. The lunatic is the man who lives in a small world but thinks it is a large one: he is the man who lives in a tenth of the truth, and thinks it is the whole. The madman cannot conceive any cosmos outside a certain tale or conspiracy or vision. Hence the more clearly we see the world divided into Saxons and non-Saxons, into our splendid selves and the rest, the more certain we may be that we are slowly and quietly going mad. The more plain and satisfying our state appears, the more we may know that we are living in an unreal world. For the real world is not satisfying. The more clear become the colours and facts of Anglo-Saxon superiority, the more surely we may know we are in a dream. For the real world is not clear or plain. The real world is full of bracing bewilderments and brutal surprises. Comfort is the blessing and the curse of the English, and of Americans of the Pogram type also. With them it is a loud comfort, a wild comfort, a screaming and capering comfort; but comfort at bottom still. For there is but an inch of difference between the cushioned chamber and the padded cell.

# Dickens and Christmas

In the July of 1844 Dickens went on an Italian tour, which he afterwards summarized in the book called 'Pictures from Italy.' They are, of course, very vivacious, but there is no great need to insist on them considered as Italian sketches; there is no need whatever to worry about them as a phase of the mind of Dickens when he travelled out of England. He never travelled out of England. There is no trace in all these amusing pages that he really felt the great foreign things which lie in wait for us in the south of Europe, the Latin civilization, the Catholic Church, the art of the centre, the endless end of Rome. His travels are not travels in Italy, but travels in Dickens-land. He sees amusing things; he describes them amusingly. But he would have seen things just as good in a street in Pimlico, and described them just as well. Few things were racier, even in his raciest novel, than his description of the marionette play of the death of Napoleon. Nothing could be more perfect than the figure of the doctor, which had something wrong with its wires, and hence 'hovered about the couch and delivered medical opinions in the air.' Nothing could be better as a catching of the spirit of all popular drama than the colossal depravity of the wooden image of 'Sir Uudson Low.' But there is nothing Italian about it. Dickens would have made just as good fun, indeed just the same fun, of a Punch and Judy show performing in Long Acre or Lincoln's Inn Fields.

Dickens uttered just and sincere satire on Plornish and Podsnap; but Dickens was as English as any Podsnap or any Plornish. He had a hearty humanitarianism, and a hearty sense of justice to all nations so far as he understood it. But that very kind of humanitarianism, that very kind of justice, were English. He was the Englishman of the type that made Free Trade, the most English of all things, since it was at once calculating and optimistic. He respected catacombs and gondolas, but that very respect was English. He wondered at brigands and volcanoes, but that very wonder was English. The very conception that Italy consists of these things was an English conception. The root things he never understood, the Roman legend, the ancient life of the Mediterranean, the world-old civilization of the vine and olive, the mystery of the immutable Church. He never understood these things, and I am glad he never understood them: he could only have understood them by ceasing to be the inspired cockney that he was, the rousing English Radical of the great Radical age in England. That spirit of his was one of the things that we have had which were truly national. All other forces we have borrowed, especially those which flatter us most. Imperialism is foreign, socialism is foreign, militarism is foreign, education is foreign, strictly even Liberalism is foreign. But Radicalism was our own; as English as the hedgerows.

Dickens abroad, then, was for all serious purposes simply the Englishman abroad; the Englishman abroad is for all serious purposes simply the Englishman at home. Of this generalization one modification must be made. Dickens did feel a direct pleasure in the bright and busy exterior of the French life, the clean caps, the coloured uniforms, the skies like blue enamel, the little green trees, the little white houses, the scene picked out in primary colours, like a child's picture-book. This he felt, and this he put (by a stroke of genius) into the mouth of Mrs Lirriper, a London landlady on a holiday: for Dickens always knew that it is the simple and not the subtle who feel differences; and he saw all his colours through the clear eyes of the poor. And in thus taking to his heart the streets, as it were, rather than the spires of the Continent, he showed beyond question that combination of which we have spoken—of common sense with uncommon sensibility. For it is for the sake of the streets and shops and the coats and hats, that we should go abroad; they are far better worth going to see than the castles and cathedrals and Roman camps. For the wonders of the world are the same all over the world, at least all over the European world. Castles that throw valleys in shadow, minsters that strike the sky, roads so old that they seem to have been made by the gods, these are in all Christian countries. The marvels of man are at all our doors. A labourer hoeing turnips in Sussex has no need to be ignorant that the bones of Europe are the Roman roads. A clerk living in Lambeth has no need not to know that there was a Christian art exuberant in the thirteenth century; for only across the river he can see the live stones of the Middle Ages surging together towards the stars. But exactly the things that do strike the traveller as extraordinary are the ordinary things, the food, the clothes, the vehicles; the strange things are cosmopolitan, the common things are national and peculiar. Cologne spire is lifted on the same arches as Canterbury; but the thing you cannot see out of Germany is a German beer-garden. There is no need for a Frenchman to go to look at Westminster Abbey as a piece of English architecture; it is not in the special sense a piece of English architecture. But a hansom cab is a piece of English architecture; a thing produced by the peculiar poetry of our cities, a symbol of a certain reckless comfort which is really English; a thing to draw a pilgrimage of the nations. The imaginative Englishman will be found all day in a *café*; the imaginative Frenchman in a hansom cab.

This sort of pleasure Dickens took in the Latin life; but no deeper kind. And the strongest of all possible indications of his fundamental detachment from it can be found in one fact. A great part of the time that he was in Italy he was engaged in writing 'The Chimes,' and such Christmas tales, tales of Christmas in the English towns, tales full of fog and snow and hail and happiness.

Dickens could find in any street divergences between man and man deeper than the divisions of nations. His fault was to exaggerate differences. He could find types almost as distinct as separate tribes of animals in his own brain and his own city, those two homes of a magnificent chaos. The only two southerners introduced prominently into his novels, the two in 'Little Dorrit,' are popular English foreigners, I had almost said stage foreigners. Villainy is, in English eyes, a southern trait, therefore one of the foreigners is villainous. Vivacity is, in English eyes, another southern trait, therefore the other foreigner is vivacious. But we can see from the outlines of both that Dickens did not have to go to Italy to get them. While poor panting million-aires, poor tired earls and poor God-forsaken American men of culture are plodding about Italy for literary inspiration, Charles Dickens made up the whole of that Italian romance (as I strongly suspect) from the faces of two London organ-grinders.

In the sunlight of the southern world, he was still dreaming of the firelight of the north. Among the palaces and the white campanili, he shut his eyes to see Marylebone and dreamed a lovely dream of chimney-pots. He was not happy, he said, without streets. The very foulness and smoke of London were lovable in his eyes and fill his Christmas tales with a vivid vapour. In the clear skies of the south he saw afar off the fog of London like a sunset cloud and longed to be in the core of it.

This Christmas tone of Dickens, in connection with his travels, is a matter that can only be expressed by a parallel with one of his other works. Much the same that has here been said of his 'Pictures from Italy,' may be said about his 'Child's History of England;' with the difference that while the 'Pictures from Italy' do in a sense add to his fame, the 'History of England' in almost every sense detracts from it. But the nature of the limitation is the same. What Dickens was travelling in distant lands, that he was travelling in distant ages; a sturdy, sentimental English Radical with a large heart and a narrow mind. He could not help falling into that besetting sin or weakness of the modern progressive, the habit of regarding the contemporary questions as the eternal questions and the latest word as the last. He could not get out of his head the instinctive conception that the real problem before St Dunstan was whether he should support Lord John Russell or Sir Robert

Peel. He could not help seeing the remotest peaks lit up by the raging bonfire of his own passionate political crisis. He lived for the instant and its urgency; that is, he did what St Dunstan did. He lived in an eternal present like all simple men. It is indeed 'A Child's History of England;' but the child is the writer and not the reader.

But Dickens in his cheapest cockney utilitarianism was not only English, but unconsciously historic. Upon him descended the real tradition of 'Merry England,' and not upon the pallid mediævalists who thought they were reviving it. The Pre-Raphaelites, the Gothicists, the admirers of the Middle Ages, had in their subtlety and sadness the spirit of the present day. Dickens had in his buffoonery and bravery the spirit of the Middle Ages. He was much more mediæval in his attacks on mediævalism than they were in their defences of it. It was he who had the things of Chaucer, the love of large jokes and long stories and brown ale and all the white roads of England. Like Chaucer he loved story within story, every man telling a tale. Like Chaucer he saw something openly comic in men's motley trades. Sam Weller would have been a great gain to the Canterbury Pilgrimage and told an admirable story. Rossetti's Damozel would have been a great bore, regarded as too fast by the Prioress and too priggish by the Wife of Bath. It is said that in the somewhat sickly Victorian revival of feudalism which was called 'Young England,' a nobleman hired a hermit to live in his grounds. It is also said that the hermit struck for more beer. Whether this anecdote be true or not, it is always told as showing a collapse from the ideal of the Middle Ages to the level of the present day. But in the mere act of striking for beer the holy man was very much more 'mediæval' than the fool who employed him.

It would be hard to find a better example of this than Dickens's great defence of Christmas. In fighting for Christmas he was fighting for the old European festival, Pagan and Christian, for that trinity of eating, drinking and praying which to moderns appears irreverent, for the holy day which is really a holiday. He had himself the most babyish ideas about the past. He supposed the Middle Ages to have consisted of tournaments and torture-chambers, he supposed himself to be a brisk man of the manufacturing age, almost a Utilitarian. But for all that he defended the mediæval feast which was going out against the Utilitarianism which was coming in. He could only see all that was bad in mediævalism. But he fought for all that was good in it. And he was all the more really in sympathy with the old strength and simplicity because he only knew that it was good and did not know that it was old. He cared as little for mediævalism as the mediævals did. He cared as much as they did for lustiness and virile laughter and sad tales of good lovers and pleasant tales of good livers. He would have been very much bored by Ruskin and Walter Pater if they had explained to him the strange sunset tints of Lippi and Botticelli. He had no pleasure in looking on the dying Middle Ages. But he looked on the living Middle Ages, on a piece of the old uproarious superstition still unbroken; and he hailed it like a new religion. The Dickens character ate pudding to an extent at which the modern mediævalists turned pale. They would do every kind of honour to an old observance, except observing it. They would pay to a Church feast every sort of compliment except feasting.

And (as I have said) as were his unconscious relations to our European past, so were his unconscious relations to England. He imagined himself to be, if anything, a sort of cosmopolitan; at any rate to be a champion of the charms and merits of continental lands against the arrogance of our island. But he was in truth very much more a champion of the old and genuine England against that comparatively cosmopolitan England which we have all lived to see. And here again the supreme example is Christmas. Christmas is, as I have said, one of numberless old European feasts of which the essence is the combination of religion with merry-making. But among those feasts it is also especially and distinctively English in the style of its merry-making and even in the style of its religion. For the character of Christmas (as distinct, for instance, from the continental Easter) lies chiefly in two things; first on the terrestrial side the note of comfort rather than the note of brightness; and on the spiritual side, Christian charity rather than Christian ecstasy. And comfort is, like charity, a very English instinct. Nay, comfort is, like charity, an English merit; though our comfort may and does degenerate into materialism, just as our charity may and does degenerate into laxity and make-believe.

This ideal of comfort belongs peculiarly to England; it belongs peculiarly to Christmas; above all, it belongs pre-eminently to Dickens. And it is astonishingly misunderstood. It is misunderstood by the continent of Europe; it is, if possible, still more misunderstood by the English of to-day. On the Continent the restaurateurs provide us with raw beef, as if we were savages; yet old English cooking takes as much care as French. And in England has arisen a parvenu patriotism which represents the English as everything but English; as a blend of Chinese stoicism, Latin militarism, Prussian rigidity, and American bad taste. And so England, whose fault is gentility and whose virtue is geniality, England with her tradition of the great gay gentlemen of Elizabeth, is represented to the four quarters of the world (as in Mr Kipling's religious poems) in the enormous image of a solemn cad. And because it is very difficult to be comfortable in the suburbs, the suburbs have voted that comfort is a gross and material thing. Comfort, especially this vision of Christmas comfort, is the reverse of a gross or material thing. It is far more poetical, properly speaking, than the Garden of Epicurus. It is far more artistic than the Palace of Art. It is more artistic because it is based upon a contrast, a contrast between the fire and wine within the house and the winter and the roaring rains without. It is far more poetical, because there is in it a note of defence, almost of war; a note of being besieged by the snow and hail; of making merry in the belly of a fort. The man who said that an Englishman's house is his castle said much more than he meant. The Englishman thinks of his house as something fortified and provisioned, and his very surliness is at root romantic. And this sense would naturally be strongest in wild winter nights, when the lowered portcullis and the lifted drawbridge do not merely bar people out, but bar people in. The Englishman's house is most sacred, not merely when the King cannot enter it, but when the Englishman cannot get out of it.

This comfort, then, is an abstract thing, a principle. The English poor shut all their doors and windows till their rooms reek like the Black Hole. They are suffering for an idea. Mere animal hedonism would not dream, as we English do, of winter feasts and little rooms, but of eating fruit in large and idle gardens. Mere sensuality would desire to please all its senses. But to our good dreams this dark and dangerous background is essential; the highest pleasure we can imagine is a defiant pleasure, a happiness that stands at bay. The word 'comfort' is not indeed the right word, it conveys too much of the slander of mere sense; the true word is 'cosiness,' a word not translatable. One, at least, of the essentials of it is smallness, smallness in preference to largeness, smallness for smallness' sake. The merry-maker wants a pleasant parlour, he would not give twopence for a pleasant continent. In our difficult time, of course, a fight for mere space has become necessary. Instead of being greedy for ale and Christmas pudding we are greedy for mere air, an equally sensual appetite. In abnormal conditions this is wise; and the illimitable veldt is an excellent thing for nervous people. But our fathers were large and healthy enough to make a thing humane, and not worry about whether it was hygienic. They were big enough to get into small rooms.

Of this quite deliberate and artistic quality in the close Christmas chamber, the standing evidence is Dickens in Italy. He created these dim firelit tales like little dim red jewels, as an artistic necessity, in the centre of an endless summer. Amid the white cities of Tuscany he hungered for something romantic, and wrote about a rainy Christmas. Amid the pictures of the Uffizi he starved for something beautiful, and fed his memory on London fog. His feeling for the fog was especially poignant and typical. In the first of his Christmas tales, the popular 'Christmas Carol,' he suggested the very soul of it in one simile, when he spoke of the dense air, suggesting that 'Nature was brewing on a large scale.' This sense of the thick atmosphere as something to eat or drink, something not only solid but satisfactory, may seem almost insane, but it is no exaggeration of Dickens's emotion. We speak of a fog 'that you could cut with a knife.' Dickens would have liked the phrase as suggesting that the fog was a colossal cake. He liked even more his own phrase of the Titanic brewery, and no dream would have given him a wilder pleasure than to grope his way to some such tremendous vats and drink the ale of the giants.

There is a current prejudice against fogs, and Dickens, perhaps, is their only poet. Considered hygienically, no doubt this may be more or less excusable. But considered poetically, fog is not undeserving, it has a real significance. We have in our great cities abolished the clean and sane darkness of the country. We have outlawed night and sent her wandering in wild meadows; we have lit eternal watch-fires against her return. We have made a new cosmos, and as a consequence our own sun and stars. And as a consequence also, and most justly, we have made our own darkness. Just as every lamp is a warm human moon, so every fog is a rich human nightfall. If it were not for this mystic accident we should never see darkness, and he who has never seen darkness has never seen the sun. Fog for us is the chief form of the outward pressure which compresses mere luxury into real comfort. It makes the world small in the same spirit as in that common and happy cry that the world is small, meaning that it is full of friends. The first man that emerges out of the mist with a light is for us Prometheus, a saviour bringing fire to men. He is that greatest and best of all men, greater than the heroes, better than the saints, Man Friday. Every rumble of a cart, every cry in the distance, marks the heart of humanity beating undaunted in the darkness. It is wholly human; man toiling in his own cloud. If real darkness is like the embrace of God, this is the dark embrace of man.

In such a sacred cloud the tale called 'The Christmas Carol' begins, the first and most typical of all his Christmas tales. It is not irrelevant to dilate upon the geniality of this darkness, because it is characteristic of Dickens that his atmospheres are more important than his stories. The Christmas atmosphere is more important than Scrooge, or the ghosts either; in a sense, the background is more important than the figures. The same thing may be noticed in his dealings with that other atmosphere (besides that of good humour) which he excelled in creating, an atmosphere of mystery and wrong, such as that which gathers round Mrs Clennam, rigid in her chair, or old Miss Havisham, ironically robed as a bride. Here again the atmosphere altogether eclipses the story, which often seems disappointing in comparison. The secrecy is sensational; the secret is tame. The surface of the thing seems more awful than the core of it. It seems almost as if these grisly figures, Mrs Chadband and Mrs Clennam, Miss Havisham, and Miss Flite, Nemo and Sally Brass, were keeping something back from the author as well as from the reader. When the book closes we do not know their real secret. They soothed the optimistic Dickens with something less terrible than the truth. The dark house of Arthur Clennam's childhood really depresses us; it is a true glimpse into that quiet street in hell, where live the children of that unique dispensation which theologians call Calvinism and Christians devil-worship. But some stranger crime had really been done there, some more monstrous blasphemy or human sacrifice than the suppression of some silly document advantageous to the silly Dorrits. Something worse than a common tale of jilting lay behind the masquerade and madness of the awful Miss Havisham. Something worse was whispered by the misshapen Quilp to the sinister Sally in that wild, wet summer-house by the river, something worse than the clumsy plot against the clumsy Kit. These dark pictures seem almost as if they were literally visions; things, that is, that Dickens saw but did not understand.

And as with his backgrounds of gloom, so with his backgrounds of good-will, in such tales as 'The Christmas Carol.' The tone of the tale is kept throughout in a happy monotony, though the tale is everywhere irregular and in some places weak. It has the same kind of artistic unity that belongs to a dream. A dream may begin with the end of the world and end with a tea-party; but either the end of the world will seem as trivial as a tea-party or that tea-party will be as terrible as the day of doom. The incidents change wildly; the story scarcely changes at all. 'The Christmas Carol' is a kind of philanthropic dream, an enjoyable nightmare, in which the scenes shift bewilderingly and seem as miscellaneous as the pictures in a scrap-book, but in which there is one constant state of the soul, a state of rowdy benediction and a hunger for human faces. The beginning is about a winter day and a miser; yet the beginning is in no way bleak. The author starts with a kind of happy howl; he bangs on our door like a drunken carol singer; his style is festive and popular, he compares the snow and hail to philanthropists who 'come down handsomely;' he compares the fog to unlimited beer. Scrooge is not really inhuman at the beginning any more than he is at the end. There is a heartiness in his inhospitable sentiments that is akin to humour and therefore to humanity; he is only a crusty old bachelor, and had (I strongly suspect) given away turkeys secretly all his life. The beauty and the real blessing of the story do not lie in the mechanical plot of it, the repentance of Scrooge, probable or improbable; they lie in the great furnace of real happiness that glows through Scrooge and everything around him; that great furnace, the heart of Dickens. Whether the Christmas visions would or would not convert Scrooge, they convert us. Whether or no the visions were evoked by real Spirits of the Past, Present, and Future, they were evoked by that truly exalted order of angels who are correctly called High Spirits. They are impelled and sustained by a quality which our contemporary artists ignore or almost deny, but which in a life decently lived is as normal and attainable as sleep, positive, passionate, conscious joy. The story sings from end to end like a happy man going home; and, like a happy and good man, when it cannot sing it yells. It is lyric and exclamatory, from the first exclamatory words of it. It is strictly a Christmas carol.

Dickens, as has been said, went to Italy with this kindly cloud still about him, still meditating on Yule mysteries. Among the olives and the orange-trees he wrote his second great Christmas tale, 'The Chimes,' at Genoa in 1844, a Christmas tale only differing from 'The Christmas Carol' in being fuller of the grey rains of winter and the north. 'The Chimes' is, like the 'Carol,' an appeal for charity and mirth, but it is a stern and fighting appeal: if the other is a Christmas carol, this a Christmas war-song. In it Dickens hurled himself with even more than his usual militant joy and scorn into an attack upon a cant, which he said made his blood boil. This cant was nothing more nor less than the whole tone taken by three-quarters of the political and economic world towards the poor. It was a vague and vulgar Bentham-ism with a rollicking Tory touch in it. It explained to the poor their duties with a cold and coarse philanthropy unendurable by any free man. It had also at its command a kind of brutal banter, a loud good humour which Dickens sketches savagely in Alderman Cute. He fell furiously on all their ideas: the cheap advice to live cheaply, the base advice to live basely, above all, the preposterous primary assumption that the rich are to advise the poor and not the poor the rich. There were and are hundreds of these benevolent bullies. Some say that the poor should give up having children, which means that they should give up their great virtue of sexual sanity. Some say that they should give up 'treating' each other, which means that they should give up all that remains to them of the virtue of hospitality. Against all of this Dickens thundered very thoroughly in 'The Chimes.' It may be remarked in passing that this affords another instance of a confusion already referred to, the confusion whereby Dickens supposed himself to be exalting the present over the past, whereas he was really dealing deadly blows at things strictly peculiar to the present. Embedded in this very book is a somewhat useless interview between Trotty Veck and the church bells, in which the latter lecture the former for having supposed (why, I don't know) that they were expressing regret for the disappearance of the Middle Ages. There is no reason why Trotty Veck or anyone else should idealize the Middle Ages, but certainly he was the last man in the world to be asked to idealize the nineteenth century, seeing that the smug and stingy philosophy, which poisons his life through the book, was an exclusive creation of that century. But, as I have said before, the fieriest mediævalist may forgive Dickens for disliking the good things the Middle Ages took away, considering how he loved whatever good things the Middle Ages left behind. It matters very little that he hated old feudal castles when they were already old. It matters very much that he hated the New Poor Law while it was still new.

The moral of this matter in 'The Chimes' is essential. Dickens had sympathy with the poor in the Greek and literal sense; he suffered with them mentally; for the things that irritated them were the things that irritated him. He did not pity the people, or even champion the people, or even merely love the people; in this matter he was the people. He alone in our literature is the voice not merely of the social substratum, but even of the subconsciousness of the substratum. He utters the secret anger of the humble. He says what the uneducated only think, or even only feel, about the educated. And in nothing is he so genuinely such a voice as in this fact of his fiercest mood being reserved for methods that are counted scientific and progressive. Pure and exalted atheists talk themselves into believing that the working-classes are turning with indignant scorn from the churches. The working-classes are not indignant against the churches in the least. The things the working-classes really are indignant against are the hospitals. The people has no definite disbelief in the temples of theology. The people has a very fiery and practical disbelief in the temples of physical science. The things the poor hate are the modern things, the rationalistic things—doctors, inspectors, poor law guardians, professional philanthropy. They never showed any reluctance to be helped by the old and corrupt monasteries. They will often die rather than be helped by the modern and efficient workhouse. Of all this anger, good or bad, Dickens is the voice of an accusing energy. When, in 'The Christmas Carol,' Scrooge refers to the surplus population, the Spirit tells him, very justly, not to speak till he knows what the surplus is and where it is. The implication is severe but sound. When a group of superciliously benevolent economists look down into the abyss for the surplus population, assuredly there is only one answer that should be given to them; and that is to say, 'If there is a surplus, you are a surplus.' And if anyone were ever cut off, they would be. If the barricades went up in our streets and the poor became masters, I think the priests would escape, I fear the gentlemen would; but I believe the gutters would be simply running with the blood of philanthropists.

Lastly, he was at one with the poor in this chief matter of Christmas, in the matter, that is, of special festivity. There is nothing on which the poor are more criticized than on the point of spending large sums on small feasts; and though there are material difficulties, there is nothing in which they are more right. It is said that a Boston paradox-monger said, 'Give us the luxuries of life and we will dispense with the necessities.' But it is the whole human race that says it, from the first savage wearing feathers instead of clothes to the last costermonger having a treat instead of three meals.

The third of his Christmas stories, 'The Cricket on the Hearth,' calls for no extensive comment, though it is very characteristic. It has all the qualities which we have called dominant qualities in his Christmas sentiment. It has cosiness, that is the comfort that depends upon a discomfort surrounding it.

It has a sympathy with the poor, and especially with the extravagance of the poor; with what may be called the temporary wealth of the poor. It has the sentiment of the hearth, that is, the sentiment of the open fire being the red heart of the room. That open fire is the veritable flame of England, still kept burning in the midst of a mean civilization of stoves. But everything that is valuable in 'The Cricket on the Hearth' is perhaps as well expressed in the title as it is in the story. The tale itself, in spite of some of those inimitable things that Dickens never failed to say, is a little too comfortable to be quite convincing. 'The Christmas Carol' is the conversion of an anti-Christmas character. 'The Chimes' is a slaughter of anti-Christmas characters. 'The Cricket,' perhaps, fails for lack of this crusading note. For everything has its weak side, and when full justice has been done to this neglected note of poetic comfort, we must remember that it has its very real weak side. The defect of it in the work of Dickens was that he tended sometimes to pile up the cushions until none of the characters could move. He is so much interested in effecting his state of static happiness that he forgets to make a story at all. His princes at the start of the story begin to live happily ever afterwards. We feel this strongly in 'Master Humphrey's Clock' and we feel it sometimes in these Christmas stories. He makes his characters so comfortable that his characters begin to dream and drivel. And he makes his reader so comfortable that his reader goes to sleep.

The actual tale of the carrier and his wife sounds somewhat sleepily in our ears; we cannot keep our attention fixed on it, though we are conscious of a kind of warmth from it as from a great wood fire. We know so well that everything will soon be all right that we do not suspect when the carrier suspects, and are not frightened when the gruff Tackleton growls. The sound of the festivities at the end come fainter on our ears than did the shout of the Cratchits or the bells of Trotty Veck. All the good figures that followed Scrooge when he came growling out of the fog fade into the fog again.

# Woman

A correspondent has written me an able and interesting letter in the matter of some allusions of mine to the subject of communal kitchens. He defends communal kitchens. He defends communal kitchens very lucidly from the standpoint of the calculating collectivist; but, like many of his school, he cannot apparently grasp that there is another test of the whole matter, with which such calculation has nothing at all to do. He knows it would be cheaper if a number of us ate at the same time, so as to use the same table. So it would. It would also be cheaper if a number of us slept at different times, so as to use the same pair of trousers. But the question is not how cheap are we buying a thing, but what are we buying? It is cheap to own a slave. And it is cheaper still to be a slave.

My correspondent also says that the habit of dining out in restaurants, etc., is growing. So, I believe, is the habit of committing suicide. I do not desire to connect the two facts together. It seems fairly clear that a man could not dine at a restaurant because he had just committed suicide; and it would be extreme, perhaps, to suggest that he commits suicide because he has just dined at a restaurant. But the two cases when put side by side are enough to indicate the falsity and poltroonery of this eternal modern argument from what is in fashion. The question for brave men is not whether a certain thing is increasing; the question is whether we are increasing it. I dine very often in restaurants because the nature of my trade makes it convenient: but if I thought that by dining in restaurants I was working for the creation of communal meals, I would never enter a restaurant again; I would carry bread and cheese in my pocket or eat chocolate out of automatic machines. For the personal element in some things is sacred. I heard Mr Will Crooks put it perfectly the other day: 'The most sacred thing is to be able to shut your own door.'

My correspondent says, 'Would not our women be spared the drudgery of cooking and all its attendant worries, leaving them free for higher culture?'

*Illustrated London News*, 24 March, 1906. Collected in All Things Considered, 1908

The first thing that occurs to me to say about this is very simple, and is, I imagine, a part of all our experience. If my correspondent can find any way of preventing women from worrying, he will indeed be a remarkable man. I think the matter is a much deeper one. First of all, my correspondent overlooks a distinction which is elementary in our human nature. Theoretically, I suppose, every one would like to be freed from worries. But nobody in the world would always like to be freed from worrying occupations. I should very much like (as far as my feelings at the moment go) to be free from the consuming nuisance of writing this article. But it does not follow that I should like to be free from the consuming nuisance of being a journalist. Because we are worried about a thing, it does not follow that we are not interested in it. The truth is the other way. If we are not interested, why on earth should we be worried? Women are worried about housekeeping, but those that are most interested are the most worried. Women are still more worried about their husbands and their children. And I suppose if we strangled the children and pole-axed the husbands it would leave women free for higher culture. That is, it would leave them free to begin to worry about that. For women would worry about higher culture as much as they worry about everything else.

I believe this way of talking about women and their higher culture is almost entirely a growth of the classes which (unlike the journalistic class to which I belong) have always a reasonable amount of money. One odd thing I specially notice. Those who write like this seem entirely to forget the existence of the working and wage-earning classes. They say eternally, like my correspondent, that the ordinary woman is always a drudge. And what, in the name of the Nine Gods, is the ordinary man? These people seem to think that the ordinary man is a Cabinet Minister. They are always talking about man going forth to wield power, to carve his own way, to stamp his individuality on the world, to command and to be obeyed. This may be true of a certain class. Dukes, perhaps, are not drudges; but, then, neither are Duchesses. The Ladies and Gentlemen of the Smart Set are quite free for the higher culture, which consists chiefly of motoring and Bridge. But the ordinary man who typifies and constitutes the millions that make up our civilization is no more free for the higher culture than his wife is.

Indeed, he is not so free. Of the two sexes the woman is in the more powerful position. For the average woman is at the head of something with which she can do as she likes; the average man has to obey orders and do nothing else. He has to put one dull brick on another dull brick, and do nothing else; he has to add one dull figure to another dull figure, and do nothing else. The woman's world is a small one, perhaps, but she can alter it. The woman can tell the tradesman with whom she deals some realistic things about himself. The clerk who does this to the manager generally gets the sack or shall we say (to avoid the vulgarism), finds himself free for higher culture. Above all ... the woman does work which is in some small degree creative and individual. She can put the flowers or the furniture in fancy arrangements of her own. I fear the bricklayer cannot put the bricks in fancy arrangements of his own, without disaster to himself and others. If the woman is only putting a patch into a carpet, she can choose the thing with regard to colour. I fear it would not do for the office boy dispatching a parcel to choose his stamps with a view to colour; to prefer the tender mauve of the sixpenny to the crude scarlet of the penny stamp. A woman cooking may not always cook artistically; still she can cook artistically. She can introduce a personal and imperceptible alteration into the composition of a soup. The clerk is not encouraged to introduce a personal and imperceptible alteration into the figures in a ledger.

The trouble is that the real question I raised is not discussed. It is argued as a problem in pennies, not as a problem in people. It is not the proposals of these reformers that I feel to be false so much as their temper and their arguments. I am not nearly so certain that communal kitchens are wrong as I am that the defenders of communal kitchens are wrong. Of course, for one thing, there is a vast difference between the communal kitchens of which I spoke and the communal meal (*monstrum horrendum, informe*) which the darker and wilder mind of my correspondent diabolically calls up. But in both the trouble is that their defenders will not defend them humanly as human institutions. They will not interest themselves in the staring psychological fact that there are some things that a man or a woman, as the case may be, wishes to do for himself or herself. He or she must do it inventively, creatively, artistically, individually—in a word, badly. Choosing your wife (say) is one of these things. Is choosing your husband's dinner one of these things? That is the whole question: it is never asked.

And then the higher culture. I know that culture. I would not set any man free for it if I could help it. The effect of it on the rich men who are free for it is so horrible that it is worse than any of the other amusements of the millionaire—worse than gambling, worse even than philanthropy. It means thinking the smallest poet in Belgium greater than the greatest poet of England. It means losing every democratic sympathy. It means being unable to talk to a navvy about sport, or about beer, or about the Bible, or about the Derby, or about patriotism or about anything whatever that he, the navvy, wants to talk about. It means taking literature seriously, a very amateurish thing to do. It means pardoning indecency only when it is gloomy indecency. Its disciples will call a spade a spade: but only when it is a grave-digger's spade. The higher culture is sad, cheap, impudent, unkind, without honesty and without ease. In short, it is 'high'. That abominable word (also applied to game) admirably describes it.

No; if you were setting women free for something else I might be more melted. If you can assure me, privately and gravely, that you are setting women free to dance on the mountains like Maenads, or to worship some monstrous goddess, I will make a note of your request. If you are quite sure that the ladies in Brixton, the moment they give up cooking, will beat great gongs and blow horns to Mumbo-Jumbo, then I will agree that the occupation is at least human and is more or less entertaining. Women have been set free to be Bacchantes; they have been set free to be Virgin Martyrs; they have been set free to be Witches. Do not ask them now to sink so low as the higher culture.

I have my own little notions of the possible emancipation of women; but I suppose I should not be taken very seriously if I propounded them. I should favour anything that would increase the present enormous authority of women and their creative action in their own homes. The average woman, as I have said, is a despot; the average man is a serf. I am for any scheme that any one can suggest that will make the average woman more of a despot. So far from wishing her to get her cooked meals from outside, I should like her to cook more wildly and at her own will than she does. So far from getting always the same meals from the same place, let her invent, if she likes, a new dish every day of her life. Let woman be more of a maker, not less. We are right to talk about 'Woman': only blackguards talk about women. Yet all men talk about men, and that is the whole difference. Men represent the deliberative and democratic element in life. Woman represents the despotic.

# The Perpetuation of Punishment

Surely something ought to be done in connection with our system of police and punishment. A case has quite recently come within my knowledge which I will describe in the strict and prosaic terms required for such a matter. It is one of the innumerable truths of human life which have come to me from the custom, the admirable and beautiful custom, of driving in hansom cabs. This habit has nothing to do with low considerations of comfort or convenience; it is a custom, and, being a custom, I, who am the most conservative of mankind, adhere to it. I know quite well that many other modern inventions have become far more cabbish than cabs. I know that motor cabs whistle by me like the wind. I know that electric trams flash by me like the thunderbolt as I toil along in this antiquated vehicle. The hansom cab has been called the gondola of London; alas! it has become as antiquated, as inconvenient, as truly national as the gondola of Venice. I cannot help the fact that Radicals alone love the past. If I had been born in the time of coaches I should still go to Brighton by coach. When the last lost hansom is wrecked upon some ruined street or shore, I shall be tipped out of it.

But I have been misled into a lyric, whereas my meaning was even practical and painful. I have got many good things out of riding in hansom cabs; incidentally the ride. I fancy that the surliness of the hansom cabman must be chiefly created by the haughtiness of indignant ladies. I could tell many stories to the everlasting credit of cabmen. Once, I remember, I was leaving the house of some politician in Berkeley Square literally without a penny in my pocket. A hansom cabman, innocently supposing that a man in evening dress must have money (which is almost infinitely untrue), came up and offered to drive me to Battersea. I told him the exact facts—that I had no money at all, and was not even very certain of getting it tomorrow. He drove me back the whole of the way by his own request for nothing. Those stories are not told as jokes in *Punch*.

Now, I knew a cabman who stole. He did his turn of imprisonment, and

*Daily News*, 1907. Collected in Lunacy and Letters, 1958

came out of it as few men do, fundamentally healthy in his aim and point of view. He had often driven me, and he still spoke to me as a free man speaks to another, and told me that he did not want, if he could help it, to be driven to such desperation again; and I made him promise always to let me know before he was so driven. He could not get a character for any employment; he could not offer what is called a 'deserving' case to any organized charity. He told me that he meant to hawk a basket of flowers, and I gave him the money to buy it as naturally as I would have given it to any of my own friends. The man's attitude was entirely human and conceivable; I did not doubt his sorrow for his first sin, and I do not doubt it now. I felt quite certain that I was simply putting straight a path that had not gone very crooked. I went away into the country; when I came back he had been put in prison again for hawking flowers without a licence; without the licence that he could not get. And his old conviction was brought up against him.

The modern world is wicked, because it is civilized. What is specially shameful and pitiless in modern punishment is not the severity of the punishment; it is the continuity of the punishment. The modern philosophers say that they do not like the idea of everlasting punishment in the other world. Let them rest content. They have created everlasting punishment in this world. What is frightful about modern punishment is exactly that it is as logical as Calvinism. Its horror is that it is rational, that it remembers, that it treats the man who has broken trust as for ever untrustworthy. There may be something in this which pleases those who have Calvinistic, Materialistic, or Theosophical minds, minds that enjoy the recurrence of an unforgiving, that is, a dead, law. But you and I only have the tradition of Christian charity, and we should say, Beat the man about with a great stick and then let him go free for ever.

In reading the old records of religious communities, even the most ferocious, such as New England or the Presbyterian Government of West Scotland in Burns's time, we always have a feeling that the sin was punished and wiped out, savagely punished, perhaps, but also savagely understood; regarded as a thing that a man might do and that a man might recover from doing. It will be a terrible thing in the modern world if the making of punishment mild only means making it eternal. To be in hot hell for ever is bad enough; to be in a tepid hell for ever and to be asked to admit the humane temperature—that is intolerable. Nobody wants a punishment to be humane; a punishment, so long as it is a punishment, cannot be humane. But everybody wants a punishment to be human; everybody want a punishment to have just these two qualities about it. First, that a man can inflict it and remain a man. Second, that a man can receive it and remain a man. If it passes these limits the victim may very well kill the executioner or the executioner may very well kill himself.

Now these limits may be crossed and doubtless have been crossed by certain horrible punishments in the past; I can well imagine a man cutting his throat merely because he had stood by and seen a woman stripped and scourged as were many women quite late in the history of England and Ireland, or some negro burnt alive as he still is in the United States. But some part of this shocking shame lies on us all. For we stand by and permit that one thing in punishment which makes it worse than any ancient torture —its perpetuation. It is exactly this that defines torture: that it goes on. It is exactly this that is in the literal and real sense of the word inhuman. This modern scientific punishment in which a man cannot get away from his past belongs to the same world as that detestable determinism which declares also that he cannot get away from his past. It is making memory stronger than will. It is a thing not natural to men; and it will not long be endured among them.

# Oxford from Without

Some time ago I ventured to defend that race of hunted and persecuted outlaws, the Bishops; but until this week I had no idea how much persecuted they were. For instance, the Bishop of Birmingham made some extremely sensible remarks in the House of Lords, to the effect that Oxford and Cambridge were (as everybody knows they are) far too much merely plutocratic playgrounds. One would have thought that an Anglican Bishop might be allowed to know something about the English University system, and even to have, if anything, some bias in its favour. But (as I pointed out) the rollicking Radicalism of Bishops has to be restrained. The man who writes the notes in the weekly paper called the *Outlook* feels that it is his business to restrain it. The passage has such simple sublimity that I must quote it:—

'Dr Gore talked unworthily of his reputation when he spoke of the older Universities as playgrounds for the rich and idle. In the first place, the rich men there are not idle. Some of the rich men are, and so are some of the poor men. On the whole, the sons of noble and wealthy families keep up the best traditions of academic life.'

So far this seems all very nice. It is a part of the universal principle on which Englishmen have acted in recent years. As you will not try to make the best people the most powerful people, persuade yourselves that the most powerful people are the best people. Mad Frenchmen and Irishmen try to realize the ideal. To you belongs the nobler (and much easier) task of idealizing the real. First give your Universities entirely into the power of the rich; then let the rich start traditions; and then congratulate yourselves on the fact that the sons of the rich keep up these traditions. All that is quite simple and jolly. But then this critic, who crushes Dr Gore from the high throne of the *Outlook*, goes on in a way that is really perplexing. 'It is distinctly advantageous', he says, 'that rich and poor—*i.e.*, young men with a

*Illustrated London News*, 3 August, 1907. Collected in All Things Considered, 1908

smooth path in life before them, and those who have to hew out a road for themselves—should be brought into association. Each class learns a great deal from the other. On the one side, social conceit and exclusiveness give way to the free spirit of competition amongst all classes; on the other side, angularities and prejudices are rubbed away.' Even this I might have swallowed. But the paragraph concludes with this extraordinary sentence: 'We get the net result in such careers as those of Lord Milner, Lord Curzon, and Mr Asquith.'

Those three names lay my intellect prostrate. The rest of the argument I understand quite well. The social exclusiveness of aristocrats at Oxford and Cambridge gives way before the free spirit of competition amongst all classes. That is to say, there is at Oxford so hot and keen a struggle, consisting of coal-heavers, London clerks, gypsies, navvies, drapers' assistants, grocers' assistants—in short, all the classes that make up the bulk of England—there is such a fierce competition at Oxford among all these people that in its presence aristocratic exclusiveness gives way. That is all quite clear. I am not quite sure about the facts but I quite understand the argument. But then, having been called upon to contemplate this bracing picture of a boisterous turmoil of all the classes of England, I am suddenly asked to accept as example of it, Lord Milner, Lord Curzon, and the present Chancellor of the Exchequer. What part do these gentlemen play in the mental process? Is Lord Curzon one of the rugged and ragged poor men whose angularities have been rubbed away? Or is he one of those whom Oxford immediately deprived of all kind of social exclusiveness? His Oxford reputation does not seem to bear out either account of him. To regard Lord Milner as a typical product of Oxford would surely be unfair. It would be to deprive the educational tradition of Germany of one of its most typical products. English aristocrats have their faults, but they are not at all like Lord Milner. What Mr Asquith was meant to prove, whether he was a rich man who lost his exclusiveness or a poor man who lost his angles, I am utterly unable to conceive.

There is, however, one mild but very evident truth that might perhaps be mentioned. And it is this: that none of those three excellent persons is or ever has been a poor man in the sense that that word is understood by the overwhelming majority of the English nation. There are no poor men at Oxford in the sense that the majority of men in the street are poor. The very fact that the writer in the *Outlook* can talk about such people as poor shows that he does not understand what the modern problem is. His kind of poor man rather reminds me of the Earl in the ballad by that great English satirist, Sir W. S. Gilbert, whose angles (very acute angles) had, I fear, never been rubbed down by an old English University. The reader will remember that when the Periwinkle-girl was adored by two Dukes the poet added:—

> 'A third adorer had the girl,
>   A man of lowly station;
> A miserable grovelling Earl
>   Besought her approbation.'

Perhaps, indeed, some allusion to our University system, and to the universal clash in it of all the classes of the community, may be found in the verse a little farther on, which says: —

> 'He'd had, it happily befell,
>   A decent education;
> His views would have befitted well
>   A far superior station.'

Possibly there was as simple a chasm between Lord Curzon and Lord Milner. But I am afraid that the chasm will become almost imperceptible, a microscopic crack, if we compare it with the chasm that separates either or both of them from the people of this country.

Of course the truth is exactly as the Bishop of Birmingham put it. I am sure that he did not put it in any unkindly or contemptuous spirit towards those old English seats of learning which, whether they are or are not seats of learning, are, at any rate, old and English, and those are two very good things to be. The old English University is a playground for the governing class. That does not prove that it is a bad thing; it might prove that it was a very good thing. Certainly if there is a governing class let there be a playground for the governing class. I would much rather be ruled by men who know how to play than by men who do not know how to play. Granted that we are to be governed by a rich section of the community, it is certainly very important that that section should be kept tolerably genial and jolly. If the sensitive man on the *Outlook* does not like the phrase, 'Playground of the rich', I can suggest a phrase that describes such a place as Oxford perhaps with more precision. It is a place for humanizing those who might otherwise be tyrants or even experts.

To pretend that the aristocrat meets all classes at Oxford is too ludicrous to be worth discussion. But it may be true that he meets more different kinds of men than he would meet under a strictly aristocratic régime of private tutors and small schools. It all comes back to the fact that the English, if they were resolved to have an aristocracy, were at least resolved to have a good-natured aristocracy. And it is due to them to say that almost alone among the peoples of the world, they have succeeded in getting one. One could almost tolerate the thing, if it were not for the praise of it. One might endure Oxford, but not the *Outlook*.

When the poor man at Oxford loses his angles (which means, I suppose, his independence), he may perhaps, even if his poverty is of that highly relative type possible at Oxford, gain a certain amount of worldly advantage from the surrender of those angles. I must confess, however, that I can imagine nothing nastier than to lose one's angles. It seems to me that a desire to retain some angles about one's person is a desire common to all those human beings who do not set their ultimate hopes upon looking like Humpty-Dumpty. Our angles are simply our shapes. I cannot imagine any phrase more full of the subtle and exquisite vileness which is poisoning and weakening our country than such a phrase as this, about the desirability of rubbing down the angularities of poor men. Reduced to permanent and practical human speech, it means nothing whatever except the corrupting of the first human sense of justice which is the critic of all human institutions.

It is not in any such spirit of facile and reckless reassurance that we should approach the really difficult problem of the delicate virtues and the deep dangers of our two historic seats of learning. A good son does not easily admit that his sick mother is dying; but neither does a good son cheerily assert that she is 'all right'. There are many good arguments for leaving the two historic Universities exactly as they are. There are many good arguments for smashing them or altering them entirely. But in either case the plain truth told by the Bishop of Birmingham remains. If these Universities were destroyed, they would not be destroyed as Universities. If they are preserved, they will not be preserved as Universities. They will be preserved strictly and literally as playgrounds; places valued for their hours of leisure more than for their hours of work. I do not say that this is unreasonable; as a matter of private temperament I find it attractive. It is not only possible to say a great deal in praise of play, it is really possible to say the highest things in praise of it. It might reasonably be maintained that the true object of all human life is play. Earth is a task garden; heaven is a playground. To be at last in such secure innocence that one can juggle with the universe and the stars, to be so good that one can treat everything as a joke—that may be, perhaps, the real end and final holiday of human souls. When we are really holy we may regard the Universe as a lark; so perhaps it is not essentially wrong to regard the University as a lark. But the plain and present fact is that our upper classes do regard the University as a lark, and do not regard it as a University. It also happens very often that through some oversight they neglect to provide themselves with that extreme degree of holiness which I have postulated as a necessary preliminary to such indulgence in the higher frivolity.

Humanity, always dreaming of a happy race, free, fantastic, and at ease, has sometimes pictured them in some mystical island, sometimes in some celestial city, sometimes as fairies, gods, or citizens of Atlantis. But one method in which it has often indulged is to picture them as aristocrats, as a special human class that could actually be seen hunting in the woods or driving about the streets. And this never was (as some silly Germans say) a worship of pride and scorn; mankind never really admired pride; mankind never had anything but a scorn for scorn. It was a worship of the spectacle of happiness; especially of the spectacle of youth. This is what the old Universities in their noblest aspect really are; and this is why there is always something to be said for keeping them as they are. Aristocracy is not a tyranny; it is not even merely a spell. It is a vision. It is a deliberate indulgence in a certain picture of pleasure painted for the purpose; every Duchess is (in an innocent sense) painted, like Gainsborough's 'Duchess of Devonshire'. She is only beautiful because, at the back of all, the English people wanted her to be beautiful. In the same way, the lads at Oxford and Cambridge are only larking because England, in the depths of its solemn soul, really wishes them to lark. All this is very human and pardonable, and would be even harmless if there were no such things in the world as danger and honour and intellectual responsibility. But if aristocracy is a vision, it is perhaps the most unpractical of all visions. It is not a working way of doing things to put all your happiest people on a lighted platform and stare only at them. It is not a working way of managing education to be entirely content with the mere fact that you have (to a degree unexampled in the world) given the luckiest boys the jolliest time. It would be easy enough, like the writer in the *Outlook*, to enjoy the pleasures and deny the perils. Oh, what a happy place England would be to live in if only one did not love it!

# Two Stubborn Pieces of Iron

In discussing such a proposal as that of the co-education of the sexes it is very desirable first of all to realize clearly what it is that we want the thing to do. The thing might be upheld for quite opposite reasons. It might be supposed to increase delicacy or to decrease it. It might be valued because it was a sphere for sentiment or because it was a damper for sentiment. My sympathies would move me in a discussion entirely according to what difference its upholders thought it would make. For myself, I doubt whether it would make much difference at all. Everyone must agree with co-education for very young children; and I cannot believe that even for older children it would do any great harm. But that is because I think the school is not so important as people think it nowadays. The home is the really important thing, and always will be. People talk about the poor neglecting their children; but a little boy in the street has more traces of having been brought up by his mother than of having been taught ethics and geography by a pupil teacher. And if we take this true parallel of the home we can see, I think, exactly what co-education can do and what it cannot do. The school will never make boys and girls ordinary comrades. The home does not make them that. The sexes can work together in a schoolroom just as they can breakfast together in a breakfast-room; but neither makes any difference to the fact that the boys go off to a boyish companionship which the girls would think disgusting, while the girls go off to a girl companionship which the boys would think literally insane. Co-educate as much as you like, there will always be a wall between the sexes until love or lust breaks it down. Your co-educative playground for pupils in their teens will not be a place of sexless camaraderie. It will be a place where boys go about in fives sulkily growling at the girls, and where the girls go about in twos turning up their noses at the boys.

Now if you accept this state of things and are content with it as the result of your co-education, I am with you; I accept it as one of the mystical first

*Daily Graphic*, September 1907. Collected in The Common Man, 1950

facts of Nature. I accept it somewhat in the spirit of Carlyle when somebody told him that Harriet Martineau had 'accepted the Universe', and he said 'By God, she'd better'. But if you have any idea that co-education would do more than parade the sexes in front of each other twice a day, if you think it would destroy their deep ignorance of each other or start them on a basis of rational understanding, then I say first that this will never happen, and second that I (for one) should be horribly annoyed if it did.

I can reach my meaning best by another route. Very few people ever state properly the strong argument in favour of marrying for love or against marrying for money. The argument is not that all lovers are heroes and heroines, nor is it that all dukes are profligates or all millionaires cads. The argument is this, that the differences between a man and a woman are at the best so obstinate and exasperating that they practically cannot be got over unless there is an atmosphere of exaggerated tenderness and mutual interest. To put the matter in one metaphor, the sexes are two stubborn pieces of iron; if they are to be welded together, it must be while they are red-hot. Every woman has to find out that her husband is a selfish beast, because every man is a selfish beast by the standard of a woman. But let her find out the beast while they are both still in the story of 'Beauty and the Beast'. Every man has to find out that his wife is cross—that is to say, sensitive to the point of madness: for every woman is mad by the masculine standard. But let him find out that she is mad while her madness is more worth considering than anyone else's sanity.

This is not a digression. The whole value of the normal relations of man and woman lies in the fact that they first begin really to criticize each other when they first begin really to admire each other. And a good thing, too. I say, with a full sense of the responsibility of the statement, that it is better that the sexes should misunderstand each other until they marry. It is better that they should not have the knowledge until they have the reverence and the charity. We want no premature and puppyish 'knowing all about girls'. We do not want the highest mysteries of a Divine distinction to be understood before they are desired, and handled before they are understood. That which Mr Shaw calls the Life Force, but for which Christianity has more philosophical terms, has created this early division of tastes and habits for that romantic purpose, which is also the most practical of all purposes. Those whom God has sundered, shall no man join.

It is, therefore, a question of what are really the co-educators' aims. If they have small aims, some convenience in organization, some slight improvement in manners, they know more about such things than I. But if they have large aims, I am against them.

## TO EDMUND CLERIHEW BENTLEY

A cloud was on the mind of men, and wailing went the weather,
Yea, a sick cloud upon the soul when we were boys together.
Science announced nonentity and art admired decay;
The world was old and ended: but you and I were gay;
Round us in antic order their crippled vices came—
Lust that had lost its laughter, fear that had lost its shame.
Like the white lock of Whistler, that lit our aimless gloom,
Men showed their own white feather as proudly as a plume.
Life was a fly that faded, and death a drone that stung;
The world was very old indeed when you and I were young.
They twisted even decent sin to shapes not to be named:
Men were ashamed of honour; but we were not ashamed.
Weak if we were and foolish, not thus we failed, not thus;
When that black Baal blocked the heavens he had no hymns from us.
Children we were—our forts of sand were even as weak as we,
High as they went we piled them up to break that bitter sea.
Fools as we were in motley, all jangling and absurd,
When all church bells were silent our cap and bells were heard.

Not all unhelped we held the fort, our tiny flags unfurled;
Some giants laboured in that cloud to lift it from the world.
I find again the book we found, I feel the hour that flings
Far out of fish-shaped Paumanok some cry of cleaner things;
And the Green Carnation withered, as in forest fires that pass,
Roared in the wind of all the world ten million leaves of grass;
Or sane and sweet and sudden as a bird sings in the rain—
Truth out of Tusitala spoke and pleasure out of pain.
Yea, cool and clear and sudden as a bird sings in the grey,
Dunedin to Samoa spoke, and darkness unto day.
But we were young; we lived to see God break their bitter charms.
God and the good Republic come riding back in arms:
We have seen the City of Mansoul, even as it rocked, relieved—
Blessed are they who did not see, but being blind, believed.

This is a tale of those old fears, even of those emptied hells,
And none but you shall understand the true thing that it tells—
Of what colossal gods of shame could cow men and yet crash,
Of what huge devils hid the stars, yet fell at a pistol flash.
The doubts that were so plain to chase, so dreadful to withstand—
Oh, who shall understand but you; yea, who shall understand?
The doubts that drove us through the night as we two talked amain,
And day had broken on the streets e'er it broke upon the brain.
Between us, by the peace of God, such truth can now be told;
Yea, there is strength in striking root, and good in growing old.
We have found common things at last, and marriage and a creed,
And I may safely write it now, and you may safely read.

G. K. C.

# The Man Who Was Thursday

## A NIGHTMARE

## I

### THE TWO POETS OF SAFFRON PARK

The suburb of Saffron Park lay on the sunset side of London, as red and ragged as a cloud of sunset. It was built of a bright brick throughout; its sky-line was fantastic, and even its ground plan was wild. It had been the outburst of a speculative builder, faintly tinged with art, who called its architecture sometimes Elizabethan and sometimes Queen Anne, apparently under the impression that the two sovereigns were identical. It was described with some justice as an artistic colony, though it never in any definable way produced any art. But although its pretensions to be an intellectual centre were a little vague, its pretensions to be a pleasant place were quite indisputable. The stranger who looked for the first time at the quaint red houses could only think how very oddly shaped the people must be who could fit in to them. Nor when he met the people was he disappointed in this respect. The place was not only pleasant, but perfect, if once he could regard it not as a deception but rather as a dream. Even if the people were not 'artists,' the whole was nevertheless artistic. That young man with the long, auburn hair and the impudent face— that young man was not really a poet; but surely he was a poem. That old gentleman with the wild, white beard and the wild, white hat—that venerable humbug was not really a philosopher; but at least he was the cause of philosophy in others. That scientific gentleman with the bald, egg-like head and the bare, bird-like neck had no real right to the airs of science that he assumed. He had not discovered anything new in biology; but what biological creature could he have discovered more singular than himself? Thus, and thus only, the whole place had properly to be regarded; it had to be considered not so much as a workshop for artists, but as a frail but finished work of art. A man who stepped into its social atmosphere felt as if he had stepped into a written comedy.

More especially this attractive unreality fell upon it about nightfall, when the extravagant roofs were dark against the afterglow and the whole insane

The Man Who Was Thursday, 1908.

127

village seemed as separate as a drifting cloud. This again was more strongly true of the many nights of local festivity, when the little gardens were often illuminated, and the big Chinese lanterns glowed in the dwarfish trees like some fierce and monstrous fruit. And this was strongest of all on one particular evening, still vaguely remembered in the locality, of which the auburn-haired poet was the hero. It was not by any means the only evening of which he was the hero. On many nights those passing by his little back garden might hear his high, didactic voice laying down the law to men and particularly to women. The attitude of women in such cases was indeed one of the paradoxes of the place. Most of the women were of the kind vaguely called emancipated, and professed some protest against male supremacy. Yet these new women would always pay to a man the extravagant compliment which no ordinary woman ever pays to him, that of listening while he is talking. And Mr Lucian Gregory, the red-haired poet, was really (in some sense) a man worth listening to, even if one only laughed at the end of it. He put the old cant of the lawlessness of art and the art of lawlessness with a certain impudent freshness which gave at least a momentary pleasure. He was helped in some degree by the arresting oddity of his appearance, which he worked, as the phrase goes, for all it was worth. His dark red hair parted in the middle was literally like a woman's, and curved into the slow curls of a virgin in a pre-Raphaelite picture. From within this almost saintly oval, however, his face projected suddenly broad and brutal, the chin carried forward with a look of cockney contempt. This combination at once tickled and terrified the nerves of a neurotic population. He seemed like a walking blasphemy, a blend of the angel and the ape.

This particular evening, if it is remembered for nothing else, will be remembered in that place for its strange sunset. It looked like the end of the world. All the heaven seemed covered with a quite vivid and palpable plumage; you could only say that the sky was full of feathers, and of feathers that almost brushed the face. Across the great part of the dome they were grey, with the strangest tints of violet and mauve and an unnatural pink or pale green; but towards the west the whole grew past description, transparent and passionate, and the last red-hot plumes of it covered up the sun like something too good to be seen. The whole was so close about the earth, as to express nothing but a violent secrecy. The very empyrean seemed to be a secret. It expressed that splendid smallness which is the soul of local patriotism. The very sky seemed small.

I say that there are some inhabitants who may remember the evening if only by that oppressive sky. There are others who may remember it because it marked the first appearance in the place of the second poet of Saffron Park. For a long time the red-haired revolutionary had reigned without a rival; it was upon the night of the sunset that his solitude suddenly ended. The new poet, who introduced himself by the name of Gabriel Syme, was a very mild-looking mortal, with a fair, pointed beard and faint, yellow hair. But an impression grew that he was less meek than he looked. He signalised his entrance by differing with the established poet, Gregory, upon the whole nature of poetry. He said that he (Syme) was a poet of law, a poet of order; nay, he said he was a poet of respectability. So all the Saffron Parkers looked at him as if he had that moment fallen out of that impossible sky.

In fact, Mr Lucian Gregory, the anarchic poet, connected the two events.

'It may well be,' he said, in his sudden lyrical manner, 'it may well be on such a night of clouds and cruel colours that there is brought forth upon the earth such a portent as a respectable poet. You say you are a poet of law; I say you are a contradiction in terms. I only wonder there were not comets and earthquakes on the night you appeared in this garden.'

The man with the meek blue eyes and the pale, pointed beard endured these thunders with a certain submissive solemnity. The third party of the group, Gregory's sister Rosamond, who had her brother's braids of red hair, but a kindlier face underneath them, laughed with such mixture of admiration and disapproval as she gave commonly to the family oracle.

Gregory resumed in high oratorical good humour.

'An artist is identical with an anarchist,' he cried. 'You might transpose the words anywhere. An anarchist is an artist. The man who throws a bomb is an artist, because he prefers a great moment to everything. He sees how much more valuable is one burst of blazing light, one peal of perfect thunder, than the mere common bodies of a few shapeless policemen. An artist disregards all governments, abolishes all conventions. The poet delights in disorder only. If it were not so, the most poetical thing in the world would be the Underground Railway.'

'So it is,' said Mr Syme.

'Nonsense!' said Gregory, who was very rational when anyone else attempted paradox. 'Why do all the clerks and navvies in the railway trains look so sad and tired, so very sad and tired? I will tell you. It is because they know that the train is going right. It is because they know that whatever place they have taken a ticket for that place they will reach. It is because after they have passed Sloane Square they know that the next station must be Victoria, and nothing but Victoria. Oh, their wild rapture! oh, their eyes like stars and their souls again in Eden, if the next station were unaccountably Baker Street!'

'It is you who are unpoetical,' replied the poet Syme. 'If what you say of clerks is true, they can only be as prosaic as your poetry. The rare, strange thing is to hit the mark; the gross, obvious thing is to miss it. We feel it is epical when man with one wild arrow strikes a distant bird. Is it not also epical when man with one wild engine strikes a distant station? Chaos is dull; because in chaos the train might indeed go anywhere, to Baker Street or to Bagdad. But man is a magician, and his whole magic is in this, that he does say Victoria, and lo! it is Victoria. No, take your books of mere poetry and prose; let me read a time table, with tears of pride. Take your Byron, who commemorates the defeats of man; give me Bradshaw, who commemorates his victories. Give me Bradshaw, I say!'

'Must you go?' inquired Gregory sarcastically.

'I tell you,' went on Syme with passion, 'that every time a train comes in I feel that it has broken past batteries of besiegers, and that man has won a battle against chaos. You say contemptuously that when one has left Sloane Square one must come to Victoria. I say that one might do a thousand things instead, and that whenever I really come there I have the sense of hair-breadth escape. And when I hear the guard shout out the word "Victoria," it is not an unmeaning word. It is to me the cry of a herald announcing conquest. It is to me indeed "Victoria"; it is the victory of Adam.'

Gregory wagged his heavy, red head with a slow and sad smile.

'And even then,' he said, 'we poets always ask the question, 'And what is Victoria now that you have got there?' You think Victoria is like the New Jerusalem. We know that the New Jerusalem will only be like Victoria. Yes, the poet will be discontented even in the streets of heaven. The poet is always in revolt.'

'There again,' said Syme irritably, 'what is there poetical about being in revolt? You might as well say that it is poetical to be sea-sick. Being sick is a revolt. Both being sick and being rebellious may be the wholesome thing on certain desperate occasions; but I'm hanged if I can see why they are poetical. Revolt in the abstract is—revolting. It's mere vomiting.'

The girl winced for a flash at the unpleasant word, but Syme was too hot to heed her.

'It is things going right,' he cried, 'that is poetical! Our digestions, for instance, going sacredly and silently right, that is the foundation of all poetry. Yes, the most poetical thing, more poetical than the flowers, more poetical than the stars—the most poetical thing in the world is not being sick.'

'Really,' said Gregory superciliously, 'the examples you choose——'

'I beg your pardon,' said Syme grimly, 'I forgot we had abolished all conventions.'

For the first time a red patch appeared on Gregory's forehead.

'You don't expect me,' he said, 'to revolutionise society on this lawn?'

Syme looked straight into his eyes and smiled sweetly.

'No, I don't,' he said; 'but I suppose that if you were serious about your anarchism, that is exactly what you would do.'

Gregory's big bull's eyes blinked suddenly like those of an angry lion, and one could almost fancy that his red mane rose.

'Don't you think, then,' he said in a dangerous voice, 'that I am serious about my anarchism?'

'I beg your pardon?' said Syme.

'Am I not serious about my anarchism?' cried Gregory, with knotted fists.

'My dear fellow!' said Syme, and strolled away.

With surprise, but with a curious pleasure, he found Rosamond Gregory still in his company.

'Mr Syme,' she said, 'do the people who talk like you and my brother often mean what they say? Do you mean what you say now?'

Syme smiled.

'Do you?' he asked.

'What do you mean?' asked the girl, with grave eyes.

'My dear Miss Gregory,' said Syme gently, 'there are many kinds of sincerity and insincerity. When you say "thank you" for the salt, do you mean what you say? No. When you say "the world is round," do you mean what you say? No. It is true, but you don't mean it. Now, sometimes a man like your brother really finds a thing he does mean. It may be only a half-truth, quarter-truth, tenth-truth; but then he says more than he means—from sheer force of meaning it.'

She was looking at him from under level brows; her face was grave and open, and there had fallen upon it the shadow of that unreasoning responsibility which is at the bottom of the most frivolous woman, the maternal watch which is as old as the world.

'Is he really an anarchist, then?' she asked.

'Only in that sense I speak of,' replied Syme; 'or if you prefer it, in that nonsense.'

She drew her broad brows together and said abruptly—

'He wouldn't really use—bombs or that sort of thing?'

Syme broke into a great laugh, that seemed too large for his slight and somewhat dandified figure.

'Good Lord, no!' he said, 'that has to be done anonymously.'

And at that the corners of her own mouth broke into a smile, and she thought with a simultaneous pleasure of Gregory's absurdity and of his safety.

Syme strolled with her to a seat in the corner of the garden, and continued to pour out his opinions. For he was a sincere man, and in spite of his superficial airs and graces, at root a humble one. And it is always the humble man who talks too much; the proud man watches himself too closely. He defended respectability with violence and exaggeration. He grew passionate in his praise of tidiness and propriety. All the time there was a smell of lilac all round him. Once he heard very faintly in some distant street a barrel-organ begin to play, and it seemed to him that his heroic words were moving to a tiny tune from under or beyond the world.

He stared and talked at the girl's red hair and amused face for what seemed to be a few minutes; and then, feeling that the groups in such a place should mix, rose to his feet. To his astonishment, he discovered the whole garden empty. Everyone had gone long ago, and he went himself with a rather hurried apology. He left with a sense of champagne in his head, which he could not afterwards explain. In the wild events which were to follow this girl had no part at all; he never saw her again until all his tale was over. And yet, in some indescribable way, she kept recurring like a motive in music through all his mad adventures afterwards, and the glory of her strange hair ran like a red thread through those dark and ill-drawn tapestries of the night. For what followed was so improbable, that it might well have been a dream.

When Syme went out into the starlit street, he found it for the moment empty. Then he realised (in some odd way) that the silence was rather a living silence than a dead one. Directly outside the door stood a street lamp, whose gleam gilded the leaves of the tree that bent out over the fence behind him. About a foot from the lamp-post stood a figure almost as rigid and motionless as the lamp-post itself. The tall hat and long frock-coat were black; the face, in an abrupt shadow, was almost as dark. Only a fringe of fiery hair against the light, and also something aggressive in the attitude, proclaimed that it was the poet Gregory. He had something of the look of a masked bravo waiting sword in hand for his foe.

He made a sort of doubtful salute, which Syme somewhat more formally returned.

'I was waiting for you,' said Gregory. 'Might I have a moment's conversation?'

'Certainly. About what?' asked Syme in a sort of weak wonder.

Gregory struck out with his stick at the lamp-post, and then at the tree.

'About *this* and *this*,' he cried; 'about order and anarchy. There is your precious order, that lean, iron lamp, ugly and barren; and there is anarchy, rich, living, reproducing itself—there is anarchy, splendid in green and gold.'

'All the same,' replied Syme patiently, 'just at present you only see the tree by the light of the lamp. I wonder when you would ever see the lamp by the light of the tree.' Then after a pause he said, 'But may I ask if you have been standing out here in the dark only to resume our little argument?'

'No,' cried out Gregory, in a voice that rang down the street, 'I did not stand here to resume our argument, but to end it for ever.'

The silence fell again, and Syme, though he understood nothing, listened instinctively for something serious. Gregory began in a smooth voice and with a rather bewildering smile.

'Mr Syme,' he said, 'this evening you succeeded in doing something rather remarkable. You did something to me that no man born of woman has ever succeeded in doing before.'

'Indeed!'

'Now I remember,' resumed Gregory reflectively, 'one other person suc-ceeded in doing it. The captain of a penny steamer (if I remember correctly) at Southend. You have irritated me.'

'I am very sorry,' replied Syme with gravity.

'I am afraid my fury and your insult are too shocking to be wiped out even with an apology,' said Gregory very calmly. 'No duel could wipe it out. If I struck you dead I could not wipe it out. There is only one way by which that insult can be erased, and that way I choose. I am going, at the possible sacrifice of my life and honour, to *prove* to you that you were wrong in what you said.'

'In what I said?'

'You said I was not serious about being an anarchist.'

'There are degrees of seriousness,' replied Syme. 'I have never doubted that you were perfectly sincere in this sense, that you thought what you said well worth saying, that you thought a paradox might wake men up to a neglected truth.'

Gregory stared at him steadily and painfully.

'And in no other sense,' he asked, 'you think me serious? You think me a *flâneur* who lets fall occasional truths. You do not think that in a deeper, a more deadly sense, I am serious.'

Syme struck his stick violently on the stones of the road.

'Serious!' he cried. 'Good Lord! is this street serious? Are these damned Chinese lanterns serious? Is the whole caboodle serious? One comes here and talks a pack of bosh, and perhaps some sense as well, but I should think very little of a man who didn't keep something in the background of his life that was more serious than all this talking—something more serious, whether it was religion or only drink.'

'Very well,' said Gregory, his face darkening, 'you shall see something more serious than either drink or religion.'

Syme stood waiting with his usual air of mildness until Gregory again opened his lips.

'You spoke just now of having a religion. Is it really true that you have one?'

'Oh,' said Syme with a beaming smile, 'we are all Catholics now.'

'Then may I ask you to swear by whatever gods or saints your religion involves that you will *not* reveal what I am now going to tell you to any son of Adam, and especially not to the police? Will you swear that! If you will take upon yourself this awful abnegation, if you will consent to burden your soul with a vow that you should never make and a knowledge you should never dream about, I will promise you in return——'

'You will promise me in return?' inquired Syme, as the other paused.

'I will promise you a very entertaining evening.' Syme suddenly took off his hat.

'Your offer,' he said, 'is far too idiotic to be declined. You say that a poet is always an anarchist. I disagree; but I hope at least that he is always a sportsman. Permit me, here and now, to swear as a Christian, and promise as a good comrade and a fellow-artist, that I will not report anything of this, whatever it is, to the police. And now, in the name of Colney Hatch, what is it?'

'I think,' said Gregory, with placid irrelevancy, 'that we will call a cab.'

He gave two long whistles, and a hansom came rattling down the road. The two got into it in silence. Gregory gave through the trap the address of an obscure public-house on the Chiswick bank of the river. The cab whisked itself away again, and in it these two fantastics quitted their fantastic town.

# II

## *THE SECRET OF GABRIEL SYME*

The cab pulled up before a particularly dreary and greasy beershop, into which Gregory rapidly conducted his companion. They seated themselves in a close and dim sort of bar-parlour, at a stained wooden table with one wooden leg. The room was so small and dark, that very little could be seen of the attendant who was summoned, beyond a vague and dark impression of something bulky and bearded.

'Will you take a little supper?' asked Gregory politely. 'The *pâté de foie gras* is not good here, but I can recommend the game.'

Syme received the remark with stolidity, imagining it to be a joke. Accepting the vein of humour, he said, with a well-bred indifference—

'Oh, bring me some lobster mayonnaise.'

To his indescribable astonishment, the man only said 'Certainly, sir!' and went away apparently to get it.

'What will you drink?' resumed Gregory, with the same careless yet apologetic air. 'I shall only have a *crême de menthe* myself; I have dined. But the champagne can really be trusted. Do let me start you with a half-bottle of Pommery at least?'

'Thank you!' said the motionless Syme. 'You are very good.'

His further attempts at conversation, somewhat disorganised in themselves, were cut short finally as by a thunderbolt by the actual appearance of the lobster. Syme tasted it, and found it particularly good. Then he suddenly began to eat with great rapidity and appetite.

'Excuse me if I enjoy myself rather obviously!' he said to Gregory, smiling.

'I don't often have the luck to have a dream like this. It is new to me for a nightmare to lead to a lobster. It is commonly the other way.'

'You are not asleep, I assure you,' said Gregory. 'You are, on the contrary, close to the most actual and rousing moment of your existence. Ah, here comes your champagne! I admit that there may be a slight disproportion, let us say, between the inner arrangements of this excellent hotel and its simple and unpretentious exterior. But that is all our modesty. We are the most modest men that ever lived on earth.'

'And who are *we*?' asked Syme, emptying his champagne glass.

'It is quite simple,' replied Gregory. '*We* are the serious anarchists, in whom you do not believe.'

'Oh!' said Syme shortly. 'You do yourselves well in drinks.'

'Yes, we are serious about everything,' answered Gregory.

Then after a pause he added—

'If in a few moments this table begins to turn round a little, don't put it down to your inroads into the champagne. I don't wish you to do yourself an injustice.'

'Well, if I am not drunk, I am mad,' replied Syme with perfect calm; 'but I trust I can behave like a gentleman in either condition. May I smoke?'

'Certainly!' said Gregory, producing a cigar-case. 'Try one of mine.'

Syme took the cigar, clipped the end off with a cigar-cutter out of his waistcoat pocket, put it in his mouth, lit it slowly, and let out a long cloud of smoke. It is not a little to his credit that he performed these rites with so much composure, for almost before he had begun them the table at which he sat had begun to revolve, first slowly, and then rapidly, as if at an insane séance.

'You must not mind it,' said Gregory; 'it's a kind of screw.'

'Quite so,' said Syme placidly, 'a kind of screw. How simple that is!'

The next moment the smoke of his cigar, which had been wavering across the room in snaky twists, went straight up as if from a factory chimney, and the two, with their chairs and table, shot down through the floor as if the earth had swallowed them. They went rattling down a kind of roaring chimney as rapidly as a lift cut loose, and they came with an abrupt bump to the bottom. But when Gregory threw open a pair of doors and let in a red subterranean light, Syme was still smoking, with one leg thrown over the other, and had not turned a yellow hair.

Gregory led him down a low, vaulted passage, at the end of which was the red light. It was an enormous crimson lantern, nearly as big as a fireplace, fixed over a small but heavy iron door. In the door there was a sort of hatchway or grating, and on this Gregory struck five times. A heavy voice with a foreign accent asked him who he was. To this he gave the more or less unexpected reply, 'Mr Joseph Chamberlain.' The heavy hinges began to move; it was obviously some kind of password.

Inside the doorway the passage gleamed as if it were lined with a network of steel. On a second glance, Syme saw that the glittering pattern was really made up of ranks and ranks of rifles and revolvers, closely packed or interlocked.

'I must ask you to forgive me all these formalities,' said Gregory; 'we have to be very strict here.'

'Oh, don't apologise,' said Syme. 'I know your passion for law and order,' and he stepped into the passage lined with the steel weapons. With his long, fair hair and rather foppish frock-coat, he looked a singularly frail and fanciful figure as he walked down that shining avenue of death.

They passed through several such passages, and came out at last into a queer steel chamber with curved walls, almost spherical in shape, but presenting, with its tiers of benches, something of the appearance of a scientific lecture-theatre. There were no rifles or pistols in this apartment, but round the walls of it were hung more dubious and dreadful shapes, things that looked like the bulbs of iron plants, or the eggs of iron birds. They were bombs, and the very room itself seemed like the inside of a bomb. Syme knocked his cigar ash off against the wall, and went in.

'And now, my dear Mr Syme,' said Gregory, throwing himself in an expansive manner on the bench under the largest bomb, 'now we are quite cosy, so let us talk properly. Now no human words can give you any notion of why I brought you here. It was one of those quite arbitrary emotions, like jumping off a cliff or falling in love. Suffice it to say that you were an inexpressibly irritating fellow, and, to do you justice, you are still. I would break twenty oaths of secrecy for the pleasure of taking you down a peg. That way you have of lighting a cigar would make a priest break the seal of confession. Well, you said that you were quite certain I was not a serious anarchist. Does this place strike you as being serious?'

'It does seem to have a moral under all its gaiety,' assented Syme; 'but may I ask you two questions? You need not fear to give me information, because, as you remember, you very wisely extorted from me a promise not to tell the police, a promise I shall certainly keep. So it is in mere curiosity that I make my queries. First of all, what is it really all about? What is it you object to? You want to abolish Government?'

'To abolish God!' said Gregory, opening the eyes of a fanatic. 'We do not only want to upset a few despotisms and police regulations; that sort of anarchism does exist, but it is a mere branch of the Nonconformists. We dig deeper and we blow you higher. We wish to deny all those arbitrary distinctions of vice and virtue, honour and treachery, upon which mere rebels base themselves. The silly sentimentalists of the French Revolution talked of the Rights of Man! We hate Rights as we hate Wrongs. We have abolished Right and Wrong.'

'And Right and Left,' said Syme with a simple eagerness, 'I hope you will abolish them too. They are much more troublesome to me.'

'You spoke of a second question,' snapped Gregory.

'With pleasure,' resumed Syme. 'In all your present acts and surroundings there is a scientific attempt at secrecy. I have an aunt who lived over a shop, but this is the first time I have found people living from preference under a public-house. You have a heavy iron door. You cannot pass it without submitting to the humiliation of calling yourself Mr Chamberlain. You surround yourself with steel instruments which make the place, if I may say so, more impressive than homelike. May I ask why, after taking all this trouble to barricade yourselves in the bowels of the earth, you then parade your whole secret by talking about anarchism to every silly woman in Saffron Park?'

Gregory smiled.

'The answer is simple,' he said. 'I told you I was a serious anarchist, and you did not believe me. Nor do *they* believe me. Unless I took them into this infernal room they would not believe me.'

Syme smoked thoughtfully, and looked at him with interest. Gregory went on.

'The history of the thing might amuse you,' he said. 'When first I became one of the New Anarchists I tried all kinds of respectable disguises. I dressed up as a bishop. I read up all about bishops in our anarchist pamphlets, in *Superstition the Vampire* and *Priests of Prey*. I certainly understood from them that bishops are strange and terrible old men keeping a cruel secret from mankind. I was misinformed. When on my first appearing in episcopal gaiters in a drawing-room I cried out in a voice of thunder, 'Down! down! presumptuous human reason!' they found out in some way that I was not a bishop at all. I was nabbed at once. Then I made up as a millionaire; but I defended Capital with so much intelligence that a fool could see that I was quite poor. Then I tried being a major. Now I am a humanitarian myself, but I have, I hope, enough intellectual breadth to understand the position of those who, like Nietzsche, admire violence—the proud, mad war of Nature and all that, you know. I threw myself into the major. I drew my sword and waved it constantly. I called out 'Blood!' abstractedly, like a man calling for wine. I often said, 'Let the weak perish; it is the Law.' Well, well, it seems majors don't do this. I was nabbed again. At last I went in despair to the President of the Central Anarchist Council, who is the greatest man in Europe.'

'What is his name?' asked Syme.

'You would not know it,' answered Gregory. 'That is his greatness. Cæsar and Napoleon put all their genius into being heard of, and they *were* heard of. He puts all his genius into not being heard of, and he is not heard of. But you cannot be for five minutes in the room with him without feeling that Cæsar and Napoleon would have been children in his hands.'

He was silent and even pale for a moment, and then resumed—

'But whenever he gives advice it is always something as startling as an epigram, and yet as practical as the Bank of England. I said to him, "What disguise will hide me from the world? What can I find more respectable than bishops and majors?" He looked at me with his large but indecipherable face. "You want a safe disguise, do you? You want a dress which will guarantee you harmless; a dress in which no one would ever look for a bomb?" I nodded. He suddenly lifted his lion's voice. "Why, then, dress up as an *anarchist,* you fool!" he roared so that the room shook. "Nobody will ever expect you to do anything dangerous then." And he turned his broad back on me without another word. I took his advice, and have never regretted it. I preached blood and murder to those women day and night, and—by God!—they would let me wheel their perambulators.'

Syme sat watching him with some respect in his large, blue eyes.

'You took me in,' he said. 'It is really a smart dodge.'

Then after a pause he added—

'What do you call this tremendous President of yours?'

'We generally call him Sunday,' replied Gregory with simplicity. 'You see, there are seven members of the Central Anarchist Council, and they are named after days of the week. He is called Sunday, by some of his admirers Bloody Sunday. It is curious you should mention the matter because the very night you have dropped in (if I may so express it) is the night on which our London branch, which assembles in this room, has to elect its own deputy to fill a vacancy in the Council. The gentleman who has for some time past played, with propriety and general applause, the difficult part of Thursday, has died quite suddenly. Consequently, we have called a meeting this very evening to elect a successor.'

He got to his feet and strolled across the room with a sort of smiling embarrassment.

'I feel somehow as if you were my mother, Syme,' he continued casually. 'I feel that I can confide anything to you, as you have promised to tell nobody. In fact, I will confide to you something that I would not say in so many words to the anarchists who will be coming to the room in about ten minutes. We shall, of course, go through a form of election; but I don't mind telling you that it is practically certain what the result will be.' He looked down for a moment modestly. 'It is almost a settled thing that I am to be Thursday.'

'My dear fellow,' said Syme heartily, 'I congratulate you. A great career!'

Gregory smiled in deprecation, and walked across the room, talking rapidly.

'As a matter of fact, everything is ready for me on this table,' he said, 'and the ceremony will probably be the shortest possible.'

Syme also strolled across to the table, and found lying across it a walking-stick, which turned out on examination to be a sword-stick, a large Colt's revolver, a sandwich case, and a formidable flask of brandy. Over the chair, beside the table, was thrown a heavy-looking cape or cloak.

'I have only to get the form of election finished,' continued Gregory with animation, 'then I snatch up this cloak and stick, stuff these other things into my pocket, step out of a door in this cavern, which opens on the river, where there is a steam-tug already waiting for me, and then—then—oh, the wild joy of being Thursday!' And he clasped his hands.

Syme, who had sat down once more with his usual insolent languor, got to his feet with an unusual air of hesitation.

'Why is it,' he asked vaguely, 'that I think you are quite a decent fellow? Why do I positively like you, Gregory?' He paused a moment, and then added with a sort of fresh curiosity, 'Is it because you are such an ass?'

There was a thoughtful silence again, and then he cried out—

'Well, damn it all! this is the funniest situation I have ever been in in my life, and I am going to act accordingly. Gregory, I gave you a promise before I came into this place. That promise I would keep under red-hot pincers. Would you give me, for my own safety, a little promise of the same kind?'

'A promise?' asked Gregory, wondering.

'Yes,' said Syme very seriously, 'a promise. I swore before God that I would not tell your secret to the police. Will you swear by Humanity, or whatever beastly thing you believe in, that you will not tell my secret to the anarchists?'

'Your secret?' asked the staring Gregory. 'Have you got a secret?'

'Yes,' said Syme, 'I have a secret.' Then after a pause, 'Will you swear?'

Gregory glared at him gravely for a few moments, and then said abruptly—

'You must have bewitched me, but I feel a furious curiosity about you. Yes, I will swear not to tell the anarchists anything you tell me. But look sharp, for they will be here in a couple of minutes.'

Syme rose slowly to his feet and thrust his long, white hands into his long, grey trousers' pockets. Almost as he did so there came five knocks on the outer grating, proclaiming the arrival of the first of the conspirators.

'Well,' said Syme slowly, 'I don't know how to tell you the truth more shortly than by saying that your expedient of dressing up as an aimless poet is not confined to you or your President. We have known the dodge for some time at Scotland Yard.'

Gregory tried to spring up straight, but he swayed thrice.

'What do you say?' he asked in an inhuman voice.

'Yes,' said Syme simply, 'I am a police detective. But I think I hear your friends coming.'

From the doorway there came a murmur of 'Mr Joseph Chamberlain.' It was repeated twice and thrice and then thirty times, and the crowd of Joseph Chamberlains (a solemn thought) could be heard trampling down the corridor.

# III

## *THE MAN WHO WAS THURSDAY*

Before one of the fresh faces could appear at the doorway, Gregory's stunned surprise had fallen from him. He was beside the table with a bound, and a noise in his throat like a wild beast. He caught up the Colt's revolver and took aim at Syme. Syme did not flinch, but he put up a pale and polite hand.

'Don't be such a silly man,' he said, with the effeminate dignity of a curate. 'Don't you see it's not necessary? Don't you see that we're both in the same boat? Yes, and jolly sea-sick.'

Gregory could not speak, but he could not fire either, and he looked his question.

'Don't you see we've checkmated each other?' cried Syme. 'I can't tell the police you are an anarchist. You can't tell the anarchists I'm a policeman. I can only watch you, knowing what you are; you can only watch me, knowing what I am. In short, it's a lonely, intellectual duel, my head against yours. I'm a policeman deprived of the help of the police. You, my poor fellow, are an anarchist deprived of the help of that law and organisation which is so essential to anarchy. The one solitary difference is in your favour. You are not surrounded by inquisitive policemen; I am surrounded by inquisitive anarchists. I cannot betray you, but I might betray myself. Come, come! wait and see me betray myself. I shall do it so nicely.'

Gregory put the pistol slowly down, still staring at Syme as if he were a sea-monster.

'I don't believe in immortality,' he said at last, 'but if, after all this, you were to break your word, God would make a hell only for you, to howl in for ever.'

'I shall not break my word,' said Syme sternly, 'nor will you break yours. Here are your friends.'

The mass of the anarchists entered the room heavily, with a slouching and somewhat weary gait; but one little man, with a black beard and glasses—a man somewhat of the type of Mr Tim Healy—detached himself, and bustled forward with some papers in his hand.

'Comrade Gregory,' he said, 'I suppose this man is a delegate?'

Gregory, taken by surprise, looked down and muttered the name of Syme; but Syme replied almost pertly—

'I am glad to see that your gate is well enough guarded to make it hard for anyone to be here who was not a delegate.'

The brow of the little man with the black beard was, however, still contracted with something like suspicion.

'What branch do you represent?' he asked sharply.

'I should hardly call it a branch,' said Syme, laughing; 'I should call it at the very least a root.'

'What do you mean?'

'The fact is,' said Syme serenely, 'the truth is I am a Sabbatarian. I have been specially sent here to see that you show a due observance of Sunday.'

The little man dropped one of his papers, and a flicker of fear went over all the faces of the group. Evidently the awful President, whose name was Sunday, did sometimes send down such irregular ambassadors to such branch meetings.

'Well, comrade,' said the man with the papers after a pause, 'I suppose we'd better give you a seat in the meeting?'

'If you ask my advice as a friend,' said Syme with severe benevolence, 'I think you'd better.'

When Gregory heard the dangerous dialogue end, with a sudden safety for his rival, he rose abruptly and paced the floor in painful thought. He was, indeed, in an agony of diplomacy. It was clear that Syme's inspired impudence was likely to bring him out of all merely accidental dilemmas. Little was to be hoped from them. He could not himself betray Syme, partly from honour, but partly also because, if he betrayed him and for some reason failed to destroy him, the Syme who escaped would be a Syme freed from all obligation of secrecy, a Syme who would simply walk to the nearest police station. After all, it was only one night's discussion, and only one detective who would know of it. He would let out as little as possible of their plans that night, and then let Syme go, and chance it.

He strode across to the group of anarchists, which was already distributing itself along the benches.

'I think it is time we began,' he said; 'the steam-tug is waiting on the river already. I move that Comrade Buttons takes the chair.'

This being approved by a show of hands, the little man with the papers slipped into the presidential seat.

'Comrades,' he began, as sharp as a pistol-shot, 'our meeting to-night is important, though it need not be long. This branch has always had the honour of electing Thursdays for the Central European Council. We have elected many and splendid Thursdays. We all lament the sad decease of the heroic worker who occupied the post until last week. As you know, his services to the cause were considerable. He organised the great dynamite coup of Brighton which, under happier circumstances, ought to have killed everybody on the pier. As you also know, his death was as self-denying as his life, for he died through his faith in a hygienic mixture of chalk and water as a substitute for milk, which beverage he regarded as barbaric, and as involving cruelty to the cow. Cruelty, or anything approaching to cruelty, revolted him always. But it is not to acclaim his virtues that we are met, but for a harder task. It is difficult properly to praise his qualities, but it is more difficult to replace them. Upon you, comrades, it devolves this evening to choose out of the company present the man who shall be Thursday. If any comrade suggests a name I will put it to the vote. If no comrade suggests a name, I can only tell myself that that dear dynamiter, who is gone from us, has carried into the unknowable abysses the last secret of his virtue and his innocence.'

There was a stir of almost inaudible applause, such as is sometimes heard in church. Then a large old man, with a long and venerable white beard, perhaps the only real working-man present, rose lumberingly and said—

'I move that Comrade Gregory be elected Thursday,' and sat lumberingly down again. 'Does anyone second?' asked the chairman.

A little man with a velvet coat and pointed beard seconded.

'Before I put the matter to the vote,' said the chairman, 'I will call on Comrade Gregory to make a statement.'

Gregory rose amid a great rumble of applause. His face was deadly pale, so that by contrast his queer red hair looked almost scarlet. But he was smiling and altogether at ease. He had made up his mind, and he saw his best policy quite plain in front of him like a white road. His best chance was to make a softened and ambiguous speech, such as would leave on the detective's mind the impression that the anarchist brotherhood was a very mild affair after all. He believed in his own literary power, his capacity for suggesting fine shades and picking perfect words. He thought that with care he could succeed, in spite of all the people around him, in conveying an impression of the institution, subtly and delicately false. Syme had once thought that anarchists, under all their bravado, were only playing the fool. Could he not now, in the hour of peril, make Syme think so again?

'Comrades,' began Gregory, in a low but penetrating voice, 'it is not necessary for me to tell you what is my policy, for it is your policy also. Our belief has been slandered, it has been disfigured, it has been utterly confused and concealed, but it has never been altered. Those who talk about anarchism and its dangers go everywhere and anywhere to get their information, except to us, except to the fountain head. They learn about anarchists from sixpenny novels; they learn about anarchists from tradesmen's newspapers; they learn about anarchists from *Ally Sloper's Half-Holiday* and the *Sporting Times*. They never learn about anarchists from anarchists. We have no chance of denying the mountainous slanders which are heaped upon our heads from one end of Europe to another. The man who has always heard that we are walking plagues has never heard our reply. I know that he will not hear it to-night, though my passion were to rend the roof. For it is deep, deep under the earth that the persecuted are permitted to assemble, as the Christians assembled in the Catacombs. But if, by some incredible accident, there were here to-night a man who all his life had thus immensely misunderstood us, I would put this question to him: "When those Christians met in those Catacombs, what sort of moral reputation had they in the streets above? What tales were told of their atrocities by one educated Roman to another? Suppose" (I would say to him), "suppose that we are only repeating that still mysterious paradox of history. Suppose we seem as shocking as the Christians because we are really as harmless as the Christians. Suppose we seem as mad as the Christians because we are really as meek."'

The applause that had greeted the opening sentences had been gradually growing fainter, and at the last word it stopped suddenly. In the abrupt silence, the man with the velvet jacket said, in a high, squeaky voice—

'I'm not meek!'

'Comrade Witherspoon tells us,' resumed Gregory, 'that he is not meek. Ah, how little he knows himself! His words are, indeed, extravagant; his appearance is ferocious, and even (to an ordinary taste) unattractive. But only the eye of a friendship as deep and delicate as mine can perceive the deep foundation of solid meekness which lies at the base of him, too deep even for himself to see. I repeat, we are the true early Christians, only that we come too late. We are simple, as they were simple—look at Comrade Witherspoon. We are modest, as they were modest—look at me. We are merciful——'

'No, no!' called out Mr Witherspoon with the velvet jacket.

'I say we are merciful,' repeated Gregory furiously, 'as the early Christians were merciful. Yet this did not prevent their being accused of eating human flesh. We do not eat human flesh——'

'Shame!' cried Witherspoon. 'Why not?'

'Comrade Witherspoon,' said Gregory, with a feverish gaiety, 'is anxious to know why nobody eats him (laughter). In our society, at any rate, which loves him sincerely, which is founded upon love——'

'No, no!' said Witherspoon, 'down with love.'

'Which is founded upon love,' repeated Gregory, grinding his teeth, 'there will be no difficulty about the aims which we shall pursue as a body, or which I should pursue were I chosen as the representative of that body. Superbly careless of the slanders that represent us as assassins and enemies of human society, we shall pursue with moral courage and quiet intellectual pressure, the permanent ideals of brotherhood and simplicity.'

Gregory resumed his seat and passed his hand across his forehead. The silence was sudden and awkward, but the chairman rose like an automaton, and said in a colourless voice—

'Does anyone oppose the election of Comrade Gregory?'

The assembly seemed vague and sub-consciously disappointed, and Comrade Witherspoon moved restlessly on his seat and muttered in his thick beard. By the sheer rush of routine, however, the motion would have been put and carried. But as the chairman was opening his mouth to put it, Syme sprang to his feet and said in a small and quiet voice—

'Yes, Mr Chairman, I oppose.'

The most effective fact in oratory is an unexpected change in the voice. Mr Gabriel Syme evidently understood oratory. Having said these first formal words in a moderated tone and with a brief simplicity, he made his next word ring and volley in the vault as if one of the guns had gone off.

'Comrades!' he cried, in a voice that made every man jump out of his boots, 'have we come here for this? Do we live underground like rats in order to listen to talk like this? This is talk we might listen to while eating buns at a Sunday School treat. Do we line these walls with weapons and bar that door with death lest anyone should come and hear Comrade Gregory saying to us, 'Be good, and you will be happy,' 'Honesty is the best policy,' and 'Virtue is its own reward'? There was not a word in Comrade Gregory's address to which a curate could not have listened with pleasure (hear, hear). But I am not a curate (loud cheers), and I did not listen to it with pleasure (renewed cheers). The man who is fitted to make a good curate is not fitted to make a resolute, forcible, and efficient Thursday (hear, hear).

'Comrade Gregory has told us, in only too apologetic a tone, that we are not the enemies of society. But I say that we are the enemies of society, and so much the worse for society. We are the enemies of society, for society is the enemy of humanity, its oldest and its most pitiless enemy (hear, hear). Comrade Gregory has told us (apologetically again) that we are not murderers. There I agree. We are not murderers, we are executioners (cheers).'

Ever since Syme had risen Gregory had sat staring at him, his face idiotic with astonishment. Now in the pause his lips of clay parted, and he said, with an automatic and lifeless distinctness—

'You damnable hypocrite!'

Syme looked straight into those frightful eyes with his own pale blue ones, and said with dignity—

'Comrade Gregory accuses me of hypocrisy. He knows as well as I do that I am keeping all my engagements and doing nothing but my duty. I do not mince words. I do not pretend to. I say that Comrade Gregory is unfit to be Thursday for all his amiable qualities. He is unfit to be Thursday because of his amiable qualities. We do not want the Supreme Council of Anarchy infected with a maudlin mercy (hear, hear). This is no time for ceremonial politeness, neither is it a time for ceremonial modesty. I set myself against Comrade Gregory as I would set myself against all the Governments of Europe, because the anarchist who has given himself to anarchy has forgotten modesty as much as he has forgotten pride (cheers). I am not a man at all. I am a cause (renewed cheers). I set myself against Comrade Gregory as impersonally and as calmly as I should choose one pistol rather than another out of that rack upon the wall; and I say that rather than have Gregory and his milk-and-water methods on the Supreme Council, I would offer myself for election——'

His sentence was drowned in a deafening cataract of applause. The faces, that had grown fiercer and fiercer with approval as his tirade grew more and more uncompromising, were now distorted with grins of anticipation or cloven with delighted cries. At the moment when he announced himself as ready to stand for the post of Thursday, a roar of excitement and assent broke forth, and became uncontrollable, and at the same moment Gregory sprang to his feet, with foam upon his mouth, and shouted against the shouting.

'Stop, you blasted madmen!' he cried, at the top of a voice that tore his throat. 'Stop, you——'

But louder than Gregory's shouting and louder than the roar of the room came the voice of Syme, still speaking in a peal of pitiless thunder—

'I do not go to the Council to rebut that slander that calls us murderers; I go to earn it (loud and prolonged cheering). To the priest who says these men are the enemies of religion, to the judge who says these men are the enemies of law, to the fat parliamentarian who says these men are the enemies of order and public decency, to all these I will reply, "You are false kings, but you are true prophets. I am come to destroy you, and to fulfil your prophecies."'

The heavy clamour gradually died away, but before it had ceased Witherspoon had jumped to his feet, his hair and beard all on end, and had said—

'I move, as an amendment, that Comrade Syme be appointed to the post.'

'Stop all this, I tell you!' cried Gregory, with frantic face and hands. 'Stop it, it is all——'

The voice of the chairman clove his speech with a cold accent.

'Does anyone second this amendment?' he said.

A tall, tired man, with melancholy eyes and an American chin beard, was observed on the back bench to be slowly rising to his feet. Gregory had been screaming for some time past; now there was a change in his accent, more shocking than any scream.

'I end all this!' he said, in a voice as heavy as stone. 'This man cannot be elected. He is a——'

'Yes,' said Syme, quite motionless, 'what is he?'

Gregory's mouth worked twice without sound; then slowly the blood began to crawl back into his dead face.

'He is a man quite inexperienced in our work,' he said, and sat down abruptly.

Before he had done so, the long, lean man with the American beard was again upon his feet, and was repeating in a high American monotone—

'I beg to second the election of Comrade Syme.'

'The amendment will, as usual, be put first,' said Mr Buttons, the chairman, with mechanical rapidity.

'The question is that Comrade Syme——'

Gregory had again sprung to his feet, panting and passionate.

'Comrades,' he cried out, 'I am not a madman.'

'Oh, oh!' said Mr Witherspoon.

'I am not a madman,' reiterated Gregory, with a frightful sincerity which for a moment staggered the room, 'but I give you a counsel which you can call mad if you like. No, I will not call it a counsel, for I can give you no reason for it. I will call it a command. Call it a mad command, but act upon it. Strike, but hear me! Kill me but obey me! Do not elect this man.'

Truth is so terrible, even in fetters, that for a moment Syme's slender and insane victory swayed like a reed. But you could not have guessed it from Syme's bleak blue eyes. He merely began—

'Comrade Gregory commands——'

Then the spell was snapped, and one anarchist called out to Gregory—

'Who are you? You are not Sunday'; and another anarchist added in a heavier voice, 'And you are not Thursday.'

'Comrades,' cried Gregory, in a voice like that of a martyr who in an ecstasy of pain has passed beyond pain, 'it is nothing to me whether you detest me as a tyrant or detest me as a slave. If you will not take my command, accept my degradation. I kneel to you. I throw myself at your feet. I implore you. Do not elect this man.'

'Comrade Gregory,' said the chairman after a painful pause, 'this is really not quite dignified.'

For the first time in the proceedings there was for a few seconds a real silence. Then Gregory fell back in his seat, a pale wreck of a man, and the chairman repeated, like a piece of clock-work suddenly started again—

'The question is that Comrade Syme be elected to the post of Thursday on the General Council.'

The roar rose like the sea, the hands rose like a forest, and three minutes afterwards Mr Gabriel Syme, of the Secret Police Service, was elected to the post of Thursday on the General Council of the Anarchists of Europe.

Everyone in the room seemed to feel the tug waiting on the river, the sword-stick and the revolver, waiting on the table. The instant the election was ended and irrevocable, and Syme had received the paper proving his election, they all sprang to their feet, and the fiery groups moved and mixed in the room. Syme found himself, somehow or other, face to face with

146

Gregory, who still regarded him with a stare of stunned hatred. They were silent for many minutes.

'You are a devil!' said Gregory at last.

'And you are a gentleman,' said Syme with gravity.

'It was you that entrapped me,' began Gregory, shaking from head to foot, 'entrapped me into——'

'Talk sense,' said Syme shortly. 'Into what sort of devils' parliament have you entrapped me, if it comes to that? You made me swear before I made you. Perhaps we are both doing what we think right. But what we think right is so damned different that there can be nothing between us in the way of concession. There is nothing possible between us but honour and death,' and he pulled the great cloak about his shoulders and picked up the flask from the table.

'The boat is quite ready,' said Mr Buttons, bustling up. 'Be good enough to step this way.'

With a gesture that revealed the shopwalker, he led Syme down a short, iron-bound passage, the still agonised Gregory following feverishly at their heels. At the end of the passage was a door, which Buttons opened sharply, showing a sudden blue and silver picture of the moonlit river, that looked like a scene in a theatre. Close to the opening lay a dark, dwarfish steam-launch, like a baby dragon with one red eye.

Almost in the act of stepping on board, Gabriel Syme turned to the gaping Gregory.

'You have kept your word,' he said gently, with his face in shadow. 'You are a man of honour, and I thank you. You have kept it even down to a small particular. There was one special thing you promised me at the beginning of the affair, and which you have certainly given me by the end of it.'

'What do you mean?' cried the chaotic Gregory. 'What did I promise you?'

'A very entertaining evening,' said Syme, and he made a military salute with the sword-stick as the steamboat slid away.

# IV

## *THE TALE OF A DETECTIVE*

Gabriel Syme was not merely a detective who pretended to be a poet; he was really a poet who had become a detective. Nor was his hatred of anarchy hypocritical. He was one of those who are driven early in life into too conservative an attitude by the bewildering folly of most revolutionists. He had not attained it by any tame tradition. His respectability was spontaneous and sudden, a rebellion against rebellion. He came of a family of cranks, in which all the oldest people had all the newest notions. One of his uncles always walked about without a hat, and another had made an unsuccessful attempt to walk about with a hat and nothing else. His father cultivated art and self-realisation; his mother went in for simplicity and hygiene. Hence the child, during his tenderer years, was wholly unacquainted with any drink between the extremes of absinth and cocoa, of both of which he had a healthy dislike. The more his mother preached a more than Puritan abstinence the more did his father expand into a more than pagan latitude; and by the time the former had come to enforcing vegetarianism, the latter had pretty well reached the point of defending cannibalism.

Being surrounded with every conceivable kind of revolt from infancy, Gabriel had to revolt into something, so he revolted into the only thing left—sanity. But there was just enough in him of the blood of these fanatics to make even his protest for common sense a little too fierce to be sensible. His hatred of modern lawlessness had been crowned also by an accident. It happened that he was walking in a side street at the instant of a dynamite outrage. He had been blind and deaf for a moment, and then seen, the smoke clearing, the broken windows and the bleeding faces. After that he went about as usual—quiet, courteous, rather gentle; but there was a spot on his mind that was not sane. He did not regard anarchists, as most of us do, as a handful of morbid men, combining ignorance with intellectualism. He regarded them as a huge and pitiless peril, like a Chinese invasion.

He poured perpetually into newspapers and their waste-paper baskets a torrent of tales, verses and violent articles, warning men of this deluge of barbaric denial. But he seemed to be getting no nearer his enemy, and what was worse, no nearer a living. As he paced the Thames embankment, bitterly biting a cheap cigar and brooding on the advance of Anarchy, there was no anarchist with a bomb in his pocket so savage or so solitary as he. Indeed, he always felt that Government stood alone and desperate, with its back to the wall. He was too quixotic to have cared for it otherwise.

He walked on the Embankment once under a dark red sunset. The red river reflected the red sky, and they both reflected his anger. The sky, indeed, was so swarthy, and the light on the river relatively so lurid, that the water almost seemed of fiercer flame than the sunset it mirrored. It looked like a stream of literal fire winding under the vast caverns of a subterranean country.

Syme was shabby in those days. He wore an old-fashioned black chimney-pot hat; he was wrapped in a yet more old-fashioned cloak, black and ragged; and the combination gave him the look of the early villains in Dickens and Bulwer Lytton. Also his yellow beard and hair were more unkempt and leonine than when they appeared long afterwards, cut and pointed, on the lawns of Saffron Park. A long, lean, black cigar, bought in Soho for twopence, stood out from between his tightened teeth, and altogether he looked a very satisfactory specimen of the anarchists upon whom he had vowed a holy war. Perhaps this was why a policeman on the Embankment spoke to him, and said 'Good evening.'

Syme, at a crisis of his morbid fears for humanity, seemed stung by the mere stolidity of the automatic official, a mere bulk of blue in the twilight.

'A good evening is it?' he said sharply. 'You fellows would call the end of the world a good evening. Look at that bloody red sun and that bloody river! I tell you that if that were literally human blood, spilt and shining, you would still be standing here as solid as ever, looking out for some poor harmless tramp whom you could move on. You policemen are cruel to the poor, but I could forgive you even your cruelty if it were not for your calm.'

'If we are calm,' replied the policeman, 'it is the calm of organised resistance.'

'Eh?' said Syme, staring.

'The soldier must be calm in the thick of the battle,' pursued the policeman. 'The composure of an army is the anger of a nation.'

'Good God, the Board Schools!' said Syme. 'Is this undenominational education?'

'No,' said the policeman sadly, 'I never had any of those advantages. The Board Schools came after my time. What education I had was very rough and old-fashioned, I am afraid.'

'Where did you have it?' asked Syme, wondering.

'Oh, at Harrow,' said the policeman.

The class sympathies which, false as they are, are the truest things in so many men, broke out of Syme before he could control them.

'But, good Lord, man,' he said, 'you oughtn't to be a policeman!'

The policeman sighed and shook his head.

'I know,' he said solemnly, 'I know I am not worthy.'

'But why did you join the police?' asked Syme with rude curiosity.

'For much the same reason that you abused the police,' replied the other. 'I found that there was a special opening in the service for those whose fears for humanity were concerned rather with the aberrations of scientific intellect than with the normal and excusable, though excessive, outbreaks of the human will. I trust I make myself clear.'

'If you mean that you make your opinion clear,' said Syme, 'I suppose you do. But as for making yourself clear, it is the last thing you do. How comes a man like you to be talking philosophy in a blue helmet on the Thames embankment?'

'You have evidently not heard of the latest development in our police system,' replied the other. 'I am not surprised at it. We are keeping it rather dark from the educated class, because that class contains most of our enemies. But you

punishment. They believe that the punishment has created the crime. They believe that if a man seduced seven women he would naturally walk away as blameless as the flowers of spring. They believe that if a man picked a pocket he would naturally feel exquisitely good. These I call the innocent section.'

'Oh!' said Syme.

'Naturally, therefore, these people talk about "a happy time coming"; "the paradise of the future"; "mankind freed from the bondage of vice and the bondage of virtue," and so on. And so also the men of the inner circle speak—the sacred priesthood. They also speak to applauding crowds of the happiness of the future, and of mankind freed at last. But in their mouths'— and the policeman lowered his voice—'in their mouths these happy phrases have a horrible meaning. They are under no illusions; they are too intellectual to think that man upon this earth can ever be quite free of original sin and the struggle. And they mean death. When they say that mankind shall be free at last, they mean that mankind shall commit suicide. When they talk of a paradise without right or wrong, they mean the grave. They have but two objects, to destroy first humanity and then themselves. That is why they throw bombs instead of firing pistols. The innocent rank and file are disappointed because the bomb has not killed the king; but the high-priesthood are happy because it has killed somebody.'

'How can I join you?' asked Syme, with a sort of passion.

'I know for a fact that there is a vacancy at the moment,' said the policeman, 'as I have the honour to be somewhat in the confidence of the chief of whom I have spoken. You should really come and see him. Or rather, I should not say see him, nobody ever sees him; but you can talk to him if you like.'

'Telephone?' inquired Syme, with interest.

'No,' said the policeman placidly, 'he has a fancy for always sitting in a pitch-dark room. He says it makes his thoughts brighter. Do come along.'

Somewhat dazed and considerably excited, Syme allowed himself to be led to a side-door in the long row of buildings of Scotland Yard. Almost before he knew what he was doing, he had been passed through the hands of about four intermediate officials, and was suddenly shown into a room, the abrupt blackness of which startled him like a blaze of light. It was not the ordinary darkness, in which forms can be faintly traced; it was like going suddenly stone-blind.

'Are you the new recruit?' asked a heavy voice.

And in some strange way, though there was not the shadow of a shape in the gloom, Syme knew two things: first, that it came from a man of massive stature; and second, that the man had his back to him.

'Are you the new recruit?' said the invisible chief, who seemed to have heard all about it. 'All right. You are engaged.'

Syme, quite swept off his feet, made a feeble fight against this irrevocable phrase.

'I really have no experience,' he began.

'No one has any experience,' said the other, 'of the Battle of Armageddon.'

'But I am really unfit—'

'You are willing, that is enough,' said the unknown.

'Well, really,' said Syme, 'I don't know any profession of which mere willingness is the final test.'

'I do,' said the other—'martyrs. I am condemning you to death. Good day.'

Thus it was that when Gabriel Syme came out again into the crimson light of evening, in his shabby black hat and shabby, lawless cloak, he came out a member of the New Detective Corps for the frustration of the great conspiracy. Acting under the advice of his friend the policeman (who was professionally inclined to neatness), he trimmed his hair and beard, bought a good hat, clad himself in an exquisite summer suit of light blue-grey, with a pale yellow flower in the button-hole, and, in short, became that elegant and rather insupportable person whom Gregory had first encountered in the little garden of Saffron Park. Before he finally left the police premises his friend provided him with a small blue card, on which was written, 'The Last Crusade,' and a number, the sign of his official authority. He put this carefully in his upper waistcoat pocket, lit a cigarette, and went forth to track and fight the enemy in all the drawing-rooms of London. Where his adventure ultimately led him we have already seen. At about half-past one on a February night he found himself steaming in a small tug up the silent Thames, armed with swordstick and revolver, the duly elected Thursday of the Central Council of Anarchists.

When Syme stepped out on to the steam-tug he had a singular sensation of stepping out into something entirely new; not merely into the landscape of a new land, but even into the landscape of a new planet. This was mainly due to the insane yet solid decision of that evening, though partly also to an entire change in the weather and the sky since he entered the little tavern some two hours before. Every trace of the passionate plumage of the cloudy sunset had been swept away, and a naked moon stood in a naked sky.

The moon was so strong and full, that (by a paradox often to be noticed) it seemed like a weaker sun. It gave, not the sense of bright moonshine, but rather of a dead daylight.

Over the whole landscape lay a luminous and unnatural discoloration, as of that disastrous twilight which Milton spoke of as shed by the sun in eclipse; so that Syme fell easily into his first thought, that he was actually on some other and emptier planet, which circled round some sadder star. But the more he felt this glittering desolation in the moonlit land, the more his own chivalric folly glowed in the night like a great fire. Even the common things he carried with him—the food and the brandy and the loaded pistol—took on exactly that concrete and material poetry which a child feels when he takes a gun upon a journey or a bun with him to bed. The sword-stick and the brandy-flask, though in themselves only the tools of morbid conspirators, became the expressions of his own more healthy romance. The sword-stick became almost the sword of chivalry, and the brandy the wine of the stirrup-cup. For even the most dehumanised modern fantasies depend on some older and simpler figure; the adventures may be mad, but the adventurer must be sane. The dragon without St George would not even be grotesque. So this inhuman landscape was only imaginative by the presence of a man really human. To Syme's exaggerative mind the bright, bleak houses and terraces by the Thames looked as empty as the mountains of the moon. But even the moon is only poetical because there is a man in the moon.

The tug was worked by two men, and with much toil went comparatively slowly. The clear moon that had lit up Chiswick had gone down by the time that they passed Battersea, and when they came under the enormous bulk of Westminster day had already begun to break. It broke like the splitting of great bars of lead, showing bars of silver; and these had brightened like white fire when the tug, changing its onward course, turned inward to a large landing stage rather beyond Charing Cross.

The great stones of the Embankment seemed equally dark and gigantic as Syme looked up at them. They were big and black against the huge white dawn. They made him feel that he was landing on the colossal steps of some Egyptian palace; and, indeed, the thing suited his mood, for he was, in his own mind, mounting to attack the solid thrones of horrible and heathen kings. He leapt out of the boat on to one slimy step, and stood, a dark and slender figure, amid the enormous masonry. The two men in the tug put her off again and turned up stream. They had never spoken a word.

# V

## *THE FEAST OF FEAR*

At first the large stone stair seemed to Syme as deserted as a pyramid; but before he reached the top he had realised that there was a man leaning over the parapet of the Embankment and looking out across the river. As a figure he was quite conventional, clad in a silk hat and frock-coat of the more formal type of fashion; he had a red flower in his buttonhole. As Syme drew nearer to him step by step, he did not even move a hair; and Syme could come close enough to notice even in the dim, pale morning light that his face was long, pale and intellectual, and ended in a small triangular tuft of dark beard at the very point of the chin, all else being clean-shaven. This scrap of hair almost seemed a mere oversight; the rest of the face was of the type that is best shaven—clear-cut, ascetic, and in its way noble. Syme drew closer and closer, noting all this, and still the figure did not stir.

At first an instinct had told Syme that this was the man whom he was meant to meet. Then, seeing that man made no sign, he had concluded that he was not. And now again he had come back to a certainty that the man had something to do with his mad adventure. For the man remained more still than would have been natural if a stranger had come so close. He was as motionless as a wax-work, and got on the nerves somewhat in the same way. Syme looked again and again at the pale, dignified and delicate face, and the face still looked blankly across the river. Then he took out of his pocket the note from Buttons proving his election, and put it before that sad and beautiful face. Then the man smiled, and his smile was a shock, for it was all on one side, going up in the right cheek and down in the left.

There was nothing, rationally speaking, to scare anyone about this. Many people have this nervous trick of a crooked smile, and in many it is even attractive. But in all Syme's circumstances, with the dark dawn and the deadly errand and the loneliness on the great dripping stones, there was something unnerving in it. There was the silent river and the silent man, a man of even classic face. And there was the last nightmare touch that his smile suddenly went wrong.

The spasm of smile was instantaneous, and the man's face dropped at once into its harmonious melancholy. He spoke without further explanation or inquiry, like a man speaking to an old colleague.

'If we walk up towards Leicester Square,' he said, 'we shall just be in time for breakfast. Sunday always insists on an early breakfast. Have you had any sleep?'

'No,' said Syme.

'Nor have I,' answered the man in an ordinary tone. 'I shall try to get to bed after breakfast.'

He spoke with casual civility, but in an utterly dead voice that contradicted the fanaticism of his face. It seemed almost as if all friendly words were to him lifeless conveniences, and that his only life was hate. After a pause the man spoke again.

'Of course, the Secretary of the branch told you everything that can be told. But the one thing that can never be told is the last notion of the President, for his notions grow like a tropical forest. So in case you don't know, I'd better tell you that he is carrying out his notion of concealing ourselves by not concealing ourselves to the most extraordinary lengths just now. Originally, of course, we met in a cell underground, just as your branch does. Then Sunday made us take a private room at an ordinary restaurant. He said that if you didn't seem to be hiding nobody hunted you out. Well, he is the only man on earth, I know; but sometimes I really think that his huge brain is going a little mad in its old age. For now we flaunt ourselves before the public. We have our breakfast on a balcony—on a balcony, if you please—overlooking Leicester Square.'

'And what do the people say?' asked Syme.

'It's quite simple what they say,' answered his guide. 'They say we are a lot of jolly gentlemen who pretend they are anarchists.'

'It seems to me a very clever idea,' said Syme.

'Clever! God blast your impudence! Clever!' cried out the other in a sudden, shrill voice which was as startling and discordant as his crooked smile. 'When you've seen Sunday for a split second you'll leave off calling him clever.'

With this they emerged out of a narrow street, and saw the early sunlight filling Leicester Square. It will never be known, I suppose, why this square itself should look so alien and in some ways so continental. It will never be known whether it was the foreign look that attracted the foreigners or the foreigners who gave it the foreign look. But on this particular morning the effect seemed singularly bright and clear. Between the open square and the sunlit leaves and the statue and the Saracenic outlines of the Alhambra, it looked the replica of some French or even Spanish public place. And this effect increased in Syme the sensation, which in many shapes he had had through the whole adventure, the eerie sensation of having strayed into a new world. As a fact, he had bought bad cigars round Leicester Square ever since he was a boy. But as he turned that corner, and saw the trees and the Moorish cupolas, he could have sworn that he was turning into an unknown Place de something or other in some foreign town.

At one corner of the square there projected a kind of angle of a prosperous but quiet hotel, the bulk of which belonged to a street behind. In the wall there was one large French window, probably the window of a large coffee-room; and outside this window, almost literally overhanging the square, was a formidably buttressed balcony, big enough to contain a dining-table. In fact it did contain a dining-table, or more strictly a breakfast-table; and round the breakfast-table, glowing in the sunlight and evident to the street, were a group of noisy and talkative men, all dressed in the insolence of fashion, with white waistcoats and expensive button-holes. Some of their jokes could almost be heard across the square. Then the grave Secretary gave his unnatural smile, and Syme knew that this boisterous breakfast party was the secret conclave of the European Dynamiters.

Then, as Syme continued to stare at them, he saw something that he had not seen before. He had not seen it literally because it was too large to see.

At the nearest end of the balcony, blocking up a great part of the perspective, was the back of a great mountain of a man. When Syme had seen him, his first thought was that the weight of him must break down the balcony of stone. His vastness did not lie only in the fact that he was abnormally tall and quite incredibly fat. This man was planned enormously in his original proportions, like a statue carved deliberately as colossal. His head, crowned with white hair, as seen from behind looked bigger than a head ought to be. The ears that stood out from it looked larger than human ears. He was enlarged terribly to scale; and this sense of size was so staggering, that when Syme saw him all the other figures seemed quite suddenly to dwindle and become dwarfish. They were still sitting there as before with their flowers and frock-coats, but now it looked as if the big man was entertaining five children to tea.

As Syme and the guide approached the side door of the hotel, a waiter came out smiling with every tooth in his head.

'The gentlemen are up there, sare,' he said. 'They do talk and they do laugh at what they talk. They do say they will throw bombs at ze king.'

And the waiter hurried away with a napkin over his arm, much pleased with the singular frivolity of the gentlemen upstairs.

The two men mounted the stairs in silence.

Syme had never thought of asking whether the monstrous man who almost filled and broke the balcony was the great President of whom the others stood in awe. He knew it was so, with an unaccountable but instantaneous certainty. Syme, indeed, was one of those men who are open to all the more nameless psychological influences in a degree a little dangerous to mental health. Utterly devoid of fear in physical dangers, he was a great deal too sensitive to the smell of spiritual evil. Twice already that night little unmeaning things had peeped out at him almost pruriently, and given him a sense of drawing nearer and nearer to the headquarters of hell. And this sense became overpowering as he drew nearer to the great President.

The form it took was a childish and yet hateful fancy. As he walked across the inner room towards the balcony, the large face of Sunday grew larger and larger; and Syme was gripped with a fear that when he was quite close the face would be too big to be possible, and that he would scream aloud. He remembered that as a child he would not look at the mask of Memnon in the British Museum, because it was a face, and so large.

By an effort, braver than that of leaping over a cliff, he went to an empty seat at the breakfast-table and sat down. The men greeted him with good-humoured raillery as if they had always known him. He sobered himself a little by looking at their conventional coats and solid, shining coffee-pot; then he looked again at Sunday. His face was very large, but it was still possible to humanity.

In the presence of the President the whole company looked sufficiently commonplace; nothing about them caught the eye at first, except that by the President's caprice they had been dressed up with a festive respectability, which gave the meal the look of a wedding breakfast. One man indeed stood out at even a superficial glance. He at least was the common or garden Dynamiter. He wore, indeed, the high white collar and satin tie that were the uniform of the occasion; but out of this collar there sprang a head quite unmanageable and quite unmistakable, a bewildering bush of brown hair and beard that almost obscured the eyes like those of a Skye terrier. But the eyes did look out of the tangle, and they were the sad eyes of some Russian serf. The effect of this figure was not terrible like that of the President, but it had every diablerie that can come from the utterly grotesque. If out of that stiff tie and collar there had come abruptly the head of a cat or a dog, it could not have been a more idiotic contrast.

The man's name, it seemed, was Gogol; he was a Pole, and in this circle of days he was called Tuesday. His soul and speech were incurably tragic; he could not force himself to play the prosperous and frivolous part demanded of him by President Sunday. And indeed, when Syme came in the President, with that daring disregard of public suspicion which was his policy, was actually chaffing Gogol upon his inability to assume conventional graces.

'Our friend Tuesday,' said the President in a deep voice at once of quietude and volume, 'our friend Tuesday doesn't seem to grasp the idea. He dresses up like a gentleman, but he seems to be too great a soul to behave like one. He insists on the ways of the stage conspirator. Now if a gentleman goes about London in a top hat and a frock-coat, no one need know that he is an anarchist. But if a gentleman puts on a top hat and a frock-coat, and then goes about on his hands and knees—well, he may attract attention. That's what Brother Gogol does. He goes about on his hands and knees with such inexhaustible diplomacy, that by this time he finds it quite difficult to walk upright.'

'I am not good at goncealment,' said Gogol sulkily, with a thick foreign accent; 'I am not ashamed of the cause.'

'Yes you are, my boy, and so is the cause of you,' said the President good-naturedly. 'You hide as much as anybody; but you can't do it, you see, you're such an ass! You try to combine two inconsistent methods. When a house-holder finds a man under his bed, he will probably pause to note the circumstance. But if he finds a man under his bed in a top hat, you will agree with me, my dear Tuesday, that he is not likely even to forget it. Now when you were found under Admiral Biffin's bed—'

'I am not good at deception,' said Tuesday gloomily, flushing.

'Right, my boy, right,' said the President with a ponderous heartiness, 'you aren't good at anything.'

While this stream of conversation continued, Syme was looking more steadily at the men around him. As he did so, he gradually felt all his sense of something spiritually queer return.

He had thought at first that they were all of common stature and costume, with the evident exception of the hairy Gogol. But as he looked at the others, he began to see in each of them exactly what he had seen in the man by the river, a demoniac detail somewhere. That lop-sided laugh, which would suddenly disfigure the fine face of his original guide, was typical of all these types. Each man had something about him, perceived perhaps at the tenth or twentieth glance, which was not normal, and which seemed hardly human. The only metaphor he could think of was this, that they all looked as men of fashion and presence would look, with the additional twist given in a false and curved mirror.

Only the individual examples will express this half-concealed eccentricity. Syme's original cicerone bore the title of Monday; he was the Secretary of the Council, and his twisted smile was regarded with more terror than anything, except the President's horrible happy laughter. But now that Syme had more space and light to observe him, there were other touches. His fine face was so emaciated, that Syme thought it must be wasted with some disease; yet somehow the very distress of his dark eyes denied this. It was no physical ill that troubled him. His eyes were alive with intellectual torture, as if pure thought was pain.

He was typical of each of the tribe; each man was subtly and differently wrong. Next to him sat Tuesday, the tousle-headed Gogol, a man more obviously mad. Next was Wednesday, a certain Marquis de St Eustache, a sufficiently characteristic figure. The first few glances found nothing un-usual about him, except that he was the only man at table who wore the fashionable clothes as if they were really his own. He had a black French beard cut square and a black English frock-coat cut even squarer. But Syme, sensitive to such things, felt somehow that the man carried a rich atmosphere with him, a rich atmosphere that suffocated. It reminded one irrationally of drowsy odours and of dying lamps in the darker poems of Byron and Poe. With this went a sense of his being clad, not in lighter colours, but in softer materials; his black seemed richer and warmer than the black shades about him, as if it were compounded of profound colour. His black coat looked as if it were only black by being too dense a purple. His black beard looked as if it were only black by being too deep a blue. And in the gloom and thickness of the beard his dark red mouth showed sensual and scornful. Whatever he was he was not a Frenchman; he might be a Jew; he might be something deeper yet in the dark heart of the East. In the bright coloured Persian tiles and pictures showing tyrants hunting, you may see just those almond eyes, those blue-black beards, those cruel, crimson lips.

Then came Syme, and next a very old man, Professor de Worms, who still kept the chair of Friday, though every day it was expected that his death would leave it empty. Save for his intellect, he was in the last dissolution of senile decay. His face was as grey as his long grey beard, his forehead was lifted and fixed finally in a furrow of mild despair. In no other case, not even that of Gogol, did the bridegroom brilliancy of the morning dress express a more painful contrast. For the red flower in his button-hole showed up against a face that was literally discoloured like lead; the whole hideous effect was as if some drunken dandies had put their clothes upon a corpse. When he rose or sat down, which was with long labour and peril, something worse was expressed than mere weakness, something indefinably connected with the horror of the whole scene. It did not express decrepitude merely, but corruption. Another hateful fancy crossed Syme's quivering mind. He could not help thinking that whenever the man moved a leg or arm might fall off.

Right at the end sat the man called Saturday, the simplest and the most baffling of all. He was a short square man with a dark, square face clean-shaven, a medical practitioner going by the name of Bull. He had that combination of *savoir-faire* with a sort of well-groomed coarseness which is not uncommon in young doctors. He carried his fine clothes with confidence rather than ease, and he mostly wore a set smile. There was nothing whatever odd about him except that he wore a pair of dark, almost opaque spectacles. It may have been merely a crescendo of nervous fancy that had gone before, but those black discs were dreadful to Syme; they reminded him of half-remembered ugly tales, of some story about pennies being put on the eyes of the dead. Syme's eye always caught the black glasses and the blind grin. Had the dying professor worn them, or even the pale Secretary, they would have been appropriate. But on the younger and grosser man they seemed only an enigma. They took away the key of the face. You could not tell what his smile or his gravity meant. Partly from this, and partly because he had a vulgar virility wanting in most of the others, it seemed to Syme that he might be the wickedest of all those wicked men. Syme even had the thought that his eyes might be covered up because they were too frightful to see.

# VI

## THE EXPOSURE

Such were the six men who had sworn to destroy the world. Again and again Syme strove to pull together his common sense in their presence. Sometimes he saw for an instant that these notions were subjective, that he was only looking at ordinary men, one of whom was old, another nervous, another short-sighted. The sense of an unnatural symbolism always settled back on him again. Each figure seemed to be, somehow, on the borderland of things, just as their theory was on the borderland of thought. He knew that each one of these men stood at the extreme end, so to speak, of some wild road of reasoning. He could only fancy, as in some old-world fable, that if a man went westward to the end of the world he would find something—say a tree—that was more or less than a tree, a tree possessed by a spirit; and that if he went east to the end of the world he would find something else that was not wholly itself—a tower, perhaps, of which the very shape was wicked. So these figures seemed to stand up, violent and unaccountable, against an ultimate horizon, visions from the verge. The ends of the earth were closing in.

Talk had been going on steadily as he took in the scene; and not the least of the contrasts of that bewildering breakfast-table was the contrast between the easy and unobtrusive tone of talk and its terrible purport. They were deep in the discussion of an actual and immediate plot. The waiter downstairs had spoken quite correctly when he said that they were talking about bombs and kings. Only three days afterwards the Czar was to meet the President of the French Republic in Paris, and over their bacon and eggs upon their sunny balcony these beaming gentleman had decided how both should die. Even the instrument was chosen; the black-bearded Marquis, it appeared, was to carry the bomb.

Ordinarily speaking, the proximity of this positive and objective crime would have sobered Syme, and cured him of all his merely mystical tremors. He would have thought of nothing but the need of saving at least two human bodies from being ripped in pieces with iron and roaring gas. But the truth was that by this time he had begun to feel a third kind of fear, more piercing and practical than either his moral revulsion or his social responsibility. Very simply, he had no fear to spare for the French President or the Czar; he had begun to fear for himself. Most of the talkers took little heed of him, debating now with their faces closer together, and almost uniformly grave, save when for an instant the smile of the Secretary ran aslant across his face as the jagged lightning runs aslant across the sky. But there was one persistent thing which first troubled Syme and at last terrified him. The President was always looking at him, steadily, and with a great and baffling interest. The enormous man was quite quiet, but his blue eyes stood out of his head. And they were always fixed on Syme.

Syme felt moved to spring up and leap over the balcony. When the President's eyes were on him he felt as if he were made of glass. He had hardly the shred of a doubt that in some silent and extraordinary way Sunday had found out that he was a spy. He looked over the edge of the balcony, and saw a policeman, standing abstractedly just beneath, staring at the bright railings and the sunlit trees.

Then there fell upon him the great temptation that was to torment him for many days. In the presence of these powerful and repulsive men, who were the princes of anarchy, he had almost forgotten the frail and fanciful figure of the poet Gregory, the mere æsthete of anarchism. He even thought of him now with an old kindness, as if they had played together when children. But he remembered that he was still tied to Gregory by a great promise. He had promised never to do the very thing that he now felt himself almost in the act of doing. He had promised not to jump over that balcony and speak to that policeman. He took his cold hand off the cold stone balustrade. His soul swayed in a vertigo of moral indecision. He had only to snap the thread of a rash vow made to a villainous society, and all his life could be as open and sunny as the square beneath him. He had, on the other hand, only to keep his antiquated honour, and be delivered inch by inch into the power of this great enemy of mankind, whose very intellect was a torture-chamber. Whenever he looked down into the square he saw the comfortable policeman, a pillar of common sense and common order. Whenever he looked back at the breakfast-table he saw the President still quietly studying him with big, unbearable eyes.

In all the torrent of his thought there were two thoughts that never crossed his mind. First, it never occurred to him to doubt that the President and his Council could crush him if he continued to stand alone. The place might be public, the project might seem impossible. But Sunday was not the man who would carry himself thus easily without having, somehow or somewhere, set open his iron trap. Either by anonymous poison or sudden street accident, by hypnotism or by fire from hell, Sunday could certainly strike him. If he defied the man he was probably dead, either struck stiff there in his chair or long afterwards as by an innocent ailment. If he called in the police promptly, arrested everyone, told all, and set against them the whole energy of England, he would probably escape; certainly not otherwise. They were a balconyful of gentlemen overlooking a bright and busy square; but he felt no more safe with them than if they had been a boatful of armed pirates overlooking an empty sea.

There was a second thought that never came to him. It never occurred to him to be spiritually won over to the enemy. Many moderns, inured to a weak worship of intellect and force, might have wavered in their allegiance under this oppression of a great personality. They might have called Sunday the super-man. If any such creature be conceivable, he looked, indeed, somewhat like it, with his earth-shaking abstraction, as of a stone statue walking. He might have been called something above man, with his large plans, which were too obvious to be detected, with his large face, which was too frank to be understood. But this was a kind of modern meanness to which Syme could not sink even in his extreme morbidity. Like any man, he

was coward enough to fear great force; but he was not quite coward enough
to admire it.

The men were eating as they talked, and even in this they were typical. Dr
Bull and the Marquis ate casually and conventionally of the best things on
the table—cold pheasant or Strasbourg pie. But the Secretary was a
vegetarian, and he spoke earnestly of the projected murder over half a raw
tomato and three quarters of a glass of tepid water. The old Professor had
such slops as suggested a sickening second childhood. And even in this
President Sunday preserved his curious predominance of mere mass. For he
ate like twenty men; he ate incredibly, with a frightful freshness of appetite,
so that it was like watching a sausage factory. Yet continually, when he had
swallowed a dozen crumpets or drunk a quart of coffee, he would be found
with his great head on one side staring at Syme.

'I have often wondered,' said the Marquis, taking a great bite out of a slice
of bread and jam, 'whether it wouldn't be better for me to do it with a knife.
Most of the best things have been brought off with a knife. And it would be a
new emotion to get a knife into a French President and wriggle it round.'

'You are wrong,' said the Secretary, drawing his black brows together.
'The knife was merely the expression of the old personal quarrel with a
personal tyrant. Dynamite is not only our best tool, but our best symbol. It is
as perfect a symbol of us as is incense of the prayers of the Christians. It
expands; it only destroys because it broadens; even so thought only destroys
because it broadens. A man's brain is a bomb,' he cried out, loosening
suddenly his strange passion and striking his own skull with violence. 'My
brain feels like a bomb, night and day. It must expand! It must expand! A
man's brain must expand, if it breaks up the universe.'

'I don't want the universe broken up just yet,' drawled the Marquis. 'I
want to do a lot of beastly things before I die. I thought of one yesterday in
bed.'

'No, if the only end of the thing is nothing,' said Dr Bull with his sphinx-
like smile, 'it hardly seems worth doing.'

The old Professor was staring at the ceiling with dull eyes.

'Every man knows in his heart,' he said, 'that nothing is worth doing.'

There was a singular silence, and then the Secretary said—

'We are wandering, however, from the point. The only question is how
Wednesday is to strike the blow. I take it we should all agree with the original
notion of a bomb. As to the actual arrangements, I should suggest that to-
morrow morning he should go first of all to——'

The speech was broken off short under a vast shadow. President Sunday
had risen to his feet, seeming to fill the sky above them.

'Before we discuss that,' he said in a small, quiet voice, 'let us go into a
private room. I have something very particular to say.'

Syme stood up before any of the others. The instant of choice had come at last, the pistol was at his head. On the pavement below he could hear the policeman idly stir and stamp, for the morning, though bright, was cold.

A barrel-organ in the street suddenly sprang with a jerk into a jovial tune. Syme stood up taut, as if it had been a bugle before the battle. He found himself filled with a supernatural courage that came from nowhere. That jingling music seemed full of the vivacity, the vulgarity, and the irrational valour of the poor, who in all those unclean streets were all clinging to the decencies and the charities of Christendom. His youthful prank of being a policeman had faded from his mind; he did not think of himself as the representative of the corps of gentlemen turned into fancy constables, or of the old eccentric who lived in the dark room. But he did feel himself as the ambassador of all these common and kindly people in the street, who every day marched into battle to the music of the barrel-organ. And this high pride in being human had lifted him unaccountably to an infinite height above the monstrous men around him. For an instant, at least, he looked down upon all their sprawling eccentricities from the starry pinnacle of the commonplace. He felt towards them all that unconscious and elementary superiority that a brave man feels over powerful beasts or a wise man over powerful errors. He knew that he had neither the intellectual nor the physical strength of President Sunday; but in that moment he minded it no more than the fact that he had not the muscles of a tiger or a horn on his nose like a rhinoceros. All was swallowed up in an ultimate certainty that the President was wrong and that the barrel-organ was right. There clanged in his mind that unanswerable and terrible truism in the song of Roland—

'Païens ont tort et Chrétiens ont droit,'

which in the old nasal French has the clang and groan of great iron. This liberation of his spirit from the load of his weakness went with a quite clear decision to embrace death. If the people of the barrel-organ could keep their old-world obligations, so could he. This very pride in keeping his word was that he was keeping it to miscreants. It was his last triumph over these lunatics to go down into their dark room and die for something that they could not even understand. The barrel-organ seemed to give the marching tune with the energy and the mingled noises of a whole orchestra; and he could hear deep and rolling, under all the trumpets of the pride of life, the drums of the pride of death.

The conspirators were already filing through the open window and into the rooms behind. Syme went last, outwardly calm, but with all his brain and body throbbing with romantic rhythm. The President led them down an irregular side stair, such as might be used by servants, and into a dim, cold, empty room, with a table and benches, like an abandoned boardroom. When they were all in, he closed and locked the door.

The first to speak was Gogol, the irreconcilable, who seemed bursting with inarticulate grievance.

'Zso! Zso!' he cried, with an obscure excitement, his heavy Polish accent becoming almost impenetrable. 'You zay you nod 'ide. You zay you show himselves. It is all nuzzinks. Ven you vant talk importance you run yourselves in a dark box!'

The President seemed to take the foreigner's incoherent satire with entire good humour.

'You can't get hold of it yet, Gogol,' he said in a fatherly way. 'When once they have heard us talking nonsense on that balcony they will not care where we go afterwards. If we had come here first, we should have had the whole staff at the keyhole. You don't seem to know anything about mankind.'

'I die for zem,' cried the Pole in thick excitement, 'and I slay zare oppressors. I care not for these games of gonzealment. I would zmite ze tyrant in ze open square.'

'I see, I see,' said the President, nodding kindly as he seated himself at the top of a long table. 'You die for mankind first, and then you get up and smite their oppressors. So that's all right. And now may I ask you to control your beautiful sentiments, and sit down with the other gentlemen at this table. For the first time this morning something intelligent is going to be said.'

Syme, with the perturbed promptitude he had shown since the original summons, sat down first. Gogol sat down last, grumbling in his brown beard about gombromise. No one except Syme seemed to have any notion of the blow that was about to fall. As for him, he had merely the feeling of a man mounting the scaffold with the intention, at any rate, of making a good speech.

'Comrades,' said the President, suddenly rising, 'we have spun out this farce long enough. I have called you down here to tell you something so simple and shocking that even the waiters upstairs (long inured to our levities) might hear some new seriousness in my voice. Comrades, we were discussing plans and naming places. I propose, before saying anything else, that those plans and places should not be voted by this meeting, but should be left wholly in the control of some one reliable member. I suggest Comrade Saturday, Dr Bull.'

They all stared at him; then they all started in their seats, for the next words, though not loud, had a living and sensational emphasis. Sunday struck the table.

'Not one word more about the plans and places must be said at this meeting. Not one tiny detail more about what we mean to do must be mentioned in this company.'

Sunday had spent his life in astonishing his followers; but it seemed as if he had never really astonished them until now. They all moved feverishly in their seats, except Syme. He sat stiff in his, with his hand in his pocket, and on the handle of his loaded revolver. When the attack on him came he would sell his life dear. He would find out at least if the President was mortal.

Sunday went on smoothly—

'You will probably understand that there is only one possible motive for forbidding free speech at this festival of freedom. Strangers overhearing us matters nothing. They assume that we are joking. But what would matter, even unto death, is this, that there should be one actually among us who is not of us, who knows our grave purpose, but does not share it, who——'

The Secretary screamed out suddenly like a woman.

'It can't be!' he cried, leaping. 'There can't——'

The President flapped his large flat hand on the table like the fin of some huge fish.

'Yes,' he said slowly, 'there is a spy in this room. There is a traitor at this table. I will waste no more words. His name——'

Syme half rose from his seat, his finger firm on the trigger.

'His name is Gogol,' said the President. 'He is that hairy humbug over there who pretends to be a Pole.'

Gogol sprang to his feet, a pistol in each hand. With the same flash three men sprang at his throat. Even the Professor made an effort to rise. But Syme saw little of the scene, for he was blinded with a beneficent darkness; he had sunk down into his seat shuddering, in a palsy of passionate relief.

# VII

## THE UNACCOUNTABLE CONDUCT OF PROFESSOR DE WORMS

'Sit down!' said Sunday in a voice that he used once or twice in his life, a voice that made men drop drawn swords.

The three who had risen fell away from Gogol, and that equivocal person himself resumed his seat.

'Well, my man,' said the President briskly, addressing him as one addresses a total stranger, 'will you oblige me by putting your hand in your upper waistcoat pocket and showing me what you have there?'

The alleged Pole was a little pale under his tangle of dark hair, but he put two fingers into the pocket with apparent coolness and pulled out a blue strip of card. When Syme saw it lying on the table, he woke up again to the world outside him. For although the card lay at the other extreme of the table, and he could read nothing of the inscription on it, it bore a startling resemblance to the blue card in his own pocket, the card which had been given to him when he joined the anti-anarchist constabulary.

'Pathetic Slav,' said the President, 'tragic child of Poland, are you prepared in the presence of that card to deny that you are in this company— shall we say *de trop*?'

'Right oh!' said the late Gogol. It made everyone jump to hear a clear, commercial and somewhat cockney voice coming out of that forest of foreign hair. It was irrational, as if a Chinaman had suddenly spoken with a Scotch accent.

'I gather that you fully understand your position,' said Sunday.

'You bet,' answered the Pole. 'I see it's a fair cop. All I say is, I don't believe any Pole could have imitated my accent like I did his.'

'I concede the point,' said Sunday. 'I believe your own accent to be inimitable, though I shall practise it in my bath. Do you mind leaving your beard with your card?'

'Not a bit,' answered Gogol; and with one finger he ripped off the whole of his shaggy head-covering, emerging with thin red hair and a pale, pert face. 'It was hot,' he added.

'I will do you the justice to say,' said Sunday, not without a sort of brutal admiration, 'that you seem to have kept pretty cool under it. Now listen to me. I like you. The consequence is that it would annoy me for just about two and a half minutes if I heard that you had died in torments. Well, if you ever tell the police or any human soul about us, I shall have that two and a half minutes of discomfort. On your discomfort I will not dwell. Good day. Mind the step.'

The red-haired detective who had masqueraded as Gogol rose to his feet without a word, and walked out of the room with an air of perfect nonchalance. Yet the astonished Syme was able to realise that this ease was suddenly assumed; for there was a slight stumble outside the door, which showed that the departing detective had not minded the step.

'Time is flying,' said the President in his gayest manner, after glancing at his watch, which like everything about him seemed bigger than it ought to be. 'I must go off at once; I have to take the chair at a Humanitarian meeting.'

The Secretary turned to him with working eyebrows.

'Would it not be better,' he said a little sharply, 'to discuss further the details of our project, now that the spy has left us?'

'No, I think not,' said the President with a yawn like an unobtrusive earthquake. 'Leave it as it is. Let Saturday settle it. I must be off. Breakfast here next Sunday.'

But the late loud scenes had whipped up the almost naked nerves of the Secretary. He was one of those men who are conscientious even in crime.

'I must protest, President, that the thing is irregular,' he said. 'It is a fundamental rule of our society that all plans shall be debated in full council. Of course, I fully appreciate your forethought when in the actual presence of a traitor——'

'Secretary,' said the President seriously, 'if you'd take your head home and boil it for a turnip it might be useful. I can't say. But it might.'

The Secretary reared back in a kind of equine anger.

'I really fail to understand——' he began in high offence.

'That's it, that's it,' said the President, nodding a great many times. 'That's where you fail right enough. You fail to understand. Why, you dancing donkey,' he roared, rising, 'you didn't want to be overheard by a spy, didn't you? How do you know you aren't overheard now?'

And with these words he shouldered his way out of the room, shaking with incomprehensible scorn.

Four of the men left behind gaped after him without any apparent glimmering of his meaning. Syme alone had even a glimmering, and such as it was it froze him to the bone. If the last words of the President meant anything, they meant that he had not after all passed unsuspected. They meant that while Sunday could not denounce him like Gogol, he still could not trust him like the others.

The other four got to their feet grumbling more or less, and betook themselves elsewhere to find lunch, for it was already well past midday. The Professor went last, very slowly and painfully. Syme sat long after the rest had gone, revolving his strange position. He had escaped a thunderbolt, but he was still under a cloud. At last he rose and made his way out of the hotel into Leicester Square. The bright, cold day had grown increasingly colder, and when he came out into the street he was surprised by a few flakes of snow. While he still carried the sword-stick and the rest of Gregory's portable luggage, he had thrown the cloak down and left it somewhere, perhaps on the steam-tug, perhaps on the balcony. Hoping, therefore, that the snow-shower might be slight, he stepped back out of the street for a moment and stood up under the doorway of a small and greasy hair-dresser's shop, the front window of which was empty, except for a sickly wax lady in evening dress.

Snow, however, began to thicken and fall fast; and Syme, having found one glance at the wax lady quite sufficient to depress his spirits, stared out instead into the white and empty street. He was considerably astonished to see, standing quite still outside the shop and staring into the window, a man. His top hat was loaded with snow like the hat of Father Christmas, the white drift was rising round his boots and ankles; but it seemed as if nothing could tear him away from the contemplation of the colourless wax doll in dirty evening dress. That any human being should stand in such weather looking into such a shop was a matter of sufficient wonder to Syme; but his idle wonder turned suddenly into a personal shock; for he realised that the man standing there was the paralytic old Professor de Worms. It scarcely seemed the place for a person of his years and infirmities.

Syme was ready to believe anything about the perversions of this dehuman-ised brotherhood; but even he could not believe that the Professor had fallen in love with that particular wax lady. He could only suppose that the man's malady (whatever it was) involved some momentary fits of rigidity or trance. He was not inclined, however, to feel in this case any very compassionate concern. On the contrary, he rather congratulated himself that the Professor's stroke and his elaborate and limping walk would make it easy to escape from him and leave him miles behind. For Syme thirsted first and last to get clear of the whole poisonous atmosphere, if only for an hour. Then he could collect his thoughts, formulate his policy, and decide finally whether he should or should not keep faith with Gregory.

He strolled away through the dancing snow, turned up two or three streets, down through two or three others, and entered a small Soho restaurant for lunch. He partook reflectively of four small and quaint courses, drank half a bottle of red wine, and ended up over black coffee and a black cigar, still thinking. He had taken his seat in the upper room of the restaurant, which was full of the chink of knives and the chatter of foreigners. He remembered that in old days he had imagined that all these harmless and kindly aliens were anarchists. He shuddered, remembering the real thing. But even the shudder had the delightful shame of escape. The wine, the common food, the familiar place, the faces of natural and talkative men, made him almost feel as if the Council of the Seven Days had been a bad dream; and although he knew it was nevertheless an objective reality, it was at least a distant one. Tall houses and populous streets lay between him and his last sight of the shameful seven; he was free in free London, and drinking wine among the free. With a somewhat easier action, he took his hat and stick and strolled down the stair into the shop below.

When he entered that lower room he stood stricken and rooted to the spot. At a small table, close up to the blank window and the white street of snow, sat the old anarchist Professor over a glass of milk, with his lifted livid face and pendent eyelids. For an instant Syme stood as rigid as the stick he leant upon. Then with a gesture as of blind hurry, he brushed past the Professor, dashing open the door and slamming it behind him, and stood outside in the snow.

'Can that old corpse be following me?' he asked himself, biting his yellow moustache. 'I stopped too long up in that room, so that even such leaden feet could catch me up. One comfort is, with a little brisk walking I can put a man like that as far away as Timbuctoo. Or am I too fanciful? Was he really following me? Surely Sunday would not be such a fool as to send a lame man?'

He set off at a smart pace, twisting and whirling his stick, in the direction of Covent Garden. As he crossed the great market the snow increased, growing blinding and bewildering as the afternoon began to darken. The snow-flakes tormented him like a swarm of silver bees. Getting into his eyes and beard, they added their unremitting futility to his already irritated nerves; and by the time that he had come at a swinging pace to the beginning of Fleet Street, he lost patience, and finding a Sunday teashop, turned into it to take shelter. He ordered another cup of black coffee as an excuse. Scarcely had he done so, when Professor de Worms hobbled heavily into the shop, sat down with difficulty and ordered a glass of milk.

Syme's walking-stick had fallen from his hand with a great clang, which confessed the concealed steel. But the Professor did not look round. Syme, who was commonly a cool character, was literally gaping as a rustic gapes at a conjuring trick. He had seen no cab following; he had heard no wheels outside the shop; to all mortal appearances the man had come on foot. But the old man could only walk like a snail, and Syme had walked like the wind. He started up and snatched his stick, half crazy with the contradiction in mere arithmetic, and swung out of the swinging doors, leaving his coffee untasted. An omnibus going to the Bank went rattling by with an unusual rapidity. He had a violent run of a hundred yards to reach it; but he managed to spring, swaying upon the splash-board and, pausing for an instant to pant, he climbed on to the top. When he had been seated for about half a minute, he heard behind him a sort of heavy and asthmatic breathing.

Turning sharply, he saw rising gradually higher and higher up the omnibus steps a top hat soiled and dripping with snow, and under the shadow of its brim the short-sighted face and shaky shoulders of Professor de Worms. He let himself into a seat with characteristic care, and wrapped himself up to the chin in the mackintosh rug.

Every movement of the old man's tottering figure and vague hands, every uncertain gesture and panic-stricken pause, seemed to put it beyond question that he was helpless, that he was in the last imbecility of the body. He moved by inches, he let himself down with little gasps of caution. And yet, unless the philosophical entities called time and space have no vestige even of a practical existence, it appeared quite unquestionable that he had run after the omnibus.

Syme sprang erect upon the rocking car, and after staring wildly at the wintry sky, that grew gloomier every moment, he ran down the steps. He had repressed an elemental impulse to leap over the side.

Too bewildered to look back or to reason, he rushed into one of the little courts at the side of Fleet Street as a rabbit rushes into a hole. He had a vague idea, if this incomprehensible old Jack-in-the-box was really pursuing him, that in that labyrinth of little streets he could soon throw him off the scent. He dived in and out of those crooked lanes, which were more like cracks than thoroughfares; and by the time that he had completed about twenty alternate angles and described an unthinkable polygon, he paused to listen for any sound of pursuit. There was none; there could not in any case have been much, for the little streets were thick with the soundless snow. Somewhere behind Red Lion Court, however, he noticed a place where some energetic citizen had cleared away the snow for a space of about twenty yards, leaving the wet, glistening cobble-stones. He thought little of this as he passed it, only plunging into yet another arm of the maze. But when a few hundred yards farther on he stood still again to listen, his heart stood still also, for he heard from that space of rugged stones the clinking crutch and labouring feet of the infernal cripple.

The sky above was loaded with the clouds of snow, leaving London in a darkness and oppression premature for that hour of the evening. On each side of Syme the walls of the alley were blind and featureless; there was no little window or any kind of eye. He felt a new impulse to break out of this hive of houses, and to get once more into the open and lamplit street. Yet he rambled and dodged for a long time before he struck the main thoroughfare. When he did so, he struck it much farther up than he had fancied. He came out into what seemed the vast and void of Ludgate Circus, and saw St Paul's Cathedral sitting in the sky.

At first he was startled to find these great roads so empty, as if a pestilence had swept through the city. Then he told himself that some degree of emptiness was natural; first because the snow-storm was even dangerously deep, and secondly because it was Sunday. And at the very word Sunday he bit his lip; the word was henceforth for him like some indecent pun. Under the white fog of snow high up in the heaven the whole atmosphere of the city was turned to a very queer kind of green twilight, as of men under the sea. The sealed and sullen sunset behind the dark dome of St Paul's had in it smoky and sinister colours—colours of sickly green, dead red or decaying bronze, that were just bright enough to emphasise the solid whiteness of the snow. But right up against these dreary colours rose the black bulk of the cathedral; and upon the top of the cathedral was a random splash and great stain of snow, still clinging as to an Alpine peak. It had fallen accidentally, but just so fallen as to half drape the dome from its very topmost point, and to pick out in perfect silver the great orb and the cross. When Syme saw it he suddenly straightened himself, and made with his sword-stick an involuntary salute.

He knew that that evil figure, his shadow, was creeping quickly or slowly behind him, and he did not care. It seemed a symbol of human faith and valour that while the skies were darkening that high place of the earth was bright. The devils might have captured heaven, but they had not yet captured the cross. He had a new impulse to tear out the secret of this dancing, jumping and pursuing paralytic; and at the entrance of the court as it opened upon the Circus he turned, stick in hand, to face his pursuer.

Professor de Worms came slowly round the corner of the irregular alley behind him, his unnatural form outlined against a lonely gas-lamp, irresistibly recalling that very imaginative figure in the nursery rhymes, 'the crooked man who went a crooked mile.' He really looked as if he had been twisted out of shape by the tortuous streets he had been threading. He came nearer and nearer, the lamplight shining on his lifted spectacles, his lifted, patient face. Syme waited for him as St George waited for the dragon, as a man waits for a final explanation or for death. And the old Professor came right up to him and passed him like a total stranger, without even a blink of his mournful eyelids.

There was something in this silent and unexpected innocence that left Syme in a final fury. The man's colourless face and manner seemed to assert that the whole following had been an accident. Syme was galvanised with an energy that was something between bitterness and a burst of boyish derision. He made a wild gesture as if to knock the old man's hat off, called out something like 'Catch me if you can,' and went racing away across the white, open Circus. Concealment was impossible now; and looking back over his shoulder, he could see the black figure of the old gentleman coming after him with long, swinging strides like a man winning a mile race. But the head upon that bounding body was still pale, grave and professional, like the head of a lecturer upon the body of a harlequin.

This outrageous chase sped across Ludgate Circus, up Ludgate Hill, round St Paul's Cathedral, along Cheapside, Syme remembering all the nightmares he had ever known. Then Syme broke away towards the river, and ended almost down by the docks. He saw the yellow panes of a low, lighted public-house, flung himself into it and ordered beer. It was a foul tavern, sprinkled with foreign sailors, a place where opium might be smoked or knives drawn.

A moment later Professor de Worms entered the place, sat down carefully, and asked for a glass of milk.

# VIII

## *THE PROFESSOR EXPLAINS*

When Gabriel Syme found himself finally established in a chair, and opposite to him, fixed and final also, the lifted eyebrows and leaden eyelids of the Professor, his fears fully returned. This incomprehensible man from the fierce council, after all, had certainly pursued him. If the man had one character as a paralytic and another character as a pursuer, the antithesis might make him more interesting, but scarcely more soothing. It would be a very small comfort that he could not find the Professor out, if by some serious accident the Professor should find him out. He emptied a whole pewter pot of ale before the professor had touched his milk.

One possibility, however, kept him hopeful and yet helpless. It was just possible that this escapade signified something other than even a slight suspicion of him. Perhaps it was some regular form or sign. Perhaps the foolish scamper was some sort of friendly signal that he ought to have understood. Perhaps it was a ritual. Perhaps the new Thursday was always chased along Cheapside, as the new Lord Mayor is always escorted along it. He was just selecting a tentative inquiry, when the old Professor opposite suddenly and simply cut him short. Before Syme could ask the first diplomatic question, the old anarchist had asked suddenly, without any sort of preparation—

'Are you a policeman?'

Whatever else Syme had expected, he had never expected anything so brutal and actual as this. Even his great presence of mind could only manage a reply with an air of rather blundering jocularity.

'A policeman?' he said, laughing vaguely. 'Whatever made you think of a policeman in connection with me?'

'The process was simple enough,' answered the Professor patiently. 'I thought you looked like a policeman. I think so now.'

'Did I take a policeman's hat by mistake out of the restaurant?' asked Syme, smiling wildly. 'Have I by any chance got a number stuck on to me somewhere? Have my boots got that watchful look? Why must I be a policeman? Do, do let me be a postman.'

The old Professor shook his head with a gravity that gave no hope, but Syme ran on with a feverish irony.

'But perhaps I misunderstood the delicacies of your German philosophy. Perhaps policeman is a relative term. In an evolutionary sense, sir, the ape fades so gradually into the policeman, that I myself can never detect the shade. The monkey is only the policeman that may be. Perhaps a maiden lady on Clapham Common is only the policeman that might have been. I don't mind being the policeman that might have been. I don't mind being anything in German thought.'

'Are you in the police service?' said the old man, ignoring all Syme's improvised and desperate raillery. 'Are you a detective?'

Syme's heart turned to stone, but his face never changed.

'Your suggestion is ridiculous,' he began. 'Why on earth——'

The old man struck his palsied hand passionately on the rickety table, nearly breaking it.

'Did you hear me ask a plain question, you paltering spy?' he shrieked in a high, crazy voice. 'Are you, or are you not, a police detective?'

'No!' answered Syme, like a man standing on the hangman's drop.

'You swear it,' said the old man, leaning across to him, his dead face becoming as it were loathsomely alive. 'You swear it! You swear it! If you swear falsely, will you be damned? Will you be sure that the devil dances at your funeral? Will you see that the nightmare sits on your grave? Will there really be no mistake? You are an anarchist, you are a dynamiter! Above all, you are not in any sense a detective? You are not in the British police?'

He leant his angular elbow far across the table, and put up his large loose hand like a flap to his ear.

'I am not in the British police,' said Syme with insane calm.

Professor de Worms fell back in his chair with a curious air of kindly collapse.

'That's a pity,' he said, 'because I am.'

Syme sprang up straight, sending back the bench behind him with a crash.

'Because you are what?' he said thickly. 'You are what?'

'I am a policeman,' said the Professor with his first broad smile, and beaming through his spectacles. 'But as you think policeman only a relative term, of course I have nothing to do with you. I am in the British police force; but as you tell me you are not in the British police force, I can only say that I met you in a dynamiters' club. I suppose I ought to arrest you.' And with these words he laid on the table before Syme an exact facsimile of the blue card which Syme had in his own waistcoat pocket, the symbol of his power from the police.

Syme had for a flash the sensation that the cosmos had turned exactly upside down, that all trees were growing downwards and that all stars were under his feet. Then came slowly the opposite conviction. For the last twenty-four hours the cosmos had really been upside down, but now the capsized universe had come right side up again. This devil from whom he had been fleeing all day was only an elder brother of his own house, who on the other side of the table lay back and laughed at him. He did not for the moment ask any questions of detail; he only knew the happy and silly fact that this shadow, which had pursued him with an intolerable oppression of peril, was only the shadow of a friend trying to catch him up. He knew simultaneously that he was a fool and a free man. For with any recovery from morbidity there must go a certain healthy humiliation. There comes a certain point in such conditions when only three things are possible: first a per-petuation of Satanic pride, secondly tears, and third laughter. Syme's egotism held hard to the first course for a few seconds, and then suddenly adopted the third. Taking his own blue police ticket from his own waistcoat pocket, he tossed it on to the table; then he flung his head back until his spike of yellow beard almost pointed at the ceiling, and shouted with a barbaric laughter.

Even in that close den, perpetually filled with the din of knives, plates, cans, clamorous voices, sudden struggles and stampedes, there was something Homeric in Syme's mirth which made many half-drunken men look round.

'What yer laughing at, guv'nor?' asked one wondering labourer from the docks.

'At myself,' answered Syme, and went off again into the agony of his ecstatic reaction.

'Pull yourself together,' said the Professor, 'or you'll get hysterical. Have some more beer. I'll join you.'

'You haven't drunk your milk,' said Syme.

'My milk!' said the other, in tones of withering and unfathomable contempt, 'my milk! Do you think I'd look at the beastly stuff when I'm out of sight of the bloody anarchists? We're all Christians in this room, though perhaps,' he added, glancing around at the reeling crowd, 'not strict ones. Finish my milk? Great blazes! yes, I'll finish it right enough!' and he knocked the tumbler off the table, making a crash of glass and a splash of silver fluid.

Syme was staring at him with a happy curiosity.

'I understand now,' he cried; 'of course, you're not an old man at all.'

'I can't take my face off here,' replied Professor de Worms. 'It's rather an elaborate make-up. As to whether I'm an old man, that's not for me to say. I was thirty-eight last birthday.'

'Yes, but I mean,' said Syme impatiently, 'there's nothing the matter with you.'

'Yes,' answered the other dispassionately. 'I am subject to colds.'

Syme's laughter at all this had about it a wild weakness of relief. He laughed at the idea of the paralytic Professor being really a young actor dressed up as if for the foot-lights. But he felt that he would have laughed as loudly if a pepper-pot had fallen over.

The false professor drank and wiped his false beard.

'Did you know,' he asked, 'that that man Gogol was one of us?'

'I? No, I didn't know it,' answered Syme in some surprise. 'But didn't you?'

'I knew no more than the dead,' replied the man who called himself de Worms. 'I thought the President was talking about me, and I rattled in my boots.'

'And I thought he was talking about me,' said Syme, with his rather reckless laughter. 'I had my hand on my revolver all the time.'

'So had I,' said the Professor grimly; 'so had Gogol evidently.'

Syme struck the table with an exclamation.

'Why, there were three of us there!' he cried.

'Three out of seven is a fighting number. If we had only known that we were three!'

The face of Professor de Worms darkened, and he did not look up.

'We were three,' he said. 'If we had been three hundred we could still have done nothing.'

'Not if we were three hundred against four?' asked Syme, jeering rather boisterously.

'No,' said the Professor with sobriety, 'not if we were three hundred against Sunday.'

And the mere name struck Syme cold and serious; his laughter had died in his heart before it could die on his lips. The face of the unforgettable President sprang into his mind as startling as a coloured photograph, and he remarked this difference between Sunday and all his satellites, that their faces, however fierce or sinister, became gradually blurred by memory like other human faces, whereas Sunday's seemed almost to grow more actual during absence, as if a man's painted portrait should slowly come alive.

They were both silent for a measure of moments and then Syme's speech came with a rush, like the sudden foaming of champagne.

'Professor,' he cried, 'it is intolerable. Are you afraid of this man?'

The Professor lifted his heavy lids, and gazed at Syme with large, wide-open, blue eyes of an almost ethereal honesty.

'Yes, I am,' he said mildly. 'So are you.'

Syme was dumb for an instant. Then he rose to his feet erect, like an insulted man, and thrust the chair away from him.

'Yes,' he said in a voice indescribable, 'you are right. I am afraid of him. Therefore I swear by God that I will seek out this man whom I fear until I find him, and strike him on the mouth. If heaven were his throne and the earth his footstool, I swear that I would pull him down.'

'How?' asked the staring Professor. 'Why?'

'Because I am afraid of him,' said Syme; 'and no man should leave in the universe anything of which he is afraid.'

De Worms blinked at him with a sort of blind wonder. He made an effort to speak, but Syme went on in a low voice, but with an undercurrent of inhuman exaltation—

'Who would condescend to strike down the mere things that he does not fear? Who would debase himself to be merely brave, like any common prizefighter? Who would stoop to be fearless—like a tree? Fight the thing that you fear. You remember the old tale of the English clergyman who gave the last rites to the brigand of Sicily, and how on his death-bed the great robber said, "I can give you no money, but I can give you advice for a lifetime: your thumb on the blade, and strike upwards." So I say to you, strike upwards, if you strike at the stars.'

The other looked at the ceiling, one of the tricks of his pose.

'Sunday is a fixed star,' he said.

'You shall see him a falling star,' said Syme, and put on his hat.

176

The decision of his gesture drew the professor vaguely to his feet.

'Have you any idea,' he asked, with a sort of benevolent bewilderment, 'exactly where you are going?'

'Yes,' replied Syme shortly, 'I am going to prevent this bomb being thrown in Paris.'

'Have you any conception how?' inquired the other.

'No,' said Syme with equal decision.

'You remember, of course,' resumed the soi-disant de Worms, pulling his beard and looking out of the window, 'that when we broke up rather hurriedly the whole arrangements for the atrocity were left in the private hands of the Marquis and Dr Bull. The Marquis is by this time probably crossing the Channel. But where he will go and what he will do it is doubtful whether even the President knows; certainly we don't. The only man who does know is Dr Bull.'

'Confound it!' cried Syme. 'And we don't know where he is.'

'Yes,' said the other in his curious, absent-minded way, 'I know where he is myself.'

'Will you tell me?' asked Syme with eager eyes.

'I will take you there,' said the Professor, and took down his own hat from a peg.

Syme stood looking at him with a sort of rigid excitement.

'What do you mean?' he asked sharply. 'Will you join me? Will you take the risk?'

'Young man,' said the Professor pleasantly, 'I am amused to observe that you think I am a coward. As to that I will say only one word, and that shall be entirely in the manner of your own philosophical rhetoric. You think that it is possible to pull down the President. I know that it is impossible, and I am going to try it,' and opening the tavern door, which let in a blast of bitter air, they went out together into the dark streets by the docks.

Most of the snow was melted or trampled to mud, but here and there a clot of it still showed grey rather than white in the gloom. The small streets were sloppy and full of pools, which reflected the flaming lamps irregularly, and by accident, like fragments of some other and fallen world. Syme felt almost dazed as he stepped through this growing confusion of lights and shadows; but his companion walked on with a certain briskness, towards where, at the end of the street, an inch or two of the lamplit river looked like a bar of flame.

'Where are you going?' Syme inquired.

'Just now,' answered the Professor, 'I am going just round the corner to see whether Dr Bull has gone to bed. He is hygienic, and retires early.'

'Dr Bull!' exclaimed Syme. 'Does he live round the corner?'

'No,' answered his friend. 'As a matter of fact he lives some way off, on the other side of the river, but we can tell from here whether he has gone to bed.'

Turning the corner as he spoke, and facing the dim river, flecked with flame, he pointed with his stick to the other bank. On the Surrey side at this point there ran out into the Thames, seeming almost to overhang it, a bulk and cluster of those tall tenements, dotted with lighted windows, and rising like factory chimneys to an almost insane height. Their special poise and position made one block of buildings especially look like a Tower of Babel with a hundred eyes. Syme had never seen any of the sky-scraping buildings in America, so he could only think of the buildings in a dream.

Even as he stared, the highest light in this innumerably lighted turret abruptly went out, as if this black Argus had winked at him with one of his innumerable eyes.

Professor de Worms swung round on his heel, and struck his stick against his boot.

'We are too late,' he said, 'the hygienic Doctor has gone to bed.'

'What do you mean?' asked Syme. 'Does he live over there, then?'

'Yes,' said de Worms, 'behind that particular window which you can't see. Come along and get some dinner. We must call on him to-morrow morning.'

Without further parley, he led the way through several by-ways until they came out into the flare and clamour of the East India Dock Road. The Professor, who seemed to know his way about the neighbourhood, proceeded to a place where the line of lighted shops fell back into a sort of abrupt twilight and quiet, in which an old white inn, all out of repair, stood back some twenty feet from the road.

'You can find good English inns left by accident everywhere, like fossils,' explained the Professor. 'I once found a decent place in the West End.'

'I suppose,' said Syme, smiling, 'that this is the corresponding decent place in the East End?'

'It is,' said the professor reverently, and went in.

In that place they dined and slept, both very thoroughly. The beans and bacon, which these unaccountable people cooked well, the astonishing emergence of Burgundy from their cellars, crowned Syme's sense of new comradeship and comfort. Through all this ordeal his root horror had been isolation, and there are no words to express the abyss between isolation and having one ally. It may be conceded to the mathematicians that four is twice two. But two is not twice one; two is two thousand times one. That is why, in spite of a hundred disadvantages, the world will always return to monogamy.

Syme was able to pour out for the first time the whole of his outrageous tale, from the time when Gregory had taken him to the little tavern by the river. He did it idly and amply, in a luxuriant monologue, as a man speaks with very old friends. On his side, also the man who had impersonated Professor de Worms was not less communicative. His own story was almost as silly as Syme's.

'That's a good get-up of yours,' said Syme, draining a glass of Mâcon; 'a lot better than old Gogol's. Even at the start I thought he was a bit too hairy.'

'A difference of artistic theory,' replied the Professor pensively. 'Gogol was an idealist. He made up as the abstract or platonic ideal of an anarchist. But I am a realist. I am a portrait painter. But, indeed, to say that I am a portrait painter is an inadequate expression. I am a portrait.'

'I don't understand you,' said Syme.

'I am a portrait,' repeated the professor. 'I am a portrait of the celebrated Professor de Worms, who is, I believe, in Naples.'

'You mean you are made up like him,' said Syme. 'But doesn't he know that you are taking his nose in vain?'

'He knows it right enough,' replied his friend cheerfully.

'Then why doesn't he denounce you?'

'I have denounced him,' answered the Professor.

'Do explain yourself,' said Syme.

'With pleasure, if you don't mind hearing my story,' replied the eminent foreign philosopher. 'I am by profession an actor, and my name is Wilks. When I was on the stage I mixed with all sorts of Bohemian and blackguard company. Sometimes I touched the edge of the turf, sometimes the riff-raff of the arts, and occasionally the political refugee. In some den of exiled dreamers I was introduced to the great German Nihilist philosopher, Professor de Worms. I did not gather much about him beyond his appearance, which was was very disgusting, and which I studied carefully. I understood that he had proved that the destructive principle in the universe was God; hence he insisted on the need for a furious and incessant energy, rending all things in pieces. Energy, he said, was the All. He was lame, shortsighted, and partially paralytic. When I met him I was in a frivolous mood, and I disliked him so much that I resolved to imitate him. If I had been a draughtsman I would have drawn a caricature. I was only an actor, I could only act a caricature. I made myself up into what was meant for a wild exaggeration of the old Professor's dirty old self. When I went into the room full of his supporters I expected to be received with a roar of laughter, or (if they were too far gone) with a roar of indignation at the insult. I cannot describe the surprise I felt when my entrance was received with a respectful silence, followed (when I had first opened my lips) with a murmur of admiration. The curse of the perfect artist had fallen upon me. I had been too subtle, I had been too true. They thought I really was the great Nihilist Professor. I was a healthy-minded young man at the time, and I confess that it was a blow. Before I could fully recover, however, two or three of these admirers ran up to me radiating indignation, and told me that a public insult had been put upon me in the next room. I inquired its nature. It seemed that an impertinent fellow had dressed himself up as a preposterous parody of myself. I had drunk more champagne than was good for me, and in a flash of folly I decided to see the situation through. Consequently it was to meet the glare of the company and my own lifted eyebrows and freezing eyes that the real Professor came into the room.

'I need hardly say there was a collision. The pessimists all round me looked anxiously from one Professor to the other Professor to see which was really the more feeble. But I won. An old man in poor health, like my rival, could not be expected to be so impressively feeble as a young actor in the prime of life. You see, he really had paralysis, and working within this definite limitation, he couldn't be so jolly paralytic as I was. Then he tried to blast my claims intellectually. I countered that by a very simple dodge. Whenever he said something that nobody but he could understand, I replied with something which I could not even understand myself. "I don't fancy," he said, "that you could have worked out the principle that evolution is only negation, since there inheres in it the introduction of lacunæ, which are an essential of differentiation." I replied quite scornfully, "You read all that up in Pinckwerts; the notion that involution functioned eugenically was exposed long ago by Glumpe." It is unnecessary for me to say that there never were such people as Pinckwerts and Glumpe. But the people all round (rather to my surprise) seemed to remember them quite well, and the Professor, finding that the learned and mysterious method left him rather at the mercy of an enemy slightly deficient in scruples, fell back upon a more popular form of wit. "I see," he sneered, "you prevail like the false pig in Æsop." "And you fail," I answered, smiling, "like the hedgehog in Montaigne." Need I say that there is no hedgehog in Montaigne? "Your clap-trap comes off," he said; "so would your beard." I had no intelligent answer to this, which was quite true and witty. But I laughed heartily, answered, "Like the Pantheist's boots," at random, and turned on my heel with all the honours of victory. The real Professor was thrown out, but not with violence, though one man tried very patiently to pull off his nose. He is now, I believe, received everywhere in Europe as a delightful impostor. His apparent earnestness and anger, you see, make him all the more entertaining.'

'Well,' said Syme, 'I can understand your putting on his dirty old beard for a night's practical joke, but I don't understand your never taking it off again.'

'That is the rest of the story,' said the impersonator. 'When I myself left the company, followed by reverent applause, I went limping down the dark street, hoping that I should soon be far enough away to be able to walk like a human being. To my astonishment, as I was turning the corner, I felt a touch on the shoulder, and turning, found myself under the shadow of an enormous policeman. He told me I was wanted. I struck a sort of paralytic attitude, and cried in a high German accent, "Yes, I am wanted—by the oppressed of the world. You are arresting me on the charge of being the great anarchist, Professor de Worms." The policeman impassively consulted a paper in his hand, "No, sir," he said civilly, "at least, not exactly, sir. I am arresting you on the charge of not being the celebrated anarchist, Professor de Worms." This charge, if it was criminal at all, was certainly the lighter of the two, and I went along with the man, doubtful, but not greatly dismayed. I was shown into a number of rooms, and eventually into the presence of a police officer, who explained that a serious campaign had been opened against the centres of anarchy, and that this, my successful masquerade, might be of considerable value to the public safety. He offered me a good salary and this little blue card. Though our conversation was short, he struck me as a man of very massive common sense and humour; but I cannot tell you much about him personally, because——'

Syme laid down his knife and fork.

'I know,' he said, 'because you talked to him in a dark room.'

Professor de Worms nodded and drained his glass.

# IX

## *THE MAN IN SPECTACLES*

'Burgundy is a jolly thing,' said the Professor sadly, as he set his glass down.

'You don't look as if it were,' said Syme; 'you drink it as if it were medicine.'

'You must excuse my manner,' said the Professor dismally, 'my position is rather a curious one. Inside I am really bursting with boyish merriment; but I acted the paralytic Professor so well, that now I can't leave off. So that when I am among friends, and have no need at all to disguise myself, I still can't help speaking slow and wrinkling my forehead—just as if it were my forehead. I can be quite happy, you understand, but only in a paralytic sort of way. The most buoyant exclamations leap up in my heart, but they come out of my mouth quite different. You should hear me say, "Buck up, old cock!" It would bring tears to your eyes.'

'It does,' said Syme; 'but I cannot help thinking that apart from all that you are really a bit worried.'

The Professor started a little and looked at him steadily.

'You are a very clever fellow,' he said, 'it is a pleasure to work with you. Yes, I have rather a heavy cloud in my head. There is a great problem to face,' and he sank his bald brow in his two hands.

Then he said in a low voice—

'Can you play the piano?'

'Yes,' said Syme in simple wonder, 'I'm supposed to have a good touch.'

Then, as the other did not speak, he added—

'I trust the great cloud is lifted.'

After a long silence, the Professor said out of the cavernous shadow of his hands—

'It would have done just as well if you could work a typewriter.'

'Thank you,' said Syme, 'you flatter me.'

'Listen to me,' said the other, 'and remember whom we have to see to-morrow. You and I are going to-morrow to attempt something which is very much more dangerous than trying to steal the Crown Jewels out of the Tower. We are trying to steal a secret from a very sharp, very strong, and very wicked man. I believe there is no man, except the President, of course, who is so seriously startling and formidable as that little grinning fellow in goggles. He has not perhaps the white-hot enthusiasm unto death, the mad martyrdom for anarchy, which marks the Secretary. But then that very fanaticism in the Secretary has a human pathos, and is almost a redeeming trait. But the little Doctor has a brutal sanity that is more shocking than the Secretary's disease. Don't you notice his detestable virility and vitality? He bounces like an india-rubber ball. Depend on it, Sunday was not asleep (I wonder if he ever sleeps?) when he locked up all the plans of this outrage in the round, black head of Dr Bull.'

'And you think,' said Syme, 'that this unique monster will be soothed if I play the piano to him?'

'Don't be an ass,' said his mentor. 'I mentioned the piano because it gives one quick and independent fingers. Syme, if we are to go through this interview and come out sane or alive, we must have some code of signals between us that this brute will not see. I have made a rough alphabetical cypher corresponding to the five fingers—like this, see,' and he rippled with his fingers on the wooden table—'B A D, bad, a word we may frequently require.'

Syme poured himself out another glass of wine, and began to study the scheme. He was abnormally quick with his brains at puzzles, and with his hands at conjuring, and it did not take him long to learn how he might convey simple messages by what would seem to be idle taps upon a table or knee. But wine and companionship had always the effect of inspiring him to a farcical ingenuity, and the Professor soon found himself struggling with the too vast energy of the new language, as it passed through the heated brain of Syme.

'We must have several word-signs,' said Syme seriously—'words that we are likely to want, fine shades of meaning. My favourite word is "coeval." What's yours?'

'Do stop playing the goat,' said the Professor plaintively. 'You don't know how serious this is.'

'"Lush," too,' said Syme, shaking his head sagaciously, 'we must have "lush"—word applied to grass, don't you know?'

'Do you imagine,' asked the Professor furiously, 'that we are going to talk to Dr Bull about grass?'

'There are several ways in which the subject could be approached,' said Syme reflectively, 'and the word introduced without appearing forced. We might say, "Dr Bull, as a revolutionist, you remember that a tyrant once advised us to eat grass; and indeed many of us, looking on the fresh lush grass of summer——"'

'Do you understand,' said the other 'that this is a tragedy?'

'Perfectly,' replied Syme; 'always be comic in a tragedy. What the deuce else can you do? I wish this language of yours had a wider scope. I suppose we could not extend it from the fingers to the toes? That would involve pulling off our boots and socks during the conversation, which however unobtrusively performed——'

'Syme,' said his friend with a stern simplicity, 'go to bed!'

Syme, however, sat up in bed for a considerable time mastering the new code. He was awakened next morning while the east was still sealed with darkness, and found his grey-bearded ally standing like a ghost beside his bed.

Syme sat up in bed blinking; then slowly collected his thoughts, threw off the bed-clothes, and stood up. It seemed to him in some curious way that all the safety and sociability of the night before fell with the bed-clothes off him, and he stood up in an air of cold danger. He still felt an entire trust and loyalty towards his companion; but it was the trust between two men going to the scaffold.

'Well,' said Syme with a forced cheerfulness as he pulled on his trousers, 'I dreamt of that alphabet of yours. Did it take you long to make it up?'

The Professor made no answer, but gazed in front of him with eyes the colour of a wintry sea; so Syme repeated his question.

'I say, did it take you long to invent all this? I'm considered good at these things, and it was a good hour's grind. Did you learn it all on the spot?'

The Professor was silent; his eyes were wide open, and he wore a fixed but very small smile.

'How long did it take you?'

The Professor did not move.

'Confound you, can't you answer?' called out Syme, in a sudden anger that had something like fear underneath. Whether or no the Professor could answer, he did not.

Syme stood staring back at the stiff face like parchment and the blank, blue eyes. His first thought was that the Professor had gone mad, but his second thought was more frightful. After all, what did he know about this queer creature whom he had heedlessly accepted as a friend? What did he know, except that the man had been at the anarchist breakfast and had told him a ridiculous tale? How improbable it was that there should be another friend there beside Gogol! Was this man's silence a sensational way of declaring war? Was this adamantine stare after all only the awful sneer of some threefold traitor, who had turned for the last time? He stood and strained his ears in this heartless silence. He almost fancied he could hear dynamiters come to capture him shifting softly in the corridor outside.

Then his eye strayed downwards, and he burst out laughing. Though the Professor himself stood there as voiceless as a statue, his five dumb fingers were dancing alive upon the dead table. Syme watched the twinkling movements of the talking hand, and read clearly the message—

'I will only talk like this. We must get used to it.'

He rapped out the answer with the impatience of relief—

'All right. Let's get out to breakfast.'

They took their hats and sticks in silence; but as Syme took his sword-stick, he held it hard.

They paused for a few minutes only to stuff down coffee and coarse thick sandwiches at a coffee stall, and then made their way across the river, which under the grey and growing light looked as desolate as Acheron. They reached the bottom of the huge block of buildings which they had seen from across the river, and began in silence to mount the naked and numberless stone steps, only pausing now and then to make short remarks on the rail of the banisters. At about every other flight they passed a window; each window showed them a pale and tragic dawn lifting itself laboriously over London. From each the innumerable roofs of slate looked like the leaden surges of a grey, troubled sea after rain. Syme was increasingly conscious that his new adventure had somehow a quality of cold sanity worse than the wild adventures of the past. Last night, for instance, the tall tenements had seemed to him like a tower in a dream. As he now went up the weary and perpetual steps, he was daunted and bewildered by their almost infinite series. But it was not the hot horror of a dream or of anything that might be exaggeration or delusion. Their infinity was more like the empty infinity of arithmetic, something unthinkable, yet necessary to thought. Or it was like the stunning statements of astronomy about the distance of the fixed stars. He was ascending the house of reason, a thing more hideous than unreason itself.

By the time they reached Dr Bull's landing, a last window showed them a harsh, white dawn edged with banks of a kind of coarse red, more like red clay than red cloud. And when they entered Dr Bull's bare garret it was full of light.

Syme had been haunted by a half historic memory in connection with these empty rooms and that austere daybreak. The moment he saw the garret and Dr Bull sitting writing at a table, he remembered what the memory was—the French Revolution. There should have been the black outline of a guillotine against that heavy red and white of the morning. Dr Bull was in his white shirt and black breeches only; his cropped, dark head might well have just come out of its wig; he might have been Marat or a more slipshod Robespierre.

Yet when he was seen properly, the French fancy fell away. The Jacobins were idealists; there was about this man a murderous materialism. His position gave him a somewhat new appearance. The strong, white light of morning coming from one side creating sharp shadows, made him seem both more pale and more angular than he had looked at the breakfast on the balcony. Thus the two black glasses that encased his eyes might really have been black cavities in his skull, making him look like a death's-head. And, indeed, if ever Death himself sat writing at a wooden table it might have been he.

He looked up and smiled brightly enough as the men came in, and rose with the resilient rapidity of which the Professor had spoken. He set chairs for both of them, and going to a peg behind the door, proceeded to put on a coat and waistcoat of rough, dark tweed; he buttoned it up neatly, and came back to sit down at his table.

The quiet good humour of his manner left his two opponents helpless. It was with some momentary difficulty that the Professor broke silence and began, 'I'm sorry to disturb you so early, comrade,' said he, with a careful resumption of the slow de Worms manner. 'You have no doubt made all the arrangements for the Paris affair?' Then he added with infinite slowness, 'We have information which renders intolerable anything in the nature of a moment's delay.'

Dr Bull smiled again, but continued to gaze on them without speaking. The Professor resumed, a pause before each weary word—

'Please do not think me excessively abrupt; but I advise you to alter those plans, or if it is too late for that, to follow your agent with all the support you can get for him. Comrade Syme and I have had an experience which it would take more time to recount than we can afford, if we are to act on it. I will, however, relate the occurence in detail, even at the risk of losing time, if you really feel that it is essential to the understanding of the problem we have to discuss.'

He was spinning out his sentences, making them intolerably long and lingering, in the hope of maddening the practical little Doctor into an explosion of impatience which might show his hand. But the little Doctor continued only to stare and smile, and the monologue was uphill work. Syme began to feel a new sickness and despair. The Doctor's smile and silence were not at all like the cataleptic stare and horrible silence which he had confronted in the Professor half an hour before. About the Professor's make-up and all his antics there was always something merely grotesque, like a gollywog. Syme remembered those wild woes of yesterday as one remembers being afraid of Bogy in childhood. But here was daylight; here was a healthy, square-shouldered man in tweeds, not odd save for the accident of his ugly spectacles, not glaring or grinning at all, but smiling steadily and not saying a word. The whole had a sense of unbearable reality. Under the increasing sunlight the colours of the Doctor's complexion, the pattern of his tweeds, grew and expanded outrageously, as such things grow too important in a realistic novel. But his smile was quite slight, the pose of his head polite; the only uncanny thing was his silence.

'As I say,' resumed the Professor, like a man toiling through heavy sand, 'the incident that has occurred to us and has led us to ask for information about the Marquis, is one which you may think it better to have narrated; but as it came in the way of Comrade Syme rather than me——'

His words he seemed to be dragging out like words in an anthem; but Syme, who was watching, saw his long fingers rattle quickly on the edge of the crazy table. He read the message, 'You must go on. This devil has sucked me dry!'

Syme plunged into the breach with that bravado of improvisation which always came to him when he was alarmed.

'Yes, the thing really happened to me,' he said hastily. 'I had the good fortune to fall into conversation with a detective who took me, thanks to my hat, for a respectable person. Wishing to clinch my reputation for respectability, I took him and made him very drunk at the Savoy. Under the influence he became friendly, and told me in so many words that within a day or two they hope to arrest the Marquis in France. So unless you or I can get on his track——'

The Doctor was still smiling in the most friendly way, and his protected eyes were still impenetrable. The Professor signalled to Syme that he would resume his explanation, and he began again with the same elaborate calm.

'Syme immediately brought this information to me, and we came here together to see what use you would be inclined to make of it. It seems to me unquestionably urgent that——'

All this time Syme had been staring at the Doctor almost as steadily as the Doctor stared at the Professor, but quite without the smile. The nerves of both comrades-in-arms were near snapping under that strain of motionless amiability, when Syme suddenly leant forward and idly tapped the edge of the table. His message to his ally ran, 'I have an intuition.'

The Professor, with scarcely a pause in his monologue, signalled back, 'Then sit on it.'

Syme telegraphed, 'It is quite extraordinary.'

The other answered, 'Extraordinary rot!'

Syme said, 'I am a poet.'

The other retorted, 'You are a dead man.'

Syme had gone quite red up to his yellow hair, and his eyes were burning feverishly. As he said, he had an intuition, and it had risen to a sort of light-headed certainty. Resuming his symbolic taps, he signalled to his friend, 'You scarcely realise how poetic my intuition is. It has that sudden quality we sometimes feel in the coming of spring.'

He then studied the answer on his friend's fingers. The answer was, 'Go to hell!'

The Professor then resumed his merely verbal monologue addressed to the Doctor.

'Perhaps I should rather say,' said Syme on his fingers, 'that it resembles that sudden smell of the sea which may be found in the heart of lush woods.'

His companion disdained to reply.

'Or yet again,' tapped Syme, 'it is positive, as is the passionate red hair of a beautiful woman.'

The Professor was continuing his speech, but in the middle of it Syme decided to act. He leant across the table, and said in a voice that could not be neglected—

'Dr Bull!'

The Doctor's sleek and smiling head did not move, but they could have sworn that under his dark glasses his eyes darted towards Syme.

'Dr Bull,' said Syme, in a voice peculiarly precise and courteous, 'would you do me a small favour? Would you be so kind as to take off your spectacles?'

The Professor swung round on his seat, and stared at Syme with a sort of frozen fury of astonishment. Syme, like a man who has thrown his life and fortune on the table, leaned forward with a fiery face. The Doctor did not move.

For a few seconds there was a silence in which one could hear a pin drop, split once by the single hoot of a distant steamer on the Thames. Then Dr Bull rose slowly, still smiling, and took off his spectacles.

Syme sprang to his feet, stepping backwards a little, like a chemical lecturer from a successful explosion. His eyes were like stars, and for an instant he could only point without speaking.

The Professor had also started to his feet, forgetful of his supposed paralysis. He leant on the back of the chair and stared doubtfully at Dr Bull, as if the Doctor had been turned into a toad before his eyes. And indeed it was almost as great a transformation scene.

The two detectives saw sitting in the chair before them a very boyish-looking young man, with very frank and happy hazel eyes, an open expression, cockney clothes like those of a city clerk, and an unquestionable breath about him of being very good and rather commonplace. The smile was still there, but it might have been the first smile of a baby.

'I knew I was a poet,' cried Syme in a sort of ecstasy. 'I knew my intuition was as infallible as the Pope. It was the spectacles that did it! It was all the spectacles. Given those beastly black eyes, and all the rest of him, his health and his jolly looks, made him a live devil among dead ones.'

'It certainly does make a queer difference,' said the Professor shakily. 'But as regards the project of Dr Bull——'

'Project be damned!' roared Syme, beside himself. 'Look at him! Look at his face, look at his collar, look at his blessed boots! You don't suppose, do you, that that thing's an anarchist?'

'Syme!' cried the other in an apprehensive agony.

'Why, by God,' said Syme, 'I'll take the risk of that myself! Dr Bull, I am a police officer. There's my card,' and he flung down the blue card upon the table.

The Professor still feared that all was lost; but he was loyal. He pulled out his own official card and put it beside his friend's. Then the third man burst out laughing, and for the first time that morning they heard his voice.

'I'm awfully glad you chaps have come so early,' he said, with a sort of schoolboy flippancy, 'for we can all start for France together. Yes, I'm in the force right enough,' and he flicked a blue card towards them lightly as a matter of form.

Clapping a brisk bowler on his head and resuming his goblin glasses, the Doctor moved so quickly towards the door, that the others instinctively followed him. Syme seemed a little distrait, and as he passed under the doorway he suddenly struck his stick on the stone passage so that it rang.

'But Lord God Almighty,' he cried out, 'if this is all right, there were more damned detectives than there were damned dynamiters at the damned Council!'

'We might have fought easily,' said Bull; 'we were four against three.'

The Professor was descending the stairs, but his voice came up from below.

'No,' said the voice, 'we were not four against three—we were not so lucky. We were four against One.'

The others went down the stairs in silence.

The young man called Bull, with an innocent courtesy characteristic of him, insisted on going last until they reached the street; but there his own robust rapidity asserted itself unconsciously, and he walked quickly on ahead towards a railway inquiry office, talking to the others over his shoulder.

'It is jolly to get some pals,' he said. 'I've been half dead with the jumps, being quite alone. I nearly flung my arms round Gogol and embraced him, which would have been imprudent. I hope you won't despise me for having been in a blue funk.'

'All the blue devils in blue hell,' said Syme, 'contributed to my blue funk! But the worst devil was you and your infernal goggles.'

The young man laughed delightedly.

'Wasn't it a rag?' he said. 'Such a simple idea—not my own. I haven't got the brains. You see, I wanted to go into the detective service, especially the anti-dynamite business. But for that purpose they wanted someone to dress up as a dynamiter; and they all swore by blazes that I could never look like a dynamiter. They said my very walk was respectable, and that seen from behind I looked like the British Constitution. They said I looked too healthy and too optimistic, and too reliable and benevolent; they called me all sorts of names at Scotland Yard. They said that if I had been a criminal, I might have made my fortune by looking so like an honest man; but as I had the misfortune to be an honest man, there was not even the remotest chance of my assisting them by ever looking like a criminal. But at last I was brought before some old josser who was high up in the force, and who seemed to have no end of a head on his shoulders. And there the others all talked hopelessly. One asked whether a bushy beard would hide my nice smile; another said that if they blacked my face I might look like a negro anarchist; but this old chap chipped in with a most extraordinary remark. "A pair of smoked spectacles will do it," he said positively. "Look at him now; he looks like an angelic office boy. Put him on a pair of smoked spectacles, and children will scream at the sight of him." And so it was, by George! When once my eyes were covered, all the rest, smile and big shoulders and short hair, made me look a perfect little devil. As I say, it was simple enough when it was done, like miracles; but that wasn't the really miraculous part of it. There was one really staggering thing about the business, and my head still turns at it.'

'What was that?' asked Syme.

'I'll tell you,' answered the man in spectacles. 'This big pot in the police who sized me up so that he knew how the goggles would go with my hair and socks—by God, he never saw me at all!'

Syme's eyes suddenly flashed on him.

'How was that?' he asked. 'I thought you talked to him.'

'So I did,' said Bull brightly; 'but we talked in a pitch-dark room like a coal-cellar. There, you would never have guessed that.'

'I could not have conceived it,' said Syme gravely.

'It is indeed a new idea,' said the Professor.

Their new ally was in practical matters a whirlwind. At the inquiry office he asked with businesslike brevity about the trains for Dover. Having got his information, he bundled the company into a cab, and put them and himself inside a railway carriage before they had properly realised the breathless process. They were already on the Calais boat before conversation flowed freely.

'I had already arranged,' he explained, 'to go to France for my lunch; but I am delighted to have someone to lunch with me. You see, I had to send that beast, the Marquis, over with his bomb, because the President had his eye on me, though God knows how. I'll tell you the story some day. It was perfectly choking. Whenever I tried to slip out of it I saw the President somewhere, smiling out of the bow-window of a club, or taking off his hat to me from the top of an omnibus. I tell you, you can say what you like, that fellow sold himself to the devil; he can be in six places at once.'

'So you sent the Marquis off, I understand,' asked the Professor. 'Was it long ago? Shall we be in time to catch him?'

'Yes,' answered the new guide, 'I've timed it all. He'll still be at Calais when we arrive.'

'But when we do catch him at Calais,' said the Professor, 'what are we going to do?'

At this question the countenance of Dr Bull fell for the first time. He reflected a little, and then said—

'Theoretically, I suppose, we ought to call the police.'

'Not I,' said Syme. 'Theoretically I ought to drown myself first. I promised a poor fellow, who was a real modern pessimist, on my word of honour not to tell the police. I'm no hand at casuistry, but I can't break my word to a modern pessimist. It's like breaking one's word to a child.'

'I'm in the same boat,' said the Professor. 'I tried to tell the police and I couldn't, because of some silly oath I took. You see, when I was an actor I was a sort of all round beast. Perjury or treason is the only crime I haven't committed. If I did that I shouldn't know the difference between right and wrong.'

'I've been through all that,' said Dr Bull, 'and I've made up my mind. I gave my promise to the Secretary—you know him, man who smiles upside down. My friends, that man is the most utterly unhappy man that was ever human. It may be his digestion, or his conscience, or his nerves, or his philosophy of the universe, but he's damned, he's in hell! Well, I can't turn on a man like that, and hunt him down. It's like whipping a leper. I may be mad, but that's how I feel; and there's jolly well the end of it.'

'I don't think you're mad,' said Syme. 'I knew you would decide like that when first you——'

'Eh?' said Dr Bull.

'When first you took off your spectacles.'

Dr Bull smiled a little, and strolled across the deck to look at the sunlit sea. Then he strolled back again, kicking his heels carelessly, and a companionable silence fell between the three men.

'Well,' said Syme, 'it seems that we have all the same kind of morality or immorality, so we had better face the fact that comes of it.'

'Yes,' assented the Professor, 'you're quite right; and we must hurry up, for I can see the Grey Nose standing out from France.'

'The fact that comes of it,' said Syme seriously, 'is this, that we three are alone on this planet. Gogol has gone, God knows where; perhaps the President has smashed him like a fly. On the Council we are three men against three, like the Romans who held the bridge. But we are worse off than that, first because they can appeal to their organisation and we cannot appeal to ours, and second because——'

'Because one of those other three men,' said the Professor, 'is not a man.'

Syme nodded and was silent for a second or two, then he said—

'My idea is this. We must do something to keep the Marquis in Calais till to-morrow midday. I have turned over twenty schemes in my head. We cannot denounce him as a dynamiter; that is agreed. We cannot get him detained on some trivial charge, for we should have to appear; he knows us, and he would smell a rat. We cannot pretend to keep him on anarchist business; he might swallow much in that way, but not the notion of stopping in Calais while the Czar went safely through Paris. We might try to kidnap him, and lock him up ourselves; but he is a well-known man here. He has a whole bodyguard of friends; he is very strong and brave, and the event is doubtful. The only thing I can see to do is actually to take advantage of the very things that are in the Marquis's favour. I am going to profit by the fact that he is a highly respected nobleman. I am going to profit by the fact that he has many friends and moves in the best society.'

'What the devil are you talking about?' asked the Professor.

'The Symes are first mentioned in the fourteenth century,' said Syme; 'but there is tradition that one of them rode behind Bruce at Bannockburn. Since 1350 the tree is quite clear.'

'He's gone off his head,' said the little Doctor, staring.

'Our bearings,' continued Syme calmly, 'are "argent a chevron gules charged with three cross crosslets of the field." The motto varies.'

The Professor seized Syme roughly by the waistcoat.

'We are just inshore,' he said. 'Are you seasick or joking in the wrong place?'

'My remarks are almost painfully practical,' answered Syme, in an unhurried manner. 'The house of St Eustache also is very ancient. The Marquis cannot deny that he is a gentleman. He cannot deny that I am a gentleman. And in order to put the matter of my social position quite beyond a doubt, I propose at the earliest opportunity to knock his hat off. But here we are in the harbour.'

They went on shore under the strong sun in a sort of daze. Syme, who had now taken the lead as Bull had taken it in London, led them along a kind of marine parade until he came to some cafés, embowered in a bulk of greenery and overlooking the sea. As he went before them his step was slightly swaggering, and he swung his stick like a sword. He was making apparently for the extreme end of the line of cafés, but he stopped abruptly. With a sharp gesture he motioned them to silence, but he pointed with one gloved finger to a café table under a bank of flowering foliage at which sat the Marquis de St Eustache, his teeth shining in his thick, black beard, and his bold, brown face shadowed by a light yellow straw hat and outlined against the violet sea.

# X

## THE DUEL

Syme sat down at a café table with his companions, his blue eyes sparkling like the bright sea below, and ordered a bottle of Saumur with a pleased impatience. He was for some reason in a condition of curious hilarity. His spirits were already unnaturally high; they rose as the Saumur sank, and in half an hour his talk was a torrent of nonsense. He professed to be making out a plan of the conversation which was going to ensue between himself and the deadly Marquis. He jotted it down wildly with a pencil. It was arranged like a printed catechism, with questions and answers, and was delivered with an extraordinary rapidity of utterance.

'I shall approach. Before taking off his hat, I shall take off my own. I shall say, "The Marquis de Saint Eustache, I believe." He will say, "The celebrated Mr Syme, I presume." He will say in the most exquisite French, "How are you?" I shall reply in the most exquisite Cockney, "Oh, just the Syme——"'

'Oh, shut it,' said the man in spectacles. 'Pull yourself together, and chuck away that bit of paper. What are you really going to do?'

'But it was lovely catechism,' said Syme pathetically. 'Do let me read it you. It has only forty-three questions and answers, and some of the Marquis's answers are wonderfully witty. I like to be just to my enemy.'

'But what's the good of it all?' asked Dr Bull in exasperation.

'It leads up to my challenge, don't you see,' said Syme, beaming. 'When the Marquis has given the thirty-ninth reply, which runs——'

'Has it by any chance occurred to you,' asked the Professor, with a ponderous simplicity, 'that the Marquis may not say all the forty-three things you have put down for him? In that case, I understand, your own epigrams may appear somewhat more forced.'

Syme struck the table with a radiant face.

'Why, how true that is,' he said, 'and I never thought of it. Sir, you have an intellect beyond the common. You will make a name.'

'Oh, you're as drunk as an owl!' said the Doctor

'It only remains,' continued Syme quite unperturbed, 'to adopt some other method of breaking the ice (if I may so express it) between myself and the man I wish to kill. And since the course of a dialogue cannot be predicted by one of its parties alone (as you have pointed out with such recondite acumen), the only thing to be done, I suppose, is for the one party, as far as possible, to do all the dialogue by himself. And so I will, by George!' And he stood up suddenly, his yellow hair blowing in the slight sea breeze.

A band was playing in a *café chantant* hidden somewhere among the trees, and a woman had just stopped singing. On Syme's heated head the bray of the brass band seemed like the jar and jingle of that barrel-organ in Leicester Square, to the tune of which he had once stood up to die. He looked across to the little table where the Marquis sat. The man had two companions now, solemn Frenchmen in frock-coats and silk hats, one of them with the red rosette of the Legion of Honour, evidently people of a solid social position. Beside these black, cylindrical costumes, the Marquis, in his loose straw hat and light spring clothes, looked Bohemian and even barbaric; but he looked the Marquis. Indeed, one might say that he looked the king, with his animal elegance, his scornful eyes, and his proud head lifted against the purple sea. But he was no Christian king, at any rate; he was, rather, some swarthy despot, half Greek, half Asiatic, who in the days when slavery seemed natural looked down on the Mediterranean, on his galley and his groaning slaves. Just so, Syme thought, would the brown-gold face of such a tyrant have shown against the dark green olives and the burning blue.

'Are you going to address the meeting?' asked the Professor peevishly, seeing that Syme still stood up without moving.

Syme drained his last glass of sparkling wine.

'I am,' he said, pointing across to the Marquis and his companions, 'that meeting. That meeting displeases me. I am going to pull that meeting's great ugly, mahogany-coloured nose.'

He stepped across swiftly, if not quite steadily. The Marquis, seeing him, arched his black Assyrian eyebrows in surprise, but smiled politely.

'You are Mr Syme, I think,' he said.

Syme bowed.

'And you are the Marquis de Saint Eustache,' he said gracefully. 'Permit me to pull your nose.'

He leant over to do so, but the Marquis started backwards, upsetting his chair, and the two men in top hats held Syme back by the shoulders.

'This man has insulted me!' said Syme, with gestures of explanation.

'Insulted you?' cried the gentleman with the red rosette, 'when?'

'Oh, just now,' said Syme recklessly. 'He insulted my mother.'

'Insulted your mother!' exclaimed the gentleman incredulously.

'Well, anyhow,' said Syme, conceding a point, 'my aunt.'

'But how can the Marquis have insulted your aunt just now?' said the second gentleman with some legitimate wonder. 'He has been sitting here all the time.'

'Ah, it was what he said!' said Syme darkly.

'I said nothing at all,' said the Marquis, 'except something about the band. I only said that I liked Wagner played well.'

'It was an allusion to my family,' said Syme firmly. 'My aunt played Wagner badly. It was a painful subject. We are always being insulted about it.'

'This seems most extraordinary,' said the gentleman who was *décoré*, looking doubtfully at the Marquis.

'Oh, I assure you,' said Syme earnestly, 'the whole of your conversation was simply packed with sinister allusions to my aunt's weaknesses.'

'This is nonsense!' said the second gentleman. 'I for one have said nothing for half an hour except that I liked the singing of that girl with black hair.'

'Well, there you are again!' said Syme indignantly. 'My aunt's was red.'

'It seems to me,' said the other, 'that you are simply seeking a pretext to insult the Marquis.'

'By George!' said Syme, facing round and looking at him, 'what a clever chap you are!'

The Marquis started up with eyes flaming like a tiger's.

'Seeking a quarrel with me!' he cried. 'Seeking a fight with me! By God! there was never a man who had to seek long. These gentlemen will perhaps act for me. There are still four hours of daylight. Let us fight this evening.'

Syme bowed with a quite beautiful graciousness.

'Marquis,' he said, 'your action is worthy of your fame and blood. Permit me to consult for a moment with the gentlemen in whose hands I shall place myself.'

In three long strides he rejoined his companions, and they, who had seen his champagne-inspired attack and listened to his idiotic explanations, were quite startled at the look of him. For now that he came back to them he was quite sober, a little pale, and he spoke in a low voice of passionate practicality.

'I have done it,' he said hoarsely. 'I have fixed a fight on the beast. But look here, and listen carefully. There is no time for talk. You are my seconds, and everything must come from you. Now you must insist, and insist absolutely, on the duel coming off after seven to-morrow, so as to give me the chance of preventing him from catching the 7.45 for Paris. If he misses that he misses his crime. He can't refuse to meet you on such a small point of time and place. But this is what he will do. He will choose a field somewhere near a

wayside station, where he can pick up the train. He is a very good swords-
man, and he will trust to killing me in time to catch it. But I can fence well
too, and I think I can keep him in play, at any rate, until the train is lost.
Then perhaps he may kill me to console his feelings. You understand? Very
well then, let me introduce you to some charming friends of mine,' and
leading them quickly across the parade, he presented them to the Marquis's
seconds by two very aristocratic names of which they had not previously
heard.

Syme was subject to spasms of singular common sense, not otherwise a
part of his character. They were (as he said of his impulse about the
spectacles) poetic intuitions, and they sometimes rose to the exaltation of
prophecy.

He had correctly calculated in this case the policy of his opponent. When
the Marquis was informed by his seconds that Syme could only fight in the
morning, he must fully have realised that an obstacle had suddenly arisen
between him and his bomb-throwing business in the capital. Naturally he
could not explain this objection to his friends, so he chose the course which
Syme had predicted. He induced his seconds to settle on a small meadow
not far from the railway, and he trusted to the fatality of the first engagement.

When he came down very coolly to the field of honour, no one could have
guessed that he had any anxiety about a journey; his hands were in his
pockets, his straw hat on the back of his head, his handsome face brazen in
the sun. But it might have struck a stranger as odd that there appeared in his
train, not only his seconds carrying the sword-case, but two of his servants
carrying a portmanteau and a luncheon basket.

Early as was the hour, the sun soaked everything in warmth, and Syme was
vaguely surprised to see so many spring flowers burning gold and silver in
the tall grass in which the whole company stood almost knee-deep.

With the exception of the Marquis, all the men were in sombre and
solemn morning-dress, with hats like black chimney-pots; the little Doctor
especially, with the addition of his black spectacles, looked like an under-
taker in a farce. Syme could not help feeling a comic contrast between this
funereal church parade of apparel and the rich and glistening meadow,
growing wild flowers everywhere. But, indeed, this comic contrast between
the yellow blossoms and the black hats was but a symbol of the tragic
contrast between the yellow blossoms and the black business. On his right
was a little wood; far away to his left lay the long curve of the railway line
which he was, so to speak, guarding from the Marquis, whose goal and
escape it was. In front of him, behind the black group of his opponents, he
could see, like a tinted cloud, a small almond bush in flower against the faint
line of the sea.

The member of the Legion of Honour, whose name it seemed was

Colonel Ducroix, approached the Professor and Dr Bull with great politeness, and suggested that the play should terminate with the first considerable hurt.

Dr Bull, however, having been carefully coached by Syme upon this point of policy, insisted, with great dignity and in very bad French, that it should continue until one of the combatants was disabled. Syme had made up his mind that he could avoid disabling the Marquis and prevent the Marquis from disabling him for at least twenty minutes. In twenty minutes the Paris train would have gone by.

'To a man of the well-known skill and valour of Monsieur de St Eustache,' said the Professor solemnly, 'it must be a matter of indifference which method is adopted, and our principal has strong reasons for demanding the longer encounter, reasons the delicacy of which prevent me from being explicit, but for the just and honourable nature of which I can——'

'*Peste!*' broke from the Marquis behind, whose face had suddenly darkened, 'let us stop talking and begin,' and he slashed off the head of a tall flower with his stick.

Syme understood his rude impatience, and instinctively looked over his shoulder to see whether the train was coming in sight. But there was no smoke on the horizon.

Colonel Ducroix knelt down and unlocked the case taking out a pair of twin swords, which took the sunlight and turned to two streaks of white fire. He offered one to the Marquis, who snatched it without ceremony, and another to Syme, who took it, bent it, and poised it with as much delay as was consistent with dignity. Then the Colonel took out another pair of blades, and taking one himself and giving another to Dr Bull, proceeded to place the men.

Both combatants had thrown off their coats and waistcoats, and stood sword in hand. The seconds stood on each side of the line of fight with drawn swords also, but still sombre in their dark frock-coats and hats. The principals saluted. The Colonel said quietly, 'Engage!' and the two blades touched and tingled.

When the jar of the joined iron ran up Syme's arm, all the fantastic fears that have been the subject of this story fell from him like dreams from a man waking up in bed. He remembered them clearly and in order as mere delusions of the nerves—how the fear of the Professor had been the fear of the tyrannic accidents of the nightmare, and how the fear of the Doctor had been the fear of the airless vacuum of science. The first was the old fear that any miracle might happen, the second the more hopeless modern fear that no miracle can ever happen. But he saw that these fears were fancies, for he found himself in the presence of the great fact of the fear of death, with its coarse and pitiless common sense. He felt like a man who had dreamed all night of falling over precipices, and had woke up on the morning when he was to be hanged. For as soon as he had seen the sunlight run down the channel of his foe's foreshortened blade, and as soon as he had felt the two tongues of steel touch, vibrating like two living things, he knew that his enemy was a terrible fighter, and that probably his last hour had come.

He felt a strange and vivid value in all the earth around him, in the grass under his feet; he felt the love of life in all living things. He could almost fancy that he heard the grass growing; he could almost fancy that even as he stood fresh flowers were springing up and breaking into blossom in the meadow—flowers blood-red and burning gold and blue, fulfilling the whole pageant of the spring. And whenever his eyes strayed for a flash from the calm, staring, hypnotic eyes of the Marquis, they saw the little tuft of almond tree against the sky-line. He had the feeling that if by some miracle he escaped he would be ready to sit for ever before that almond tree, desiring nothing else in the world.

But while earth and sky and everything had the living beauty of a thing lost, the other half of his head was as clear as glass, and he was parrying his enemy's point with a kind of clockwork skill of which he had hardly supposed himself capable. Once his enemy's point ran along his wrist, leaving a slight streak of blood, but it either was not noticed or was tacitly ignored. Every now and then he *riposted*, and once or twice he could almost fancy that he felt his point go home, but as there was no blood on blade or shirt he supposed he was mistaken. Then came an interruption and a change.

At the risk of losing all, the Marquis, interrupting his quiet stare, flashed one glance over his shoulder at the line of railway on his right. Then he turned on Syme a face transfigured to that of a fiend, and began to fight as if with twenty weapons. The attack came so fast and furious, that the one shining sword seemed a shower of shining arrows. Syme had no chance to look at the railway; but also he had no need. He could guess the reason of the Marquis's sudden madness of battle—the Paris train was in sight.

But the Marquis's morbid energy over-reached itself. Twice Syme, parrying, knocked his opponent's point far out of the fighting circle; and the third time his *riposte* was so rapid, that there was no doubt about the hit this time. Syme's sword actually bent under the weight of the Marquis's body, which it had pierced. Syme was as certain that he had struck his blade into his enemy as a gardener that he has stuck his spade into the ground. Yet the Marquis sprang back from the stroke without a stagger, and Syme stood staring at his own sword-point like an idiot. There was no blood on it at all.

There was an instant of rigid silence, and then Syme in his turn fell furiously on the other, filled with a flaming curiosity. The Marquis was probably, in a general sense, a better fencer than he, as he had surmised at the beginning, but at the moment the Marquis seemed distraught and at a disadvantage. He fought wildly and even weakly, and he constantly looked away at the railway line, almost as if he feared the train more than the pointed steel. Syme, on the other hand, fought fiercely but still carefully, in an intellectual fury, eager to solve the riddle of his own bloodless sword. For this purpose, he aimed less at the Marquis's body, and more at his throat and head. A minute and a half afterwards he felt his point enter the man's neck below the jaw. It came out clean. Half mad, he thrust again, and made what should have been a bloody scar on the Marquis's cheek. But there was no scar.

For one moment the heaven of Syme again grew black with supernatural terrors. Surely the man had a charmed life. But this new spiritual dread was a more awful thing than had been the mere spiritual topsy-turvydom symbolised by the paralytic who pursued him. The Professor was only a goblin; this man was a devil—perhaps he was the Devil! Anyhow, this was certain, that three times had a human sword been driven into him and made no mark. When Syme had that thought he drew himself up, and all that was good in him sang high up in the air as a high wind sings in the trees. He thought of all the human things in his story—of the Chinese lanterns in Saffron Park, of the girl's red hair in the garden, of the honest, beer-swilling sailors down by the dock, of his loyal companions standing by. Perhaps he had been chosen as a champion of all these fresh and kindly things to cross swords with the enemy of all creation. 'After all,' he said to himself, 'I am more than a devil; I am a man. I can do the one thing which Satan himself cannot do—I can die,' and as the word went through his head, he heard a faint and far-off hoot, which would soon be the roar of the Paris train.

He fell to fighting again with a supernatural levity, like a Mohammedan panting for Paradise. As the train came nearer and nearer he fancied he could see people putting up the floral arches in Paris; he joined in the growing noise and the glory of the great Republic whose gate he was guarding against Hell. His thoughts rose higher and higher with the rising roar of the train, which ended, as if proudly, in a long and piercing whistle. The train stopped.

Suddenly, to the astonishment of everyone the Marquis sprang back quite out of sword reach and threw down his sword. The leap was wonderful, and not the less wonderful because Syme had plunged his sword a moment before into the man's thigh.

'Stop!' said the Marquis in a voice that compelled a momentary obedience. 'I want to say something.'

'What is the matter?' asked Colonel Ducroix, staring. 'Has there been foul play?'

'There has been foul play somewhere,' said Dr Bull, who was a little pale. 'Our principal has wounded the Marquis four times at least, and he is none the worse.'

The Marquis put up his hand with a curious air of ghastly patience.

'Please let me speak,' he said. 'It is rather important. Mr Syme,' he continued, turning to his opponent, 'we are fighting to-day, if I remember right, because you expressed a wish (which I thought irrational) to pull my nose. Would you oblige me by pulling my nose now as quickly as possible? I have to catch a train.'

'I protest that this is most irregular,' said Dr Bull indignantly.

'It is certainly somewhat opposed to precedent,' said Colonel Ducroix, looking wistfully at his principal. 'There is, I think, one case on record (Captain Bellegarde and the Baron Zumpt) in which the weapons were changed in the middle of the encounter at the request of one of the combatants. But one can hardly call one's nose a weapon.'

'Will you or will you not pull my nose?' said the Marquis in exasperation. 'Come, come, Mr Syme! You wanted to do it, do it! You can have no conception of how important it is to me. Don't be so selfish! Pull my nose at once, when I ask you!' and he bent slightly forward with a fascinating smile. The Paris train, panting and groaning, had grated into a little station behind the neighbouring hill.

Syme had the feeling he had more than once had in these adventures— the sense that a horrible and sublime wave lifted to heaven was just toppling over. Walking in a world he half understood, he took two paces forward and seized the Roman nose of this remarkable nobleman. He pulled it hard, and it came off in his hand.

He stood for some seconds with a foolish solemnity, with the pasteboard proboscis still between his fingers, looking at it, while the sun and the clouds and the wooded hills looked down upon this imbecile scene.

The Marquis broke the silence in a loud and cheerful voice.

'If anyone has any use for my left eyebrow,' he said, 'he can have it. Colonel Ducroix, do accept my left eyebrow! It's the kind of thing that might come in useful any day,' and he gravely tore off one of his swarthy Assyrian brows, bringing about half his brown forehead with it, and politely offered it to the Colonel, who stood crimson and speechless with rage.

'If I had known,' he spluttered, 'that I was acting for a poltroon who pads himself to fight——'

'Oh, I know, I know!' said the Marquis, recklessly throwing various parts of himself right and left about the field. 'You are making a mistake; but it can't be explained just now. I tell you the train has come into the station!'

'Yes,' said Dr Bull fiercely, 'and the train shall go out of the station. It shall go out without you. We know well enough for what devil's work——'

The mysterious Marquis lifted his hands with a desperate gesture. He was a strange scarecrow, standing there in the sun with half his old face peeled off, and half another face glaring and grinning from underneath.

'Will you drive me mad?' he cried. 'The train——'

'You shall not go by the train,' said Syme firmly, and grasped his sword.

The wild figure turned towards Syme, and seemed to be gathering itself for a sublime effort before speaking.

'You great fat, blasted, blear-eyed, blundering, thundering, brainless, God-forsaken, doddering, damned fool!' he said without taking breath. 'You great silly, pink-faced, towheaded turnip! You——'

'You shall not go by this train,' repeated Syme.

'And why the infernal blazes,' roared the other, 'should I want to go by the train?'

'We know all,' said the Professor sternly. 'You are going to Paris to throw a bomb!'

'Going to Jericho to throw a Jabberwock!' cried the other, tearing his hair, which came off easily.

'Have you all got softening of the brain, that you don't realise what I am? Did you really think I wanted to catch that train? Twenty Paris trains might go by for me. Damn Paris trains!'

'Then what did you care about?' began the Professor.

'What did I care about? I didn't care about catching the train; I cared about whether the train caught me, and now, by God! it has caught me.'

'I regret to inform you,' said Syme with restraint, 'that your remarks convey no impression to my mind. Perhaps if you were to remove the remains of your original forehead and some portion of what was once your chin, your meaning would become clearer. Mental lucidity fulfils itself in many ways. What do you mean by saying that the train has caught you? It may be my literary fancy, but somehow I feel that it ought to mean something.'

'It means everything,' said the other, 'and the end of everything. Sunday has us now in the hollow of his hand.'

'Us!' repeated the Professor, as if stupefied. 'What do you mean by "us"?'

'The police, of course!' said the Marquis, and tore off his scalp and half his face.

The head which emerged was the blonde, well brushed, smooth-haired head which is common in the English constabulary, but the face was terribly pale.

'I am Inspector Ratcliffe,' he said, with a sort of haste that verged on harshness. 'My name is pretty well known to the police, and I can see well enough that you belong to them. But if there is any doubt about my position, I have a card——' and he began to pull a blue card from his pocket.

The Professor gave a tired gesture.

'Oh don't show it us,' he said wearily; 'we've got enough of them to equip a paper-chase.'

The little man named Bull, had, like many men who seem to be of a mere vivacious vulgarity, sudden movements of good taste. Here he certainly saved the situation. In the midst of this staggering transformation scene he stepped forward with all the gravity and responsibility of a second, and addressed the two seconds of the Marquis.

'Gentlemen,' he said, 'we all owe you a serious apology; but I assure you that you have not been made the victims of such a low joke as you imagine, or indeed of anything undignified in a man of honour. You have not wasted your time; you have helped to save the world. We are not buffoons, but very desperate men at war with a vast conspiracy. A secret society of anarchists is hunting us like hares; not such unfortunate madmen as may here or there throw a bomb through starvation or German philosophy, but a rich and powerful and fanatical church, a church of eastern pessimism which holds it holy to destroy mankind like vermin. How hard they hunt us you can gather from the fact that we are driven to such disguises as those for which I apologise, and to such pranks as this one by which you suffer.'

The younger second of the Marquis, a short man with a black moustache, bowed politely, and said—

'Of course, I accept the apology; but you will in your turn forgive me if I decline to follow you further into your difficulties, and permit myself to say good morning! The sight of an acquaintance and distinguished fellow-townsman coming to pieces in the open air is unusual, and, upon the whole, sufficient for one day. Colonel Ducroix, I would in no way influence your actions, but if you feel with me that our present society is a little abnormal, I am now going to walk back to the town.'

Colonel Ducroix moved mechanically, but then tugged abruptly at his white moustache and broke out—

'No, by George! I won't. If these gentlemen are really in a mess with a lot of low wreckers like that, I'll see them through it. I have fought for France, and it is hard if I can't fight for civilisation.'

Dr Bull took of his hat and waved it, cheering as at a public meeting.

'Don't make too much noise,' said Inspector Ratcliffe, 'Sunday may hear you.'

'Sunday!' cried Bull, and dropped his hat.

'Yes,' retorted Ratcliffe, 'he may be with them.'

'With whom?' asked Syme.

'With the people out of that train,' said the other.

'What you say seems utterly wild,' began Syme. 'Why, as a matter of fact—— But, my God,' he cried out suddenly, like a man who sees an explosion a long way off, 'by God! if this is true the whole bally lot of us on the Anarchist Council were against anarchy! Every born man was a detective except the President and his personal secretary. What can it mean?'

'Mean!' said the new policeman with incredible violence. 'It means that we are struck dead! Don't you know Sunday? Don't you know that his jokes are always so big and simple that one has never thought of them? Can you think of anything more like Sunday than this, that he should put all his powerful enemies on the Supreme Council, and then take care that it was not supreme? I tell you he has bought every trust, he has captured every cable, he has control of every railway line—especially of *that* railway line!' and he pointed a shaking finger towards the small wayside station. 'The whole movement was controlled by him; half the world was ready to rise for him. But there were just five people, perhaps, who would have resisted him ... and the old devil put them on the Supreme Council, to waste their time in watching each other. Idiots that we are, he planned the whole of our idiocies! Sunday knew that the Professor would chase Syme through London, and that Syme would fight me in France. And he was combining great masses of capital, and seizing great lines of telegraphy, while we five idiots were running after each other like a lot of confounded babies playing blind man's buff.'

'Well?' asked Syme with a sort of steadiness.

'Well,' replied the other with sudden serenity, 'he has found us playing blind man's buff to-day in a field of great rustic beauty and extreme solitude. He has probably captured the world; it only remains to him to capture this field and all the fools in it. And since you really want to know what was my objection to the arrival of that train, I will tell you. My objection was that Sunday or his Secretary has just this moment got out of it.'

Syme uttered an involuntary cry, and they all turned their eyes towards the far-off station. It was quite true that a considerable bulk of people seemed to be moving in their direction. But they were too distant to be distinguished in any way.

'It was a habit of the late Marquis de St Eustache,' said the new policeman, producing a leather case, 'always to carry a pair of opera glasses. Either the President or the Secretary is coming after us with that mob. They have caught us in a nice quiet place where we are under no temptations to break our oaths by calling the police. Dr Bull, I have a suspicion that you will see better through these than through your own highly decorative spectacles.'

He handed the field-glasses to the Doctor, who immediately took off his spectacles and put the apparatus to his eyes.

'It cannot be as bad as you say,' said the Professor, somewhat shaken. 'There are a good number of them certainly, but they may easily be ordinary tourists.'

'Do ordinary tourists,' asked Bull, with the field-glasses to his eyes, 'wear black masks half-way down the face?'

Syme almost tore the glasses out of his hand, and looked through them.

Most men in the advancing mob really looked ordinary enough; but it was quite true that two or three of the leaders in front wore black half-masks almost down to their mouths. This disguise is very complete, especially at such a distance, and Syme found it impossible to conclude anything from the clean-shaven jaws and chins of the men talking in the front. But presently as they talked they all smiled, and one of them smiled on one side.

# XI

## *THE CRIMINALS CHASE THE POLICE*

Syme put the field-glasses from his eyes with an almost ghastly relief.

'The President is not with them, anyhow,' he said, and wiped his forehead.

'But surely they are right away on the horizon,' said the bewildered Colonel, blinking and but half recovered from Bull's hasty though polite explanation. 'Could you possibly know your President among all those people?'

'Could I know a white elephant among all those people?' answered Syme somewhat irritably. 'As you very truly say, they are on the horizon; but if he were walking with them ... by God! I believe this ground would shake.'

After an instant's pause the new man called Ratcliffe said with gloomy decision—

'Of course the President isn't with them. I wish to Gemini he were. Much more likely the President is riding in triumph through Paris, or sitting on the ruins of St Paul's Cathedral.'

'This is absurd!' said Syme. 'Something may have happened in our absence; but he cannot have carried the world with a rush like that. It is quite true,' he added, frowning dubiously at the distant fields that lay towards the little station, 'it is certainly true that there seems to be a crowd coming this way; but they are not all the army that you make out.'

'Oh, they,' said the new detective contemptuously; 'no they are not a very valuable force. But let me tell you frankly that they are precisely calculated to our value—we are not much, my boy, in Sunday's universe. He had got hold of all the cables and telegraphs himself. But to kill the Supreme Council he regards as a trivial matter, like a post card; it may be left to his private secretary,' and he spat on the grass.

Then he turned to the others and said somewhat austerely—

'There is a great deal to be said for death; but if anyone has any preference for the other alternative, I strongly advise him to walk after me.'

With these words, he turned his broad back and strode with silent energy towards the wood. The others gave one glance over their shoulders, and saw that the dark cloud of men had detached itself from the station and was moving with a mysterious discipline across the plain. They saw already, even with the naked eye, black blots on the foremost faces, which marked the masks they wore. They turned and followed their leader, who had already struck the wood, and disappeared among the twinkling trees.

The sun on the grass was dry and hot. So in plunging into the wood they had a cool shock of shadow, as of divers who plunge into a dim pool. The inside of the wood was full of shattered sunlight and shaken shadows. They made a sort of shuddering veil, almost recalling the dizziness of a cinematograph. Even the solid figures walking with him Syme could hardly see for the patterns of sun and shade that danced upon them. Now a man's head was lit as with a light of Rembrandt, leaving all else obliterated; now again he had strong and staring white hands with the face of a negro. The ex-Marquis had pulled the old straw hat over his eyes, and the black shade of the brim cut his face so squarely in two that it seemed to be wearing one of the black half-masks of their pursuers. The fancy tinted Syme's overwhelming sense of wonder. Was he wearing a mask? Was anyone wearing a mask? Was anyone anything? This wood of witchery, in which men's faces turned black and white by turns, in which their figures first swelled into sunlight and then faded into formless night, this mere chaos of chiaroscuro (after the clear daylight outside), seemed to Syme a perfect symbol of the world in which he had been moving for three days, this world where men took off their beards and their spectacles and their noses, and turned into other people. That tragic self-confidence which he had felt when he believed that the Marquis was a devil had strangely disappeared now that he knew that the Marquis was a friend. He felt almost inclined to ask after all these bewilderments what was a friend and what an enemy. Was there anything that was apart from what it seemed? The Marquis had taken off his nose and turned out to be a detective. Might he not just as well take off his head and turn out to be a hobgoblin? Was not everything, after all, like this bewildering woodland, this dance of dark and light? Everything only a glimpse, the glimpse always unforeseen, and always forgotten. For Gabriel Syme had found in the heart of that sun-splashed wood what many modern painters had found there. He had found the thing which the modern people call Impressionism, which is another name for that final scepticism which can find no floor to the universe.

As a man in an evil dream strains himself to scream and wake, Syme strove with a sudden effort to fling off this last and worst of his fancies. With two impatient strides he overtook the man in the Marquis's straw hat, the man whom he had come to address at Ratcliffe. In a voice exaggeratively loud and cheerful, he broke the bottomless silence and made conversation.

'May I ask,' he said, 'where on earth we are all going to?'

So genuine had been the doubts of his soul, that he was quite glad to hear his companion speak in an easy, human voice.

'We must get down through the town of Lancy to the sea,' he said. 'I think that part of the country is least likely to be with them.'

'What can you mean by all this?' cried Syme. 'They can't be running the real world in that way. Surely not many working men are anarchists, and surely if they were, mere mobs could not beat modern armies and police.'

'Mere mobs!' repeated his new friend with a snort of scorn. 'So you talk about mobs and the working classes as if they were the question. You've got that eternal idiotic idea that if anarchy came it would come from the poor. Why should it? The poor have been rebels, but they have never been anarchists; they have more interest than anyone else in there being some decent government. The poor man really has a stake in the country. The rich man hasn't; he can go away to New Guinea in a yacht. The poor have sometimes objected to being governed badly; the rich have always objected to being governed at all. Aristocrats were always anarchists, as you can see from the barons' wars.'

'As a lecture on English history for the little ones,' said Syme, 'this is all very nice; but I have not yet grasped its application.'

'Its application is,' said his informant, 'that most of old Sunday's right-hand men are South African and American millionaires. That is why he has got hold of all the communications; and that is why the last four champions of the anti-anarchist police force are running through a wood like rabbits.'

'Millionaires I can understand,' said Syme thoughtfully, 'they are nearly all mad. But getting hold of a few wicked old gentlemen with hobbies is one thing; getting hold of great Christian nations is another. I would bet the nose off my face (forgive the allusion) that Sunday would stand perfectly helpless before the task of converting any ordinary healthy person anywhere.'

'Well,' said the other, 'it rather depends what sort of person you mean.'

'Well, for instance,' said Syme, 'we could never convert that person,' and he pointed straight in front of him.

They had come to an open space of sunlight, which seemed to express to Syme the final return of his own good sense; and in the middle of this forest clearing was a figure that might well stand for that common sense in an almost awful actuality. Burnt by the sun and stained with perspiration, and grave with the bottomless gravity of small necessary toils, a heavy French peasant was cutting wood with a hatchet. His cart stood a few yards off, already half full of timber; and the horse that cropped the grass was, like his master, valorous but not desperate; like his master, he was even prosperous, but yet was almost sad. The man was a Norman, taller than the average of the French and very angular; and his swarthy figure stood dark against a square of sunlight, almost like some allegoric figure of labour frescoed on a ground of gold.

'Mr Syme is saying,' called out Ratcliffe to the French Colonel, 'that this man, at least, will never be an anarchist.'

'Mr Syme is right enough there,' answered Colonel Ducroix, laughing, 'if only for the reason that he has plenty of property to defend. But I forgot that in your country you are not used to peasants being wealthy.'

'He looks poor,' said Dr Bull doubtfully.

'Quite so,' said the Colonel; 'that is why he is rich.'

'I have an idea,' called out Dr Bull suddenly; 'how much would he take to give us a lift in his cart? Those dogs are all on foot, and we could soon leave them behind.'

'Oh, give him anything!' said Syme eagerly. 'I have piles of money on me.'

'That will never do,' said the Colonel; 'he will never have any respect for you unless you drive a bargain.'

'Oh, if he haggles!' began Bull impatiently.

'He haggles because he is a free man,' said the other. 'You do not understand; he would not see the meaning of generosity. He is not being tipped.'

And even while they seemed to hear the heavy feet of their strange pursuers behind them, they had to stand and stamp while the French Colonel talked to the French wood-cutter with all the leisurely badinage and bickering of market-day. At the end of the four minutes, however, they saw that the Colonel was right, for the wood-cutter entered into their plans, not with the vague servility of a tout too-well paid, but with the seriousness of a solicitor who had been paid the proper fee. He told them that the best thing they could do was to make their way down to the little inn on the hills above Lancy, where the innkeeper, an old soldier who had become *dévot* in his latter years, would be certain to sympathise with them, and even to take risks in their support. The whole company, therefore, piled themselves on top of the stacks of wood, and went rocking in the rude cart down the other and steeper side of the woodland. Heavy and ramshackle as was the vehicle, it was driven quickly enough, and they soon had the exhilarating impression of distancing altogether those, whoever they were, who were hunting them. For, after all, the riddle as to where the anarchists had got all these followers was still unsolved. One man's presence had sufficed for them; they had fled at the first sight of the deformed smile of the Secretary. Syme every now and then looked back over his shoulder at the army on their track.

As the wood grew first thinner and then smaller with distance, he could see the sunlit slopes beyond it and above it; and across these was still moving the square black mob like one monstrous beetle. In the very strong sunlight and with his own very strong eyes, which were almost telescopic, Syme could see this mass of men quite plainly. He could see them as separate human figures; but he was increasingly surprised by the way in which they moved as one man. They seemed to be dressed in dark clothes and plain hats, like any common crowd out of the streets; but they did not spread and sprawl and trail by various lines to the attack, as would be natural in an ordinary mob. They moved with a sort of dreadful and wicked woodenness, like a staring army of automatons.

Syme pointed this out to Ratcliffe.

'Yes,' replied the policeman, 'that's discipline. That's Sunday. He is perhaps five hundred miles off, but the fear of him is on all of them, like the finger of God. Yes, they are walking regularly; and you bet your boots that they are talking regularly, yes, and thinking regularly. But the one important thing for us is that they are disappearing regularly.'

Syme nodded. It was true that the black patch of the pursuing men was growing smaller and smaller as the peasant belaboured his horse.

The level of the sunlit landscape, though flat as a whole, fell away on the farther side of the wood in billows of heavy slope towards the sea, in a way not unlike the lower slopes of the Sussex downs. The only difference was that in Sussex the road would have been broken and angular like a little brook, but here the white French road fell sheer in front of them like a waterfall. Down this direct descent the cart clattered at a considerable angle, and in a few minutes, the road growing yet steeper, they saw below them the little harbour of Lancy and a great blue arc of the sea. The travelling cloud of their enemies had wholly disappeared from the horizon. The horse and cart took a sharp turn round a clump of elms, and the horse's nose nearly struck the face of an old gentleman who was sitting on the benches outside the little café of 'Le Soleil d'Or.' The peasant grunted an apology, and got down from his seat. The others also descended one by one, and spoke to the old gentleman with fragmentary phrases of courtesy, for it was quite evident from his expansive manner that he was the owner of the little tavern.

He was a white-haired, apple-faced old boy, with sleepy eyes and a grey moustache; stout, sedentary, and very innocent, of a type that may often be found in France, but is still commoner in Catholic Germany. Everything about him, his pipe, his pot of beer, his flowers, and his beehive, suggested an ancestral peace; only when his visitors looked up as they entered the inn-parlour, they saw the sword upon the wall.

The Colonel, who greeted the innkeeper as an old friend, passed rapidly into the inn-parlour, and sat down ordering some ritual refreshment. The military decision of his action interested Syme, who sat next to him, and he took the opportunity when the old innkeeper had gone out of satisfying his curiosity.

'May I ask you, Colonel,' he said in a low voice, 'why we have come here?'

Colonel Ducroix smiled behind his bristly white moustache.

'For two reasons, sir,' he said; 'and I will give first, not the most important, but the most utilitarian. We came here because this is the only place within twenty miles in which we can get horses.'

'Horses!' repeated Syme, looking up quickly.

'Yes,' replied the other; 'if you people are really to distance your enemies it is horses or nothing for you, unless of course you have bicycles and motor-cars in your pocket.'

'And where do you advise us to make for?' asked Syme doubtfully.

'Beyond question,' replied the Colonel, 'you had better make all haste to the police station beyond the town. My friend, whom I seconded under somewhat deceptive circumstances, seems to me to exaggerate very much the possibilities of a general rising; but even he would hardly maintain, I suppose, that you were not safe with the gendarmes.'

Syme nodded gravely; then he said abruptly—

'And your other reason for coming here?'

'My other reason for coming here,' said Ducroix soberly, 'is that it is just as well to see a good man or two when one is possibly near to death.'

Syme looked up at the wall, and saw a crudely-painted and pathetic religious picture. Then he said—

'You are right,' and then almost immediately afterwards, 'Has anyone seen about the horses?'

'Yes,' answered Ducroix, 'you may be quite certain that I gave orders the moment I came in. Those enemies of yours gave no impression of hurry, but they were really moving wonderfully fast, like a well-trained army. I had no idea that the anarchists had so much discipline. You have not a moment to waste.'

Almost as he spoke, the old innkeeper with the blue eyes and white hair came ambling into the room, and announced that six horses were saddled outside.

By Ducroix's advice the five others equipped themselves with some portable form of food and wine, and keeping their duelling swords as the only weapons available, they clattered away down the steep, white road. The two servants, who had carried the Marquis's luggage when he was a marquis, were left behind to drink at the café by common consent, and not at all against their own inclination.

By this time the afternoon sun was slanting westward, and by its rays Syme could see the sturdy figure of the old innkeeper growing smaller and smaller, but still standing and looking after them quite silently, the sunshine in his silver hair. Syme had a fixed, superstitious fancy, left in his mind by the chance phrase of the Colonel, that this was indeed, perhaps, the last honest stranger whom he should ever see upon the earth.

He was still looking as this dwindling figure, which stood as a mere grey blot touched with a white flame against the great green wall of the steep down behind him. And as he stared over the top of the down behind the innkeeper, there appeared an army of black-clad and marching men. They seemed to hang above the good man and his house like a black cloud of locusts. The horses had been saddled none too soon.

# XII

## *THE EARTH IN ANARCHY*

Urging the horses to a gallop, without respect to the rather rugged descent of the road, the horsemen soon regained their advantage over the men on the march, and at last the bulk of the first buildings of Lancy cut off the sight of their pursuers. Nevertheless, the ride had been a long one, and by the time they reached the real town the west was warming with the colour and quality of sunset. The Colonel suggested that before making finally for the police station, they should make the effort, in passing, to attach to themselves one more individual who might be useful.

'Four out of the five rich men in this town,' he said 'are common swindlers. I suppose the proportion is pretty equal all over the world. The fifth is a friend of mine, and a very fine fellow; and what is even more important from our point of view, he owns a motor-car.'

'I am afraid,' said the Professor in his mirthful way, looking back along the white road on which the black, crawling patch might appear at any moment, 'I am afraid we have hardly time for afternoon calls.'

'Doctor Renard's house is only three minutes off,' said the Colonel.

'Our danger,' said Dr Bull, 'is not two minutes off.'

'Yes,' said Syme, 'if we ride on fast we must leave them behind, for they are on foot.'

'He has a motor-car,' said the Colonel.

'But we may not get it,' said Bull.

'Yes, he is quite on your side.'

'But he might be out.'

'Hold your tongue,' said Syme suddenly. 'What is that noise?'

For a second they all sat as still as equestrian statues, and for a second—for two or three or four seconds—heaven and earth seemed equally still. Then all their ears, in an agony of attention, heard along the road that indescribable thrill and throb that means only one thing—horses!

The Colonel's face had an instantaneous change, as if lightning had struck it, and yet left it scatheless.

'They have done us,' he said, with brief military irony. 'Prepare to receive cavalry!'

'Where can they have got the horses?' asked Syme, as he mechanically urged his steed to a canter.

The Colonel was silent for a little, then he said in a strained voice—

'I was speaking with strict accuracy when I said that the "Soleil d'Or" was the only place where one can get horses within twenty miles.'

'No!' said Syme violently, 'I don't believe he'd do it. Not with all that white hair.'

'He may have been forced,' said the Colonel gently. 'They must be at least a hundred strong, for which reason we are all going to see my friend Renard, who has a motor-car.'

With these words he swung his horse suddenly round a street corner, and went down the street with such thundering speed, that the others, though already well at the gallop, had difficulty in following the flying tail of his horse.

Dr Renard inhabited a high and comfortable house at the top of a steep street, so that when the riders alighted at his door they could once more see the solid green ridge of the hill, with the white road across it, standing up above all the roofs of the town. They breathed again to see that the road as yet was clear, and they rang the bell.

Dr Renard was a beaming, brown-bearded man, a good example of that silent but very busy professional class which France has preserved even more perfectly than England. When the matter was explained to him he pooh-poohed the panic of the ex-Marquis altogether; he said, with the solid French scepticism, that there was no conceivable probability of a general anarchist rising. 'Anarchy,' he said, shrugging his shoulders, 'it is childishness!'

'*Et ça*,' cried out the Colonel suddenly, pointing over the other's shoulder, 'and that is childishness, isn't it?'

They all looked round, and saw a curve of black cavalry come sweeping over the top of the hill with all the energy of Attila. Swiftly as they rode, however, the whole rank still kept well together, and they could see the black vizards of the first line as level as a line of uniforms. But although the main black square was the same, though travelling faster, there was now one sensational dif-ference which they could see clearly upon the slope of the hill, as if upon a slanted map. The bulk of the riders were in one block; but one rider flew far ahead of the column, and with frantic movements of hand and heel urged his horse faster and faster, so that one might have fancied that he was not the pursuer but the pursued. But even at that great distance they could see something so fanatical, so unquestionable in his figure, that they knew it was the Secretary himself.

'I am sorry to cut short a cultured discussion,' said the Colonel, 'but can you lend me your motor-car now, in two minutes?'

'I have a suspicion that you are all mad,' said Dr Renard, smiling sociably; 'but God forbid that madness should in any way interrupt friendship. Let us go round to the garage.'

Dr Renard was a mild man with monstrous wealth; his rooms were like the Musée de Cluny, and he had three motor-cars. These, however, he seemed to use very sparingly, having the simple tastes of the French middle class, and when his impatient friends came to examine them, it took them some time to assure themselves that one of them even could be made to work. This with some difficulty they brought round into the street before the Doctor's house. When they came out of the dim garage they were startled to find that twilight had already fallen with the abruptness of night in the tropics. Either they had been longer in the place than they imagined, or some unusual canopy of cloud had gathered over the town. They looked down the steep streets, and seemed to see a slight mist coming up from the sea.

'It is now or never,' said Dr Bull. 'I hear horses.'

'No,' corrected the Professor, 'a horse.'

And as they listened, it was evident that the noise, rapidly coming nearer on the rattling stones, was not the noise of the whole cavalcade but that of the one horseman, who had left it far behind—the insane Secretary.

Syme's family, like most of those who end in the simple life, had once owned a motor, and he knew all about them. He had leapt at once into the chauffeur's seat, and with flushed face was wrenching and tugging at the disused machinery. He bent his strength upon one handle, and then said quite quietly—

'I am afraid it's no go.'

As he spoke, there swept round the corner a man rigid on his rushing horse, with the rush and rigidity of an arrow. He had a smile that thrust out his chin as if it were dislocated. He swept alongside of the stationary car, into which its company had crowded, and laid his hand on the front. It was the Secretary, and his mouth went quite straight in the solemnity of triumph.

Syme was leaning hard upon the steering wheel, and there was no sound but the rumble of the other pursuers riding into the town. Then there came quite suddenly a scream of scraping iron, and the car leapt forward. It plucked the Secretary clean out of his saddle, as a knife is whipped out of its sheath, trailed him kicking terribly for twenty yards, and left him flung flat upon the road far in front of his frightened horse. As the car took the corner of the street with a splendid curve, they could just see the other anarchists filling the street and raising their fallen leader.

'I can't understand why it has grown so dark,' said the Professor at last in a low voice.

'Going to be a storm, I think,' said Dr Bull. 'I say, it's a pity we haven't got a light on this car, if only to see by.'

'We have,' said the Colonel, and from the floor of the car he fished up a heavy, old-fashioned carved iron lantern with a light inside it. It was obviously an antique, and it would seem as if its original use had been in some way semi-religious, for there was a rude moulding of a cross upon one of its sides.

'Where on earth did you get that?' asked the Professor.

'I got it where I got the car,' answered the Colonel, chuckling, 'from my best friend. While our friend here was fighting with the steering wheel, I ran up the front steps of the house and spoke to Renard, who was standing in his own porch, you will remember. 'I suppose,' I said, 'there's no time to get a lamp.' He looked up, blinking amiably at the beautiful arched ceiling of his own front hall. From this was suspended, by chains of exquisite ironwork, this lantern, one of the hundred treasures of his treasure house. By sheer force he tore the lamp out of his own ceiling, shattering the painted panels, and bringing down two blue vases with his violence. Then he handed me the iron lantern, and I put it in the car. Was I not right when I said that Dr Renard was worth knowing?'

'You were,' said Syme seriously, and hung the heavy lantern over the front. There was a certain allegory of their whole position in the contrast between the modern automobile and its strange ecclesiastical lamp.

Hitherto they had passed through the quietest part of the town, meeting at most one or two pedestrians, who could give them no hint of the peace or the hostility of the place. Now, however, the windows in the houses began one by one to be lit up, giving a greater sense of habitation and humanity. Dr Bull turned to the new detective who had led their flight, and permitted himself one of his natural and friendly smiles.

'These lights make one feel more cheerful.'

Inspector Ratcliffe drew his brows together.

'There is only one set of lights that make me more cheerful,' he said, 'and they are those lights of the police station which I can see beyond the town. Please God we may be there in ten minutes.'

Then all Bull's boiling good sense and optimism broke suddenly out of him.

'Oh, this is all raving nonsense!' he cried. 'If you really think that ordinary people in ordinary houses are anarchists, you must be madder than an anarchist yourself. If we turned and fought these fellows, the whole town would fight for us.'

'No,' said the other with an immovable simplicity, 'the whole town would fight for them. We shall see.'

While they were speaking the Professor had leant forward with sudden excitement.

'What is that noise?' he said.

'Oh, the horses behind us, I suppose,' said the Colonel. 'I thought we had got clear of them.'

'The horses behind us! No,' said the Professor, 'it is not horses, and it is not behind us.'

Almost as he spoke, across the end of the street before them two shining and rattling shapes shot past. They were gone almost in a flash, but everyone could see that they were motor-cars, and the Professor stood up with a pale face and swore that they were the other two motor-cars from Dr Renard's garage.

'I tell you they were his,' he repeated, with wild eyes, 'and they were full of men in masks!'

'Absurd!' said the Colonel angrily. 'Dr Renard would never give them his cars.'

'He may have been forced,' said Ratcliffe quietly. 'The whole town is on their side.'

'You still believe that?' asked the Colonel incredulously.

'You will all believe it soon,' said the other with a hopeless calm.

There was a puzzled pause for some little time, and then the Colonel began again abruptly—

'No, I can't believe it. The thing is nonsense. The plain people of a peaceable French town——'

He was cut short by a bang and a blaze of light, which seemed close to his eyes. As the car sped on it left a floating patch of white smoke behind it, and Syme had heard a shot shriek past his ear.

'My God!' said the Colonel, 'someone has shot at us.'

'It need not interrupt conversation,' said the gloomy Ratcliffe. 'Pray resume your remarks, Colonel. You were talking, I think, about the plain people of a peaceable French town.'

The staring Colonel was long past minding satire. He rolled his eyes all round the street.

'It is extraordinary,' he said, 'most extraordinary.'

'A fastidious person,' said Syme, 'might even call it unpleasant. However, I suppose those lights out in the field beyond this street are the Gendarmerie. We shall soon get there.'

'No,' said Inspector Ratcliffe, 'we shall never get there.'

He had been standing up and looking keenly ahead of him. Now he sat down and smoothed his sleek hair with a weary gesture.

'What do you mean?' asked Bull sharply.

'I mean that we shall never get there,' said the pessimist placidly. 'They have two rows of armed men across the road already; I can see them from here. The town is in arms, as I said it was. I can only wallow in the exquisite comfort of my own exactitude.'

And Ratcliffe sat down comfortably in the car and lit a cigarette, but the others rose excitedly and stared down the road. Syme had slowed down the car as their plans became doubtful, and he brought it finally to a standstill just at the corner of a side street that ran down very steeply to the sea.

The town was mostly in shadow, but the sun had not sunk; wherever its level light could break through, it painted everything a burning gold. Up this side street the last sunset light shone as sharp and narrow as the shaft of artificial light at the theatre. It struck the car of the five friends, and lit it like a burning chariot. But the rest of the street, especially the two ends of it, was in the deepest twilight, and for some seconds they could see nothing. Then Syme, whose eyes were the keenest, broke into a little bitter whistle, and said——

'It is quite true. There is a crowd or an army or some such thing across the end of that street.'

'Well, if there is,' said Bull impatiently, 'it must be something else—a sham fight or the mayor's birthday or something. I cannot and will not believe that plain, jolly people in a place like this walk about with dynamite in their pockets. Get on a bit, Syme, and let us look at them.'

The car crawled about a hundred yards farther, and then they were all startled by Dr Bull breaking into a high crow of laughter.

'Why, you silly mugs!' he cried, 'what did I tell you. That crowd's as law-abiding as a cow, and if it weren't, it's on our side.'

'How do you know?' asked the Professor, staring.

'You blind bat,' cried Bull, 'don't you see who is leading them?'

They peered again, and then the Colonel, with a catch in his voice, cried out—

'Why, it's Renard!'

There was, indeed, a rank of dim figures running across the road, and they could not be clearly seen; but far enough in front to catch the accident of the evening light was stalking up and down the unmistakable Dr Renard, in a white hat, stroking his long brown beard, and holding a revolver in his left hand.

'What a fool I've been!' exclaimed the Colonel. 'Of course, the dear old boy has turned out to help us.'

Dr Bull was bubbling over with laughter, swinging the sword in his hand as carelessly as a cane. He jumped out of the car and ran across the intervening space, calling out—

'Dr Renard! Dr Renard!'

An instant after Syme thought his own eyes had gone mad in his head. For the philanthropic Dr Renard had deliberately raised his revolver and fired twice at Bull, so that the shots rang down the road.

Almost at the same second as the puff of white cloud went up from this atrocious explosion a long puff of white cloud went up also from the cigarette of the cynical Ratcliffe. Like all the rest he turned a little pale, but he smiled. Dr Bull, at whom the bullets had been fired, just missing his scalp, stood quite still in the middle of the road without a sign of fear, and then turned very slowly and crawled back to the car, and climbed in with two holes through his hat.

'Well,' said the cigarette smoker slowly, 'what do you think now?'

'I think,' said Dr Bull with precision, 'that I am lying in bed at No. 217 Peabody Buildings, and that I shall soon wake up with a jump; or, if that's not it, I think that I am sitting in a small cushioned cell in Hanwell, and that the doctor can't make much of my case. But if you want to know what I don't think, I'll tell you. I don't think what you think. I don't think, and I never shall think, that the mass of ordinary men are a pack of dirty modern thinkers. No, sir, I'm a democrat, and I still don't believe that Sunday could convert one average navvy or counter-jumper. No, I may be mad, but humanity isn't.'

Syme turned his bright blue eyes on Bull with an earnestness which he did not commonly make clear.

'You are a very fine fellow,' he said. 'You can believe in a sanity which is not merely your sanity. And you're right enough about humanity, about peasants and people like that jolly old innkeeper. But you're not right about Renard. I suspected him from the first. He's rationalistic, and, what's worse, he's rich. When duty and religion are really destroyed, it will be by the rich.'

'They are really destroyed now,' said the man with a cigarette, and rose with his hands in his pockets. 'The devils are coming on!'

The men in the motor-car looked anxiously in the direction of his dreamy gaze, and they saw that the whole regiment at the end of the road was advancing upon them, Dr Renard marching furiously in front, his beard flying in the breeze.

The Colonel sprang out of the car with an intolerant exclamation.

'Gentlemen,' he cried, 'the thing is incredible. It must be a practical joke. If you knew Renard as I do—it's like calling Queen Victoria a dynamiter. If you had got the man's character into your head——'

'Dr Bull,' said Syme sardonically, 'has at least got it into his hat.'

'I tell you it can't be!' cried the Colonel, stamping. 'Renard shall explain it. He shall explain it to me,' and he strode forward.

'Don't be in such a hurry,' drawled the smoker. 'He will very soon explain it to all of us.'

But the impatient Colonel was already out of earshot, advancing towards the advancing enemy. The excited Dr Renard lifted his pistol again, but perceiving his opponent, hesitated, and the Colonel came face to face with him with frantic gestures of remonstrance.

'It is no good,' said Syme. 'He will never get anything out of that old heathen. I vote we drive bang through the thick of them, bang as the bullets went through Bull's hat. We may all be killed, but we must kill a tidy number of them.'

'I won't 'ave it,' said Dr Bull, growing more vulgar in the sincerity of his virtue. 'The poor chaps may be making a mistake. Give the Colonel a chance.'

'Shall we go back, then?' asked the Professor.

'No,' said Ratcliffe in a cold voice, 'the street behind us is held too. In fact, I seem to see there another friend of yours, Syme.'

Syme spun round smartly, and stared backwards at the track which they had travelled. He saw an irregular body of horsemen gathering and galloping towards them in the gloom. He saw above the foremost saddle the silver gleam of a sword, and then as it grew nearer the silver gleam of an old man's hair. The next moment, with shattering violence, he had swung the motor round and sent it dashing down the steep side street to the sea, like a man that desired only to die.

'What the devil is up?' cried the Professor, seizing his arm.

'The morning star has fallen!' said Syme, as his own car went down the darkness like a falling star.

The others did not understand his words, but when they looked back at the street above they saw the hostile cavalry coming round the corner and down the slopes after them; and foremost of all rode the good innkeeper, flushed with the fiery innocence of the evening light.

'The world is insane!' said the Professor, and buried his face in his hands.

'No,' said Dr Bull in adamantine humility, 'it is I.'

'What are we going to do?' asked the Professor.

'At this moment,' said Syme, with a scientific detachment, 'I think we are going to smash into a lamp-post.'

The next instant the automobile had come with a catastrophic jar against an iron object. The instant after that four men had crawled out from under a chaos of metal, and a tall lean lamp-post that had stood up straight on the edge of the marine parade stood out, bent and twisted, like the branch of a broken tree.

'Well, we smashed something,' said the Professor, with a faint smile. 'That's some comfort.'

'You're becoming an anarchist,' said Syme dusting his clothes with his instinct of daintiness.

'Everyone is,' said Ratcliffe.

As they spoke, the white-haired horseman and his followers came thundering from above, and almost at the same moment a dark string of men ran shouting along the sea-front. Syme snatched a sword, and took it in his teeth; he stuck two others under his arm-pits, took a fourth in his left hand and the lantern in his right, and leapt off the high parade on to the beach below.

The others leapt after him, with a common acceptance of such decisive action, leaving the débris and the gathering mob above them.

'We have one more chance,' said Syme, taking the steel out of his mouth. 'Whatever all this pandemonium means, I suppose the police station will help us. We can't get there, for they hold the way. But there's a pier or breakwater runs out into the sea just here, which we could defend longer than anything else, like Horatius and his bridge. We must defend it till the gendarmerie turn out. Keep after me.'

They followed him as he went crunching down the beach, and in a second or two their boots broke not on the sea gravel, but on broad, flat stones. They marched down a long, low jetty, running out in one arm into the dim, boiling sea, and when they came to the end of it they felt that they had come to the end of their story. They turned and faced the town.

That town was transfigured with uproar. All along the high parade from which they had just descended was a dark and roaring stream of humanity, with tossing arms and fiery faces, groping and glaring towards them. The long dark line was dotted with torches and lanterns; but even where no flame lit up a furious face, they could see in the farthest figure, in the most shadowy gesture, an organised hate. It was clear that they were the accursed of all men, and they knew not why.

Two or three men, looking little and black like monkeys, leapt over the edge as they had done and dropped on to the beach. These came ploughing down the deep sand, shouting horribly, and strove to wade into the sea at random. The example was followed, and the whole black mass of men began to run and drip over the edge like black treacle.

Foremost among the men on the beach Syme saw the peasant who had driven their cart. He splashed into the surf on a huge cart-horse, and shook his axe at them.

'The peasant!' cried Syme. 'They have not risen since the Middle Ages.'

'Even if the police do come now,' said the Professor mournfully, 'they can do nothing with this mob.'

'Nonsense!' said Bull desperately; 'there must be some people left in the town who are human.'

'No,' said the hopeless Inspector, 'the human being will soon be extinct. We are the last of mankind.'

'It may be,' said the Professor absently. Then he added in his dreamy voice, 'What is all that at the end of the "Dunciad"?

"Nor public flame, nor private, dares to shine;
Nor human light is left, nor glimpse divine!
Lo! thy dread Empire, Chaos, is restored;
Light dies before thine uncreating word:

Thy hand, great Anarch, lets the curtain fall;
And universal darkness buries all.'''

'Stop!' cried Bull suddenly, 'the gendarmes are out.'

The low lights of the police station were indeed blotted and broken with hurrying figures, and they heard through the darkness the clash and jingle of a disciplined cavalry.

'They are charging the mob!' cried Bull in ecstasy or alarm.

'No,' said Syme, 'they are formed along the parade.'

'They have unslung their carbines,' cried Bull dancing with excitement.

'Yes,' said Ratcliffe, 'and they are going to fire on us.'

As he spoke there came a long crackle of musketry, and bullets seemed to hop like hailstones on the stones in front of them.

'The gendarmes have joined them!' cried the Professor, and struck his forehead.

'I am in the padded cell,' said Bull solidly.

There was a long silence, and then Ratcliffe said, looking out over the swollen sea, all a sort of grey purple—

'What does it matter who is mad or who is sane? We shall all be dead soon.'

Syme turned to him and said—

'You are quite hopeless, then?'

Mr Ratcliffe kept a stony silence; then at last he said quietly—

'No; oddly enough I am not quite hopeless. There is one insane little hope that I cannot get out of my mind. The power of this whole planet is against us, yet I cannot help wondering whether this one silly little hope is hopeless yet.'

'In what or whom is your hope?' asked Syme with curiosity.

'In a man I never saw,' said the other, looking at the leaden sea.

'I know what you mean,' said Syme in a low voice, 'the man in the dark room. But Sunday must have killed him by now.'

'Perhaps,' said the other steadily; 'but if so, he was the only man whom Sunday found it hard to kill.'

'I heard what you said,' said the Professor, with his back turned. 'I also am holding hard on to the thing I never saw.'

All of a sudden Syme, who was standing as if blind with introspective thought, swung round and cried out, like a man waking from sleep—

'Where is the Colonel? I thought he was with us!'

'The Colonel! Yes,' cried Bull, 'where on earth is the Colonel?'

'He went to speak to Renard,' said the Professor.

'We cannot leave him among all those beasts,' cried Syme. 'Let us die like gentlemen if——'

'Do not pity the Colonel,' said Ratcliffe, with a pale sneer. 'He is extremely comfortable. He is——'

'No! no! no!' cried Syme in a kind of frenzy, 'not the Colonel too! I will never believe it!'

'Will you believe your eyes?' asked the other, and pointed to the beach.

Many of their pursuers had waded into the water shaking their fists, but the sea was rough, and they could not reach the pier. Two or three figures, however, stood on the beginning of the stone footway, and seemed to be cautiously advancing down it. The glare of a chance lantern lit up the faces of the two foremost. One face wore a black half-mask, and under it the mouth was twisting about in such a madness of nerves that the black tuft of beard wriggled round and round like a restless, living thing. The other was the red face and white moustache of Colonel Ducroix. They were in earnest consultation.

'Yes, he is gone too,' said the Professor, and sat down on a stone. 'Everything's gone. I'm gone! I can't trust my own bodily machinery. I feel as if my own hand might fly up and strike me.'

'When my hand flies up,' said Syme, 'it will strike somebody else,' and he strode along the pier towards the Colonel, the sword in one hand and the lantern in the other.

As if to destroy the last hope or doubt, the Colonel, who saw him coming, pointed his revolver at him and fired. The shot missed Syme, but struck his sword, breaking it short at the hilt. Syme rushed on, and swung the iron lantern above his head.

'Judas before Herod!' he said, and struck the Colonel down upon the stones. Then he turned to the Secretary, whose frightful mouth was almost foaming now, and held the lamp high with so rigid and arresting a gesture, that the man was, is it were, frozen for a moment, and forced to hear.

'Do you see this lantern?' cried Syme in a terrible voice. 'Do you see the cross carved on it, and the flame inside? You did not make it. You did not light it. Better men than you, men who could believe and obey, twisted the entrails of iron and preserved the legend of fire. There is not a street you walk on, there is not a thread you wear, that was not made as this lantern was, by denying your philosophy of dirt and rats. You can make nothing. You can only destroy. You will destroy mankind; you will destroy the world. Let that suffice you. Yet this one old Christian lantern you shall not destroy. It shall go where your empire of apes will never have the wit to find it.'

He struck the Secretary once with the lantern so that he staggered; and then, whirling it twice round his head, sent it flying far out to sea, where it flared like a roaring rocket and fell.

'Swords!' shouted Syme, turning his flaming face to the three behind him. 'Let us charge these dogs, for our time has come to die.'

His three companions came after him sword in hand. Syme's sword was broken, but he rent a bludgeon from the fist of a fisherman, flinging him down. In a moment they would have flung themselves upon the face of the mob and perished, when an interruption came. The Secretary, ever since Syme's speech, had stood with his hand to his stricken head as if dazed; now he suddenly pulled off his black mask.

The pale face thus peeled in the lamplight revealed not so much rage as astonishment. He put up his hand with an anxious authority.

'There is some mistake,' he said. 'Mr Syme, I hardly think you understand your position. I arrest you in the name of the law.'

'Of the law?' said Syme, and dropped his stick.

'Certainly!' said the Secretary. 'I am a detective from Scotland Yard,' and he took a small blue card from his pocket.

'And what do you suppose we are?' asked the Professor, and threw up his arms.

'You,' said the Secretary stiffly, 'are, as I know for a fact, members of the Supreme Anarchist Council. Disguised as one of you, I——'

Dr Bull tossed his sword into the sea.

'There never was any Supreme Anarchist Council,' he said. 'We were all a lot of silly policemen looking at each other. And all these nice people who have been peppering us with shot thought we were the dynamiters. I knew I couldn't be wrong about the mob,' he said, beaming over the enormous multitude, which stretched away to the distance on both sides. 'Vulgar people are never mad. I'm vulgar myself, and I know. I am now going on shore to stand a drink to everybody here.'

# XIII

### THE PURSUIT OF THE PRESIDENT

Next morning five bewildered but hilarious people took the boat for Dover. The poor old Colonel might have had some cause to complain, having been first forced to fight for two factions that didn't exist, and then knocked down with an iron lantern. But he was a magnanimous old gentleman, and being much relieved that neither party had anything to do with dynamite, he saw them off on the pier with great geniality.

The five reconciled detectives had a hundred details to explain to each other. The Secretary had to tell Syme how they had come to wear masks originally in order to approach the supposed enemy as fellow-conspirators; Syme had to explain how they had fled with such swiftness through a civilised country. But above all these matters of detail which could be explained, rose the central mountain of the matter that they could not explain. What did it all mean? If they were all harmless officers, what was Sunday? If he had not seized the world, what on earth had he been up to? Inspector Ratcliffe was still gloomy about this.

'I can't make head or tail of old Sunday's little game any more than you can,' he said. 'But whatever else Sunday is, he isn't a blameless citizen. Damn it! do you remember his face?'

'I grant you,' answered Syme, 'that I have never been able to forget it.'

'Well,' said the Secretary, 'I suppose we can find out soon, for to-morrow we have our next general meeting. You will excuse me,' he said, with a rather ghastly smile, 'for being well acquainted with my secretarial duties.'

'I suppose you are right,' said the Professor reflectively. 'I suppose we might find it out from him; but I confess that I should feel a bit afraid of asking Sunday who he really is.'

'Why,' asked the Secretary, 'for fear of bombs?'

'No,' said the Professor, 'for fear he might tell me.'

'Let us have some drinks,' said Dr Bull, after a silence.

Throughout their whole journey by boat and train they were highly convivial, but they instinctively kept together. Dr Bull, who had always been the optimist of the party, endeavoured to persuade the other four that the whole company could take the same hansom cab from Victoria; but this was over-ruled, and they went in a four-wheeler, with Dr Bull on the box, singing. They finished their journey at an hotel in Piccadilly Circus, so as to be close to the early breakfast next morning in Leicester Square. Yet even then the adventures of the day were not entirely over. Dr Bull, discontented with the general proposal to go to bed, had strolled out of the hotel at about eleven to see and taste some of the beauties of London. Twenty minutes afterwards, however, he came back and made quite a clamour in the hall. Syme, who tried at first to soothe him, was forced at last to listen to his communication with quite new attention.

'I tell you I've seen him!' said Dr Bull, with thick emphasis.

'Whom?' asked Syme quickly. 'Not the President?'

'Not so bad as that,' said Dr Bull, with unnecessary laughter, 'not so bad as that. I've got him here.'

'Got whom here?' asked Syme impatiently.

'Hairy man,' said the other lucidly, 'man that used to be hairy man— Gogol. Here he is,' and he pulled forward by a reluctant elbow the identical young man who five days before had marched out of the Council with thin red hair and a pale face, the first of all the sham anarchists who had been exposed.

'Why do you worry with me?' he cried. 'You have expelled me as a spy.'

'We are all spies!' whispered Syme.

'We're all spies!' shouted Dr Bull. 'Come and have a drink.'

Next morning the battalion of the reunited six marched stolidly towards the hotel in Leicester Square.

'This is more cheerful,' said Dr Bull;'we are six men going to ask one man what he means.'

'I think it is a bit queerer than that,' said Syme. 'I think it is six men going to ask one man what they mean.'

They turned in silence into the Square, and though the hotel was in the opposite corner, they saw at once the little balcony and a figure that looked too big for it. He was sitting alone with bent head, poring over a newspaper. But all his councillors, who had come to vote him down, crossed that Square as if they were watched out of heaven by a hundred eyes.

They had disputed much upon their policy, about whether they should leave the unmasked Gogol without and begin diplomatically, or whether they should bring him in and blow up the gunpowder at once. The influence of Syme and Bull prevailed for the latter course, though the Secretary to the last asked them why they attacked Sunday so rashly.

'My reason is quite simple,' said Syme. 'I attack him rashly because I am afraid of him.'

They followed Syme up the dark stair in silence, and they all came out simultaneously into the broad sunlight of the morning and the broad sunlight of Sunday's smile.

'Delightful!' he said. 'So pleased to see you all. What an exquisite day it is. Is the Czar dead?'

The Secretary, who happened to be foremost, drew himself together for a dignified outburst.

'No, sir,' he said sternly, 'there has been no massacre. I bring you news of no such disgusting spectacles.'

'Disgusting spectacles?' repeated the President, with a bright, inquiring smile. 'You mean Dr Bull's spectacles?'

The Secretary choked for a moment, and the President went on with a sort of smooth appeal—

'Of course, we all have our opinions and even our eyes, but really to call them disgusting before the man himself——'

Dr Bull tore off his spectacles and broke them on the table.

'My spectacles are blackguardly,' he said, 'but I'm not. Look at my face.'

'I dare say it's the sort of face that grows on one,' said the President, 'in fact, it grows on you; and who am I to quarrel with the wild fruits upon the Tree of Life? I dare say it will grow on me some day.'

'We have no time for tomfoolery,' said the Secretary, breaking in savagely. 'We have come to know what all this means. Who are you? What are you? Why did you get us all here? Do you know who and what we are? Are you a half-witted man playing the conspirator, or are you a clever man playing the fool? Answer me, I tell you.'

'Candidates,' murmured Sunday, 'are only required to answer eight out of the seventeen questions on the paper. As far as I can make out, you want me to tell you what I am, and what you are, and what this table is, and what this Council is, and what this world is for all I know. Well, I will go so far as to rend the veil of one mystery. If you want to know what you are, you are a set of highly well-intentioned young jackasses.'

'And you,' said Syme, leaning forward, 'what are you?'

'I? What am I?' roared the President, and he rose slowly to an incredible height, like some enormous wave about to arch above them and break. 'You want to know what I am, do you? Bull, you are a man of science. Grub in the roots of those trees and find out the truth about them. Syme, you are a poet. Stare at those morning clouds. But I tell you this, that you will have found out the truth of the last tree and the topmost cloud before the truth about me. You will understand the sea, and I shall be still a riddle; you shall know what the stars are, and not know what I am. Since the beginning of the world all men have hunted me like a wolf—kings and sages, and poets and lawgivers, all the churches, and all the philosophies. But I have never been caught yet, and the skies will fall in the time I turn to bay. I have given them a good run for their money, and I will now.'

Before one of them could move, the monstrous man had swung himself like some huge orang-outang over the balustrade of the balcony. Yet before he dropped he pulled himself up again as on a horizontal bar, and thrusting his great chin over the edge of the balcony, said solemnly—

'There's one thing I'll tell you though about who I am. I am the man in the dark room, who made you all policemen.'

With that he fell from the balcony, bouncing on the stones below like a great ball of india-rubber, and went bounding off towards the corner of the Alhambra, where he hailed a hansom-cab and sprang inside it. The six detectives had been standing thunderstruck and livid in the light of his last assertion; but when he disappeared into the cab, Syme's practical senses returned to him, and leaping over the balcony so recklessly as almost to break his legs, he called another cab.

He and Bull sprang into the cab together, the Professor and the Inspector into another, while the Secretary and the late Gogol scrambled into a third just in time to pursue the flying Syme, who was pursuing the flying President. Sunday led them a wild chase towards the north-west, his cabman, evidently under the influence of more than common inducements, urging the horse at breakneck speed. But Syme was in no mood for delicacies, and he stood up in his own cab shouting, 'Stop thief!' until crowds ran along beside his cab, and policemen began to stop and ask questions. All this had its influence upon the President's cabman, who began to look dubious, and to slow down to a trot. He opened the trap to talk reasonably to his fare, and in so doing let the long whip droop over the front of the cab. Sunday leant forward, seized it and jerked it violently out of the man's hand. Then standing up in front of the cab himself, he lashed the horse and roared aloud so that they went down the streets like a flying storm. Through street after street and square after square went whirling this preposterous vehicle, in which the fare was urging the horse and the driver trying desperately to stop it. The other three cabs came after it (if the phrase be permissible of a cab) like panting hounds. Shops and streets shot by like rattling arrows.

At the highest ecstasy of speed, Sunday turned round on the splashboard where he stood, and sticking his great grinning head out of the cab, with white hair whistling in the wind, he made a horrible face at his pursuers, like some colossal urchin. Then raising his right hand swiftly, he flung a ball of paper in Syme's face and vanished. Syme caught the thing while instinctively warding it off, and discovered that it consisted of two crumpled papers. One was addressed to himself, and the other to Dr Bull, with a very long, and it is to be feared partly ironical, string of letters after his name. Dr Bull's address was, at any rate, considerably longer than his communication, for the communication consisted entirely of the words:—

'What about Martin Tupper *now?*'

'What does the old maniac mean?' asked Bull, staring at the words. 'What does yours say, Syme?'

Syme's message was, at any rate, longer, and ran as follows:—

'No one would regret anything in the nature of an interference by the Archdeacon more than I. I trust it will not come to that. But, for the last time, where are your goloshes? The thing is too bad, especially after what uncle said.'

The President's cabman seemed to be regaining some control over his horse, and the pursuers gained a little as they swept round into the Edgware Road. And here there occurred what seemed to the allies a providential stoppage. Traffic of every kind was swerving to right or left or stopping, for down the long road was coming the unmistakable roar announcing the fire-engine, which in a few seconds went by like a brazen thunderbolt. But quick as it went by, Sunday had bounded out of his cab, sprung at the fire-engine, caught it, slung himself on to it, and was seen as he disappeared in the noisy distance talking to the astonished fireman with explanatory gestures.

'After him!' howled Syme. 'He can't go astray now. There's no mistaking a fire-engine.'

The three cabmen, who had been stunned for a moment, whipped up their horses and slightly decreased the distance between themselves and their disappearing prey. The President acknowledged this proximity by coming to the back of the car, bowing repeatedly, kissing his hand, and finally flinging a neatly-folded note into the bosom of Inspector Ratcliffe. When that gentleman opened it, not without impatience, he found it contained the words:—

'Fly at once. The truth about your trouser-stretchers is known. —A FRIEND.'

The fire-engine had struck still farther to the north, into a region that they did not recognise; and as it ran by a line of high railings shadowed with trees, the six friends were startled, but somewhat relieved, to see the President leap from the fire-engine, though whether through another whim or the increasing protest of his entertainers they could not see. Before the three cabs, however, could reach up to the spot, he had gone up the high railings like a huge grey cat, tossed himself over, and vanished in a darkness of leaves.

Syme with a furious gesture stopped his cab, jumped out, and sprang also to the escalade. When he had one leg over the fence and his friends were following, he turned a face on them which shone quite pale in the shadow.

'What place can this be?' he asked. 'Can it be the old devil's house? I've heard he has a house in North London.'

'All the better,' said the Secretary grimly, planting a foot in a foothold, 'we shall find him at home.'

'No, but it isn't that,' said Syme, knitting his brows. 'I hear the most horrible noises, like devils laughing and sneezing and blowing their devilish noses!'

'His dogs barking, of course,' said the Secretary.

'Why not say his black-beetles barking!' said Syme furiously, 'snails barking! geraniums barking! Did you ever hear a dog bark like that?'

He held up his hand, and there came out of the thicket a long growling roar that seemed to get under the skin and freeze the flesh—a low thrilling roar that made a throbbing in the air all about them.

'The dogs of Sunday would be no ordinary dogs,' said Gogol, and shuddered.

Syme had jumped down on the other side, but he still stood listening impatiently.

'Well, listen to that,' he said, 'is that a dog—anybody's dog?'

There broke upon their ear a hoarse screaming as of things protesting and clamouring in sudden pain; and then, far off like an echo, what sounded like a long nasal trumpet.

'Well, his house ought to be hell!' said the Secretary; 'and if it is hell, I'm going in!' and he sprang over the tall railings almost with one swing.

The others followed. They broke through a tangle of plants and shrubs, and came out on an open path. Nothing was in sight, but Dr Bull suddenly struck his hands together.

'Why, you asses,' he cried, 'it's the Zoo!'

As they were looking round wildly for any trace of their wild quarry, a keeper in uniform came running along the path with a man in plain clothes.

'Has it come this way?' gasped the keeper.

'Has what?' asked Syme.

'The elephant!' cried the keeper. 'An elephant has gone mad and run away!'

'He has run away with an old gentleman,' said the other stranger breathlessly, 'a poor old gentleman with white hair!'

'What sort of old gentleman?' asked Syme, with great curiosity.

'A very large and fat old gentleman in light grey clothes,' said the keeper eagerly.

'Well,' said Syme, 'if he's that particular kind of old gentleman, if you're quite sure that he's a large and fat old gentleman in grey clothes, you may take my word for it that the elephant has not run away with him. He has run away with the elephant. The elephant is not made by God that could run away with him if he did not consent to the elopement. And, by thunder, there he is!'

There was no doubt about it this time. Clean across the space of grass, about two hundred yards away, with a crowd screaming and scampering vainly at his heels, went a huge grey elephant at an awful stride, with his trunk thrown out as rigid as a ship's bowsprit, and trumpeting like the trumpet of doom. On the back of the bellowing and plunging animal sat President Sunday with all the placidity of a sultan, but goading the animal to a furious speed with some sharp object in his hand.

'Stop him!' screamed the populace. 'He'll be out of the gate!'

'Stop a landslide!' said the keeper. 'He is out of the gate!'

And even as he spoke, a final crash and roar of terror announced that the great grey elephant had broken out of the gates of the Zoological Gardens, and was careering down Albany Street like a new and swift sort of omnibus.

'Great Lord!' cried Bull, 'I never knew an elephant could go so fast. Well, it must be hansom-cabs again if we are to keep him in sight.'

As they raced along to the gate out of which the elephant had vanished, Syme felt a glaring panorama of the strange animals in the cages which they passed. Afterwards he thought it queer that he should have seen them so clearly. He remembered especially seeing pelicans, with their preposterous, pendant throats. He wondered why the pelican was the symbol of charity, except it was that it wanted a good deal of charity to admire a pelican. He remembered a hornbill, which was simply a huge yellow beak with a small bird tied on behind it. The whole gave him a sensation, the vividness of which he could not explain, that Nature was always making quite mysterious jokes. Sunday had told them that they would understand him when they had understood the stars. He wondered whether even the archangels understood the hornbill.

The six unhappy detectives flung themselves into the cabs and followed the elephant, sharing the terror which he spread through the long stretch of the streets. This time Sunday did not turn round, but offered them the solid stretch of his unconscious back, which maddened them, if possible, more than his previous mockeries. Just before they came to Baker Street, however, he was seen to throw something far up into the air, as a boy does a ball meaning to catch it again. But at their rate of racing it fell far behind, just by the cab containing Gogol; and in faint hope of a clue or for some impulse unexplainable, he stopped his cab so as to pick it up. It was addressed to himself, and was quite a bulky parcel. On examination, however, its bulk was found to consist of thirty-three pieces of paper of no value wrapped one round the other. When the last covering was torn away it reduced itself to a small slip of paper, on which was written:—

'The word, I fancy, should be "pink".'

The man once known as Gogol said nothing, but the movements of his hands and feet were like those of a man urging a horse to renewed efforts.

Through street after street, through district after district, went the prodigy of the flying elephant, calling crowds to every window, and driving the traffic left and right. And still through all this insane publicity the three cabs toiled after it, until they came to be regarded as part of a procession, and perhaps the advertisement of a circus. They went at such a rate that distances were shortened beyond belief, and Syme saw the Albert Hall in Kensington when he thought that he was still in Paddington. The animal's pace was even more fast and free through the empty, aristocratic streets of South Kensington, and he finally headed towards that part of the sky-line where the enormous Wheel of Earl's Court stood up in the sky. The wheel grew larger and larger, till it filled heaven like the wheel of stars.

The beast outstripped the cabs. They lost him round several corners, and when they came to one of the gates of the Earl's Court Exhibition they found themselves finally blocked. In front of them was an enormous crowd; in the midst of it was an enormous elephant, heaving and shuddering as such shapeless creatures do. But the President had disappeared.

'Where has he gone to?' asked Syme, slipping to the ground.

'Gentleman rushed into the Exhibition, sir!' said an official in a dazed manner. Then he added in an injured voice: 'Funny gentleman, sir. Asked me to hold his horse, and gave me this.'

He held out with distaste a piece of folded paper, addressed: 'To the Secretary of the Central Anarchist Council.'

The Secretary, raging, rent it open, and found written inside it:—

> 'When the herring runs a mile,
> Let the Secretary smile;
> When the herring tries to *fly*
> Let the Secretary die.
>
> Rustic Proverb.'

'Why the eternal crikey,' began the Secretary, 'did you let the man in? Do people commonly come to your Exhibition riding on mad elephants? Do——'

'Look!' shouted Syme suddenly. 'Look over there!'

'Look at what?' asked the Secretary savagely.

'Look at the captive balloon!' said Syme, and pointed in a frenzy.

'Why the blazes should I look at a captive balloon?' demanded the Secretary. 'What is there queer about a captive balloon?'

'Nothing,' said Syme, 'except that it isn't captive!'

They all turned their eyes to where the balloon swung and swelled above the Exhibition on a string, like a child's balloon. A second afterwards the string came in two just under the car, and the balloon, broken loose, floated away with the freedom of a soap bubble.

'Ten thousand devils!' shrieked the Secretary. 'He's got into it!' and he shook his fists at the sky.

The balloon, borne by some chance wind, came right above them, and they could see the great white head of the President peering over the side and looking benevolently down on them.

'God bless my soul!' said the Professor with the elderly manner that he could never disconnect from his bleached beard and parchment face. 'God bless my soul! I seemed to fancy that something fell on the top of my hat!'

He put up a trembling hand and took from that shelf a piece of twisted paper, which he opened absently only to find it inscribed with a true lover's knot and, the words:—

'Your beauty has not left me indifferent.—From LITTLE SNOWDROP.'

There was a short silence, and then Syme said, biting his beard—

'I'm not beaten yet. The blasted thing must come down somewhere. Let's follow it!'

# XIV

## THE SIX PHILOSOPHERS

Across green fields, and breaking through blooming hedges, toiled six drag-gled detectives, about five miles out of London. The optimist of the party had at first proposed that they should follow the balloon across South England in hansom-cabs. But he was ultimately convinced of the persistent refusal of the balloon to follow the roads, and the still more persistent refusal of the cabmen to follow the balloon. Consequently the tireless though exasperated travellers broke through black thickets and ploughed through ploughed fields till each was turned into a figure too outrageous to be mistaken for a tramp. Those green hills of Surrey saw the final collapse and tragedy of the admirable light grey suit in which Syme had set out from Saffron Park. His silk hat was broken over his nose by a swinging bough, his coat-tails were torn to the shoulder by arresting thorns, the clay of England was splashed up to his collar; but he still carried his yellow beard forward with a silent and furious determination, and his eyes were still fixed on that floating ball of gas, which in the full flush of sunset seemed coloured like a sunset cloud.

'After all,' he said, 'it is very beautiful!'

'It is singularly and strangely beautiful!' said the Professor. 'I wish the beastly gas-bag would burst!'

'No,' said Dr Bull, 'I hope it won't. It might hurt the old boy.'

'Hurt him!' said the vindictive Professor, 'hurt him! Not as much as I'd hurt him if I could get up with him. Little Snowdrop!'

'I don't want him hurt, somehow,' said Dr Bull.

'What!' cried the Secretary bitterly. 'Do you believe all that tale about his being our man in the dark room? Sunday would say he was anybody.'

'I don't know whether I believe it or not,' said Dr Bull. 'But it isn't that that I mean. I can't wish old Sunday's balloon to burst because——'

'Well,' said Syme impatiently, 'because?'

'Well, because he's so jolly like a balloon himself,' said Dr Bull desperately. 'I don't understand a word of all that idea of his being the same man who gave us all our blue cards. It seems to make everything nonsense. But I don't care who knows it, I always had a sympathy for old Sunday himself, wicked as he was. Just as if he was a great bouncing baby. How can I explain what my queer sympathy was? It didn't prevent my fighting him like hell! Shall I make it clear if I say that I liked him because he was so fat?'

'You will not,' said the Secretary.

'I've got it now,' cried Bull, 'it was because he was so fat and so light. Just like a balloon. We always think of fat people as heavy, but he could have danced against a sylph. I see now what I mean. Moderate strength is shown in violence, supreme strength is shown in levity. It was like the old speculations— what would happen if an elephant could leap up in the sky like a grasshopper?'

'Our elephant,' said Syme, looking upwards, 'has leapt into the sky like a grasshopper.'

'And somehow,' concluded Bull, 'that's why I can't help liking old Sunday. No, it's not an admiration of force, or any silly thing like that. There is a kind of gaiety in the thing, as if he were bursting with some good news. Haven't you sometimes felt it on a spring day? You know Nature plays tricks, but somehow that day proves they are good-natured tricks. I never read the Bible myself, but that part they laugh at is literal truth, "Why leap ye, ye high hills?" The hills do leap—at least, they try to. . . . Why do I like Sunday? . . . how can I tell you? . . . because he's such a Bounder.'

There was a long silence, and then the Secretary said in a curious, strained voice—

'You do not know Sunday at all. Perhaps it is because you are better than I, and do not know hell. I was a fierce fellow, and a trifle morbid from the first. The man who sits in darkness, and who chose us all, chose me because I had all the crazy look of a conspirator—because my smile went crooked, and my eyes were gloomy, even when I smiled. But there must have been something in me that answered to the nerves in all these anarchic men. For when I first saw Sunday he expressed to me, not your airy vitality, but something both gross and sad in the Nature of Things. I found him smoking in a twilight room, a room with brown blind down, infinitely more depressing than the genial darkness in which our master lives. He sat there on a bench, a huge heap of a man, dark and out of shape. He listened to all my words without speaking or even stirring. I poured out my most passionate appeals, and asked my most eloquent questions. Then, after a long silence, the Thing began to shake, and I thought it was shaken by some secret malady. It shook like a loathsome and living jelly. It reminded me of everything I had ever read about the base bodies that are the origin of life—the deep sea lumps and protoplasm. It seemed like the final form of matter, the most shapeless and the most shameful. I could only tell myself, from its shudderings, that it was something at least that such a monster could be miserable. And then it broke upon me that the bestial mountain was shaking with a lonely laughter, and the laughter was at me. Do you ask me to forgive him that? It is no small thing to be laughed at by something at once lower and stronger than oneself.'

'Surely you fellows are exaggerating wildly,' cut in the clear voice of Inspector Ratcliffe. 'President Sunday is a terrible fellow for one's intellect, but he is not such a Barnum's freak physically as you make out. He received me in an ordinary office, in a grey check coat, in broad daylight. He talked to me in an ordinary way. But I'll tell you what is a trifle creepy about Sunday. His room is neat, his clothes are neat, everything seems in order; but he's absent-minded. Sometimes his great bright eyes go quite blind. For hours he forgets that you are there. Now absent-mindedness is just a bit too awful in a bad man. We think of a wicked man as vigilant. We can't think of a wicked man who is honestly and sincerely dreamy, because we daren't think of a wicked man alone with himself. An absent-minded man means a good-natured man. It means a man who, if he happens to see you, will apologise. But how will you bear an absent-minded man who, if he happens to see you, will kill you? That is what tries the nerves, abstraction combined with cruelty. Men have felt it sometimes when they went through wild forests, and felt that the animals there were at once innocent and pitiless. They might ignore or slay. How would you like to pass ten mortal hours in a parlour with an absent-minded tiger?'

'And what do you think of Sunday, Gogol?' asked Syme.

'I don't think of Sunday on principle,' said Gogol simply, 'any more than I stare at the sun at noonday.'

'Well, that is a point of view,' said Syme thoughtfully. 'What do you say, Professor?'

The Professor was walking with bent head and trailing stick, and he did not answer at all.

'Wake up, Professor!' said Syme genially. 'Tell us what you think of Sunday.'

The Professor spoke at last very slowly.

'I think something,' he said, 'that I cannot say clearly. Or, rather, I think something that I cannot even think clearly. But it is something like this. My early life, as you know, was a bit too large and loose. Well, when I saw Sunday's face I thought it was too large—everybody does, but I also thought it was too loose. The face was so big, that one couldn't focus it or make it a face at all. The eye was so far away from the nose, that it wasn't an eye. The mouth was so much by itself, that one had to think of it by itself. The whole thing is too hard to explain.'

He paused for a little, still trailing his stick, and then went on—

'But put it this way. Walking up a road at night, I have seen a lamp and a lighted window and a cloud make together a most complete and unmistakable face. If anyone in heaven has that face I shall know him again. Yet when I walked a little farther I found that there was no face, that the window was ten yards away, the lamp ten hundred yards, the cloud beyond the world. Well, Sunday's face escaped me; it ran away to right and left, as such chance pictures run away. And so his face has made me, somehow, doubt whether there are any faces. I don't know whether your face, Bull, is a face or a combination in perspective. Perhaps one black disc of your beastly glasses is quite close and another fifty miles away. Oh, the doubts of a materialist are not worth a dump. Sunday has taught me the last and the worst doubts, the doubts of a spiritualist. I am a Buddhist, I suppose; and Buddhism is not a creed, it is a doubt. My poor dear Bull, I do not believe that you really have a face. I have not faith enough to believe in matter.'

Syme's eyes were still fixed upon the errant orb, which, reddened in the evening light, looked like some rosier and more innocent world.

'Have you noticed an odd thing,' he said, 'about all your descriptions? Each man of you finds Sunday quite different, yet each man of you can only find one thing to compare him to—the universe itself. Bull finds him like the earth in spring, Gogol like the sun at noon-day. The Secretary is reminded of the shapeless protoplasm, and the Inspector of the carelessness of virgin forests. The Professor says he is like a changing landscape. This is queer, but it is queerer still that I also have had my odd notion about the President, and I also find that I think of Sunday as I think of the whole world.'

'Get on a little faster, Syme,' said Bull; 'never mind the balloon.'

'When I first saw Sunday,' said Syme slowly, 'I only saw his back; and when I saw his back, I knew he was the worst man in the world. His neck and shoulders were brutal, like those of some apish god. His head had a stoop that was hardly human, like the stoop of an ox. In fact, I had at once the revolting fancy that this was not a man at all, but a beast dressed up in men's clothes.'

'Get on,' said Dr Bull.

'And then the queer thing happened. I had seen his back from the street, as he sat in the balcony. Then I entered the hotel, and coming round the other side of him, saw his face in the sunlight. His face frightened me, as it did everyone; but not because it was brutal, not because it was evil. On the contrary, it frightened me because it was so beautiful, because it was so good.'

'Syme,' exclaimed the Secretary, 'are you ill?'

'It was like the face of some ancient archangel, judging justly after heroic wars. There was laughter in the eyes, and in the mouth honour and sorrow. There was the same white hair, the same great, grey-clad shoulders that I had seen from behind. But when I saw him from behind I was certain he was an animal, and when I saw him in front I knew he was a god.'

'Pan,' said the Professor dreamily, 'was a god and an animal.'

'Then, and again and always,' went on Syme like a man talking to himself, 'that has been for me the mystery of Sunday, and it is also the mystery of the world. When I see the horrible back, I am sure the noble face is but a mask. When I see the face but for an instant, I know the back is only a jest. Bad is so bad, that we cannot but think good an accident; good is so good, that we feel certain that evil could be explained. But the whole came to a kind of crest yesterday when I raced Sunday for the cab, and was just behind him all the way.'

'Had you time for thinking then?' asked Ratcliffe.

'Time,' replied Syme, 'for one outrageous thought. I was suddenly possessed with the idea that the blind, blank back of his head really was his face—an awful, eyeless face staring at me! And I fancied that the figure running in front of me was really a figure running backwards, and dancing as he ran.'

'Horrible!' said Dr Bull, and shuddered.

'Horrible is not the word,' said Syme. 'It was exactly the worst instant of my life. And yet ten minutes afterwards, when he put his head out of the cab and made a grimace like a gargoyle, I knew that he was only like a father playing hide-and-seek with his children.'

'It is a long game,' said the Secretary, and frowned at his broken boots.

'Listen to me,' cried Syme with extraordinary emphasis. 'Shall I tell you the secret of the whole world? It is that we have only known the back of the world. We see everything from behind, and it looks brutal. That is not a tree, but the back of a tree. That is not a cloud, but the back of a cloud. Cannot you see that everything is stooping and hiding a face? If we could only get round in front——'

'Look!' cried out Bull clamorously, 'the balloon is coming down!'

There was no need to cry out to Syme, who had never taken his eyes off it. He saw the great luminous globe suddenly stagger in the sky, right itself, and then sink slowly behind the trees like a setting sun.

The man called Gogol, who had hardly spoken through all their weary travels, suddenly threw up his hands like a lost spirit.

'He is dead!' he cried. 'And now I know he was my friend—my friend in the dark!'

'Dead!' snorted the Secretary. 'You will not find him dead easily. If he has been tipped out of the car, we shall find him rolling as a colt rolls in a field, kicking his legs for fun.'

'Clashing his hoofs,' said the Professor. 'The colts do, and so did Pan.'

'Pan again!' said Dr Bull irritably. 'You seem to think Pan is everything.'

'So he is,' said the Professor, 'in Greek. He means everything.'

'Don't forget,' said the Secretary, looking down, 'that he also means Panic.'

Syme had stood without hearing any of the exclamations.

'It fell over there,' he said shortly. 'Let us follow it!'

Then he added with an indescribable gesture—

'Oh, if he has cheated us all by getting killed! It would be like one of his larks.'

233

He strode off towards the distant trees with a new energy, his rags and ribbons fluttering in the wind. The others followed him in a more footsore and dubious manner. And almost at the same moment all six men realised that they were not alone in the little field.

Across the square of turf a tall man was advancing towards them, leaning on a strange long staff like a sceptre. He was clad in a fine but old-fashioned suit with knee-breeches; its colour was that shade between blue, violet and grey which can be seen in certain shadows of the woodland. His hair was whitish grey, and at the first glance, taken along with his knee-breeches, looked as if it was powdered. His advance was very quiet; but for the silver frost upon his head, he might have been one of the shadows of the wood.

'Gentlemen,' he said, 'my master has a carriage waiting for you in the road just by.'

'Who is your master?' asked Syme, standing quite still.

'I was told you knew his name,' said the man respectfully.

There was a silence, and then the Secretary said—

'Where is this carriage?'

'It has been waiting only a few moments,' said the stranger. 'My master has only just come home.'

Syme looked left and right upon the patch of green field in which he found himself. The hedges were ordinary hedges, the trees seemed ordinary trees; yet he felt like a man entrapped in fairyland.

He looked the mysterious ambassador up and down, but he could discover nothing except that the man's coat was the exact colour of the purple shadows, and that the man's face was the exact colour of the red and brown and golden sky.

'Show us the place,' Syme said briefly, and without a word the man in the violet coat turned his back and walked towards a gap in the hedge, which let in suddenly the light of a white road.

As the six wanderers broke out upon this thoroughfare, they saw the white road blocked by what looked like a long row of carriages, such a row of carriages as might close the approach to some house in Park Lane. Along the side of these carriages stood a rank of splendid servants, all dressed in the grey-blue uniform, and all having a certain quality of stateliness and freedom which would not commonly belong to the servants of a gentleman, but rather to the officials and ambassadors of a great king. There were no less than six carriages waiting, one for each of the tattered and miserable band. All the attendants (as if in court-dress) wore swords, and as each man crawled into his carriage they drew them, and saluted with a sudden blaze of steel.

'What can it all mean?' asked Bull of Syme as they separated. 'Is this another joke of Sunday's?'

'I don't know,' said Syme as he sank wearily back in the cushions of his carriage; 'but if it is, it's one of the jokes you talk about. It's a good-natured one.'

The six adventurers had passed through many adventures, but not one had carried them so utterly off their feet as this last adventure of comfort. They had all become inured to things going roughly; but things suddenly going smoothly swamped them. They could not even feebly imagine what the carriages were; it was enough for them to know that they were carriages, and carriages with cushions. They could not conceive who the old man was who had led them; but it was quite enough that he had certainly led them to the carriages.

Syme drove through a drifting darkness of trees in utter abandonment. It was typical of him that while he had carried his bearded chin forward fiercely so long as anything could be done, when the whole business was taken out of his hands he fell back on the cushions in a frank collapse.

Very gradually and very vaguely he realised into what rich roads the carriage was carrying him. He saw that they passed the stone gates of what might have been a park, that they began gradually to climb a hill which, while wooded on both sides, was somewhat more orderly than a forest. Then there began to grow upon him, as upon a man slowly waking from a healthy sleep, a pleasure in everything. He felt that the hedges were what hedges should be, living walls; that a hedge is like a human army, disciplined, but all the more alive. He saw high elms behind the hedges, and vaguely thought how happy boys would be climbing there. Then his carriage took a turn of the path, and he saw suddenly and quietly, like a long, low, sunset cloud, a long, low house, mellow in the mild light of sunset. All the six friends compared notes afterwards and quarrelled; but they all agreed that in some unaccountable way the place reminded them of their boyhood. It was either this elm-top or that crooked patch, it was either this scrap of orchard or that shape of a window; but each man of them declared that he could remember this place before he could remember his mother.

When the carriages eventually rolled up to a large, low, cavernous gateway, another man in the same uniform, but wearing a silver star on the grey breast of his coat, came out to meet them. This impressive person said to the bewildered Syme—

'Refreshments are provided for you in your room.'

Syme, under the influence of the same mesmeric sleep of amazement, went up the large oaken stairs after the respectful attendant. He entered a splendid suite of apartments that seemed to be designed specially for him. He walked up to a long mirror with the ordinary instinct of his class, to pull his tie straight or to smooth his hair; and there he saw the frightful figure that he was—blood running down his face from where the bough had struck him, his hair standing out like yellow rags of rank grass, his clothes torn into long, wavering tatters. At once the whole enigma sprang up, simply as the question of how he had got there, and how he was to get out again. Exactly at the same moment a man in blue, who had been appointed as his valet, said very solemnly—

'I have put out your clothes, sir.'

'Clothes!' said Syme sardonically. 'I have no clothes except these,' and he lifted two long strips of his frock-coat in fascinating festoons, and made a movement as if to twirl like a ballet girl.

'My master asks me to say,' said the attendant, 'that there is a fancy dress ball to-night, and that he desires you to put on the costume that I have laid out. Meanwhile, sir, there is a bottle of Burgundy and some cold pheasant, which he hopes you will not refuse, as it is some hours before supper.'

'Cold pheasant is a good thing,' said Syme reflectively, 'and Burgundy is a spanking good thing. But really I do not want either of them so much as I want to know what the devil all this means, and what sort of costume you have got laid out for me. Where is it?'

The servant lifted off a kind of ottoman a long peacock-blue drapery, rather of the nature of a domino, on the front of which was emblazoned a large golden sun, and which was splashed here and there with flaming stars and crescents.

'You're to be dressed as Thursday, sir,' said the valet somewhat affably.

'Dressed as Thursday!' said Syme in meditation. 'It doesn't sound a warm costume.'

'Oh, yes, sir,' said the other eagerly, 'the Thursday costume is quite warm, sir. It fastens up to the chin.'

'Well, I don't understand anything,' said Syme, sighing. 'I have been used so long to uncomfortable adventures that comfortable adventures knock me out. Still, I may be allowed to ask why I should be particularly like Thursday in a green frock spotted all over with the sun and moon. Those orbs, I think, shine on other days. I once saw the moon on Tuesday, I remember.'

'Beg pardon, sir,' said the valet, 'Bible also provided for you,' and with a respectful and rigid finger he pointed out a passage in the first chapter of Genesis. Syme read it wondering. It was that in which the fourth day of the week is associated with the creation of the sun and moon. Here, however, they reckoned from a Christian Sunday.

'This is getting wilder and wilder,' said Syme, as he sat down in a chair. 'Who are these people who provide cold pheasant and Burgundy, and green clothes and Bibles? Do they provide everything?'

'Yes, sir, everything,' said the attendant gravely. 'Shall I help you on with your costume?'

'Oh, hitch the bally thing on!' said Syme impatiently.

But though he affected to despise the mummery, he felt a curious freedom and naturalness in his movements as the blue and gold garment fell about him; and when he found that he had to wear a sword, it stirred a boyish dream. As he passed out of the room he flung the folds across his shoulder with a gesture, his sword stood out at an angle, and he had all the swagger of a troubadour. For these disguises did not disguise, but reveal.

# XV

## THE ACCUSER

As Syme strode along the corridor he saw the Secretary standing at the top of a great flight of stairs. The man had never looked so noble. He was draped in a long robe of starless black, down the centre of which fell a band or broad stripe of pure white, like a single shaft of light. The whole looked like some very severe ecclesiastical vestment. There was no need for Syme to search his memory or the Bible in order to remember that the first day of creation marked the mere creation of light out of darkness. The vestment itself would alone have suggested the symbol; and Syme felt also how perfectly this pattern of pure white and black expressed the soul of the pale and austere Secretary, with his inhuman veracity and his cold frenzy, which made him so easily make war on the anarchists, and yet so easily pass for one of them. Syme was scarcely surprised to notice that, amid all the ease and hospitality of their new surroundings, this man's eyes were still stern. No smell of ale or orchards could make the Secretary cease to ask a reasonable question.

If Syme had been able to see himself, he would have realised that he, too, seemed to be for the first time himself and no one else. For if the Secretary stood for that philosopher who loves the original and formless light, Syme was a type of the poet who seeks always to make the light in special shapes, to split it up into sun and star. The philosopher may sometimes love the infinite; the poet always loves the finite. For him the great moment is not the creation of light, but the creation of the sun and moon.

As they descended the broad stairs together they overtook Ratcliffe, who was clad in spring green like a huntsman, and the pattern upon whose garment was a green tangle of trees. For he stood for that third day on which the earth and green things were made, and his square, sensible face, with its not unfriendly cynicism, seemed appropriate enough to it.

They were led out of another broad and low gateway into a very large old English garden, full of torches and bonfires, by the broken light of which a vast carnival of people were dancing in motley dress. Syme seemed to see every shape in Nature imitated in some crazy costume. There was a man dressed as a windmill with enormous sails, a man dressed as an elephant, a man dressed as a balloon; the two last, together, seemed to keep the thread of their farcical adventures. Syme even saw, with a queer thrill, one dancer dressed like an enormous hornbill, with a beak twice as big as himself—the queer bird which had fixed itself on his fancy like a living question while he was rushing down the long road at the Zoological Gardens. There were a thousand other such objects, however. There was a dancing lamp-post, a dancing apple tree, a dancing ship. One would have thought that the untamable tune of some mad musician had set all the common objects of field and street dancing an eternal jig. And long afterwards, when Syme was middle-aged and at rest, he could never see one of those particular objects— a lamp-post, or an apple tree, or a windmill—without thinking that it was a strayed reveller from that revel of masquerade.

On one side of this lawn, alive with dancers, was a sort of green bank, like the terrace in such old-fashioned gardens.

Along this, in a kind of crescent, stood seven great chairs, the thrones of the seven days. Gogol and Dr Bull were already in their seats; the Professor was just mounting to his. Gogol, or Tuesday, had his simplicity well symbolised by a dress designed upon the division of the waters, a dress that separated upon his forehead and fell to his feet, grey and silver, like a sheet of rain. The Professor, whose day was that on which the birds and fishes— the ruder forms of life—were created, had a dress of dim purple, over which sprawled goggle-eyed fishes and outrageous tropical birds, the union in him of unfathomable fancy and of doubt. Dr Bull, the last day of Creation, wore a coat covered with heraldic animals in red and gold, and on his crest a man rampant. He lay back in his chair with a broad smile, the picture of an optimist in his element.

One by one the wanderers ascended the bank and sat in their strange seats. As each of them sat down a roar of enthusiasm rose from the carnival, such as that with which crowds receive kings. Cups were clashed and torches shaken, and feathered hats flung in the air. The men for whom these thrones were reserved were men crowned with some extraordinary laurels. But the central chair was empty.

Syme was on the left hand of it and the Secretary on the right. The Secretary looked across the empty throne at Syme, and said, compressing his lips—

'We do not know yet that he is not dead in a field.'

Almost as Syme heard the words, he saw on the sea of human faces in front of him a frightful and beautiful alteration, as if heaven had opened behind his head. But Sunday had only passed silently along the front like a shadow, and had sat in the central seat. He was draped plainly, in a pure and terrible white, and his hair was like a silver flame on his forehead.

For a long time—it seemed for hours—that huge masquerade of mankind swayed and stamped in front of them to marching and exultant music. Every couple dancing seemed a separate romance; it might be a fairy dancing with a pillar-box, or a peasant girl dancing with the moon; but in each case it was, somehow, as absurd as Alice in Wonderland, yet as grave and kind as a love story. At last, however, the thick crowd began to thin itself. Couples strolled away into the garden-walks, or began to drift towards that end of the building where stood smoking, in huge pots like fish-kettles, some hot and scented mixtures of old ale or wine. Above all these, upon a sort of black framework on the roof of the house, roared in its iron basket a gigantic bonfire, which lit up the land for miles. It flung the homely effect of firelight over the face of vast forests of grey or brown, and it seemed to fill with warmth even the emptiness of upper night. Yet this also, after a time, was allowed to grow fainter; the dim groups gathered more and more round the great cauldrons, or passed, laughing and clattering, into the inner passages of that ancient house. Soon there were only some ten loiterers in the garden; soon only four. Finally the last stray merry-maker ran into the house whooping to his companions. The fire faded, and the slow, strong stars came out. And the seven strange men were left alone, like seven stone statues on their chairs of stone. Not one of them had spoken a word.

They seemed in no haste to do so, but heard in silence the hum of insects and the distant song of one bird. Then Sunday spoke, but so dreamily that he might have been continuing a conversation rather than beginning one.

'We will eat and drink later,' he said. 'Let us remain together a little, we who have loved each other so sadly, and have fought so long. I seem to remember only centuries of heroic war, in which you were always heroes— epic on epic, iliad on iliad, and you always brothers in arms. Whether it was but recently (for time is nothing), or at the beginning of the world, I sent you out to war. I sat in the darkness, where there is not any created thing, and to you I was only a voice commanding valour and an unnatural virtue. You heard the voice in the dark, and you never heard it again. The sun in heaven denied it, the earth and sky denied it, all human wisdom denied it. And when I met you in the daylight I denied it myself.'

Syme stirred sharply in his seat, but otherwise there was silence, and the incomprehensible went on.

'But you were men. You did not forget your secret honour, though the whole cosmos turned an engine of torture to tear it out of you. I knew how near you were to hell. I know how you, Thursday, crossed swords with King Satan, and how you, Wednesday, named me in the hour without hope.'

There was complete silence in the starlit garden, and then the black-browed Secretary, implacable, turned in his chair towards Sunday, and said in a harsh voice—

'Who and what are you?'

'I am the Sabbath,' said the other without moving. 'I am the peace of God.'

The Secretary started up, and stood crushing his costly robe in his hand.

'I know what you mean,' he cried, 'and it is exactly that that I cannot forgive you. I know you are contentment, optimism, what do they call the thing, an ultimate reconciliation. Well, I am not reconciled. If you were the man in the dark room, why were you also Sunday, an offence to the sunlight? If you were from the first our father and our friend, why were you also our greatest enemy? We wept, we fled in terror; the iron entered into our souls—and you are the peace of God! Oh, I can forgive God His anger, though it destroyed nations; but I cannot forgive Him His peace.'

Sunday answered not a word, but very slowly he turned his face of stone upon Syme as if asking a question.

'No,' said Syme, 'I do not feel fierce like that. I am grateful to you, not only for wine and hospitality here, but for many a fine scamper and free fight. But I should like to know. My soul and heart are as happy and quiet here as this old garden, but my reason is still crying out. I should like to know.'

Sunday looked at Ratcliffe, whose clear voice said—

'It seems so *silly* that you should have been on both sides and fought yourself.'

Bull said—

'I understand nothing, but I am happy. In fact, I am going to sleep.'

'I am not happy,' said the Professor with his head in his hands, 'because I do not understand. You let me stray a little too near to hell.'

And then Gogol said, with the absolute simplicity of a child—

'I wish I knew why I was hurt so much.'

Still Sunday said nothing, but only sat with his mighty chin upon his hand, and gazed at the distance. Then at last he said—

'I have heard your complaints in order. And here, I think, comes another to complain, and we will hear him also.'

The falling fire in the great cresset threw a last long gleam, like a bar of burning gold, across the dim grass. Against this fiery band was outlined in utter black the advancing legs of a black-clad figure. He seemed to have a fine close suit with knee-breeches such as that which was worn by the servants of the house, only that it was not blue, but of this absolute sable. He had, like the servants, a kind of sword by his side. It was only when he had come quite close to the crescent of the seven and flung up his face to look at them, that Syme saw, with thunder-struck clearness, that the face was the broad, almost ape-like face of his old friend Gregory, with its rank red hair and its insulting smile.

'Gregory!' gasped Syme, half-rising from his seat. 'Why, this is the real anarchist!'

'Yes,' said Gregory, with a great and dangerous restraint, 'I am the real anarchist.'

'"Now there was a day,"'murmured Bull, who seemed really to have fallen asleep, '"when the sons of God came to present themselves before the Lord, and Satan came also among them."'

'You are right,' said Gregory, and gazed all round. 'I am a destroyer. I would destroy the world if I could.'

A sense of a pathos far under the earth stirred up in Syme, and he spoke brokenly and without sequence.

'Oh, most unhappy man,' he cried, 'try to be happy! You have red hair like your sister.'

'My red hair, like red flames, shall burn up the world,' said Gregory. 'I thought I hated everything more than common men can hate anything; but I find that I do not hate everything so much as I hate you!'

'I never hated you,' said Syme very sadly.

Then out of this unintelligible creature the last thunders broke.

'You!' he cried. 'You never hated because you never lived. I know what you are all of you, from first to last—you are the people in power! You are the police—the great fat, smiling men in blue and buttons! You are the Law, and you have never been broken. But is there a free soul alive that does not long to break you, only because you have never been broken? We in revolt talk all kind of nonsense doubtless about this crime or that crime of the Government. It is all folly! The only crime of the Government is that it governs. The unpardonable sin of the supreme power is that it is supreme. I do not curse you for being cruel. I do not curse you (though I might) for being kind. I curse you for being safe! You sit in your chairs of stone, and have never come down from them. You are the seven angels of heaven, and you have had no troubles. Oh, I could forgive you everything, you that rule all mankind, if I could feel for once that you had suffered for one hour a real agony such as I——'

Syme sprang to his feet, shaking from head to foot.

'I see everything,' he cried, 'everything that there is. Why does each thing on the earth war against each other thing? Why does each small thing in the world have to fight against the world itself? Why does a fly have to fight the whole universe? Why does a dandelion have to fight the whole universe? For the same reason that I had to be alone in the dreadful Council of the Days. So that each thing that obeys law may have the glory and isolation of the anarchist. So that each man fighting for order may be as brave and good a man as the dynamiter. So that the real lie of Satan may be flung back in the face of this blasphemer, so that by tears and torture we may earn the right to say to this man, "You lie!" No agonies can be too great to buy the right to say to this accuser, "We also have suffered."

'It is not true that we have never been broken. We have been broken upon the wheel. It is not true that we have never descended from these thrones. We have descended into hell. We were complaining of unforgettable miseries even at the very moment when this man entered insolently to accuse us of happiness. I repel the slander; we have not been happy. I can answer for every one of the great guards of Law whom he has accused. At least——'

He had turned his eyes so as to see suddenly the great face of Sunday, which wore a strange smile.

'Have you,' he cried in a dreadful voice, 'have you ever suffered?'

As he gazed, the great face grew to an awful size, grew larger than the colossal mask of Memnon, which had made him scream as a child. It grew larger and larger, filling the whole sky; then everything went black. Only in the blackness before it entirely destroyed his brain he seemed to hear a distant voice saying a commonplace text that he had heard somewhere, 'Can ye drink of the cup that I drink of?'

*　　*　　*　　*　　*

When men in books awake from a vision, they commonly find themselves in some place in which they might have fallen asleep; they yawn in a chair, or lift themselves with bruised limbs from a field. Syme's experience was something much more psychologically strange if there was indeed anything unreal, in the earthly sense, about the things he had gone through. For while he could always remember afterwards that he had swooned before the face of Sunday, he could not remember having ever come to at all. He could only remember that gradually and naturally he knew that he was and had been walking along a country lane with an easy and conversational companion. That companion had been a part of his recent drama; it was the red-haired poet Gregory. They were walking like old friends, and were in the middle of a conversation about some triviality. But Syme could only feel an unnatural buoyancy in his body and a crystal simplicity in his mind that seemed to be superior to everything that he said or did. He felt he was in possession of some impossible good news, which made every other thing a triviality, but an adorable triviality.

Dawn was breaking over everything in colours at once clear and timid; as if Nature made a first attempt at yellow and a first attempt at rose. A breeze blew so clean and sweet, that one could not think that it blew from the sky; it blew rather through some hole in the sky. Syme felt a simple surprise when he saw rising all round him on both sides of the road the red, irregular buildings of Saffron Park. He had no idea that he had walked so near London. He walked by instinct along one white road, on which early birds hopped and sang, and found himself outside a fenced garden. There he saw the sister of Gregory, the girl with the gold-red hair, cutting lilac before breakfast, with the great unconscious gravity of a girl.

THE END

# The Voice of Shelley

I have recently been remonstrated with upon two points—first, that I called Nero an artist; and second, that I called Shelley a typical aristocrat. The first query is somewhat easily answered. I called Nero an artist because he was an artist. He loved art in every form all his life, and his last words were a poetical quotation. If he fiddled while Rome was burning, he thought quite as much of the fiddle as he did of the fire. And if he thought a great deal of the fire, it was from the simple, and from his point of view unanswerable, reason that a fire is a very artistic thing. Mr Max Beerbohm in one of his most delightful and absurd essays has denounced the fire brigade as a band of vandals who destroy a 'fair thing'. He has threatened to start an opposition fire brigade whose pipes shall be filled not with water but with oil. Nero was only Max made serious; Nero was only Max without his good nature; Nero was only Max in action.

But the aim I had in mentioning him is very simple. A defender of undenominationalism spoke of giving his hand to every man who was working for his highest, thereby implying, as it seemed to me, that if a man put something or other highest it did not in practice matter very much what it was. To this I replied that it seemed to me a very awful and urgent matter whether a man put the right thing or the wrong thing highest; that to put the right thing highest was very difficult, and to put the wrong thing very deadly. A salient example of this is the pursuit of mere art or beauty. The moment a man puts beauty higher than love Nero becomes a logical possibility.

The other matter, it may be, is less obvious, but not, I think, less true. When I call Shelley a typical aristocrat, I have fully in remembrance all his revolutionary ardour and his almost anarchic ideality; I do not call Shelley an aristocrat in spite of these things; I call him an aristocrat because of them. The true aristocrat is by nature an anarchist. The aristocrat was and is the person desiring to do as he liked. His castle was a defiance of the decent orders of the king. His motor-car was a defiance of the decent orders of the

*Daily News*, 1905. Collected in The Apostle and the Wild Ducks, 1975

democracy. The gentlemen of real history were never anything but rowdy. They were admired for being rowdy. They were hanged for being rowdy. They are no longer hanged which seems to me to mark a considerable falling-off in the fullness of the control of the democracy. They are still admired.

Now all this patrician rebelliousness seems to me to have been built into the blood and bone of Shelley, as into the blood and bone of Byron. It was the subconscious foundation upon which he erected his republican idealism. Shelley loved liberty as all aristocrats love liberty. Shelley hated kings as all aristocrats hated kings; the feud between them has flamed since the beginning of the world. Shelley hated priests, and hated them most of all; for priests represent a startling and supernatural denial of the gradations of mankind; an aristocracy can submit to a king or humour a democracy, but another aristocracy is too much for them. Of course, Shelley, a man of quite crystalline sincerity, did not know that his anarchism had this feudal foundation; he imagined, I have no doubt, that he was a veritable voice of the people. His voice is the voice of liberty, it is the voice of beauty, it is the voice of change, and even the voice of revolution, but whatever it is it is never the voice of the people. There is not enough pain in it, and there is not enough laughter. There is not enough of that clean thing which Shelley and many other fine gentlemen would call coarseness. Shelley was idealistic; he was lyric; he was a hundred things, but there were two things that he never was. He was never comic and he was never tragic. Everything that comes out of the common heart, the heart of the real people, is comic and tragic.

There are only two kinds of ballads, recurrent and permanent, coming from the community itself. There are sad ballads about broken hearts and cheerful ballads about broken heads. There is not a trace of this popular quality in Shelley anywhere. It is not necessary, however, in order to indicate this truth to compare Shelley with any folk literature of other times or places. We can compare him with another poet, another democratic idealist, another man moved by the French Revolution, living almost in Shelley's time, and almost in Shelley's country, a man who differed from Shelley in nothing except that he was really a man of the people. To think of him after Shelley is like swallowing fire after swallowing water. It is not so easy to get out of one's mouth the stinging taste of the sweetness and bitterness of Burns.

Shelley never came to that queer common place where grand passion meets the grotesque; where the cross is a sublime gibbet and the gibbet a caricature of the cross. That is the first and best reason why he was never of the people. But there were other reasons as well. One wholly non-popular element in him was his anarchism. The poor are not anarchists, and never can be anarchists. They live too close to life for such artistic trifling. When I speak of anarchism, of course I do not use the term in the exact sense which indicates a political programme. I do not mean that Shelley disapproved of all government though he sometimes used phrases which might be taken in this sense. But his trend and tone was to offer liberty and an escape from rule as a panacea for the misfortunes of the people; and this is not a genuine popular trend or tone. The people know that life cannot be conducted without rules. The people is the maker and keeper of all custom, tradition and convention, just as it is the maker and (except, perhaps, in modern England) the keeper of all religion. Shelley never understood any of these deep tides in the *profanum vulgus*. And with all his many princely virtues I do not think I am doing him any injustice if I say that he never tried to understand them.

# A Theory of Tyrants

I have come to be convinced of late of a certain theory of the nature of tyranny. It may be right or wrong, but I think it is at least worthy of thought in connection with a highly interesting matter. Broadly speaking, the common theory of tyranny has been this: That men have groaned under some system for centuries, and have at last rebelled against it. But I think that men have actually done quite otherwise; they have rebelled against the system against which they have not groaned. But the matter is so mixed and also so acute that I may be permitted to state it in a more explanatory manner.

Let us take, for the sake of argument, the two risings against tyranny most commonly considered in current literature—the English rebellion of the early seventeenth century and the French Revolution. According to the common theory, Charles I should have been the heir of at least twenty intolerable despots. The truth is that he was the heir of one tolerable despot (who had not quite effected despotism), and beyond that everything was different. Queen Elizabeth was not tolerable, and she was not tolerated. In so far as she was endured she was adored. Cavaliers and Puritans alike looked back to her reign (most mistakenly, doubtless, but most certainly) as a midsummer of popular monarchy.

In short the English Puritans did not rebel against an old system; whatever else it was it was not old. Even if Charles I had been a much worse king than he was there would not have been enough time for him to have created a complete and cruel tradition against the tradition of Elizabeth. A few years before Charles's head was cut off, most Englishmen would have died to keep Elizabeth's on. If you turn to the case of the French Monarchy before the French Revolution you will find exactly the same thing. A very short time before the Revolution the French Monarchy was the generally accepted French symbol. The King before Louis the Guillotined was Louis the Well-Beloved. The Monarchy (in France as in England) became the most unpopular thing very soon after it had been the most popular thing. There

*Daily News*, 1908. Collected in The Apostle and the Wild Ducks, 1975

was no weakness, there was no long decline: the defeat of the thing followed swiftly on its first victory. Charles I was not the last of the English despots. He was one of the first of the English despots—only there happened to have been no more of them. Encouraged by the arrogance and popularity of Elizabeth, who had stood for patriotism and Protestantism and the defiance of Spain, Charles tried to work with Elizabethan England and found that Elizabethan England was not there. It was not too old to last, it was too new to last. Louis XVI was not the last of a line of unpopular kings. On the contrary, he was the first of a line of popular kings to be unpopular.

I can only explain all this by my private theory of tyrants; which is this. Men do not rebel against the old; rather they rebel against the new. They turn upon something when they find that it has them in a trap. They do not revolt against something that has been unpopular. They revolt (and very rightly) against something that has been popular. They hated Charles I because they had loved Elizabeth. They killed Louis XVI because they had been killed for Louis XIV. In fact, this is probably what is meant by that seemingly meaningless phrase, the fickleness of the mob. It probably means that the mob is quicker than other people in discovering that man has walked into a man-trap. England went mad with joy for the English Monarchy, because the Armada had not conquered England. And then England suddenly went mad with rage because it discovered that (during that exciting interlude) the English Monarchy had conquered England. We had escaped the snare of Philip; we walked into the snare of Elizabeth; we broke out of the snare of Charles I.

This is the essential mark of tyranny: that it is always new. Tyranny always enters by the unguarded gate. The tyrant is always shy and unobtrusive. The tyrant is always a traitor. He has always come there on the pretence that he was protecting something which people really wanted protected—religion, or public justice, or patriotic glory. Men staring at the Armada did not watch the King; so they strengthened the King. Later when they watched the King they unconsciously strengthened the aristocracy. Again, when they attacked the aristocracy, they did not watch the big merchants who were attacking it—and who wanted watching. All tyrannies are new tyrannies. There are no such things really as old tyrannies; there are hardly any such things as old superstitions.

There is one moral to these evident facts of history. When you look for tyrants, do not look for them among the obvious types that have oppressed men in the past—the King, the priest, or the soldier. If you do, you are merely looking at the Spanish Armada while England is being turned into a despotism behind your back. Monarchy was once a popular organ; yet it was turned against the people. Remember that newspapers are popular organs that may be turned against the people. Whatever the new tyrant is, he will not wear the exact uniform of the old tyrant.

# Tommy and the Traditions

A little while ago I was trying to convince the writers and readers of an excellent Socialist paper that the democracy was very decent after all. I did not succeed. The Socialist writers and readers were really delightful, and even playful people; but they could not swallow such a paradox as the statement that the poor are really right and the rich really wrong. In those quarters (in consequence) there has ever since been a disposition to connect my name with gin, a drink which I dislike, and with wife-beating, a pastime for which I lack the adequate energy. I have often wondered whether it would be worth while to try and explain again why I think that the poor are really quite right; and I was suddenly precipitated into the enterprise this morning. The impulse was only this— that as I walked past a dreary row of dwellings I heard a slatternly woman say to a very big child, 'Now, Tommy, run away and play.' She did not say it brutally, but with a hearty and healthy impatience, such as is natural to her sex.

I want to make one more attempt to revive the dead tradition of democracy by discussing what was involved in that remark. First, we must get it into our heads that a thing can be a superstition and still be true. Ten thousand people may recite a thing as a lie, and it may still be a truth, in spite of their saying it. Thus Liberalism is true; but many Liberals are mere myths. Christianity can be believed; but some Christians are quite incredible. A hypocrite can hand on a truth. The Whigs of the early eighteenth century handed on the theory of liberty and self-government, though there was practically not one of them who was not a dirty courtier and a corrupt tyrant. The fashionable French priests of the later eighteenth century handed on the tradition of Catholicism, though there was hardly one of them who was not an atheist. But when democracy came, it was glad the Whigs had kept the tradition of Algernon Sydney. When the Catholic revival came, it was glad the French clergy had kept the tradition of St Louis. Therefore, when I say that the poor have the right tradition I do not mean necessarily that they are

*Daily News*, 1908. Collected in Lunacy and Letters, 1958

going on in exactly the right way. I do not even mean that they think they are going on in the right way. As a matter of fact, they don't. The great difficulty is to persuade the poor that they are as right as they are.

I mean that just as there was an important truth in the Whig Parliaments even when they were corrupt, just as there was an important truth in the Christian religion even when the Christians did not think so, so there is a truth which the poor possess in their misery and confusion, which we do not possess in our largest schemes of social reform. The point is not that they have gone specially right; but that they have stayed tolerably right while we have gone specially wrong.

I have often urged instances of this. For the sake of clearness I will repeat one of them only. The very poor are always despised and rebuked because of their fuss and expenditure on funerals. Only to-day I saw that a public body refused aid to those who had gone any length in such expenditure. Now I do not mean that their crape is my abstract conception of robes of mourning, or that the conversation of Mrs Brown with Mrs Jones over the coffin has the dignity of 'Lycidas'. I do not even say that educated people could not do it better. I say that they are not trying to do it at all. Educated people have got some chilly fad to the effect that making a fuss about death is morbid or vulgar. The educated people are entirely wrong on the fundamental point of human psychology. The uneducated people are entirely right on the point.

The one way to make bereavement tolerable is to make it important. To gather your friends, to have a gloomy festival, to talk, to cry, to praise the dead—all that does change the atmosphere, and carry human nature over the open grave. The nameless torture is to try and treat it as something private and casual, as our elegant stoics do. That is at once pride and pain and hypocrisy. The only way to make less of death is to make more of it. The poor have this blind tradition, and will not be torn away from it. They do it in a bad social system; they do it in a bad way; but they have all humanity behind them, and in the noise and heat of their houses of mourning is the smoke of the baked meats of Hamlet and the dust and echo of the funeral games of Patroclus.

Now take a more cheerful instance: the poor have, in practice, a certain view of work and play. And it is the right view; the root view of all mankind. I do not mean that their work and play are better; they are not. They do not play specially well; and they work as little as they can, and so should I in their shoes. What they have got right is the philosophy; the original principle of the thing. They differ from us and from the aristocracy (pardon the distinction) simply in this: that their work is work and their play is play. Work is doing what you do not like; play is doing what you like. The whole point of work is law; the whole point of play is liberty. There should be hours of labour, and they should be laborious; there should be hours of freedom, and they should be free.

That sounds simple enough: but the educated classes cannot understand it. The educationalists cannot understand it. The public schools cannot understand it. The whole English upper class is built on the negation of it. A gentleman is taught to treat half his work as play (diplomacy, Parliament, finance), and then to treat more than half his play as work, by training for matches and bursting blood vessels in a race. He is taught to play at politics and work at cricket. At the English schools (as Mr Maurice Baring sketched very cleverly in an article), a game has practically ceased to be a game; it has become a specially dull lesson, where boys are bored by having to look interested. But the athletic school is not alone to blame; the intellectual educationalists are quite as bad. They want to make children's play significant and instructive. They arrange children in Pre-Raphaelite patterns. They make them dance ethically or yell aesthetically. They want to follow children when they play, and make their games useful. They might as well follow them when they sleep, and make their dreams useful. Play is a rest, like sleep.

The woman who said 'Run away and play' to Tommy on the doorstep was the weary guardian of an eternal commonsense. Probably Tommy had a bad time sometimes; probably she made him work; but at least she did not make him play. She let him play. He fed on loneliness and liberty. That hour of play at least was not Froebel's contribution or Dr Arnold's contribution to Tommy. That hour was Tommy's contribution to Tommy. I do not know whether I have succeeded, or ever shall succeed, in conveying what I mean about these people, and how they hold a battered shape of truth, while we hold perfected forms of error. But at least my work for this Friday evening is done. I shall run away and play.

# Oscar Wilde

The time has certainly come when this extraordinary man, Oscar Wilde, may be considered merely as a man of letters. He sometimes pretended that art was more important than morality, but that was mere play-acting. Morality or immorality was more important than art to him and everyone else. But the very cloud of tragedy that rested on his career makes it easier to treat him as a mere artist now. His was a complete life, in that awful sense in which your life and mine are incomplete; since we have not yet paid for our sins. In that sense one might call it a perfect life, as one speaks of a perfect equation; it cancels out. On the one hand we have the healthy horror of the evil; on the other the healthy horror of the punishment. We have it all the more because both sin and punishment were highly civilized; that is, nameless and secret. Some have said that Wilde was sacrificed; let it be enough for us to insist on the literal meaning of the word. Any ox that is really sacrificed is made sacred.

But the very fact that monstrous wrong and monstrous revenge cancel each other actually does leave this individual artist in that very airy detachment which he professed to desire. We can really consider him solely as a man of letters.

About Oscar Wilde, as about other wits, Disraeli or Bernard Shaw, men wage a war of words, some calling him a great artist and others a mere charlatan. But this controversy misses the really extraordinary thing about Wilde: the thing that appears rather in the plays than the poems. He was a great artist. He also was really a charlatan. I mean by a charlatan one sufficiently dignified to despise the tricks that he employs. A vulgar demagogue is not a charlatan; he is as coarse as his crowd. He may be lying in every word, but he is sincere in his style. Style (as Wilde might have said) is only another name for spirit. Again, a man like Mr Bernard Shaw is not a charlatan. I can understand people thinking his remarks hurried or shallow or senselessly perverse, or blasphemous, or merely narrow. But I cannot

*Daily News*, 1909. Collected in A Handful of Authors, 1953

understand anyone failing to feel that Mr Shaw is being as suggestive as he can, is giving his brightest and boldest speculations to the rabble, is offering something which he honestly thinks valuable. Now Wilde often uttered remarks which he must have known to be literally valueless. Shaw may be high or low, but he never talks down to the audience. Wilde did talk down, sometimes very far down.

Wilde and his school professed to stand as solitary artistic souls apart from the public. They professed to scorn the middle class, and declared that the artist must not work for the bourgeois. The truth is that no artist so really great ever worked so much for the bourgeois as Oscar Wilde. No man, so capable of thinking about truth and beauty, ever thought so constantly about his own effect on the middle classes. He studied them with exquisite attention, and knew exactly how to shock and how to please them. Mr Shaw often gets above them in seraphic indignation, and often below them in sterile and materialistic explanations. He disgusts them with new truths or he bores them with old truths; but they are always living truths to Bernard Shaw. Wilde knew how to say the precise thing which, whether true or false, is irresistible. As, for example, 'I can resist everything but temptation.'

But he sometimes sank lower. One might go through his swift and sparkling plays with a red and blue pencil marking two kinds of epigrams; the real epigram which he wrote to please his own wild intellect, and the sham epigram which he wrote to thrill the very tamest part of our tame civilization. This is what I mean by saying that he was strictly a charlatan—among other things. He descended below himself to be on top of others. He became purposely stupider than Oscar Wilde that he might seem cleverer than the nearest curate. He lowered himself to superiority; he stooped to conquer.

One might easily take examples of the phrase meant to lightly touch the truth and the phrase meant only to bluff the bourgeoisie. For instance, in *A Woman of No Importance*, he makes his chief philosopher say that all thought is immoral, being essentially destructive; 'Nothing survives being thought of.' That is nonsense, but nonsense of the nobler sort; there is an idea in it. It is, like most professedly modern ideas, a death-dealing idea not a life-giving one; but it is an idea. There is truly a sense in which all definition is deletion. Turn a few pages of the same play and you will find somebody asking, 'What is an immoral woman?' The philosopher answers, 'The kind of woman a man never gets tired of.' Now that is not nonsense, but rather rubbish. It is without value of any sort or kind. It is not symbolically true; it is not fantastically true; it is not true at all.

Anyone with the mildest knowledge of the world knows that nobody can be such a consuming bore as a certain kind of immoral woman. That vice never tires men might be a tenable and entertaining lie; that the individual instrument of vice never tires them is not, even as a lie, tenable enough to be entertaining. Here the great wit was playing the cheap dandy to the in-credibly innocent; as much as if he had put on paper cuffs and collars. He is simply shocking a tame curate; and he must be rather a specially tame curate even to be shocked. This irritating duplication of real brilliancy with snob-bish bluff runs through all his three comedies. 'Life is much too important to be taken seriously'; that is the true humorist. 'A well-tied tie is the first serious step in life'; that is the charlatan. 'Man can believe the impossible, but man can never believe the improbable'; that is said by a fine philosopher. 'Nothing is so fatal to a personality as the keeping of promises, unless it be telling the truth'; that is said by a tired quack. 'A man can be happy with any woman so long as he does not love her'; that is wild truth. 'Good intentions are invariably ungrammatical'; that is tame trash.

But while he had a strain of humbug in him, which there is not in the demagogues of wit like Bernard Shaw, he had, in his own strange way, a much deeper and more spiritual nature than they. Queerly enough, it was the very multitude of his falsities that prevented him from being entirely false. Like a many-coloured humming top, he was at once a bewilderment and a balance. He was so fond of being many-sided that among his sides he even admitted the right side. He loved so much to multiply his souls that he had among them one soul at least that was saved. He desired all beautiful things—even God.

His frightful fallacy was that he would not see that there is reason in everything, even in religion and morality. Universality is a contradiction in terms. You cannot be everything if you are anything. If you wish to be white all over, you must austerely resist the temptation to have green spots or yellow stripes. If you wish to be good all over, you must resist the spots of sin or the stripes of servitude. It may be great fun to be many-sided; but however many sides one has there cannot be one of them which is complete and rounded innocence. A polygon can have an infinite number of sides; but no one of its sides can be a circle.

GKC

# The Ethics of Elfland

When the businessman rebukes the idealism of his office-boy, it is commonly in some such speech as this: 'Ah, yes, when one is young, one has these ideals in the abstract and these castles in the air; but in middle age they all break up like clouds, and one comes down to a belief in practical politics, to using the machinery one has and getting on with the world as it is.' Thus, at least, venerable and philanthropic old men now in their honoured graves used to talk to me when I was a boy. But since then I have grown up and have discovered that these philanthropic old men were telling lies. What has really happened is exactly the opposite of what they said would happen. They said that I should lose my ideals and begin to believe in the methods of practical politicians. Now, I have not lost my ideals in the least; my faith in fundamentals is exactly what it always was. What I have lost is my old childlike faith in practical politics. I am still as much concerned as ever about the Battle of Armageddon; but I am not so much concerned about the General Election. As a babe I leapt up on my mother's knee at the mere mention of it. No; the vision is always solid and reliable. The vision is always a fact. It is the reality that is often a fraud. As much as I ever did, more than I ever did, I believe in Liberalism. But there was a rosy time of innocence when I believed in Liberals.

I take this instance of one of the enduring faiths because, having now to trace the roots of my personal speculation, this may be counted, I think, as the only positive bias. I was brought up a Liberal, and have always believed in democracy, in the elementary liberal doctrine of a self-governing humanity. If any one finds the phrase vague or threadbare, I can only pause for a moment to explain that the principle of democracy, as I mean it, can be stated in two propositions. The first is this: that the things common to all men are more important than the things peculiar to any men. Ordinary things are more valuable than extraordinary things; nay, they are more extraordinary. Man is something more awful than men; something more strange. The sense of the miracle of humanity itself

Orthodoxy, 1908

should be always more vivid to us than any marvels of power, intellect, art or civilization. The mere man on two legs, as such, should be felt as something more heart-breaking than any music and more startling than any caricature. Death is more tragic even than death by starvation. Having a nose is more comic even than having a Norman nose.

This is the first principle of democracy: that the essential things in men are the things they hold in common, not the things they hold separately. And the second principle is merely this: that the political instinct or desire is one of these things which they hold in common. Falling in love is more poetical than dropping into poetry. The democratic contention is that government (helping to rule the tribe) is a thing like falling in love, and not a thing like dropping into poetry. It is not something analogous to playing the church organ, painting on vellum, discovering the North Pole (that insidious habit), looping the loop, being Astronomer Royal and so on. For these things we do not wish a man to do at all unless he does them well. It is, on the contrary, a thing analogous to writing one's own love-letters or blowing one's own nose. These things we want a man to do for himself, even if he does them badly. I am not here arguing the truth of any of these conceptions; I know that some moderns are asking to have their wives chosen by scientists, and they may soon be asking, for all I know, to have their noses blown by nurses. I merely say that mankind does recognize these universal human functions, and that democracy classes government among them. In short, the democratic faith is this: that the most terribly important things must be left to ordinary men themselves—the mating of the sexes, the rearing of the young, the laws of the state. This is democracy; and in this I have always believed.

But there is one thing that I have never from my youth up been able to understand. I have never been able to understand where people got the idea that democracy was in some way opposed to tradition. It is obvious that tradition is only democracy extended through time. It is trusting to a consensus of common human voices rather than to some isolated or arbitrary record. The man who quotes some German historian against the tradition of the Catholic Church, for instance, is strictly appealing to aristocracy. He is appealing to the superiority of one expert against the awful authority of a mob. It is quite easy to see why a legend is treated, and ought to be treated, more respectfully than a book of history. The legend is generally made by the majority of people in the village, who are sane. The book is generally written by the one man in the village who is mad. Those who urge against tradition that men in the past were ignorant may go and urge it at the Carlton Club, along with the statement that voters in the slums are ignorant. It will not do for us. If we attach great importance to the opinion of ordinary men in great unanimity when we are dealing with daily matters, there is no reason why we should disregard it when we are dealing with history or fable.

Tradition may be defined as an extension of the franchise. Tradition means giving votes to the most obscure of all classes, our ancestors. It is the democracy of the dead. Tradition refuses to submit to the small and arrogant oligarchy of those who merely happen to be walking about. All democrats object to men being disqualified by the accident of birth; tradition objects to their being disqualified by the accident of death. Democracy tells us not to neglect a good man's opinion, even if he is our groom; tradition asks us not to neglect a good man's opinion, even if he is our father. I, at any rate, cannot separate the two ideas of democracy and tradition; it seems evident to me that they are the same idea. We will have the dead at our councils. The ancient Greeks voted by stones; these shall vote by tombstones. It is all quite regular and official, for most tombstones, like most ballot papers, are marked with a cross.

I have first to say, therefore, that if I have had a bias, it was always a bias in favour of democracy, and therefore of tradition. Before we come to any theoretic or logical beginnings I am content to allow for that personal equation; I have always been more inclined to believe the ruck of hard-working people than to believe that special and troublesome literary class to which I belong. I prefer even the fancies and prejudices of the people who see life from the inside to the clearest demonstrations of the people who see life from the outside. I would always trust the old wives' fables against the old maids' facts. As long as wit is mother wit it can be as wild as it pleases.

Now, I have to put together a general position, and I pretend to no training in such things. I propose to do it, therefore, by writing down one after another the three or four fundamental ideas which I have found for myself, pretty much in the way that I found them. Then I shall roughly synthesise them, summing up my personal philosophy or natural religion; then I shall describe my startling discovery that the whole thing had been discovered before. It had been discovered by Christianity. But of these profound persuasions which I have to recount in order, the earliest was concerned with this element of popular tradition. And without the foregoing explanation touching tradition and democracy I could hardly make my mental experience clear. As it is, I do not know whether I can make it clear, but I now propose to try.

My first and last philosophy, that which I believe in with unbroken certainty, I learnt in the nursery. I generally learnt it from a nurse; that is, from the solemn and star-appointed priestess at once of democracy and tradition. The things I believed most then, the things I believe most now, are the things called fairy tales. They seem to me to be the entirely reasonable things. They are not fantasies: compared with them other things are fantastic. Compared with them religion and rationalism are both abnormal, though religion is abnormally right and rationalism abnormally wrong.

Fairyland is nothing but the sunny country of common sense. It is not earth that judges heaven, but heaven that judges earth; so for me at least it was not earth that criticised elfland, but elfland that criticised the earth. I knew the magic beanstalk before I had tasted beans; I was sure of the Man in the Moon before I was certain of the moon. This was at one with all popular tradition. Modern minor poets are naturalists, and talk about the bush or the brook; but the singers of the old epics and fables were supernaturalists, and talked about the gods of brook and bush. That is what the moderns mean when they say that the ancients did not 'appreciate Nature,' because they said that Nature was divine. Old nurses do not tell children about the grass, but about the fairies that dance on the grass; and the old Greeks could not see the trees for the dryads.

But I deal here with what ethic and philosophy come from being fed on fairy tales. If I were describing them in detail I could note many noble and healthy principles that arise from them. There is the chivalrous lesson of 'Jack the Giant Killer'; that giants should be killed because they are gigantic. It is a manly mutiny against pride as such. For the rebel is older than all the kingdoms, and the Jacobin has more tradition than the Jacobite. There is the lesson of 'Cinderella', which is the same as that of the Magnificat—*exaltavit humiles*. There is the great lesson of 'Beauty and the Beast'; that a thing must be loved *before* it is loveable. There is the terrible allegory of the 'Sleeping Beauty', which tells how the human creature was blessed with all birthday gifts, yet cursed with death; and how death also may perhaps be softened to a sleep. But I am not concerned with any of the separate statutes of elfland, but with the whole spirit of its law, which I learnt before I could speak, and shall retain when I cannot write. I am concerned with a certain way of looking at life, which was created in me by the fairy tales, but has since been meekly ratified by the mere facts.

It might be stated this way. There are certain sequences or developments (cases of one thing following another), which are, in the true sense of the word, reasonable. They are, in the true sense of the word, necessary. Such are mathematical and merely logical sequences. We in fairyland (who are the most reasonable of all creatures) admit that reason and that necessity. For instance, if the Ugly Sisters are older than Cinderella, it is (in an iron and awful sense) *necessary* that Cinderella is younger than the Ugly Sisters. There is no getting out of it. Haeckel may talk as much fatalism about that fact as he pleases: it really must be. If Jack is the son of a miller, a miller is the father of Jack. Cold reason decrees it from her awful throne: and we in fairyland submit. If the three brothers all ride horses, there are six animals and eighteen legs involved: that is true rationalism, and fairyland is full of it. But as I put my head over the hedge of the elves and began to take notice of the natural world, I observed an extraordinary thing. I observed that learned men in spectacles were talking of the actual things that happened—dawn and death and so on—as if *they* were rational and inevitable. They talked as if the fact that trees bear fruit were just as *necessary* as the fact that two and one trees make three. But it is not. There is an enormous difference by the test of fairyland; which is the test of the imagination. You cannot *imagine* two and one not making three. But you can easily imagine trees not growing fruit; you can imagine them growing golden candlesticks or tigers hanging on by the tail. These men in spectacles spoke much of a man named Newton, who was hit by an apple, and who discovered a law. But they could not be got to see the distinction between a true law, a law of reason, and the mere fact of apples falling. If the apple hit Newton's nose, Newton's nose hit the apple. That is a true necessity: because we cannot conceive the one occurring without the other. But we can quite well conceive the apple not falling on his nose; we can fancy it flying ardently through the air to hit some other nose, of which it had a more definite dislike. We have always in our fairy tales kept this sharp distinction between the science of mental relations, in which there really are laws, and the science of physical facts, in which there are no laws, but only weird repetitions. We believe in bodily miracles, but not in mental impossibilities. We believe that a Bean-stalk climbed up to Heaven; but that does not at all confuse our convictions on the philosophical question of how many beans make five.

Here is the peculiar perfection of tone and truth in the nursery tales. The man of science says, 'Cut the stalk, and the apple will fall'; but he says it calmly, as if the one idea really led up to the other. The witch in the fairy tale says, 'Blow the horn, and the ogre's castle will fall'; but she does not say it as if it were something in which the effect obviously arose out of the cause. Doubtless she has given the advice to many champions, and has seen many castles fall, but she does not lose either her wonder or her reason. She does not muddle her head until it imagines a necessary mental connection between a horn and a falling tower. But the scientific men do muddle their heads, until they imagine a necessary mental connection between an apple leaving the tree and an apple reaching the ground. They do really talk as if they had found not only a set of marvellous facts, but a truth connecting those facts. They do talk as if the connection of two strange things physically connected them philosophically. They feel that because one incomprehensible thing constantly follows another incomprehensible thing the two together somehow make up a comprehensible thing. Two black riddles make a white answer.

In fairyland we avoid the word 'law'; but in the land of science they are singularly fond of it. Thus they will call some interesting conjecture about how forgotten folks pronounced the alphabet, Grimm's Law. But Grimm's Law is far less intellectual than Grimm's Fairy Tales. The tales are, at any rate, certainly tales; while the law is not a law. A law implies that we know the nature of the generalisation and enactment; not merely that we have noticed some of the effects. If there is a law that pick-pockets shall go to prison, it implies that there is an imaginable mental connection between the idea of prison and the idea of picking pockets. And we know what the idea is. We can say why we take liberty from a man who takes liberties. But we cannot say why an egg can turn into a chicken any more than we can say why a bear could turn into a fairy prince. As *ideas*, the egg and the chicken are further off each other than the bear and the prince; for no egg in itself suggests a chicken, whereas some princes do suggest bears. Granted, then, that certain transformations do happen, it is essential that we should regard them in the philosophic manner of fairy tales, not in the unphilosophic manner of science and the 'Laws of Nature'. When we are asked why eggs turn to birds or fruits fall in autumn, we must answer exactly as the fairy godmother would answer if Cinderella asked her why mice turned to horses or her clothes fell from her at twelve o'clock. We must answer that it is *magic*. It is not a 'law', for we do not understand its general formula. It is not a necessity, for though we can count on it happening practically, we have no right to say that it must always happen. It is no argument for unalterable law (as Huxley fancied) that we count on the ordinary course of things. We do not count on it; we bet on it. We risk the remote possibility of a miracle as we do that of a poisoned pancake or a world-destroying comet. We leave it out of account, not because it is a miracle, and therefore an impossibility, but because it is a miracle, and therefore an exception. All the terms used in the science books, 'law', 'necessity', 'order', 'tendency' and so on, are really unintellectual, because they assume an inner synthesis which we do not possess. The only words that ever satisfied me as describing Nature are the terms used in the fairy books, 'charm', 'spell', 'enchantment'. They express the arbitrariness of the fact and its mystery. A tree grows fruit because it is a *magic* tree. Water runs downhill because it is bewitched. The sun shines because it is bewitched.

I deny altogether that this is fantastic or even mystical. We may have some mysticism later on; but this fairy-tale language about things is simply rational and agnostic. It is the only way I can express in words my clear and definite perception that one thing is quite distinct from another; that there is no logical connection between flying and laying eggs. It is the man who talks about 'a law' that he has never seen who is the mystic. Nay, the ordinary scientific man is strictly a sentimentalist. He is a sentimentalist in this essential sense, that he is soaked and swept away by mere associations. He has so often seen birds fly and lay eggs that he feels as if there must be some dreamy, tender connection between the two ideas, whereas there is none. A forlorn lover might be unable to dissociate the moon from lost love; so the materialist is unable to dissociate the moon from the tide. In both cases there is no connection, except that one has seen them together. A sentimentalist might shed tears at the smell of apple-blossom, because, by a dark association of his own, it reminded him of his boyhood. So the materialist professor (though he conceals his tears) is yet a sentimentalist, because, by a dark association of his own, apple-blossoms remind him of apples. But the cool rationalist from fairyland does not see why, in the abstract, the apple tree should not grow crimson tulips; it sometimes does in his country.

This elementary wonder, however, is not a mere fancy derived from the fairy tales; on the contrary, all the fire of the fairy tales is derived from this. Just as we all like love tales because there is an instinct of sex, we all like astonishing tales because they touch the nerve of the ancient instinct of astonishment. This is proved by the fact that when we are very young children we do not need fairy tales: we only need tales. Mere life is interesting enough. A child of seven is excited by being told that Tommy opened a door and saw a dragon. But a child of three is excited by being told that Tommy opened a door. Boys like romantic tales; but babies like realistic tales—because they find them romantic. In fact, a baby is about the only person, I should think, to whom a modern realistic novel could be read without boring him. This proves that even nursery tales only echo an almost pre-natal leap of interest and amazement. These tales say that apples were golden only to refresh the forgotten moment when we found that they were green. They make rivers run with wine only to make us remember, for one wild moment, that they run with water. I have said that this is wholly reasonable and even agnostic. And, indeed, on this point I am all for the higher agnosticism; its better name is Ignorance. We have all read in scientific books, and, indeed, in all romances, the story of the man who has forgotten his name. This man walks about the streets and can see and appreciate everything; only he cannot remember who he is. Well, every man is that man in the story. Every man has forgotten who he is. One may understand the cosmos, but never the ego; the self is more distant than any star. Thou shalt love the Lord thy God; but thou shalt not know thyself. We are all under the same mental calamity; we have all forgotten our names. We have all forgotten what we really are. All that we call common sense and rationality and practicality and positivism only means that for certain dead levels of our life we forget that we have forgotten. All that we call spirit and art and ecstacy only means that for one awful instant we remember that we forget.

But though (like the man without memory in the novel) we walk the streets with a sort of half-witted admiration, still it is admiration. It is admiration in English and not only admiration in Latin. The wonder has a positive element of praise. This is the next milestone to be definitely marked on our road through fairyland. I shall speak in the next chapter about optimists and pessimists in their intellectual aspect, so far as they have one. Here I am only trying to describe the enormous emotions which cannot be described. And the strongest emotion was that life was as precious as it was puzzling. It was an ecstacy because it was an adventure; it was an adventure because it was an opportunity. The goodness of the fairy tale was not affected by the fact that there might be more dragons than princesses; it was good to be in a fairy tale. The test of all happiness is gratitude; and I felt grateful, though I hardly knew to whom. Children are grateful when Santa Claus puts in their stockings gifts of toys or sweets. Could I not be grateful to Santa Claus when he put in my stockings the gift of two miraculous legs? We thank people for birthday presents of cigars and slippers. Can I thank no one for the birthday present of birth?

There were, then, these two first feelings, indefensible and indisputable. The world was a shock, but it was not merely shocking; existence was a surprise, but it was a pleasant surprise. In fact, all my first views were exactly uttered in a riddle that stuck in my brain from boyhood. The question was, 'What did the first frog say?' And the answer was, 'Lord, how you made me jump!' That says succinctly all that I am saying. God made the frog jump; but the frog prefers jumping. But when these things are settled there enters the second great principle of the fairy philosophy.

Any one can see it who will simply read 'Grimm's Fairy Tales' or the fine collections of Mr Andrew Lang. For the pleasure of pedantry I will call it the Doctrine of Conditional Joy. Touchstone talked of much virtue in an 'if'; according to elfin ethics all virtue is an 'if'. The note of the fairy utterance always is, 'You may live in a palace of gold and sapphire, *if* you do not say the word "cow"'; or 'You may live happily with the King's daughter, *if* you do not show her an onion.' The vision always hangs upon a veto. All the dizzy and colossal things conceded depend upon one small thing withheld. All the wild and whirling things that are let loose depend upon one thing that is forbidden. Mr W. B. Yeats, in his exquisite and piercing elfin poetry, describes the elves as lawless; they plunge in innocent anarchy on the unbridled horses of the air—

'Ride on the crest of the dishevelled tide,
And dance upon the mountains like a flame.'

It is a dreadful thing to say that Mr W. B. Yeats does not understand fairyland. But I do say it. He is an ironical Irishman, full of intellectual reactions. He is not stupid enough to understand fairyland. Fairies prefer people of the yokel type like myself; people who gape and grin and do as they are told. Mr Yeats reads into elfland all the righteous insurrection of his own race. But the lawlessness of Ireland is a Christian lawlessness, founded on reason and justice. The Fenian is rebelling against something he understands only too well; but the true citizen of fairyland is obeying something that he does not understand at all. In the fairy tale an incomprehensible happiness rests upon an incomprehensible condition. A box is opened, and all evils fly out. A word is forgotten, and cities perish. A lamp is lit, and love flies away. A flower is plucked, and human lives are forfeited. An apple is eaten, and the hope of God is gone.

This is the tone of fairy tales, and it is certainly not lawlessness or even liberty, though men under a mean modern tyranny may think it liberty by comparison. People out of Portland Gaol might think Fleet Street free; but closer study will prove that both fairies and journalists are the slaves of duty. Fairy godmothers seem at least as strict as other godmothers. Cinderella received a coach out of Wonderland and a coachman out of nowhere, but she received a command—which might have come out of Brixton—that she should be back by twelve. Also, she had a glass slipper; and it cannot be a coincidence that glass is so common a substance in folk-lore. This princess lives in a glass castle, that princess on a glass hill; this one sees all things in a mirror; they may all live in glass houses if they will not throw stones. For this thin glitter of glass everywhere is the expression of the fact that the happiness is bright but brittle, like the substance most easily smashed by a housemaid or a cat. And this fairy-tale sentiment also sank into me and became my sentiment towards the whole world. I felt and feel that life itself is as bright as the diamond, but as brittle as the window-pane; and when the heavens were compared to the terrible crystal I can remember a shudder. I was afraid that God would drop the cosmos with a crash.

Remember, however, that to be breakable is not the same as to be perishable. Strike a glass, and it will not endure an instant; simply do not strike it, and it will endure a thousand years. Such, it seemed, was the joy of man, either in elfland or on earth; the happiness depended on *not doing something* which you could at any moment do and which, very often, it was not obvious why you should not do. Now, the point here is that to *me* this did not seem unjust. If the miller's third son said to the fairy, 'Explain why I must not stand on my head in the fairy palace,' the other might fairly reply, 'Well, if it comes to that, explain the fairy palace.' If Cinderella says, 'How is it that I must leave the ball at twelve?' her godmother might answer, 'How is it that you are going there till twelve?' If I leave a man in my will ten talking elephants and a hundred winged horses, he cannot complain if the conditions partake of the slight eccentricity of the gift. He must not look a winged horse in the mouth. And it seemed to me that existence was itself so very eccentric a legacy that I could not complain of not understanding the limitations of the vision when I did not understand the vision they limited. The frame was no stranger than the picture. The veto might well be as wild as the vision; it might be as startling as the sun, as elusive as the waters, as fantastic and terrible as the towering trees.

For this reason (we may call it the fairy godmother philosophy) I never could join the young men of my time in feeling what they called the general sentiment of *revolt*. I should have resisted, let us hope, any rules that were evil, and with these and their definition I shall deal in another chapter. But I did not feel disposed to resist any rule merely because it was mysterious. Estates are sometimes held by foolish forms, the breaking of a stick or the payment of a peppercorn: I was willing to hold the huge estate of earth and heaven by any such feudal fantasy. It could not well be wilder than the fact that I was allowed to hold it at all. At this stage I give only one ethical instance to show my meaning. I could never mix in the common murmur of that rising generation against monogamy, because no restriction on sex seemed so odd and unexpected as sex itself. To be allowed, like Endymion, to make love to the moon and then to complain that Jupiter kept his own moons in a harem seemed to me (bred on fairy tales like Endymion's) a vulgar anti-climax. Keeping to one woman is a small price for so much as seeing one woman. To complain that I could only be married once was like complaining that I had only been born once. It was incommensurate with the terrible excitement of which one was talking. It showed, not an exaggerated sensibility to sex, but a curious insensibility to it. A man is a fool who complains that he cannot enter Eden by five gates at once. Polygamy is a lack of the realization of sex; it is like a man plucking five pears in mere absence of mind. The æsthetes touched the last insane limits of language in their eulogy on lovely things. The thistledown made them weep; a burnished beetle brought them to their knees. Yet their emotion never impressed me for an instant, for this reason, that it never occurred to them to pay for their pleasure in any sort of symbolic sacrifice. Men (I felt) might fast forty days for the sake of hearing a blackbird sing. Men might go through fire to find a cowslip. Yet these lovers of beauty could not even keep sober for the blackbird. They would not go through common Christian marriage by way of recompense to the cowslip. Surely one might pay for extraordinary joy in ordinary morals. Oscar Wilde said that sunsets were not valued because we could not pay for sunsets. But Oscar Wilde was wrong; we can pay for sunsets. We can pay for them by not being Oscar Wilde.

Well, I left the fairy tales lying on the floor of the nursery, and I have not found any books so sensible since. I left the nurse guardian of tradition and democracy, and I have not found any modern type so sanely radical or so sanely conservative. But the matter for important comment was here; that when I first went out into the mental atmosphere of the modern world, I found that the modern world was positively opposed on two points to my nurse and to the nursery tales. It has taken me a long time to find out that the modern world is wrong and my nurse was right. The really curious thing was this: that modern thought contradicted this basic creed of my boyhood on its two most essential doctrines. I have explained that the fairy tales founded in me two convictions; first, that this world is a wild and startling place, which might have been quite different, but which is quite delightful; second, that before this wildness and delight one may well be modest and submit to the queerest limitations of so queer a kindness. But I found the whole modern world running like a high tide against both my tendernesses; and the shock of that collision created two sudden and spontaneous sentiments, which I have had ever since and which, crude as they were, have since hardened into convictions.

First, I found the whole modern world talking scientific fatalism; saying that everything is as it must always have been, being unfolded without fault from the beginning. The leaf on the tree is green because it could never have been anything else. Now, the fairy-tale philosopher is glad that the leaf is green precisely because it might have been scarlet. He feels as if it had turned green an instant before he looked at it. He is pleased that snow is white on the strictly reasonable ground that it might have been black. Every colour has in it a bold quality as of choice; the red of garden roses is not only decisive but dramatic, like suddenly spilt blood. He feels that something has been *done*. But the great determinists of the nineteenth century were strongly against this native feeling that something had happened an instant before. In fact, according to them, nothing ever really had happened since the beginning of the world. Nothing ever had happened since existence had happened; and even about the date of that they were not very sure.

The modern world as I found it was solid for modern Calvinism, for the necessity of things being as they are. But when I came to ask them I found they had really no proof of this unavoidable repetition in things except the fact that the things were repeated. Now, the mere repetition made the things to me rather more weird than more rational. It was as if, having seen a curiously shaped nose in the street and dismissed it as an accident, I had then seen six other noses of the same astonishing shape. I should have fancied for a moment that it must be some local secret society. So one elephant having a trunk was odd; but all elephants having trunks looked like a plot. I speak here only of an emotion, and of an emotion at once stubborn and subtle. But the repetition in Nature seemed sometimes to be an excited repetition, like that of an angry schoolmaster saying the same thing over and over again. The grass seemed signalling to me with all its fingers at once; the crowded stars seemed bent upon being understood. The sun would make me see him if he rose a thousand times. The recurrences of the universe rose to the maddening rhythm of an incantation, and I began to see an idea.

All the towering materialism which dominates the modern mind rests ultimately upon one assumption; a false assumption. It is supposed that if a thing goes on repeating itself it is probably dead; a piece of clockwork.

People feel that if the universe was personal it would vary; if the sun were alive it would dance. This is a fallacy even in relation to known fact. For the variation in human affairs is generally brought into them, not by life, but by death; by the dying down or breaking off of their strength or desire. A man varies his movements because of some slight element of failure or fatigue. He gets into an omnibus because he is tired of walking; or he walks because he is tired of sitting still. But if his life and joy were so gigantic that he never tired of going to Islington, he might go to Islington as regularly as the Thames goes to Sheerness. The very speed and ecstasy of his life would have the stillness of death. The sun rises every morning. I do not rise every morning; but the variation is due not to my activity, but to my inaction. Now, to put the matter in a popular phrase, it might be true that the sun rises regularly because he never gets tired of rising. His routine might be due, not to a lifelessness, but to a rush of life. The thing I mean can be seen, for instance, in children, when they find some game or joke that they specially enjoy. A child kicks his legs rhythmically through excess, not absence, of life. Because children have abounding vitality, because they are in spirit fierce and free, therefore they want things repeated and unchanged. They always say, 'Do it again'; and the grown-up person does it again until he is nearly dead. For grown-up people are not strong enough to exult in monotony. But perhaps God is strong enough to exult in monotony. It is possible that God says every morning, 'Do it again' to the sun; and every evening, 'Do it again' to the moon. It may not be automatic necessity that makes all daisies alike; it may be that God makes every daisy separately, but has never got tired of making them. It may be that He has the eternal appetite of infancy; for we have sinned and grown old, and our Father is younger than we. The repetition in Nature may not be a mere recurrence; it may be a theatrical *encore*. Heaven may *encore* the bird who laid an egg. If the human being conceives and brings forth a human child instead of bringing forth a fish, or a bat, or a griffin, the reason may not be that we are fixed in an animal fate without life or purpose. It may be that our little tragedy has touched the gods, that they admire it from their starry galleries, and that at the end of every human drama man is called again and again before the curtain. Repetition may go on for millions of years, by mere choice, and at any instant it may stop. Man may stand on the earth generation after generation, and yet each birth be his positively last appearance.

This was my first conviction; made by the shock of my childish emotions meeting the modern creed in mid-career. I had always vaguely felt facts to be miracles in the sense that they are wonderful: now I began to think them miracles in the stricter sense that they were *wilful*. I mean that they were, or might be, repeated exercises of some will. In short, I had always believed that the world involved magic: now I thought that perhaps it involved a magician.

And this pointed a profound emotion always present and sub-conscious; that this world of ours has some purpose; and if there is a purpose, there is a person. I had always felt life first as a story: and if there is a story there is a story-teller.

But modern thought also hit my second human tradition. It went against the fairy feeling about strict limits and conditions. The one thing it loved to talk about was expansion and largeness. Herbert Spencer would have been greatly annoyed if any one had called him an imperialist, and therefore it is highly regrettable that nobody did. But he was an imperialist of the lowest type. He popularized this contemptible notion that the size of the solar system ought to over-awe the spiritual dogma of man. Why should a man surrender his dignity to the solar system any more than to a whale? If mere size proves that man is not the image of God, then a whale may be the image of God; a somewhat formless image; what one might call an impressionist portrait. It is quite futile to argue that man is small compared to the cosmos; for man was always small compared to the nearest tree. But Herbert Spencer, in his headlong imperialism, would insist that we had in some way been conquered and annexed by the astronomical universe. He spoke about men and their ideals exactly as the most insolent Unionist talks about the Irish and their ideals. He turned mankind into a small nationality. And his evil influence can be seen even in the most spirited and honourable of later scientific authors; notably in the early romances of Mr H. G. Wells. Many moralists have in an exaggerated way represented the earth as wicked. But Mr Wells and his school made the heavens wicked. We should lift up our eyes to the stars from whence would come our ruin.

But the expansion of which I speak was much more evil than all this. I have remarked that the materialist, like the madman, is in prison; in the prison of one thought. These people seemed to think it singularly inspiring to keep on saying that the prison was very large. The size of this scientific universe gave one no novelty, no relief. The cosmos went on for ever, but not in its wildest constellation could there be anything really interesting; anything, for instance, such as forgiveness or free will. The grandeur or infinity of the secret of its cosmos added nothing to it. It was like telling a prisoner in Reading gaol that he would be glad to hear that the gaol now covered half the county. The warder would have nothing to show the man except more and more long corridors of stone lit by ghastly lights and empty of all that is human. So these expanders of the universe had nothing to show us except more and more infinite corridors of space lit by ghastly suns and empty of all that is divine.

In fairyland there had been a real law; a law that could be broken, for the definition of a law is something that can be broken. But the machinery of this cosmic prison was something that could not be broken; for we ourselves were only a part of its machinery. We were either unable to do things or we were destined to do them. The idea of the mystical condition quite disappeared; one can neither have the firmness of keeping laws nor the fun of breaking them. The largeness of this universe had nothing of that freshness and airy outbreak which we have praised in the universe of the poet. This modern universe is literally an empire; that is, it is vast, but it is not free. One went into larger and larger windowless rooms, rooms big with Babylonian perspective; but one never found the smallest window or a whisper of outer air.

Their infernal parallels seemed to expand with distance; but for me all good things come to a point, swords for instance. So finding the boast of the big cosmos so unsatisfactory to my emotions I began to argue about it a little; and I soon found that the whole attitude was even shallower than could have been expected. According to these people the cosmos was one thing since it had one unbroken rule. Only (they would say) while it is one thing it is also the only thing there is. Why, then, should one worry particularly to call it large? There is nothing to compare it with. It would be just as sensible to call it small. A man may say, 'I like this vast cosmos, with its throng of stars and its crowd of varied creatures'. But if it comes to that why should not a man say, 'I like this cosy little cosmos, with its decent number of stars and as neat a provision of live stock as I wish to see'? One is as good as the other; they are both mere sentiments. It is mere sentiment to rejoice that the sun is larger than the earth; it is quite as sane a sentiment to rejoice that the sun is no larger than it is. A man chooses to have an emotion about the largeness of the world; why should he not choose to have an emotion about its smallness?

It happened that I had that emotion. When one is fond of anything one addresses it by diminutives, even if it is an elephant or a lifeguardsman. The reason is, that anything, however huge, that can be conceived of as complete, can be conceived of as small. If military moustaches did not suggest a sword or tusks a tail, then the object would be vast because it would be immeasurable. But the moment you can imagine a guardsman you can imagine a small guardsman. The moment you really see an elephant you can call it 'Tiny'. If you can make a statue of a thing you can make a statuette of it. These people professed that the universe was one coherent thing; but they were not fond of the universe. But I was frightfully fond of the universe and wanted to address it by a diminutive. I often did so; and it never seemed to mind. Actually and in truth I did feel that these dim dogmas of vitality were better expressed by calling the world small than by calling it large. For about infinity there was a sort of carelessness which was the reverse of the fierce and pious care which I felt touching the pricelessness and the peril of life. They showed only a dreary waste; but I felt a sort of sacred thrift. For economy is far more romantic than extravagance. To them stars were an unending income of halfpence; but I felt about the golden sun and the silver moon as a schoolboy feels if he has one sovereign and one shilling.

These subconscious convictions are best hit off by the colour and tone of certain tales. Thus I have said that stories of magic alone can express my sense that life is not only a pleasure but a kind of eccentric privilege. I may express this other feeling of cosmic cosiness by allusion to another book always read in boyhood, *Robinson Crusoe*, which I read about this time, and which owes its eternal vivacity to the fact that it celebrates the poetry of limits, nay, even the wild romance of prudence. Crusoe is a man on a small rock with a few comforts just snatched from the sea: the best thing in the book is simply the list of things saved from the wreck. The greatest of poems is an inventory. Every kitchen tool becomes ideal because Crusoe might have dropped it in the sea. It is a good exercise, in empty or ugly hours of the day, to look at anything, the coal-scuttle or the book-case, and think how happy one could be to have brought it out of the sinking ship on to the solitary island. But it is a better exercise still to remember how all things have had this hair-breadth escape: everything has been saved from a wreck. Every man has had one horrible adventure: as a hidden untimely birth he had not been, as infants that never see the light. Men spoke much in my boyhood of restricted or ruined men of genius: and it was common to say that many a man was a Great Might-Have-Been. To me it is a more solid and startling fact that any man in the street is a Great Might-Not-Have-Been.

But I really felt (the fancy may seem foolish) as if all the order and number of things were the romantic remnant of Crusoe's ship. That there are two sexes and one sun, was like the fact that there were two guns and one axe. It was poignantly urgent that none should be lost; but somehow, it was rather fun that none could be added. The trees and the planets seemed like things saved from the wreck: and when I saw the Matterhorn I was glad that it had not been overlooked in the confusion. I felt economical about the stars as if they were sapphires (they are called so in Milton's Eden): I hoarded the hills. For the universe is a single jewel, and while it is a natural cant to talk of a jewel as peerless and priceless, of this jewel it is literally true. This cosmos is indeed without peer and without price: for there cannot be another one.

Thus ends, in unavoidable inadequacy, the attempt to utter the unutterable things. These are my ultimate attitudes towards life; the soils for the seeds of doctrine. These in some dark way I thought before I could write, and felt before I could think: that we may proceed more easily afterwards, I will roughly recapitulate them now. I felt in my bones; first, that this world does not explain itself. It may be a miracle with a supernatural explanation; it may be a conjuring trick, with a natural explanation. But the explanation of the conjuring trick, if it is to satisfy me, will have to be better than the natural explanations I have heard. The thing is magic, true or false. Second, I came to feel as if magic must have a meaning, and meaning must have some one to mean it. There was something personal in the world, as in a work of art; whatever it meant it meant violently. Third, I thought this purpose beautiful in its old design, in spite of its defects, such as dragons. Fourth, that the proper form of thanks to it is some form of humility and restraint: we should thank God for beer and Burgundy by not drinking too much of them. We owed, also, an obedience to whatever made us. And last, and strangest, there had come into my mind a vague and vast impression that in some way all good was a remnant to be stored and held sacred out of some primordial ruin. Man had saved his good as Crusoe saved his goods: he had saved them from a wreck. All this I felt and the age gave me no encouragement to feel it. And all this time I had not even thought of Christian theology.

# The Flag of the World

When I was a boy there were two curious men running about who were called the optimist and the pessimist. I constantly used the words myself, but I cheerfully confess that I never had any very special idea of what they meant. The only thing which might be considered evident was that they could not mean what they said; for the ordinary verbal explanation was that the optimist thought this world as good as it could be, while the pessimist thought it as bad as it could be. Both these statements being obviously raving nonsense, one had to cast about for other explanations. An optimist could not mean a man who thought everything right and nothing wrong. For that is meaningless; it is like calling everything right and nothing left. Upon the whole, I came to the conclusion that the optimist thought everything good except the pessimist, and that the pessimist thought everything bad, except himself. It would be unfair to omit altogether from the list the mysterious but suggestive definition said to have been given by a little girl, 'An optimist is a man who looks after your eyes, and a pessimist is a man who looks after your feet.' I am not sure that this is not the best definition of all. There is even a sort of allegorical truth in it. For there might, perhaps, be a profitable distinction drawn between that more dreary thinker who thinks merely of our contact with the earth from moment to moment, and that happier thinker who considers rather our primary power of vision and of choice of road.

But there is a deep mistake in this alternative of the optimist and the pessimist. The assumption of it is that a man criticises this world as if he were house-hunting, as if he were being shown over a new suite of apartments. If a man came to this world from some other world in full possession of his powers he might discuss whether the advantage of midsummer woods made up for the disadvantage of mad dogs, just as a man looking for lodgings might balance the presence of a telephone against the absence of a sea view. But no man is in that position. A man belongs to this world before he begins to ask if it is nice to belong to it. He has fought for the flag, and often won

Orthodoxy, 1908

heroic victories for the flag long before he has ever enlisted. To put shortly what seems the essential matter, he has a loyalty long before he has any admiration.

In the last chapter it has been said that the primary feeling that this world is strange and yet attractive is best expressed in fairy tales. The reader may, if he likes, put down the next stage to that bellicose and even jingo literature which commonly comes next in the history of a boy. We all owe much sound morality to the penny dreadfuls. Whatever the reason, it seemed and still seems to me that our attitude towards life can be better expressed in terms of a kind of military loyalty than in terms of criticism and approval. My acceptance of the universe is not optimism, it is more like patriotism. It is a matter of primary loyalty. The world is not a lodging-house at Brighton, which we are to leave because it is miserable. It is the fortress of our family, with the flag flying on the turret, and the more miserable it is the less we should leave it. The point is not that this world is too sad to love or too glad not to love; the point is that when you do love a thing, its gladness is a reason for loving it, and its sadness a reason for loving it more. All optimistic thoughts about England and all pessimistic thoughts about her are alike reasons for the English patriot. Similarly, optimism and pessimism are alike arguments for the cosmic patriot.

Let us suppose we are confronted with a desperate thing—say Pimlico. If we think what is really best for Pimlico we shall find the thread of thought leads to the throne of the mystic and the arbitrary. It is not enough for a man to disapprove of Pimlico: in that case he will merely cut his throat or move to Chelsea. Nor, certainly, is it enough for a man to approve of Pimlico: for then it will remain Pimlico, which would be awful. The only way out of it seems to be for somebody to love Pimlico: to love it with a transcendental tie and without any earthly reason. If there arose a man who loved Pimlico, then Pimlico would rise into ivory towers and golden pinnacles; Pimlico would attire herself as a woman does when she is loved. For decoration is not given to hide horrible things; but to decorate things already adorable. A mother does not give her child a blue bow because he is so ugly without it. A lover does not give a girl a necklace to hide her neck. If men loved Pimlico as mothers love children, arbitrarily, because it is *theirs*, Pimlico in a year or two might be fairer than Florence. Some readers will say that this is a mere fantasy. I answer that this is the actual history of mankind. This, as a fact, is how cities did grow great. Go back to the darkest roots of civilisation and you will find them knotted round some sacred stone or encircling some sacred well. People first paid honour to a spot and afterwards gained glory for it. Men did not love Rome because she was great. She was great because they had loved her.

The eighteenth-century theories of the social contract have been exposed to much clumsy criticism in our time; in so far as they meant that there is at the back of all historic government an idea of content and co-operation, they were demonstrably right. But they really were wrong in so far as they suggested that men had ever aimed at order or ethics directly by a conscious exchange of interests. Morality did not begin by one man saying to another, 'I will not hit you if you do not hit me'; there is no trace of such a transaction. There *is* a trace of both men having said, 'We must not hit each other in the holy place.' They gained their morality by guarding their religion. They did not cultivate courage. They fought for the shrine, and found they had become courageous. They did not cultivate cleanliness. They purified themselves for the altar, and found that they were clean. The history of the Jews is the only early document known to most Englishmen, and the facts can be judged sufficiently from that. The Ten Commandments which have been found substantially common to mankind were merely military commands; a code of regimental orders, issued to protect a certain ark across a certain desert. Anarchy was evil because it endangered the sanctity. And only when they made a holy day for God did they find they had made a holiday for men.

If it be granted that this primary devotion to a place or thing is a source of creative energy, we can pass on to a very peculiar fact. Let us reiterate for an instant that the only right optimism is a sort of universal patriotism. What is the matter with the pessimist? I think it can be stated by saying that he is the cosmic anti-patriot. And what is the matter with the anti-patriot? I think it can be stated, without undue bitterness, by saying that he is the candid friend. And what is the matter with the candid friend? There we strike the rock of real life and immutable human nature.

I venture to say that what is bad in the candid friend is simply that he is not candid. He is keeping something back—his own gloomy pleasure in saying unpleasant things. He has a secret desire to hurt, not merely to help. This is certainly, I think, what makes a certain sort of anti-patriot irritating to healthy citizens. I do not speak (of course) of the anti-patriotism which only irritates feverish stockbrokers and gushing actresses; that is only patriotism speaking plainly. A man who says that no patriot should attack the Boer War until it is over is not worth answering intelligently; he is saying that no good son should warn his mother off a cliff until she has fallen over it. But there is an anti-patriot who honestly angers honest men, and the explanation of him is, I think, what I have suggested: he is the uncandid candid friend; the man who says, 'I am sorry to say we are ruined,' and is not sorry at all. And he may be said, without rhetoric, to be a traitor; for he is using that ugly knowledge which was allowed him to strengthen the army, to discourage people from joining it. Because he is allowed to be pessimistic as a military adviser he is being pessimistic as a recruiting sergeant. Just in the same way the pessimist (who is the cosmic anti-patriot) uses the freedom that life allows to her counsellors to lure away the people from her flag. Granted that he states only facts, it is still essential to know what are his emotions, what is his motive. It may be that twelve hundred men in Tottenham are down with smallpox; but we want to know whether this is stated by some great philosopher who wants to curse the gods, or only by some common clergyman who wants to help the men.

The evil of the pessimist is, then, not that he chastises gods and men, but that he does not love what he chastises—he has not this primary and supernatural loyalty to things. What is the evil of the man commonly called an optimist? Obviously, it is felt that the optimist, wishing to defend the honour of this world, will defend the indefensible. He is the jingo of the universe; he will say, 'My cosmos, right or wrong.' He will be less inclined to the reform of things; more inclined to a sort of front-bench official answer to all attacks, soothing every one with assurances. He will not wash the world, but whitewash the world. All this (which is true of a type of optimist) leads us to the one really interesting point of psychology, which could not be explained without it.

We say there must be a primal loyalty to life: the only question is, shall it be a natural or a supernatural loyalty? If you like to put it so, shall it be a reasonable or an unreasonable loyalty? Now, the extraordinary thing is that the bad optimism (the whitewashing, the weak defence of everything) comes in with the reasonable optimism. Rational optimism leads to stagnation: it is irrational optimism that leads to reform. Let me explain by using once more the parallel of patriotism. The man who is most likely to ruin the place he loves is exactly the man who loves it with a reason. The man who will improve the place is the man who loves it without a reason. If a man loves some feature of Pimlico (which seems unlikely), he may find himself defending that feature against Pimlico itself. But if he simply loves Pimlico itself, he may lay it waste and turn it into the New Jerusalem. I do not deny that reform may be excessive; I only say that it is the mystic patriot who reforms. Mere jingo self-contentment is commonest among those who have some pedantic reason for their patriotism. The worst jingoes do not love England, but a theory of England. If we love England for being an empire, we may overrate the success with which we rule the Hindoos. But if we love it only for being a nation, we can face all events: for it would be a nation even if the Hindoos ruled us. Thus also only those will permit their patriotism to falsify history whose patriotism depends on history. A man who loves England for being English will not mind how she arose. But a man who loves England for being Anglo-Saxon may go against all facts for his fancy. He may end (like Carlyle and Freeman) by maintaining that the Norman Conquest was a Saxon Conquest. He may end in utter unreason—because he has a reason. A man who loves France for being military will palliate the army of 1870. But a man who loves France for being France will improve the army of 1870. This is exactly what the French have done, and France is a good instance of the working paradox. Nowhere else is patriotism more purely abstract and arbitrary; and nowhere else is reform more drastic and sweeping. The more transcendental is your patriotism, the more practical are your politics.

Perhaps the most everyday instance of this point is in the case of women, and their strange and strong loyalty. Some stupid people started the idea that because women obviously back up their own people through everything, therefore women are blind and do not see anything. They can hardly have known any women. The same women who are ready to defend their men through thick and thin are (in their personal intercourse with the man) almost morbidly lucid about the thinness of his excuses or the thickness of his head. A man's friend likes him but leaves him as he is: his wife loves him and is always trying to turn him into somebody else. Women who are utter mystics in their creed are utter cynics in their criticism. Thackeray expressed this well when he made Pendennis' mother, who worshipped her son as a god, yet assume that he would go wrong as a man. She underrated his virtue, though she overrated his value. The devotee is entirely free to criticise; the fanatic can safely be a sceptic. Love is not blind; that is the last thing that it is. Love is bound; and the more it is bound the less it is blind.

This at least had come to be my position about all that was called optimism, pessimism, and improvement. Before any cosmic act of reform we must have a cosmic oath of allegiance. A man must be interested in life, then he could be disinterested in his views of it. 'My son give me thy heart'; the heart must be fixed on the right thing: the moment we have a fixed heart we have a free hand. I must pause to anticipate an obvious criticism. It will be said that a rational person accepts the world as mixed of good and evil with a decent satisfaction and a decent endurance. But this is exactly the attitude which I maintain to be defective. It is, I know, very common in this age; it was perfectly put in those quiet lines of Matthew Arnold which are more piercingly blasphemous than the shrieks of Schopenhauer—

'Enough we live:—and if a life,
With large results so little rife,
Though bearable, seem hardly worth
This pomp of worlds, this pain of birth.'

I know this feeling fills our epoch, and I think it freezes our epoch. For our Titanic purposes of faith and revolution, what we need is not the cold acceptance of the world as a compromise, but some way in which we can heartily hate and heartily love it. We do not want joy and anger to neutralise each other and produce a surly contentment; we want a fiercer delight and a fiercer discontent. We have to feel the universe at once as an ogre's castle, to be stormed, and yet as our own cottage, to which we can return at evening.

No one doubts that an ordinary man can get on with this world: but we demand not strength enough to get on with it, but strength enough to get it on. Can he hate it enough to change it, and yet love it enough to think it worth changing? Can he look up at its colossal good without once feeling acquiescence? Can he look up at its colossal evil without once feeling despair? Can he, in short, be at once not only a pessimist and an optimist, but a fanatical pessimist and a fanatical optimist? Is he enough of a pagan to die for the world, and enough of a Christian to die to it? In this combination, I maintain, it is the rational optimist who fails, the irrational optimist who succeeds. He is ready to smash the whole universe for the sake of itself.

I put these things not in their mature logical sequence, but as they came: and this view was cleared and sharpened by an accident of the time. Under the lengthening shadow of Ibsen, an argument arose whether it was not a very nice thing to murder one's self. Grave moderns told us that we must not even say 'poor fellow', of a man who had blown his brains out, since he was an enviable person, and had only blown them out because of their exceptional excellence. Mr William Archer even suggested that in the golden age there would be penny-in-the-slot machines, by which a man could kill himself for a penny. In all this I found myself utterly hostile to many who called themselves liberal and humane. Not only is suicide a sin, it is the sin. It is the ultimate and absolute evil, the refusal to take an interest in existence; the refusal to take the oath of loyalty to life. The man who kills a man, kills a man. The man who kills himself, kills all men; as far as he is concerned he wipes out the world. His act is worse (symbolically considered) than any rape or dynamite outrage. For it destroys all buildings: it insults all women. The thief is satisfied with diamonds; but the suicide is not: that is his crime. He cannot be bribed, even by the blazing stones of the Celestial City. The thief compliments the things he steals, if not the owner of them. But the suicide insults everything on earth by not stealing it. He defiles every flower by refusing to live for its sake. There is not a tiny creature in the cosmos at whom his death is not a sneer. When a man hangs himself on a tree, the leaves might fall off in anger and the birds fly away in fury: for each has received a personal affront. Of course there may be pathetic emotional excuses for the act. There often are for rape, and there almost always are for dynamite. But if it comes to clear ideas and the intelligent meaning of things, then there is much more rational and philosophic truth in the burial at the cross-roads and the stake driven through the body, than in Mr Archer's suicidal automatic machines. There is a meaning in burying the suicide apart. The man's crime is different from other crimes—for it makes even crimes impossible.

About the same time I read a solemn flippancy by some free thinker: he said that a suicide was only the same as a martyr. The open fallacy of this helped to clear the question. Obviously a suicide is the opposite of a martyr. A martyr is a man who cares so much for something outside him, that he forgets his own personal life. A suicide is a man who cares so little for anything outside him, that he wants to see the last of everything. One wants something to begin: the other wants everything to end. In other words, the martyr is noble, exactly because (however he renounces the world or execrates all humanity) he confesses this ultimate link with life; he sets his heart outside himself: he dies that something may live. The suicide is ignoble because he has not this link with being: he is a mere destroyer; spiritually, he destroys the universe. And then I remembered the stake and the cross-roads, and the queer fact that Christianity had shown this weird harshness to the suicide. For Christianity had shown a wild encouragement of the martyr. Historic Christianity was accused, not entirely without reason, of carrying martyrdom and asceticism to a point, desolate and pessimistic. The early Christian martyrs talked of death with a horrible happiness. They blasphemed the beautiful duties of the body: they smelt the grave afar off like a field of flowers. All this has seemed to many the very poetry of pessimism. Yet there is the stake at the cross-roads to show what Christianity thought of the pessimist.

This was the first of the long train of enigmas with which Christianity entered the discussion. And there went with it a peculiarity of which I shall have to speak more markedly, as a note of all Christian notions, but which distinctly began in this one. The Christian attitude to the martyr and the suicide was not what is so often affirmed in modern morals. It was not a matter of degree. It was not that a line must be drawn somewhere, and that the self-slayer in exaltation fell within the line, the self-slayer in sadness just beyond it. The Christian feeling evidently was not merely that the suicide was carrying martyrdom too far. The Christian feeling was furiously for one and furiously against the other: these two things that looked so much alike were at opposite ends of heaven and hell. One man flung away his life; he was so good that his dry bones could heal cities in pestilence. Another man flung away life; he was so bad that his bones would pollute his brethren's. I am not saying this fierceness was right; but why was it so fierce?

Here it was that I first found that my wandering feet were in some beaten track. Christianity had also felt this opposition of the martyr to the suicide: had it perhaps felt it for the same reason? Had Christianity felt what I felt, but could not (and cannot) express—this need for a first loyalty to things, and then for a ruinous reform of things? Then I remembered that it was actually the charge against Christianity that it combined these two things which I was wildly trying to combine. Christianity was accused, at one and the same time, of being too optimistic about the universe and of being too pessimistic about the world. The coincidence made me suddenly stand still.

An imbecile habit has arisen in modern controversy of saying that such and such a creed can be held in one age but cannot be held in another. Some dogma, we are told, was credible in the twelfth century, but is not credible in the twentieth. You might as well say that a certain philosophy can be believed on Mondays, but cannot be believed on Tuesdays. You might as well say of a view of the cosmos that it was suitable to half-past three, but not suitable to half-past four. What a man can believe depends upon his philosophy, not upon the clock or the century. If a man believes in unalterable natural law, he cannot believe in any miracle in any age. If a man believes in a will behind law, he can believe in any miracle in any age. Suppose, for the sake of argument, we are concerned with a case of thaumaturgic healing. A materialist of the twelfth century could not believe it any more than a materialist of the twentieth century. But a Christian Scientist of the twentieth century can believe it as much as a Christian of the twelfth century. It is simply a matter of a man's theory of things. Therefore in dealing with any historical answer, the point is not whether it was given in our time, but whether it was given in answer to our question. And the more I thought about when and how Christianity had come into the world, the more I felt that it had actually come to answer this question.

It is commonly the loose and latitudinarian Christians who pay quite indefensible compliments to Christianity. They talk as if there had never been any piety or pity until Christianity came, a point on which any mediæval would have been eager to correct them. They represent that the remarkable thing about Christianity was that it was the first to preach simplicity or self-restraint, or inwardness and sincerity. They will think me very narrow (whatever that means) if I say that the remarkable thing about Christianity was that it was the first to preach Christianity. Its peculiarity was that it was peculiar, and simplicity and sincerity are not peculiar, but obvious ideals for all mankind. Christianity was the answer to a riddle, not the last truism uttered after a long talk. Only the other day I saw in an excellent weekly paper of Puritan tone this remark, that Christianity when stripped of its armour of dogma (as who should speak of a man stripped of his armour of bones), turned out to be nothing but the Quaker doctrine of the Inner Light. Now, if I were to say that Christianity came into the world specially to destroy the doctrine of the Inner Light, that would be an exaggeration. But it would be very much nearer to the truth. The last Stoics, like Marcus Aurelius, were exactly the people who did believe in the Inner Light. Their dignity, their weariness, their sad external care for others, their incurable internal care for themselves, were all due to the Inner Light, and existed only by that dismal illumination. Notice that Marcus Aurelius insists, as such introspective moralists always do, upon small things done or undone; it is because he has not hate or love enough to make a moral revolution. He gets up early in the morning, just as our own aristocrats living the Simple Life get up early in the morning; because such altruism is much easier than stopping the games of the amphitheatre or giving the English people back their land. Marcus Aurelius is the most intolerable of human types. He is an unselfish egoist. An unselfish egoist is a man who has pride without the excuse of passion. Of all conceivable forms of enlightenment the worst is what these people call the Inner Light. Of all horrible religions the most horrible is the worship of the god within. Any one who knows any body knows how it would work; any one who knows any one from the Higher Thought Centre knows how it does work. That Jones shall worship the god within him turns out ultimately to mean that Jones shall worship Jones. Let Jones worship the sun or moon, anything rather than the Inner Light; let Jones worship cats or crocodiles, if he can find any in his street, but not the god within. Christianity came into the world firstly in order to assert with violence that a man had not only to look inwards, but to look outwards, to behold with astonishment and enthusiasm a divine company and a divine captain. The only fun of being a Christian was that a man was not left alone with the Inner Light, but definitely recognised an outer light, fair as the sun, clear as the moon, terrible as an army with banners.

All the same, it will be as well if Jones does not worship the sun and moon. If he does, there is a tendency for him to imitate them; to say, that because the sun burns insects alive, he may burn insects alive. He thinks that because the sun gives people sun-stroke, he may give his neighbour measles. He thinks that because the moon is said to drive men mad, he may drive his wife mad. This ugly side of mere external optimism had also shown itself in the ancient world. About the time when the Stoic idealism had begun to show the weaknesses of pessimism, the old nature worship of the ancients had begun to show the enormous weaknesses of optimism. Nature worship is natural enough while the society is young, or, in other words, Pantheism is all right as long as it is the worship of Pan. But Nature has another side which experience and sin are not slow in finding out, and it is no flippancy to say of the god Pan that he soon showed the cloven hoof. The only objection to Natural Religion is that somehow it always becomes unnatural. A man loves Nature in the morning for her innocence and amiability, and at nightfall, if he is loving her still, it is for her darkness and her cruelty. He washes at dawn in clear water as did the Wise Man of the Stoics, yet, somehow at the dark end of the day, he is bathing in hot bull's blood, as did Julian the Apostate. The mere pursuit of health always leads to something unhealthy. Physical nature must not be made the direct object of obedience; it must be enjoyed, not worshipped. Stars and mountains must not be taken seriously. If they are, we end where the pagan nature worship ended. Because the earth is kind, we can imitate all her cruelties. Because sexuality is sane, we can all go mad about sexuality. Mere optimism had reached its insane and appropriate termination. The theory that everything was good had become an orgy of everything that was bad.

On the other side our idealist pessimists were represented by the old remnant of the Stoics. Marcus Aurelius and his friends had really given up the idea of any god in the universe and looked only to the god within. They had no hope of any virtue in nature, and hardly any hope of any virtue in society. They had not enough interest in the outer world really to wreck or revolutionise it. They did not love the city enough to set fire to it. Thus the ancient world was exactly in our own desolate dilemma. The only people who really enjoyed this world were busy breaking it up; and the virtuous people did not care enough about them to knock them down. In this dilemma (the same as ours) Christianity suddenly stepped in and offered a singular answer, which the world eventually accepted as *the* answer. It was the answer then, and I think it is the answer now.

This answer was like the slash of a sword; it sundered; it did not in any sense sentimentally unite. Briefly, it divided God from the cosmos. That transcendence and distinctness of the deity which some Christians now want to remove from Christianity, was really the only reason why any one wanted to be a Christian. It was the whole point of the Christian answer to the unhappy pessimist and the still more unhappy optimist. As I am here only concerned with their particular problem I shall indicate only briefly this great metaphysical suggestion. All descriptions of the creating or sustaining principle in things must be metaphorical, because they must be verbal. Thus the pantheist is forced to speak of God *in* all things as if he were in a box. Thus the evolutionist has, in his very name, the idea of being unrolled like a carpet. All terms, religious and irreligious, are open to this charge. The only question is whether all terms are useless, or whether one can, with such a phrase, cover a distinct *idea* about the origin of things. I think one can, and so evidently does the evolutionist, or he would not talk about evolution. And the root phrase for all Christian theism was this, that God was a creator, as an artist is a creator. A poet is so separate from his poem that he himself speaks of it as a little thing he has 'thrown off'. Even in giving it forth he has flung it away. This principle that all creation and procreation is a breaking off is at least as consistent through the cosmos as the evolutionary principle that all growth is a branching out. A woman loses a child even in having a child. All creation is separation. Birth is as solemn a parting as death.

It was the prime philosophic principle of Christianity that this divorce in the divine act of making (such as severs the poet from the poem or the mother from the new-born child) was the true description of the act whereby the absolute energy made the world. According to most philosophers, God in making the world enslaved it. According to Christianity, in making it, He set it free. God had written, not so much a poem, but rather a play; a play He had planned as perfect, but which had necessarily been left to human actors and stage-managers, who had since made a great mess of it. I will discuss the truth of this theorem later. Here I have only to point out with what a startling smoothness it passed the dilemma we have discussed in this chapter. In this way at least one could be both happy and indignant without degrading one's self to be either a pessimist or an optimist. On this system one could fight all the forces of existence without deserting the flag of existence. One could be at peace with the universe and yet be at war with the world. St George could still fight the dragon, however big the monster bulked in the cosmos, though he were bigger than the mighty cities or bigger than the everlasting hills. If he were as big as the world he could yet be killed in the name of the world. St George had not to consider any obvious odds or proportions in the scale of things, but only the original secret of their design. He can shake his sword at the dragon, even if it is everything; even if the empty heavens over his head are only the huge arch of its open jaws.

And then followed an experience impossible to describe. It was as if I had been blundering about since my birth with two huge and unmanageable machines, of different shapes and without apparent connection—the world and the Christian tradition. I had found this hole in the world: the fact that one must somehow find a way of loving the world without trusting it; somehow one must love the world without being worldly. I found this projecting feature of Christian theology, like a sort of hard spike, the dogmatic insistence that God was personal, and had made a world separate from Himself. The spike of dogma fitted exactly into the hole in the world—it had evidently been meant to go there—and then the strange thing began to happen. When once these two parts of the two machines had come together, one after another, all the other parts fitted and fell in with an eerie exactitude. I could hear bolt after bolt over all the machinery falling into its place with a kind of click of relief. Having got one part right, all the other parts were repeating that rectitude, as clock after clock strikes noon. Instinct after instinct was answered by doctrine after doctrine. Or, to vary the metaphor, I was like one who had advanced into a hostile country to take one high fortress. And when that fort had fallen the whole country surrendered and turned solid behind me. The whole land was lit up, as it were, back to the first fields of my childhood. All those blind fancies of boyhood which in the fourth chapter I have tried in vain to trace on the darkness, became suddenly transparent and sane. I was right when I felt that roses were red by some sort of choice: it was the divine choice. I was right when I felt that I would almost rather say that grass was the wrong colour than say that it must by necessity have been that colour: it might verily have been any other. My sense that happiness hung on the crazy thread of a condition did mean something when all was said: it meant the whole doctrine of the Fall. Even those dim and shapeless monsters of notions which I have not been able to describe, much less defend, stepped quietly into their places like colossal caryatides of the creed. The fancy that the cosmos was not vast and void, but small and cosy, had a fulfilled significance now, for anything that is a work of art must be small in the sight of the artist; to God the stars might be only small and dear, like diamonds. And my haunting instinct that somehow good was not merely a tool to be used, but a relic to be guarded, like the goods from Crusoe's ship—even that had been the wild whisper of something originally wise, for, according to Christianity, we were indeed the survivors of a wreck, the crew of a golden ship that had gone down before the beginning of the world.

But the important matter was this, that it entirely reversed the reason for optimism. And the instant the reversal was made it felt like the abrupt ease when a bone is put back in the socket. I had often called myself an optimist, to avoid the too evident blasphemy of pessimism. But all the optimism of the age had been false and disheartening for this reason, that it had always been trying to prove that we fit in to the world. The Christian optimism is based on the fact that we do *not* fit in to the world. I had tried to be happy by telling myself that man is an animal, like any other which sought its meat from God. But now I really was happy, for I had learnt that man is a monstrosity. I had been right in feeling all things as odd, for I myself was at once worse and better than all things. The optimist's pleasure was prosaic, for it dwelt on the naturalness of everything; the Christian pleasure was poetic, for it dwelt on the unnaturalness of everything in the light of the supernatural. The modern philosopher had told me again and again that I was in the right place, and I had still felt depressed even in acquiescence. But I had heard that I was in the *wrong* place, and my soul sang for joy, like a bird in spring. The knowledge found out and illuminated forgotten chambers in the dark house of infancy. I knew now why grass had always seemed to me as queer as the green beard of a giant, and why I could feel homesick at home.

# The Paradoxes of Christianity

The real trouble with this world of ours is not that it is an unreasonable world, nor even that it is a reasonable one. The commonest kind of trouble is that it is nearly reasonable, but not quite. Life is not an illogicality; yet it is a trap for logicians. It looks just a little more mathematical and regular than it is; its exactitude is obvious, but its inexactitude is hidden; its wildness lies in wait. I give one coarse instance of what I mean. Suppose some mathematical creature from the moon were to reckon up the human body; he would at once see that the essential thing about it was that it was duplicate. A man is two men, he on the right exactly resembling him on the left. Having noted that there was an arm on the right and one on the left, a leg on the right and one on the left, he might go further and still find on each side the same number of fingers, the same number of toes, twin eyes, twin ears, twin nostrils and even twin lobes of the brain. At last he would take it as a law; and then, where he found a heart on one side, would deduce that there was another heart on the other. And just then, where he most felt he was right, he would be wrong.

It is this silent swerving from accuracy by an inch that is the uncanny element in everything. It seems a sort of secret treason in the universe. An apple or an orange is round enough to get itself called round, and yet is not round after all. The earth itself is shaped like an orange in order to lure some simple astronomer into calling it a globe. A blade of grass is called after the blade of a sword, because it comes to a point; but it doesn't. Everywhere in things there is this element of the quiet and incalculable. It escapes the rationalists, but it never escapes till the last moment. From the grand curve of our earth it could easily be inferred that every inch of it was thus curved. It would seem rational that as a man has a brain on both sides, he should have a heart on both sides. Yet scientific men are still organising expeditions to find the North Pole, because they are so fond of flat country. Scientific men are also still organising expeditions to find a man's heart; and when they try to find it, they generally get on the wrong side of him.

Orthodoxy, 1908

Now, actual insight or inspiration is best tested by whether it guesses these hidden malformations or surprises. If our mathematician from the moon saw the two arms and the two ears, he might deduce the two shoulder-blades and the two halves of the brain. But if he guessed that the man's heart was in the right place, then I should call him something more than a mathematician. Now, this is exactly the claim which I have since come to propound for Christianity. Not merely that it deduces logical truths, but that when it suddenly becomes illogical, it has found, so to speak, an illogical truth. It not only goes right about things, but it goes wrong (if one may say so) exactly where the things go wrong. Its plan suits the secret irregularities, and expects the unexpected. It is simple about the simple truth; but it is stubborn about the subtle truth. It will admit that a man has two hands, it will not admit (though all the Modernists wail to it) the obvious deduction that he has two hearts. It is my only purpose in this chapter to point this out; to show that whenever we feel there is something odd in Christian theology, we shall generally find that there is something odd in the truth.

I have alluded to an unmeaning phrase to the effect that such and such a creed cannot be believed in our age. Of course, anything can be believed in any age. But, oddly enough, there really is a sense in which a creed, if it is believed at all, can be believed more fixedly in a complex society than in a simple one. If a man finds Christianity true in Birmingham, he has actually clearer reasons for faith than if he had found it true in Mercia. For the more complicated seems the coincidence, the less it can be a coincidence. If snowflakes fell in the shape, say, of the heart of Midlothian, it might be an accident. But if snowflakes fell in the exact shape of the maze at Hampton Court, I think one might call it a miracle. It is exactly as of such a miracle that I have since come to feel of the philosophy of Christianity. The complication of our modern world proves the truth of the creed more perfectly than any of the plain problems of the ages of faith. It was in Notting Hill and Battersea that I began to see that Christianity was true. This is why the faith has that elaboration of doctrines and details which so much distresses those who admire Christianity without believing in it. When once one believes in a creed, one is proud of its complexity, as scientists are proud of the complexity of science. It shows how rich it is in discoveries. If it is right at all, it is a compliment to say that it's elaborately right. A stick might fit a hole or a stone a hollow by accident. But a key and a lock are both complex. And if a key fits a lock, you know it is the right key.

But this involved accuracy of the thing makes it very difficult to do what I now have to do, to describe this accumulation of truth. It is very hard for a man to defend anything of which he is entirely convinced. It is comparatively easy when he is only partially convinced. He is partially convinced because he has found this or that proof of the thing, and he can expound it. But a

man is not really convinced of a philosophic theory when he finds that
something proves it. He is only really convinced when he finds that everything
proves it. And the more converging reasons he finds pointing to this conviction, the more bewildered he is if asked suddenly to sum them up. Thus, if one
asked an ordinary intelligent man, on the spur of the moment, 'Why do you
prefer civilisation to savagery?' he would look wildly round at object after
object, and would only be able to answer vaguely, 'Why, there is that bookcase
... and the coals in the coal-scuttle ... and pianos ... and policemen.' The
whole case for civilisation is that the case for it is complex. It has done so many
things. But that very multiplicity of proof which ought to make reply overwhelming makes reply impossible.

There is, therefore, about all complete conviction a kind of huge helplessness. The belief is so big that it takes a long time to get it into action. And this
hesitation chiefly arises, oddly enough, from an indifference about where one
should begin. All roads lead to Rome; which is one reason why many people
never get there. In the case of this defence of the Christian conviction I
confess that I would as soon begin the argument with one thing as another; I
would begin it with a turnip or a taximeter cab. But if I am to be at all careful
about making my meaning clear, it will, I think, be wiser to continue the
current arguments of the last chapter, which was concerned to urge the first of
these mystical coincidences, or rather ratifications. All I had hitherto heard of
Christian theology had alienated me from it. I was a pagan at the age of twelve,
and a complete agnostic by the age of sixteen; and I cannot understand any one
passing the age of seventeen without having asked himself so simple a
question. I did, indeed, retain a cloudy reverence for a cosmic deity and a great
historical interest in the Founder of Christianity. But I certainly regarded Him
as a man; though perhaps I thought that, even in that point, He had an
advantage over some of His modern critics. I read the scientific and sceptical
literature of my time — all of it, at least, that I could find written in English and
lying about; and I read nothing else; I mean I read nothing else on any other
note of philosophy. The penny dreadfuls which I also read were indeed in a
healthy and heroic tradition of Christianity; but I did not know this at the time.
I never read a line of Christian apologetics. I read as little as I can of them now.
It was Huxley and Herbert Spencer and Bradlaugh who brought me back to
orthodox theology. They sowed in my mind my first wild doubts of doubt. Our
grandmothers were quite right when they said that Tom Paine and the freethinkers unsettled the mind. They do. They unsettled mine horribly. The
rationalist made me question whether reason was of any use whatever; and
when I had finished Herbert Spencer I had got as far as doubting (for the first
time) whether evolution had occurred at all. As I laid down the last of Colonel
Ingersoll's atheistic lectures the dreadful thought broke across my mind,
'Almost thou persuadest me to be a Christian.' I was in a desperate way.

This odd effect of the great agnostics in arousing doubts deeper than their own might be illustrated in many ways. I take only one. As I read and re-read all the non-Christian or anti-Christian accounts of the faith, from Huxley to Bradlaugh, a slow and awful impression grew gradually but graphically upon my mind—the impression that Christianity must be a most extraordinary thing. For not only (as I understood) had Christianity the most flaming vices, but it had apparently a mystical talent for combining vices which seemed inconsistent with each other. It was attacked on all sides and for all contradictory reasons. No sooner had one rationalist demonstrated that it was too far to the east than another demonstrated with equal clearness that it was much too far to the west. No sooner had my indignation died down at its angular and aggressive squareness than I was called up again to notice and condemn its enervating and sensual roundness. In case any reader has not come across the thing I mean, I will give such instances as I remember at random of this self-contradiction in the sceptical attack. I give four or five of them; there are fifty more.

Thus, for instance, I was much moved by the eloquent attack on Christianity as a thing of inhuman gloom; for I thought (and still think) sincere pessimism the unpardonable sin. Insincere pessimism is a social accomplishment, rather agreeable than otherwise; and fortunately nearly all pessimism is insincere. But if Christianity was, as these people said, a thing purely pessimistic and opposed to life, then I was quite prepared to blow up St Paul's Cathedral. But the extraordinary thing is this. They did prove to me in Chapter I (to my complete satisfaction) that Christianity was too pessimistic; and then, in Chapter II, they began to prove to me that it was a great deal too optimistic. One accusation against Christianity was that it prevented men, by morbid tears and terrors, from seeking joy and liberty in the bosom of Nature. But another accusation was that it comforted men with a fictitious providence, and put them in a pink-and-white nursery. One great agnostic asked why Nature was not beautiful enough, and why it was hard to be free. Another great agnostic objected that Christian optimism, 'the garment of make-believe woven by pious hands,' hid from us the fact that Nature was ugly, and that it was impossible to be free. One rationalist had hardly done calling Christianity a nightmare before another began to call it a fool's paradise. This puzzled me; the charges seemed inconsistent. Christianity could not at once be the black mask on a white world, and also the white mask on a black world. The state of the Christian could not be at once so comfortable that he was a coward to cling to it, and so uncomfortable that he was a fool to stand it. If it falsified human vision it must falsify it one way or another; it could not wear both green and rose-coloured spectacles. I rolled on my tongue with a terrible joy, as did all young men of that time, the taunts which Swinburne hurled at the dreariness of the creed—

'Thou hast conquered, O pale Galilæan, the world has grown gray with Thy breath.'

But when I read the same poet's accounts of paganism (as in 'Atalanta'), I gathered that the world was, if possible, more gray before the Galilæan breathed on it than afterwards. The poet maintained, indeed, in the abstract, that life itself was pitch dark. And yet, somehow, Christianity had darkened it. The very man who denounced Christianity for pessimism was himself a pessimist. I thought there must be something wrong. And it did for one wild moment cross my mind that, perhaps, those might not be the very best judges of the relation of religion to happiness who, by their own account, had neither one nor the other.

It must be understood that I did not conclude hastily that the accusations were false or the accusers fools. I simply deduced that Christianity must be something even weirder and wickeder than they made out. A thing might have these two opposite vices; but it must be a rather queer thing if it did. A man might be too fat in one place and too thin in another; but he would be an odd shape. At this point my thoughts were only of the odd shape of the Christian religion; I did not allege any odd shape in the rationalistic mind.

Here is another case of the same kind. I felt that a strong case against Christianity lay in the charge that there is something timid, monkish and unmanly about all that is called 'Christian', especially in its attitude towards resistance and fighting. The great sceptics of the nineteenth century were largely virile. Bradlaugh in an expansive way, Huxley in a reticent way, were decidedly men. In comparison, it did seem tenable that there was something weak and over patient about Christian counsels. The Gospel paradox about the other cheek, the fact that priests never fought, a hundred things made plausible the accusation that Christianity was an attempt to make a man too like a sheep. I read it and believed it, and if I had read nothing different, I should have gone on believing it. But I read something very different. I turned the next page in my agnostic manual, and my brain turned up-side down. Now I found that I was to hate Christianity not for fighting too little, but for fighting too much. Christianity, it seemed, was the mother of wars. Christianity had deluged the world with blood. I had got thoroughly angry with the Christian, because he never was angry. And now I was told to be angry with him because his anger had been the most huge and horrible thing in human history; because his anger had soaked the earth and smoked to the sun. The very people who reproached Christianity with the meekness and non-resistance of the monasteries were the very people who reproached it also with the violence and valour of the Crusades. It was the fault of poor old Christianity (somehow or other) both that Edward the Confessor did not fight and that Richard Cœur de Lion did. The Quakers (we were told) were the only characteristic Christians; and yet the massacres of Cromwell and Alva were characteristic Christian crimes. What could it all mean? What was this Christianity which always forbade war and always produced wars? What could be the nature of the thing which one could abuse first because it would not fight, and second because it was always fighting? In what world of riddles was born this monstrous murder and this monstrous meekness? The shape of Christianity grew a queerer shape every instant.

I take a third case; the strangest of all, because it involves the one real objection to the faith. The one real objection to the Christian religion is simply that it is one religion. The world is a big place, full of very different kinds of people. Christianity (it may reasonably be said) is one thing confined to one kind of people; it began in Palestine, it has practically stopped with Europe. I was duly impressed with this argument in my youth, and I was much drawn towards the doctrine often preached in Ethical Societies—I mean the doctrine that there is one great unconscious church of all humanity founded on the omnipresence of the human conscience. Creeds, it was said, divided men; but at least morals united them. The soul might seek the strangest and most remote lands and ages and still find essential ethical common sense. It might find Confucius under Eastern trees, and he would be writing 'Thou shalt not steal.' It might decipher the darkest hieroglyphic on the most primeval desert, and the meaning when deciphered would be 'Little boys should tell the truth.' I believed this doctrine of the brotherhood of all men in the possession of a moral sense, and I believe it still—with other things. And I was thoroughly annoyed with Christianity for suggesting (as I supposed) that whole ages and empires of men had utterly escaped this light of justice and reason. But then I found an astonishing thing. I found that the very people who said that mankind was one church from Plato to Emerson were the very people who said that morality had changed altogether, and that what was right in one age was wrong in another. If I asked, say, for an altar, I was told that we needed none, for men our brothers gave us clear oracles and one creed in their universal customs and ideals. But if I mildly pointed out that one of men's universal customs was to have an altar, then my agnostic teachers turned clean round and told me that men had always been in darkness and the superstitions of savages. I found it was their daily taunt against Christianity that it was the light of one people and had left all others to die in the dark. But I also found that it was their special boast for themselves that science and progress were the discovery of one people, and that all other peoples had died in the dark. Their chief insult to Christianity was actually their chief compliment to themselves, and there seemed to be a strange unfairness about all their relative insistence on the two things. When considering some pagan or agnostic, we were to remember that all men had one religion; when considering some mystic or spiritualist, we were only to consider what absurd religions some men had. We could trust the ethics of Epictetus, because ethics had never changed. We must not trust the ethics of Bossuet, because ethics had changed. They changed in two hundred years, but not in two thousand.

This began to be alarming. It looked not so much as if Christianity was bad enough to include any vices, but rather as if any stick was good enough to beat Christianity with. What again could this astonishing thing be like which people were so anxious to contradict, that in doing so they did not mind contradicting themselves? I saw the same thing on every side. I can give no further space to this discussion of it in detail; but lest any one supposes that I have unfairly selected three accidental cases I will run briefly through a few others. Thus, certain sceptics wrote that the great crime of Christianity had been its attack on the family; it had dragged women to the loneliness and contemplation of the cloister, away from their homes and their children. But, then, other sceptics (slightly more advanced) said that the great crime of Christianity was forcing the family and marriage upon us; that it doomed women to the drudgery of their homes and children, and forbade them loneliness and contemplation. The charge was actually reversed. Or, again, certain phrases in the Epistles or the Marriage Service, were said by the anti-Christians to show contempt for woman's intellect. But I found that the anti-Christians themselves had a contempt for woman's intellect; for it was their great sneer at the Church on the Continent that 'only women' went to it. Or again, Christianity was reproached with its naked and hungry habits; with its sackcloth and dried peas. But the next minute Christianity was being reproached with its pomp and its ritualism; its shrines of porphyry and its robes of gold. It was abused for being too plain and for being too coloured. Again Christianity had always been accused of restraining sexuality too much, when Bradlaugh the Malthusian discovered that it restrained it too little. It is often accused in the same breath of prim respectability and of religious extravagance. Between the covers of the same atheistic pamphlet I have found the faith rebuked for its disunion, 'One thinks one thing, and one another,' and rebuked also for its union, 'It is difference of opinion that prevents the world from going to the dogs.' In the same conversation a free-thinker, a friend of mine, blamed Christianity for despising Jews, and then despised it himself for being Jewish.

I wished to be quite fair then, and I wish to be quite fair now; and I did not conclude that the attack on Christianity was all wrong. I only concluded that if Christianity was wrong, it was very wrong indeed. Such hostile horrors might be combined in one thing, but that thing must be very strange and solitary. There are men who are misers, and also spendthrifts; but they are rare. There are men sensual and also ascetic; but they are rare. But if this mass of mad contradictions really existed, quakerish and bloodthirsty, too gorgeous and too thread-bare, austere, yet pandering preposterously to the lust of the eye, the enemy of women and their foolish refuge, a solemn pessimist and a silly optimist, if this evil existed, then there was in this evil something quite supreme and unique. For I found in my rationalist teachers no explanation of such exceptional corruption. Christianity (theoretically speaking) was in their eyes only one of the ordinary myths and errors of mortals. *They* gave me no key to this twisted and unnatural badness. Such a paradox of evil rose to the stature of the supernatural. It was, indeed, almost as supernatural as the infallibility of the Pope. An historic institution, which never went right, is really quite as much of a miracle as an institution that cannot go wrong. The only explanation which immediately occurred to my mind was that Christianity did not come from heaven, but from hell. Really, if Jesus of Nazareth was not Christ, He must have been Antichrist.

And then in a quiet hour a strange thought struck me like a still thunder-bolt. There had suddenly come into my mind another explanation. Suppose we heard an unknown man spoken of by many men. Suppose we were puzzled to hear that some men said he was too tall and some too short; some objected to his fatness, some lamented his leanness; some thought him too dark, and some too fair. One explanation (as has been already admitted) would be that he might be an odd shape. But there is another explanation. He might be the right shape. Outrageously tall men might feel him to be short. Very short men might feel him to be tall. Old bucks who are growing stout might consider him insufficiently filled out; old beaux who were growing thin might feel that he expanded beyond the narrow lines of elegance. Perhaps Swedes (who have pale hair like tow) called him a dark man, while negroes considered him distinctly blond. Perhaps (in short) this extraordinary thing is really the ordinary thing; at least the normal thing, the centre. Perhaps, after all, it is Christianity that is sane and all its critics that are mad—in various ways. I tested this idea by asking myself whether there was about any of the accusers anything morbid that might explain the accusation. I was startled to find that this key fitted a lock. For instance, it was certainly odd that the modern world charged Christianity at once with bodily austerity and with artistic pomp. But then it was also odd, very odd, that the modern world itself combined extreme bodily luxury with an extreme absence of artistic pomp. The modern man thought Becket's robes too rich and his meals too poor. But then the modern man was really exceptional in history; no man before ever ate such elaborate dinners in such ugly clothes. The modern man found the church too simple exactly where modern life is too complex; he found the church too gorgeous exactly where modern life is too dingy. The man who disliked the plain fasts and feasts was mad on *entrées*. The man who disliked vestments wore a pair of preposterous trousers. And surely if there was any insanity involved in the matter at all it was in the trousers, not in the simply falling robe. If there was any insanity at all, it was in the extravagant *entrées*, not in the bread and wine.

I went over all the cases, and I found the key fitted so far. The fact that Swinburne was irritated at the unhappiness of Christians and yet more irritated at their happiness was easily explained. It was no longer a complication of diseases in Christianity, but a complication of diseases in Swinburne. The restraints of Christians saddened him simply because he was more hedonist than a healthy man should be. The faith of Christians angered him because he was more pessimist than a healthy man should be. In the same way the Malthusians by instinct attacked Christianity; not because there is anything especially anti-Malthusian about Christianity, but because there is something a little anti-human about Malthusianism.

Nevertheless it could not, I felt, be quite true that Christianity was merely sensible and stood in the middle. There was really an element in it of emphasis and even frenzy which had justified the secularists in their superficial criticism. It might be wise, I began more and more to think that it was wise, but it was not merely worldly wise; it was not merely temperate and respectable. Its fierce crusaders and meek saints might balance each other; still, the crusaders were very fierce and the saints were very meek, meek beyond all decency. Now, it was just at this point of the speculation that I remembered my thoughts about the martyr and the suicide. In that matter there had been this combination between two almost insane positions which yet somehow amounted to sanity. This was just such another contradiction; and this I had already found to be true. This was exactly one of the paradoxes in which sceptics found the creed wrong; and in this I had found it right. Madly as Christians might love the martyr or hate the suicide, they never felt these passions more madly than I had felt them long before I dreamed of Christianity. Then the most difficult and interesting part of the mental process opened, and I began to trace this idea darkly through all the enormous thoughts of our theology. The idea was that which I had outlined touching the optimist and the pessimist; that we want not an amalgam or compromise, but both things at the top of their energy; love and wrath both burning. Here I shall only trace it in relation to ethics. But I need not remind the reader that the idea of this combination is indeed central in orthodox theology. For orthodox theology has specially insisted that Christ was not a being apart from God and man, like an elf, nor yet a being half human and half not, like a centaur, but both things at once and both things thoroughly, very man and very God. Now let me trace this notion as I found it.

All sane men can see that sanity is some kind of equilibrium; that one may be mad and eat too much, or mad and eat too little. Some moderns have indeed appeared with vague versions of progress and evolution which seeks to destroy the μέσον or balance of Aristotle. They seem to suggest that we are meant to starve progressively, or to go on eating larger and larger breakfasts every morning for ever. But the great truism of the μέσον remains for all thinking men, and these people have not upset any balance except their own. But granted that we have all to keep a balance, the real interest comes in with the question of how that balance can be kept. That was the problem which Paganism tried to solve: that was the problem which I think Christianity solved and solved in a very strange way.

Paganism declared that virtue was in a balance; Christianity declared it was in a conflict: the collision of two passions apparently opposite. Of course they were not really inconsistent; but they were such that it was hard to hold simultaneously. Let us follow for a moment the clue of the martyr and the suicide; and take the case of courage. No quality has ever so much addled the brains and tangled the definitions of merely rational sages. Courage is almost a contradiction in terms. It means a strong desire to live taking the form of a readiness to die. 'He that will lose his life, the same shall save it,' is not a piece of mysticism for saints and heroes. It is a piece of everyday advice for sailors or mountaineers. It might be printed in an Alpine guide or a drill book. This paradox is the whole principle of courage; even of quite earthly or quite brutal courage. A man cut off by the sea may save his life if he will risk it on the precipice. He can only get away from death by continually stepping within an inch of it. A soldier surrounded by enemies, if he is to cut his way out, needs to combine a strong desire for living with a strange carelessness about dying. He must not merely cling to life, for then he will be a coward, and will not escape. He must not merely wait for death, for then he will be a suicide, and will not escape. He must seek his life in a spirit of furious indifference to it; he must desire life like water and yet drink death like wine. No philosopher, I fancy, has ever expressed this romantic riddle with adequate lucidity, and I certainly have not done so. But Christianity has done more: it has marked the limits of it in the awful graves of the suicide and the hero, showing the distance between him who dies for the sake of living and him who dies for the sake of dying. And it has held up ever since above the European lances the banner of the mystery of chivalry: the Christian courage, which is a disdain of death; not the Chinese courage, which is a disdain of life.

And now I began to find that this duplex passion was the Christian key to ethics everywhere. Everywhere the creed made a moderation out of the still crash of two impetuous emotions. Take, for instance, the matter of modesty, of the balance between mere pride and mere prostration. The average pagan, like the average agnostic, would merely say that he was content with himself, but not insolently self-satisfied, that there were many better and many worse, that his deserts were limited, but he would see that he got them. In short, he would walk with his head in the air; but not necessarily with his nose in the air. This is a manly and rational position, but it is open to the objection we noted against the compromise between optimism and pessimism—the 'resignation' of Matthew Arnold. Being a mixture of two things, it is a dilution of two things; neither is present in its full strength or contributes its full colour. This proper pride does not lift the heart like the tongue of trumpets; you cannot go clad in crimson and gold for this. On the other hand, this mild rationalist modesty does not cleanse the soul with fire and make it clear like crystal; it does not (like a strict and searching humility) make a man as a little child, who can sit at the feet of the grass. It does not make him look up and see marvels; for Alice must grow small if she is to be Alice in Wonderland. Thus it loses both the poetry of being proud and the poetry of being humble. Christianity sought by this same strange expedient to save both of them.

It separated the two ideas and then exaggerated them both. In one way Man was to be haughtier than he had ever been before; in another way he was to be humbler than he had ever been before. In so far as I am Man I am the chief of creatures. In so far as I am *a* man I am the chief of sinners. All humility that had meant pessimism, that had meant man taking a vague or mean view of his whole destiny—all that was to go. We were to hear no more the wail of Ecclesiastes that humanity had no pre-eminence over the brute, or the awful cry of Homer that man was only the saddest of all the beasts of the field. Man was a statue of God walking about the garden. Man had pre-eminence over all the brutes; man was only sad because he was not a beast, but a broken god. The Greek had spoken of men creeping on the earth, as if clinging to it. Now Man was to tread on the earth as if to subdue it. Christianity thus held a thought of the dignity of man that could only be expressed in crowns rayed like the sun and fans of peacock plumage. Yet at the same time it could hold a thought about the abject smallness of man that could only be expressed in fasting and fantastic submission, in the grey ashes of St Dominic and the white snows of St Bernard. When one came to think of *one's self*, there was vista and void enough for any amount of bleak abnegation and bitter truth. There the realistic gentleman could let himself go—as long as he let himself go at himself. There was an open playground for the happy pessimist. Let him say anything against himself short of blaspheming the original aim of his being; let him call himself a fool and even a damned fool (though that is Calvinistic); but he must not say that fools are not worth saving. He must not say that a man, *quâ* man, can be valueless. Here again, in short, Christianity got over the difficulty of combining furious opposites, by keeping them both, and keeping them both furious. The Church was positive on both points. One can hardly think too little of one's self. One can hardly think too much of one's soul.

Take another case: the complicated question of charity, which some highly uncharitable idealists seem to think quite easy. Charity is a paradox, like modesty and courage. Stated baldly, charity certainly means one of two things—pardoning unpardonable acts, or loving unlovable people. But if we ask ourselves (as we did in the case of pride) what a sensible pagan would feel about such a subject, we shall probably be beginning at the bottom of it. A sensible pagan would say that there were some people one could forgive, and some one couldn't: a slave who stole wine could be laughed at; a slave who betrayed his benefactor could be killed, and cursed even after he was killed. In so far as the act was pardonable, the man was pardonable. That again is rational, and even refreshing; but it is a dilution. It leaves no place for a pure horror of injustice, such as that which is a great beauty in the innocent. And it leaves no place for a mere tenderness for men as men, such as is the whole fascination of the charitable. Christianity came in here as before. It came in startlingly with a sword, and clove one thing from another. It divided the crime from the criminal. The criminal we must forgive unto seventy times seven. The crime we must not forgive at all. It was not enough that slaves who stole wine inspired partly anger and partly kindness. We must be much more angry with theft than before, and yet much kinder to thieves than before. There was room for wrath and love to run wild. And the more I considered Christianity, the more I found that while it had established a rule and order, the chief aim of that order was to give room for good things to run wild.

Mental and emotional liberty are not so simple as they look. Really they require almost as careful a balance of laws and conditions as do social and political liberty. The ordinary æsthetic anarchist who sets out to feel every-thing freely gets knotted at last in a paradox that prevents him feeling at all. He breaks away from home limits to follow poetry. But in ceasing to feel home limits he has ceased to feel the *Odyssey*. He is free from national prejudices and outside patriotism. But being outside patriotism he is outside *Henry V*. Such a literary man is simply outside all literature: he is more of a prisoner than any bigot. For if there is a wall between you and the world, it makes little difference whether you describe yourself as locked in or as locked out. What we want is not the universality that is outside all normal sentiments; we want the universality that is inside all normal sentiments. It is all the difference between being free from them, as a man is free from a prison, and being free of them as a man is free of a city. I am free from Windsor Castle (that is, I am not forcibly detained there), but I am by no means free of that building. How can man be approximately free of fine emotions, able to swing them in a clear space without breakage or wrong? *This* was the achievement of this Christian paradox of the parallel passions. Granted the primary dogma of the war between divine and diabolic, the revolt and ruin of the world, their optimism and pessimism, as pure poetry, could be loosened like cataracts.

St Francis, in praising all good, could be a more shouting optimist than Walt Whitman. St Jerome, in denouncing all evil, could paint the world blacker than Schopenhauer. Both passions were free because both were kept in their place. The optimist could pour out all the praise he liked on the gay music of the march, the golden trumpets, and the purple banners going into battle. But he must not call the fight needless. The pessimist might draw as darkly as he chose the sickening marches or the sanguine wounds. But he must not call the fight hopeless. So it was with all the other moral problems, with pride, with protest, and with compassion. By defining its main doctrine, the Church not only kept seemingly inconsistent things side by side, but, what was more, allowed them to break out in a sort of artistic violence otherwise possible only to anarchists. Meekness grew more dramatic than madness. Historic Christianity rose into a high and strange *coup de théâtre* of morality—things that are to virtue what the crimes of Nero are to vice. The spirits of indignation and of charity took terrible and attractive forms, ranging from that monkish fierceness that scourged like a dog the first and greatest of the Plantagenets, to the sublime pity of St Catherine, who, in the official shambles, kissed the bloody head of the criminal. Poetry could be acted as well as composed. This heroic and monumental manner in ethics has entirely vanished with supernatural religion. They, being humble, could parade themselves; but we are too proud to be prominent. Our ethical teachers write reasonably for prison reform; but we are not likely to see Mr Cadbury, or any eminent philanthropist, go into Reading Gaol and embrace the strangled corpse before it is cast into the quicklime. Our ethical teachers write mildly against the power of millionaires; but we are not likely to see Mr Rockefeller, or any modern tyrant, publicly whipped in Westminster Abbey.

Thus, the double charges of the secularists, though throwing nothing but darkness and confusion on themselves, throw a real light on the faith. It *is* true that the historic Church has at once emphasised celibacy and emphasised the family; has at once (if one may put it so) been fiercely for having children and fiercely for not having children. It has kept them side by side like two strong colours, red and white, like the red and white upon the shield of St George. It has always had a healthy hatred of pink. It hates that combination of two colours which is the feeble expedient of the philosophers. It hates that evolution of black into white which is tantamount to a dirty grey. In fact, the whole theory of the Church on virginity might be symbolized in the statement that white is a colour: not merely the absence of a colour. All that I am urging here can be expressed by saying that Christianity sought in most of these cases to keep two colours co-existent but pure. It is not a mixture like russet or purple; it is rather like a shot silk, for a shot silk is always at right angles, and is in the pattern of the cross.

So it is also, of course, with the contradictory charges of the anti-Christians about submission and slaughter. It *is* true that the Church told some men to fight and others not to fight; and it *is* true that those who fought were like thunderbolts and those who did not fight were like statues. All this simply means that the Church preferred to use its Supermen and to use its Tolstoyans. There must be *some* good in the life of battle, for so many good men have enjoyed being soldiers. There must be *some* good in the idea of non-resistance, for so many good men seem to enjoy being Quakers. All that the Church did (so far as that goes) was to prevent either of these good things from ousting the other. They existed side by side. The Tolstoyans, having all the scruples of monks, simply became monks. The Quakers became a club instead of becoming a sect. Monks said all that Tolstoy says; they poured out lucid lamentations about the cruelty of battles and the vanity of revenge. But the Tolstoyans are not quite right enough to run the whole world; and in the ages of faith they were not allowed to run it. The world did not lose the last charge of Sir James Douglas or the banner of Joan the Maid. And sometimes this pure gentleness and this pure fierceness met and justified their juncture; the paradox of all the prophets was fulfilled, and, in the soul of St Louis, the lion lay down with the lamb. But remember that this text is too lightly interpreted. It is constantly assured, especially in our Tolstoyan tendencies, that when the lion lies down with the lamb the lion becomes lamb-like. But that is brutal annexation and imperialism on the part of the lamb. That is simply the lamb absorbing the lion instead of the lion eating the lamb. The real problem is—Can the lion lie down with the lamb and still retain his royal ferocity? *That* is the problem the Church attempted; *that* is the miracle she achieved.

This is what I have called guessing the hidden eccentricities of life. This is knowing that a man's heart is to the left and not in the middle. This is knowing not only that the earth is round, but knowing exactly where it is flat. Christian doctrine detected the oddities of life. It not only discovered the law, but it foresaw the exceptions. Those underrate Christianity who say that it discovered mercy; any one might discover mercy. In fact every one did. But to discover a plan for being merciful and also severe—*that* was to anticipate a strange need of human nature. For no one wants to be forgiven for a big sin as if it were a little one. Any one might say that we should be neither quite miserable nor quite happy. But to find out how far one *may* be quite miserable without making it impossible to be quite happy—that was a discovery in psychology. Any one might say, 'Neither swagger nor grovel'; and it would have been a limit. But to say, 'Here you can swagger and there you can grovel'—that was an emancipation.

This was the big fact about Christian ethics; the discovery of the new balance. Paganism had been like a pillar of marble, upright because proportioned with symmetry. Christianity was like a huge and ragged and romantic rock, which, though it sways on its pedestal at a touch, yet, because its exaggerated excrescences exactly balance each other, is enthroned there for a thousand years. In a Gothic cathedral the columns were all different, but they were all necessary. Every support seemed an accidental and fantastic support; every buttress was a flying buttress. So in Christendom apparent accidents balanced. Becket wore a hair shirt under his gold and crimson, and there is much to be said for the combination; for Becket got the benefit of the hair shirt while the people in the street got the benefit of the crimson and gold. It is at least better than the manner of the modern millionaire, who has the black and the drab outwardly for others, and the gold next his heart. But the balance was not always in one man's body as in Becket's; the balance was often distributed over the whole body of Christendom. Because a man prayed and fasted on the Northern snows, flowers could be flung at his festival in the Southern cities; and because fanatics drank water on the sands of Syria, men could still drink cider in the orchards of England. This is what makes Christendom at once so much more perplexing and so much more interesting than the Pagan empire; just as Amiens Cathedral is not better but more interesting than the Parthenon. If any one wants a modern proof of all this, let him consider the curious fact that, under Christianity, Europe (while remaining a unity) has broken up into individual nations. Patriotism is a perfect example of this deliberate balancing of one emphasis against another emphasis. The instinct of the Pagan empire would have said, 'You shall all be Roman citizens, and grow alike; let the German grow less slow and reverent; the Frenchmen less experimental and swift.' But the instinct of Christian Europe says, 'Let the German remain slow and reverent, that the Frenchman may the more safely be swift and experimental. We will make an equipoise out of these excesses. The absurdity called Germany shall correct the insanity called France.'

Last and most important, it is exactly this which explains what is so inexplicable to all the modern critics of the history of Christianity. I mean the monstrous wars about small points of theology, the earthquakes of emotion about a gesture or a word. It was only a matter of an inch; but an inch is everything when you are balancing. The Church could not afford to swerve a hair's breadth on some things if she was to continue her great and daring experiment of the irregular equilibrium. Once let one idea become less powerful and some other idea would become too powerful. It was no flock of sheep the Christian shepherd was leading, but a herd of bulls and tigers, of terrible ideals and devouring doctrines, each one of them strong enough to turn to a false religion and lay waste the world. Remember that the Church went in specifically for dangerous ideas; she was a lion tamer. The idea of birth through a Holy Spirit, of the death of a divine being, of the forgiveness of sins, or the fulfilment of prophecies, are ideas which, any one can see, need but a touch to turn them into something blasphemous or ferocious. The smallest link was let drop by the artificers of the Mediterranean, and the lion of ancestral pessimism burst his chain in the forgotten forests of the north. Of these theological equalisations I have to speak afterwards. Here it is enough to notice that if some small mistake were made in doctrine, huge blunders might be made in human happiness. A sentence phrased wrong about the nature of symbolism would have broken all the best statues in Europe. A slip in the definitions might stop all the dances; might wither all the Christmas trees or break all the Easter eggs. Doctrines had to be defined within strict limits, even in order that man might enjoy general human liberties. The Church had to be careful, if only that the world might be careless.

This is the thrilling romance of Orthodoxy. People have fallen into a foolish habit of speaking of orthodoxy as something heavy, humdrum, and safe. There never was anything so perilous or so exciting as orthodoxy. It was sanity: and to be sane is more dramatic than to be mad. It was the equilibrium of a man behind madly rushing horses, seeming to stoop this way and to sway that, yet in every attitude having the grace of statuary and the accuracy of arithmetic. The Church in its early days went fierce and fast with any warhorse; yet it is utterly unhistoric to say that she merely went mad along one idea, like a vulgar fanaticism. She swerved to left and right, so as exactly to avoid enormous obstacles. She left on one hand the huge bulk of Arianism, buttressed by all the worldly powers to make Christianity too worldly. The next instant she was swerving to avoid an orientalism, which would have made it too unworldly. The orthodox Church never took the tame course or accepted the conventions; the orthodox Church was never respectable. It would have been easier to have accepted the earthly power of the Arians. It would have been easy, in the Calvinistic seventeenth century, to fall into the bottomless pit of predestination. It is easy to be a madman: it is easy to be a heretic. It is always easy to let the age have its head; the difficult thing is to keep one's own. It is always easy to be a modernist; as it is easy to be a snob. To have fallen into any of those open traps of error and exaggeration which fashion after fashion and sect after sect set along the historic path of Christendom—that would indeed have been simple. It is always simple to fall; there are an infinity of angles at which one falls, only one at which one stands. To have fallen into any one of the fads from Gnosticism to Christian Science would indeed have been obvious and tame. But to have avoided them all has been one whirling adventure; and in my vision the heavenly chariot flies thundering through the ages, the dull heresies sprawling and prostrate, the wild truth reeling but erect.

# The Romance of Orthodoxy

It is customary to complain of the bustle and strenuousness of our epoch. But in truth the chief mark of our epoch is a profound laziness and fatigue; and the fact is that the real laziness is the cause of the apparent bustle. Take one quite external case; the streets are noisy with taxicabs and motorcars; but this is not due to human activity but to human repose. There would be less bustle if there were more activity, if people were simply walking about. Our world would be more silent if it were more strenuous. And this which is true of the apparent physical bustle is true also of the apparent bustle of the intellect. Most of the machinery of modern language is labour-saving machinery; and it saves mental labour very much more than it ought. Scientific phrases are used like scientific wheels and piston-rods to make swifter and smoother yet the path of the comfortable. Long words go rattling by us like long railway trains. We know they are carrying thousands who are too tired or too indolent to walk and think for themselves. It is a good exercise to try for once in a way to express any opinion one holds in words of one syllable. If you say 'The social utility of the indeterminate sentence is recognised by all criminologists as a part of our sociological evolution towards a more humane and scientific view of punishment,' you can go on talking like that for hours with hardly a movement of the grey matter inside your skull. But if you begin 'I wish Jones to go to gaol and Brown to say when Jones shall come out,' you will discover, with a thrill of horror, that you are obliged to think. The long words are not the hard words, it is the short words that are hard. There is much more metaphysical subtlety in the word 'damn' than in the word 'degeneration'.

But these long comfortable words that save modern people the toil of reasoning have one particular aspect in which they are especially ruinous and confusing. This difficulty occurs when the same long word is used in different connections to mean quite different things. Thus, to take a well-known instance, the word 'idealist' has one meaning as a piece of philosophy

Orthodoxy, 1908

298

and quite another as a piece of moral rhetoric. In the same way the scientific materialists have had just reason to complain of people mixing up 'materialist' as a term of cosmology with 'materialist' as a moral taunt. So, to take a cheaper instance, the man who hates 'progressives' in London always calls himself a 'progressive' in South Africa.

A confusion quite as unmeaning as this has arisen in connection with the word 'liberal' as applied to religion and as applied to politics and society. It is often suggested that all Liberals ought to be freethinkers, because they ought to love everything that is free. You might just as well say that all idealists ought to be High Churchmen, because they ought to love everything that is high. You might as well say that Low Churchmen ought to like Low Mass, or that Broad Churchmen ought to like broad jokes. The thing is a mere accident of words. In actual modern Europe a free-thinker does not mean a man who thinks for himself. It means a man who, having thought for himself, has come to one particular class of conclusions, the material origin of phenomena, the impossibility of miracles, the improbability of personal immortality and so on. And none of these ideas are particularly liberal. Nay, indeed almost all these ideas are definitely illiberal, as it is the purpose of this chapter to show.

In the few following pages I propose to point out as rapidly as possible that on every single one of the matters most strongly insisted on by liberalisers of theology their effect upon social practice would be definitely illiberal. Almost every contemporary proposal to bring freedom into the church is simply a proposal to bring tyranny into the world. For freeing the church now does not even mean freeing it in all directions. It means freeing that peculiar set of dogmas loosely called scientific, dogmas of monism, of pantheism, or of Arianism, or of necessity. And every one of these (and we will take them one by one) can be shown to be the natural ally of oppression. In fact, it is a remarkable circumstance (indeed not so very remarkable when one comes to think of it) that most things are the allies of oppression. There is only one thing that can never go past a certain point in its alliance with oppression— and that is orthodoxy. I may, it is true, twist orthodoxy so as partly to justify a tyrant. But I can easily make up a German philosophy to justify him entirely.

Now let us take in order the innovations that are the notes of the new theology or the modernist church. We concluded the last chapter with the discovery of one of them. The very doctrine which is called the most old-fashioned was found to be the only safeguard of the new democracies of the earth. The doctrine seemingly most unpopular was found to be the only strength of the people. In short, we found that the only logical negation of oligarchy was in the affirmation of original sin. So it is, I maintain, in all the other cases.

I take the most obvious instance first, the case of miracles. For some extraordinary reason, there is a fixed notion that it is more liberal to disbelieve in miracles than to believe in them. Why, I cannot imagine, nor can anybody tell me. For some inconceivable cause a 'broad' or 'liberal' clergyman always means a man who wishes at least to diminish the number of miracles; it never means a man who wishes to increase that number. It always means a man who is free to disbelieve that Christ came out of His grave; it never means a man who is free to believe that his own aunt came out of her grave. It is common to find trouble in a parish because the parish priest cannot admit that St Peter walked on water; yet how rarely do we find trouble in a parish because the clergyman says that his father walked on the Serpentine? And this is not because (as the swift secularist debater would immediately retort) miracles cannot be believed in our experience. It is not because 'miracles do not happen,' as in the dogma which Matthew Arnold recited with simple faith. More supernatural things are *alleged* to have happened in our time than would have been possible eighty years ago. Men of science believe in such marvels much more than they did: the most perplexing, and even horrible, prodigies of mind and spirit are always being unveiled in modern psychology. Things that the old science at least would frankly have rejected as miracles are hourly being asserted by the new science. The only thing which is still old-fashioned enough to reject miracles is the New Theology. But in truth this notion that it is 'free' to deny miracles has nothing to do with the evidence for or against them. It is a lifeless verbal prejudice of which the original life and beginning was not in the freedom of thought, but simply in the dogma of materialism. The man of the nineteenth century did not disbelieve in the Resurrection because his liberal Christianity allowed him to doubt it. He disbelieved in it because his very strict materialism did not allow him to believe it. Tennyson, a very typical nineteenth-century man, uttered one of the instinctive truisms of his contemporaries when he said that there was faith in their honest doubt. There was indeed. Those words have a profound and even a horrible truth. In their doubt of miracles there was a faith in a fixed and godless fate; a deep and sincere faith in the incurable routine of the cosmos. The doubts of the agnostic were only the dogmas of the monist.

Of the fact and evidence of the supernatural I will speak afterwards. Here we are only concerned with this clear point; that in so far as the liberal idea of freedom can be said to be on either side in the discussion about miracles, it is obviously on the side of miracles. Reform or (in the only tolerable sense) progress means simply the gradual control of matter by mind. A miracle simply means the swift control of matter by mind. If you wish to feed the people, you may think that feeding them miraculously in the wilderness is impossible—but you cannot think it illiberal. If you really want poor children to go to the seaside, you cannot think it illiberal that they should go there on flying dragons; you can only think it unlikely. A holiday, like Liberalism, only means the liberty of man. A miracle only means the liberty of God. You may conscientiously deny either of them, but you cannot call your denial a triumph of the liberal idea. The Catholic Church believed that man and God both had a sort of spiritual freedom. Calvinism took away the freedom from man, but left it to God. Scientific materialism binds the Creator Himself; it chains up God as the Apocalypse chained the devil. It leaves nothing free in the universe. And those who assist this process are called the 'liberal theologians'.

This, as I say, is the lightest and most evident case. The assumption that there is something in the doubt of miracles akin to liberality or reform is literally the opposite of the truth. If a man cannot believe in miracles there is an end of the matter; he is not particularly liberal, but he is perfectly honourable and logical, which are much better things. But if he can believe in miracles, he is certainly the more liberal for doing so; because they mean first, the freedom of the soul, and secondly, its control over the tyranny of circumstance. Sometimes this truth is ignored in a singularly naïve way, even by the ablest men. For instance, Mr Bernard Shaw speaks with a hearty old-fashioned contempt for the idea of miracles, as if they were a sort of breach of faith on the part of nature: he seems strangely unconscious that miracles are only the final flowers of his own favourite tree, the doctrine of the omnipotence of will. Just in the same way he calls the desire for immortality a paltry selfishness, forgetting that he has just called the desire for life a healthy and heroic selfishness. How can it be noble to wish to make one's life infinite and yet mean to wish to make it immortal? No, if it is desirable that man should triumph over the cruelty of nature or custom, then miracles are certainly desirable; we will discuss afterwards whether they are possible.

But I must pass on to the larger cases of this curious error; the notion that the 'liberalising' of religion in some way helps the liberation of the world. The second example of it can be found in the question of pantheism—or rather of a certain modern attitude which is often called immanentism, and which often is Buddhism. But this is so much more difficult a matter that I must approach it with rather more preparation.

The things said most confidently by advanced persons to crowded audiences are generally those quite opposite to the fact; it is actually our truisms that are untrue. Here is a case. There is a phrase of facile liberality uttered again and again at ethical societies and parliaments of religion: 'the religions of the earth differ in rites and forms, but they are the same in what they teach'. It is false; it is the opposite of the fact. The religions of the earth do *not* greatly differ in rites and forms; they do greatly differ in what they teach. It is as if a man were to say, 'Do not be misled by the fact that the *Church Times* and the *Freethinker* look utterly different, that one is painted on vellum

and the other carved on marble, that one is triangular and the other hec-
tagonal; read them and you will see that they say the same thing.' The truth
is, of course, that they are alike in everything except in the fact that they
don't say the same thing. An atheist stockbroker in Surbiton looks exactly
like a Swedenborgian stockbroker in Wimbledon. You may walk round and
round them and subject them to the most personal and offensive study
without seeing anything Swedenborgian in the hat or anything particularly
godless in the umbrella. It is exactly in their souls that they are divided. So
the truth is that the difficulty of all the creeds of the earth is not as alleged in
this cheap maxim: that they agree in meaning, but differ in machinery. It is
exactly the opposite. They agree in machinery; almost every great religion on
earth works with the same external methods, with priests, scriptures, altars,
sworn brotherhoods, special feasts. They agree in the mode of teaching;
what they differ about is the thing to be taught. Pagan optimists and Eastern
pessimists would both have temples, just as Liberals and Tories would both
have newspapers. Creeds that exist to destroy each other both have scriptures, just as armies that exist to destroy each other both have guns.

The great example of this alleged spiritual identity of all human religions
is the alleged spiritual identity of Buddhism and Christianity. Those who
adopt this theory generally avoid the ethics of most other creeds, except,
indeed, Confucianism, which they like because it is not a creed. But they are
cautious in their praises of Mahommedanism, generally confining themselves to imposing its morality only upon the refreshment of the lower
classes. They seldom suggest the Mahommedan view of marriage (for which
there is a great deal to be said), and towards Thugs and fetish worshippers
their attitude may even be called cold. But in the case of the great religion of
Gautama they feel sincerely a similarity.

Students of popular science, like Mr Blatchford, are always insisting that
Christianity and Buddhism are very much alike, especially Buddhism. This
is generally believed, and I believed it myself until I read a book giving the
reasons for it. The reasons were of two kinds: resemblances that meant
nothing because they were common to all humanity, and resemblances
which were not resemblances at all. The author solemnly explained that the
two creeds were alike in things in which all creeds are alike, or else he
described them as alike in some point in which they are quite obviously
different. Thus, as a case of the first class, he said that both Christ and
Buddha were called by the divine voice coming out of the sky, as if you would
expect the divine voice to come out of the coal-cellar. Or, again, it was
gravely urged that these two Eastern teachers, by a singular coincidence,
both had to do with the washing of feet. You might as well say that it was a
remarkable coincidence that they both had feet to wash. And the other class
of similarities were those which simply were not similar. Thus this reconciler

of the two religions draws earnest attention to the fact that at certain religious feasts the robe of the Lama is rent in pieces out of respect, and the remnants highly valued. But this is the reverse of a resemblance, for the garments of Christ were not rent in pieces out of respect, but out of derision; and the remnants were not highly valued except for what they would fetch in the rag shops. It is rather like alluding to the obvious connection between the two ceremonies of the sword: when it taps a man's shoulder, and when it cuts off his head. It is not at all similar for the man. These scraps of puerile pedantry would indeed matter little if it were not also true that the alleged philosophical resemblances are also of these two kinds, either proving too much or not proving anything. That Buddhism approves of mercy or of self-restraint is not to say that it is specially like Christianity; it is only to say that it is not utterly unlike all human existence. Buddhists disapprove in theory of cruelty or excess because all sane human beings disapprove in theory of cruelty or excess. But to say that Buddhism and Christianity give the same philosophy of these things is simply false. All humanity does agree that we are in a net of sin. Most of humanity agrees that there is some way out. But as to what is the way out, I do not think that there are two institutions in the universe which contradict each other so flatly as Buddhism and Christianity.

Even when I thought, with most other well-informed, though unscholarly, people, that Buddhism and Christianity were alike, there was one thing about them that always perplexed me; I mean the startling difference in their type of religious art. I do not mean in its technical style of representation, but in the things that it was manifestly meant to represent. No two ideals could be more opposite than a Christian saint in a Gothic cathedral and a Buddhist saint in a Chinese temple. The opposition exists at every point; but perhaps the shortest statement of it is that the Buddhist saint always has his eyes shut, while the Christian saint always has them very wide open. The Buddhist saint has a sleek and harmonious body, but his eyes are heavy and sealed with sleep. The mediæval saint's body is wasted to its crazy bones, but his eyes are frightfully alive. There cannot be any real community of spirit between forces that produced symbols so different as that. Granted that both images are extravagances, are perversions of the pure creed, it must be a real divergence which could produce such opposite extravagances. The Buddhist is looking with a peculiar intentness inwards. The Christian is staring with a frantic intentness outwards. If we follow that clue steadily we shall find some interesting things.

A short time ago Mrs Besant, in an interesting essay, announced that there was only one religion in the world, that all faiths were only versions or perversions of it, and that she was quite prepared to say what it was. According to Mrs Besant this universal Church is simply the universal self. It is the doctrine that we are really all one person; that there are no real walls of individuality between man and man. If I may put it so, she does not tell us to love our neighbours; she tells us to be our neighbours. That is Mrs Besant's thoughtful and suggestive description of the religion in which all men must find themselves in agreement. And I never heard of any suggestion in my life with which I more violently disagree. I want to love my neighbour not because he is I, but precisely because he is not I. I want to adore the world, not as one likes a looking-glass, because it is one's self, but as one loves a woman, because she is entirely different. If souls are separate love is possible. If souls are united love is obviously impossible. A man may be said loosely to love himself, but he can hardly fall in love with himself, or, if he does, it must be a monotonous courtship. If the world is full of real selves, they can be really unselfish selves. But upon Mrs Besant's principle the whole cosmos is only one enormously selfish person.

It is just here that Buddhism is on the side of modern pantheism and immanence. And it is just here that Christianity is on the side of humanity and liberty and love. Love desires personality; therefore love desires division. It is the instinct of Christianity to be glad that God has broken the universe into little pieces, because they are living pieces. It is her instinct to say 'little children love one another' rather than to tell one large person to love himself. This is the intellectual abyss between Buddhism and Christianity; that for the Buddhist or Theosophist personality is the fall of man, for the Christian it is the purpose of God, the whole point of his cosmic idea. The world-soul of the Theosophists asks man to love it only in order that man may throw himself into it. But the divine centre of Christianity actually threw man out of it in order that he might love it. The oriental deity is like a giant who should have lost his leg or hand and be always seeking to find it; but the Christian power is like some giant who in a strange generosity should cut off his right hand, so that it might of its own accord shake hands with him. We come back to the same tireless note touching the nature of Christianity; all modern philosophies are chains which connect and fetter; Christianity is a sword which separates and sets free. No other philosophy makes God actually rejoice in the separation of the universe into living souls. But according to orthodox Christianity this separation between God and man is sacred, because this is eternal. That a man may love God it is necessary that there should be not only a God to be loved, but a man to love him. All those vague theosophical minds for whom the universe is an immense melting-pot are exactly the minds which shrink instinctively from that earthquake saying of our Gospels, which declare that the Son of God came not with peace but with a sundering sword. The saying rings entirely true even considered as what it obviously is; the statement that any man who preaches real love is bound to beget hate. It is as true of democratic fraternity as of divine love; sham love ends in compromise and common philosophy; but real love has always ended in bloodshed. Yet there is another and yet more awful truth behind the obvious meaning of this utterance of our Lord. According to Himself the Son was a sword separating brother and brother that they should for an æon hate each other. But the Father also was a sword, which in the black beginning separated brother and brother, so that they should love each other at last.

This is the meaning of that almost insane happiness in the eyes of the mediæval saint in the picture. This is the meaning of the sealed eyes of the superb Buddhist image. The Christian saint is happy because he has verily been cut off from the world; he is separate from things and is staring at them in astonishment. But why should the Buddhist saint be astonished at things? Since there is really only one thing, and that being impersonal can hardly be astonished at itself. There have been many pantheist poems suggesting wonder, but no really successful ones. The pantheist cannot wonder, for he cannot praise God or praise anything as really distinct from himself. Our immediate business here however is with the effect of this Christian admiration (which strikes outwards, towards a deity distinct from the worshipper) upon the general need for ethical activity and social reform. And surely its effect is sufficiently obvious. There is no real possibility of getting out of pantheism any special impulse to moral action. For pantheism implies in its nature that one thing is as good as another; whereas action implies in its nature that one thing is greatly preferable to another. Swinburne in the high summer of his scepticism tried in vain to wrestle with this difficulty. In 'Songs before Sunrise', written under the inspiration of Garibaldi and the revolt of Italy, he proclaimed the newer religion and the purer God which should wither up all the priests of the world.

> 'What doest thou now
> Looking Godward to cry
> I am I, thou art thou,
> I am low, thou art high,
> I am thou that thou seekest to find him, find thou
> but thyself, thou art I.'

Of which the immediate and evident deduction is that tyrants are as much the sons of God as Garibaldis; and that King Bomba of Naples having, with the utmost success, 'found himself' is identical with the ultimate good in all things. The truth is that the western energy that dethrones tyrants has been directly due to the western theology that says 'I am I, thou art thou'. The same spiritual separation which looked up and saw a good king in the universe looked up and saw a bad king in Naples. The worshippers of Bomba's god dethroned Bomba. The worshippers of Swinburne's god have covered Asia for centuries and have never dethroned a tyrant. The Indian saint may reasonably shut his eyes because he is looking at that which is I and Thou and We and They and It. It is a rational occupation: but it is not true in theory and not true in fact that it helps the Indian to keep an eye on Lord Curzon. That external vigilance which has always been the mark of Christianity (the command that we should *watch* and pray) has expressed itself both in typical western orthodoxy and in typical western politics: but both depend on the idea of a divinity transcendent, different from ourselves, a deity that disappears. Certainly the most sagacious creeds may suggest that we should pursue God into deeper and deeper rings of the labyrinth of our own ego. But only we of Christendom have said that we should hunt God like an eagle upon the mountains: and we have killed all monsters in the chase.

Here again, therefore, we find that in so far as we value democracy and the self renewing energies of the west, we are much more likely to find them in the old theology than the new. If we want reform, we must adhere to orthodoxy: especially in this matter (so much disputed in the counsels of Mr R. J. Campbell), the matter of insisting on the immanent or the transcendent deity. By insisting specially on the immanence of God we get introspection, self-isolation, quietism, social indifference—Tibet. By insisting specially on the transcendence of God we get wonder, curiosity, moral and political adventure, righteous indignation—Christendom. Insisting that God is inside man, man is always inside himself. By insisting that God transcends man, man has transcended himself.

If we take any other doctrine that has been called old-fashioned we shall find the case the same. It is the same, for instance, in the deep matter of the Trinity. Unitarians (a sect never to be mentioned without a special respect for their distinguished intellectual dignity and high intellectual honour) are often reformers by the accident that throws so many small sects into such an attitude. But there is nothing in the least liberal or akin to reform in the substitution of pure monotheism for the Trinity. The complex God of the Athanasian Creed may be an enigma for the intellect; but He is far less likely to gather the mystery and cruelty of a Sultan than the lonely god of Omar or Mahomet. The god who is a mere awful unity is not only a king but an Eastern king. The *heart* of humanity, especially of European humanity, is certainly much more satisfied by the strange hints and symbols that gather round the Trinitarian idea, the image of a council at which mercy pleads as well as justice, the conception of a sort of liberty and variety existing even in the inmost chamber of the world. For Western religion has always felt keenly the idea 'it is not well for man to be alone'. The social instinct asserted itself everywhere as when the Eastern idea of hermits was practically expelled by the Western idea of monks. So even asceticism became brotherly; and the Trappists were sociable even when they were silent. If this love of a living complexity be our test, it is certainly healthier to have the Trinitarian religion than the Unitarian. For to us Trinitarians (if I may say it with reverence)—to us God Himself is a society. It is indeed a fathomless mystery of theology, and even if I were theologian enough to deal with it directly, it would not be relevant to do so here. Suffice it to say here that this triple enigma is as comforting as wine and open as an English fireside; that this thing that bewilders the intellect utterly quiets the heart: but out of the desert, from the dry places and the dreadful suns, come the cruel children of the lonely God; the real Unitarians who with scimitar in hand have laid waste the world. For it is not well for God to be alone.

Again, the same is true of that difficult matter of the danger of the soul, which has unsettled so many just minds. To hope for all souls is imperative; and it is quite tenable that their salvation is inevitable. It is tenable, but it is not specially favourable to activity or progress. Our fighting and creative society ought rather to insist on the danger of everybody, on the fact that every man is hanging by a thread or clinging to a precipice. To say that all will be well anyhow is a comprehensible remark: but it cannot be called the blast of a trumpet. Europe ought rather to emphasise possible perdition; and Europe always has emphasised it. Here its highest religion is at one with all its cheapest romances. To the Buddhist or the eastern fatalist existence is a science or a plan, which must end up in a certain way. But to a Christian existence is a *story*, which may end up in any way. In a thrilling novel (that purely Christian product) the hero is not eaten by cannibals; but it is essential to the existence of the thrill that he *might* be eaten by cannibals. The hero must (so to speak) be an eatable hero. So Christian morals have always said to the man, not that he would lose his soul, but that he must take care that he didn't. In Christian morals, in short, it is wicked to call a man 'damned': but it is strictly religious and philosophic to call him damnable.

All Christianity concentrates on the man at the cross-roads. The vast and shallow philosophies, the huge syntheses of humbug, all talk about ages and evolution and ultimate developments. The true philosophy is concerned with the instant. Will a man take this road or that? That is the only thing to think about, if you enjoy thinking. The æons are easy enough to think about, any one can think about them. The instant is really awful: and it is because our religion has intensely felt the instant, that it has in literature dealt much with battle and in theology dealt much with hell. It is full of *danger*, like a boy's book: it is at an immortal crisis. There is a great deal of real similarity between popular fiction and the religion of the western people. If you say that popular fiction is vulgar and tawdry, you only say what the dreary and well-informed say also about the images in the Catholic churches. Life (according to the faith) is very like a serial story in a magazine: life ends with the promise (or menace) 'to be continued in our next'. Also, with a noble vulgarity, life imitates the serial and leaves off at the exciting moment. For death is distinctly an exciting moment.

But the point is that a story is exciting because it has in it so strong an element of will, of what theology calls free-will. You cannot finish a sum how you like. But you can finish a story how you like. When somebody discovered the Differential Calculus there was only one Differential Calculus he could discover. But when Shakespeare killed Romeo he might have married him to Juliet's old nurse if he had felt inclined. And Christendom has excelled in the narrative romance exactly because it has insisted on the theological free-will. It is a large matter and too much to one side of the road to be discussed adequately here; but this is the real objection to that torrent of modern talk about treating crime as disease, about making a prison merely a hygienic environment like a hospital, of healing sin by slow scientific methods. The fallacy of the whole thing is that evil is a matter of active choice, whereas disease is not. If you say that you are going to cure a profligate as you cure an asthmatic, my cheap and obvious answer is, 'Produce the people who want to be asthmatics as many people want to be profligates.' A man may lie still and be cured of a malady. But he must not lie still if he wants to be cured of a sin; on the contrary, he must get up and jump about violently. The whole point indeed is perfectly expressed in the very word which we use for a man in hospital; 'patient' is in the passive mood; 'sinner' is in the active. If a man is to be saved from influenza, he may be a patient. But if he is to be saved from forging, he must be not a patient but an *impatient*. He must be personally impatient with forgery. All moral reform must start in the active not the passive will.

Here again we reach the same substantial conclusion. In so far as we desire the definite reconstructions and the dangerous revolutions which have distinguished European civilisation, we shall not discourage the thought of possible ruin; we shall rather encourage it. If we want, like the Eastern saints, merely to contemplate how right things are, of course we shall only say that they must go right. But if we particularly want to *make* them go right, we must insist that they may go wrong.

Lastly, this truth is yet again true in the case of the common modern attempts to diminish or to explain away the divinity of Christ. The thing may be true or not; that I shall deal with before I end. But if the divinity is true it is certainly terribly revolutionary. That a good man may have his back to the wall is no more than we knew already; but that God could have his back to the wall is a boast for all insurgents for ever. Christianity is the only religion on earth that has felt that omnipotence made God incomplete. Christianity alone has felt that God, to be wholly God, must have been a rebel as well as a king. Alone of all creeds, Christianity has added courage to the virtues of the Creator. For the only courage worth calling courage must necessarily mean that the soul passes a breaking point—and does not break. In this indeed I approach a matter more dark and awful than it is easy to discuss; and I apologise in advance if any of my phrases fall wrong or seem irreverent touching a matter which the greatest saints and thinkers have justly feared to approach. But in that terrific tale of the Passion there is a distinct emotional suggestion that the author of all things (in some unthinkable way) went not only through agony, but through doubt. It is written, 'Thou shalt not tempt the Lord thy God.' No; but the Lord thy God may tempt Himself; and it seems as if this was what happened in Gethsemane. In a garden Satan tempted man: and in a garden God tempted God. He passed in some superhuman manner through our human horror of pessimism. When the world shook and the sun was wiped out of heaven, it was not at the crucifixion, but at the cry from the cross: the cry which confessed that God was forsaken of God. And now let the revolutionists choose a creed from all the creeds and a god from all the gods of the world, carefully weighing all the gods of inevitable recurrence and of unalterable power. They will not find another god who has himself been in revolt. Nay (the matter grows too difficult for human speech), but let the atheists themselves choose a god. They will find only one divinity who ever uttered their isolation; only one religion in which God seemed for an instant to be an atheist.

These can be called the essentials of the old orthodoxy, of which the chief merit is that it is the natural fountain of revolution and reform; and of which the chief defect is that it is obviously only an abstract assertion. Its main advantage is that it is the most adventurous and manly of all theologies. Its chief disadvantage is simply that it is a theology. It can always be urged against it that it is in its nature arbitrary and in the air. But it is not so high in the air but that great archers spend their whole lives in shooting arrows at it—yes, and their last arrows; there are men who will ruin themselves and ruin their civilisation if they may ruin also this old fantastic tale. This is the last and most astounding fact about this faith; that its enemies will use any weapon against it, the swords that cut their own fingers, and the firebrands that burn their own homes. Men who begin to fight the Church for the sake of freedom and humanity end by flinging away freedom and humanity if only they may fight the Church. This is no exaggeration; I could fill a book with the instances of it. Mr Blatchford set out, as an ordinary Bible-smasher to prove that Adam was guiltless of sin against God; in manœuvring so as to maintain this he admitted, as a mere side issue, that all the tyrants, from Nero to King Leopold, were guiltless of any sin against humanity. I know a man who has such a passion for proving that he will have no personal existence after death that he falls back on the position that he has no personal existence now. He invokes Buddhism and says that all souls fade into each other; in order to prove that he cannot go to heaven he proves that he cannot go to Hartlepool. I have known people who protested against religious education with arguments against any education, saying that the child's mind must grow freely or that the old must not teach the young. I have known people who showed that there could be no divine judgment by showing that there can be no human judgment, even for practical purposes, They burned their own corn to set fire to the church; they smashed their own tools to smash it; any stick was good enough to beat it with, though it were the last stick of their own dismembered furniture. We do not admire, we hardly excuse, the fanatic who wrecks this world for love of the other. But what are we to say of the fanatic who wrecks this world out of hatred of the other? He sacrifices the very existence of humanity to the non-existence of God. He offers his victims not to the altar, but merely to assert the idleness of the altar and the emptiness of the throne. He is ready to ruin even that primary ethic by which all things live, for his strange and eternal vengeance upon some one who never lived at all.

And yet the thing hangs in the heavens unhurt. Its opponents only succeed in destroying all that they themselves justly hold dear. They do not destroy orthodoxy; they only destroy political courage and common sense. They do not prove that Adam was not responsible to God; how could they prove it? They only prove (from their premises) that the Czar is not responsible to Russia. They do not prove that Adam should not have been punished by God; they only prove that the nearest sweater should not be punished by men. With their oriental doubts about personality they do not make certain that we shall have no personal life hereafter; they only make certain that we shall not have a very jolly or complete one here. With their paralysing hints of all conclusions coming out wrong they do not tear the book of the Recording Angel; they only make it a little harder to keep the books of Marshall and Snelgrove. Not only is the faith the mother of all wordly energies, but its foes are the fathers of all worldly confusion. The secularists have not wrecked divine things; but the secularists have wrecked secular things, if that is any comfort to them. The Titans did not scale heaven; but they laid waste the world.

# Authority and the Adventurer

The last chapter has been concerned with the contention that orthodoxy is not only (as is often urged) the only safe guardian of morality or order, but is also the only logical guardian of liberty, innovation and advance. If we wish to pull down the prosperous oppressor we cannot do it with the new doctrine of human perfectibility; we can do it with the old doctrine of Original Sin. If we want to uproot inherent cruelties or lift up lost populations we cannot do it with the scientific theory that matter precedes mind; we can do it with the supernatural theory that mind precedes matter. If we wish specially to awaken people to social vigilance and tireless pursuit of practice, we cannot help it much by insisting on the Immanent God and the Inner Light: for these are at best reasons for contentment; we can help it much by insisting on the transcendent God and the flying and escaping gleam; for that means divine discontent. If we wish particularly to assert the idea of a generous balance against that of a dreadful autocracy we shall instinctively be Trinitarian rather than Unitarian. If we desire European civilisation to be a raid and a rescue, we shall insist rather that souls are in real peril than that their peril is ultimately unreal. And if we wish to exalt the outcast and the crucified, we shall rather wish to think that a veritable God was crucified, rather than a mere sage or hero. Above all, if we wish to protect the poor we shall be in favour of fixed rules and clear dogmas. The *rules* of a club are occasionally in favour of the poor member. The drift of a club is always in favour of the rich one.

And now we come to the crucial question which truly concludes the whole matter. A reasonable agnostic, if he has happened to agree with me so far, may justly turn round and say, 'You have found a practical philosophy in the doctrine of the Fall; very well. You have found a side of democracy now dangerously neglected wisely asserted in Original Sin; all right. You have found a truth in the doctrine of hell; I congratulate you. You are convinced that worshippers of a personal God look outwards and are progressive; I

Orthodoxy, 1908

311

congratulate them. But even supposing that those doctrines do include those truths, why cannot you take the truths and leave the doctrines? Granted that all modern society is trusting the rich too much because it does not allow for human weakness; granted that orthodox ages have had a great advantage because (believing in the Fall) they did allow for human weakness, why cannot you simply allow for human weakness without believing in the Fall? If you have discovered that the idea of damnation represents a healthy idea of danger, why can you not simply take the idea of danger and leave the idea of damnation? If you see clearly the kernel of common-sense in the nut of Christian orthodoxy, why cannot you simply take the kernel and leave the nut? Why cannot you (to use that cant phrase of the newspapers which I, as a highly scholarly agnostic, am a little ashamed of using) why cannot you simply take what is good in Christianity, what you can define as valuable, what you can comprehend, and leave all the rest, all the absolute dogmas that are in their nature incomprehensible?' This is the real question; this is the last question; and it is a pleasure to try to answer it.

The first answer is simply to say that I am a rationalist. I like to have some intellectual justification for my intuitions. If I am treating man as a fallen being it is an intellectual convenience to me to believe that he fell; and I find, for some odd psychological reason, that I can deal better with a man's exercise of freewill if I believe that he has got it. But I am in this matter yet more definitely a rationalist. I do not propose to turn this book into one of ordinary Christian apologetics; I should be glad to meet at any other time the enemies of Christianity in that more obvious arena. Here I am only giving an account of my own growth in spiritual certainty. But I may pause to remark that the more I saw of the merely abstract arguments against the Christian cosmology the less I thought of them. I mean that having found the moral atmosphere of the Incarnation to be common sense, I then looked at the established intellectual arguments against the Incarnation and found them to be common nonsense. In case the argument should be thought to suffer from the absence of the ordinary apologetic I will here very briefly summarise my own arguments and conclusions on the purely objective or scientific truth of the matter.

If I am asked, as a purely intellectual question, why I believe in Christianity, I can only answer, 'For the same reason that an intelligent agnostic disbelieves in Christianity.' I believe in it quite rationally upon the evidence. But the evidence in my case, as in that of the intelligent agnostic, is not really in this or that alleged demonstration; it is in an enormous accumulation of small but unanimous facts. The secularist is not to be blamed because his objections to Christianity are miscellaneous and even scrappy; it is precisely such scrappy evidence that does convince the mind. I mean that a man may well be less convinced of a philosophy from four books, than from one book, one battle, one landscape and one old friend. The very fact that the things are of different kinds increases the importance of the fact that they all point to one conclusion. Now, the non-Christianity of the average educated man to-day is almost always, to do him justice, made up of these loose but living experiences. I can only say that my evidences for Christianity are of the same vivid but varied kind as his evidences against it. For when I look at these various anti-Christian truths, I simply discover that none of them are true. I discover that the true tide and force of all the facts flows the other way. Let us take cases. Many a sensible modern man must have abandoned Christianity under the pressure of three such converging convictions as these: first, that men, with their shape, structure and sexuality, are, after all, very much like beasts, a mere variety of the animal kingdom; second, that primeval religion arose in ignorance and fear; third, that priests have blighted societies with bitterness and gloom. Those three anti-Christian arguments are very different; but they are all quite logical and legitimate; and they all converge. The only objection to them (I discover) is that they are all untrue. If you leave off looking at books about beasts and men, if you begin to look at beasts and men then (if you have any humour or imagination, any sense of the frantic or the farcical) you will observe that the startling thing is not how like man is to the brutes, but how unlike he is. It is the monstrous scale of his divergence that requires an explanation. That man and brute are like is, in a sense, a truism; but that being so like they should then be so insanely unlike, that is the shock and the enigma. That an ape has hands is far less interesting to the philosopher than the fact that having hands he does next to nothing with them; does not play knuckle-bones or the violin; does not carve marble or carve mutton. People talk of barbaric architecture and debased art. But elephants do not build colossal temples of ivory even in a rococo style; camels do not paint even bad pictures, though equipped with the material of many camel's-hair brushes. Certain modern dreamers say that ants and bees have a society superior to ours. They have, indeed, a civilisation; but that very truth only reminds us that it is an inferior civilisation. Who ever found an ant-hill decorated with the statues of celebrated ants? Who has seen a bee-hive carved with the images of gorgeous queens of old? No; the chasm between man and other creatures may have a natural explanation, but it is a chasm. We talk of wild animals; but man is the only wild animal. It is man that has broken out. All other animals are tame animals; following the rugged respectability of the tribe or type. All other animals are domestic animals; man alone is ever undomestic, either as a profligate or a monk. So that this first superficial reason for materialism is, if anything, a reason for its opposite; it is exactly where biology leaves off that all religion begins.

It would be the same if I examined the second of the three chance rationalist arguments; the argument that all that we call divine began in some darkness and terror. When I did attempt to examine the foundations of this modern idea I simply found that there were none. Science knows nothing whatever about pre-historic man; for the excellent reason that he is pre-historic. A few professors choose to conjecture that such things as human sacrifice were once innocent and general and that they gradually dwindled; but there is no direct evidence of it, and the small amount of indirect evidence is very much the other way. In the earliest legends we have, such as the tales of Isaac and of Iphigenia, human sacrifice is not introduced as something old, but rather as something new; as a strange and frightful exception darkly demanded by the gods. History says nothing; and legends all say that the earth was kinder in its earliest time. There is no tradition of progress; but the whole human race has a tradition of the Fall. Amusingly enough, indeed, the very dissemination of this idea is used against its authenticity. Learned men literally say that this pre-historic calamity cannot be true because every race of mankind remembers it. I cannot keep pace with these paradoxes.

And if we took the third chance instance, it would be the same; the view that priests darken and embitter the world. I look at the world and simply discover that they don't. Those countries in Europe which are still influenced by priests, are exactly the countries where there is still singing and dancing and coloured dresses and art in the open-air. Catholic doctrine and discipline may be walls; but they are the walls of a play-ground. Christianity is the only frame which has preserved the pleasure of Paganism. We might fancy some children playing on the flat grassy top of some tall island in the sea. So long as there was a wall round the cliff's edge they could fling themselves into every frantic game and make the place the noisiest of nurseries. But the walls were knocked down, leaving the naked peril of the precipice. They did not fall over; but when their friends returned to them they were all huddled in terror in the centre of the island; and their song had ceased.

Thus these three facts of experience, such facts as go to make an agnostic, are, in this view, turned totally round. I am left saying, 'Give me an explanation, first, of the towering eccentricity of man among the brutes; second, of the vast human tradition of some ancient happiness; third, of the partial perpetuation of such pagan joy in the countries of the Catholic Church.' One explanation, at any rate, covers all three: the theory that twice was the natural order interrupted by some explosion or revelation such as people now call 'psychic'. Once Heaven came upon the earth with a power or seal called the image of God, whereby man took command of Nature; and once again (when in empire after empire men had been found wanting) Heaven came to save mankind in the awful shape of a man. This would explain why the mass of men always look backwards; and why the only corner where they in any sense look forwards is the little continent where Christ has His Church. I know it will be said that Japan has become progressive. But how can this be an answer when even in saying 'Japan has become progressive', we really only mean, 'Japan has become European'? But I wish here not so much to insist on my own explanation as to insist on my original remark. I agree with the ordinary unbelieving man in the street in being guided by three or four odd facts all pointing to something; only when I came to look at the facts I always found they pointed to something else.

I have given an imaginary triad of such ordinary anti-Christian arguments; if that be too narrow a basis I will give on the spur of the moment another. These are the kind of thoughts which in combination create the impression that Christianity is something weak and diseased. First, for instance, that Jesus was a gentle creature, sheepish and unworldly, a mere ineffectual appeal to the world; second, that Christianity arose and flourished in the dark ages of ignorance, and that to these the Church would drag us back; third, that the people still strongly religious or (if you will) superstitious— such people as the Irish—are weak, unpractical and behind the times. I only mention these ideas to affirm the same thing: that when I looked into them independently I found, not that the conclusions were unphilosophical, but simply that the facts were not facts. Instead of looking at books and pictures about the New Testament I looked at the New Testament. There I found an account, not in the least of a person with his hair parted in the middle or his hands clasped in appeal, but of an extraordinary being with lips of thunder and acts of lurid decision, flinging down tables, casting out devils, passing with the wild secrecy of the wind from mountain isolation to a sort of dreadful demagogy; a being who often acted like an angry god—and always like a god. Christ had even a literary style of his own, not to be found, I think, elsewhere; it consists of an almost furious use of the, *a fortiori*. His 'how much more' is piled one upon another like castle upon castle in the clouds. The diction used *about* Christ has been, and perhaps wisely, sweet and submissive. But the diction used by Christ is quite curiously gigantesque; it is full of camels leaping through needles and mountains hurled into the sea. Morally it is equally terrific; he called himself a sword of slaughter, and told men to buy swords if they sold their coats for them. That he used other even wilder words on the side of non-resistance greatly increases the mystery; but it also, if anything, rather increases the violence. We cannot even explain it by calling such a being insane; for insanity is usually along one consistent channel. The maniac is generally a monomaniac. Here we must remember the difficult definition of Christianity already given; Christianity is a superhuman paradox whereby two opposite passions may blaze beside each other. The one explanation of the Gospel language that does explain it, is that it is the survey of one who from some supernatural height beholds some more startling synthesis.

I take in order the next instance offered: the idea that Christianity belongs to the dark ages. Here I did not satisfy myself with reading modern generalisations; I read a little history. And in history I found that Christianity, so far from belonging to the dark ages, was the one path across the dark ages that was not dark. It was a shining bridge connecting two shining civilisations. If any one say that the faith arose in ignorance and savagery the answer is simple: it didn't. It arose in the Mediterranean civilisation in the full summer of the Roman Empire. The world was swarming with sceptics, and pantheism was as plain as the sun, when Constantine nailed the cross to the mast. It is perfectly true that afterwards the ship sank; but it is far more extraordinary that the ship came up again: repainted and glittering, with the cross still at the top. This is the amazing thing the religion did: it turned a sunken ship into a submarine. The ark lived under the load of waters; after being buried under the débris of dynasties and clans, we arose and remembered Rome. If our faith had been a mere fad of the fading empire, fad would have followed fad in the twilight, and if the civilisation ever re-emerged (and many such have never re-emerged) it would have been under some new barbaric flag. But the Christian Church was the last life of the old society and was also the first life of the new. She took the people who were forgetting how to make an arch and she taught them to invent the Gothic arch. In a word, the most absurd thing that could be said of the Church is the thing we have all heard said of it. How can we say that the Church wishes to bring us back into the Dark Ages? The Church was the only thing that ever brought us out of them.

I added in this second trinity of objections an idle instance taken from those who feel such people as the Irish to be weakened or made stagnant by superstition. I only added it because this is a peculiar case of a statement of fact that turns out to be a statement of falsehood. It is constantly said of the Irish that they are impractical. But if we refrain for a moment from looking at what is said about them and look at what is *done* about them, we shall see that the Irish are not only practical, but quite painfully successful. The poverty of their country, the minority of their members are simply the conditions under which they were asked to work; but no other group in the British Empire has done so much with such conditions. The Nationalists were the only minority that ever succeeded in twisting the whole British Parliament sharply out of its path. The Irish peasants are the only poor men in these islands who have forced their masters to disgorge. These people, whom we call priest-ridden, are the only Britons who will not be squire-ridden. And when I came to look at the actual Irish character, the case was the same. Irishmen are best at the specially *hard* professions—the trades of iron, the lawyer, and the soldier. In all these cases, therefore, I came back to the same conclusion: the sceptic was quite right to go by the facts, only he had not looked at the facts. The sceptic is too credulous; he believes in newspapers or even in encyclopædias. Again the three questions left me with three very antagonistic questions. The average sceptic wanted to know how I explained the namby-pamby note in the Gospel, the connection of the creed with mediæval darkness and the political impracticability of the Celtic Christians. But I wanted to ask, and to ask with an earnestness amounting to urgency, 'What is this incomparable energy which appears first in one walking the earth like a living judgment and this energy which can die with a dying civilisation and yet force it to a resurrection from the dead; this energy which last of all can inflame a bankrupt peasantry with so fixed a faith in justice that they get what they ask, while others go empty away; so that the most helpless island of the Empire can actually help itself?'

There is an answer: it is an answer to say that the energy is truly from outside the world; that it is psychic, or at least one of the results of a real psychical disturbance. The highest gratitude and respect are due to the great human civilisations such as the old Egyptian or the existing Chinese. Nevertheless it is no injustice for them to say that only modern Europe has exhibited incessantly a power of self-renewal recurring often at the shortest intervals and descending to the smallest facts of building or costume. All other societies die finally and with dignity. We die daily. We are always being born again with almost indecent obstetrics. It is hardly an exaggeration to say that there is in historic Christendom a sort of unnatural life: it could be explained as a supernatural life. It could be explained as an awful galvanic life working in what would have been a corpse. For our civilisation *ought* to have died, by all parallels, by all sociological probability, in the Ragnorak of the end of Rome. That is the weird inspiration of our estate: you and I have no business to be here at all. We are all *revenants*; all living Christians are dead pagans walking about. Just as Europe was about to be gathered in silence to Assyria and Babylon, something entered into its body. And Europe has had a strange life—it is not too much to say that it has had the *jumps*—ever since.

I have dealt at length with such typical triads of doubt in order to convey the main contention—that my own case for Christianity is rational; but it is not simple. It is an accumulation of varied facts, like the attitude of the ordinary agnostic. But the ordinary agnostic has got his facts all wrong. He is a non-believer for a multitude of reasons; but they are untrue reasons. He doubts because the Middle Ages were barbaric, but they weren't; because Darwinism is demonstrated, but it isn't; because miracles do not happen, but they do; because monks were lazy, but they were very industrious; because nuns are unhappy, but they are particularly cheerful; because Christian art was sad and pale, but it was picked out in peculiarly bright colours and gay with gold; because modern science is moving away from the supernatural, but it isn't, it is moving towards the supernatural with the rapidity of a railway train.

But among these million facts all flowing one way there is, of course, one question sufficiently solid and separate to be treated briefly, but by itself; I mean the objective occurrence of the supernatural. In another chapter I have indicated the fallacy of the ordinary supposition that the world must be impersonal because it is orderly. A person is just as likely to desire an orderly thing as a disorderly thing. But my own positive conviction that personal creation is more conceivable than material fate, is, I admit, in a sense, undiscussable. I will not call it a faith or an intuition, for those words are mixed up with mere emotion, it is strictly an intellectual conviction; but it is a *primary* intellectual conviction like the certainty of self or the good of living. Any one who likes, therefore, may call my belief in God merely mystical; the phrase is not worth fighting about. But my belief that miracles have happened in human history is not a mystical belief at all; I believe in them upon human evidence as I do in the discovery of America. Upon this point there is a simple logical fact that only requires to be stated and cleared up. Somehow or other an extraordinary idea has arisen that the disbelievers in miracles consider them coldly and fairly, while believers in miracles accept them only in connection with some dogma. The fact is quite the other way. The believers in miracles accept them (rightly or wrongly) because they have evidence for them. The disbelievers in miracles deny them (rightly or wrongly) because they have a doctrine against them. The open, obvious, democratic thing is to believe an old apple-woman when she bears testimony to a miracle, just as you believe an old apple-woman when she bears testimony to a murder. The plain, popular course is to trust the peasant's word about the ghost exactly as far as you trust the peasant's word about the landlord. Being a peasant he will probably have a great deal of healthy agnosticism about both. Still you could fill the British Museum with evidence uttered by the peasant, and given in favour of the ghost. If it comes to human testimony there is a choking cataract of human testimony in favour of the supernatural. If you reject it, you can only mean one of two things. You reject the peasant's story about the ghost either because the man is a peasant or because the story is a ghost story. That is, you either deny the main principle of democracy, or you affirm the main principle of materialism— the abstract impossibility of miracle. You have a perfect right to do so; but in that case you are the dogmatist. It is we Christians who accept all actual evidence—it is you rationalists who refuse actual evidence, being constrained to do so by your creed. But I am not constrained by any creed in the matter, and looking impartially into certain miracles of mediæval and modern times, I have come to the conclusion that they occurred. All argument against these plain facts is always argument in a circle. If I say,

'Mediæval documents attest certain miracles as much as they attest certain battles,' they answer, 'But mediævals were superstitious;' if I want to know in what they were superstitious, the only ultimate answer is that they believed in the miracles. If I say 'a peasant saw a ghost,' I am told, 'But peasants are so credulous.' If I ask, 'Why credulous?' the only answer is—that they see ghosts. Iceland is impossible because only stupid sailors have seen it; and the sailors are only stupid because they say they have seen Iceland. It is only fair to add that there is another argument that the unbeliever may rationally use against miracles, though he himself generally forgets to use it.

He may say that there has been in many miraculous stories a notion of spiritual preparation and acceptance: in short, that the miracle could only come to him who believed in it. It may be so, and if it is so how are we to test it? If we are inquiring whether certain results follow faith, it is useless to repeat wearily that (if they happen) they do follow faith. If faith is one of the conditions, those without faith have a most healthy right to laugh. But they have no right to judge. Being a believer may be, if you like, as bad as being drunk; still if we were extracting psychological facts from drunkards, it would be absurd to be always taunting them with having been drunk. Suppose we were investigating whether angry men really saw a red mist before their eyes. Suppose sixty excellent house-holders swore that when angry they had seen this crimson cloud: surely it would be absurd to answer 'Oh, but you admit you were angry at the time.' They might reasonably rejoin (in a stentorian chorus), 'How the blazes could we discover, without being angry, whether angry people see red?' So the saints and ascetics might rationally reply, 'Suppose that the question is whether believers can see visions—even then, if you are interested in visions it is no point to object to believers.' You are still arguing in a circle—in that old mad circle with which this book began.

The question of whether miracles ever occur is a question of common sense and of ordinary historical imagination: not of any final physical experiment. One may here surely dismiss that quite brainless piece of pedantry which talks about the need for 'scientific conditions' in connection with alleged spiritual phenomena. If we are asking whether a dead soul can communicate with a living it is ludicrous to insist that it shall be under conditions in which no two living souls in their senses would seriously communicate with each other. The fact that ghosts prefer darkness no more disproves the existence of ghosts than the fact that lovers prefer darkness disproves the existence of love. If you choose to say, 'I will believe that Miss Brown called her *fiancé* a periwinkle or any other endearing term, if she will repeat the word before seventeen psychologists,' then I shall reply, 'Very well, if those are your conditions, you will never get the truth, for she certainly will not say it.' It is just as unscientific as it is unphilosophical to be

319

surprised that in an unsympathetic atmosphere certain extraordinary sympathies do not arise. It is as if I said that I could not tell if there was a fog because the air was not clear enough; or as if I insisted on perfect sunlight in order to see a solar eclipse.

As a common-sense conclusion, such as those to which we come about sex or about midnight (well knowing that many details must in their own nature be concealed) I conclude that miracles do happen. I am forced to it by a conspiracy of facts: the fact that the men who encounter elves or angels are not the mystics and the morbid dreamers, but fishermen, farmers, and all men at once coarse and cautious; the fact that we all know men who testify to spiritualist incidents but are not spiritualists; the fact that science itself admits such things more and more every day. Science will even admit the Ascension if you call it Levitation, and will very likely admit the Resurrection when it has thought of another word for it. I suggest the Regalvanisation. But the strongest of all is the dilemma above mentioned, that these supernatural things are never denied except on the basis either of anti-democracy or of materialist dogmatism—I may say materialist mysticism. The sceptic always takes one of the two positions; either an ordinary man need not be believed, or an extraordinary event must not be believed. For I hope we may dismiss the argument against wonders attempted in the mere recapitulation of frauds, of swindling mediums or trick miracles. That is not an argument at all, good or bad. A false ghost disproves the reality of ghosts exactly as much as a forged banknote disproves the existence of the Bank of England—if anything, it proves its existence.

Given this conviction that the spiritual phenomena do occur (my evidence for which is complex but rational), we then collide with one of the worst mental evils of the age. The greatest disaster of the nineteenth century was this: that men began to use the word 'spiritual' as the same as the word 'good'. They thought that to grow in refinement and uncorporeality was to grow in virtue. When scientific evolution was announced, some feared that it would encourage mere animality. It did worse: it encouraged mere spirituality. It taught men to think that so long as they were passing from the ape they were going to the angel. But you can pass from the ape and go to the devil. A man of genius, very typical of that time of bewilderment, expressed it perfectly. Benjamin Disraeli was right when he said he was on the side of the angels. He was indeed; he was on the side of the fallen angels. He was not on the side of any mere appetite or animal brutality; but he was on the side of all the imperialism of the princes of the abyss; he was on the side of arrogance and mystery, and contempt of all obvious good. Between this sunken pride and the towering humilities of heaven there are, one must suppose, spirits of shapes and sizes. Man, in encountering them, must make much the same mistakes that he makes in encountering any other varied types in any other distant continent. It must be hard at first to know who is supreme and who is subordinate. If a shade arose from the under world, and stared at Piccadilly, that shade would not quite understand the idea of an ordinary closed carriage. He would suppose that the coachman on the box was a triumphant conqueror, dragging behind him a kicking and imprisoned captive. So, if we see spiritual facts for the first time, we may mistake who is uppermost. It is not enough to find the gods; they are obvious; we must find God, the real chief of the gods. We must have a long historic experience in supernatural phenomena—in order to discover which are really natural. In this light I find the history of Christianity, and even of its Hebrew origins, quite practical and clear. It does not trouble me to be told that the Hebrew god was one among many. I know he was, without any research to tell me so. Jehovah and Baal looked equally important, just as the sun and the moon looked the same size. It is only slowly that we learn that the sun is immeasurably our master, and the small moon only our satellite. Believing that there is a world of spirits, I shall walk in it as I do in the world of men, looking for the thing that I like and think good. Just as I should seek in a desert for clean water, or toil at the North Pole to make a comfortable fire, so I shall search the land of void and vision until I find something fresh like water, and comforting like fire; until I find some place in eternity, where I am literally at home. And there is only one such place to be found.

I have now said enough to show (to any one to whom such an explanation is essential) that I have in the ordinary arena of apologetics, a ground of belief. In pure records of experiment (if these be taken democratically without contempt or favour) there is evidence first, that miracles happen, and second that the nobler miracles belong to our tradition. But I will not pretend that this curt discussion is my real reason for accepting Christianity instead of taking the moral good of Christianity as I should take it out of Confucianism.

I have another far more solid and central ground for submitting to it as a faith, instead of merely picking up hints from it as a scheme. And that is this: that the Christian Church in its practical relation to my soul is a living teacher, not a dead one. It not only certainly taught me yesterday, but will almost certainly teach me to-morrow. Once I saw suddenly the meaning of the shape of the cross; some day I may see suddenly the meaning of the shape of the mitre. One fine morning I saw why windows were pointed; some fine morning I may see why priests were shaven. Plato has told you a truth; but Plato is dead. Shakespeare has startled you with an image; but Shakespeare will not startle you with any more. But imagine what it would be to live with such men still living, to know that Plato might break out with an original lecture to-morrow, or that at any moment Shakespeare might shatter everything with a single song. The man who lives in contact with what he believes to be a living Church is a man always expecting to meet Plato and Shake-speare to-morrow at breakfast. He is always expecting to see some truth that he has never seen before. There is one only other parallel to this position; and that is the parallel of the life in which we all began. When your father told you, walking about the garden, that bees stung or that roses smelt sweet, you did not talk of taking the best out of his philosophy. When the bees stung you, you did not call it an entertaining coincidence. When the rose smelt sweet you did not say 'My father is a rude, barbaric symbol, enshrining (perhaps unconsciously) the deep delicate truths that flowers smell.' No: you believed your father, because you had found him to be a living fountain of facts, a thing that really knew more than you; a thing that would tell you truth to-morrow, as well as to-day. And if this was true of your father, it was even truer of your mother, at least it was true of mine, to whom this book is dedicated. Now, when society is in a rather futile fuss about the subjection of women, will no one say how much every man owes to the tyranny and privilege of women, to the fact that they alone rule education until education becomes futile: for a boy is only sent to be taught at school when it is too late to teach him anything. The real thing has been done already, and thank God it is nearly always done by women. Every man is womanised, merely by being born. They talk of the masculine woman; but every man is a feminised man. And if ever men walk to Westminster to protest against this female privilege, I shall not join their procession.

For I remember with certainty this fixed psychological fact; that the very time when I was most under a woman's authority, I was most full of flame and adventure. Exactly because when my mother said that ants bit they did bite, and because snow did come in winter (as she said); therefore the whole world was to me a fairyland of wonderful fulfilments, and it was like living in some Hebraic age, when prophecy after prophecy came true. I went out as a child into the garden, and it was a terrible place to me, precisely because I had a clue to it: if I had held no clue it would not have been terrible, but tame. A mere unmeaning wilderness is not even impressive. But the garden of childhood was fascinating, exactly because everything had a fixed meaning which could be found out in its turn. Inch by inch I might discover what was the object of the ugly shape called a rake; or form some shadowy conjecture as to why my parents kept a cat.

So, since I have accepted Christendom as a mother and not merely as a chance example, I have found Europe and the world once more like the little garden where I stared at the symbolic shapes of cat and rake; I look at everything with the old elvish ignorance and expectancy. This or that rite or doctrine may look as ugly and extraordinary as a rake; but I have found by experience that such things end somehow in grass and flowers. A clergyman may be apparently as useless as a cat, but he is also as fascinating, for there must be some strange reason for his existence. I give one instance out of a hundred; I have not myself any instinctive kinship with that enthusiasm for physical virginity, which has certainly been a note of historic Christianity. But when I look not at myself but at the world, I perceive that this enthusiasm is not only a note of Christianity, but a note of Paganism, a note of high human nature in many spheres. The Greeks felt virginity when they carved Artemis, the Romans when they robed the vestals, the worst and wildest of the great Elizabethen playwrights clung to the literal purity of a woman as to the central pillar of the world. Above all, the modern world (even while mocking sexual innocence) has flung itself into a generous idolatry of sexual innocence—the great modern worship of children. For any man who loves children will agree that their peculiar beauty is hurt by a hint of physical sex. With all this human experience, allied with the Christian authority, I simply conclude that I am wrong, and the church right; or rather that I am defective, while the church is universal. It takes all sorts to make a church; she does not ask me to be celibate. But the fact that I have no appreciation of the celibates, I accept like the fact that I have no ear for music. The best human experience is against me, as it is on the subject of Bach. Celibacy is one flower in my father's garden, of which I have not been told the sweet or terrible name. But I may be told it any day.

This, therefore, is, in conclusion, my reason for accepting the religion and not merely the scattered and secular truths out of the religion. I do it because the thing has not merely told this truth or that truth, but has revealed itself as a truth-telling thing. All other philosophies say the things that plainly seem to be true; only this philosophy has again and again said the thing that does not seem to be true, but is true. Alone of all creeds it is convincing where it is not attractive; it turns out to be right, like my father in the garden. Theosophists, for instance, will preach an obviously attractive idea like re-incarnation; but if we wait for its logical results, they are spiritual superciliousness and the cruelty of caste. For if a man is a beggar by his own pre-natal sins, people will tend to despise the beggar. But Christianity preaches an obviously unattractive idea, such as original sin; but then we wait for its results, they are pathos and brotherhood, and a thunder of laughter and pity; for only with original sin we can at once pity the beggar and distrust the king. Men of science offer us health, an obvious benefit; it is only afterwards that we discover that by health, they mean bodily slavery and spiritual tedium. Orthodoxy makes us jump by the sudden brink of hell; it is only afterwards that we realise that jumping was an athletic exercise highly beneficial to our health. It is only afterwards that we realise that this danger is the root of all drama and romance. The strongest argument for the divine grace is simply its ungraciousness. The unpopular parts of Christianity turn out when examined to be the very props of the people. The outer ring of Christianity is a rigid guard of ethical abnegations and professional priests; but inside that inhuman guard you will find the old human life dancing like children, and drinking wine like men; for Christianity is the only frame for pagan freedom. But in the modern philosophy the case is opposite; it is its outer ring that is obviously artistic and emancipated; its despair is within.

And its despair is this, that it does not really believe that there is any meaning in the universe; therefore it cannot hope to find any romance; its romances will have no plots. A man cannot expect any adventures in the land of anarchy. But a man can expect any number of adventures if he goes travelling in the land of authority. One can find no meanings in a jungle of scepticism; but the man will find more and more meanings who walks through a forest of doctrine and design. Here everything has a story tied to its tail, like the tools or pictures in my father's house; for it is my father's house. I end where I began—at the right end. I have entered at least the gate of all good philosophy. I have come into my second childhood.

But this larger and more adventurous Christian universe has one final mark difficult to express, yet as a conclusion of the whole matter I will attempt to express it. All the real argument about religion turns on the question of whether a man who was born upside down can tell when he comes right way up. The primary paradox of Christianity is that the ordinary condition of man is not his sane or sensible condition; that the normal itself is an abnormality. That is the inmost philosophy of the Fall. In Sir Oliver Lodge's interesting new Catechism, the first two questions were: 'What are you?' and 'What, then, is the meaning of the Fall of Man?' I remember amusing myself by writing my own answers to the questions; but I soon found that they were very broken and agnostic answers. To the question, 'What are you?' I could only answer, 'God knows.' And to the question, 'What is meant by the Fall?' I could answer with complete sincerity, 'That whatever I am, I am not myself.' This is the prime paradox of our religion; something that we have never in any full sense known, is not only better than ourselves, but even more natural to us than ourselves. And there is really no test of this except the merely experimental one with which these pages began, the test of the padded cell and the open door. It is only since I have known orthodoxy that I have known mental emancipation. But, in conclusion, it has one special application to the ultimate idea of joy.

It is said that Paganism is a religion of joy and Christianity of sorrow; it would be just as easy to prove that Paganism is pure sorrow and Christianity pure joy. Such conflicts mean nothing and lead nowhere. Everything human must have in it both joy and sorrow; the only matter of interest is the manner in which the two things are balanced or divided. And the really interesting thing is this, that the pagan was (in the main) happier and happier as he approached the earth, but sadder and sadder as he approached the heavens.

The gaiety of the best Paganism, as in the playfulness of Catullus or Theocritus, is, indeed, an eternal gaiety never to be forgotten by a grateful humanity. But it is all a gaiety about the facts of life, not about its origin. To the pagan the small things are as sweet as the small brooks breaking out of the mountain; but the broad things are as bitter as the sea. When the pagan looks at the very core of the cosmos he is struck cold. Behind the gods, who are merely despotic, sit the fates, who are deadly. Nay, the fates are worse than deadly; they are dead. And when rationalists say that the ancient world was more enlightened than the Christian, from their point of view they are right. For when they say 'enlightened' they mean darkened with incurable despair. It is profoundly true that the ancient world was more modern than the Christian. The common bond is in the fact that ancients and moderns have both been miserable about existence, about everything, while mediævals were happy about that at least. I freely grant that the pagans, like the moderns, were only miserable about everything—they were quite jolly about everything else. I concede that the Christians of the Middle Ages were only at peace about everything—they were at war about everything else. But if the question turn on the primary pivot of the cosmos, then there was more cosmic contentment in the narrow and bloody streets of Florence than in the theatre of Athens or the open garden of Epicurus. Giotto lived in a gloomier town than Euripides, but he lived in a gayer universe.

The mass of men have been forced to be gay about the little things, but sad about the big ones. Nevertheless (I offer my last dogma defiantly) it is not native to man to be so. Man is more himself, man is more manlike, when joy is the fundamental thing in him, and grief the superficial. Melancholy should be an innocent interlude, a tender and fugitive frame of mind; praise should be the permanent pulsation of the soul. Pessimism is at best an emotional half-holiday; joy is the uproarious labour by which all things live. Yet, according to the apparent estate of man as seen by the pagan or the agnostic, this primary need of human nature can never be fulfilled. Joy ought to be expansive; but for the agnostic it must be contracted, it must cling to one corner of the world. Grief ought to be a concentration; but for the agnostic its desolation is spread through an unthinkable eternity. This is what I call being born upside down. The sceptic may truly be said to be topsy-turvy; for his feet are dancing upwards in idle ecstasies, while his brain is in the abyss. To the modern man the heavens are actually below the earth. The explanation is simple; he is standing on his head; which is a very weak pedestal to stand on. But when he has found his feet again he knows it. Christianity satisfies suddenly and perfectly man's ancestral instinct for being the right way up; satisfies it supremely in this; that by its creed joy becomes something gigantic and sadness something special and small. The vault above us is not deaf because the universe is an idiot; the silence is not the heartless silence of an endless and aimless world. Rather the silence around us is a small and pitiful stillness like the prompt stillness in a sick room. We are perhaps permitted tragedy as a sort of merciful comedy: because the frantic energy of divine things would knock us down like a drunken farce. We can take our own tears more lightly than we could take the tremendous levities of the angels. So we sit perhaps in a starry chamber of silence, while the laughter of the heavens is too loud for us to hear.

Joy, which was the small publicity of the pagan, is the gigantic secret of the Christian. And as I close this chaotic volume I open again the strange small book from which all Christianity came; and I am again haunted by a kind of confirmation. The tremendous figure which fills the Gospels towers in this respect, as in every other, above all the thinkers who ever thought themselves tall. His pathos was natural, almost casual. The Stoics, ancient and modern, were proud of concealing their tears. He never concealed His tears; He showed them plainly on His open face at any daily sight, such as the far sight of His native city. Yet He concealed something. Solemn supermen and imperial diplomatists are proud of restraining their anger. He never restrained His anger. He flung furniture down the front steps of the Temple, and asked men how they expected to escape the damnation of Hell. Yet He restrained something. I say it with reverence; there was in that shattering personality a thread that must be called shyness. There was something that He hid from all men when He went up a mountain to pray. There was something that He covered constantly by abrupt silence or impetuous isolation. There was some one thing that was too great for God to show us when He walked upon our earth; and I have sometimes fancied that it was His mirth.

# The Queer Feet

If you meet a member of that select club, 'The Twelve True Fishermen,' entering the Vernon Hotel for the annual club dinner, you will observe, as he takes off his overcoat, that his evening coat is green and not black. If (supposing that you have the star-defying audacity to address such a being) you ask him why, he will probably answer that he does it to avoid being mistaken for a waiter. You will then retire crushed. But you will leave behind you a mystery as yet unsolved and a tale worth telling.

If (to pursue the same vein of improbable conjecture) you were to meet a mild, hard-working little priest, named Father Brown, and were to ask him what he thought was the most singular luck of his life, he would probably reply that upon the whole his best stroke was at the Vernon Hotel, where he had averted a crime and, perhaps, saved a soul, merely by listening to a few footsteps in a passage. He is perhaps a little proud of this wild and wonderful guess of his, and it is possible that he might refer to it. But since it is immeasurably unlikely that you will ever rise high enough in the social world to find 'The Twelve True Fishermen,' or that you will ever sink low enough among slums and criminals to find Father Brown, I fear you will never hear the story at all unless you hear it from me.

The Vernon Hotel, at which the Twelve True Fishermen held their annual dinners, was an institution such as can only exist in an oligarchical society which has almost gone mad on good manners. It was that topsy-turvy product—an 'exclusive' commercial enterprise. That is, it was a thing which paid, not by attracting people, but actually by turning people away. In the heart of a plutocracy tradesmen become cunning enough to be more fastidious than their customers. They positively create difficulties so that their wealthy and weary clients may spend money and diplomacy in over-coming them. If there were a fashionable hotel in London which no man could enter who was under six foot, society would meekly make up parties of six-foot men to dine in it. If there were an expensive restaurant which by a

The Innocence of Father Brown, 1910

mere caprice of its proprietor was only open on Thursday afternoon, it would be crowded on Thursday afternoon. The Vernon Hotel stood, as if by accident, in the corner of a square in Belgravia. It was a small hotel; and a very inconvenient one. But its very inconveniences were considered as walls protecting a particular class. One inconvenience, in particular, was held to be of vital importance: the fact that practically only twenty-four people could dine in the place at once. The only big dinner table was the celebrated terrace table, which stood open to the air on a sort of veranda overlooking one of the most exquisite old gardens in London. Thus it happened that even the twenty-four seats at this table could only be enjoyed in warm weather; and this making the enjoyment yet more difficult made it yet more desired. The existing owner of the hotel was a Jew named Lever; and he made nearly a million out of it, by making it difficult to get into. Of course he combined with this limitation in the scope of his enterprise the most careful polish in its performance. The wines and cooking were really as good as any in Europe, and the demeanour of the attendants exactly mirrored the fixed mood of the English upper class. The proprietor knew all his waiters like the fingers on his hand; there were only fifteen of them all told. It was much easier to become a member of Parliament than to become a waiter in that hotel. Each waiter was trained in terrible silence and smoothness, as if he were a gentleman's servant. And, indeed, there was generally at least one waiter to every gentleman who dined.

The club of The Twelve True Fishermen would not have consented to dine anywhere but in such a place, for it insisted on a luxurious privacy; and would have been quite upset by the mere thought that any other club was even dining in the same building. On the occasion of their annual dinner the Fishermen were in the habit of exposing all their treasures, as if they were in a private house, especially the celebrated set of fish knives and forks which were, as it were, the insignia of the society, each being exquisitely wrought in silver in the form of a fish, and each loaded at the hilt with one large pearl. These were always laid out for the fish course, and the fish course was always the most magnificent in that magnificent repast. The society had a vast number of ceremonies and observances, but it had no history and no object; that was where it was so very aristocratic. You did not have to be anything in order to be one of the Twelve Fishers; unless you were already a certain sort of person, you never even heard of them. It had been in existence twelve years. Its president was Mr Audley. Its vice-president was the Duke of Chester.

If I have in any degree conveyed the atmosphere of this appalling hotel, the reader may feel a natural wonder as to how I came to know anything about it, and may even speculate as to how so ordinary a person as my friend Father Brown came to find himself in that golden gallery. As far as that is concerned, my story is simple, or even vulgar. There is in the world a very aged rioter and demagogue who breaks into the most refined retreats with the dreadful information that all men are brothers, and wherever this leveller went on his pale horse it was Father Brown's trade to follow. One of the waiters, an Italian, had been struck down with a paralytic stroke that afternoon; and his Jewish employer, marvelling mildly at such superstitions, had consented to send for the nearest Popish priest. With what the waiter confessed to Father Brown we are not concerned, for the excellent reason that the cleric kept it to himself; but apparently it involved him in writing out a note or statement for the conveying of some message or the righting of some wrong. Father Brown, therefore, with a meek impudence which he would have shown equally in Buckingham Palace, asked to be provided with a room and writing materials. Mr Lever was torn in two. He was a kind man, and had also that bad imitation of kindness, the dislike of any difficulty or scene. At the same time the presence of one unusual stranger in his hotel that evening was like a speck of dirt on something just cleaned. There was never any borderland or ante-room in the Vernon Hotel, no people waiting in the hall, no customers coming in on chance. There were fifteen waiters. There were twelve guests. It would be as startling to find a new guest in the hotel that night as to find a new brother taking breakfast or tea in one's own family. Moreover, the priest's appearance was second-rate and his clothes muddy; a mere glimpse of him afar off might precipitate a crisis in the club. Mr Lever at last hit on a plan to cover, since he might not obliterate, the disgrace. When you enter (as you never will) the Vernon Hotel, you pass down a short passage decorated with a few dingy but important pictures, and come to the main vestibule and lounge which opens on your right into passages leading to the public rooms, and on your left to a similar passage pointing to the kitchens and offices of the hotel. Immediately on your left hand is the corner of a glass office, which abuts upon the lounge—a house within a house, so to speak, like the old hotel bar which probably once occupied its place.

In this office sat the representative of the proprietor (nobody in this place ever appeared in person if he could help it), and just beyond the office, on the way to the servants' quarters, was the gentlemen's cloak-room, the last boundary of the gentlemen's domain. But between the office and the cloak-room was a small private room without other outlet, sometimes used by the proprietor for delicate and important matters, such as lending a duke a thousand pounds or declining to lend him sixpence. It is a mark of the magnificent tolerance of Mr Lever that he permitted this holy place to be for about half an hour profaned by a mere priest, scribbling away on a piece of paper. The story which Father Brown was writing down was very likely a much better story than this one, only it will never be known. I can merely state that it was very nearly as long, and that the last two or three paragraphs of it were the least exciting and absorbing.

For it was by the time that he had reached these that the priest began a little to allow his thoughts to wander and his animal senses, which were commonly keen, to awaken. The time of darkness and dinner was drawing on; his own forgotten little room was without a light, and perhaps the gathering gloom, as occasionally happens, sharpened the sense of sound. As Father Brown wrote the last and least essential part of his document, he caught himself writing to the rhythm of a recurrent noise outside, just as one sometimes thinks to the tune of a railway train. When he became conscious of the thing he found what it was: only the ordinary patter of feet passing the door, which in an hotel was no very unlikely matter. Nevertheless, he stared at the darkened ceiling, and listened to the sound. After he had listened for a few seconds dreamily, he got to his feet and listened intently, with his head a little on one side. Then he sat down again and buried his brow in his hands, now not merely listening, but listening and thinking also.

The footsteps outside at any given moment were such as one might hear in any hotel; and yet, taken as a whole, there was something very strange about them. There were no other footsteps. It was always a very silent house, for the few familiar guests went at once to their own apartments, and the well-trained waiters were told to be almost invisible until they were wanted. One could not conceive any place where there was less reason to apprehend anything irregular. But these footsteps were so odd that one could not decide to call them regular or irregular. Father Brown followed them with his finger on the edge of the table, like a man trying to learn a tune on the piano.

First, there came a long rush of rapid little steps, such as a light man might make in winning a walking race. At a certain point they stopped and changed to a sort of slow, swinging stamp, numbering not a quarter of the steps, but occupying about the same time. The moment the last echoing stamp had died, away would come again the run or ripple of light, hurrying feet, and then again the thud of the heavier walking. It was certainly the same pair of boots, partly because (as has been said) there were no other boots about, and partly because they had a small but unmistakable creak in them. Father Brown had the kind of head that cannot help asking questions; and on this apparently trivial question his head almost split. He had seen men run in order to jump. He had seen men run in order to slide. But why on earth should a man run in order to walk? Or, again, why should he walk in order to run? Yet no other description would cover the antics of this invisible pair of legs. The man was either walking very fast down one-half of the corridor in order to walk very slow down the other half; or he was walking very slow at one end to have the rapture of walking fast at the other. Neither suggestion seemed to make much sense. His brain was growing darker and darker, like his room.

Yet, as he began to think steadily, the very blackness of his cell seemed to make his thoughts more vivid; he began to see as in a kind of vision the fantastic feet capering along the corridor in unnatural or symbolic attitudes. Was it a heathen religious dance? Or some entirely new kind of scientific exercise? Father Brown began to ask himself with more exactness what the steps suggested. Taking the slow step first; it certainly was not the step of the proprietor. Men of his type walk with a rapid waddle, or they sit still. It could not be any servant or messenger waiting for directions. It did not sound like it. The poorer orders (in an oligarchy) sometimes lurch about when they are slightly drunk, but generally, and especially in such gorgeous scenes, they stand or sit in constrained attitudes. No; that heavy yet springy step, with a kind of careless emphasis, not specially noisy, yet not caring what noise it made, belonged to only one of the animals of this earth. It was a gentleman of western Europe, and probably one who had never worked for his living.

Just as he came to this solid certainty, the step changed to the quicker one, and ran past the door as feverishly as a rat. The listener remarked that though this step was much swifter it was also much more noiseless, almost as if the man were walking on tip-toe. Yet it was not associated in his mind with secrecy, but with something else—something that he could not remember. He was maddened by one of those half-memories that make a man feel half-witted. Surely he had heard that strange, swift walking somewhere. Suddenly he sprang to his feet with a new idea in his head, and walked to the door. His room had no direct outlet on the passage, but let on one side into the glass office, and on the other into the cloak-room beyond. He tried the door into the office, and found it locked. Then he looked at the window, now a square pane full of purple cloud cleft by livid sunset, and for an instant he smelt evil as a dog smells rats.

The rational part of him (whether the wiser or not) regained its supremacy. He remembered that the proprietor had told him that he should lock the door, and would come later to release him. He told himself that twenty things he had not thought of might explain the eccentric sounds outside; he reminded himself that there was just enough light left to finish his own proper work. Bringing his paper to the window so as to catch the last stormy evening light, he resolutely plunged once more into the almost completed record. He had written for about twenty minutes, bending closer and closer to his paper in the lessening light; then suddenly he sat upright. He had heard the strange feet once more.

This time they had a third oddity. Previously the unknown man had walked, with levity indeed and lightning quickness, but he had walked. This time he ran. One could hear the swift, soft, bounding steps coming along the corridor, like the pads of a fleeing and leaping panther. Whoever was coming was a very strong, active man, in still yet tearing excitement. Yet, when the sound had swept up to the office like a sort of whispering whirlwind, it suddenly changed again to the old slow, swaggering stamp.

Father Brown flung down his paper, and, knowing the office door to be locked, went at once into the cloak-room on the other side. The attendant of this place was temporarily absent, probably because the only guests were at dinner, and his office was a sinecure. After groping through a grey forest of overcoats, he found that the dim cloak-room opened on the lighted corridor in the form of a sort of counter or half-door, like most of the counters across which we have all handed umbrellas and received tickets. There was a light immediately above the semi-circular arch of this opening. It threw little illumination on Father Brown himself, who seemed a mere dark outline against the dim sunset window behind him. But it threw an almost theatrical light on the man who stood outside the cloak-room in the corridor.

He was an elegant man in very plain evening-dress; tall, but with an air of not taking up much room; one felt that he could have slid along like a shadow where many smaller men would have been obvious and obstructive. His face, now flung back in the lamplight, was swarthy and vivacious, the face of a foreigner. His figure was good, his manners good-humoured and confident; a critic could only say that his black coat was a shade below his figure and manners, and even bulged and bagged in an odd way. The moment he caught sight of Brown's black silhouette against the sunset, he tossed down a scrap of paper with a number and called out with amiable authority: 'I want my hat and coat, please; I find I have to go away at once.'

Father Brown took the paper without a word, and obediently went to look for the coat; it was not the first menial work he had done in his life. He brought it and laid it on the counter; meanwhile, the strange gentleman who had been feeling in his waistcoat pocket, said, laughing: 'I haven't got any silver; you can keep this.' And he threw down half a sovereign, and caught up his coat.

Father Brown's figure remained quite dark and still; but in that instant he had lost his head. His head was always most valuable when he had lost it. In such moments he put two and two together and made four million. Often the Catholic Church (which is wedded to common sense) did not approve of it. Often he did not approve of it himself. But it was a real inspiration— important at rare crises—when whosoever shall lose his head the same shall save it.

'I think, sir,' he said civilly, 'that you have some silver in your pocket.'

The tall gentleman stared. 'Hang it,' he cried. 'If I give you gold, why should you complain?'

'Because silver is sometimes more valuable than gold,' said the priest mildly; 'that is, in large quantities.'

The stranger looked at him curiously. Then he looked still more curiously up the passage towards the main entrance. Then he looked back at Brown again, and then he looked very carefully at the window beyond Brown's head, still coloured with the afterglow of the storm. Then he seemed to make up his mind. He put one hand on the counter, vaulted over as easily as an acrobat and towered above the priest, putting one tremendous hand upon his collar.

'Stand still,' he said, in a hacking whisper. 'I don't want to threaten you, but——'

'I don't want to threaten you,' said Father Brown, in a voice like a rolling drum. 'I want to threaten you with the worm that dieth not, and the fire that is not quenched.'

'You're a rum sort of cloak-room clerk,' said the other.

'I am a priest, Monsieur Flambeau,' said Brown, 'and I am ready to hear your confession.'

The other stood gasping for a few moments, and then staggered back into a chair.

The first two courses of the dinner of the Twelve True Fishermen had proceeded with placid success. I do not possess a copy of the menu; and if I did it would not convey anything to anybody. It was written in a sort of super-French employed by cooks, but quite unintelligible to Frenchmen. There was a tradition in the club that the *hors d'œuvres* should be various and manifold to the point of madness. They were taken seriously because they were avowedly useless extras, like the whole dinner and the whole club. There was also a tradition that the soup course should be light and unpre-tending—a sort of simple and austere vigil for the feast of fish that was to come. The talk was that strange, slight talk which governs the British Empire, which governs it in secret, and yet would scarcely enlighten an ordinary Englishman even if he could overhear it. Cabinet Ministers on both sides were alluded to by their Christian names with a sort of bored benignity. The Radical Chancellor of the Exchequer, whom the whole Tory party was supposed to be cursing for his extortions, was praised for his minor poetry, or his saddle in the hunting-field. The Tory leader, whom all Liberals were supposed to hate as a tyrant, was discussed and, on the whole, praised—as a Liberal. It seemed somehow that politicians were very important. And yet, anything seemed important about them except their politics. Mr Audley, the chairman, was an amiable, elderly man who still wore Gladstone collars; he was a kind of symbol of all that phantasmal and yet fixed society. He had never done anything—not even anything wrong. He was not fast; he was not even particularly rich. He was simply in the thing; and there was an end of it. No party could ignore him, and if he had wished to be in the Cabinet he certainly would have been put there. The Duke of Chester, the vice-president, was a young and rising politician. That is to say, he was a pleasant youth, with flat, fair hair and a freckled face, with moderate intelligence and enormous estates. In public his appearances were always successful and his principle was simple enough. When he thought of a joke he made it, and was called brilliant. When he could not think of a joke he said that this was no time for trifling, and was called able. In private, in a club of his own class, he was simply quite pleasantly frank and silly, like a schoolboy. Mr Audley, never having been in politics, treated them a little more seriously. Sometimes he even embarrassed the company by phrases suggesting that there was some difference between a Liberal and a Conservative. He, himself, was a Conservative, even in private life. He had a roll of grey hair over the back of his collar like certain old-fashioned statesmen, and seen from behind he looked like the man the empire wants. Seen from the front he looked like a mild, self-indulgent bachelor, with rooms in the Albany—which he was.

As has been remarked, there were twenty-four seats at the terrace table, and only twelve members of the club. Thus they could occupy the terrace in the most luxurious style of all, being ranged along the inner side of the table, with no one opposite, commanding an uninterrupted view of the garden, the colours of which were still vivid, though evening was closing in somewhat luridly for the time of year. The chairman sat in the centre of the line, and the vice-president at the right-hand end of it. When the twelve guests first trooped into their seats it was the custom (for some unknown reason) for all the fifteen waiters to stand lining the wall like troops presenting arms to the king, while the fat proprietor stood and bowed to the club with radiant surprise, as if he had never heard of them before. But before the first chink of knife and fork this army of retainers had vanished, only the one or two required to collect and distribute the plates darting about in deathly silence. Mr Lever, the proprietor, of course had disappeared in convulsions of courtesy long before. It would be exaggerative, indeed irreverent, to say that he ever positively appeared again. But when the important course, the fish course, was being brought on there was—how shall I put it?—a vivid shadow, a projection of his personality, which told that he was hovering near. The sacred fish course consisted (to the eyes of the vulgar) in a sort of monstrous pudding, about the size and shape of a wedding cake, in which some considerable number of interesting fishes had finally lost the shapes which God had given to them. The Twelve True Fishermen took up their celebrated fish knives and fish forks, and approached it as gravely as if every inch of the pudding cost as much as the silver fork it was eaten with. So it did, for all I know. This course was dealt with in eager and devouring silence; and it was only when his plate was nearly empty that the young duke made the ritual remark: 'They can't do this anywhere but here.'

'Nowhere,' said Mr Audley, in a deep bass voice, turning to the speaker and nodding his venerable head a number of times. 'Nowhere, assuredly, except here. It was represented to me that at the Café Anglais——'

Here he was interrupted and even agitated for a moment by the removal of his plate, but he recaptured the valuable thread of his thoughts. 'It was represented to me that the same could be done at the Café Anglais. Nothing like it, sir,' he said, shaking his head ruthlessly, like a hanging judge. 'Nothing like it.'

'Overrated place,' said a certain Colonel Pound, speaking (by the look of him) for the first time for some months.

'Oh, I don't know,' said the Duke of Chester, who was an optimist, 'it's jolly good for some things. You can't beat it at——'

A waiter came swiftly along the room, and then stopped dead. His stoppage was as silent as his tread; but all those vague and kindly gentlemen were so used to the utter smoothness of the unseen machinery which surrounded and supported their lives, that a waiter doing anything unexpected was a start and a jar. They felt as you and I would feel if the inanimate world disobeyed —if a chair ran away from us.

The waiter stood staring a few seconds, while there deepened on every face at table a strange shame which is wholly the product of our time. It is the combination of modern humanitarianism with the horrible modern abyss between the souls of the rich and poor. A genuine historic aristocrat would have thrown things at the waiter, beginning with empty bottles, and very probably ending with money. A genuine democrat would have asked him, with a comrade-like clearness of speech, what the devil he was doing. But these modern plutocrats could not bear a poor man near to them, either as a slave or as a friend. That something had gone wrong with the servants was merely a dull, hot embarrassment. They did not want to be brutal, and they dreaded the need to be benevolent. They wanted the thing, whatever it was, to be over. It was over. The waiter, after standing for some seconds rigid, like a cataleptic, turned round and ran madly out of the room.

When he reappeared in the room, or rather in the doorway, it was in company with another waiter, with whom he whispered and gesticulated with southern fierceness. Then the first waiter went away, leaving the second waiter, and reappeared with a third waiter. By the time a fourth waiter had joined this hurried synod, Mr Audley felt it necessary to break the silence in the interests of Tact. He used a very loud cough, instead of a presidential hammer, and said: 'Splendid work young Moocher's doing in Burmah. Now, no other nation in the world could have——'

A fifth waiter had sped towards him like an arrow and was whispering in his ear: 'So sorry. Important! Might the proprietor speak to you?'

The chairman turned in disorder, and with a dazed stare saw Mr Lever coming towards them with his lumbering quickness. The gait of the good proprietor was indeed his usual gait, but his face was by no means usual. Generally it was a genial copper-brown; now it was a sickly yellow.

'You will pardon me, Mr Audley,' he said, with asthmatic breathlessness. 'I have great apprehensions. Your fish-plates, they are cleared away with the knife and fork on them!'

'Well, I hope so,' said the chairman, with some warmth.

'You see him?' panted the excited hotel keeper; 'you see the waiter who took them away? You know him?'

'Know the waiter?' answered Mr Audley indignantly. 'Certainly not!'

Mr Lever opened his hands with a gesture of agony. 'I never send him,' he said. 'I know not when or why he come. I send my waiter to take away the plates, and he find them already away.'

Mr Audley still looked rather too bewildered to be really the man the empire wants; none of the company could say anything except the man of wood—Colonel Pound—who seemed galvanized into an unnatural life. He rose rigidly from his chair, leaving all the rest sitting, screwed his eyeglass into his eye, and spoke in a raucous undertone as if he had half-forgotten how to speak. 'Do you mean,' he said, 'that somebody has stolen our silver fish service?'

The proprietor repeated the open-handed gesture with even greater helplessness; and in a flash all the men at the table were on their feet.

'Are all your waiters here?' demanded the colonel, in his low, harsh accent.

'Yes; they're all here. I noticed it myself,' cried the young duke, pushing his boyish face into the inmost ring. 'Always count 'em as I come in; they look so queer standing up against the wall.'

'But surely one cannot exactly remember,' began Mr Audley, with heavy hesitation.

'I remember exactly, I tell you,' cried the duke excitedly. 'There never have been more than fifteen waiters at this place, and there were no more than fifteen to-night, I'll swear; no more and no less.'

The proprietor turned upon him, quaking in a kind of palsy of surprise. 'You say—you say,' he stammered, 'that you see all my fifteen waiters?'

'As usual,' assented the duke. 'What is the matter with that?'

'Nothing,' said Lever, with a deepening accent, 'only you did not. For one of zem is dead upstairs.'

There was a shocking stillness for an instant in that room. It may be (so supernatural is the word death) that each of those idle men looked for a second at his soul, and saw it as a small dried pea. One of them—the duke, I think—even said with the idiotic kindness of wealth: 'Is there anything we can do?'

'He has had a priest,' said the Jew, not untouched.

Then, as to the clang of doom, they awoke to their own position. For a few weird seconds they had really felt as if the fifteenth waiter might be the ghost of the dead man upstairs. They had been dumb under that oppression, for ghosts were to them an embarrassment, like beggars. But the remembrance of the silver broke the spell of the miraculous; broke it abruptly and with a brutal reaction. The colonel flung over his chair and strode to the door. 'If there was a fifteenth man here, friends,' he said, 'that fifteenth fellow was a thief. Down at once to the front and back doors and secure everything; then we'll talk. The twenty-four pearls are worth recovering.'

Mr Audley seemed at first to hesitate about whether it was gentlemanly to be in such a hurry about anything; but, seeing the duke dash down the stairs with youthful energy, he followed with a more mature motion.

At the same instant a sixth waiter ran into the room, and declared that he had found the pile of fish plates on a sideboard, with no trace of the silver.

The crowd of diners and attendants that tumbled helter-skelter down the passages divided into two groups. Most of the Fishermen followed the proprietor to the front room to demand news of any exit. Colonel Pound, with the chairman, the vice-president, and one or two others darted down the corridor leading to the servants' quarters, as the more likely line of escape. As they did so they passed the dim alcove or cavern of the cloak-room, and saw a short, black-coated figure, presumably an attendant, stand-ing a little way back in the shadow of it.

'Hallo there!' called out the duke. 'Have you seen anyone pass?'

The short figure did not answer the question directly, but merely said: 'Perhaps I have got what you are looking for, gentlemen.'

They paused, wavering and wondering, while he quietly went to the back of the cloak-room, and came back with both hands full of shining silver, which he laid out on the counter as calmly as a salesman. It took the form of a dozen quaintly shaped forks and knives.

'You—you——' began the colonel, quite thrown off his balance at last. Then he peered into the dim little room and saw two things: first, that the short, black-clad man was dressed like a clergyman; and second, that the window of the room behind him was burst, as if someone had passed violently through.

'Valuable things to deposit in a cloak-room, aren't they?' remarked the clergyman, with cheerful composure.

'Did—did you steal those things?' stammered Mr Audley, with staring eyes.

'If I did,' said the cleric pleasantly, 'at least I am bringing them back again.'

'But you didn't,' said Colonel Pound, still staring at the broken window.

'To make a clean breast of it, I didn't,' said the other, with some humour. And he seated himself quite gravely on a stool.

'But you know who did,' said the colonel.

'I don't know his real name,' said the priest placidly; 'but I know something of his fighting weight, and a great deal about his spiritual difficulties. I formed the physical estimate when he was trying to throttle me, and the moral estimate when he repented.'

'Oh, I say—repented!' cried young Chester, with a sort of crow of laughter.

Father Brown got to his feet, putting his hands behind him. 'Odd, isn't it,' he said, 'that a thief and a vagabond should repent, when so many who are rich and secure remain hard and frivolous, and without fruit for God or man? But there, if you will excuse me, you trespass a little upon my province. If you doubt the penitence as a practical fact, there are your knives and forks. You are The Twelve True Fishers, and there are all your silver fish. But He has made me a fisher of men.'

'Did you catch this man?' asked the colonel, frowning.

Father Brown looked him full in his frowning face. 'Yes,' he said, 'I caught him, with an unseen hook and an invisible line which is long enough to let him wander to the ends of the world, and still to bring him back with a twitch upon the thread.'

There was a long silence. All the other men present drifted away to carry the recovered silver to their comrades, or to consult the proprietor about the queer condition of affairs. But the grim-faced colonel still sat sideways on the counter, swinging his long, lank legs and biting his dark moustache.

At last he said quietly to the priest: 'He must have been a clever fellow, but I think I know a cleverer.'

'He was a clever fellow,' answered the other, 'but I am not quite sure of what other you mean.'

'I mean you,' said the colonel, with a short laugh. 'I don't want to get the fellow jailed; make yourself easy about that. But I'd give a good many silver forks to know exactly how you fell into this affair, and how you got the stuff out of him. I reckon you're the most up-to-date devil of the present company.'

Father Brown seemed rather to like the saturnine candour of the soldier. 'Well,' he said, smiling, 'I mustn't tell you anything of the man's identity, or his own story, of course; but there's no particular reason why I shouldn't tell you of the mere outside facts which I found out for myself.'

He hopped over the barrier with unexpected activity, and sat beside Colonel Pound, kicking his short legs like a little boy on a gate. He began to tell the story as easily as if he were telling it to an old friend by a Christmas fire.

'You see, colonel,' he said, 'I was shut up in that small room there doing some writing, when I heard a pair of feet in this passage doing a dance that was as queer as the dance of death. First came quick, funny little steps, like a man walking on tip-toe for a wager; then came slow, careless, creaking steps, as of a big man walking about with a cigar. But they were both made by the same feet, I swear, and they came in rotation; first the run and then the walk, and then the run again. I wondered at first idly, and then wildly why a man should act these two parts at once. One walk I knew; it was just like yours, colonel. It was the walk of a well-fed gentleman waiting for something, who strolls about rather because he is physically alert than because he is mentally impatient. I knew that I knew the other walk, too, but I could not remember what it was. What wild creature had I met on my travels that tore along on tiptoe in that extraordinary style? Then I heard a clink of plates somewhere; and the answer stood up as plain as St Peter's. It was the walk of a waiter—that walk with the body slanted forward, the eyes looking down, the ball of the toe spurning away the ground, the coat tails and napkin flying. Then I thought for a minute and a half more. And I believe I saw the manner of the crime, as clearly as if I were going to commit it.'

Colonel Pound looked at him keenly, but the speaker's mild grey eyes were fixed upon the ceiling with almost empty wistfulness.

'A crime,' he said slowly, 'is like any other work of art. Don't look surprised; crimes are by no means the only works of art that come from an infernal workshop. But every work of art, divine or diabolic, has one indispensable mark—I mean, that the centre of it is simple, however much the fulfilment may be complicated. Thus, in *Hamlet*, let us say, the grotesqueness of the grave-digger, the flowers of the mad girl, the fantastic finery of Osric, the pallor of the ghost and the grin of the skull are all oddities in a sort of tangled wreath round one plain tragic figure of a man in black. Well, this also,' he said, getting slowly down from his seat with a smile, 'this also is the plain tragedy of a man in black. Yes,' he went on, seeing the colonel look up in some wonder, 'the whole of this tale turns on a black coat. In this, as in *Hamlet*, there are the rococo excrescences—yourselves, let us say. There is the dead waiter, who was there when he could not be there. There is the invisible hand that swept your table clear of silver and melted into air. But every clever crime is founded ultimately on some one quite simple fact—some fact that is not itself mysterious. The mystification comes in covering it up, in leading men's thoughts away from it. This large and subtle and (in the ordinary course) most profitable crime, was built on the plain fact that a gentleman's evening-dress is the same as a waiter's. All the rest was acting, and thundering good acting, too.'

'Still,' said the colonel, getting up and frowning at his boots. 'I am not sure that I understand.'

339

'Colonel,' said Father Brown, 'I tell you that this archangel of impudence who stole your forks walked up and down this passage twenty times in the blaze of all the lamps, in the glare of all the eyes. He did not go and hide in dim corners where suspicion might have searched for him. He kept constantly on the move in the lighted corridors, and everywhere that he went he seemed to be there by right. Don't ask me what he was like; you have seen him yourself six or seven times to-night. You were waiting with all the other grand people in the reception room at the end of the passage there, with the terrace just beyond. Whenever he came among you gentlemen, he came in the lightning style of a waiter, with bent head, flapping napkin and flying feet. He shot out on to the terrace, did something to the tablecloth, and shot back again towards the office and the waiters' quarters. By the time he had come under the eye of the office clerk and the waiters he had become another man in every inch of his body, in every instinctive gesture. He strolled among the servants with the absent-minded insolence which they have all seen in their patrons. It was no new thing to them that a swell from the dinner party should pace all parts of the house like an animal at the Zoo; they know that nothing marks the Smart Set more than a habit of walking where one chooses. When he was magnificently weary of walking down that particular passage he would wheel round and pace back past the office; in the shadow of the arch just beyond he was altered as by a blast of magic, and went hurrying forward again among the Twelve Fishermen, an obsequious attendant. Why should the gentlemen look at a chance waiter? Why should the waiters suspect a first-rate walking gentleman? Once or twice he played the coolest tricks. In the proprietor's private quarters he called out breezily for a syphon of soda water, saying he was thirsty. He said genially that he would carry it himself, and he did; he carried it quickly and correctly through the thick of you, a waiter with an obvious errand. Of course, it could not have been kept up long, but it only had to be kept up till the end of the fish course.

'His worst moment was when the waiters stood in a row; but even then he contrived to lean against the wall just around the corner in such a way that for that important instant the waiters thought him a gentleman, while the gentlemen thought him a waiter. The rest went like winking. If any waiter caught him away from the table, that waiter caught a languid aristocrat. He had only to time himself two minutes before the fish was cleared, become a swift servant, and clear it himself. He put the plates down on a sideboard, stuffed the silver in his breast pocket, giving it a bulgy look, and ran like a hare (I heard him coming) till he came to the cloak-room. There he had only to be a plutocrat again—a plutocrat called away suddenly on business. He had only to give his ticket to the cloak-room attendant, and go out again elegantly as he had come in. Only—only I happened to be the cloak-room attendant.'

'What did you do to him?' cried the colonel, with unusual intensity. 'What did he tell you?'

'I beg your pardon,' said the priest immovably, 'that is where the story ends.'

'And the interesting story begins,' muttered Pound. 'I think I understand his professional trick. But I don't seem to have got hold of yours.'

'I must be going,' said Father Brown.

They walked together along the passage to the entrance hall, where they saw the fresh, freckled face of the Duke of Chester, who was bounding buoyantly along towards them.

'Come along, Pound,' he cried breathlessly. 'I've been looking for you everywhere. The dinner's going again in spanking style, and old Audley has got to make a speech in honour of the forks being saved. We want to start some new ceremony, don't you know, to commemorate the occasion. I say, you really got the goods back, what do you suggest?'

'Why,' said the colonel, eyeing him with a certain sardonic approval. 'I should suggest that henceforward we wear green coats instead of black. One never knows what mistakes may arise when one looks so like a waiter.'

'Oh, hang it all!' said the young man; 'a gentleman never looks like a waiter.'

'Nor a waiter like a gentleman, I suppose,' said Colonel Pound, with the same lowering laughter on his face. 'Reverend sir, your friend must have been very smart to act the gentleman.'

Father Brown buttoned up his commonplace overcoat to the neck, for the night was stormy, and took his commonplace umbrella from the stand.

'Yes,' he said; 'it must be very hard work to be a gentleman; but, do you know, I have sometimes thought that it may be almost as laborious to be a waiter.'

And saying 'Good evening,' he pushed open the heavy doors of that palace of pleasures. The golden gates closed behind him, and he went at a brisk walk through the damp, dark streets in search of a penny omnibus.

# What is Right With the World

The above excellent title is not of my own invention. It was suggested to me by the Editor of this paper and I consented to fill up the bill, partly because of the pleasure I have always had from the paper itself, and partly because it gives me an opportunity of telling an egotistical story, a story which may enlighten the public about the general origin of such titles.

I have always heard of the brutality of publishers and how they crush and obscure the author; but my complaint has always been that they push him forward far too much. I will not say that, so far from making too little of the author, they make too much of him; that this phrase is capable of a dark financial interpretation which I do not intend. But I do say that the prominent personalities of the literary world are very largely the creations of their publishers, in so far as they are not solely the creations of their wives. Here is a small incident out of my own existence. I designed to write a sort of essay, divided into sections, on one particular point of political error. This fallacy, though small and scholastic at first sight, seemed to me to be the real mistake in most modern sociological works. It was, briefly, the idea that things that have been tried have been found wanting. It was my purpose to point out that in the entanglements of practice this is untrue; that an old expedient may easily be the best thing for a new situation; that its principle may be useful though its practice failed; that its practice may have failed because its principle was abandoned; and so on. Therefore, I claimed, we should look for the best method, the ideal, whether it is in the future or the past. I imagined this book as a drab-coloured, decorous little philosophical treatise, with no chapters, but the page occasionally broken by section-headings at the side. I proposed to call my analysis of a radical error 'What is wrong', meaning where the mistake is in our logical calculation. But I had highly capable and sympathetic publishers, whose only weakness was that they thought my unhappy monologue much more important than I did. By some confusion of ecstasy (which entirely through my own fault I failed to check)

*T. P.'s Weekly*, 1910. Collected in The Apostle and the Wild Ducks, 1975 the title was changed into the apocalyptic trumpet-blast 'What's Wrong With the World'. It was divided up into three short, fierce chapters, like proclamations in a French riot. Outside there was an enormous portrait of myself looking like a depressed hairdresser, and the whole publication had somehow got the violence and instancy of a bombshell. Let it be understood that I do not blame the publishers in the least for this. I could have stopped it if I had minded my own affairs, and it came out of their beautiful and ardent souls. I merely mention it as an instance of the error about publishers. They are always represented as cold and scornful merchants, seeking to keep your writers in the background. Alas (as Wordsworth so finely says), alas! the enthusiasm of publishers has oftener left me mourning.

Upon the whole, I am rather inclined to approve of this method of the publisher or editor making up the title, while the author makes up the remarks about it. Any man with a large mind ought to be able to write about anything. Any really free man ought to be able to write to order. Some of the greatest books in the world—*Pickwick*, for instance—were written to fulfil a scheme partly sketched out by a publisher. But I only brought together these two cases of titles that came to me from outside because they do illustrate the necessity of some restatement in such a case. For these two titles are, when it comes to the fulfilment, at once too complex and too simple. I would never have dreamed of announcing, like some discovery of my own, what is wrong with the world. What is wrong with the world is the devil, and what is right with it is God; the human race will travel for a few more million years in all sorts of muddle and reform, and when it perishes of the last cold or heat it will still be within the limits of that very simple definition. But in an age that has confused itself with such phrases as 'optimist' and 'pessimist', it is necessary to distinguish along more delicate lines. One of the strangest things about the use of the word 'optimist' is that it is now so constantly used about the future. The house of man is criticised not as a house, but as a kind of caravan; not by what it is, but by where it is going to. None are more vitally and recklessly otherworldly than those modern progressives who do not believe in another world.

Now, for the matter of that, I do think the world is getting very much better in very many vital respects. In some of them, I think, the fact could hardly be disputed. The one perfectly satisfactory element at the present crisis is that all the prophecies have failed. At least the people who have been clearly proved to be wrong are the people who were quite sure they were right. That is always a gratifying circumstance. Now why is it that all these prophecies of the wise have been confounded and why has the destiny of men taken so decisive and so different a course? It is because of the very simple fact that the human race consists of many millions of two-legged and tolerably cheerful, reasonably unhappy beings who never read any books at all and certainly never hear of any scientific predictions. If they act in opposition to the scheme which science has foreseen for them, they must be excused. They sin in ignorance. They have no notion that they are avoiding what was really unavoidable. But, indeed, the phrases loosely used of the obscure mass of mankind are a little misleading. To say of the bulk of human beings that they are uneducated is like saying of a Red Indian hunter that he has not yet taken his degree. He has taken many other things. And so, sincerely speaking, there are no uneducated men. They may escape the trivial examinations, but not the tremendous examinations of existence. The dependence of infancy, the enjoyment of animals, the love of woman, and the fear of death—these are more frightful and more fixed than all conceivable forms of the cultivation of the mind. It is idle to complain of schools and colleges being trivial. Schools and colleges must always be trivial. In no case will a college ever teach the important things. For before a man is twenty he has always learnt the important things. He has learnt them right or wrong, and he has learnt them all alone.

We therefore come back to the primary truth, that what is right with the world has nothing to do with future changes, but is rooted in original realities. If groups or peoples show an unexpected independence or creative power; if they do things no one had dreamed of their doing; if they prove more ferocious or more self-sacrificing than the wisdom of the world had ever given them credit for, then such inexplicable outbursts can always be referred back to some elementary and absolute doctrine about the nature of men. No traditions in this world are so ancient as the traditions that lead to modern upheaval and innovation. Nothing nowadays is so conservative as a revolution. The men who call themselves Republicans are men walking the streets of deserted and tiny city-states, and digging up the great bones of pagans. And when we ask on what republicanism really rests, we come back to that great undemonstrable dogma of the native dignity of man. And when we come back to the lord of creation, we come back of necessity to creation; and we ask ourselves that ultimate question which St Thomas of Aquinas (an extreme optimist) answered in the affirmative: Are these things ultimately of value at all?

What is right with the world is the world. In fact, nearly everything else is wrong with it. This is that great truth in the tremendous tale of Creation, a truth that our people must remember or perish. It is at the *beginning* that things are good, and not (as the more pallid progressives say) only at the end. The primordial things—existence, energy, fruition—are good so far as they go. You cannot have evil life, though you can have notorious evil livers. Manhood and womanhood are good things, though men and woman are often perfectly pestilent. You can use poppies to drug people, or birch trees to beat them, or stones to make an idol, or corn to make a corner; but it remains true that, in the abstract, before you have done anything, each of these four things is in strict truth a glory, a beneficent speciality and variety. We do praise the Lord that there are birch trees growing amongst the rocks and poppies amongst the corn; we do praise the Lord, even if we do not believe in Him. We do admire and applaud the *project* of a world, just as if we had been called to council in the primal darkness and seen the first starry plan of the skies. We are, as a matter of fact, far more certain that this life of ours is a magnificent and amazing enterprise than we are that it will succeed. These evolutionary optimists who call themselves Meliorists (a patient and poor-spirited lot they are) always talk as if we were certain of the end, though not of the beginning. In other words, they don't know what life is aiming at, but they are quite sure it will get there. Why anybody who has avowedly forgotten where he came from should be quite so certain of where he is going to I have never been able to make out; but Meliorists are like that. They are ready to talk of existence itself as the product of purely evil forces. They never mention animals except as perpetually tearing each other in pieces; but a month in the country would cure that. They have a real giddy horror of stars and seas, as a man has on the edge of a hopelessly high precipice. They sometimes instinctively shrink from clay, fungoids, and the fresh young of animals with a quivering gesture that reveals the fundamental pessimist. Life itself, crude, uncultivated life, is horrible to them. They belong very largely to the same social class and creed as the lady who objected that the milk came to her from a dirty cow, and not from a nice clean shop. But they are sure how everything will end.

I am in precisely the opposite position. I am much more sure that everything is good at the beginning than I am that everything will be good at the end. That all this frame of things, this flesh, these stones, are good things, of that I am more brutally certain than I can say. But as for what will happen to them, that is to take a step into dogma and prophecy. I speak here, of course, solely of my personal feelings, not even of my reasoned creed. But on my instincts alone I should have no notion what would ultimately happen to this material world I think so magnificent. For all I know it may be literally and not figuratively true that the tares are tied into bundles for burning, and that as the tree falleth so shall it lie. I am an agnostic, like most people with a positive theology. But I do affirm, with the full weight of sincerity, that trees and flowers are good at the beginning, whatever happens to them in the end. The ordinary modern progressive position is that this is a bad universe, but will certainly get better. I say it is certainly a good universe, even if it gets worse. I say that these trees and flowers, stars and sexes, are primarily, not merely ultimately, good. In the Beginning the power beyond words created heaven and earth. In the Beginning He looked on them and saw that they were good.

All this unavoidable theory (for theory is always unavoidable) may be popularly pulled together thus. We are to regard existence as a raid or great adventure; it is to be judged, therefore, not by what calamities it encounters, but by what flag it follows and what high town it assaults. The most dangerous thing in the world is to be alive; one is always in danger of one's life. But anyone who shrinks from this is a traitor to the great scheme and experiment of being. The pessimist of the ordinary type, the pessimist who thinks he would be better dead, is blasted with the crime of Iscariot. Spiritually speaking, we should be justified in punishing him with death. Only, out of polite deference to his own philosophy, we punish him with life.

But this faith (that existence was fundamentally and purposely good) is not attacked only by the black, consistent pessimist. The man who says that he would sooner die is best answered by a sudden blow with the poker, for the reply is rightly logical, as well as physically very effective. But there has crept through the culture of modern Europe another notion that is equally in its own way an attack on the essential rightness of the world. It is not avowedly pessimistic, though the source from which it comes (which is Buddhism) is pessimistic for those who really understand it. It can offer itself—as it does among some of the high-minded and distinguished Theosophists—with an air of something highly optimistic. But this disguised pessimism is what is really wrong with the world—at least, especially with the modern world. It is essential to arrest and to examine it.

There has crept into our thoughts, through a thousand small openings, a curious and unnatural idea. I mean the idea that unity is itself a good thing; that there is something high and spiritual about things being blended and absorbed into each other. That all rivers should run into one river, that all vegetables should go into one pot—that is spoken of as the last and best fulfilment of being. Boys are to be 'at one' with girls; all sects are to be 'at one' in the New Theology; beasts fade into men and men fade into God; union in itself is a noble thing. Now union in itself is not a noble thing. Love is a noble thing; but love is not union. Nay, it is rather a vivid sense of separation and identity. Maudlin, inferior love poetry does, indeed, talk of lovers being 'one soul', just as maudlin, inferior religious poetry talks of being lost in God; but the best poetry does not. When Dante meets Beatrice, he feels his distance from her, not his proximity; and all the greatest saints have felt their lowness, not their highness, in the moment of ecstasy. And what is true of these grave and heroic matters (I do not say, of course, that saints and lovers have never used the language of union too, true enough in its own place and proper limitation of meaning)—what is true of these is equally true of all the lighter and less essential forms of appreciation of surprise. Division and variety are essential to praise; division and variety *are* what is right with the world. There is nothing specially right about mere contact and coalescence.

In short, this vast, vague idea of unity is the one 'reactionary' thing in the world. It is perhaps the only connection in which that foolish word 're-actionary' can be used with significance and truth. For this blending of men and women, nations and nations, is truly a return to the chaos and un-consciousness that were before the world was made. There is, of course, another kind of unity of which I do not speak here; unity in the possession of truth and the perception of the need for these varieties. But the varieties themselves; the reflection of man and woman in each other, as in two distinct mirrors; the wonder of man at nature as a strange thing at once above and below him; the quaint and solitary kingdom of childhood; the local affections and the colour of certain landscapes—these actually are the things that are the grace and honour of the earth; these are the things that make life worth living and the whole framework of things well worthy to be sustained. And the best thing remains; that this view, whether conscious or not, always has been and still is the view of the living and labouring millions. While a few prigs on platforms are talking about 'oneness' and absorption in 'The All', the folk that dwell in all the valleys of this ancient earth are renewing the varieties for ever. With them a woman is loved for being unmanly, and a man loved for being unwomanly. With them the church and the home are both beautiful, because they are both different; with them fields are personal and flags are sacred; they are the virtue of existence, for they are not mankind but men.

The rooted hope of the modern world is that all these dim democracies do still believe in that romance of life, that variation of man, woman and child upon which all poetry has hitherto been built. The danger of the modern world is that these dim democracies are so very dim, and that they are especially dim where they are right. The danger is that the world may fall under a new oligarchy—the oligarchy of prigs. And if anyone should promptly ask (in the manner of the debating clubs) for the definition of a prig, I can only reply that a prig is an oligarch who does not even know he is an oligarch. A circle of small pedants sit on an upper platform, and pass unanimously (in a meeting of none) that there is no difference between the social duties of men and of women, the social instruction of men or of children. Below them boils that multitudinous sea of millions that think differently, that have always thought differently, that will always think dif-ferently. In spite of the overwhelming majority that maintains the old theory of life, I am in some real doubt about which will win. Owing to the decay of theology and all the other clear systems of thought, men have been thrown back very much upon their instincts, as with animals. As with animals, their instincts are right; but, as with animals, they can be cowed. Between the agile scholars and the stagnant mob, I am really doubtful about which will be triumphant. I have no doubt at all about which ought to be.

Europe at present exhibits a concentration upon politics which is partly the unfortunate result of our loss of religion, partly the just and needful result of our loss of our social inequality and iniquity. These causes, however, will not remain in operation for ever. Religion is returning from her exile; it is more likely that the future will be crazily and corruptly superstitious than that it will be merely rationalist.

On the other hand, our attempts to right the extreme ill-balance of wealth must soon have some issue; something will be done to lessen the perpetual torture of incompetent compassion; some scheme will be substituted for our malevolent anarchy, if it be only one of benevolent servitude. And as these two special unrests about the universe and the State settle down into a more silent and enduring system, there will emerge more and more those primary and archaic truths which the dust of these two conflicts has veiled. The secondary questions relatively solved, we shall find ourselves all the more in the presence of the primary questions of Man.

For at present we all tend to one mistake; we tend to make politics too important. We tend to forget how huge a part of a man's life is the same under a Sultan and a Senate, under Nero or St Louis. Daybreak is a never-ending glory, getting out of bed is a never-ending nuisance; food and friends will be welcomed; work and strangers must be accepted and endured; birds will go bedwards and children won't, to the end of the last evening. And the worst peril is that in our just modern revolt against intolerable accidents we may have unsettled those things that alone make daily life tolerable. It will be an ironic tragedy if, when we have toiled to find rest, we find we are incurably restless. It will be sad if, when we have worked for our holiday, we find we have unlearnt everything but work. The typical modern man is the insane millionaire who has drudged to get money, and then finds he cannot enjoy even money. There is danger that the social reformer may silently and occultly develop some of the madness of the millionaire whom he denounces. He may find that he has learnt how to build playgrounds but forgotten how to play. He may agitate for peace and quiet, but only propagate his own mental agitation. In his long fight to get a slave a half-holiday he may angrily deny those ancient and natural things, the zest of being, the divinity of man, the sacredness of simple things, the health and humour of the earth, which alone make a half-holiday even half a holiday or a slave even half a man.

There is danger in that modern phrase 'divine discontent'. There is truth in it also, of course; but it is only truth of a special and secondary kind. Much of the quarrel between Christianity and the world has been due to this fact; that there are generally two truths, as it were, at any given moment of revolt or reaction, and the ancient underlying truism which is nevertheless true all the time. It is sometimes worth while to point out that black is not so black as it is painted; but black is still black, and not white. So with the merits of content and discontent. It is true that in certain acute and painful crises of oppression or disgrace, discontent is a duty and shame could call us like a trumpet. But it is not true that man should look at life with an eye of discontent, however high-minded. It is not true that in his primary, naked relation to the world, in his relation to sex, to pain, to comradeship, to the grave or to the weather, man ought to make discontent his ideal; it is black lunacy. Half his poor little hopes of happiness hang on his thinking a small house pretty, a plain wife charming, a lame foot not unbearable, and bad cards not so bad. The voice of the special rebels and prophets, recommending discontent, should, as I have said, sound now and then suddenly, like a trumpet. But the voices of the saints and sages, recommending contentment, should sound unceasingly, like the sea.

# Poems

### A BALLADE OF SUICIDE

The gallows in my garden, people say,
Is new and neat and adequately tall.
I tie the noose on in a knowing way
As one that knots his necktie for a ball;
But just as all the neighbours—on the wall—
Are drawing a long breath to shout 'Hurray!'
The strangest whim has seized me. . . . After all
I think I will not hang myself to-day.

To-morrow is the time I get my pay—
My uncle's sword is hanging in the hall—
I see a little cloud all pink and grey—
Perhaps the Rector's mother will *not* call—
I fancy that I heard from Mr Gall
That mushrooms could be cooked another way—
I never read the works of Juvenal—
I think I will not hang myself to-day.

The world will have another washing day;
The decadents decay; the pedants pall;
And H. G. Wells has found that children play,
And Bernard Shaw discovered that they squall;
Rationalists are growing rational—
And through thick woods one finds a stream astray,
So secret that the very sky seems small—
I think I will not hang myself to-day.

Collected Poems, 1915

ENVOI

Prince, I can hear the trumpet of Germinal,
The tumbrils toiling up the terrible way;
Even to-day your royal head may fall—
I think I will not hang myself to-day.

[1911]

## ANTICHRIST, OR THE REUNION OF
## CHRISTENDOM: AN ODE

'A BILL WHICH HAS SHOCKED THE CONSCIENCE
OF EVERY CHRISTIAN COMMUNITY IN EUROPE.'
*Mr F. E. Smith*, ON THE WELSH DISESTABLISHMENT BILL.

Are they clinging to their crosses,
   F. E. Smith,
 Where the Breton boat-fleet tosses,
    Are they, Smith?
Do they, fasting, trembling, bleeding,
 Wait the news from this our city?
Groaning 'That's the Second Reading!'
 Hissing 'There is still Committee!'
If the voice of Cecil falters,
 If McKenna's point has pith,
Do they tremble for their altars?
    Do they, Smith?

Russian peasants round their pope
   Huddled, Smith,
Hear about it all, I hope,
    Don't they, Smith?
In the mountain hamlets clothing
 Peaks beyond Caucasian pales,
Where Establishment means nothing
 And they never heard of Wales,

351

Do they read it all in Hansard
   With a crib to read it with—
'Welsh Tithes: Dr Clifford Answered.'
        Really, Smith?

In the lands where Christians were,
        F. E. Smith,
In the little lands laid bare,
        Smith, O Smith!
Where the Turkish bands are busy,
   And the Tory name is blessed
Since they hailed the Cross of Dizzy
   On the banners from the West!
Men don't think it half so hard if
   Islam burns their kin and kith,
Since a curate lives in Cardiff
        Saved by Smith.

It would greatly, I must own,
        Soothe me, Smith!
If you left this theme alone,
        Holy Smith!
For your legal cause or civil
   You fight well and get your fee;
For your God or dream or devil
   You will answer, not to me.
Talk about the pews and steeples
   And the Cash that goes therewith!
But the souls of Christian peoples ...
        Chuck it, Smith!

        [1912]

## THE ROLLING ENGLISH ROAD

Before the Roman came to Rye or out to Severn strode,
The rolling English drunkard made the rolling English road.
A reeling road, a rolling road, that rambles round the shire,
And after him the parson ran, the sexton and the squire;
A merry road, a mazy road, and such as we did tread
The night we went to Birmingham by way of Beachy Head.

I knew no harm of Bonaparte and plenty of the Squire,
And for to fight the Frenchman I did not much desire;
But I did bash their baggonets because they came arrayed
To straighten out the crooked road an English drunkard made,
Where you and I went down the lane with ale-mugs in our hands,
The night we went to Glastonbury by way of Goodwin Sands.

His sins they were forgiven him; or why do flowers run
Behind him; and the hedges all strengthening in the sun?
The wild thing went from left to right and knew not which was which,
But the wild rose was above him when they found him in the ditch.
God pardon us, nor harden us; we did not see so clear
The night we went to Bannockburn by way of Brighton Pier.

My friends, we will not go again or ape an ancient rage,
Or stretch the folly of our youth to be the shame of age,
But walk with clearer eyes and ears this path that wandereth,
And see undrugged in evening light the decent inn of death;
For there is good news yet to hear and fine things to be seen,
Before we go to Paradise by way of Kensal Green.

[1913]


## WINE AND WATER

Old Noah he had an ostrich farm and fowls on the largest scale,
He ate his egg with a ladle in a egg-cup big as a pail,
And the soup he took was Elephant Soup and the fish he took was Whale,
But they all were small to the cellar he took when he set out to sail,
And Noah he often said to his wife when he sat down to dine,
'I don't care where the water goes if it doesn't get into the wine.'

The cataract of the cliff of heaven fell blinding off the brink
As if it would wash the stars away as suds go down a sink,
The seven heavens came roaring down for the throats of hell to drink,
And Noah he cocked his eye and said, 'It looks like rain, I think,
The water has drowned the Matterhorn as deep as a Mendip mine,
But I don't care where the water goes if it doesn't get into the wine.'

But Noah he sinned, and we have sinned; on tipsy feet we trod,
Till a great big black teetotaller was sent to us for a rod,
And you can't get wine at a PSA, or chapel, or Eisteddfod,
For the Curse of Water has come again because of the wrath of God,
And water is on the Bishop's board and the Higher Thinker's shrine,
But I don't care where the water goes if it doesn't get into the wine.

[1914]

## A HYMN

O God of earth and altar,
  Bow down and hear our cry,
Our earthly rulers falter,
  Our people drift and die;
The walls of gold entomb us,
  The swords of scorn divide,
Take not thy thunder from us,
  But take away our pride.

From all that terror teaches,
  From lies of tongue and pen,
From all the easy speeches
  That comfort cruel men,
For sale and profanation
  Of honour and the sword,
From sleep and from damnation,
  Deliver us, good Lord.

Tie in a living tether
  The prince and priest and thrall,
Bind all our lives together,
  Smite us and save us all;
In ire and exultation
  Aflame with faith, and free,
Lift up a living nation,
  A single sword to thee.

[1915]

## THE BEATIFIC VISION

Then Bernard smiled at me, that I should gaze
   But I had gazed already; caught the view,
Faced the unfathomable ray of rays
   Which to itself and by itself is true.

Then was my vision mightier than man's speech;
   Speech snapt before it like a flying spell;
And memory and all that time can teach
   Before that splendid outrage failed and fell.

As when one dreameth and remembereth not
   Waking, what were his pleasures or his pains,
With every feature of the dream forgot,
   The printed passion of the dream remains:—

Even such am I; within whose thoughts resides
   No picture of that sight nor any part,
Nor any memory: in whom abides
   Only a happiness within the heart,

A secret happiness that soaks the heart
   As hills are soaked by slow unsealing snow,
Or secret as that wind without a chart
   Whereon did the wild leaves of Sibyl go.

O light uplifted from all mortal knowing,
   Send back a little of that glimpse of thee,
That of its glory I may kindle glowing
   One tiny spark for all men yet to be.

[1915]

## THE SECRET PEOPLE

Smile at us, pay us, pass us; but do not quite forget.
For we are the people of England, that never have spoken yet.
There is many a fat farmer that drinks less cheerfully,
There is many a free French peasant who is richer and sadder than we.
There are no folk in the whole world so helpless or so wise.
There is hunger in our bellies, there is laughter in our eyes;
You laugh at us and love us, both mugs and eyes are wet:
Only you do not know us. For we have not spoken yet.

The fine French kings came over in a flutter of flags and dames.
We liked their smiles and battles, but we never could say their names.
The blood ran red to Bosworth and the high French lords went down;
There was naught but a naked people under a naked crown.
And the eyes of the King's Servants turned terribly every way,
And the gold of the King's Servants rose higher every day.
They burnt the homes of the shaven men, that had been quaint and kind,
Till there was no bed in a monk's house, nor food that man could find.
The inns of God where no man paid, that were the wall of the weak,
The King's Servants ate them all. And still we did not speak.

And the face of the King's Servants grew greater than the King:
He tricked them, and they trapped him, and stood round him in a ring.
The new grave lords closed round him, that had eaten the abbey's fruits,
And the men of the new religion, with their bibles in their boots,
We saw their shoulders moving, to menace or discuss,
And some were pure and some were vile; but none took heed of us.
We saw the King as they killed him, and his face was proud and pale;
And a few men talked of freedom, while England talked of ale.

A war that we understood not came over the world and woke
Americans, Frenchmen, Irish; but we knew not the things they spoke.
They talked about rights and nature and peace and the people's reign:
And the squires, our masters, bade us fight; and never scorned us again.
Weak if we be for ever, could none condemn us then;
Men called us serfs and drudges; men knew that we were men.
In foam and flame at Trafalgar, on Albeura plains,
We did and died like lions, to keep ourselves in chains
We lay in living ruins; firing and fearing not
The strange fierce face of the Frenchman who knew for what they fought,
And the man who seemed to be more than man we strained against and
    broke;
And we broke our own rights with him. And still we never spoke.

Our patch of glory ended; we never heard guns again.
But the squire seemed struck in the saddle; he was foolish, as if in pain.
He leaned on a staggering lawyer, he clutched a cringing Jew,
He was stricken; it may be, after all, he was stricken at Waterloo.
Or perhaps the shades of the shaven men, whose spoil is in his house,
Come back in shining shapes at last to spoil his last carouse:
We only know the last sad squires ride slowly towards the sea,
And a new people takes the land: and still it is not we.

They have given us into the hand of new unhappy lords,
Lords without anger and honour, who dare not carry their swords.
They fight by shuffling papers; they have bright dead alien eyes;
They look at our labour and laughter as a tired man looks at flies.
And the load of their loveless pity is worse than the ancient wrongs,
Their doors are shut in the evening; and they know no songs.

We hear men speaking for us of new laws strong and sweet,
Yet is there no man speaketh as we speak in the street.
It may be we shall rise the last as Frenchmen rose the first,
Our wrath come after Russia's wrath and our wrath be the worst.
It may be we are meant to mark with our riot and our rest
God's scorn for all men governing. It may be beer is best.
But we are the people of England; and we have not spoken yet.
Smile at us, pay us, pass us. But do not quite forget.

[1915]

# The Mad Official

Going mad is the slowest and dullest business in the world. I have very nearly done it more than once in my boyhood, and so have nearly all my friends, born under the general doom of mortals, but especially of moderns; I mean the doom that makes a man come almost to the end of thinking before he comes to the first chance of living.

But the process of going mad is dull, for the simple reason that a man does not know that it is going on. Routine and literalism and a certain dry-throated earnestness and mental thirst, these are the very atmosphere of morbidity. If once the man could become conscious of his madness, he would cease to be mad. He studies certain texts in Daniel or cryptograms in Shakespeare through monstrously magnifying spectacles, which are on his nose night and day. If once he could take off the spectacles he would smash them. He deduces all his fantasies about the Sixth Seal or the Anglo-Saxon Race from one unexamined and invisible first principle. If he could once see the first principle, he would see that it is not there.

This slow and awful self-hypnotism of errors is a process that can occur not only with individuals, but also with whole societies. It is hard to pick out and prove; that is why it is hard to cure. But this mental degeneration may be brought to one test, which I truly believe to be a real test. A nation is not going mad when it does extravagant things, so long as it does them in an extravagant spirit. Crusaders not cutting their beards till they found Jerusalem, Jacobins calling each other Harmodius and Epaminondas when their names were Jacques and Jules; these are wild things, but they were done in wild spirits at a wild moment.

But whenever we see things done wildly, but taken tamely, then the State is growing insane. For instance, I have a gun licence. For all I know, this would logically allow me to fire off fifty-nine enormous field guns day and night in my back garden. I should not be surprised at a man doing it; for it would be great fun. But I should be surprised at the neighbours putting up

*Daily News*, 18 February, 1911. Collected in A Miscellany of Men, 1912

with it, and regarding it as an ordinary thing merely because it might happen to fulfil the letter of my licence.

Or, again, I have a dog licence; and I may have the right (for all I know) to turn ten thousand wild dogs loose in Buckinghamshire. I should not be surprised if the law were like that; because in modern England there is practically no law to be surprised at. I should not be surprised even at the man who did it; for a certain kind of man, if he lived long under the English landlord system, might do anything. But I should be surprised at the people who consented to stand it. I should, in other words, think the world a little mad if the incident were received in silence.

Now things every bit as wild as this are being received in silence every day. All strokes slip on the smoothness of a polished wall. All blows fall soundless on the softness of a padded cell. For madness is a passive as well as an active state; it is a paralysis, a refusal of the nerves to respond to the normal stimuli, as well as an unnatural stimulation. There are commonwealths, plainly to be distinguished here and there in history, which pass from prosperity to squalor, or from glory to insignificance, or from freedom to slavery, not only in silence, but with serenity. The face still smiles while the limbs, literally and loathsomely, are dropping from the body. These are peoples that have lost the power of astonishment at their own actions. When they give birth to a fantastic fashion or a foolish law, they do not start or stare at the monster they have brought forth. They have grown used to their own unreason; chaos is their cosmos; and the whirlwind is the breath of their nostrils. These nations are really in danger of going off their heads *en masse*; of becoming one vast vision of imbecility, with toppling cities and crazy countrysides, all dotted with industrious lunatics. One of these countries is modern England.

Now here is an actual instance, a small case of how our social conscience really works: tame in spirit, wild in result, blank in realisation; a thing without the light of mind in it. I take this paragraph from a daily paper:

'At Epping, yesterday, Thomas Woolbourne, a Lambourne labourer, and his wife were summoned for neglecting their five children. Dr Alpin said he was invited by the inspector of the NSPCC to visit defendants' cottage. Both the cottage and the children were dirty. The children looked exceedingly well in health, but the conditions would be serious in case of illness. Defendants were stated to be sober. The man was discharged. The woman, who said she was hampered by the cottage having no water supply and that she was ill, was sentenced to six weeks' imprisonment. The sentence caused surprise and the woman was removed crying, "Lord, save me!"'

I know no name for this but Chinese. It calls up the mental picture of some archaic and changeless Eastern Court, in which men with dried faces and stiff ceremonial costumes perform some atrocious cruelty to the accompaniment of formal proverbs and sentences of which the very meaning has been forgotten. In both cases the only thing in the whole farrago that can be called real is the wrong. If we apply the lightest touch of reason to the whole Epping prosecution it dissolves into nothing.

I here challenge any person in his five wits to tell me what that woman was sent to prison for. Either it was for being poor, or it was for being ill. Nobody could suggest, nobody will suggest, nobody, as a matter of fact, did suggest, that she had committed any other crime. The doctor was called in by a Society for the Prevention of Cruelty to Children. Was this woman guilty of cruelty to children? Not in the least. Did the doctor say she was guilty of cruelty to children? Not in the least. Was there any evidence even remotely bearing on the sin of cruelty? Not a rap. The worst that the doctor could work himself up to saying was that though the children were 'exceedingly' well, the conditions would be serious in case of illness. If the doctor will tell me any conditions that would be comic in case of illness, I shall attach more weight to his argument.

Now this is the worst effect of modern worry. The mad doctor has gone mad. He is literally and practically mad; and still he is quite literally and practically a doctor. The only question is the old one, *Quis docebit ipsum doctorem?* Now cruelty to children is an utterly unnatural thing; instinctively accursed of earth and heaven. But neglect of children is a natural thing; like neglect of any other duty. It is a mere difference of degree that divides extending arms and legs in calisthenics and extending them on the rack. It is a mere difference of degree that separates any operation from any torture. The thumb-screw can easily be called Manicure. Being pulled about by wild horses can easily be called Massage. The modern problem is not so much what people will endure as what they will not endure. But I fear I interrupt. ... The boiling oil is boiling; and the Tenth Mandarin is already reciting the 'Seventeen Serious Principles and the Fifty-three Virtues of the Sacred Emperor'.

# A SHORT HISTORY OF ENGLAND
## Introduction to a New Edition

When I was invited, some years ago, to write the little volume that bears the title of *A Short History of England*, I was well aware that there would seem to be a certain impudence in accepting the challenge; though in reality the title is more impudent than the book. I had intended it to be called *A Sketch of English History*, or *An Essay on English History*, though I did not think either the title or the book a worthy subject for solemn dispute. But the task as I conceived it involved no swagger of sham scholarship. The neglected side of English history does not consist of little things which the learned obscurely conceal, but rather of large things which the learned frequently ignore. Much of it can be learned, not only without any prodigy of book-learning, but practically without any books. It can be learned from large and obvious things, like the size of Gothic churches or the style of classical country houses. It needs no very abstruse learning to know that a squire is not an abbot, while his house is called an abbey. It needs no very elaborate logic to deduce that a place called a Common was common land. The difference is not about the facts but about the importance of the facts; and that must be left to a general criticism of the general view.

In my original introduction I disclaimed any particular historical learning, and it would not be surprising if I fell into particular historical errors. Curiously enough, however, most of the errors I have since discovered were not concerned with things I did not know, but with things I did know. An interesting psychological essay might be written about such mistakes; the mistakes that are made in spite of knowledge. For instance, I find that I referred to King John as the second son of Henry of Anjou. It is impossible for anybody who ever read the ordinary nursery histories, with their royal anecdotes, not to know quite well that Henry the Second had more sons than he knew what to do with, so to speak, and that John was the youngest. Everybody knows the story of his father's bitterness over the desertion of that unsatisfactory Benjamin. But the context will probably show that I was not

A Short History of England, 1917. 1924 edition

counting sons but counting kings; and meant that he was the second son to succeed. There are other errors of the sort equally easy to make and easy to correct. On page 129 'widow of Henry V' ought obviously to be 'widow of Henry VI,' or rather 'wife of Henry VI'; for in contradiction of the creed of Mr Weller she was not formidable through being a widow. But I vaguely thought of her as a widow, or at least a mourning woman left alone with her child, because my memory rested at the moment on an old story of her solitary adventure with the little prince. I found a misprint in the Benedictine anecdote: obviously it should be 'Franciscere' or 'Franciscet,' if it be worth while to conjugate a verb that does not exist, in the mouth of a man talking dog Latin. There are probably only too many mistakes that are not misprints. I am told that I have attributed one remark about the sun to Sir Thomas More which was really made by one of his companions in the same school of martyrs; and this is possible, for I remember reading all the stories in the same collection of martyrological anecdotes. These are the more doubtful details that have come to my notice; I apologise for them very heartily, but they are rather fewer than I feared.

I say I apologise for any such details; because I have no apology at all to offer about the general thesis or design. Everything I have since learned, especially from more learned people, has led me to think that I was much more right than I thought I was. Such amateur history must be a little like guesswork; but I have almost a retrospective shiver at my own good luck in having so often guessed right. I could now give a great deal more evidence than I possessed then of the general propositions; that mediæval England possessed many democratic ideals; that it might have moved and was even moving towards a more really democratic progress; that it was thwarted by the oligarchy which had grown too strong under the too fitful and personal authority of the kings; that it was oligarchy that triumphed in the sixteenth and seventeenth centuries, trampling out the last popular elements in the colleges, the guilds, the law and the holding of the land; and that the aristocracy is now changing to a plutocracy without having really given the people a glimpse of the popular vision without which they perish. I have not only grown more convinced of the truth of this general view, but I have lived to see the world grow more and more disposed to consider it. When this book was written, for instance, all that world which regarded Mr Bernard Shaw as the supreme modernist regarded me as a sort of moonstruck antiquary for being a mediævalist. Yet I only praised the best of medi- ævalism, and especially the morning of mediævalism; I definitely admitted that in its last twilight were many monsters: and I particularly instanced the perverted zeal of the priests who persecuted St Joan. I have lived to see Bernard Shaw the Modernist complete the case for Chesterton the Medi- ævalist. I have lived to see him, of all men, proving that there was something to be said even for the monsters of mediævalism. Where I defended its glory he has defended even its decay; and defended it triumphantly. For he has defended it on the fundamental ground; the fact that has to be grasped by everybody before he is fit to discuss the question; the fact that the mediæval men's vision of Christendom was something much larger than our empires and races and vested interests; and that where our best can only die gloriously for the flag, they could commit even their crimes for the Cross.

In becoming more and more solidly certain of such a thing as a truth, one loses the temptation to exaggerate it as a challenge. A fair statement of the transition from the Middle Ages would, I think, be something like this. With that change the world improved in many things, but not in the one thing needful; the one thing that can make them all one. It did not become more universal; it became much less universal; for it only picked up and polished the fragments of a shattered universe. In other words, the improvement was the sort of improvement which is seen when medicine becomes purely specialist or football becomes purely professional. The mediæval man was really ruder and more ineffective in many ways; but his outlook on life was really larger and more human. Thus the revival of learning was not an extension of learning; the public schools ceased to be popular schools. More gentlemen learnt Greek, but fewer peasants learnt Latin. Thus the Reformation intensified religion into sects; but it was no longer possible to reconcile men through religion. Thus in the drama, it is obvious that greater plays were produced, but fewer people produced them. Shakespeare emerged to make fun of Snout and Snug producing a play; but there was something to be said for the old guild theatre in which all the Snouts and Snugs could produce plays. Literature grew more finished because language grew more finished; but for good and evil it was narrowed into national languages; there was no longer a really European Esperanto. In a hundred ways human beings had lost the conception of a complete humanity. The application of this to English history can easily be made by an example in English literature. One of the very greatest and most human geniuses of the not very human seventeenth century was John Bunyan. His work is rightly regarded as a model and monument of completed English. But compare for one moment the moral atmosphere of the allegorist who wrote the *Pilgrim's Progress* with that of the allegorist who wrote *Piers Plowman*. They are both symbolical pageants of human life under the light of religion. Nobody will deny that the Puritan masterpiece is a more complete and coherent work of art; for the national language and literature have become more complete and coherent. But if it comes to broadmindedness, to brotherhood, to a survey of the mighty world, of every class, every problem, every political ideal, then Bunyan is burrowing in a hole while Langland is standing on a mountain. It is very right and even very glorious that Bunyan's statue at Bedford should 'stand facing the place where he lay in gaol'; but there stands no statue on the Malvern Heights, where the great tribune of the Middle Ages saw his vision of justice for the whole world; the corporate common people gathered into one gigantic figure, labouring through clouds and confusions: till, in the last phase of mystery, he turns on us the terrible face of Christ.

# The Province of Britain

The land on which we live once had the highly poetic privilege of being the end of the world. Its extremity was *ultima Thule*, the other end of nowhere. When these islands, lost in a night of northern seas, were lit up at last by the long searchlights of Rome, it was felt that the remotest remnant of things had been touched; and more for pride than possession.

The sentiment was not unsuitable, even in geography. About these realms upon the edge of everything there was really something that can only be called edgy. Britain is not so much an island as an archipelago; it is at least a labyrinth of peninsulas. In few of the kindred countries can one so easily and so strangely find sea in the fields or fields in the sea. The great rivers seem not only to meet in the ocean, but barely to miss each other in the hills: the whole land, though low as a whole, leans towards the west in shouldering mountains; and a prehistoric tradition has taught it to look towards the sunset for islands yet dreamier than its own. The islanders are of a kind with their islands. Different as are the nations into which they are now divided, the Scots, the English, the Irish, the Welsh of the western uplands, have something altogether different from the humdrum docility of the inland Germans, or from the *bon sens français* which can be at will trenchant or trite. There is something common to all the Britons, which even Acts of Union have not torn asunder. The nearest name for it is insecurity, something fitting in men walking on cliffs and the verge of things. Adventure, a lonely taste in liberty, a humour without wit, perplex their critics and perplex themselves. Their souls are fretted like their coasts. They have an embarrassment, noted by all foreigners: it is expressed, perhaps, in the Irish by a confusion of speech and in the English by a confusion of thought. For the Irish bull is a licence with the symbol of language. But Bull's own bull, the English bull, is 'a dumb ox of thought'; a standing mystification in the mind. There is something double in the thoughts as of the soul mirrored in many waters. Of all peoples they are least attached to the purely classical; the

A Short History of England, 1917

365

imperial plainness which the French do finely and the Germans coarsely, but the Britons hardly at all. They are constantly colonists and emigrants; they have the name of being at home in every country. But they are in exile in their own country. They are torn between love of home and love of something else; of which the sea may be the explanation or may be only the symbol. It is also found in a nameless nursery rhyme which is the finest line in English literature and the dumb refrain of all English poems—'Over the hills and far away.'

The great rationalist hero who first conquered Britain, whether or no he was the detached demigod of 'Cæsar and Cleopatra,' was certainly a Latin of the Latins, and described these islands when he found them with all the curt positivism of his pen of steel. But even Julius Cæsar's brief account of the Britons leaves on us something of this mystery, which is more than ignorance of fact. They were apparently ruled by that terrible thing, a pagan priesthood. Stones now shapeless yet arranged in symbolic shapes bear witness to the order and labour of those that lifted them. Their worship was probably Nature-worship; and while such a basis may count for something in the elemental quality that has always soaked the island arts, the collision between it and the tolerant Empire suggests the presence of something which generally grows out of Nature-worship—I mean the unnatural. But upon nearly all the matters of modern controversy Cæsar is silent. He is silent about whether the language was 'Celtic'; and some of the place-names have even given rise to a suggestion that, in parts at least, it was already Teutonic. I am not capable of pronouncing upon the truth of such speculations, but I am of pronouncing upon their importance; at least, to my own very simple purpose. And indeed their importance has been very much exaggerated. Cæsar professed to give no more than the glimpse of a traveller; but when, some considerable time after, the Romans returned and turned Britain into a Roman province, they continued to display a singular indifference to questions that have excited so many professors. What they cared about was getting and giving in Britain what they had got and given in Gaul. We do not know whether the Britons then, or for that matter the Britons now, were Iberian or Cymric or Teutonic. We do know that in a short time they were Roman.

Every now and then there is discovered in modern England some fragment such as a Roman pavement. Such Roman antiquities rather diminish than increase the Roman reality. They make something seem distant which is still very near, and something seem dead that is still alive. It is like writing a man's epitaph on his front door. The epitaph would probably be a compliment, but hardly a personal introduction. The important thing about France and England is not that they have Roman remains. They are Roman remains. In truth they are not so much remains as relics; for they are still

366

working miracles. A row of poplars is a more Roman relic than a row of pillars. Nearly all that we call the works of nature have but grown like fungoids upon this original work of man; and our woods are mosses on the bones of a giant. Under the seed of our harvests and the roots of our trees is a foundation of which the fragments of tile and brick are but emblems; and under the colours of our wildest flowers are the colours of a Roman pavement.

Britain was directly Roman for fully four hundred years; longer than she has been Protestant, and very much longer than she has been industrial. What was meant by being Roman it is necessary in a few lines to say, or no sense can be made of what happened after, especially of what happened immediately after. Being Roman did *not* mean being subject, in the sense that one savage tribe will enslave another, or in the sense that the cynical politicians of recent times watched with a horrible hopefulness for the evanescence of the Irish. Both conquerors and conquered were heathen, and both had the institutions which seem to us to give an inhumanity to heathenism: the triumph, the slave-market, the lack of all the sensitive nationalism of modern history. But the Roman Empire did not destroy nations; if anything, it created them. Britons were not originally proud of being Britons; but they were proud of being Romans. The Roman steel was at least as much a magnet as a sword. In truth it was rather a round mirror of steel, in which every people came to see itself. For Rome as Rome the very smallness of the civic origin was a warrant for the largeness of the civic experiment. Rome itself obviously could not rule the world, any more than Rutland. I mean it could not rule the other races as the Spartans ruled the Helots or the Americans ruled the negroes. A machine so huge had to be human; it had to have a handle that fitted any man's hand. The Roman Empire necessarily became less Roman as it became more of an Empire; until not very long after Rome gave conquerors to Britain, Britain was giving emperors to Rome. Out of Britain, as the Britons boasted, came at length the great Empress Helena, who was the mother of Constantine. And it was Constantine, as all men know, who first nailed up that proclamation which all after generations have in truth been struggling either to protect or to tear down.

About that revolution no man has ever been able to be impartial. The present writer will make no idle pretence of being so. That it was the most revolutionary of all revolutions, since it identified the dead body on a servile gibbet with the fatherhood in the skies, has long been a commonplace without ceasing to be a paradox. But there is another historic element that must also be realised. Without saying anything more of its tremendous essence, it is very necessary to note why even pre-Christian Rome was regarded as something mystical for long afterwards by all European men. The extreme view of it was held, perhaps, by Dante; but it pervaded mediævalism, and therefore still haunts modernity. Rome was regarded as Man, mighty, though fallen, because it was the utmost that Man had done. It was divinely necessary that the Roman Empire should succeed—if only that it might fail. Hence the school of Dante implied the paradox that the Roman soldiers killed Christ, not only by right, but even by divine right. That mere law might fail at its highest test it had to be real law, and not mere military lawlessness. Therefore God worked by Pilate as by Peter. Therefore the mediæval poet is eager to show that Roman government was simply good government, and not a usurpation. For it was the whole point of the Christian revolution to maintain that in this, good government was as bad as bad. Even good government was not good enough to know God among the thieves. This is not only generally important as involving a colossal change in the conscience; the loss of the whole heathen repose in the complete sufficiency of the city or the state. It made a sort of eternal rule enclosing an eternal rebellion. It must be incessantly remembered through the first half of English history; for it is the whole meaning in the quarrel of the priests and kings.

The double rule of the civilisation and the religion in one sense remained for centuries; and before its first misfortunes came it must be conceived as substantially the same everywhere. And however it began it largely ended in equality. Slavery certainly existed, as it had in the most democratic states of ancient times. Harsh officialism certainly existed, as it exists in the most democratic states of modern times. But there was nothing of what we mean in modern times by aristocracy, still less of what we mean by racial domination. In so far as any change was passing over that society with its two levels of equal citizens and equal slaves, it was only the slow growth of the power of the Church at the expense of the power of the Empire. Now it is important to grasp that the great exception to equality, the institution of Slavery, was slowly modified by both causes. It was weakened both by the weakening of the Empire and by the strengthening of the Church.

Slavery was for the Church not a difficulty of doctrine, but a strain on the imagination. Aristotle and the pagan sages who had defined the servile or 'useful' arts, had regarded the slave as a tool, an axe to cut wood or whatever wanted cutting. The Church did not denounce the cutting; but she felt as if she was cutting glass with a diamond. She was haunted by the memory that the diamond is so much more precious than the glass. So Christianity could not settle down into the pagan simplicity that the man was made for the work, when the work was so much less immortally momentous than the man. At about this stage of a history of England there is generally told the anecdote of a pun of Gregory the Great; and this is perhaps the true point of it. By the Roman theory the barbarian bondmen were meant to be useful. The saint's mysticism was moved at finding them ornamental; and 'Non

Angli sed Angeli' meant more nearly 'Not slaves, but souls.' It is to the point, in passing, to note that in the modern country most collectively Christian, Russia, the serfs were always referred to as 'souls'. The great Pope's phrase, hackneyed as it is, is perhaps the first glimpse of the golden halos in the best Christian Art. Thus the Church, with whatever other faults, worked of her own nature towards greater social equality; and it is a historical error to suppose that the Church hierarchy worked with aristocracies, or was of a kind with them. It was an inversion of aristocracy; in the ideal of it, at least, the last were to be first. The Irish bull that 'One man is as good as another and a great deal better' contains a truth, like many contradictions; a truth that was the link between Christianity and citizenship. Alone of all superiors, the saint does not depress the human dignity of others. He is not conscious of his superiority to them; but only more conscious of his inferiority than they are.

But while a million little priests and monks like mice were already nibbling at the bonds of the ancient servitude, another process was going on, which has here been called the weakening of the Empire. It is a process which is to this day very difficult to explain. But it affected all the institutions of all the provinces, especially the institution of Slavery. But of all the provinces its effect was heaviest in Britain, which lay on or beyond the borders. The case of Britain, however, cannot possibly be considered alone. The first half of English history has been made quite unmeaning in the schools by the attempt to tell it without reference to that corporate Christendom in which it took part and pride. I fully accept the truth in Mr Kipling's question of 'What can they know of England who only England know?' and merely differ from the view that they will best broaden their minds by the study of Wagga-Wagga and Timbuctoo. It is therefore necessary, though very difficult, to frame in few words some idea of what happened to the whole European race.

Rome itself, which had made all that strong world, was the weakest thing in it. The centre had been growing fainter and fainter, and now the centre disappeared. Rome had as much freed the world as ruled it, and now she could rule no more. Save for the presence of the Pope and his constantly increasing supernatural prestige, the eternal city became like one of her own provincial towns. A loose localism was the result rather than any conscious intellectual mutiny. There was anarchy, but there was no rebellion. For rebellion must have a principle, and therefore (for those who can think) an authority. Gibbon called his great pageant of prose 'The Decline and Fall of the Roman Empire.' The Empire did decline, but it did not fall. It remains to this hour.

By a process very much more indirect even than that of the Church, this decentralisation and drift also worked against the slave-state of antiquity. The localism did indeed produce that choice of territorial chieftains which came to be called Feudalism, and of which we shall speak later. But the direct possession of man by man the same localism tended to destroy; though this negative influence upon it bears no kind of proportion to the positive influence of the Catholic Church. The later pagan slavery, like our own industrial labour which increasingly resembles it, was worked on a larger and larger scale; and it was at last too large to control. The bondman found the visible Lord more distant than the new invisible one. The slave became the serf; that is, he could be shut in, but not shut out. When once he belonged to the land, it could not be long before the land belonged to him. Even in the old and rather fictitious language of chattel slavery, there is here a difference. It is the difference between a man being a chair and a man being a house. Canute might call for his throne; but if he wanted his throne-room he must go and get it himself. Similarly, he could tell his slave to run, but he could only tell his serf to stay. Thus the two slow changes of the time both tended to transform the tool into a man. His status began to have roots; and whatever has roots will have rights.

What the decline did involve everywhere was decivilisation; the loss of letters, of laws, of roads and means of communication, the exaggeration of local colour into caprice. But on the edges of the Empire this decivilisation became a definite barbarism, owing to the nearness of wild neighbours who were ready to destroy as deafly and blindly as things are destroyed by fire. Save for the lurid and apocalyptic locust-flight of the Huns, it is perhaps an exaggeration to talk, even in those darkest ages, of a deluge of the barbarians; at least when we are speaking of the old civilisation as a whole. But a deluge of barbarians is not entirely an exaggeration of what happened on some of the borders of the Empire; of such edges of the known world as we began by describing in these pages. And on the extreme edge of the world lay Britain.

It may be true, though there is little proof of it, that the Roman civilisation itself was thinner in Britain than in the other provinces; but it was a very civilised civilisation. It gathered round the great cities like York and Chester and London; for the cities are older than the counties, and indeed older even than the countries. These were connected by a skeleton of great roads which were and are the bones of Britain. But with the weakening of Rome the bones began to break under barbarian pressure, coming at first from the north; from the Picts who lay beyond Agricola's boundary in what is now the Scotch Lowlands. The whole of this bewildering time is full of temporary tribal alliances, generally mercenary; of barbarians paid to come on or barbarians paid to go away. It seems certain that in this welter Roman Britain bought help from ruder races living about that neck of Denmark where is now the duchy of Schleswig. Having been chosen only to fight somebody they naturally fought anybody; and a century of fighting followed, under the trampling of which the Roman pavement was broken into yet smaller pieces.

It is perhaps permissible to disagree with the historian Green when he says that no spot should be more sacred to modern Englishmen than the neighbourhood of Ramsgate, where the Schleswig people are supposed to have landed; or when he suggests that their appearance is the real beginning of our island story. It would be rather more true to say that it was nearly, though prematurely, the end of it.

# The Age of the Crusades

The last chapter began, in an apparent irrelevance, with the name of St Edward; and this one might very well begin with the name of St George. His first appearance, it is said, as a patron of our people, occurred at the instance of Richard Cœur de Lion during his campaign in Palestine; and this, as we shall see, really stands for a new England which might well have a new saint. But the Confessor is a character in English history; whereas St George, apart from his place in martyrology as a Roman soldier, can hardly be said to be a character in any history. And if we wish to understand the noblest and most neglected of human revolutions, we can hardly get closer to it than by considering this paradox, of how much progress and enlightenment was represented by thus passing from a chronicle to a romance.

In any intellectual corner of modernity can be found such a phrase as I have just read in a newspaper controversy: 'Salvation, like other good things, must not come from outside.' To call a spiritual thing external and not internal is the chief mode of modernist excommunication. But if our subject of study is mediæval and not modern, we must pit against this apparent platitude the very opposite idea. We must put ourselves in the posture of men who thought that almost every good thing came from outside—like good news. I confess that I am not impartial in my sympathies here; and that the newspaper phrase I quoted strikes me as a blunder about the very nature of life. I do not, in my private capacity, believe that a baby gets his best physical food by sucking his thumb; nor that a man gets his best moral food by sucking his soul, and denying its dependence on God or other good things. I would maintain that thanks are the highest form of thought; and that gratitude is happiness doubled by wonder. But this faith in receptiveness, and in respect for things outside oneself, need here do no more than help me in explaining what any version of this epoch ought in any case to explain. In nothing is the modern German more modern, or more mad, than in his dream of finding a German name for everything; eating his language,

A Short History of England, 1917

or in other words biting his tongue. And in nothing were the mediævals more free and sane than in their acceptance of names and emblems from outside their most beloved limits. The monastery would often not only take in the stranger but almost canonise him. A mere adventurer like Bruce was enthroned and thanked as if he had really come as a knight errant. And a passionately patriotic community more often than not had a foreigner for a patron saint. Thus crowds of saints were Irishmen, but St Patrick was not an Irishman. Thus as the English gradually became a nation, they left the numberless Saxon saints in a sense behind them, passed over by comparison not only the sanctity of Edward but the solid fame of Alfred, and invoked a half mythical hero, striving in an eastern desert against an impossible monster.

That transition and that symbol stand for the Crusades. In their romance and reality they were the first English experience of learning, not only from the external, but the remote. England, like every Christian thing, had thriven on outer things without shame. From the roads of Cæsar to the churches of Lanfranç, it had sought its meat from God. But now the eagles were on the wing, scenting a more distant slaughter; they were seeking the strange things instead of receiving them. The English had stepped from acceptance to adventure, and the epic of their ships had begun. The scope of the great religious movement which swept England along with all the West would distend a book like this into huge disproportion, yet it would be much better to do so than to dismiss it in the distant and frigid fashion common in such short summaries. The inadequacy of our insular method in popular history is perfectly shown in the treatment of Richard Cœur de Lion. His tale is told with the implication that his departure for the Crusade was something like the escapade of a schoolboy running away to sea. It was, in this view, a pardonable or lovable prank; whereas in truth it was more like a responsible Englishman now going to the Front. Christendom was nearly one nation, and the Front was the Holy Land. That Richard himself was of an adventurous and even romantic temper is true, though it is not unreasonably romantic for a born soldier to do the work he does best. But the point of the argument against insular history is particularly illustrated here by the absence of a continental comparison. In this case we have only to step across the Straits of Dover to find the fallacy. Philip Augustus, Richard's contemporary in France, had the name of a particularly cautious and coldly public-spirited statesman; yet Philip Augustus went on the same Crusade. The reason was, of course, that the Crusades were, for all thoughtful Europeans, things of the highest statesmanship and the purest public spirit.

Some six hundred years after Christianity sprang up in the East and swept westwards, another great faith arose in almost the same eastern lands and followed it like its gigantic shadow. Like a shadow, it was at once a copy and a contrary. We call it Islam, or the creed of the Moslems; and perhaps its most explanatory description is that it was the final flaming up of the accumulated Orientalisms, perhaps of the accumulated Hebraisms, gradually rejected as the Church grew more European, or as Christianity turned into Christendom. Its highest motive was a hatred of idols, and in its view Incarnation was itself an idolatry. The two things it persecuted were the idea of God being made flesh and of His being afterwards made wood or stone. A study of the questions smouldering in the track of the prairie fire of the Christian conversion favours the suggestion that this fanaticism against art or mythology was at once a development and a reaction from that conversion, a sort of minority report of the Hebraists. In this sense Islam was something like a Christian heresy. The early heresies had been full of mad reversals and evasions of the Incarnation, rescuing their Jesus from the reality of his body even at the expense of the sincerity of his soul. And the Greek Iconoclasts had poured into Italy, breaking the popular statues and denouncing the idolatry of the Pope, until routed, in a style sufficiently symbolic, by the sword of the father of Charlemagne. It was all these disappointed negations that took fire from the genius of Mahomet, and launched out of the burning lands a cavalry charge that nearly conquered the world. And if it be suggested that a note on such Oriental origins is rather remote from a history of England, the answer is that this book may, alas! contain many digressions, but that this is not a digression. It is quite peculiarly necessary to keep in mind that this Semite god haunted Christianity like a ghost; to remember it in every European corner, but especially in our corner. If any one doubts the necessity, let him take a walk to all the parish churches in England within a radius of thirty miles, and ask why this stone virgin is headless or that coloured glass is gone. He will soon learn that it was lately, and in his own lanes and homesteads, that the ecstasy of the deserts returned, and his bleak northern island was filled with the fury of the Iconoclasts.

It was an element in this sublime and yet sinister simplicity of Islam that it knew no boundaries. Its very home was homeless. For it was born in a sandy waste among nomads, and it went everywhere because it came from nowhere. But in the Saracens of the early Middle Ages this nomadic quality in Islam was masked by a high civilisation, more scientific if less creatively artistic than that of contemporary Christendom. The Moslem monotheism was, or appeared to be, the more rationalist religion of the two. This rootless refinement was characteristically advanced in abstract things, of which a memory remains in the very name of algebra. In comparison the Christian civilisation was still largely instinctive, but its instincts were very strong and very much the other way. It was full of local affections, which found form in that system of *fences* which runs like a pattern through everything mediæval, from heraldry to the holding of land. There was a shape and colour in all their customs and statutes which can be seen in all their tabards and escutcheons; something at once strict and gay. This is not a departure from the interest in external things, but rather a part of it. The very welcome they would often give to a stranger from beyond the wall was a recognition of the wall. Those who think their own life all-sufficient do not see its limit as a wall, but as the end of the world. The Chinese called the white man 'a sky-breaker'. The mediæval spirit loved its part in life as a part, not a whole; its charter for it came from something else. There is a joke about a Benedictine monk who used the common grace of *Benedictus benedicat*, whereupon the unlettered Franciscan triumphantly retorted *Franciscus Franciscat*. It is something of a parable of mediæval history; for if there were a verb *Franciscare* it would be an approximate description of what St Francis afterwards did. But that more individual mysticism was only approaching its birth, and *Benedictus benedicat* is very precisely the motto of the earliest mediævalism. I mean that everything is blessed from beyond, by something which has in its turn been blessed from beyond again; only the blessed bless. But the point which is the clue to the Crusades is this: that for them the beyond was not the infinite, as in a modern religion. Every beyond was a place. The mystery of locality, with all its hold on the human heart, was as much present in the most ethereal things of Christendom as it was absent from the most practical things of Islam. England would derive a thing from France, France from Italy, Italy from Greece, Greece from Palestine, Palestine from Paradise. It was not merely that a yeoman of Kent would have his house hallowed by the priest of the parish church, which was confirmed by Canterbury, which was confirmed by Rome. Rome herself did not worship herself, as in the pagan age. Rome herself looked eastward to the mysterious cradle of her creed, to a land of which the very earth was called holy. And when she looked eastward for it she saw the face of Mahound. She saw standing in the place that was her earthly heaven a devouring giant out of the deserts, to whom all places were the same.

It has been necessary thus to pause upon the inner emotions of the Crusade, because the modern English reader is widely cut off from these particular feelings of his fathers; and the real quarrel of Christendom and Islam, the fire-baptism of the young nations, could not otherwise be seized in its unique character. It was nothing so simple as a quarrel between two men who both wanted Jerusalem. It was the much deadlier quarrel between one man who wanted it and another man who could not see why it was wanted. The Moslem, of course, had his own holy places; but he has never felt about them as Westerns can feel about a field or a roof-tree; he thought of the holiness as holy, not of the places as places. The austerity which forbade him imagery, the wandering war that forbade him rest, shut him off from all that was breaking out and blossoming in our local patriotisms; just as it has given the Turks an empire without ever giving them a nation.

Now, the effect of this adventure against a mighty and mysterious enemy was simply enormous in the transformation of England, as of all the nations that were developing side by side with England. Firstly, we learnt enormously from what the Saracen did. Secondly, we learnt yet more enormously from what the Saracen did not do. Touching some of the good things which we lacked, we were fortunately able to follow him. But in all the good things which he lacked, we were confirmed like adamant to defy him. It may be said that Christians never knew how right they were till they went to war with Moslems. At once the most obvious and the most representative reaction was the reaction which produced the best of what we call Christian Art; and especially those grotesques of Gothic architecture, which are not only alive but kicking. The East as an environment, as an impersonal glamour, certainly stimulated the Western mind, but stimulated it rather to break the Moslem commandment than to keep it. It was as if the Christian were impelled, like a caricaturist, to cover all that faceless ornament with faces; to give heads to all those headless serpents and birds to all those lifeless trees. Statuary quickened and came to life under the veto of the enemy as under a benediction. The image, merely because it was called an idol, became not only an ensign but a weapon. A hundredfold host of stone sprang up all over the shrines and streets of Europe. The Iconoclasts made more statues than they destroyed.

The place of Cœur de Lion in popular fable and gossip is far more like his place in true history than the place of the mere denationalised ne'er-do-weel given him in our utilitarian school books. Indeed the vulgar rumour is nearly always much nearer the historical truth than the 'educated' opinion of to-day; for tradition is truer than fashion. King Richard, as the typical Crusader, did make a momentous difference to England by gaining glory in the East, instead of devoting himself conscientiously to domestic politics in the exemplary manner of King John. The accident of his military genius and prestige gave England something which it kept for four hundred years, and without which it is incomprehensible throughout that period—the reputation of being in the very vanguard of chivalry. The great romances of the Round Table, the attachment of knighthood to the name of a British king, belong to this period. Richard was not only a knight but a troubadour; and culture and courtesy were linked up with the idea of English valour. The mediæval Englishman was even proud of being polite; which is at least no worse than being proud of money and bad manners, which is what many Englishmen in our later centuries have meant by their common sense.

Chivalry might be called the baptism of Feudalism. It was an attempt to bring the justice and even the logic of the Catholic creed into a military system which already existed; to turn its discipline into an initiation and its inequalities into a hierarchy. To the comparative grace of the new period belongs, of course, that considerable cultus of the dignity of woman, to which the word 'chivalry' is often narrowed, or perhaps exalted. This also was a revolt against one of the worst gaps in the more polished civilisation of the Saracens. The Moslems naturally suffered from the older Oriental sentiment about women; and were, of course, without the special inspiration given by the cult of the Virgin. It is false to say that the chivalric view of women was merely an affectation, except in the sense in which there must always be an affectation where there is an ideal. It is the worst sort of superficiality not to see the pressure of a general sentiment merely because it is always broken up by events; the Crusade itself, for example, is more present and potent as a dream even than as a reality. From the first Plantagenet to the last Lancastrian it haunts the minds of English kings, giving as a background to their battles a mirage of Palestine. So a devotion like that of Edward I to his queen was quite a real motive in the lives of multitudes of his contemporaries. When crowds of enlightened tourists, setting forth to sneer at the superstitions of the continent, are taking tickets and labelling luggage at the large railway station at the west end of the Strand, I do not know whether they all speak to their wives with a more flowing courtesy than their fathers in Edward's time, or whether they pause to meditate on the legend of a husband's sorrow, to be found in the very name of Charing Cross.

But it is a huge historical error to suppose that the Crusades concerned only that crust of society for which heraldry was an art and chivalry an etiquette. The direct contrary is the fact. The First Crusade especially was much more an unanimous popular rising than most that are called riots and revolutions. The Guilds, the great democratic systems of the time, often owed their increasing power to corporate fighting for the Cross; but I shall deal with such things later. Often it was not so much a levy of men as a trek of whole families, like new gipsies moving eastwards. And it has passed into a proverb that children by themselves often organised a crusade as they now organise a charade. But we shall best realise the fact by fancying every Crusade as a Children's Crusade. They were full of all that the modern world worships in children, because it has crushed it out of men. Their lives were full, as the rudest remains of their vulgarest arts are full, of something that we all saw out of the nursery window. It can best be seen later, for instance, in the lanced and latticed interiors of Memling, but it is ubiquitous in the older and more unconscious contemporary art; something that domesticated distant lands and made the horizon at home. They fitted into the corners of small houses the ends of the earth and edges of the sky. Their perspective is rude and crazy, but it is perspective; it is not the decorative flatness of orientalism. In a word, their world, like a child's, is full of foreshortening, as of a short cut to fairyland. Their maps are more provocative than pictures. Their half-fabulous animals are monsters, and yet are pets. It is impossible to state verbally this very vivid atmosphere; but it was an atmosphere as well as an adventure. It was precisely these outlandish visions that truly came home to everybody; it was the royal councils and feudal quarrels that were comparatively remote. The Holy Land was much nearer to a plain man's house than Westminster, and immeasurably nearer than Runymede. To give a list of English kings and parliaments, without pausing for a moment upon this prodigious presence of a religious transfiguration in common life, is something the folly of which can but faintly be conveyed by a more modern parallel, with secularity and religion reversed. It is as if some Clericalist or Royalist writer should give a list of the Archbishops of Paris from 1750 to 1850, noting how one died of small-pox, another of old age, another by a curious accident of decapitation, and throughout all his record should never once mention the nature, or even the name, of the French Revolution.

# The Problem of the Plantagenets

It is a point of prestige with what is called the Higher Criticism in all branches to proclaim that certain popular texts and authorities are 'late', and therefore apparently worthless. Two similar events are always the same event, and the later alone is even credible. This fanaticism is often in mere fact mistaken; it ignores the most common coincidences of human life: and some future critic will probably say that the tale of the Tower of Babel cannot be older than the Eiffel Tower, because there was certainly a confusion of tongues at the Paris Exhibition. Most of the mediæval remains familiar to the modern reader are necessarily 'late', such as Chaucer or the Robin Hood ballads; but they are none the less, to a wiser criticism, worthy of attention and even trust. That which lingers after an epoch is generally that which lived most luxuriantly in it. It is an excellent habit to read history backwards. It is far wiser for a modern man to read the Middle Ages backwards from Shakespeare, whom he can judge for himself, and who yet is crammed with the Middle Ages, than to attempt to read them forwards from Cædmon, of whom he can know nothing, and of whom even the authorities he must trust know very little. If this be true of Shakespeare, it is even truer, of course, of Chaucer. If we really want to know what was strongest in the twelfth century, it is no bad way to ask what remained of it in the fourteenth. When the average reader turns to the *Canterbury Tales*, which are still as amusing as Dickens yet as mediæval as Durham Cathedral, what is the very first question to be asked? Why, for instance, are they called Canterbury Tales; and what were the pilgrims doing on the road to Canterbury? They were, of course, taking part in a popular festival like a modern public holiday, though much more genial and leisurely. Nor are we, perhaps, prepared to accept it as a self-evident step in progress that their holidays were derived from saints, while ours are dictated by bankers.

It is almost necessary to say nowadays that a saint means a very good man. The notion of an eminence merely moral, consistent with complete stupidity

A Short History of England, 1917

379

or unsuccess, is a revolutionary image grown unfamiliar by its very familiarity, and needing, as do so many things of this older society, some almost preposterous modern parallel to give its original freshness and point. If we entered a foreign town and found a pillar like the Nelson Column, we should be surprised to learn that the hero on the top of it had been famous for his politeness and hilarity during a chronic toothache. If a procession came down the street with a brass band and a hero on a white horse, we should think it odd to be told that he had been very patient with a half-witted maiden aunt. Yet some such pantomime impossibility is the only measure of the innovation of the Christian idea of a popular and recognised saint. It must especially be realised that while this kind of glory was the highest, it was also in a sense the lowest. The materials of it were almost the same as those of labour and domesticity: it did not need the sword or sceptre, but rather the staff or spade. It was the ambition of poverty. All this must be approximately visualised before we catch a glimpse of the great effects of the story which lay behind the Canterbury Pilgrimage.

The first few lines of Chaucer's poem, to say nothing of thousands in the course of it, make it instantly plain that it was no case of secular revels still linked by a slight ritual to the name of some forgotten god, as may have happened in the pagan decline. Chaucer and his friends did think about St Thomas, at least more frequently than a clerk at Margate thinks about St Lubbock. They did definitely believe in the bodily cures wrought for them through St Thomas, at least as firmly as the most enlightened and progressive modern can believe in those of Mrs Eddy. Who was St Thomas, to whose shrine the whole of that society is thus seen in the act of moving; and why was he so important? If there be a streak of sincerity in the claim to teach social and democratic history, instead of a string of kings and battles, this is the obvious and open gate by which to approach the figure which disputed England with the first Plantagenet. A real popular history should think more of his popularity even than his policy. And unquestionably thousands of ploughmen, carpenters, cooks and yeomen, as in the motley crowd of Chaucer, knew a great deal about St Thomas when they had never even heard of Becket.

It would be easy to detail what followed the Conquest as the feudal tangle that it was, till a prince from Anjou repeated the unifying effort of the Conqueror. It is found equally easy to write of the Red King's hunting instead of his building, which has lasted longer, and which he probably loved much more. It is easy to catalogue the questions he disputed with Anselm—leaving out the question Anselm cared most about, and which he asked with explosive simplicity, as, 'Why was God a man?' All this is as simple as saying that a king died of eating lampreys, from which, however, there is little to learn nowadays, unless it be that when a modern monarch perishes of gluttony the newspapers seldom say so. But if we want to know what really happened to England in this dim epoch, I think it can be dimly but truly traced in the story of St Thomas of Canterbury.

Henry of Anjou, who brought fresh French blood into the monarchy, brought also a refreshment of the idea for which the French have always stood: the idea in the Roman Law of something impersonal and omnipresent. It is the thing we smile at even in a small French detective story; when Justice opens a handbag or Justice runs after a cab. Henry II really produced this impression of being a police force in person; a contemporary priest compared his restless vigilance to the bird and the fish of scripture whose way no man knoweth. Kinghood, however, meant law and not caprice; its ideal at least was a justice cheap and obvious as daylight, an atmosphere which lingers only in popular phrases about the King's English or the King's highway. But though it tended to be egalitarian it did not, of itself, tend to be humanitarian. In modern France, as in ancient Rome, the other name of Justice has sometimes been Terror. The Frenchman especially is always a Revolutionist—and never an Anarchist. Now this effort of kings like Henry II to rebuild on a plan like that of the Roman Law was not only, of course, crossed and entangled by countless feudal fancies and feelings in themselves as well as others, it was also conditioned by what was the corner-stone of the whole civilisation. It had to happen not only with but within the Church. For a Church was to these men rather a world they lived in than a building to which they went. Without the Church the Middle Ages would have had no law, as without the Church the Reformation would have had no Bible. Many priests expounded and embellished the Roman Law, and many priests supported Henry II. And yet there was another element in the Church, stored in its first foundations like dynamite, and destined in every age to destroy and renew the world. An idealism akin to impossibilism ran down the ages parallel to all its political compromises. Monasticism itself was the throwing off of innumerable Utopias, without posterity yet with perpetuity. It had, as was proved recurrently after corrupt epochs, a strange secret of getting poor quickly; a mushroom magnificence of destitution. This wind of revolution in the crusading time caught Francis in Assisi and stripped him of his rich garments in the street. The same wind of revolution suddenly smote Thomas Becket, King Henry's brilliant and luxurious Chancellor, and drove him on to an unearthly glory and a bloody end.

Becket was a type of those historic times in which it is really very practical to be impracticable. The quarrel which tore him from his friend's side cannot be appreciated in the light of those legal and constitutional debates which the misfortunes of the seventeenth century have made so much of in more recent history. To convict St Thomas of illegality and clerical intrigue, when he set the law of the Church against that of the State, is about as adequate as to convict St Francis of bad heraldry when he said he was the brother of the sun and moon. There may have been heralds stupid enough to say so even in that much more logical age, but it is no sufficient way of dealing with visions or with revolutions. St Thomas of Canterbury was a great visionary and a great revolutionist, but so far as England was concerned his revolution failed and his vision was not fulfilled. We are therefore told in the text-books little more than that he wrangled with the King about certain regulations; the most crucial being whether 'criminous clerks' should be punished by the State or the Church. And this was indeed the chief text of the dispute; but to realise it we must reiterate what is hardest for modern England to understand—the nature of the Catholic Church when it was itself a government, and the permanent sense in which it was itself a revolution.

It is always the first fact that escapes notice; and the first fact about the Church was that it created a machinery of pardon, where the State could only work with a machinery of punishment. It claimed to be a divine detective who helped the criminal to escape by a plea of guilty. It was, therefore, in the very nature of the institution, that when it did punish materially it punished more lightly. If any modern man were put back in the Becket quarrel, his sympathies would certainly be torn in two; for if the King's scheme was the more rational, the Archbishop's was the more humane. And despite the horrors that darkened religious disputes long afterwards, this character was certainly in the bulk of the historic character of Church government. It is admitted, for instance, that things like eviction, or the harsh treatment of tenants, were practically unknown wherever the Church was landlord. The principle lingered into more evil days in the form by which the Church authorities handed over culprits to the secular arm to be killed, even for religious offences. In modern romances this is treated as a mere hypocrisy; but the man who treats every human inconsistency as a hypocrisy is himself a hypocrite about his own inconsistencies.

Our world, then, cannot understand St Thomas, any more than St Francis, without accepting very simply a flaming and even fantastic charity, by which the great Archbishop undoubtedly stands for the victims of this world, where the wheel of fortune grinds the faces of the poor. He may well have been too idealistic; he wished to protect the Church as a sort of earthly paradise, of which the rules might seem to him as paternal as those of heaven, but might well seem to the King as capricious as those of fairyland. But if the priest was too idealistic, the King was really too practical; it is intrinsically true to say he was too practical to succeed in practice. There re-enters here, and runs, I think, through all English history, the rather indescribable truth that I have suggested about the Conqueror; that perhaps he was hardly impersonal enough for a pure despot. The real moral of our mediæval story is, I think, subtly contrary to Carlyle's vision of a stormy strong man to hammer and weld the state like a smith. Our strong men were too strong for us, and too strong for themselves. They were too strong for their own aim of a just and equal monarchy. The smith broke upon the anvil the sword of state that he was hammering for himself. Whether or no this will serve as a key to the very complicated story of our kings and barons, it is the exact posture of Henry II to his rival. He became lawless out of sheer love of law. He also stood, though in a colder and more remote manner, for the whole people against feudal oppression; and if his policy had succeeded in its purity, it would at least have made impossible the privilege and capitalism of later times. But that bodily restlessness which stamped and spurned the furniture was a symbol of him; it was some such thing that prevented him and his heirs from sitting as quietly on their throne as the heirs of St Louis. He thrust again and again at the tough intangibility of the priests' Utopianism like a man fighting a ghost; he answered transcendental defiances with baser material persecutions; and at last, on a dark and, I think, decisive day in English history, his word sent four feudal murderers into the cloisters of Canterbury, who went there to destroy a traitor and who created a saint.

At the grave of the dead man broke forth what can only be called an epidemic of healing. For miracles so narrated there is the same evidence as for half the facts of history; and any one denying them must deny them upon a dogma. But something followed which would seem to modern civilisation even more monstrous than a miracle. If the reader can imagine Mr Cecil Rhodes submitting to be horsewhipped by a Boer in St Paul's Cathedral, as an apology for some indefensible death incidental to the Jameson Raid, he will form but a faint idea of what was meant when Henry II was beaten by monks at the tomb of his vassal and enemy. The modern parallel called up is comic, but the truth is that mediæval actualities have a violence that does seem comic to our conventions. The Catholics of that age were driven by two dominant thoughts: the all-importance of penitence as an answer to sin, and the all-importance of vivid and evident external acts as a proof of penitence. Extravagant humiliation after extravagant pride for them restored the balance of sanity. The point is worth stressing, because without it moderns make neither head nor tail of the period. Green gravely suggests, for instance, of Henry's ancestor Fulk of Anjou, that his tyrannies and frauds were further blackened by 'low superstition', which led him to be dragged in a halter round a shrine, scourged and screaming for the mercy of God. Mediævals would simply have said that such a man might well scream for it, but his scream was the only logical comment he could make. But they would have quite refused to see why the scream should be added to the sins and not subtracted from them. They would have thought it simply muddle-headed to have the same horror at a man for being horribly sinful and for being horribly sorry.

But it may be suggested, I think, though with the doubt proper to ignorance, that the Angevin ideal of the King's justice lost more by the death of St Thomas than was instantly apparent in the horror of Christendom, the canonisation of the victim and the public penance of the tyrant. These things indeed were in a sense temporary; the King recovered the power to judge clerics, and many later kings and justiciars continued the monarchical plan. But I would suggest, as a possible clue to puzzling after events, that here and by this murderous stroke the crown lost what should have been the silent and massive support of its whole policy. I mean that it lost the people.

It need not be repeated that the case for despotism is democratic. As a rule its cruelty to the strong is kindness to the weak. An autocrat cannot be judged as a historical character by his relations with other historical characters. His true applause comes not from the few actors on the lighted stage of aristocracy, but from that enormous audience which must always sit in darkness throughout the drama. The king who helps numberless helps nameless men, and when he flings his widest largesse he is a Christian doing good by stealth. This sort of monarchy was certainly a mediæval ideal, nor need it necessarily fail as a reality. French kings were never so merciful to the people as when they were merciless to the peers; and it is probably true that a Czar who was a great lord to his intimates was often a little father in innumerable little homes. It is overwhelmingly probable that such a central power, though it might at last have deserved destruction in England as in France, would in England as in France have prevented the few from seizing and holding all the wealth and power to this day. But in England it broke off short, through something of which the slaying of St Thomas may well have been the supreme example. It was something overstrained and startling and against the instincts of the people. And of what was meant in the Middle Ages by that very powerful and rather peculiar thing, the people, I shall speak in the next chapter.

In any case this conjecture finds support in the ensuing events. It is not merely that, just as the great but personal plan of the Conqueror collapsed after all into the chaos of the Stephen transition, so the great but personal plan of the first Plantagenet collapsed into the chaos of the Barons' Wars. When all allowance is made for constitutional fictions and afterthoughts, it does seem likely that here for the first time some moral strength deserted the monarchy. The character of Henry's second son John (for Richard belongs rather to the last chapter) stamped it with something accidental and yet symbolic. It was not that John was a mere black blot on the pure gold of the Plantagenets, the texture was much more mixed and continuous; but he really was a discredited Plantagenet, and as it were a damaged Plantagenet. It was not that he was much more of a bad man than many opposed to him, but he was the kind of bad man whom bad men and good do combine to oppose. In a sense subtler than that of the legal and parliamentary logic-chopping invented long afterwards, he certainly managed to put the Crown in the wrong. Nobody suggested that the barons of Stephen's time starved men in dungeons to promote political liberty, or hung them up by the heels as a symbolic request for a free parliament. In the reign of John and his son it was still the barons, and not in the least the people, who seized the power; but there did begin to appear a *case* for their seizing it, for contemporaries as well as constitutional historians afterwards. John, in one of his diplomatic doublings, had put England into the papal care, as an estate is put in Chancery. And unluckily the Pope, whose counsels had generally been mild and liberal, was then in his death-grapple with the Germanic Emperor and wanted every penny he could get to win. His winning was a blessing to Europe, but a curse to England, for he used the island as a mere treasury for this foreign war. In this and other matters the baronial party began to have something like a principle, which is the backbone of a policy. Much conventional history that connects their councils with a thing like our House of Commons is as far-fetched as it would be to say that the Speaker wields a Mace like those which the barons brandished in battle. Simon de Montfort was not an enthusiast for the Whig theory of the British Constitution, but he was an enthusiast for something. He founded a parliament in a fit of considerable absence of mind; but it was with true presence of mind, in the responsible and even religious sense which had made his father so savage a Crusader against heretics, that he laid about him with his great sword before he fell at Evesham.

Magna Carta was not a step towards democracy, but it was a step away from despotism. If we hold that double truth firmly, we have something like a key to the rest of English history. A rather loose aristocracy not only gained but often deserved the name of liberty. And the history of the English can be most briefly summarised by taking the French motto of 'Liberty, Equality, and Fraternity', and noting that the English have sincerely loved the first and lost the other two.

In the contemporary complication much could be urged both for the Crown and the new and more national rally of the nobility. But it was a complication, whereas a miracle is a plain matter that any man can understand. The possibilities or impossibilities of St Thomas Becket were left a riddle for history; the white flame of his audacious theocracy was frustrated, and his work cut short like a fairy tale left untold. But his memory passed into the care of the common people, and with them he was more active dead than alive—yes, even more busy. In the next chapter we shall consider what was meant in the Middle Ages by the common people, and how uncommon we should think it to-day. And in the last chapter we have already seen how in the Crusading age the strangest things grew homely, and men fed on travellers' tales when there were no national newspapers. A many-coloured pageant of martyrology on numberless walls and windows had familiarised the most ignorant with alien cruelties in many climes; with a bishop flayed by Danes or a virgin burned by Saracens, with one saint stoned by Jews and another hewn in pieces by negroes. I cannot think it was a small matter that among these images one of the most magnificent had met his death but lately at the hands of an English monarch. There was at least something akin to the primitive and epical romances of that period in the tale of those two mighty friends, one of whom struck too hard and slew the other. It may even have been so early as this that something was judged in silence; and for the multitude rested on the Crown a mysterious seal of insecurity like that of Cain, and of exile on the English kings.

# The Meaning of Merry England

The mental trick by which the first half of English history has been wholly dwarfed and dehumanised is a very simple one. It consists in telling only the story of the professional destroyers and then complaining that the whole story is one of destruction. A king is at the best a sort of crowned executioner; all government is an ugly necessity; and if it was then uglier it was for the most part merely because it was more difficult. What we call the Judges' circuits were first rather the King's raids. For a time the criminal class was so strong that ordinary civil government was conducted by a sort of civil war. When the social enemy was caught at all he was killed or savagely maimed. The King could not take Pentonville Prison about with him on wheels. I am far from denying that there was a real element of cruelty in the Middle Ages; but the point here is that it was concerned with one side of life, which is cruel at the best; and that this involved more cruelty for the same reason that it involved more courage. When we think of our ancestors as the men who inflicted tortures, we ought sometimes to think of them as the men who defied them. But the modern critic of mediævalism commonly looks only at these crooked shadows and not at the common daylight of the Middle Ages. When he has got over his indignant astonishment at the fact that fighters fought and that hangmen hanged, he assumes that any other ideas there may have been were ineffectual and fruitless. He despises the monk for avoiding the very same activities which he despises the warrior for cultivating. And he insists that the arts of war were sterile, without even admitting the possibility that the arts of peace were productive. But the truth is that it is precisely in the arts of peace, and in the type of production, that the Middle Ages stand singular and unique. This is not eulogy but history; an informed man must recognise this productive peculiarity even if he happens to hate it. The melodramatic things currently called mediæval are much older and more universal; such as the sport of tournament or the use of torture. The tournament was indeed a Christian and liberal advance on the gladiatorial

A Short History of England, 1917

show, since the lords risked themselves and not merely their slaves. Torture, so far from being peculiarly mediæval, was copied from pagan Rome and its most rationalist political science; and its application to others besides slaves was really part of the slow mediæval extinction of slavery. Torture, indeed, is a logical thing common in states innocent of fanaticism, as in the great agnostic empire of China. What was really arresting and remarkable about the Middle Ages, as the Spartan discipline was peculiar to Sparta, or the Russian communes typical of Russia, was precisely its positive social scheme of production, of the making, building and growing of all the good things of life.

For the tale told in a book like this cannot really touch on mediæval England at all. The dynasties and the parliaments passed like a changing cloud and across a stable and fruitful landscape. The institutions which affected the masses can be compared to corn or fruit trees in one practical sense at least, that they grew upwards from below. There may have been better societies, and assuredly we have not to look far for worse; but it is doubtful if there was ever so spontaneous a society. We cannot do justice, for instance, to the local government of that epoch, even where it was very faulty and fragmentary, by any comparisons with the plans of local government laid down today. Modern local government always comes from above; it is at best granted; it is more often merely imposed. The modern English oligarchy, the modern German Empire, are necessarily more efficient in making munici-palities upon a plan, or rather a pattern. The mediævals not only had self-government, but their self-government was self-made. They did indeed, as the central powers of the national monarchies grew stronger, seek and procure the stamp of state approval; but it was approval of a popular fact already in existence. Men banded together in guilds and parishes long before Local Government Acts were dreamed of. Like charity, which has worked in the same way, their Home Rule began at home. The reactions of recent centuries have left most educated men bankrupt of the corporate imagina-tion required even to imagine this. They only think of a mob as a thing that breaks things—even if they admit it is right to break them. But the mob made these things. An artist mocked as many-headed, an artist with many eyes and hands, created these masterpieces. And if the modern sceptic, in his detestation of the democratic ideal, complains of my calling them master-pieces, a simple answer will for the moment serve. It is enough to reply that the very word 'masterpiece' is borrowed from the terminology of the medi-æval craftsmen. But such points in the Guild System can be considered a little later; here we are only concerned with the quite spontaneous springing upwards of all these social institutions, such as they were. They rose in the streets like a silent rebellion; like a still and statuesque riot. In modern constitutional countries there are practically no political institutions thus given by the people; all are received by the people. There is only one thing that stands in our midst, attenuated and threatened, but enthroned in some power like a ghost of the Middle Ages: the Trades Unions.

In agriculture, what had happened to the land was like a universal landslide. But by a prodigy beyond the catastrophes of geology it may be said that the land had slid uphill. Rural civilisation was on a wholly new and much higher level; yet there were no great social convulsions or apparently even great social campaigns to explain it. It is possibly a solitary instance in history of men thus falling upwards; at least of outcasts falling on their feet or vagrants straying into the promised land. Such a thing could not be and was not a mere accident; yet, if we go by conscious political plans, it was something like a miracle. There had appeared, like a subterranean race cast up to the sun, something unknown to the august civilisation of the Roman Empire—a peasantry. At the beginning of the Dark Ages the great pagan cosmopolitan society now grown Christian was as much a slave state as old South Carolina. By the fourteenth century it was almost as much a state of peasant proprietors as modern France. No laws had been passed against slavery; no dogmas even had condemned it by definition; no war had been waged against it, no new race or ruling caste had repudiated it; but it was gone. This startling and silent transformation is perhaps the best measure of the pressure of popular life in the Middle Ages, of how fast it was making new things in its spiritual factory. Like everything else in the mediæval revolution, from its cathedrals to its ballads, it was as anonymous as it was enormous. It is admitted that the conscious and active emancipators everywhere were the parish priests and the religious brotherhoods; but no name among them has survived and no man of them has reaped his reward in this world. Countless Clarksons and innumerable Wilberforces, without political machinery or public fame, worked at death-beds and confessionals in all the villages of Europe; and the vast system of slavery vanished. It was probably the widest work ever done which was voluntary on both sides; and the Middle Ages was in this and other things the age of volunteers. It is possible enough to state roughly the stages through which the thing passed; but such a statement does not explain the loosening of the grip of the great slave-owners; and it cannot be explained except psychologically. The Catholic type of Christianity was not merely an element, it was a climate; and in that climate the slave would not grow. I have already suggested, touching that transformation of the Roman Empire which was the background of all these centuries, how a mystical view of man's dignity must have this effect. A table that walked and talked, or a stool that flew with wings out of the window, would be about as workable a thing as an immortal chattel. But though here as everywhere the spirit explains the processes, and the processes cannot even plausibly explain the spirit, these processes involve two very practical points, without which we cannot understand how this great popular civilisation was created—or how it was destroyed.

What we call the manors were originally the *villae* of the pagan lords, each with its population of slaves. Under this process, however it be explained, what had occurred was the diminishment of the lords' claim to the whole profit of a slave estate, by which it became a claim to the profit of part of it, and dwindled at last to certain dues or customary payments to the lord, having paid which the slave could enjoy not only the use of the land but the profit of it. It must be remembered that over a great part, and especially very important parts, of the whole territory, the lords were abbots, magistrates elected by a mystical communism and themselves often of peasant birth. Men not only obtained a fair amount of justice under their care, but a fair amount of freedom even from their carelessness. But two details of the development are very vital. First, as has been hinted elsewhere, the slave was long in the intermediate status of a serf. This meant that while the land was entitled to the services of the man, he was equally entitled to the support of the land. He could not be evicted; he could not even, in the modern fashion, have his rent raised. At the beginning it was merely that the slave was owned, but at least he could not be disowned. At the end he had really become a small landlord, merely because it was not the lord that owned him, but the land. It is hardly unsafe to suggest that in this (by one of the paradoxes of this extraordinary period) the very fixity of serfdom was a service to freedom. The new peasant inherited something of the stability of the slave. He did not come to life in a competitive scramble where everybody was trying to snatch his freedom from him. He found himself among neighbours who already regarded his presence as normal and his frontiers as natural frontiers, and among whom all-powerful customs crushed all experiments in competition. By a trick or overturn no romancer has dared to put in a tale, this prisoner had become the governor of his own prison. For a little time it was almost true that an Englishman's house was his castle, because it had been built strong enough to be his dungeon.

The other notable element was this: that when the produce of the land began by custom to be cut up and only partially transmitted to the lord, the remainder was generally subdivided into two types of property. One the serfs enjoyed severally, in private patches, while the other they enjoyed in common, and generally in common with the lord. Thus arose the momentously important mediæval institutions of the Common Land, owned side by side with private land. It was an alternative and a refuge. The mediævals, except when they were monks, were none of them Communists; but they were all, as it were, potential Communists. It is typical of the dark and dehumanised picture now drawn of the period that our romances constantly describe a broken man as falling back on the forests and the outlaw's den, but never describe him as falling back on the common land, which was a much more common incident. Mediævalism believed in mending its broken men; and as the idea existed in the communal life for monks, it existed in the communal land for peasants. It was their great green hospital, their free and airy workhouse. A Common was not a naked and negative thing like the scrub or heath we call a Common on the edges of the suburbs. It was a reserve of wealth like a reserve of grain in a barn; it was deliberately kept back as a balance, as we talk of a balance at the bank. Now these provisions for a healthier distribution of property would by themselves show any man of imagination that a real moral effort had been made towards social justice; that it could not have been mere evolutionary accident that slowly turned the slave into a serf, and the serf into a peasant proprietor. But if anybody still thinks that mere blind luck, without any groping for the light, had somehow brought about the peasant condition in place of the agrarian slave estate, he has only to turn to what was happening in all the other callings and affairs of humanity. Then he will cease to doubt. For he will find the same mediæval men busy upon a social scheme which points as plainly in effect to pity and a craving for equality. And it is a system which could no more be produced by accident than one of their cathedrals could be built by an earthquake.

Most work beyond the primary work of agriculture was guarded by the egalitarian vigilance of the Guilds. It is hard to find any term to measure the distance between this system and modern society; one can only approach it first by the faint traces it has left. Our daily life is littered with a debris of the Middle Ages, especially of dead words which no longer carry their meaning. I have already suggested one example. We hardly call up the picture of a return to Christian Communism whenever we mention Wimbledon Common. This truth descends to such trifles as the titles which we write on letters and postcards. The puzzling and truncated monosyllable 'Esq.' is a pathetic relic of a remote evolution from chivalry to snobbery. No two historic things could well be more different than an esquire and a squire. The first was above all things an incomplete and probationary position—the tadpole of knighthood; the second is above all things a complete and assured position—the status of the owners and rulers of rural England throughout recent centuries. Our esquires did not win their estates till they had given up any particular fancy for winning their spurs. Esquire does not mean squire, and esq. does not mean anything. But it remains on our letters a little wriggle in pen and ink and an indecipherable hieroglyph twisted by the strange turns of our history, which have turned a military discipline into a pacific oligarchy, and that into a mere plutocracy at last. And there are similar historic riddles to be unpicked in the similar forms of social address. There is something singularly forlorn about the modern word 'Mister'. Even in sound it has a simpering feebleness which marks the shrivelling of the strong word from which it came. Nor, indeed, is the symbol of the mere sound inaccurate. I remember seeing a German story of Samson in which he bore the unassuming name of Simson, which surely shows Samson very much shorn. There is something of the same dismal *diminuendo* in the evolution of a Master into a Mister.

The very vital importance of the word 'Master' is this. A Guild was, very broadly speaking, a Trade Union in which every man was his own employer. That is, a man could not work at any trade unless he would join the league and accept the laws of that trade; but he worked in his own shop with his own tools, and the whole profit went to himself. But the word 'employer' marks a modern deficiency which makes the modern use of the word 'master' quite inexact. A master meant something quite other and greater than a 'boss'. It meant a master of the work, where it now means only a master of the workmen. It is an elementary character of Capitalism that a shipowner need not know the right end of a ship, or a landowner have even seen the landscape, that the owner of a goldmine may be interested in nothing but old pewter, or the owner of a railway travel exclusively in balloons. He may be a more successful capitalist if he has a hobby of his own business; he is often a more successful capitalist if he has the sense to leave it to a manager; but economically he can control the business because he is a capitalist, not because he has any kind of hobby or any kind of sense. The highest grade in the Guild system was a Master, and it meant a mastery of the business. To take the term created by the colleges in the same epoch, all the mediæval bosses were Masters of Arts. The other grades were the journeyman and the apprentice; but like the corresponding degrees at the universities, they were grades through which every common man could pass. They were not social classes; they were degrees and not castes. This is the whole point of the recurrent romance about the apprentice marrying his master's daughter. The master would not be surprised at such a thing, any more than an M.A. would swell with aristocratic indignation when his daughter married a B.A.

When we pass from the strictly educational hierarchy to the strictly egalitarian ideal, we find again that the remains of the thing today are so distorted and disconnected as to be comic. There are City Companies which inherit the coats of arms and the immense relative wealth of the old Guilds, and inherit nothing else. Even what is good about them is not what was good about the Guilds. In one case we shall find something like a Worshipful Company of Bricklayers, in which, it is unnecessary to say, there is not a single bricklayer or anybody who has ever known a bricklayer, but in which the senior partners of a few big businesses in the City, with a few faded military men with a taste in cookery, tell each other in after-dinner speeches that it has been the glory of their lives to make allegorical bricks without straw. In another case we shall find a Worshipful Company of Whitewashers who do deserve their name, in the sense that many of them employ a large number of other people to whitewash. These Companies support large charities and often doubtless very valuable charities; but their object is quite different from that of the old charities of the Guilds. The aim of the Guild charities was the same as the aim of the Common Land. It was to resist inequality—or, as some earnest old gentlemen of the last generation would probably put it, to resist evolution. It was to ensure, not only that bricklaying should survive and succeed, but that every bricklayer should survive and succeed. It sought to rebuild the ruins of any bricklayer, and to give any faded whitewasher a new white coat. It was the whole aim of the Guilds to cobble their cobblers like their shoes and clout their clothiers with their clothes; to strengthen the weakest link, or go after the hundredth sheep; in short, to keep the row of little shops unbroken like a line of battle. It resisted the growth of a big shop like the growth of a dragon. Now even the whitewashers of the Whitewashers Company will not pretend that it exists to prevent a small shop being swallowed by a big shop, or that it has done anything whatever to prevent it. At the best the kindness it would show to a bankrupt whitewasher would be a kind of compensation; it would not be reinstatement; it would not be the restoration of status in an industrial system. So careful of the type it seems, so careless of the single life; and by that very modern evolutionary philosophy the type itself has been destroyed. The old Guilds, with the same object of equality, of course, insisted peremptorily upon the same level system of payment and treatment which is a point of complaint against the modern Trades Unions. But they insisted also, as the Trades Unions cannot do, upon a high standard of craftsmanship, which still astonishes the world in the corners of perishing buildings or the colours of broken glass. There is no artist or art critic who will not concede, however distant his own style from the Gothic school, that there was in this time a nameless but universal artistic touch in the moulding of the very tools of life. Accident has preserved the rudest sticks and stools and pots and pans which have suggestive shapes as if they were possessed not by devils but by elves. For they were, indeed, as compared with subsequent systems, produced in the incredible fairyland of a free country.

That the most mediæval of modern institutions, the Trades Unions, do not fight for the same ideal of æsthetic finish is true and certainly tragic; but to make it a matter of blame is wholly to misunderstand the tragedy. The Trades Unions are confederations of men without property, seeking to balance its absence by numbers and the necessary character of their labour. The Guilds were confederations of men with property, seeking to ensure each man in the possession of that property. This is, of course, the only condition of affairs in which property can properly be said to exist at all. We should not speak of a negro community in which most men were white, but the rare negroes were giants. We should not conceive a married community in which most men were bachelors, and three men had harems. A married community means a community where most people are married; not a community where one or two people are very much married. A propertied community means a community where most people have property; not a community where there are a few capitalists. But in fact the Guildsmen (as also, for that matter, the serfs, semi-serfs and peasants) were much richer than can be realised even from the fact that the Guilds protected the possession of houses, tools, and just payment. The surplus is self-evident upon any just study of the prices of the period, when all deductions have been made, of course, for the different value of the actual coinage. When a man could get a goose or a gallon of ale for one or two of the smallest and commonest coins, the matter is in no way affected by the name of those coins. Even when the individual wealth was severely limited, the collective wealth was very large—the wealth of the Guilds, of the parishes, and especially of the monastic estates. It is important to remember this fact in the subsequent history of England.

The next fact to note is that the local government grew out of things like the Guild system, and not the system from the government. In sketching the sound principles of this lost society, I shall not, of course, be supposed by any sane person to be describing a moral paradise, or to be implying that it was free from the faults and fights and sorrows that harass human life in all times, and certainly not least in our own time. There was a fair amount of rioting and fighting in connection with the Guilds; and there was especially for some time a combative rivalry between the guilds of merchants who sold things and those of craftsmen who made them, a conflict in which the craftsmen on the whole prevailed. But whichever party may have been predominant, it was the heads of the Guild who became the heads of the town, and not vice versa. The stiff survivals of this once very spontaneous uprising can again be seen in the now anomalous constitution of the Lord Mayor and the Livery of the City of London. We are told so monotonously that the government of our fathers reposed upon arms, that it is valid to insist that this, their most intimate, and everyday sort of government, was wholly based upon tools; a government in which the workman's tool became the sceptre. Blake, in one of his symbolic fantasies, suggests that in the Golden Age the gold and gems should be taken from the hilt of the sword and put upon the handle of the plough. But something very like this did happen in the interlude of this mediæval democracy, fermenting under the crust of mediæval monarchy and aristocracy; where productive implements often took on the pomp of heraldry. The Guilds often exhibited emblems and pageantry so compact of their most prosaic uses, that we can only parallel them by imagining armorial tabards, or even religious vestments, woven out of a navvy's corduroys or a coster's pearl buttons.

Two more points must be briefly added: and the rough sketch of this now foreign and even fantastic state will be as complete as it can be made here. Both refer to the links between this popular life and the politics which are conventionally the whole of history. The first, and for that age the most evident, is the Charter. To recur once more to the parallel of Trades Unions, as convenient for the casual reader of today, the Charter of a Guild roughly corresponded to that 'recognition' for which the railwaymen and other trades unionists asked some years ago, without success. By this they had the authority of the King, the central or national government; and this was of great moral weight with mediævals who always conceived of freedom as a positive status, not as a negative escape: they had none of the modern romanticism which makes liberty akin to loneliness. Their view remains in the phrase about giving a man the freedom of a city: they had no desire to give him the freedom of a wilderness. To say that they had also the authority of the Church is something of an understatement; for religion ran like a rich thread through the rude tapestry of these popular things while they were still merely popular; and many a trade society must have had a patron saint long before it had a royal seal. The other point is that it was from these municipal groups already in existence that the first men were chosen for the largest and perhaps the last of the great mediæval experiments: the Parliament.

We have all read at school that Simon de Montfort and Edward I, when they first summoned Commons to council, chiefly as advisers on local taxation, called 'two burgesses' from every town. If we had read a little more closely, those simple words would have given away the whole secret of the lost mediæval civilisation. We had only to ask what burgesses were, and whether they grew on trees. We should immediately have discovered that England was full of little parliaments, out of which the great parliament was made. And if it be a matter of wonder that the great council (still called in quaint archaism by its old title of the House of Commons) is the only one of these popular or elective corporations of which we hear much in our books of history, the explanation, I fear, is simple and a little sad. It is that the Parliament was the one among these mediæval creations which ultimately consented to betray and to destroy the rest.

# The Rebellion of The Rich

Sir Thomas More, apart from any arguments about the more mystical meshes in which he was ultimately caught and killed, will be hailed by all as a hero of the New Learning; that great dawn of a more rational daylight which for so many made mediævalism seem a mere darkness. Whatever we think of his appreciation of the Reformation, there will be no dispute about his appreciation of the Renascence. He was above all things a Humanist and a very human one. He was even in many ways very modern, which some rather erroneously suppose to be the same as being human; he was also humane, in the sense of humanitarian. He sketched an ideal, or rather perhaps a fanciful social system, with something of the ingenuity of Mr H. G. Wells, but essentially with much more than the flippancy attributed to Mr Bernard Shaw. It is not fair to charge the Utopian notions upon his morality; but their subjects and suggestions mark what (for want of a better word) we can only call his modernism. Thus the immortality of animals is the sort of transcendentalism which savours of evolution; and the grosser jest about the preliminaries of marriage might be taken quite seriously by the students of Eugenics. He suggested a sort of pacifism—though the Utopians had a quaint way of achieving it. In short, while he was, with his friend Erasmus, a satirist of mediæval abuses, few would now deny that Protestantism would be too narrow rather than too broad for him. If he was obviously not a Protestant, there are few Protestants who would deny him the name of a Reformer. But he was an innovator in things more alluring to modern minds than theology; he was partly what we should call a Neo-Pagan. His friend Colet summed up that escape from mediævalism which might be called the passage from bad Latin to good Greek. In our loose modern debates they are lumped together; but Greek learning was the growth of this time; there had always been a popular Latin, if a dog-Latin. It would be nearer the truth to call the mediævals bi-lingual than to call their Latin a dead language. Greek never, of course, became so general a possession; but for the man who got it,

A Short History of England, 1917

396

it is not too much to say that he felt as if he were in the open air for the first time. Much of this Greek spirit was reflected in More; its universality, its urbanity, its balance of buoyant reason and cool curiosity. It is even probable that he shared some of the excesses and errors of taste which inevitably infected the splendid intellectualism of the reaction against the Middle Ages; we can imagine him thinking gargoyles Gothic, in the sense of barbaric, or even failing to be stirred, as Sydney was, by the trumpet of 'Chevy Chase.' The wealth of the ancient heathen world, in wit, loveliness, and civic heroism, had so recently been revealed to that generation in its dazzling profusion and perfection, that it might seem a trifle if they did here and there an injustice to the relics of the Dark Ages. When, therefore, we look at the world with the eyes of More we are looking from the widest windows of that time; looking over an English landscape seen for the first time very equally, in the level light of the sun at morning. For what he saw was England of the Renascence; England passing from the mediæval to the modern. Thus he looked forth, and saw many things and said many things; they were all worthy and many witty; but he noted one thing which is at once a horrible fancy and a homely and practical fact. He who looked over that landscape said: 'Sheep are eating men.'

This singular summary of the great epoch of our emancipation and enlightenment is not the fact usually put first in such very curt historical accounts of it. It has nothing to do with the translation of the Bible, or the character of Henry VIII, or the characters of Henry VIII's wives, or the triangular debates between Henry and Luther and the Pope. It was not Popish sheep who were eating Protestant men, or *vice versa*; nor did Henry, at any period of his own brief and rather bewildering papacy, have martyrs eaten by lambs as the heathen had them eaten by lions. What was meant, of course, by this picturesque expression, was that an intensive type of agriculture was giving way to a very extensive type of pasture. Great spaces of England which had hitherto been cut up into the commonwealth of a number of farmers were being laid under the sovereignty of a solitary shepherd. The point has been put, by a touch of epigram rather in the manner of More himself, by Mr J. Stephen, in a striking essay now, I think, only to be found in the back files of *The New Witness*. He enunciated the paradox that the very much admired individual who made two blades of grass grow instead of one, was a murderer. In the same article, Mr Stephen traced the true moral origins of this movement, which led to the growing of so much grass and the murder, or at any rate the destruction, of so much humanity. He traced it, and every true record of that transformation traces it, to the growth of a new refinement, in a sense a more rational refinement, in the governing class. The mediæval lord had been, by comparison, a coarse fellow; he had merely lived in the largest kind of farm-house after the fashion of the largest kind of farmer. He drank wine when he could, but he was quite ready to drink ale; and science had not yet smoothed his paths with petrol. At a time later than this, one of the greatest ladies of England writes to her husband that she cannot come to him because her carriage horses are pulling the plough. In the true Middle Ages the greatest men were even more rudely hampered, but in the time of Henry VIII the transformation was beginning. In the next generation a phrase was common which is one of the keys of the time, and is very much the key to these more ambitious territorial schemes. This or that great lord was said to be 'Italianate.' It meant subtler shapes of beauty, delicate and ductile glass, gold and silver not treated as barbaric stones but rather as stems and wreaths of molten metal, mirrors, cards and such trinkets bearing a load of beauty; it meant the perfection of trifles. It was not, as in popular Gothic craftsmanship, the almost unconscious touch of art upon all necessary things: rather it was the pouring of the whole soul of passionately conscious art especially into unnecessary things. Luxury was made alive with a soul. We must remember this real thirst for beauty; for it is an explanation—and an excuse.

The old barony had indeed been thinned by the civil wars that closed at Bosworth, and curtailed by the economical and crafty policy of that unkingly king, Henry VII. He was himself a 'new man,' and we shall see the barons largely give place to a whole nobility of new men. But even the older families already had their faces set in the newer direction. Some of them, the Howards, for instance, may be said to have figured both as old and new families. In any case the spirit of the whole upper class can be described as increasingly new. The English aristocracy, which is the chief creation of the Reformation, is undeniably entitled to a certain praise, which is now almost universally regarded as very high praise. It was always progressive. Aristocrats are accused of being proud of their ancestors; it can truly be said that English aristocrats have rather been proud of their descendants. For their descendants they planned huge foundations and piled mountains of wealth; for their descendants they fought for a higher and higher place in the government of the state; for their descendants, above all, they nourished every new science or scheme of social philosophy. They seized the vast economic chances of pasturage; but they also drained the fens. They swept away the priests, but they condescended to the philosophers. As the new Tudor house passes through its generations a new and more rationalist civilisation is being made; scholars are criticising authentic texts; sceptics are discrediting not only popish saints but pagan philosophers; specialists are analysing and rationalising traditions, and sheep are eating men.

We have seen that in the fourteenth century in England there was a real revolution of the poor. It very nearly succeeded; and I need not conceal the conviction that it would have been the best possible thing for all of us if it had entirely succeeded. If Richard II had really sprung into the saddle of Wat Tyler, or rather if his parliament had not unhorsed him when he had got there, if he had confirmed the fact of the new peasant freedom by some form of royal authority, as it was already common to confirm the fact of the Trade Unions by the form of a royal charter, our country would probably have had as happy a history as is possible to human nature. The Renascence, when it came, would have come as popular education and not the culture of a club of æsthetics. The New Learning might have been as democratic as the old learning in the old days of mediæval Paris and Oxford. The exquisite artistry of the school of Cellini might have been but the highest grade of the craft of a guild. The Shakespearean drama might have been acted by workmen on wooden stages set up in the street like Punch and Judy, the finer fulfilment of the miracle play as it was acted by a guild. The players need not have been 'the king's servants,' but their own masters. The great Renascence might have been liberal with its liberal education. If this be a fancy, it is at least one that cannot be disproved; the mediæval revolution was too unsuccessful at the beginning for any one to show that it need have been unsuccessful in the end. The feudal parliament prevailed, and pushed back the peasants at least into their dubious and half-developed status. More than this it would be exaggerative to say, and a mere anticipation of the really decisive events afterwards. When Henry VIII came to the throne the guilds were perhaps checked but apparently unchanged, and even the peasants had probably regained ground; many were still theoretically serfs, but largely under the easy landlordism of the abbots; the mediæval system still stood. It might, for all we know, have begun to grow again; but all such speculations are swamped in new and very strange things. The failure of the revolution of the poor was ultimately followed by a counter-revolution; a successful revolution of the rich.

The apparent pivot of it was in certain events, political and even personal. They roughly resolve themselves into two: the marriages of Henry VIII and the affair of the monasteries. The marriages of Henry VIII have long been a popular and even a stale joke; and there is a truth of tradition in the joke, as there is in almost any joke if it is sufficiently popular, and indeed if it is sufficiently stale. A jocular thing never lives to be stale unless it is also serious. Henry was popular in his first days, and even foreign contemporaries give us quite a glorious picture of a young prince of the Renascence, radiant with all the new accomplishments. In his last days he was something very like a maniac; he no longer inspired love, and even when he inspired fear, it was rather the fear of a mad dog than of a watch-dog. In this change doubtless the inconsistency and even ignominy of his Bluebeard weddings played a great part. And it is but just to him to say that, perhaps with the exception of the first and the last, he was almost as unlucky in his wives as they were in their husband. But it was undoubtedly the affair of the first divorce that broke the back of his honour, and incidentally broke a very large number of other more valuable and universal things. To feel the meaning of his fury we must realize that he did not regard himself as the enemy but rather as the friend of the Pope; there is a shadow of the old story of Becket. He had defended the Pope in diplomacy and the Church in controversy; and when he wearied of his queen and took a passionate fancy to one of her ladies, Anne Boleyn, he vaguely felt that a rather cynical concession, in that age of cynical concessions, might very well be made to him by a friend. But it is part of that high inconsistency which is the fate of the Christian faith in human hands, that no man knows when the higher side of it will really be uppermost, if only for an instant; and that the worst ages of the Church will not do or say something, as if by accident, that is worthy of the best. Anyhow, for whatever reason, Henry sought to lean upon the cushions of Leo and found he had struck his arm upon the rock of Peter. The Pope denied the new marriage; and Henry, in a storm and darkness of anger, dissolved all the old relations with the Papacy. It is probable that he did not clearly know how much he was doing then; and it is very tenable that we do not know it now. He certainly did not think he was Anti-Catholic; and, in one rather ridiculous sense, we can hardly say that he thought he was anti-papal, since he apparently thought he was a pope. From this day really dates something that played a certain part in history, the more modern doctrine of the divine right of kings, widely different from the mediæval one. It is a matter which further embarrasses the open question about the continuity of Catholic things in Anglicanism, for it was a new note and yet one struck by the older party. The supremacy of the King over the English national church was not, unfortunately, merely a fad of the King, but became partly, and for one period, a fad of the Church. But apart from all controverted questions, there is at least a human and historic sense in which the continuity of our past is broken perilously at this point. Henry not only cut off England from Europe, but what was even more important, he cut off England from England.

The great divorce brought down Wolsey, the mighty minister who had held the scales between the Empire and the French Monarchy, and made the modern balance of power in Europe. He is often described under the dictum of *Ego et Rex Meus*; but he marks a stage in the English story rather because he suffered for it than because he said it. *Ego et Rex Meus* might be the motto of any modern Prime Minister; for we have forgotten the very fact that the word minister merely means servant. Wolsey was the last great servant who could be, and was, simply dismissed; the mark of a monarchy still absolute; the English were amazed at it in modern Germany, when Bismarck was turned away like a butler. A more awful act proved the new force was already inhuman; it struck down the noblest of the Humanists.

Thomas More, who seemed sometimes like an Epicurean under Augustus, died the death of a saint under Diocletian. He died gloriously jesting; and the death has naturally drawn out for us rather the sacred savours of his soul; his tenderness and his trust in the truth of God. But for Humanism it must have seemed a monstrous sacrifice; it was somehow as if Montaigne were a martyr. And that is indeed the note; something truly to be called unnatural had already entered the naturalism of the Renascence; and the soul of the great Christian rose against it. He pointed to the sun, saying 'I shall be above that fellow' with Franciscan familiarity, which can love nature because it will not worship her. So he left to his king the sun, which for so many weary days and years was to go down only on his wrath.

But the more impersonal process which More himself had observed (as noted at the beginning of this chapter) is more clearly defined, and less clouded with controversies, in the second of the two parts of Henry's policy. There is indeed a controversy about the monasteries; but it is one that is clarifying and settling every day. Now it is true that the Church, by the Renascence period, had reached a considerable corruption; but the real proofs of it are utterly different both from the contemporary despotic pretence and from the common Protestant story. It is wildly unfair, for instance, to quote the letters of bishops and such authorities denouncing the sins of monastic life, violent as they often are. They cannot possibly be more violent than the letters of St Paul to the purest and most primitive churches; the apostle was there writing to those Early Christians whom all churches idealise; and he talks to them as to cut-throats and thieves. The explanation, for those concerned for such subtleties, may possibly be found in the fact that Christianity is not a creed for good men, but for men. Such letters had been written in all centuries; and even in the sixteenth century they do not prove so much that there were bad abbots as that there were good bishops. Moreover, even those who profess that the monks were profligates dare not profess that they were oppressors; there is truth in Cobbett's point that where monks were landlords, they did not become rack-renting landlords, and could not become absentee landlords. Nevertheless, there was a weakness in the good institutions as well as a mere strength in the bad ones; and that weakness partakes of the worst element of the time. In the fall of good things there is almost always a touch of betrayal from within; and the abbots were destroyed more easily because they did not stand together. They did not stand together because the spirit of the age (which is very often the worst enemy of the age) was the increasing division between rich and poor; and it had partly divided even the rich and poor clergy. And the betrayal came, as it nearly always comes, from that servant of Christ who holds the bag.

To take a modern attack on liberty, on a much lower plane, we were familiar with the picture of a politician going to the great brewers, or even the great hotel proprietors, and pointing out the uselessness of a litter of little public-houses. That is what the Tudor politicians did first with the monasteries. They went to the heads of the great houses and proposed the extinction of the small ones. The great monastic lords did not resist, or at any rate, did not resist enough; and the sack of the religious houses began. But if the lord abbots acted for a moment as lords, that could not excuse them, in the eyes of much greater lords, for having frequently acted as abbots. A momentary rally to the cause of the rich did not wipe out the disgrace of a thousand petty interferences which had told only to the advantage of the poor; and they were soon to learn that it was no epoch for their easy rule and their careless hospitality. The great houses, now isolated, were themselves brought down one by one; and the beggar, whom the monastery had served as a sort of sacred tavern, came to it at evening and found it a ruin. For a new and wide philosophy was in the world, which still rules our society. By this creed most of the mystical virtues of the old monks have simply been turned into great sins; and the greatest of these is charity.

But the populace which had risen under Richard II was not yet disarmed. It was trained in the rude discipline of bow and bill, and organised into local groups of town and guild and manor. Over half the counties of England the people rose, and fought one final battle for the vision of the Middle Ages. The chief tool of the new tyranny, a dirty fellow named Thomas Cromwell, was specially singled out as the tyrant, and he was indeed rapidly turning all government into a nightmare. The popular movement was put down partly by force; and there is the new note of modern militarism in the fact that it was put down by cynical professional troops, actually brought in from foreign countries, who destroyed English religion for hire. But, like the old popular rising, it was even more put down by fraud. Like the old rising, it was sufficiently triumphant to force the government to a parley; and the government had to resort to the simple expedient of calming the people with promises, and then proceeding to break first the promises and then the people, after the fashion made familiar to us by the modern politicians in their attitude towards the great strikes. The revolt bore the name of the Pilgrimage of Grace, and its programme was practically the restoration of the old religion. In connection with the fancy about the fate of England if Tyler had triumphed, it proves, I think, one thing; that his triumph, while it might or might not have led to something that could be called a reform, would have rendered quite impossible everything that we now know as the Reformation.

The reign of terror established by Thomas Cromwell became an Inquis-ition of the blackest and most unbearable sort. Historians, who have no shadow of sympathy with the old religion, are agreed that it was uprooted by means more horrible than have ever, perhaps, been employed in England before or since. It was a government by torturers rendered ubiquitous by spies. The spoliation of the monasteries especially was carried out, not only with a violence which recalled barbarism, but with a minuteness for which there is no other word but meanness. It was as if the Dane had returned in the character of a detective. The inconsistency of the King's personal attitude to Catholicism did indeed complicate the conspiracy with new brutalities towards Protestants; but such reaction as there was in this was wholly theological. Cromwell lost that fitful favour and was executed, but the terrorism went on the more terribly for being simplified to the single vision of the wrath of the King. It culminated in a strange act which rounds off symbolically the story told on an earlier page. For the despot revenged himself on a rebel whose defiance seemed to him to ring down three centuries. He laid waste the most popular shrine of the English, the shrine to which Chaucer had once ridden singing, because it was also the shrine where King Henry had knelt to repent. For three centuries the Church and the people had called Becket a saint, when Henry Tudor arose and called him a traitor. This might well be thought the topmost point of autocracy; and yet it was not really so.

For then rose to its supreme height of self-revelation that still stranger something of which we have, perhaps fancifully, found hints before in this history. The strong king was weak. He was immeasurably weaker than the strong kings of the Middle Ages; and whether or no his failure had been foreshadowed, he failed. The breach he had made in the dyke of the ancient doctrines let in a flood that may almost be said to have washed him away. In a sense he disappeared before he died; for the drama that filled his last days is no longer the drama of his own character. We may put the matter most practically by saying that it is unpractical to discuss whether Froude finds any justification for Henry's crimes in the desire to create a strong national monarchy. For whether or no it was desired, it was not created. Least of all our princes did the Tudors leave behind them a secure central government, and the time when monarchy was at its worst comes only one or two generations before the time when it was weakest. But a few years afterwards, as history goes, the relations of the Crown and its new servants were to be reversed on a high stage so as to horrify the world; and the axe which had been sanctified with the blood of More and soiled with the blood of Cromwell was, at the signal of one of that slave's own descendants, to fall and to kill an English king.

The tide which thus burst through the breach and overwhelmed the King as well as the Church was the revolt of the rich, and especially of the new rich. They used the King's name, and could not have prevailed without his power, but the ultimate effect was rather as if they had plundered the King after he had plundered the monasteries. Amazingly little of the wealth, considering the name and theory of the thing, actually remained in royal hands. The chaos was increased, no doubt, by the fact that Edward VI succeeded to the throne as a mere boy, but the deeper truth can be seen in the difficulty of drawing any real line between the two reigns. By marrying into the Seymour family, and thus providing himself with a son, Henry had also provided the country with the very type of powerful family which was to rule merely by pillage. An enormous and unnatural tragedy, the execution of one of the Seymours by his own brother, was enacted during the impotence of the childish king, and the successful Seymour figured as Lord Protector though even he would have found it hard to say what he was protecting, since it was not even his own family. Anyhow, it is hardly too much to say that every human thing was left unprotected from the greed of such cannibal protectors. We talk of the dissolution of the monasteries, but what occurred was the dissolution of the whole of the old civilisation. Lawyers and lackeys and money-lenders, the meanest of lucky men, looted the art and economics of the Middle Ages like thieves robbing a church. Their names (when they did not change them) became the names of the great dukes and marquises of our own day. But if we look back and forth in our history, perhaps the most fundamental act of destruction occurred when the armed men of the Seymours and their sort passed from the sacking of the Monasteries to the sacking of the Guilds. The mediæval Trade Unions were struck down, their buildings broken into by the soldiery, and their funds seized by the new nobility. And this simple incident takes all its common meaning out of the assertion (in itself plausible enough) that the Guilds, like everything else at that time, were probably not at their best. Proportion is the only practical thing; and it may be true that Cæsar was not feeling well on the morning of the Ides of March. But simply to say that the Guilds declined, is about as true as saying that Cæsar quietly decayed from purely natural causes at the foot of the statue of Pompey.

# Spain and the Schism of Nations

The revolution that arose out of what is called the Renascence, and ended in some countries in what is called the Reformation, did in the internal politics of England one drastic and definite thing. That thing was destroying the institutions of the poor. It was not the only thing it did, but it was much the most practical. It was the basis of all the problems now connected with Capital and Labour. How much the theological theories of the time had to do with it is a perfectly fair matter for difference of opinion. But neither party, if educated about the facts, will deny that the same time and temper which produced the religious schism also produced this new lawlessness in the rich. The most extreme Protestant will probably be content to say that Protestantism was not the motive, but the mask. The most extreme Catholic will probably be content to admit that Protestantism was not the sin, but rather the punishment. The most sweeping and shameless part of the process was not complete, indeed, until the end of the eighteenth century, when Protestantism was already passing into scepticism. Indeed a very decent case could be made out for the paradox that Puritanism was first and last a veneer on Paganism; that the thing began in the inordinate thirst for new things in the *noblesse* of the Renascence and ended in the Hell-Fire Club. Anyhow, what was first founded at the Reformation was a new and abnormally powerful aristocracy, and what was destroyed, in an ever-increasing degree, was everything that could be held, directly or indirectly, by the people *in spite of* such an aristocracy. This fact has filled all the subsequent history of our country; but the next particular point in that history concerns the position of the Crown. The King, in reality, had already been elbowed aside by the courtiers who had crowded behind him just before the bursting of the door. The King is left behind in the rush for wealth, and already can do nothing alone. And of this fact the next reign, after the chaos of Edward VI's, affords a very arresting proof.

Mary Tudor, daughter of the divorced Queen Katherine, has a bad name

A Short History of England, 1917

even in popular history; and popular prejudice is generally more worthy of study than scholarly sophistry. Her enemies were indeed largely wrong about her character, but they were not wrong about her effect. She was, in the limited sense, a good woman, convinced, conscientious, rather morbid. But it is true that she was a bad queen; bad for many things, but especially bad for her own most beloved cause. It is true, when all is said, that she set herself to burn out 'No Popery' and managed to burn it in. The concentration of her fanaticism into cruelty, especially its concentration in particular places and in a short time, did remain like something red-hot in the public memory. It was the first of the series of great historical accidents that separated a real, if not universal, public opinion from the old *régime*. It has been summarised in the death by fire of the three famous martyrs at Oxford; for one of them at least, Latimer, was a reformer of the more robust and human type, though another of them, Cranmer, had been so smooth a snob and coward in the councils of Henry VIII, as to make Thomas Cromwell seem by comparison a man. But of what may be called the Latimer tradition, the saner and more genuine Protestantism, I shall speak later. At the time even the Oxford Martyrs probably produced less pity and revulsion than the massacre in the flames of many more obscure enthusiasts, whose very ignorance and poverty made their cause seem more popular than it really was. But this last ugly feature was brought into sharper relief, and produced more conscious or unconscious bitterness, because of that other great fact of which I spoke above, which is the determining test of this time of transition.

What made all the difference was this: that even in this Catholic reign the property of the Catholic Church could not be restored. The very fact that Mary was a fanatic, and yet this act of justice was beyond the wildest dreams of fanaticism—that is the point. The very fact that she was angry enough to commit wrongs for the Church, and yet not bold enough to ask for the rights of the Church—that is the test of the time. She was allowed to deprive small men of their lives, she was not allowed to deprive great men of their property—or rather of other people's property. She could punish heresy, she could not punish sacrilege. She was forced into the false position of killing men who had not gone to church, and sparing men who had gone there to steal the church ornaments. What forced her into it? Not certainly her own religious attitude, which was almost maniacally sincere; not public opinion, which had naturally much more sympathy for the religious humanities which she did not restore than for the religious inhumanities which she did. The force came, of course, from the new nobility and the new wealth they refused to surrender; and the success of this early pressure proves that the nobility was already stronger than the Crown. The sceptre had only been used as a crowbar to break open the door of a treasure-house, and was itself broken, or at least bent, with the blow.

There is a truth also in the popular insistence on the story of Mary having 'Calais' written on her heart, when the last relic of the mediæval conquests reverted to France. Mary had the solitary and heroic half-virtue of the Tudors: she was a patriot. But patriots are often pathetically behind the times; for the very fact that they dwell on old enemies often blinds them to new ones. In a later generation Cromwell exhibited the same error reversed, and continued to keep a hostile eye on Spain when he should have kept it on France. In our own time the Jingoes of Fashoda kept it on France when they ought already to have had it on Germany. With no particular anti-national intention, Mary nevertheless got herself into an anti-national position towards the most tremendous international problem of her people. It is the second of the coincidences that confirmed the sixteenth-century change, and the name of it was Spain. The daughter of a Spanish queen, she married a Spanish prince, and probably saw no more in such an alliance than her father had done. But by the time she was succeeded by her sister Elizabeth, who was more cut off from the old religion (though very tenuously attached to the new one), and by the time the project of a similar Spanish marriage for Elizabeth herself had fallen through, something had matured which was wider and mightier than the plots of princes. The Englishman, standing on his little island as on a lonely boat, had already felt falling across him the shadow of a tall ship.

Wooden *clichés* about the birth of the British Empire and the spacious days of Queen Elizabeth have not merely obscured but contradicted the crucial truth. From such phrases one would fancy that England, in some imperial fashion, now first realised that she was great. It would be far truer to say that she now first realised that she was small. The great poet of the spacious days does not praise her as spacious, but only as small, like a jewel. The vision of universal expansion was wholly veiled until the eighteenth century; and even when it came it was far less vivid and vital than what came in the sixteenth. What came then was not Imperialism; it was Anti-Imperialism. England achieved, at the beginning of her modern history, that one thing human imagination will always find heroic—the story of a small nationality. The business of the Armada was to her what Bannockburn was to the Scots, or Majuba to the Boers—a victory that astonished even the victors. What was opposed to them was Imperialism in its complete and colossal sense, a thing unthinkable since Rome. It was, in no overstrained sense, civilisation itself. It was the greatness of Spain that was the glory of England. It is only when we realise that the English were, by comparison, as dingy, as undeveloped, as petty and provincial as Boers, that we can appreciate the height of their defiance or the splendour of their escape. We can only grasp it by grasping that for a great part of Europe the cause of the Armada had almost the cosmopolitan common sense of a crusade. The Pope had declared Elizabeth illegitimate—logically, it is hard so see what else he could say, having declared her mother's marriage invalid; but the fact was another and perhaps a final stroke sundering England from the elder world. Meanwhile those picturesque English privateers who had plagued the Spanish Empire of the New World were spoken of in the South simply as pirates, and technically the description was true; only technical assaults by the weaker party are in retrospect rightly judged with some generous weakness. Then, as if to stamp the contrast in an imperishable image, Spain, or rather the empire with Spain for its centre, put forth all its strength, and seemed to cover the sea with a navy like the legendary navy of Xerxes. It bore down on the doomed island with the weight and solemnity of a day of judgment; sailors or pirates struck at it with small ships staggering under large cannon, fought it with mere masses of flaming rubbish, and in that last hour of grapple a great storm arose out of the sea and swept round the island, and the gigantic fleet was seen no more. The uncanny completeness and abrupt silence that swallowed this prodigy touched a nerve that has never ceased to vibrate. The hope of England dates from that hopeless hour, for there is no real hope that has not once been a forlorn hope. The breaking of that vast naval net remained like a sign that the small thing which escaped would survive the greatness. And yet there is truly a sense in which we may never be so small or so great again.

For the splendour of the Elizabethan age, which is always spoken of as a sunrise, was in many ways a sunset. Whether we regard it as the end of the Renascence or the end of the old mediæval civilisation, no candid critic can deny that its chief glories ended with it. Let the reader ask himself what strikes him specially in the Elizabethan magnificence, and he will generally find it is something of which there were at least traces in mediæval times, and far fewer traces in modern times. The Elizabethan drama is like one of its own tragedies—its tempestuous torch was soon to be trodden out by the Puritans. It is needless to say that the chief tragedy was the cutting short of the comedy; for the comedy that came to England after the Restoration was by comparison both foreign and frigid. At the best it is comedy in the sense of being humorous, but not in the sense of being happy. It may be noted that the givers of good news and good luck in the Shakespearian love-stories nearly all belong to a world which was passing, whether they are friars or fairies. It is the same with the chief Elizabethan ideals, often embodied in the Elizabethan drama. The national devotion to the Virgin Queen must not be wholly discredited by its incongruity with the coarse and crafty character of the historical Elizabeth. Her critics might indeed reasonably say that in replacing the Virgin Mary by the Virgin Queen, the English reformers merely exchanged a true virgin for a false one. But this truth does not dispose of a true, though limited, contemporary cult. Whatever we think of that particular Virgin Queen, the tragic heroines of the time offer us a whole procession of virgin queens. And it is certain that the mediævals would have understood much better than the moderns the martyrdom of *Measure for Measure*. And as with the title of Virgin, so with the title of Queen. The mystical monarchy glorified in *Richard II* was soon to be dethroned much more ruinously than in *Richard II*. The same Puritans who tore off the pasteboard crowns of the stage players were also to tear off the real crowns of the kings whose parts they played. All mummery was to be forbidden, and all monarchy to be called mummery.

Shakespeare died upon St George's Day, and much of what St George had meant died with him. I do not mean that the patriotism of Shakespeare or of England died; that remained and even rose steadily, to be the noblest pride of the coming times. But much more than patriotism had been involved in that image of St George to whom the Lion Heart had dedicated England long ago in the deserts of Palestine. The conception of a patron saint had carried from the Middle Ages one very unique and as yet unreplaced idea. It was the idea of variation without antagonism. The Seven Champions of Christendom were multiplied by seventy times seven in the patrons of towns, trades and social types; but the very idea that they were all saints excluded the possibility of ultimate rivalry in the fact that they were all patrons. The Guild of the Shoemakers and the Guild of the Skinners, carrying the badges of St Crispin and St Bartholomew, might fight each other in the streets; but they did not believe that St Crispin and St Bartholomew were fighting each other in the skies. Similarly the English would cry in battle on St George and the French on St Denis; but they did not seriously believe that St George hated St Denis or even those who cried upon St Denis. Joan of Arc, who was on the point of patriotism what many modern people would call very fanatical, was yet upon this point what most modern people would call very enlightened. Now, with the religious schism, it cannot be denied, a deeper and more inhuman division appeared. It was no longer a scrap between the followers of saints who were themselves at peace, but a war between the followers of gods who were themselves at war. That the great Spanish ships were named after St Francis or St Philip was already beginning to mean little to the new England; soon it was to mean something almost cosmically conflicting, as if they were named after Baal or Thor. These are indeed mere symbols; but the process of which they are symbols was very practical and must be seriously followed. There entered with the religious wars the idea which modern science applies to racial wars; the idea of *natural* wars, not arising from a special quarrel but from the nature of the people quarrelling. The shadow of racial fatalism first fell across our path, and far away in distance and darkness something moved that men had almost forgotten.

Beyond the frontiers of the fading Empire lay that outer land, as loose and drifting as a sea, which had boiled over in the barbarian wars. Most of it was now formally Christian, but barely civilized; a faint awe of the culture of the south and west lay on its wild forces like a light frost. This semi-civilized world had long been asleep; but it had begun to dream. In the generation before Elizabeth a great man who, with all his violence, was vitally a dreamer, Martin Luther, had cried out in his sleep in a voice like thunder, partly against the place of bad customs, but largely also against the place of good works in the Christian scheme. In the generation after Elizabeth the spread of the new wild doctrines in the old wild lands had sucked Central Europe into a cyclic war of creeds. In this the house which stood for the legend of the Holy Roman Empire, Austria, the Germanic partner of Spain, fought for the old religion against a league of other Germans fighting for the new. The continental conditions were indeed complicated, and grew more and more complicated as the dream of restoring religious unity receded. They were complicated by the firm determination of France to be a nation in the full modern sense; to stand free and foursquare from all combinations; a purpose which led her, while hating her own Protestants at home, to give diplomatic support to many Protestants abroad, simply because it preserved the balance of power against the gigantic confederation of Spaniards and Austrians. It is complicated by the rise of a Calvinistic and commercial power in the Netherlands, logical, defiant, defending its own independence valiantly against Spain. But on the whole we shall be right if we see the first throes of the modern international problems in what is called the Thirty Years' War; whether we call it the revolt of half-heathens against the Holy Roman Empire, or whether we call it the coming of new sciences, new philosophies and new ethics from the north. Sweden took a hand in the struggle, and sent a military hero to the help of the newer Germany. But the sort of military heroism everywhere exhibited offered a strange combination of more and more complex strategic science with the most naked and cannibal cruelty. Other forces besides Sweden found a career in the carnage. Far away to the north-east, in a sterile land of fens, a small ambitious family of money-lenders who had become squires, vigilant, thrifty, thoroughly selfish, rather thinly adopted the theories of Luther, and began to lend their almost savage hinds as soldiers on the Protestant side. They were well paid for it by step after step of promotion; but at this time their principality was only the old Mark of Brandenburg. Their own name was Hohenzollern.

# Poems

SONGS OF EDUCATION

### III. FOR THE CRÊCHE

*Form 8277059, Sub-Section K*

I remember my mother, the day that we met,
A thing I shall never entirely forget;
And I toy with the fancy that, young as I am,
I should know her again if we met in a tram.
　　But mother is happy in turning a crank
　　That increases the balance at somebody's bank;
　　And I feel satisfaction that mother is free
　　From the sinister task of attending to me.

They have brightened our room, that is spacious and cool,
With diagrams used in the Idiot School,
And Books for the Blind that will teach us to see;
But mother is happy, for mother is free.
　　For mother is dancing up forty-eight floors.
　　For love of the Leeds International Stores,
　　And the flame of that faith might perhaps have grown cold,
　　With the care of a baby of seven weeks old.

For mother is happy in greasing a wheel
For somebody else, who is cornering Steel;
And though our one meeting was not very long,
She took the occasion to sing me this song:
   'O, hush thee, my baby, the time will soon come
   When thy sleep will be broken with hooting and hum;
   There are handles want turning and turning all day,
   And knobs to be pressed in the usual way;

O, hush thee, my baby, take rest while I croon,
For Progress comes early, and Freedom too soon.'

*New Witness*, 25 July, 1919

## ELEGY IN A COUNTRY CHURCHYARD

The men that worked for England
They have their graves at home:
And bees and birds of England
About the cross can roam.

But they that fought for England,
Following a falling star,
Alas, alas for England
They have their graves afar.

And they that rule in England,
In stately conclave met,
Alas, alas for England
They have no graves as yet.

The Ballad of St Barbara, 1922

## A SECOND CHILDHOOD

When all my days are ending
And I have no song to sing,
I think I shall not be too old
To stare at everything;
As I stared once at a nursery door
Or a tall tree and a swing.

Wherein God's ponderous mercy hangs
On all my sins and me,
Because He does not take away
The terror from the tree
And stones still shine along the road
That are and cannot be.

Men grow too old for love, my love,
Men grow too old for wine,
But I shall not grow too old to see
Unearthly daylight shine,
Changing my chamber's dust to snow
Till I doubt if it be mine.

Behold, the crowning mercies melt,
The first surprises stay;
And in my dross is dropped a gift
For which I dare not pray:
That a man grow used to grief and joy
But not to night and day.

Men grow too old for love, my love,
Men grow too old for lies;
But I shall not grow too old to see
Enormous night arise,
A cloud that is larger than the world
And a monster made of eyes.

Nor am I worthy to unloose
The latchet of my shoe;
Or shake the dust from off my feet
Or the staff that bears me through
On ground that is too good to last,
Too solid to be true.

Men grow too old to woo, my love,
Men grow too old to wed:
But I shall not grow too old to see
Hung crazily overhead
Incredible rafters when I wake
And find I am not dead.

A thrill of thunder in my hair:
Though blackening clouds be plain,
Still I am stung and startled
By the first drop of the rain:
Romance and pride and passion pass
And these are what remain.

Strange crawling carpets of the grass,
Wide windows of the sky:
So in this perilous grace of God
With all my sins go I:
And things grow new though I grow old,
Though I grow old and die.

*The Ballad of St Barbara, 1922*


## THE MYSTERY

If sunset clouds could grow on trees
It would but match the may in flower;
And skies be underneath the seas
No topsyturvier than a shower.

If mountains rose on wings to wander
They were no wilder than a cloud;
Yet all my praise is mean as slander,
Mean as these mean words spoken aloud.

And never more than now I know
That man's first heaven is far behind;
Unless the blazing seraph's blow
Has left him in the garden blind.

Witness, O Sun that blinds our eyes,
Unthinkable and unthankable King,
That though all other wonder dies
I wonder at not wondering.

*The Ballad of St Barbara, 1922*

## *ANSWERS TO THE POETS*

### THE FAT WHITE WOMAN SPEAKS

Why do you rush through the field in trains,
Guessing so much and so much,
Why do you flash through the flowery meads,
Fat-head poet that nobody reads;
And why do you know such a frightful lot
About people in gloves as such?

And how the devil can you be sure,
Guessing so much and so much,
How do you know but what someone who loves
Always to see me in nice white gloves
At the end of the field you are rushing by,
Is waiting for his Old Dutch?

### LUCASTA REPLIES TO LOVELACE

Tell me not, friend, you are unkind,
   If ink and books laid by,
You turn up in a uniform
   Looking all smart and spry.

I thought your ink one horrid smudge,
   Your books one pile of trash,
And with less fear of smear embrace
   A sword, a belt, a sash.

Yet this inconstancy forgive,
   Though gold lace I adore,
I could not love the lace so much
   Loved I not Lovelace more.

G.K.W., 9 May, 1925

415

# The Riddles of the Gospel

To understand the nature of this chapter, it is necessary to recur to the nature of this book. The argument which is meant to be the backbone of the book is of the kind called the *reductio ad absurdum*. It suggests that the results of assuming the rationalist thesis are more irrational than ours; but to prove it we must assume that thesis. Thus in the first section I often treated man as merely an animal, to show that the effect was more impossible than if he were treated as an angel. In the sense in which it was necessary to treat man merely as an animal, it is necessary to treat Christ merely as a man. I have to suspend my own beliefs, which are much more positive; and assume this limitation even in order to remove it. I must try to imagine what would happen to a man who did really read the story of Christ as the story of a man; and even of a man of whom he had never heard before. And I wish to point out that a really impartial reading of that kind would lead, if not immediately to belief, at least to a bewilderment of which there is really no solution except in belief. In this chapter, for this reason, I shall bring in nothing of the spirit of my own creed; I shall exclude the very style of diction, and even of lettering, which I should think fitting in speaking in my own person. I am speaking as an imaginary heathen human being, honestly, staring at the Gospel story for the first time.

Now it is not at all easy to regard the New Testament as a New Testament. It is not at all easy to realise the good news as new. Both for good and evil familiarity fills us with assumptions and associations; and no man of our civilisation, whatever he thinks of our religion, can really read the thing as if he had never heard of it before. Of course it is in any case utterly unhistorical to talk as if the New Testament were a neatly bound book that had fallen from heaven. It is simply the selection made by the authority of the Church from a mass of early Christian literature. But apart from any such question, there is a psychological difficulty in feeling the New Testament as new. There is a psychological difficulty in seeing those well-known words simply

The Everlasting Man, 1925

416

as they stand and without going beyond what they intrinsically stand for. And this difficulty must indeed be very great; for the result of it is very curious. The result of it is that most modern critics and most current criticism, even popular criticism, makes a comment that is the exact reverse of the truth. It is so completely the reverse of the truth that one could almost suspect that they had never read the New Testament at all.

We have all heard people say a hundred times over, for they seem never to tire of saying it, that the Jesus of the New Testament is indeed a most merciful and humane lover of humanity, but that the Church has hidden this human character in repellent dogmas and stiffened it with ecclesiastical terrors till it has taken on an inhuman character. This is, I venture to repeat, very nearly the reverse of the truth. The truth is that it is the image of Christ in the churches that is almost entirely mild and merciful. It is the image of Christ in the Gospels that is a good many other things as well. The figure in the Gospels does indeed utter in words of almost heart-breaking beauty his pity for our broken hearts. But they are very far from being the only sort of words that he utters. Nevertheless they are almost the only kind of words that the Church in its popular imagery ever represents him as uttering. That popular imagery is inspired by a perfectly sound popular instinct. The mass of the poor are broken, and the mass of the people are poor, and for the mass of mankind the main thing is to carry the conviction of the incredible compassion of God. But nobody with his eyes open can doubt that it is chiefly this idea of compassion that the popular machinery of the Church does seek to carry. The popular imagery carries a great deal to excess the sentiment of 'Gentle Jesus, meek and mild.' It is the first thing that the outsider feels and criticises in a Pietà or a shrine of the Sacred Heart. As I say, while the art may be insufficient, I am not sure that the instinct is unsound. In any case there is something appalling, something that makes the blood run cold, in the idea of having a statue of Christ in wrath. There is something insupportable even to the imagination in the idea of turning the corner of a street or coming out into the spaces of a market-place, to meet the petrifying petrifaction of *that* figure as it turned upon a generation of vipers, or that face as it looked at the face of a hypocrite. The Church can reasonably be justified therefore if she turns the most merciful face or aspect towards men; but it is certainly the most merciful aspect that she does turn. And the point is here that it is very much more specially and exclusively merciful than any impression that could be formed by a man merely reading the New Testament for the first time. A man simply taking the words of the story as they stand would form quite another impression; an impression full of mystery and possibly of inconsistency; but certainly not merely an impression of mildness. It would be intensely interesting; but part of the interest would consist in its leaving a good deal to be guessed at or explained. It is full of sudden gestures evidently significant except that we hardly know what they signify; of enigmatic silences; of ironical replies. The outbreaks of wrath, like storms above our atmosphere, do not seem to break out exactly where we should expect them, but to follow some higher weather-chart of their own. The Peter whom popular Church teaching presents is very rightly the Peter to whom Christ said in forgiveness, 'Feed my lambs.' He is not the Peter upon whom Christ turned as if he were the devil, crying in that obscure wrath, 'Get thee behind me, Satan.' Christ lamented with nothing but love and pity over Jerusalem which was to murder him. We do not know what strange spiritual atmosphere or spiritual insight led him to sink Bethsaida lower in the pit than Sodom. I am putting aside for the moment all questions of doctrinal inferences or expositions, orthodox or otherwise; I am simply imagining the effect on a man's mind if he did really do what these critics are always talking about doing; if he did really read the New Testament without reference to orthodoxy and even without reference to doctrine. He would find a number of things which fit in far less with the current unorthodoxy than they do with the current orthodoxy. He would find, for instance, that if there are any descriptions that deserved to be called realistic, they are precisely the descriptions of the supernatural. If there is one aspect of the New Testament Jesus in which he may be said to present himself eminently as a practical person, it is in the aspect of an exorcist. There is nothing meek and mild, there is nothing even in the ordinary sense mystical, about the tone of the voice that says 'Hold thy peace and come out of him.' It is much more like the tone of a very business-like lion-tamer or a strong-minded doctor dealing with a homicidal maniac. But this is only a side issue for the sake of illustration; I am not now raising these controversies; but considering the case of the imaginary man from the moon to whom the New Testament is new.

Now the first thing to note is that if we take it merely as a human story, it is in some ways a very strange story. I do not refer here to its tremendous and tragic culmination or to any implications involving triumph in that tragedy. I do not refer to what is commonly called the miraculous element; for on that point philosophies vary and modern philosophies very decidedly waver. Indeed the educated Englishman of to-day may be said to have passed from an old fashion, in which he would not believe in any miracles unless they were ancient, and adopted a new fashion in which he will not believe in any miracles unless they are modern. He used to hold that miraculous cures stopped with the first Christians and is now inclined to suspect that they began with the first Christian Scientists. But I refer here rather specially to unmiraculous and even to unnoticed and inconspicuous parts of the story. There are a great many things about it which nobody would have invented, for they are things that nobody has ever made any particular use of; things which if they were remarked at all have remained rather as puzzles. For instance, there is that long stretch of silence in the life of Christ up to the age of thirty. It is of all silences the most immense and imaginatively impressive. But it is not the sort of thing that anybody is particularly likely to invent in order to prove something; and nobody so far as I know has ever tried to prove anything in particular from it. It is impressive, but it is only impressive as a fact; there is nothing particularly popular or obvious about it as a fable. The ordinary trend of hero-worship and myth-making is much more likely to say the precise opposite. It is much more likely to say (as I believe some of the gospels rejected by the Church do say) that Jesus displayed a divine precocity and began his mission at a miraculously early age. And there is indeed something strange in the thought that he who of all humanity needed least preparation seems to have had most. Whether it was some mode of the divine humility, or some truth of which we see the shadow in the longer domestic tutelage of the higher creatures of the earth, I do not propose to speculate; I mention it simply as an example of the sort of thing that does in any case give rise to speculations, quite apart from recognised religious speculations. Now the whole story is full of these things. It is not by any means, as badly presented in print, a story that it is easy to get to the bottom of. It is anything but what these people talk of as a simple Gospel. Relatively speaking, it is the Gospel that has the mysticism and the Church that has the rationalism. As I should put it, of course, it is the Gospel that is the riddle and the Church that is the answer. But whatever be the answer, the Gospel as it stands is almost a book of riddles.

First, a man reading the Gospel sayings would not find platitudes. If he had read even in the most respectful spirit the majority of ancient philosophers and of modern moralists, he would appreciate the unique importance of saying that he did not find platitudes. It is more than can be said even of Plato. It is much more than can be said of Epictetus or Seneca or Marcus Aurelius or Apollonius of Tyana. And it is immeasurably more than can be said of most of the agnostic moralists and the preachers of the ethical societies: with their songs of service and their religion of brotherhood. The morality of most moralists, ancient and modern, has been one solid and polished cataract of platitudes flowing forever and ever. That would certainly not be the impression of the imaginary independent outsider studying the New Testament. He would be conscious of nothing so commonplace and in a sense of nothing so continuous as that stream. He would find a number of strange claims that might sound like the claim to be the brother of the sun and moon; a number of very startling pieces of advice; a number of stunning rebukes; a number of strangely beautiful stories. He would see some very gigantesque figures of speech about the impossibility of threading a needle with a camel or the possibility of throwing a mountain into the sea. He would see a number of very daring simplifications of the difficulties of life; like the advice to shine upon everybody indifferently as does the sunshine or not to worry about the future any more than the birds. He would find on the other hand some passages of almost impenetrable darkness, so far as he is concerned, such as the moral of the parable of the Unjust Steward. Some of these things might strike him as fables and some as truths; but none as truisms. For instance, he would not find the ordinary platitudes in favour of peace. He would find several paradoxes in favour of peace. He would find several ideals of non-resistance, which taken as they stand would be rather too pacific for any pacifist. He would be told in one passage to treat a robber *not* with passive resistance, but rather with positive and enthusiastic encouragement, if the terms be taken literally; heaping up gifts upon the man who had stolen goods. But he would not find a word of all that obvious rhetoric against war which has filled countless books and odes and orations; not a word about the wickedness of war, the wastefulness of war, the appalling scale of the slaughter in war and all the rest of the familiar frenzy; indeed not a word about war at all. There is nothing that throws any particular light on Christ's attitude towards organised warfare, except that he seems to have been rather fond of Roman soldiers. Indeed it is another perplexity, speaking from the same external and human standpoint, that he seems to have got on much better with Romans than he did with Jews. But the question here is a certain tone to be appreciated by merely reading a certain text; and we might give any number of instances of it.

The statement that the meek shall inherit the earth is very far from being a meek statement. I mean it is not meek in the ordinary sense of mild and moderate and inoffensive. To justify it, it would be necessary to go very deep into history and anticipate things undreamed of then and by many unrealised even now; such as the way in which the mystical monks reclaimed the lands which the practical kings had lost. If it was a truth at all, it was because it was a prophecy. But certainly it was not a truth in the sense of a truism. The blessing upon the meek would seem to be a very violent statement; in the sense of doing violence to reason and probability. And with this we come to another important stage in the speculation. As a prophecy it really was fulfilled; but it was only fulfilled long afterwards. The monasteries were the most practical and prosperous estates and experiments in reconstruction after the barbaric deluge; the meek did really inherit the earth. But nobody could have known anything of the sort at the time—unless indeed there was one who knew. Something of the same thing may be said about the incident of Martha and Mary; which has been interpreted in retrospect and from the inside by the mystics of the Christian contemplative life. But it was not at all an obvious view of it; and most moralists, ancient and modern, could be trusted to make a rush for the obvious. What torrents of effortless eloquence would have flowed from them to swell any slight superiority on the part of Martha; what splendid sermons about the Joy of Service and the Gospel of Work and the World Left Better Than We Found It, and generally all the ten thousand platitudes that can be uttered in favour of taking trouble—by people who need take no trouble to utter them. If in Mary the mystic and child of love Christ was guarding the seed of something more subtle, who was likely to understand it at the time? Nobody else could have seen Clare and Catherine and Teresa shining above the little roof at Bethany. It is so in another way with that magnificent menace about bringing into the world a sword to sunder and divide. Nobody could have guessed then either how it could be fulfilled or how it could be justified. Indeed some freethinkers are still so simple as to fall into the trap and be shocked at a phrase so deliberately defiant. They actually complain of the paradox for not being a platitude.

But the point here is that if we *could* read the Gospel reports as things as new as newspaper reports, they would puzzle us and perhaps terrify us much *more* than the same things as developed by historical Christianity. For instance: Christ, after a clear allusion to the eunuchs of eastern courts, said there would be eunuchs of the kingdom of heaven. If this does not mean the voluntary enthusiasm of virginity, it could only be made to mean something much more unnatural or uncouth. It is the historical religion that humanises it for us by the experience of Franciscans or of Sisters of Mercy. The mere statement standing by itself might very well suggest a rather dehumanised atmosphere; the sinister and inhuman silence of the Asiatic harem and divan. This is but one instance out of scores; but the moral is that the Christ of the Gospel might actually seem more strange and terrible than the Christ of the Church.

I am dwelling on the dark or dazzling or defiant or mysterious side of the Gospel words, not because they had not obviously a more obvious and popular side, but because this is the answer to a common criticism on a vital point. The freethinker frequently says that Jesus of Nazareth was a man of his time, even if he was in advance of his time; and that we cannot accept his ethics as final for humanity. The freethinker then goes on to criticise his ethics, saying plausibly enough that men cannot turn the other cheek, or that they must take thought for the morrow, or that the self-denial is too ascetic or the monogamy too severe. But the Zealots and the Legionaries did not turn the other cheek any more than we do, if so much. The Jewish traders and Roman tax-gatherers took thought for the morrow as much as we, if not more. We cannot pretend to be abandoning the morality of the past for one more suited to the present. It is certainly not the morality of another age, but it might be of another world.

In short, we can say that these ideals are impossible in themselves. Exactly what we cannot say is that they are impossible for us. They are rather notably marked by a mysticism which, if it be a sort of madness, would always have struck the same sort of people as mad. Take, for instance, the case of marriage and the relations of the sexes. It might very well have been true that a Galilean teacher taught things natural to a Galilean environment; but it is not. It might rationally be expected that a man in the time of Tiberius would have advanced a view conditioned by the time of Tiberius; but he did not. What he advanced was something quite different; something very difficult; but something no more difficult now than it was then. When, for instance, Mahomet made his polygamous compromise we may reasonably say that it was conditioned by a polygamous society. When he allowed a man four wives he was really doing something suited to the circumstances, which might have been less suited to other circumstances. Nobody will pretend that the four wives were like the four winds, something seemingly a part of the order of nature; nobody will say that the figure four was written forever in stars upon the sky. But neither will anyone say that the figure four is an inconceivable ideal; that it is beyond the power of the mind of man to count up to four; or to count the number of his wives and see whether it amounts to four. It is a practical compromise carrying with it the character of a particular society. If Mahomet had been born in Acton in the nineteenth century, we may well doubt whether he would instantly have filled that suburb with harems of four wives apiece. As he was born in Arabia in the sixth century, he did in his conjugal arrangements suggest the conditions of Arabia in the sixth century. But Christ in his view of marriage does not in the least suggest the conditions of Palestine in the first century. He does not suggest anything at all, except the sacramental view of marriage as developed long afterwards by the Catholic Church. It was quite as difficult for people then as for people now. It was much more puzzling to people then than to people now. Jews and Romans and Greeks did not believe, and did not even understand enough to disbelieve, the mystical idea that the man and the woman had become one sacramental substance. We may think it an incredible or impossible ideal; but we cannot think it any more incredible or impossible than they would have thought it. In other words, whatever else is true, it is not true that the controversy has been altered by time. Whatever else is true, it is emphatically not true that the ideas of Jesus of Nazareth were suitable to his time, but are no longer suitable to our time. Exactly how suitable they were to his time is perhaps suggested in the end of his story.

The same truth might be stated in another way by saying that if the story be regarded as merely human and historical, it is extraordinary how very little there is in the recorded words of Christ that ties him at all to his own time. I do not mean the details of a period, which even a man of the period knows to be passing. I mean the fundamentals which even the wisest man often vaguely assumes to be eternal. For instance, Aristotle was perhaps the wisest and most wide-minded man who ever lived. He founded himself entirely upon fundamentals, which have been generally found to remain rational and solid through all social and historical changes. Still, he lived in a world in which it was thought as natural to have slaves as to have children. And therefore he did permit himself a serious recognition of a difference between slaves and free men. Christ as much as Aristotle lived in a world that took slavery for granted. He did not particularly denounce slavery. He started a movement that could exist in a world with slavery. But he started a movement that could exist in a world without slavery. He never used a phrase that made his philosophy depend even upon the very existence of the social order in which he lived. He spoke as one conscious that everything was ephemeral, including the things that Aristotle thought eternal. By that time the Roman Empire had come to be merely the *orbis terrarum*, another name for the world. But he never made his morality dependent on the existence of the Roman Empire or even on the existence of the world. 'Heaven and earth shall pass away; but my words shall not pass away.'

The truth is that, when critics have spoken of the local limitations of the Galilean, it has always been a case of the local limitations of the critics. He did undoubtedly believe in certain things that one particular modern sect of materialists do not believe. But they were not things particularly peculiar to his time. It would be nearer the truth to say that the denial of them is quite peculiar to our time. Doubtless it would be nearer still to the truth to say merely that a certain solemn social importance, in the minority disbelieving them, is peculiar to our time. He believed, for instance, in evil spirits or in the psychic healing of bodily ills; but not because he was a Galilean born under Augustus. It is absurd to say that a man believed things because he was a Galilean under Augustus when he might have believed the same things if he had been an Egyptian under Tutankhamen or an Indian under Gengis Khan. But with this general question of the philosophy of diabolism or of divine miracles I deal elsewhere. It is enough to say that the materialists have to prove the impossibility of miracles against the testimony of all mankind, not against the prejudices of provincials in North Palestine under the first Roman Emperors. What they have to prove, for the present argument, is the presence in the Gospels of those particular prejudices of those particular provincials. And, humanly speaking, it is astonishing how little they can produce even to make a beginning of proving it.

So it is in this case of the sacrament of marriage. We may not believe in sacraments, as we may not believe in spirits, but it is quite clear that Christ believed in this sacrament in his own way and not in any current or contemporary way. He certainly did not get his argument against divorce from the Mosaic law or the Roman law or the habits of the Palestinian people. It would appear to his critics then exactly what it appears to his critics now; an arbitrary and transcendental dogma coming from nowhere save in the sense that it came from him. I am not at all concerned here to defend that dogma; the point here is that it is just as easy to defend it now as it was to defend it then. It is an ideal altogether outside time; difficult at any period; impossible at no period. In other words, if anyone says it is what might be expected of a man walking about in that place at that period, we can quite fairly answer that it is much *more* like what might be the mysterious utterance of a being beyond man, if he walked alive among men.

I maintain therefore that a man reading the New Testament frankly and freshly would *not* get the impression of what is now often meant by a human Christ. The merely human Christ is a made-up figure, a piece of artificial selection, like the merely evolutionary man. Moreover there have been too many of these human Christs found in the same story, just as there have been too many keys to mythology found in the same stories. Three or four separate schools of rationalism have worked over the ground and produced three or four equally rational explanations of his life. The first rational explanation of his life was that he never lived. And this in turn gave an opportunity for three or four different explanations; as that he was a sun-myth or a corn-myth, or any other kind of myth that is also a monomania. Then the idea that he was a divine being who did not exist gave place to the idea that he was a human being who did exist. In my youth it was the fashion to say that he was merely an ethical teacher in the manner of the Essenes, who had apparently nothing very much to say that Hillel or a hundred other Jews might not have said; as that it is a kindly thing to be kind and an assistance to purification to be pure. Then somebody said he was a madman with a Messianic delusion. Then others said he was indeed an original teacher because he cared about nothing but Socialism; or (as others said) about nothing but Pacifism. Then a more grimly scientific character appeared who said that Jesus would never have been heard of at all except for his prophecies of the end of the world. He was important merely as a Millennarian like Dr Cumming; and created a provincial scare by announcing the exact date of the crack of doom. Among other variants on the same theme was the theory that he was a spiritual healer and nothing else; a view implied by Christian Science, which has really to expound a Christianity without the Crucifixion in order to explain the curing of Peter's wife's mother or the daughter of a centurion. There is another theory that concentrates entirely on the business of diabolism and what it would call the contemporary superstition about demoniacs; as if Christ, like a young deacon taking his first orders, had got as far as exorcism and never got any further. Now each of these explanations in itself seems to me singularly inadequate; but taken together they do suggest something of the very mystery which they miss. There must surely have been something not only mysterious but many-sided about Christ if so many smaller Christs can be carved out of him. If the Christian Scientist is satisfied with him as a spiritual healer and the Christian Socialist is satisfied with him as a social reformer, so satisfied that they do not even expect him to be anything else, it looks as if he really covered rather more ground than they could be expected to expect. And it does seem to suggest that there might be more than they fancy in these other mysterious attributes of casting out devils or prophesying doom.

Above all, would not such a new reader of the New Testament stumble over something that would startle him much more than it startles us? I have here more than once attempted the rather impossible task of reversing time and the historic method; and in fancy looking forward to the facts, instead of backward through the memories. So I have imagined the monster that man might have seemed at first to the mere nature around him. We should have a worse shock if we really imagined the nature of Christ named for the first time. What should we feel at the first whisper of a certain suggestion about a certain man? Certainly it is not for us to blame anybody who should find that first wild whisper merely impious and insane. On the contrary, stumbling on that rock of scandal is the first step. Stark staring incredulity is a far more loyal tribute to that truth than a modernist metaphysic that would make it out merely a matter of degree. It were better to rend our robes with a great cry against blasphemy, like Caiaphas in the judgment, or to lay hold of the man as a maniac possessed of devils like the kinsmen and the crowd, rather than to stand stupidly debating fine shades of pantheism in the presence of so catastrophic a claim. There is more of the wisdom that is one with surprise in any simple person, full of the sensitiveness of simplicity, who should expect the grass to wither and the birds to drop dead out of the air, when a strolling carpenter's apprentice said calmly and almost carelessly, like one looking over his shoulder: 'Before Abraham was, I am.'

# A Self-made Man

It is now rather more than a century and a half since a small boy of the poorer sort was occupied in scaring rooks where they rose, as they still rise, in black flotillas flecking the great white clouds that roll up against the great ridges of Surrey and the southern shires. Yet further south where the Sussex hills take on an outline at once more opulent and more bare there was repeated a rhyme that might run like a refrain through much of his story.

> 'Bees are bees of Paradise,
> Do the work of Jesus Christ,
> Do the work that no man can;
> God made bees and bees make honey,
> God made man and man makes money,
> God made man to plough and reap and sow,
> And God made little boys to scare away the crow.'

And so the little boy in question continued to scare away the crow, in obedience to that providential arrangement.

The little boy was destined to grow up into a tall and vigorous man, who was to travel far and into strange places, into exile and into prison and into Parliament; but his heart never wandered very far from the simple ideals that are summed up in that verse. He was no mere dreamer or more or less lovable loafer, of the sort sometimes associated with the village genius. He would have been as ready as any man of the utilitarian school to admit that men would do well to imitate the industry of bees. Only, those who look at his literary industry may be tempted to say that he had more sting than honey. Similarly he was no mere romantic or sentimentalist, such as is sometimes associated with a love of the rural scene. He would have been as ready as any merchant or trader to face the fact that man, as God has made him, must make money. But he had a vivid sense that the money must be as

William Cobbett, 1925

solid and honest as the corn and fruit for which it stood, that it must be closely in touch with the realities that it represented; and he waged a furious war on all those indirect and sometimes imaginary processes of debts and shares and promises and percentages which make the world of wealth to-day a world at the worst unreal and at the best unseen. He was most immediately concerned, in the conditions of the hour, with what he regarded as the fugitive and wasteful paper-chase of paper money. But what he was at once predicting and denouncing, like a small cloud that had not yet become a universal fog, was that vast legal fiction that we call finance. In any case, against a world in which such financial mysteries were multiplying every day, in which machinery was everywhere on the march, and the new towns spreading with the swiftness of a landslide, in which England was already well on the way to becoming merely the workshop of the world, against the whole great crawling labyrinth of the modern state which is almost one with the modern city, there remained in him unaltered, cut deep into the solitary rock of his soul, the single clause of his single creed: that God made man to plough and reap and sow.

For this was William Cobbett, who was born in 1762 at a little farm at Farnham in Surrey. His grandfather had been an ordinary agricultural labourer, one of a class drudging for a miserable wage, and fallen so far from anything resembling the pride of a peasantry that in English history it had utterly sunk out of sight. It was something that has hardly been known since heathen times; there rests on all its records the ancient silence of slavery. It was to these slaves that the heart of Cobbett continually turned, in what seemed to many its dizzy and incalculable turnings. Those that were trampled and forgotten alike by the Tory squire and the Radical merchant were those whom Cobbett cared to remember; exactly as both Patrician and Plebeian citizens might have been puzzled by a sage whose first thought was of the slaves. And if ever in this land of ours the poor are truly lifted up, if ever the really needy find a tongue for their own needs, if ever progressives and reactionaries alike realise upon what ruins were built both their order and their reform, how many failures went to make their success, and what crimes have set their house in order, if they see the under-side of their own history with its secrets of sealed-up wrath and irrevocable injustice—in a word, if a great people can ever repent, then posterity may see achieved by this agency also, by this one lonely and angry bee in whom society saw nothing but a hornet, the work of Jesus Christ.

His father was a small farmer and evidently no fool; but the son could have but a very rudimentary and rustic schooling. The son was perhaps all his life a little too prone to play the schoolmaster; and from an early age he played the schoolmaster to himself. We have many notes of his first reading; notably a glimpse which shows him gaping at the broad farcical title of *The Tale of a*

*Tub*, so much in his own verbal fashion, and buying it and trying to understand it. He read it under a haystack, and it was so that there fell across him in his first sunshine the shadow of that dark but not ignoble spirit who a hundred years before had seen the first victory of our Venetian oligarchy and despaired. For many have discussed whether Cobbett owed anything to Swift's style, but few have sufficiently considered his connection with Swift's cause or creed. Anyhow, precious little of either could have been made out by a farmer's boy reading *The Tale of a Tub* under a haystack. For the rest, there is something of the boy's adventure story running through his boyhood. He embodied the recognised romance of England by running away to sea. He also embodied his own rather recurrent and fitful sagacity by running back again.

He was a character from his earliest years. There was a sort of calm impetuosity about his movements. He set out one day to escort some girls to the village fair, dressed up in all his village finery. He saw a coach with 'London' on it, and inconsequently got on to it and went careering away, leaving his lady friends, his fair, his farm and his family behind him like things of the past. Fortunately he met a friend of his father's in London, who got him a post as clerk in a lawyer's office. He hated the lawyer's office, as he hated lawyers and law all his life; as he hated long words and pedantry and petty tyranny. He took another plunge with the same placid abruptness; he took the King's shilling and enlisted as a private soldier. Here he was more successful; for there was much more of a soldier than a lawyer about him. Moreover, he was none the less a country boy because he had played the traditional part of the country boy who comes up to London where the streets are paved with gold. He was tall and strong, with a stride for which there seemed to be no room in the narrow streets, which went with a better swing on the long marches over the hills and far away. His lungs, which in every sense played so large a part in his life, demanded the deep air of the open places. Fifty years afterwards, at Westminster, as he would have said, he was to find himself dying in another den of lawyers. He was much happier anyhow in the camp of soldiers; indeed, he was not only happy but fortunate. He was recognised as a good soldier, and rose to be corporal and sergeant and eventually a sort of secretary to the whole regiment, assisting the adjutant. All this time he had been teaching himself grammar; and also (what is pleasingly characteristic) teaching the adjutant grammar. Anyhow it is obvious that he was trustworthy and that he was trusted. He was strict in his duty; rose early, an early bird ready to catch the earliest worm; he kept an eye on everything; he was as busy as a business man. Such a man generally dies rich and respected; but it is just here that there appears that little twist or bias which decided how William Cobbett was to live and die.

Cobbett began to note something queer and quite wrong about the regimental accounts. He soon discovered that a number of officers were simply pocketing money meant for the regimental food. Then it was that there appeared the deplorable difference between Cobbett and a really respectable and successful man. All his life long he never could leave things alone. He was a business man: but he could not mind his own business. He kept an eye on things; but he had never learnt to wink the other eye. He was the early bird; but he fell into the melancholy mistake of supposing that all worms ought really to be treated as worms. He had not the fine instinct which makes the really successful secretary-bird distinguish between the earth-worms of the underworld and the silk-worms of the smart set. It is not suggested that he was a pure altruist, a spotless saint of patriotism; then as always his action involved a vast amount of vanity, of self-assertion, of sensationalism and crudity, also a vast amount of inconsistency and incon-sequence. The point is that, whatever his other vices, he did not really know how to rise in the world. He made a scene; and discovered too late that in denouncing what he supposed to be a detail of individual swindling in his own regiment he had really challenged a system running through the whole British Army, or for that matter through the whole British Constitution. Where his restless meddling thought to let the regimental cat out of the bag, or out of one particular knapsack, he found he had roused from its lair a sort of Tammany Tiger. He was not by any means clear or consistent about it. The truth is he was quite out of his depth; yet he was perfectly right in feeling that there were depths of degradation. While he was in the Army his protest was easily crushed; when he had left it the Government granted some sort of enquiry; but as Cobbett could not get what he demanded as the conditions of that enquiry, he refused even to attend it himself, and the whole protest went by default. In a society like ours, it is very common for scandals that are too big to be cured to fizzle out like that, as if they were too small to be considered.

It was while he was a soldier that he took another of those characteristic steps, that might seem to many like steps over a precipice. But it is essential to realise about him that the very first step always had about it something almost stiff and automatic in its composure, however stormy might be the consequences or however much he might rave back against the storm. In this connection we must try to remember what is so entirely forgotten: the Stoic ideal of the end of the eighteenth century. The secular ideals of humanity fossilise very fast, and nothing but religion ever remains. Stoicism is strati-fied amid layers of lost moral fashions; but it was a fine thing in its day, when it stiffened with heathen virtues the Revolutionists of France and America. Our luxurious and orientalised fashions and fictions have a great deal to learn from the Roman virtues advocated in *Sandford and Merton*. That is why they certainly will not learn it. It must be admitted that in Mr Cobbett there was a touch of Mr Barlow. All his life he admired people who did things for themselves; especially if they did them under difficulties. He admired home-made bread or home-brewed ale even if some would call it the bread of affliction or consider it very bitter beer. Very early one morning he was going some of his military rounds in his sergeant's uniform, when the grey day was just breaking over fields of snow. He had a great power of sketching a landscape in simple words; and somehow such a twilight of grey and silver remains long in the reader's memory. At the end of a small yard he saw a girl with dark hair scouring out some pots and pans. He looked at her again and saw she was very beautiful. Then he said with a sort of fatal finality: 'That's the girl for me.' And indeed she was the wife who was with him when he died fifty years afterwards, on those Surrey hills that were his home.

Another incident attaches itself to her memory which is very significant of Cobbett's career from its earliest days. Doubtless he had before and since taken many girls to fairs, or failed to take them to fairs, like those who must have waited wondering after the incident of the coach. But like many combative, objective men he was really by nature very faithful in relations of mere affection; and he makes us believe it by a very convincing account of his one serious temptation to unfaithfulness. Unfaithfulness is never so vivid to an unfaithful man. By the time he returned to England, it was with the perfectly simple and concentrated purpose of seeking out the girl he had seen in the snow. In the old days he had come to a sort of understanding with her; and had solemnly placed in her hands a sealed packet of money, telling her to use it whenever she was in need. Then his regiment crossed the Atlantic and she was lost in the labyrinth of the poverty of a modern town. For a long time he could find no trace; at last he tracked her to a slum where she was working as the poorest sort of servant; and she handed him back his packet of money with the seal unbroken.

It is clear that for Cobbett that small gesture of repayment seemed as splendid as the throwing of the gauntlet. To enter into his sense of triumph we must understand something that is found in him through life, and especially found in him, when it is generally rarest, in youth. It is something seldom understood in a society without peasants; an oligarchy which can only understand what we call 'honour' as it is understood by gentlemen. It was the self-respect of the poor, which all modern industrial society has been slowly crushing to death. To find it anywhere uncrushed and even uncowed was to Cobbett like the noise of a great victory in a war of the world. When the poor servant-girl stood up and handed him back his little handful, there were things in it that neither snobs nor Bohemians will ever understand. There was at once fidelity and defiance, there was at once loyalty and solitude, there was a hard pride in work and a fine shade of delicacy; there was dignity, there was justice, above all there was triumph. Not here at least had the almighty meanness of the modern world prevailed, that lopped all lofty simplicities and lamed all lovers' quests; here was a romance rounded and complete and solid as the sealed packet in his hand; here in this unhappy world was a story with a happy ending. In all the long comedy of the contrast between the heart of man and its surroundings, never has there been a stranger disproportion than between the outside and the inside of that one small incident; of a young man finding his first love left alone with her honour and her pride. To any one passing in the street there could have been nothing visible but a tall and shabby soldier staring at a servant-girl on a door-step; but in his own narration it becomes easy to understand that she came back to him with all the beauty of banners.

I have dwelt on this one case of the contrast between the external homeliness of poverty and the internal glow of its occasional festivals and triumphs, because this is something very near to the whole secret of the man's life. It was always of such small tragedies and small triumphs that he was thinking when he talked about the problem of poverty. He differed from many modern social reformers and from most modern philanthropists, in the fact that he was not merely concerned with what is called the welfare of the workers. He was very much concerned for their dignity, their good name, their honour, and even their glory. Any humane man may desire the well-being of his servants, as he may the well-being of his horses or his sheep. But he does not commonly expect a horse to bring back a nosebag, full of oats, to which the conscientious quadruped does not think himself entitled by the terms of the contract. He does not expect a sheep to fire up and take offence, either at being bribed with grass or water, or at being criticised as the black sheep of the flock. He does not expect the sheep to offer to fight the sheep-dog, when accused of running away from the wolf. In short, he does not expect horses and sheep to have a sense of honour; but Cobbett, always so eccentric and paradoxical, did really desire peasants and working-men to have a sense of honour. The agony of rage in which so much of his life was passed was due to the consciousness that this popular sense of honour was everywhere being broken down by a cruel and ignoble industrialism. His whole life was a resistance to the degradation of the poor; to their degradation in the literal sense of the loss of a step, of a standing, of a status. There lay on his mind, like a nightmare of machinery crushing and crunching millions of bones, all the detailed destruction of the private property and domestic traditions of destitute families; all the selling up and breaking up of furniture, all the pawning of heirlooms and keepsakes; all that is meant by the awful sacrifice of the wedding-ring. He thought of a thousand stories like the story of the servant-girl: except that these stories did not have a happy ending.

His wife was soon to discover that if she had married (as she had) one of the most constant and considerate of husbands, she had also married one of the most restless and incalculable of men. It would be instructive to have a diary of Mrs Cobbett, as well as the endless autobiographies of Mr Cobbett. But she remains in the background of his life in a sort of powerful silence; and is known to us only by the praises that he never ceased to give her. She was soon called upon to go on some of his interminable travels. When he found in the case of Army corruption, to use one of his own homely sort of figures, that he had bitten off more than he could chew, he retired in disgust to France, and remained there through some of the most thrilling days of the French Revolution. Yet it is typical of him that he took with immense seriousness to the subject of French grammar, as a pendant to his devouring hobby of English grammar. When he set sail again from France it was not for England but for America, where he and his wife remained in exile for seven years. Their travels were not without their tragedies; for his first child died and his second was still-born, and it was not until he was more finally established that a living child rejoiced the most enthusiastic of fathers. But through all these early days we have the same vigilant activity in private things; as in the touching story of his striding up and down all night and driving away the howling dogs that his wife might sleep.

But there is another moral affecting the man and his work and arising in this connection out of an incident like that of his courtship and marriage. From the start we find him standing up sternly and almost priggishly for ideals of thrift and self-control. He might almost have been mistaken for a supporter of Smiles and Self-Help, if it were not for his second phase in raising a riot far more reckless than that of Wilkes and Liberty. But he enormously strengthened his case for Liberty by being the very antithesis of Wilkes. He justified his riot precisely because it could not be mistaken merely for riotous living. No sane person could pretend that Cobbett only sympathised with poverty because he sympathised with profligacy; because he sympathised with improvidence and irresponsibility and imbecile waste. Nobody could say *he* was merely an idler sympathising with idlers, or a wastrel sympathising with wastrels, or a man who loved ignorance preferring those who were ignorant. He was not even a man like Byron or Burns, whose sincere love of public liberty could be confused with a love of private licence. His case against industrialism was immensely strengthened by the fact that he himself was quite cut out to be the industrious apprentice. When he said that thousands were not only unlucky but unjustly oppressed, he said it with the authority of one who might quite well have been the hundredth lucky man who was the only hope of industrial competition. He who was so obviously a self-educated man might surely have been a self-made man. At least he stood a better chance of it than the thousands who were told to live only for that remote chance. When he said that the chance was worthless he was a reasonable and valid witness; when he said that most men were unfairly equipped for the struggle, he was better equipped than most. It was a much wiser Mr Smiles, himself entirely capable of self-help, who saw that the poor were really and truly helpless. And this second consideration comes back to the same truth as the first. It comes back to the fundamental truth of the modern state. Our commercialism does not punish the vices of the poor, but the virtues of the poor. It hampers the human character at its best and not merely at its worst; and makes impossible even the merits that it vainly recommends. Capitalism has prevented the poor man from saving more than it has prevented him from spending. It has restrained him from respectable marriage more than from casual immorality. It may be that Socialism threatens to destroy domesticity; but it is capitalism that destroys it. This is doubtless what is meant by saying that capitalism is the more practical of the two.

Cobbett was eminently and emphatically a respectable man. He was denounced as a demagogue, he was thrown in prison like a felon, he was all his life in the midst of riot and abuse, he was regarded as the inaugurator of red ruin and the breaking up of laws; but he remained to the last a highly respectable person, in the sense that he valued what are called the respectable virtues. That he was respectable to the last is perhaps less remarkable than that he was respectable from the first; and perhaps especially respectable at the first. That period of youth, which is commonly excused as the irresponsible period, was with him by far the most responsible period. It was during that period that he was improving his mind, limiting his luxuries, schooling himself in simple habits and rising in his military profession. He married the girl whose independence and probity he so much admired: and he was all his life a model husband and father. He was respectable and he might easily have been respected. It is his great virtue that he preferred to be reviled. It is his great glory that having taken the first steps in the successful life as it has been lived by so many successful men, he preferred to make himself a mockery and a cockshy for every worldly wit or comfortable critic to laugh at as a failure for a hundred years. He might have been a self-made man; but he died unfinished, trying to make something better than himself.

Finally, he was by nature a traditionalist and he was by tradition a Tory. He appeared first as a solid and loyal supporter of Church and King; and he appeared with complete success. As we shall see, his place was prepared for him as a good party man; his path was straight before him to the position of a great party leader. It seemed to most honest people, it seemed to him quite honestly, his logical and legitimate goal. It is his glory that he never reached his goal. It is his merit that his fallen figure was found far astray, and picked up, so to speak, like a dead vagabond; a puzzle for pedants and a sort of suicidal wreck to politicians; when he had set out on his journey stiff with so many strict loyalties and so many respectable conventions. For there dwelt within him a divine spirit more restless than a devil; a spirit that could not feed on fictions or sleep at the dictation of any drug; an insomnia of intelligence that could not choose but understand; a lidless eye that could not escape from seeing; a surge of spontaneous protest almost as involuntary as vomiting and stronger than the strength of fear; a voice not to be strangled, which for ever, in a fashion so fierce and unfamiliar that it startled men like the roar of a blind beast, appealed from tyranny to God.

# The Runaway Abbot

Thomas Aquinas, in a strange and rather symbolic manner, sprang out of the very centre of the civilised world of his time; the central knot or coil of the powers then controlling Christendom. He was closely connected with all of them; even with some of them that might well be described as destroying Christendom. The whole religious quarrel, the whole international quarrel, was for him a family quarrel. He was born in the purple: almost literally on the hem of the imperial purple: for his own cousin was the Holy Roman Emperor. He could have quartered half the kingdoms of Europe on his shield—if he had not thrown away the shield. He was Italian and French and German and in every way European. On one side, he inherited from the energy that made the episode of the Normans, whose strange organising raids rang and rattled like flights of arrows in the corners of Europe and the ends of the earth: one flight of them following Duke William far northward through the blinding snows to Chester; another treading in Greek and Punic footsteps through the island of Sicily to the gates of Syracuse. Another bond of blood bound him to the great Emperors of the Rhine and Danube who claimed to wear the crown of Charlemagne; Red Barbarossa, who sleeps under the rushing river, was his great uncle and Frederick II, the Wonder of the World, his second cousin; and yet he held by a hundred more intimate ties to the lively inner life, the local vivacity, the little walled nations and the thousand shrines of Italy. While inheriting this physical kinship with the Emperor, he maintained far more firmly his spiritual kinship with the Pope. He understood the meaning of Rome, and in what sense it was still ruling the world; and was not likely to think that the German Emperors of his time, any more than the Greek Emperors of a previous time, would be able to be really Roman in defiance of Rome. To this cosmopolitan comprehensiveness in his inherited position, he afterwards added many things of his own, that made for mutual understanding among the peoples, and gave him something of the character of an ambassador and interpreter. He travelled a great deal; he was

St Thomas Aquinas, 1933

not only well known in Paris and the German universities, but he almost certainly visited England; probably he went to Oxford and London; and it has been said that we may be treading in the footsteps of him and his Dominican companions, whenever we go down by the river to the railway station that still bears the name of Blackfriars. But the truth applies to the travels of his mind as well as his body. He studied the literature even of the opponents of Christianity much more carefully and impartially than was then the fashion; he really tried to understand the Arabian Aristotelianism of the Moslems; and wrote a highly humane and reasonable treatise on the problem of the treatment of the Jews. He always attempted to look at everything from the inside; but he was certainly lucky in having been born in the inside of the state system and the high politics of his day. What he thought of them may perhaps be inferred from the next passage in his history.

St Thomas might thus stand very well for the International Man, to borrow the title of a modern book. But it is only fair to remember that he lived in the International Age; in a world that was international in a sense not to be suggested in any modern book, or by any modern man. If I remember right, the modern candidate for the post of International Man was Cobden, who was an almost abnormally national man; a narrowly national man; a very fine type, but one which can hardly be imagined except as moving between Midhurst and Manchester. He had an international policy, and he indulged in international travel; but if he always remained a national person, it was because he remained a normal person; that is, normal to the nineteenth century. But it was not so in the thirteenth century. There a man of international influence, like Cobden, could be also almost a man of inter-national nationality. The names of nations and cities and places of origin did not connote that deep division that is the mark of the modern world. Aquinas as a student was nicknamed the ox of Sicily, though his birthplace was near Naples; but this did not prevent the city of Paris regarding him so simply and solidly as a Parisian, because he had been a glory of the Sorbonne, that it proposed to bury his bones when he was dead. Or take a more obvious contrast with modern times. Consider what is meant in most modern talk by a German Professor. And then realise that the greatest of all German Professors, Albertus Magnus, was himself one of the glories of the University of Paris; and it was in Paris that Aquinas supported him. Think of the modern German Professor being famous throughout Europe for his popularity when lecturing in Paris.

Thus, if there was war in Christendom, it was international war in the special sense in which we speak of international peace. It was not the war of two nations; but the war of two internationalisms: of two World States: the Catholic Church and the Holy Roman Empire. The political crisis in

Christendom affected the life of Aquinas at the start in one sharp disaster, and afterwards in many indirect ways. It had many elements: the Crusades; the embers of the Albigensian pessimism, over which St Dominic had triumphed in argument and Simon de Montfort in arms; the dubious experiment of an Inquisition which started from it; and many other things. But, broadly speaking, it is the period of the great duel between the Popes and the Emperors, that is the German Emperors who called themselves Holy Roman Emperors; the House of Hohenstaufen. The particular period of the life of Aquinas, however, is entirely overshadowed by the particular Emperor who was himself more an Italian than a German; the brilliant Frederick II who was called the Wonder of the World. It may be remarked, in passing, that Latin was the most living of languages at this time, and we often feel a certain weakness in the necessary translation. For I seem to have read somewhere that the word used was stronger than the Wonder of the World; that his mediæval title was *Stupor Mundi*, which is more exactly the Stupefaction of the World. Something of the sort may be noted later of philosophical language, and the weakness of translating a word like *Ens* by a word like Being. But for the moment the parenthesis has another application; for it might well be said that Frederick did indeed stupefy the world; that there was something stunning and blinding about the blows he struck at religion, as in that blow which almost begins the biography of Thomas Aquinas. He may also be called stupefying in another sense; in that his very brilliancy has made some of his modern admirers very stupid.

For Frederick II is the first figure, and that a rather fierce and ominous figure, who rides across the scene of his cousin's birth and boyhood: a scene of wild fighting and of fire. And it may be allowable to pause for a parenthesis upon his name; for two particular reasons: first that his romantic reputation, even among modern historians, covers and partly conceals the true background of the time; and second that the tradition in question directly involves the whole status of St Thomas Aquinas. The nineteenth-century view, still so strangely called the modern view by many moderns, touching such a man as Frederick II, was well summed up by some solid Victorian, I think by Macaulay; Frederick was 'a statesman in an age of Crusaders; a philosopher in an age of monks.' It may be noted that the antithesis involves the assumption that a Crusader cannot easily be a statesman; and that a monk cannot easily be a philosopher. Yet, to take only that special instance, it would be easy to point out that the cases of two famous men in the age of Frederick II would alone be strong enough to upset both the assumption and the antithesis. St Louis, though a Crusader and even an unsuccessful Crusader, was really a far more successful statesman than Frederick II. By the test of practical politics, he popularised, solidified and sanctified the most powerful government in Europe, the order and concentration of the French Monarchy; the single dynasty that steadily increased in strength for five hundred years up to the glories of the Grand Siècle; whereas Frederick went down in ruin before the Papacy and the Republics and a vast combination of priests and peoples. The Holy Roman Empire he wished to found was an ideal rather in the sense of a dream; it was certainly never a fact like the square and solid State which the French statesman did found. Or, to take another example from the next generation, one of the most strictly practical statesmen in history, our own Edward I, was also a Crusader.

The other half of the antithesis is even more false and here even more relevant. Frederick II was not a philosopher in the age of monks. He was a gentleman dabbling in philosophy in the age of the monk Thomas Aquinas. He was doubtless an intelligent and even brilliant gentleman; but if he did leave any notes on the nature of Being and Becoming, or the precise sense in which realities can be relative to Reality, I do not imagine those notes are now exciting undergraduates at Oxford or literary men in Paris, let alone the little groups of Thomists who have already sprung up even in New York and Chicago. It is no disrespect to the Emperor to say that he certainly was not a philosopher in the sense in which Thomas Aquinas was a philosopher, let alone so great or so universal or so permanent a philosopher. And Thomas Aquinas lived in that very age of monks, and in that very world of monks, which Macaulay talks of as if it were incapable of producing philosophy.

We need not dwell on the causes of this Victorian prejudice, which some still think so very advanced. It arose mainly from one narrow or insular notion; that no man could possibly be building up the best of the modern world, if he went with the main movement of the mediæval world. These Victorians thought that only the heretic had ever helped humanity; only the man who nearly wrecked mediæval civilisation could be of any use in constructing modern civilisation. Hence came a score of comic fables; as that the cathedrals must have been built by a secret society of Freemasons; or that the epic of Dante must be a cryptogram referring to the political hopes of Garibaldi. But the generalisation is not in its nature probable and it is not in fact true. This mediæval period was rather specially the period of communal or corporate thinking, and in some matters it was really rather larger than the individualistic modern thinking. This could be proved in a flash from the mere fact of the use of the word 'statesman'. To a man of Macaulay's period, a statesman *always* meant a man who maintained the more narrow national interests of his own state against other states, as Richelieu maintained those of France, or Chatham of England, or Bismarck of Prussia. But if a man actually wanted to defend all these states, to combine all these states, to make a living brotherhood of all these states, to resist some outer peril as from the Mongolian millions—then that poor devil, of course, could not really be called a statesman. He was only a Crusader.

In this way it is but fair to Frederick II to say that he was a Crusader; if he was also rather like an Anti-Crusader. Certainly he was an international statesman. Indeed, he was a particular type, which may be called an international soldier. The international soldier is always very much disliked by internationalists. They disliked Charlemagne and Charles V and Napoleon, and everybody who tried to create the World State for which they cry aloud day and night. But Frederick is more dubious and less doubted; he was supposed to be the head of the Holy Roman Empire; and accused of wanting to be the head of a very Unholy Roman Empire. But even if he were Antichrist, he would still be a witness to the unity of Christendom.

Nevertheless, there is a queer quality in that time; which, while it was international, was also internal and intimate. War, in the wide modern sense, is possible, not because more men disagree, but because more men agree. Under the peculiarly modern coercions, such as Compulsory Education and Conscription, there are such very large *peaceful* areas, that they can all agree upon War. In that age men disagreed even about war; and peace might break out anywhere. Peace was interrupted by feuds and feuds by pardons. Individuality wound in and out of a maze; spiritual extremes were walled up with one another in one little walled town; and we see the great soul of Dante divided, a cloven flame; loving and hating his own city. This individual complexity is intensely vivid in the particular story we have here to tell, in a very rough outline. If anyone wishes to know what is meant by saying that action was more individual, and indeed incalculable, he may well note some of the stages in the story of the great feudal house of Aquino, which had its castle not far from Naples. In the mere hasty anecdote we have now to tell, we shall note in succession five or six stages of this sort. Landulf of Aquino, a heavy feudal fighter typical of the time, rode in armour behind the imperial banners, and attacked a monastery, because the Emperor regarded the monastery as a fortress held for his enemy the Pope. Later, we shall see, the same feudal lord sent his own son to the same monastery; probably on the friendly advice of the same Pope. Later still, another of his sons, entirely on his own, rebelled against the Emperor, and went over to the armies of the Pope. For this he was executed by the Emperor, with promptitude and despatch. I wish we knew more about that brother of Thomas Aquinas who risked and lost his life to support the cause of the Pope; which was in all human essentials the cause of the People. He may not have been a saint; but he must have had some qualities of a martyr. Meanwhile, two other brothers, still ardent and active, apparently, in the service of the Emperor who killed the third brother, themselves proceeded to kidnap another brother, because they did not approve of his sympathy with the new social movements in religion. That is the sort of tangle in which this one distinguished mediæval family found itself. It was not a war of nations; but it was a rather widespread family quarrel.

The reason for dwelling here, however, upon the position of the Emperor Frederick, as a type of his time, in his culture and his violence, in his concern for philosophy and his quarrel with religion, is not merely concerned with these things. He may here be the first figure that crosses the stage, because one of his very typical actions precipitated the first action, or obstinate inaction, which began the personal adventures of Thomas Aquinas in this world. The story also illustrates the extraordinary tangle in which a family like that of the Count of Aquino found itself; being at once so close to the Church and so much at odds with it. For Frederick II, in the course of those remarkable manœuvres, military and political, which ranged from burning heretics to allying himself with Saracens, made a swoop as of a predatory eagle (and the Imperial eagle was rather predatory) upon a very large and wealthy monastery; the Benedictine Abbey of Monte Cassino; and stormed and sacked the place.

Some miles from the monastery of Monte Cassino stood a great crag or cliff, standing up like a pillar of the Apennines. It was crowned with a castle that bore the name of the Dry Rock, and was the eyrie in which the eaglets of the Aquino branch of the Imperial family were nursed to fly. Here lived Count Landulf of Aquino, who was the father of Thomas Aquinas and some seven other sons. In military affairs he doubtless rode with his family, in the feudal manner; and apparently had something to do with the destruction of the monastery. But it was typical of the tangle of the time, that Count Landulf seems afterwards to have thought that it would be a tactful and delicate act to put in his son Thomas as Abbot of the monastery. This would be of the nature of a graceful apology to the Church; and also, it would appear, the solution of a family difficulty.

For it had been long apparent to Count Landulf that nothing could be done with his seventh son Thomas, except to make him an Abbot or something of that kind. Born in 1226, he had from childhood a mysterious objection to becoming a predatory eagle, or even to taking an ordinary interest in falconry or tilting or any other gentlemanly pursuits. He was a large and heavy and quiet boy, and phenomenally silent; scarcely opening his mouth except to say suddenly to his schoolmaster in an explosive manner, 'What is God?' The answer is not recorded; but it is probable that the asker went on worrying out answers for himself. The only place for a person of this kind was the Church and presumably the cloister; and so far as that went, there was no particular difficulty. It was easy enough for a man in Count Landulf's position to arrange with some monastery for his son to be received there; and in this particular case he thought it would be a good idea if he were received in some official capacity, that would be worthy of his worldly rank. So everything was smoothly arranged for Thomas Aquinas becoming a monk, which would seem to be what he himself wanted; and sooner or later becoming Abbot of Monte Cassino. And then the curious thing happened.

In so far as we may follow rather dim and disputed events, it would seem that the young Thomas Aquinas walked into his father's castle one day and calmly announced that he had become one of the Begging Friars, of the new order founded by Dominic the Spaniard; much as the eldest son of the squire might go home and airily inform the family that he had married a gypsy; or the heir of a Tory Duke state that he was walking tomorrow with the Hunger Marchers organised by alleged Communists. By this, as has been noted already, we may pretty well measure the abyss between the old monasticism and the new, and the earthquake of the Dominican and Franciscan revolution. Thomas had appeared to wish to be a Monk; and the gates were silently opened to him, and the long avenues of the abbey, the very carpet, so to speak, laid for him up to the throne of the mitred abbot. He said he wished to be a Friar; and his family flew at him like wild beasts; his brothers pursued him along the public roads, half-rent his friar's frock from his back and finally locked him up in a tower like a lunatic.

It is not very easy to trace the course of this furious family quarrel, and how it eventually spent itself against the tenacity of the young Friar; according to some stories, his mother's disapproval was short-lived and she went over to his side; but it was not only his relatives that were embroiled. We might say that the central governing class of Europe, which partly consisted of his family, were in a turmoil over the deplorable youth; even the Pope was asked for tactful intervention; and it was at one time proposed that Thomas should be allowed to wear the Dominican habit while acting as Abbot in the Benedictine Abbey. To many this would seem a tactful compromise; but it did not commend itself to the narrow mediæval mind of Thomas Aquinas. He indicated sharply that he wished to be a Dominican in the Dominican Order, and not at a fancy-dress ball; and the diplomatic proposal appears to have been dropped.

Thomas of Aquino wanted to be a Friar. It was a staggering fact to his contemporaries; and it is rather an intriguing fact even to us; for this desire, limited literally and strictly to this statement, was the one practical thing to which his will was clamped with adamantine obstinacy till his death. He would not be an Abbot; he would not be a Monk; he would not even be a Prior or ruler in his own fraternity; he would not be a prominent or important Friar; he would be a Friar. It is as if Napoleon had insisted on remaining a private soldier all his life. Something in this heavy, quiet, cultivated, rather academic gentleman would not be satisfied till he was, by fixed authoritative proclamation and official pronouncement, established and appointed to be a Beggar. It is all the more interesting because, while he did more than his duty a thousand times over, he was not at all like a Beggar; nor at all likely to be a good Beggar. He had nothing of the native vagabond about him, as had his great precursors; he was not born with something of the wandering minstrel, like St Francis; or something of the tramping missionary, like St Dominic. But he insisted upon putting himself under military orders, to do these things at the will of another, if required. He may be compared with some of the more magnanimous aristocrats who have enrolled themselves in revolutionary armies; or some of the best of the poets and scholars who volunteered as private soldiers in the Great War. Something in the courage and consistency of Dominic and Francis had challenged his deep sense of justice; and while remaining a very reasonable person, and even a diplomatic one, he never let anything shake the iron immobility of this one decision of his youth; nor was he to be turned from his tall and towering ambition to take the lowest place.

The first effect of his decision, as we have seen, was much more stimulating and even startling. The General of the Dominicans, under whom Thomas had enrolled himself, was probably well aware of the diplomatic attempts to dislodge him and the worldly difficulties of resisting them. His expedient was to take his young follower out of Italy altogether; bidding him proceed with a few other Friars to Paris. There was something prophetic even about this first progress of the travelling teacher of the nations; for Paris was indeed destined to be in some sense the goal of his spiritual journey; since it was there that he was to deliver both his great defence of the Friars and his great defiance to the antagonists of Aristotle. But this his first journey to Paris was destined to be broken off very short indeed. The Friars had reached a turn of the road by a wayside fountain, a little way north of Rome, when they were overtaken by a wild cavalcade of captors, who seized on Thomas like brigands, but who were in fact only rather needlessly agitated brothers. He had a large number of brothers: perhaps only two were here involved. Indeed he was the seventh; and friends of Birth Control may lament that this philosopher was needlessly added to the noble line of ruffians who kidnapped him. It was an odd affair altogether. There is something quaint and picturesque in the idea of kidnapping a begging Friar; who might in a sense be called a runaway abbot. There is a comic and tragic angle in the motives and purposes of such a trio of strange kinsmen. There is a sort of Christian cross-purposes in the contrast between the feverish illusion of the importance of things, always marking men who are called practical; and the much more practical pertinacity of the man who is called theoretical.

Thus at least did those three strange brethren stagger or trail along their tragic road, tied together, as it were, like criminal and constable; only that the criminals were making the arrest. So their figures are seen for an instant against the horizon of history; brothers as sinister as any since Cain and Abel. For this queer outrage in the great family of Aquino does really stand out symbolically, as representing something that will for ever make the Middle Ages a mystery and a bewilderment; capable of sharply contrasted interpretations like darkness and light. For in two of those men there raged, we might say screamed, a savage pride of blood and blazonry of arms, though they were princes of the most refined world of their time, which would seem more suitable to a tribe dancing round a totem. For the moment they had forgotten everything except the name of a family, that is narrower than a tribe, and far narrower than a nation. And the third figure of that trio, born of the same mother and perhaps visibly one with the others in face or form, had a conception of brotherhood broader than most modern democracy, for it was not national but international; a faith in mercy and modesty far deeper than any mere mildness of manners in the modern world; and a drastic oath of poverty, which would now be counted quite a mad exaggeration of the revolt against plutocracy and pride. Out of the same Italian castle came two savages and one sage; or one saint more pacific than most modern sages. That is the double aspect confusing a hundred controversies. That is what makes the riddle of the mediæval age; that it was not one age but two ages. We look into the moods of some men, and it might be the Stone Age; we look into the minds of other men, and they might be living in the Golden Age; in the most modern sort of Utopia. There were always good men and bad men; but in this time good men who were subtle lived with bad men who were simple. They lived in the same family; they were brought up in the same nursery; and they came out to struggle, as the brothers of Aquino struggled by the wayside when they dragged the new Friar along the road and shut him up in the castle on the hill.

When his relations tried to despoil him of his Friar's frock he seems to have laid about them in the fighting manner of his fathers; and it would seem successfully, since this attempt was abandoned. He accepted the imprisonment itself with his customary composure, and probably did not mind very much whether he was left to philosophise in a dungeon or in a cell. Indeed there is something in the way the whole tale is told, which suggests that through a great part of that strange abduction, he had been carried about like a lumbering stone statue. Only one tale told of his captivity shows him merely in anger; and that shows him angrier than he ever was before or after. It struck the imagination of his own time for more important reasons; but it has an interest that is psychological as well as moral. For once in his life, for the first time and the last, Thomas of Aquino was really *hors de lui*; riding a storm outside that tower of intellect and contemplation in which he commonly lived. And that was when his brothers introduced into his room some specially gorgeous and painted courtesan, with the idea of surprising him by a sudden temptation; or at least involving him in a scandal. His anger was justified, even by less strict moral standards than his own; for the meanness was even worse than the foulness of the expedient. Even on the lowest grounds, he knew his brothers knew, and they knew that he knew, that it was an insult to him as a gentleman to suppose that he would break his pledge upon so base a provocation; and he had behind him a far more terrible sensibility: all that huge ambition of humility which was to him the voice of God out of heaven. In this one flash alone we see that huge unwieldy figure in an attitude of activity, or even animation; and he was very animated indeed. He sprang from his seat and snatched a brand out of the fire, and stood brandishing it like a flaming sword. The woman not unnaturally shrieked and fled, which was all that he wanted; but it is quaint to think of what she must have thought of that madman of monstrous stature juggling with flames and apparently threatening to burn down the house. All he did, however, was to stride after her to the door and bang and bar it behind her; and then, with a sort of impulse of violent ritual, he rammed the burning brand into the door, blackening and blistering it with one big black sign of the cross. Then he returned, and dropped it again into the fire; and sat down on that seat of sedentary scholarship, that chair of philosophy, that secret throne of contemplation, from which he never rose again.

# A Meditation on the Manichees

There is one casual anecdote about St Thomas Aquinas which illuminates him like a lightning-flash, not only without, but within. For it not only shows him as a character, and even as a comedy character, and shows the colours of his period and social background; but also, as if for an instant, makes a transparency of his mind. It is a trivial incident which occurred one day when he was reluctantly dragged from his work; and we might almost say from his play. For both were for him found in the unusual hobby of thinking; which is for some men a thing much more intoxicating than mere drinking. He had declined any number of society invitations, to the courts of kings and princes, not because he was unfriendly, for he was not; but because he was always glowing within with the really gigantic plans of exposition and argument which filled his life. On one occasion, however, he was invited to the court of King Louis IX of France, more famous as the great St Louis; and for some reason or other, the Dominican authorities of his Order told him to accept; so he immediately did so, being an obedient friar even in his sleep; or rather in his permanent trance of reflection.

It is a real case against conventional hagiography that it sometimes tends to make all saints seem to be the same. Whereas in fact no men are more different than saints; not even murderers. And there could hardly be a more complete contrast, given the essentials of holiness, than between St Thomas and St Louis. St Louis was born a knight and a king; but he was one of those men in whom a certain simplicity, combined with courage and activity, makes it natural, and in a sense easy, to fulfil directly and promptly any duty or office, however official. He was a man in whom holiness and healthiness had no quarrel; and their issue was in action. He did not go in for thinking much; in the sense of theorising much. But, even in theory, he had that sort of presence of mind which belongs to the rare and really practical man when he has to think. He never said the wrong thing; and he was orthodox by instinct. In the old pagan proverb about kings being philosophers or

St Thomas Aquinas, 1933

philosophers kings, there was a certain miscalculation, connected with a mystery that only Christianity could reveal. For while it is possible for a king to wish very much to be a saint, it is not possible for a saint to wish very much to be a king. A good man will hardly dream always of being a great monarch; but, such is the liberality of the Church, that she cannot forbid even a great monarch to dream of being a good man. But Louis was a straightforward, soldierly sort of person who did not particularly mind being a king, any more than he would have minded being a captain or a sergeant or any other rank in his army. Now a man like St Thomas would definitely dislike being a king, or being entangled with the pomp and politics of kings; not only his humility, but a sort of subconscious fastidiousness and fine dislike of futility, often found in leisurely and learned men with large minds, would really have prevented him making contact with the complexity of court life. Also, he was anxious all his life to keep out of politics; and there was no political symbol more striking, or in a sense more challenging, at that moment, than the power of the King in Paris.

Paris was truly at that time an *aurora borealis*; a Sunrise in the North. We must realise that lands much nearer to Rome had rotted with paganism and pessimism and Oriental influences, of which the most respectable was that of Mahound. Provence and all the South had been full of a fever of nihilism or negative mysticism, and from Northern France had come the spears and swords that swept away the unchristian thing. In Northern France also sprang up that splendour of building that shines like swords and spears: the first spires of the Gothic. We talk now of grey Gothic buildings; but they must have been very different when they went up white and gleaming into the northern skies, partly picked out with gold and bright colours; a new flight of architecture, as startling as flying-ships. The new Paris ultimately left behind by St Louis must have been a thing white like lilies and splendid as the oriflamme. It was the beginning of the great new thing: the nation of France, which was to pierce and overpower the old quarrel of Pope and Emperor in the lands from which Thomas came. But Thomas came very unwillingly, and, if we may say it of so kindly a man, rather sulkily. As he entered Paris, they showed him from the hill that splendour of new spires beginning, and somebody said something like 'How grand it must be to own all this'. And Thomas Aquinas only muttered, 'I would rather have that Chrysostom MS. I can't get hold of'.

Somehow they steered that reluctant bulk of reflection to a seat in the royal banquet-hall; and all that we know of Thomas tells us that he was perfectly courteous to those who spoke to him, but spoke little, and was soon forgotten in the most brilliant and noisy clatter in the world: the noise of French talking. What the Frenchmen were talking about we do not know; but they forgot all about the large fat Italian in their midst, and it seems only too possible that he forgot all about them. Sudden silences will occur even in French conversation; and in one of these the interruption came. There had long been no word or motion in that huge heap of black and white weeds, like motley in mourning, which marked him as a mendicant friar out of the streets, and contrasted with all the colours and patterns and quarterings of that first and freshest dawn of chivalry and heraldry. The triangular shields and pennons and pointed spears, the triangular swords of the Crusade, the pointed windows and the conical hoods, repeated everywhere that fresh French mediæval spirit that did, in every sense, come to the point. But the colours of the coats were gay and varied, with little to rebuke their richness; for St Louis, who had himself a special quality of coming to the point, had said to his courtiers, 'Vanity should be avoided; but every man should dress well, in the manner of his rank; that his wife may the more easily love him'.

And then suddenly the goblets leapt and rattled on the board and the great table shook, for the friar had brought down his huge fist like a club of stone, with a crash that startled everyone like an explosion; and had cried out in a strong voice, but like a man in the grip of a dream, 'And *that* will settle the Manichees!'

The palace of a king, even when it is the palace of a saint, has its conventions. A shock thrilled through the court, and every one felt as if the fat friar from Italy had thrown a plate at King Louis, or knocked his crown sideways. They all looked timidly at the terrible seat, that was for a thousand years the throne of the Capets; and many there were presumably prepared to pitch the big black-robed beggar-man out of the window. But St Louis, simple as he seemed, was no mere mediæval fountain of honour or even fountain of mercy; but also the fountain of two eternal rivers; the irony and the courtesy of France. And he turned to his secretaries, asking them in a low voice to take their tablets round to the seat of the absent-minded controversialist, and take a note of the argument that had just occurred to him; because it must be a very good one and he might forget it. I have paused upon this anecdote, first, as has been said, because it is the one which gives us the most vivid snapshot of a great mediæval character; indeed of two great mediæval characters. But it is also specially fitted to be taken as a type or a turning-point, because of the glimpse it gives of the man's main preoccupation; and the sort of thing that might have been found in his thoughts, if they had been thus surprised at any moment by a philosophical eavesdropper or through a psychological keyhole. It was not for nothing that he was still brooding, even in the white court of St Louis, upon the dark cloud of the Manichees.

This book is meant only to be the sketch of a man; but it must at least lightly touch, later on, upon a method and a meaning; or what our journalism has an annoying way of calling a message. A few very inadequate pages must be given to the man in relation to his theology and his philosophy; but the thing of which I mean to speak here is something at once more general and more personal even than his philosophy. I have therefore introduced it here, before we come to anything like technical talk about his philosophy. It was something that might alternatively be called his moral attitude, or his temperamental predisposition, or the purpose of his life so far as social and human effects were concerned; for he knew better than most of us that there is but one purpose in this life, and it is one that is beyond this life. But if we wanted to put in a picturesque and simplified form what he wanted for the world, and what was his work in history, apart from theoretical and theological definitions, we might well say that it really was to strike a blow and settle the Manichees.

The full meaning of this may not be apparent to those who do not study theological history; and perhaps even less apparent to those who do. Indeed, it may seem equally irrelevant to the history and the theology. In history St Dominic and Simon de Montfort between them had already pretty well settled the Manichees. And in theology, of course, an encyclopædic doctor like Aquinas dealt with a thousand other heresies besides the Manichean heresy. Nevertheless, it does represent his main position and the turn he gave to the whole history of Christendom.

I think it well to interpose this chapter, though its scope may seem more vague than the rest, because there is a sort of big blunder about St Thomas and his creed, which is an obstacle for most modern people in even beginning to understand them. It arises roughly thus. St Thomas, like other monks, and especially other saints, lived a life of renunciation and austerity; his fasts, for instance, being in marked contrast to the luxury in which he might have lived if he chose. This element stands high in his religion, as a manner of asserting the will against the power of nature, of thanking the Redeemer by partially sharing his sufferings, of making a man ready for anything as a missionary or martyr, and similar ideals. These happen to be rare in the modern industrial society of the West, outside his communion; and it is therefore assumed that they are the whole meaning of that communion. Because it is uncommon for an alderman to fast forty days, or a politician to take a Trappist vow of silence, or a man about town to live a life of strict celibacy, the average outsider is convinced, not only that Catholicism is nothing except asceticism, but that asceticism is nothing except pessimism. He is so obliging as to explain to Catholics why they hold this heroic virtue in respect; and is ever ready to point out that the philosophy behind it is an Oriental hatred of anything connected with Nature, and a purely Schopenhauerian disgust with the Will to Live. I read in a 'high-class' review of Miss Rebecca West's book on St Augustine, the astounding statement that the Catholic Church regards sex as having the nature of sin. How marriage can be a sacrament if sex is a sin, or why it is the Catholics who are in favour of birth and their foes who are in favour of birth-control, I will leave the critic to worry out for himself. My concern is not with that part of the argument; but with another.

The ordinary modern critic, seeing this ascetic ideal in an authoritative Church, and not seeing it in most other inhabitants of Brixton or Brighton, is apt to say, 'This is the result of Authority; it would be better to have Religion without Authority'. But in truth, a wider experience outside Brixton or Brighton would reveal the mistake. It is rare to find a fasting alderman or a Trappist politician; but it is still more rare to see nuns suspended in the air on hooks or spikes; it is unusual for a Catholic Truth Society orator in Hyde Park to begin his speech by gashing himself all over with knives; a stranger calling at an ordinary presbytery will seldom find the parish priest lying on the floor with a fire lighted on his chest and scorching him, while he utters spiritual ejaculations. Yet all these things are done all over Asia, for instance, by voluntary enthusiasts acting solely on the great impulse of Religion; of Religion, in their case, not commonly imposed by any immediate Authority; and certainly not imposed by this particular Authority. In short, a real knowledge of mankind will tell anybody that Religion is a very terrible thing; that it is truly a raging fire; and that Authority is often quite as much needed to restrain it as to impose it. Asceticism, or the war with the appetites, is itself an appetite. It can never be eliminated from among the strange ambitions of Man. But it can be kept in some reasonable control; and it is indulged in much saner proportion under Catholic Authority than in Pagan or Puritan anarchy. Meanwhile, the whole of this ideal, though an essential part of Catholic idealism when it is understood, is in some ways entirely a side issue. It is not the primary principle of Catholic philosophy; it is only a particular deduction from Catholic ethics. And when we begin to talk about primary philosophy, we realise the full and flat contradiction between the monk fasting and the fakir hanging himself on hooks.

Now nobody will begin to understand the Thomist philosophy, or indeed the Catholic philosophy, who does not realise that the primary and fundamental part of it is entirely the praise of Life; the praise of Being; the praise of God as the Creator of the World. Everything else follows a long way after that, being conditioned by various complications like the Fall or the vocation of heroes. The trouble occurs because the Catholic mind moves upon two planes; that of the Creation and that of the Fall. The nearest parallel is, for instance, that of England invaded; there might be strict martial law in Kent because the enemy had landed in Kent, and relative liberty in Hereford; but this would not affect the affection of an English patriot for Hereford or Kent, and strategic caution in Kent would not affect the love of Kent. For the love of England would remain, both of the parts to be redeemed by discipline and the parts to be enjoyed in liberty. Any extreme of Catholic asceticism is a wise, or unwise, precaution against the evil of the Fall; it is *never* a doubt about the good of the Creation. And *that* is where it really does differ, not only from the rather excessive eccentricity of the gentleman who hangs himself on hooks, but from the whole cosmic theory which is the hook on which he hangs. In the case of many Oriental religions, it really is true that the asceticism is pessimism; that the ascetic tortures himself to death out of an abstract hatred of life; that he does not merely mean to control Nature as he should, but to contradict Nature as much as he can. And though it takes a milder form than hooks in millions of the religious populations of Asia, it is a fact far too little realised, that the dogma of the denial of life does really rule as a first principle on so vast a scale. One historic form it took was that great enemy of Christianity from its beginnings: the Manichees.

What is called the Manichean philosophy has had many forms; indeed, it has attacked what is immortal and immutable with a very curious kind of immortal mutability. It is like the legend of the magician who turns himself into a snake or a cloud; and the whole has that nameless note of irresponsibility, which belongs to much of the metaphysics and morals of Asia, from which the Manichean mystery came. But it is always in one way or another a notion that nature is evil; or that evil is at least rooted in nature. The essential point is that as evil has roots in nature, so it has rights in nature. Wrong has as much right to exist as right. As already stated, this notion took many forms. Sometimes it was a dualism, which made evil an equal partner with good; so that neither could be called a usurper. More often it was a general idea that demons had made the material world; and if there were any good spirits, they were concerned only with the spiritual world. Later, again, it took the form of Calvinism, which held that God had indeed made the world, but in a special sense, made the evil as well as the good: had made an evil will as well as an evil world. On this view, if a man chooses to damn his soul alive, he is not thwarting God's will, but rather fulfilling it. In these two forms of the early Gnosticism and the later Calvinism, we see the superficial variety and fundamental unity of Manichæism. The old Manicheans taught that Satan originated the whole work of creation commonly attributed to God. The new Calvinists taught that God originated the whole work of damnation commonly attributed to Satan. One looked back to the first day when a devil acted like a god; the other looked forward to a last day when a god acted like a devil. But both had the idea that the creator of the earth was primarily the creator of the evil, whether we call him a devil or a god.

Since there are a good many Manicheans among the Moderns, as we may remark in a moment, some may agree with this view; some may be puzzled about it; some may only be puzzled about why we should object to it. To understand the mediæval controversy, a word must be said of the Catholic doctrine, which is as modern as it is mediæval. That 'God looked on all things and saw that they were good' contains a subtlety which the popular pessimist cannot follow; or is too hasty to notice. It is the thesis that there are no bad things; but only bad uses of things. If you will, there are no bad things but only bad thoughts; and especially bad intentions. Only Calvinists can really believe that hell is paved with good intentions. That is exactly the one thing it cannot be paved with. But it is possible to have bad intentions about good things; and good things, like the world and the flesh, have been twisted by a bad intention called the devil. But he cannot make *things* bad; they remain as on the first day of creation. The work of heaven alone was material; the making of a material world. The work of hell is entirely spiritual.

This error then had many forms; but especially, like nearly every error, it had two forms; a fiercer one which was outside the Church and attacking the Church, and a subtler one, which was inside the Church and corrupting the Church. There has never been a time when the Church was not torn between that invasion and that treason. It was so, for instance, in the Victorian time. Darwinian 'competition', in commerce or race-conflict, was every bit as brazen an atheist assault in the nineteenth century, as the Bolshevist No-God movement in the twentieth century. To brag of brute prosperity, to admire the most muddy millionaires who had cornered wheat by a trick, to talk about the 'unfit' (in imitation of the scientific thinker who would finish them off because he cannot even finish his own sentence—unfit for what?) all that is as simply and openly Anti-Christian as the Black Mass. Yet some weak and worldly Catholics did use this cant in defence of Capitalism, in their first rather feeble resistance to Socialism. At least they did, until the great Encyclical of the Pope on the Rights of Labour put a stop to all their nonsense. The evil is always both within and without the Church; but in a wilder form outside and a milder form inside. So it was again in the seventeenth century, when there was Calvinism outside and Jansenism inside. And so it was in the thirteenth century, when the obvious danger outside was in the revolution of the Albigensians; but the potential danger inside was in the very traditionalism of the Augustinians. For the Augustinians derived only from Augustine; and Augustine derived partly from Plato; and Plato was right, but not quite right. It is a mathematical fact that if a line be not perfectly directed towards a point, it will actually go further away from it as it comes nearer to it. After a thousand years of extension, the miscalculation of Platonism had come very near to Manichæism.

Popular errors are nearly always right. They nearly always refer to some ultimate reality, about which those who correct them are themselves incorrect. It is a very queer thing that 'Platonic Love' has come to mean for the unlettered something rather purer and cleaner than it means for the learned.

Yet even those who realise the great Greek evil may well realise that perversity often comes out of the wrong sort of purity. Now it was the inmost lie of the Manichees that they identified purity with sterility. It is singularly contrasted with the language of St Thomas, which always connects purity with fruitfulness; whether it be natural or supernatural. And, queerly enough, as I have said, there does remain a sort of reality in the vulgar colloquialism that the affair between Sam and Susan is 'quite platonic'. It is true that, quite apart from the local perversion, there was in Plato a sort of idea that people would be better without their bodies; that their heads might fly off and meet in the sky in merely intellectual marriage, like cherubs in a picture. The ultimate phase of this 'Platonic' philosophy was what inflamed poor D. H. Lawrence into talking nonsense, and he was probably unaware that the Catholic doctrine of marriage would say much of what he said, without talking nonsense. Anyhow, it is historically important to see that Platonic love did somewhat distort both human and divine love, in the theory of the early theologians. Many mediæval men, who would indignantly deny the Albigensian doctrine of sterility, were yet in an emotional mood to abandon the body in despair; and some of them to abandon everything in despair.

In truth, this vividly illuminates the provincial stupidity of those who object to what they call 'creeds and dogmas'. It was precisely the creed and dogma that saved the sanity of the world. These people generally propose an alternative religion of intuition and feeling. If, in the really Dark Ages, there had been a religion of feeling, it would have been a religion of black and suicidal feeling. It was the rigid creed that resisted the rush of suicidal feeling. The critics of asceticism are probably right in supposing that many a Western hermit did *feel* rather like an Eastern fakir. But he could not really *think* like an Eastern fakir; because he was an orthodox Catholic. And what kept his thought in touch with healthier and more humanistic thought was simply and solely the Dogma. He could not deny that a good God had created the normal and natural world; he could not say that the devil had made the world; because he was not a Manichee. A thousand enthusiasts for celibacy, in the day of the great rush to the desert or the cloister, might have called marriage a sin, if they had only considered their individual ideals, in the modern manner, and their own immediate feelings about marriage. Fortunately, they had to accept the Authority of the Church, which had definitely said that marriage was not a sin. A modern emotional religion might at any moment have turned Catholicism into Manichæism. But when Religion would have maddened men, Theology kept them sane.

In this sense St Thomas stands up simply as the great orthodox theologian, who reminded men of the creed of Creation, when many of them were still in the mood of mere destruction. It is futile for the critics of mediævalism to quote a hundred mediæval phrases that may be supposed to sound like mere pessimism, if they will not understand the central fact; that mediæval men did not care about being mediæval and did not accept the authority of a mood, because it was melancholy, but did care very much about orthodoxy, which is not a mood. It was because St Thomas could *prove* that his glorification of the Creator and His creative joy was more orthodox than any atmospheric pessimism, that he dominated the Church and the world, which accepted that truth as a test. But when this immense and impersonal importance is allowed for, we may agree that there was a personal element as well. Like most of the great religious teachers, he was fitted individually for the task that God had given him to do. We can if we like call that talent instinctive; we can even descend to calling it temperamental.

Anybody trying to popularise a mediæval philosopher must use language that is very modern and very unphilosophical. Nor is this a sneer at modernity; it arises from the moderns having dealt so much in moods and emotions, especially in the arts, that they have developed a large but loose vocabulary, which deals more with atmosphere than with actual attitude or position. As noted elsewhere, even the modern philosophers are more like the modern poets; in giving an individual tinge even to truth, and often looking at all life through different coloured spectacles. To say that Schopenhauer had the blues, or that William James had a rather rosier outlook, would often convey more than calling the one a Pessimist or the other a Pragmatist. This modern moodiness has its value, though the moderns overrate it; just as mediæval logic had its value, though it was overrated in the later Middle Ages. But the point is that to explain the mediævals to the moderns, we must often use this modern language of mood. Otherwise the character will be missed, through certain prejudices and ignorances about all such mediæval characters. Now there is something that lies all over the work of St Thomas Aquinas like a great light; which is something quite primary and perhaps unconscious with him, which he would perhaps have passed over as an irrelevant personal quality, and which can now only be expressed by a rather cheap journalistic term which he would probably have thought quite senseless.

Nevertheless, the only working word for that atmosphere is Optimism. I know that the word is now even more degraded in the twentieth century than it was in the nineteenth century. Men talked lately of being Optimists about the issue of War; they talk now of being Optimists about the revival of Trade; they may talk tomorrow of being Optimists about the International Ping-pong Tournament. But men in the Victorian time did mean a little more than that, when they used the word Optimist of Browning or Stevenson or Walt Whitman. And in a rather larger and more luminous sense than in the case of these men, the term was basically true of Thomas Aquinas. He did, with a most solid and colossal conviction, believe in Life; and in something like what Stevenson called the great theorem of the livableness of life. It breathes somehow in his very first phrases about the reality of Being. If the morbid Renaissance intellecual is supposed to say, 'To be or not to be—that is the question', then the massive mediæval doctor does most certainly reply in a voice of thunder, 'To be—that is the answer.'

The point is important; many not unnaturally talk of the Renaissance as the time when certain men began to believe in Life. The truth is that it was the time when a few men, for the first time, began to disbelieve in Life. The mediævals had put many restrictions, and some excessive restrictions, upon the universal human hunger and even fury for Life. Those restrictions had often been expressed in fanatical and rabid terms; the terms of those resisting a great natural force; the force of men who desired to live. Never until modern thought began, did they really have to fight with men who desired to die. That horror had threatened them in Asiatic Albigensianism, but it never became normal to them—until now.

But this fact becomes very vivid indeed, when we compare the greatest of Christian philosophers with the only men who were anything like his equals, or capable of being his rivals. They were people with whom he did not directly dispute; most of them he had never seen; some of them he had never heard of. Plato and Augustine were the only two with whom he could confer as he did with Bonaventure or even Averrhoes. But we must look elsewhere for his real rivals; and the only real rivals of the Catholic theory. They are the heads of the great heathen systems; some of them very ancient, some very modern, like Buddha on the one hand or Nietzsche on the other. It is when we see his gigantic figure against this vast and cosmic background, that we realise: first, that he was the only optimist theologian; and second, that Catholicism is the only optimist theology. Something milder and more amiable may be made out of the deliquescence of theology, and the mixture of the creed with everything that contradicts it; but among consistent cosmic creeds, this is the only one that is entirely on the side of Life.

Comparative religion has indeed allowed us to compare religions—and to contrast them. Fifty years ago, it set out to prove that all religions were much the same; generally proving, alternately, that they were all equally worthy and that they were all equally worthless. Since then this scientific process has suddenly begun to be scientific, and discovered the depths of the chasms as well as the heights of the hills. It is indeed an excellent improvement that sincerely religious people should respect each other. But respect has discovered difference, where contempt knew only indifference. The more we really appreciate the noble revulsion and renunciation of Buddha, the more we see that intellectually it was the converse and almost the contrary of the salvation of the world by Christ. The Christian would escape from the world into the universe; the Buddhist wishes to escape from the universe even more than from the world. One would uncreate himself; the other would return to his Creation: to his Creator. Indeed, it was so genuinely the converse of the idea of the Cross as the Tree of Life, that there is some excuse for setting up the two things side by side, as if they were of equal significance. They are in one sense parallel and equal; as a mound and a hollow, as a valley and a hill. There is a sense in which that sublime despair is the only alternative to that divine audacity. It is even true that the truly spiritual and intellectual man sees it as a sort of dilemma; a very hard and terrible choice. There is little else on earth that can compare with these for completeness. And he who will not climb the mountain of Christ does indeed fall into the abyss of Buddha.

The same is true, in a less lucid and dignified fashion, of most other alternatives of heathen humanity; nearly all are sucked back into that whirlpool of recurrence which all the ancients knew. Nearly all return to the one idea of returning. That is, what Buddha described so darkly as the Sorrowful Wheel. It is true that the sort of recurrence which Buddha described as the Sorrowful Wheel, poor Nietzsche actually managed to describe as the Joyful Wisdom. I can only say that if bare repetition was his idea of Joyful Wisdom, I should be curious to know what was his idea of Sorrowful Wisdom. But as a fact, in the case of Nietzsche, this did not belong to the moment of his breaking out, but to the moment of his breaking down. It came at the end of his life, when he was near to mental collapse; and it is really quite contrary to his earlier and finer inspirations of wild freedom or fresh and creative innovation. Once at least he had tried to break out; but he also was only broken—on the wheel.

Alone upon the earth, and lifted and liberated from all the wheels and whirlpools of the earth, stands up the faith of St Thomas; weighted and balanced indeed with more than Oriental metaphysics and more than Pagan pomp and pageantry; but vitally and vividly alone in declaring that life is a living story, with a great beginning and a great close; rooted in the primeval joy of God and finding its fruition in the final happiness of humanity; opening with the colossal chorus in which the sons of God shouted for joy, and ending in that mystical comradeship, shown in a shadowy fashion in those ancient words that move like an archaic dance; 'For His delight is with the sons of men'.

It is the fate of this sketch to be sketchy about philosophy, scanty or rather empty about theology, and to achieve little more than a decent silence on the subject of sanctity. And yet it must none the less be the recurrent burden of this little book, to which it must return with some monotony, that in this story the philosophy did depend on the theology, and the theology did depend on the sanctity. In other words, it must repeat the first fact, which was emphasised in the first chapter: that this great intellectual creation was a Christian and Catholic creation, and cannot be understood as anything else. It was Aquinas who baptised Aristotle, when Aristotle could not have baptised Aquinas; it was a purely Christian miracle which raised the great pagan from the dead. And this is proved in three ways (as St Thomas himself might say), which it will be well to summarise as a sort of summary of this book.

First, in the life of St Thomas, it is proved in the fact that only his huge and solid orthodoxy could have supported so many things which then seemed to be unorthodox. Charity covers a multitude of sins; and in that sense orthodoxy covers a multitude of heresies; or things which are hastily mistaken for heresies. It was precisely because his personal Catholicism was so convincing, that his impersonal Aristotelianism was given the benefit of the doubt. He did not smell of the faggot because he did smell of the firebrand; of the firebrand he had so instantly and instinctively snatched up, under a real assault on essential Catholic ethics. A typically cynical modern phrase refers to the man who is so good that he is good for nothing. St Thomas was so good that he was good for everything; that his warrant held good for what others considered the most wild and daring speculations, ending in the worship of nothing. Whether or no he baptised Aristotle, he was truly the godfather of Aristotle; he was his sponsor; he swore that the old Greek would do no harm; and the whole world trusted his word.

Second, in the philosophy of St Thomas, it is proved by the fact that everything depended on the new Christian *motive* for the study of facts, as distinct from truths. The Thomist philosophy began with the lowest roots of thought, the senses and the truisms of the reason; and a Pagan sage might have scorned such things, as he scorned the servile arts. But the materialism, which is merely cynicism in a Pagan, can be Christian humility in a Christian. St Thomas was willing to begin by recording the facts and sensations of the material world, just as he would have been willing to begin by washing up the plates and dishes in the monastery. The point of his Aristotelianism was that even if common sense about concrete things really was a sort of servile labour, he must not be ashamed to be *servus servorum Dei*. Among heathens the mere sceptic might become the mere cynic; Diogenes in his tub had always a touch of the tub-thumper; but even the dirt of the cynics was dignified into dust and ashes among the saints. If we miss that, we miss the whole meaning of the greatest revolution in history. There was a new *motive* for beginning with the most material, and even with the meanest things.

Third, in the theology of St Thomas, it is proved by the tremendous truth that supports all that theology; or any other Christian theology. There really was a new reason for regarding the senses, and the sensations of the body, and the experiences of the common man, with a reverence at which great Aristotle would have stared, and no man in the ancient world could have begun to understand. The Body was no longer what it was when Plato and Porphyry and the old mystics had left it for dead. It had hung upon a gibbet. It had risen from a tomb. It was no longer possible for the soul to despise the senses, which had been the organs of something that was more than man. Plato might despise the flesh; but God had not despised it. The senses had truly become sanctified; as they are blessed one by one at a Catholic baptism. 'Seeing is believing' was no longer the platitude of a mere idiot, or common individual, as in Plato's world; it was mixed up with real conditions of real belief. Those revolving mirrors that send messages to the brain of man, that light that breaks upon the brain, these had truly revealed to God himself the path to Bethany or the light on the high rock of Jerusalem. These ears that resound with common noises had reported also to the secret knowledge of God the noise of the crowd that strewed palms and the crowd that cried for Crucifixion. After the Incarnation had become the idea that is central in our civilisation, it was inevitable that there should be a return to materialism; in the sense of the serious value of matter and the making of the body. When once Christ has risen, it was inevitable that Aristotle should rise again.

Those are three real reasons, and very sufficient reasons, for the general support given by the saint to a solid and objective philosophy. And yet there was something else, very vast and vague, to which I have tried to give a faint expression by the interposition of this chapter. It is difficult to express it fully, without the awful peril of being popular, or what the Modernists quite wrongly imagine to be popular; in short, passing from religion to religiosity. But there is a general tone and temper of Aquinas, which it is as difficult to avoid as daylight in a great house of windows. It is that *positive* position of his mind, which is filled and soaked as with sunshine, with the warmth of the wonder of created things. There is a certain private audacity, in his communion, by which men add to their private names the tremendous titles of the Trinity and the Redemption; so that some nun may be called 'of the Holy Ghost'; or a man bear such a burden as the title of St John of the Cross. In this sense, the man we study may specially be called St Thomas of the Creator.

The Arabs have a phrase about the hundred names of God; but they also inherit the tradition of a tremendous name unspeakable, because it expresses Being itself; dumb and yet dreadful as an instant inaudible shout; the proclamation of the Absolute. And perhaps no other man ever came so near to calling the Creator by His own name; which can only be written I Am.

# The Permanent Philosophy

It is a pity the word Anthropology has been degraded to the study of Anthropoids. It is now incurably associated with squabbles between pre-historic professors (in more senses than one) about whether a chip of stone is the tooth of a man or an ape; sometimes settled as in that famous case, when it was found to be the tooth of a pig. It is very right that there should be a purely physical science of such things; but the name commonly used might well, by analogy, have been dedicated to things not only wider and deeper, but rather more relevant. Just as, in America, the new Humanists have pointed out to the old Humanitarians that their humanitarianism has been largely concentrated on things that are *not* specially human, such as physical conditions, appetites, economic needs, environment and so on—so in practice those who are called Anthropologists have to narrow their minds to the materialistic things that are *not* notably anthropic. They have to hunt through history and pre-history something which emphatically is not *Homo Sapiens*, but is always in fact regarded as *Simius Insipiens*. *Homo Sapiens* can only be considered in relation to *Sapientia*; and only a book like that of St Thomas is really devoted to the intrinsic idea of *Sapientia*. In short, there ought to be a real study called Anthropology corresponding to Theology. In this sense St Thomas Aquinas, perhaps more than he is anything else, is a great Anthropologist.

I apologise for the opening words of this chapter to all those excellent and eminent men of science, who are engaged in the real study of humanity in its relation to biology. But I rather fancy that they will be the last to deny that there has been a somewhat disproportionate disposition, in popular science, to turn the study of human beings into the study of savages. And savagery is not history: it is either the beginning of history or the end of it. I suspect that the greatest scientists would agree that only too many professors have thus been lost in the bush or the jungle; professors who wanted to study anthro-pology and never got any further than anthropophagy. But I have a particular

St Thomas Aquinas, 1933

reason for prefacing this suggestion of a higher anthropology by an apology to any genuine biologists who might seem to be included, but are certainly not included, in a protest against cheap popular science. For the first thing to be said about St Thomas as an Anthropologist, is that he is really remarkably like the best sort of modern biological Anthropologists; of the sort who would call themselves Agnostics. This fact is so sharp and decisive a turning point in history, that the history really needs to be recalled and recorded.

St Thomas Aquinas closely resembles the great Professor Huxley, the Agnostic who invented the word Agnosticism. He is like him in his way of starting the argument, and he is unlike everybody else, before and after, until the Huxleyan age. He adopts almost literally the Huxleyan definition of the Agnostic method; 'To follow reason as far as it will go'; the only question is—where does it go? He lays down the almost startlingly modern or materialist statement; 'Everything that is in the intellect has been in the senses'. This is where he began, as much as any modern man of science, nay, as much as any modern materialist who can now hardly be called a man of science; at the very opposite end of inquiry from that of the mere mystic. The Platonists, or at least the Neo-Platonists, all tended to the view that the mind was lit entirely from within; St Thomas insisted that it was lit by five windows, that we call the windows of the senses. But he wanted the light from without to shine on what was within. He wanted to study the nature of Man, and not merely of such moss and mushrooms as he might see through the window, and which he valued as the first enlightening experience of man. And starting from this point, he proceeds to climb the House of Man, step by step and story by story, until he has come out on the highest tower and beheld the largest vision.

In other words, he is an Anthropologist, with a complete theory of Man, right or wrong. Now the modern Anthropologists, who called themselves Agnostics, completely failed to be Anthropologists at all. Under their limitations, they could not get a complete theory of Man, let alone a complete theory of Nature. They began by ruling out something which they called the Unknowable. The incomprehensibility was almost comprehensible, if we could really understand the Unknowable in the sense of the Ultimate. But it rapidly became apparent that all sorts of things were Unknowable, which were exactly the things that a man has got to know. It is necessary to know whether he is responsible or irresponsible, perfect or imperfect, perfectible or unperfectible, mortal or immortal, doomed or free: not in order to understand God, but in order to understand Man. Nothing that leaves these things under a cloud of religious doubt can possibly pretend to be a Science of Man; it shrinks from anthropology as completely as from theology. Has a man free will; or is his sense of choice an illusion? Has he a conscience, or has his conscience any authority; or is it only the prejudice of the tribal past?

Is there any real hope of settling these things by human reason; and has *that* any authority? Is he to regard death as final; and is he to regard miraculous help as possible? Now it is all nonsense to say that these are unknowable in any remote sense, like the distinction between the Cherubim and the Seraphim, or the Procession of the Holy Ghost. The Schoolmen may have shot too far beyond our limits in pursuing the Cherubim and Seraphim. But in asking whether a man can choose or whether a man will die, they were asking ordinary questions in natural history; like whether a cat can scratch or whether a dog can smell. Nothing calling itself a complete Science of Man can shirk them. And the great Agnostics did shirk them. They may have said they had no scientific evidence; in that case they failed to produce even a scientific hypothesis. What they generally did produce was a wildly unscientific contradiction. Most Monist moralists simply said that Man has no choice; but he must think and act heroically as if he had. Huxley made morality, and even Victorian morality, in the exact sense, supernatural. He said it had arbitrary rights above nature; a sort of theology without theism.

I do not know for certain why St Thomas was called the Angelic Doctor: whether it was that he had an angelic temper, or the intellectualism of an Angel; or whether there was a later legend that he concentrated on Angels— especially on the points of needles. If so, I do not quite understand how this idea arose; history has many examples of an irritating habit of labelling somebody in connection with something, as if he never did anything else. Who was it who began the inane habit of referring to Dr Johnson as 'our lexicographer'; as if he never did anything but write a dictionary? Why do most people insist on meeting the large and far-reaching mind of Pascal at its very narrowest point; the point at which it was sharpened into a spike by the spite of the Jansenists against the Jesuits? It is just possible, for all I know, that this labelling of Aquinas as a specialist was an obscure depreciation of him as a universalist. For that is a very common trick for the belittling of literary or scientific men. St Thomas must have made a certain number of enemies, though he hardly ever treated them as enemies. Unfortunately, good temper is sometimes more irritating than bad temper. And he had, after all, done a great deal of damage, as many mediæval men would have thought; and, what is more curious, a good deal of damage to both sides. He had been a revolutionist against Augustine and a traditionalist against Averrhoes. He might appear to some to have tried to wreck that ancient beauty of the City of God, which bore some resemblance to the Republic of Plato. He might appear to others to have inflicted a blow on the advancing and levelling forces of Islam, as dramatic as that of Godfrey storming Jerusalem. It is possible that these enemies, by way of damning with faint praise, talked about his very respectable little work on Angels; as a man might say that Darwin was really reliable when writing on coral insects, or that some of

Milton's Latin poems were very creditable indeed. But this is only a conjecture, and many other conjectures are possible. And I am disposed to think that St Thomas really was rather specially interested in the nature of Angels, for the same reason that made him even more interested in the nature of Men. It was a part of that strong personal interest in things subordinate and semi-dependent, which runs through his whole system; a hierarchy of higher and lower liberties. He was interested in the problem of the Angel, as he was interested in the problem of the Man, because it was a problem; and especially because it was a problem of an intermediate creature. I do not pretend to deal here with this mysterious quality, as he conceives it to exist in that inscrutable intellectual being, who is less than God but more than Man. But it was this quality of a link in the chain, or a rung in the ladder, which mainly concerned the theologian in developing his own particular theory of degrees. Above all, it is this which chiefly moves him when he finds so fascinating the central mystery of Man. And for him the point is always that Man is not a balloon going up into the sky, nor a mole burrowing merely in the earth; but rather a thing like a tree, whose roots are fed from the earth, while its highest branches seem to rise almost to the stars.

I have pointed out that mere modern free-thought has left everything in a fog, including itself. The assertion that thought is free led first to the denial that will is free; but even about that there was no real determination among the Determinists. In practice, they told men that they must treat their will as free though it was not free. In other words, Man must live a double life; which is exactly the old heresy of Siger of Brabant about the Double Mind. In other words, the nineteenth century left everything in chaos; and the importance of Thomism to the twentieth century is that it may give us back a cosmos. We can give here only the rudest sketch of how Aquinas, like the Agnostics, beginning in the cosmic cellars, yet climbed to the cosmic towers.

Without pretending to span within such limits the essential Thomist idea, I may be allowed to throw out a sort of rough version of the fundamental question, which I think I have known myself, consciously or unconsciously, since my childhood. When a child looks out of the nursery window and sees anything, say the green lawn of the garden, what does he actually know; or does he know anything? There are all sorts of nursery games of negative philosophy played round this question. A brilliant Victorian scientist delighted in declaring that the child does not see any grass at all; but only a sort of green mist reflected in a tiny mirror of the human eye. This piece of rationalism has always struck me as almost insanely irrational. If he is not sure of the existence of the grass, which he sees through the glass of a window, how on earth can he be sure of the existence of the retina, which he sees through the glass of a microscope? If sight deceives, why can it not go on deceiving? Men of another school answer that grass is a mere green impression on the mind; and that the child can be sure of nothing except the mind. They declare that he can only be conscious of his own consciousness; which happens to be the one thing that we know the child is not conscious of at all. In that sense, it would be far truer to say that there is grass and no child, than to say that there is a conscious child but no grass. St Thomas Aquinas, suddenly intervening in this nursery quarrel, says emphatically that the child is aware of *Ens*. Long before he knows that grass is grass, or self is self, he knows that something is something. Perhaps it would be best to say very emphatically (with a blow on the table), 'There *is* an Is'. That is as much monkish credulity as St Thomas asks of us at the start. Very few unbelievers start by asking us to believe so little. And yet, upon this sharp pinpoint of reality, he rears by long logical processes that have never really been success-fully overthrown, the whole cosmic system of Christendom.

Thus, Aquinas insists very profoundly, but very practically, that there *instantly* enters, with this idea of affirmation, the idea of contradiction. It is instantly apparent, even to the child, that there cannot be both affirmation and contradiction. Whatever you call the thing he sees, a lawn or a mirage or a sensation or a state of consciousness, when he sees it, he knows it is not true that he does not see it. Or whatever you call what he is supposed to be doing, seeing or dreaming or being conscious of an impression, he knows that if he is doing it, it is a lie to say he is not doing it. Therefore there has already entered *something* beyond even the first fact of being; there follows it like its shadow the first fundamental creed or commandment; that a thing cannot be and not be. Henceforth, in common or popular language, there is a false and true. I say in popular language, because Aquinas is nowhere more subtle than in pointing out that being is not strictly the same as truth; seeing truth must mean the appreciation of being by some mind capable of appreci-ating it. But in a general sense there has entered that primeval world of pure actuality, the division and dilemma that brings the ultimate sort of war into the world; the everlasting duel between Yes and No. This is the dilemma that many sceptics have darkened the universe and dissolved the mind, solely in order to escape. They are those who maintain that there is something that is both Yes and No. I do not know whether they pronounce it Yo.

The next step following on this acceptance of actuality or certainty, or whatever we call it in popular language, is much more difficult to explain in that language. But it represents exactly the point at which nearly all other systems go wrong; and in taking the third step abandon the first. Aquinas has affirmed that our first sense of fact is a fact; and he cannot go back on it without falsehood. But when we come to look at the fact or facts, as we know them, we observe that they have a rather queer character, which has made many moderns grow strangely and restlessly sceptical about them. For instance, they are largely in a state of change, from being one thing to being another; or their qualities are relative to other things; or they appear to move incessantly; or they appear to vanish entirely. At this point, as I say, many sages lose hold of the first principle of reality, which they would concede at first; and fall back on saying that there is nothing except change; or nothing except comparison; or nothing except flux; or in effect that there is nothing at all. Aquinas turns the whole argument the other way, keeping in line with his first realisation of reality. There is no doubt about the being of being, even if it does sometimes look like becoming; that is because what we see is not the fullness of being; or (to continue a sort of colloquial slang) we never see being being as much as it can. Ice is melted into cold water and cold water is heated into hot water; it cannot be all three at once. But this does not make water unreal or even relative; it only means that its being is limited to being one thing at a time. But the fullness of being is everything that it can be; and without it the lesser or approximate forms of being cannot be explained as anything; unless they are explained away as nothing.

This crude outline can only at the best be historical rather than philosophical. It is impossible to compress into it the metaphysical proofs of such an idea; especially in the mediæval metaphysical language. But this distinction in philosophy is tremendous as a turning-point in history. Most thinkers, on realising the apparent mutability of being, have really forgotten their own realisation of the being, and believed only in the mutability. They cannot even say that a thing changes into another thing; for them there is no instant in the process at which it is a thing at all. It is only a change. It would be more logical to call it nothing changing into nothing, than to say (on these principles) that there ever was or will be a moment when the thing is itself. St Thomas maintains that the ordinary thing at any moment is something; but it is not everything that it could be. There is a fullness of being, in which it could be everything that it can be. Thus, while most sages come at last to nothing but naked change, he comes to the ultimate thing that is unchangeable, because it is all the other things at once. While they describe a change which is really a change in nothing, he describes a changelessness which includes the changes of everything. Things change because they are not complete; but their reality can only be explained as part of something that is complete. It is God.

Historically, at least, it was round this sharp and crooked corner that all the sophists have followed each other, while the great Schoolman went up the high road of experience and expansion; to the beholding of cities; to the building of cities. They all failed at this early stage because, in the words of the old game, they took away the number they first thought of. The recognition of something, of a thing or things, is the first act of the intellect. But because the examination of a thing shows it is not a fixed or final thing, they inferred that there is nothing fixed or final. Thus, in various ways, they all began to see a thing as something thinner than a thing; a wave; a weakness; an abstract instability. St Thomas, to use the same rude figure, saw a thing that was thicker than a thing; that was even more solid than the solid but secondary facts he had started by admitting as facts. Since we know them to be real, any elusive or bewildering element in their reality cannot really be unreality; and must be merely their relation to the real reality. A hundred human philosophies, ranging over the earth from Nominalism to Nirvana and Maya, from formless Evolutionism to mindless Quietism, all come from this first break in the Thomist chain; the notion that, because what we see does not satisfy us, or explain itself, it is not even what we see. That cosmos is a contradiction in terms and strangles itself; but Thomism cuts itself free. The defect we see, in what is, is simply that it is not all that is. God is more actual even than Man; more actual even than Matter; for God with all His powers at every instant is immortally in action.

A cosmic comedy of a very curious sort occurred recently; involving the views of very brilliant men, such as Mr Bernard Shaw and the Dean of St Paul's. Briefly, freethinkers of many sorts had often said they had no need of a Creation, because the cosmos had always existed and always would exist. Mr Bernard Shaw said he had become an atheist because the universe had gone on making itself from the beginning, or without a beginning; Dean Inge later displayed consternation at the very idea that the universe could have an end. Most modern Christians, living by tradition where mediæval Christians could live by logic or reason, vaguely felt that it was a dreadful idea to deprive them of the Day of Judgment. Most modern agnostics (who are delighted to have their ideas called dreadful) cried out all the more, with one accord, that the self-producing, self-existent, truly scientific universe had never needed to have a beginning and could not come to an end. At this very instant, quite suddenly, like the look-out man on a ship who shouts a warning about a rock, the *real* man of science, the expert who was examining the facts, announced in a loud voice that the universe *was* coming to an end. He had not been listening, of course, to the talk of the amateurs; he had been actually examining the texture of matter; and he said it was disintegrating; the world was apparently blowing itself up by a gradual explosion called energy; the whole business would certainly have an end and had presumably had a beginning. This was very shocking indeed; not to the orthodox, but rather specially to the unorthodox, who are rather more easily shocked. Dean Inge, who had been lecturing the orthodox for years on their stern duty of accepting all scientific discoveries, positively wailed aloud over this truly tactless scientific discovery; and practically implored the scientific discoverers to go away and discover something different. It seems almost incredible; but it is a fact that he asked what God would have to amuse Him, if the universe ceased. That is a measure of how much the modern mind needs Thomas Aquinas. But even without Aquinas, I can hardly conceive any educated man, let alone such a learned man, believing in God at all without assuming that God contains in Himself every perfection including eternal joy; and does not require the solar system to entertain Him like a circus.

To step out of these presumptions, prejudices and private disappointments, into the world of St Thomas, is like escaping from a scuffle in a dark room into the broad daylight. St Thomas says, quite straightforwardly, that he himself believes this world has a beginning and end; because such seems to be the teaching of the Church; the validity of which mystical message to mankind he defends elsewhere with dozens of quite different arguments. Anyhow, the Church said the world would end, and apparently the Church was right; always supposing (as we are always supposed to suppose) that the latest men of science are right. But Aquinas says he sees no particular reason, in reason, why this world should not be a world without end; or even without beginning. And he is quite certain that, if it were entirely without end or beginning, there would still be exactly the same logical need of a Creator. Anybody who does not see that, he gently implies, does not really understand what is meant by a Creator.

For what St Thomas means is not a mediæval picture of an old king; but this second step in the great argument about *Ens* or Being; the second point which is so desperately difficult to put correctly in popular language. That is why I have introduced it here in the particular form of the argument that there must be a Creator even if there is no Day of Creation. Looking at Being as it is now, as the baby looks at the grass, we see a second thing about it; in quite popular language, it *looks* secondary and dependent. Existence exists; but it is not sufficiently self-existent; and would never become so merely by going on existing. The same primary sense which tells us it is Being, tells us that it is not perfect Being; not merely imperfect in the popular controversial sense of containing sin or sorrow; but imperfect as Being; less actual than the actuality it implies. For instance, its Being is often only Becoming; beginning to Be or ceasing to Be; it implies a more constant or complete thing of which it gives in itself no example. That is the meaning of that basic mediæval phrase, 'Everything that is moving is moved by another'; which, in the clear subtlety of St Thomas, means inexpressibly more than the mere Deistic 'somebody wound up the clock' with which it is probably often confounded. Anyone who thinks deeply will see that motion has about it an essential incompleteness, which approximates to something more complete. The actual argument is rather technical; and concerns the fact that potentiality does not explain itself; moreover, in any case unfolding must be of something folded. Suffice it to say that the mere modern evolutionists, who would ignore the argument, do not do so because they have discovered any flaw in the argument; for they have never discovered the argument itself. They do so because they are too shallow to see the flaw in their own argument; for the weakness of their thesis is covered by fashionable phraseology, as the strength of the old thesis is covered by old-fashioned phraseology. But, for those who really think, there is always something really unthinkable about the whole evolutionary cosmos, as they conceive it; because it is something coming out of nothing; an ever-increasing flood of water pouring out of an empty jug. Those who can simply accept that, without even seeing the difficulty, are not likely to go so deep as Aquinas and see the solution of his difficulty. In a word, the world does not explain itself, and cannot do so merely by continuing to expand itself. But anyhow it is absurd for the Evolutionist to complain that it is unthinkable for an admittedly unthinkable God to make everything out of nothing; and then pretend that it is *more* thinkable that nothing should turn itself into everything.

We have seen that most philosophers simply fail to philosophise about things because they change; they also fail to philosophise about things because they differ. We have no space to follow St Thomas through all these negative heresies; but a word must be said about Nominalism, or the doubt founded on the things that differ. Everyone knows that the Nominalist declared that things differ too much to be really classified; so that they are only labelled. Aquinas was a firm but moderate Realist, and therefore held that there really are general qualities; as that human beings are human, and other paradoxes. To be an extreme Realist would have taken him too near to being a Platonist. He recognised that individuality is real, but said that it coexists with a common character making some generalisation possible; in fact, as in most things, he said exactly what all common sense would say, if no intelligent heretics had ever disturbed it. Nevertheless, they still continue to disturb it. I remember when Mr H. G. Wells had an alarming fit of Nominalist philosophy, and poured forth book after book to argue that everything is unique and untypical; as that a man is so much an individual that he is not even a man. It is a quaint and almost comic fact, that this chaotic negation especially attracts those who are always complaining of social chaos, and who propose to replace it by the most sweeping social regulations. It is the very men, who say that nothing can be classified, who say that everything must be codified. Thus Mr Bernard Shaw said that the only golden rule is that there is no golden rule. He prefers an iron rule; as in Russia.

But this is only a small inconsistency in some moderns as individuals. There is a much deeper inconsistency in them as theorists in relation to the general theory called Creative Evolution. They seem to imagine that they avoid the metaphysical doubt about mere change by assuming (it is not very clear why) that the change will always be for the better. But the mathematical difficulty of finding a corner in a curve is not altered by turning the chart upside down, and saying that a downward curve is now an upward curve. The point is that there is no point in the curve; no place at which we have a logical right to say that the curve has reached its climax, or revealed its origin, or come to its end. It makes no difference that they choose to be cheerful about it, and say, 'It is enough that there is always a beyond'; instead of lamenting, like the more realistic poets of the past, over the tragedy of mere Mutability. It is not enough that there is always a beyond; because it might be beyond bearing. Indeed the only defence of this view is that sheer boredom is such an agony, that any movement is a relief. But the truth is that they have never read St Thomas; or they would find, with no little terror, that they really agree with him. What they really mean is that change is not mere change, but is the unfolding of something; and if it is thus unfolded, though the unfolding takes twelve million years, it must be there already. In other words, they agree with Aquinas that there is everywhere potentiality that has not reached its end in act. But if it is a definite potentiality, and if it can only end in a definite act, why then there is a Great Being, in whom all potentialities already exist as a plan of action. In other words, it is impossible even to say that the change is for the better, unless the best exists somewhere, both before and after the change. Otherwise it is indeed mere change; as the blankest sceptics or the blackest pessimists would see it. Suppose two entirely new paths open before the progress of Creative Evolution. How is the evolutionist to know which Beyond is the better; unless he accepts from the past and present some standard of the best? By their superficial theory everything can change; everything can improve, even the nature of improvement. But in their submerged common sense, they do not really think that an ideal of kindness could change to an ideal of cruelty. It is typical of them that they will sometimes rather timidly use the word Purpose; but blush at the very mention of the word Person.

St Thomas is the very reverse of anthropomorphic, in spite of his shrewdness as an anthropologist. Some theologians have even claimed that he is too much of an agnostic; and has left the nature of God too much of an intellectual abstraction. But we do not need even St Thomas, we do not need anything but our own common sense, to tell us that if there has been from the beginning anything that can possibly be called a Purpose, it must reside in something that has the essential elements of a Person. There cannot be an intention hovering in the air all by itself, any more than a memory that nobody remembers or a joke that nobody has made. The only chance for those supporting such suggestions is to take refuge in blank and bottomless irrationality; and even then it is impossible to prove that anybody has any right to be unreasonable, if St Thomas has no right to be reasonable.

In a sketch that aims only at the baldest simplification, this does seem to me the simplest truth about St Thomas the philosopher. He is one, so to speak, who is faithful to his first love; and it is love at first sight. I mean that he immediately recognised a real quality in things; and afterwards resisted all the disintegrating doubts arising from the nature of those things. That is why I emphasise, even in the first few pages, the fact that there is a sort of purely Christian humility and fidelity underlying his philosophic realism. St Thomas could as truly say, of having seen merely a stick or a stone, what St Paul said of having seen the rending of the secret heavens, 'I was not disobedient to the heavenly vision'. For though the stick or the stone is an earthly vision, it is through them that St Thomas finds his way to heaven; and the point is that he is obedient to the vision; he does not go back on it. Nearly all the other sages who have led or misled mankind do, on one excuse or another, go back on it. They dissolve the stick or the stone in chemical solutions of scepticism; either in the medium of mere time and change; or in the difficulties of classification of unique units; or in the difficulty of recognising variety while admitting unity. The first of these three is called debate about flux or formless transition; the second is the debate about Nominalism and Realism, or the existence of general ideas; the third is called the ancient metaphysical riddle of the One and the Many. But they can all be reduced under a rough image to this same statement about St Thomas. He is still true to the first truth and refusing the first treason. He will not deny what he has seen, though it be a secondary and diverse reality. He will not take away the numbers he first thought of, though there may be quite a number of them.

He has seen grass; and will not say he has not seen grass, because it today is and tomorrow is cast into the oven. That is the substance of all scepticism about change, transition, transformism and the rest. He will not say that there is no grass but only growth. If grass grows and withers, it can only mean that it is part of a greater thing, which is even more real; not that the grass is less real than it looks. St Thomas has a really logical right to say, in the words of the modern mystic, A. E.: 'I begin by the grass to be bound again to the Lord.'

He has seen grass and grain; and he will not say that they do not differ, because there is something common to grass and grain. Nor will he say that, because there is something common to grass and grain, they do not really differ. He will not say, with the extreme Nominalists, that because grain can be differentiated into all sorts of fruitage, or grass trodden into mire with any kind of weed, therefore there can be no *classification* to distinguish weeds from slime or to draw a fine distinction between cattle-food and cattle. He will not say with the extreme Platonists, on the other hand, that he saw the perfect fruit in his own head by shutting his eyes, *before* he saw any difference between grain and grass. He saw one thing and then another thing, and then a common quality; but he does not really pretend that he saw the quality before the thing.

He has seen grass and gravel; that is to say, he has seen things really different; things not classified together like grass and grain. The first flash of fact shows us a world of really strange things; not merely strange to us, but strange to each other. The separate things need have nothing in common except Being. Everything is Being; but it is not true that everything is Unity. It is here, as I have said, that St Thomas does definitely, one might say defiantly, part company with the Pantheist and the Monist. All things are; but among the things that are is the thing called difference, quite as much as the thing called similarity. And here again we begin to be bound again to the Lord, not only by the universality of grass, but by the incompatibility of grass and gravel. For this world of different and varied beings is especially the world of the Christian Creator; the world of created things, like things made by an artist; as compared with the world that is only one thing, with a sort of shimmering and shifting veil of misleading change, which is the conception of so many of the ancient religions of Asia and the modern sophistries of Germany. In the face of these, St Thomas still stands stubborn in the same obstinate objective fidelity. He has seen grass and gravel; and he is not disobedient to the heavenly vision.

To sum up; the reality of things, the mutability of things, the diversity of things, and all other such things that can be attributed to things, is followed carefully by the mediæval philosopher, without losing touch with the original point of the reality. There is no space in this book to specify the thousand steps of thought, by which he shows that he is right. But the point is that, even apart from being right, he is real. He is a realist in a rather curious sense of his own, which is a third thing, distinct from the almost contrary mediæval and modern meanings of the word. Even the doubts and difficulties about reality have driven him to believe in more reality rather than less. The *deceitfulness* of things which has had so sad an effect on so many sages, has almost a contrary effect on this sage. If things deceive us, it is by being more real than they seem. As ends in themselves they always deceive us; but as things tending to a greater end, they are even more real than we think them. If they seem to have a relative unreality (so to speak) it is because they are potential and not actual; they are unfulfilled, like packets of seeds or boxes of fireworks. They have it in them to be more real than they are. And there is an upper world of what the Schoolman called Fruition, or Fulfilment, in which all this relative relativity becomes actuality; in which the trees burst into flower or the rockets into flame.

Here I leave the reader, on the very lowest rung of those ladders of logic, by which St Thomas besieged and mounted the House of Man. It is enough to say that by arguments as honest and laborious, he climbed up to the turrets and talked with angels on the roofs of gold. This is, in a very rude outline, his philosophy; it is impossible in such an outline to describe his theology. Anyone writing so small a book about so big a man, must leave out something. Those who know him best will best understand why, after some considerable consideration, I have left out the only important thing.

# The Sequel to St Thomas

It is often said that St Thomas, unlike St Francis, did not permit in his work the indescribable element of poetry. As, for instance, that there is little reference to any pleasure in the actual flowers and fruit of natural things, though any amount of concern with the buried roots of nature. And yet I confess that, in reading his philosophy, I have a very peculiar and powerful impression analogous to poetry. Curiously enough, it is in some ways more analogous to painting, and reminds me very much of the effect produced by the *best* of the modern painters, when they throw a strange and almost crude light upon stark and rectangular objects, or seem to be groping for rather than grasping the very pillars of the subconscious mind. It is probably because there is in his work a quality which is Primitive, in the best sense of a badly misused word; but anyhow, the pleasure is definitely not only of the reason, but also of the imagination.

Perhaps the impression is connected with the fact that painters deal with things without words. An artist draws quite gravely the grand curves of a pig; because he is not thinking of the *word* pig. There is no thinker who is so unmistakably thinking about things, and not being misled by the indirect influence of words, as St Thomas Aquinas. It is true in that sense that he has not the advantage of words, any more than the disadvantage of words. Here he differs sharply, for instance, from St Augustine, who was, among other things, a wit. He was also a sort of prose poet, with a power over words in their atmospheric and emotional aspect; so that his books abound with beautiful passages that rise in the memory like strains of music; the *illi in vos saeviant*; or the unforgettable cry, 'Late I have loved thee, O Ancient Beauty!' It is true that there is little or nothing of this kind in St Thomas; but if he was without the higher uses of the mere magic of words, he was also free from that abuse of it, by mere sentimentalists or self-centred artists, which can become merely morbid and a very black magic indeed. And truly it is by some such comparison with the purely introspective intellectual, that we may

St Thomas Aquinas, 1933

471

find a hint about the real nature of the thing I describe, or rather fail to describe; I mean the elemental and primitive poetry that shines through all his thoughts, and especially through the thought with which all his thinking begins. It is the intense rightness of his sense of the relation between the mind and the real thing outside the mind.

That *strangeness* of things, which is the light in all poetry, and indeed in all art, is really connected with their otherness, or what is called their objectivity. What is subjective must be stale; it is exactly what is objective that is in this imaginative manner strange. In this the great contemplative is the complete contrary of that false contemplative, the mystic who looks only into his own soul, the selfish artist who shrinks from the world and lives only in his own mind. According to St Thomas, the mind acts freely of itself, but its freedom exactly consists in finding a way out to liberty and the light of day; to reality and the land of the living. In the subjectivist, the pressure of the world forces the imagination inwards. In the Thomist, the energy of the mind forces the imagination outwards, but because the images it seeks are real things. All their romance and glamour, so to speak, lie in the fact that they are real things; things *not* to be found by staring inwards at the mind. The flower is a vision because it is not only a vision. Or, if you will, it is a vision because it is not a dream. This is for the poet the strangeness of stones and trees and solid things; they are strange because they are solid. I am putting it first in the poetical manner, and indeed it needs much more technical subtlety to put it in the philosophical manner. According to Aquinas, the object becomes a part of the mind; nay, according to Aquinas, the mind actually becomes the object. But, as one commentator acutely puts it, it only becomes the object and does not create the object. In other words, the object *is* an object; it can and does exist outside the mind, or in the absence of the mind. And *therefore* it enlarges the mind of which it becomes a part. The mind conquers a new province like an emperor; but only because the mind has answered the bell like a servant. The mind has opened the doors and windows, because it is the natural activity of what is inside the house to find out what is outside the house. If the mind is sufficient to itself, it is insufficient for itself. For this feeding upon fact *is* itself; as an organ it has an object which is objective; this eating of the strange strong meat of reality.

Note how this view avoids both pitfalls; the alternative abysses of impotence. The mind is not merely receptive, in the sense that it absorbs sensations like so much blotting-paper; on that sort of softness has been based all that cowardly materialism, which conceives man as wholly servile to his environment. On the other hand, the mind is not purely creative, in the sense that it paints pictures on the windows and then mistakes them for a landscape outside. But the mind is active, and its activity consists in following, so far as the will chooses to follow, the light outside that does really shine upon real landscapes. That is what gives the indefinably virile and even adventurous quality to this view of life; as compared with that which holds that material influences pour in upon an utterly helpless mind, or that which holds that psychological influences pour out and create an entirely baseless phantasmagoria. In other words, the essence of the Thomist common sense is that two agencies are at work; reality and the recognition of reality; and their meeting is a sort of marriage. Indeed it is very truly a marriage, because it is fruitful; the only philosophy now in the world that really is fruitful. It produces practical results, precisely because it is the combination of an adventurous mind and a strange fact. M. Maritain has used an admirable metaphor, in his book *Theonas*, when he says that the external fact *fertilises* the internal intelligence, as the bee fertilises the flower. Anyhow, upon that marriage, or whatever it may be called, the whole system of St Thomas is founded; God made Man so that he was capable of coming in contact with reality; and those whom God hath joined, let no man put asunder.

Now, it is worthy of remark that it is the only working philosophy. Of nearly all other philosophies it is strictly true that their followers work in spite of them; or do not work at all. No sceptics work sceptically; no fatalists work fatalistically; all without exception work on the principle that it is possible to assume what it is not possible to believe. No materialist who thinks his mind was made up for him, by mud and blood and heredity, has any hesitation in making up his mind. No sceptic who believes that truth is subjective has any hesitation about treating it as objective.

Therefore his work has a constructive quality absent from almost all cosmic systems after him. For he is already building a house, while the newer speculators are still at the stage of testing the rungs of a ladder, demonstrating the hopeless softness of the unbaked bricks, chemically analysing the spirit in the spirit-level, and generally quarrelling about whether they can even make the tools that will make the house. Aquinas is whole intellectual æons ahead of them, over and above the common chronological sense of saying a man is in advance of his age; he is ages in advance of our age. For he has thrown out a bridge across the abyss of the first doubt, and found reality beyond and begun to build on it. Most modern philosophies are not philosophy but philosophic doubt; that is, doubt about whether there can be any philosophy. If we accept St Thomas's fundamental act or argument in the acceptance of reality, the further deductions from it will be equally real; they will be things and not words. Unlike Kant and most of the Hegelians, he has a faith that is not merely a doubt about doubt. It is not merely what is commonly called a faith about faith; it is a faith about fact. From this point he can go forward, and deduce and develop and decide, like a man planning a city and sitting in a judgment-seat. But never since that time has any thinking man of that eminence thought that there is any real evidence for anything, not even the evidence of his senses, that was strong enough to bear the weight of a definite deduction.

From all this we may easily infer that this philosopher does not merely touch on social things, or even take them in his stride to spiritual things; though that is always his direction. He takes hold of them, he has not only a grasp of them, but a grip. As all his controversies prove, he was perhaps a perfect example of the iron hand in the velvet glove. He was a man who always turned his full attention to anything; and he seems to fix even passing things as they pass. To him even what was momentary was momentous. The reader feels that any small point of economic habit or human accident is for the moment almost scorched under the converging rays of a magnifying lens. It is impossible to put in these pages a thousandth part of the decisions on details of life that may be found in his work; it would be like reprinting the law-reports of an incredible century of just judges and sensible magistrates. We can only touch on one or two obvious topics of this kind.

I have noted the need to use modern atmospheric words for certain ancient atmospheric things; as in saying that St Thomas was what most modern men vaguely mean by an Optimist. In the same way, he was very much what they vaguely mean by a Liberal. I do not mean that any of his thousand political suggestions would suit any such definite political creed; if there are nowadays any definite political creeds. I mean, in the same sense, that he has a sort of atmosphere of believing in breadth and balance and debate. He may not be a Liberal by the extreme demands of the moderns, for we seem always to mean by the moderns the men of the last century, rather than this. He was very much of a Liberal compared with the most modern of all moderns; for they are nearly all of them turning into Fascists and Hitlerites. But the point is that he obviously preferred the sort of decisions that are reached by deliberation rather than despotic action; and while, like all his contemporaries and co-religionists, he has no doubt that true authority may be authoritative, he is rather averse to the whole savour of its being arbitrary. He is much less of an Imperialist than Dante, and even his Papalism is not very Imperial. He is very fond of phrases like 'a mob of free men' as the essential material of a city; and he is emphatic upon the fact that law, when it ceases to be justice, ceases even to be law.

If this work were controversial, whole chapters could be given to the economics as well as to the ethics of the Thomist system. It would be easy to show that, in this matter, he was a prophet as well as a philosopher. He foresaw from the first the peril of that mere reliance on trade and exchange, which was beginning about his time; and which has culminated in a universal commercial collapse in our time. He did not merely assert that Usury is unnatural, though in saying that he only followed Aristotle and obvious common sense, which was never contradicted by anybody until the time of the commercialists, who have involved us in the collapse. The modern world began by Bentham writing the Defence of Usury, and it has ended after a hundred years in even the vulgar newspaper opinion finding Finance indefensible. But St Thomas struck much deeper than that. He even mentioned the truth, ignored during the long idolatry of trade, that things which men produce only to sell are likely to be worse in quality than the things they produce in order to consume. Something of our difficulty about the fine shades of Latin will be felt when we come to his statement that there is always a certain *inhonestas* about trade. For *inhonestas* does not exactly mean dishonesty. It means approximately 'something unworthy,' or, more nearly perhaps, 'something not quite handsome.' And he was right; for trade, in the modern sense, does mean selling something for a little more than it is worth, nor would the nineteenth century economists have denied it. They would only have said that he was not practical; and this seemed sound while their view led to practical prosperity. Things are a little different now that it has led to universal bankruptcy.

Here, however, we collide with a colossal paradox of history. The Thomist philosophy and theology, quite fairly compared with other philosophies like the Buddhist or the Monist, with other theologies like the Calvinist or the Christian Scientist, is quite obviously a working and even a fighting system; full of common sense and constructive confidence, and therefore normally full of hope and promise. Nor is this hope vain or this promise unfulfilled. In this not very hopeful modern moment, there are no men so hopeful as those who are today looking to St Thomas as a leader in a hundred crying questions of craftsmanship and ownership and economic ethics. There is undoubtedly a hopeful and creative Thomism in our time. But we are none the less puzzled by the fact that this did not immediately follow on St Thomas's time. It is true that there was a great march of progress in the thirteenth century; and in some things, such as the status of the peasant, matters had greatly improved by the end of the Middle Ages. But nobody can honestly say that Scholasticism had greatly improved by the end of the Middle Ages. Nobody can tell how far the popular spirit of the Friars had helped the later popular mediæval movements; or how far this great Friar, with his luminous rules of justice and his lifelong sympathy with the poor, may have indirectly contributed to the improvement that certainly occurred. But those who followed his method, as distinct from his moral spirit, degenerated with a strange rapidity; and it was certainly not in the Scholastics that the improvement occurred. Of some of the Scholastics we can only say that they took everything that was worst in Scholasticism and made it worse. They continued to count the steps of logic; but every step of logic took them further from common sense. They forgot how St Thomas had started almost as an agnostic; and they seemed resolved to leave nothing in heaven or hell about which anybody could be agnostic. They were a sort of rabid rationalist, who would have left no mysteries in the Faith at all. In the earliest Scholasticism there is something that strikes a modern as fanciful and pedantic; but, properly understood, it has a fine spirit in its fancy. It is the spirit of freedom; and especially the spirit of free will. Nothing seems more quaint, for instance, than the speculations about what would have happened to every vegetable or animal or angel, if Eve had chosen *not* to eat the fruit of the tree. But this was originally full of the thrill of choice; and the feeling that she might have chosen otherwise. It was this detailed detective method that was followed, without the thrill of the original detective story. The world was cumbered with countless tomes, proving by logic a thousand things that can be known only to God. They developed all that was really sterile in Scholasticism; and left for us all that is really fruitful in Thomism.

There are many historical explanations. There is the Black Death, which broke the back of the Middle Ages; the consequent decline in clerical culture, which did so much to provoke the Reformation. But I suspect that there was another cause also; which can only be stated by saying that the contemporary fanatics, who controverted with Aquinas, left their own school behind them; and in a sense that school triumphed after all. The really narrow Augustinians, the men who saw the Christian life only as the narrow way, the men who could not even comprehend the great Dominican's exultation in the blaze of Being, or the glory of God in all his creatures, the men who continued to insist feverishly on every text, or even on every truth, that appeared pessimistic or paralysing, these gloomy Christians could not be extirpated from Christendom; and they remained and waited for their chance. The narrow Augustinians, the men who would have no science or reason or rational use of secular things, might have been defeated in controversy, but they had an accumulated passion of conviction. There was an Augustinian monastery in the North where it was near to explosion.

Thomas Aquinas had struck his blow; but he had not entirely settled the Manichees. The Manichees are not so easily settled; in the sense of settled for ever. He had insured that the main outline of the Christianity that has come down to us should be supernatural but not anti-natural; and should never be darkened with a false spirituality to the oblivion of the Creator and the Christ who was made Man. But as his tradition trailed away into less liberal or less creative habits of thought, and as his mediæval society fell away and decayed through other causes, the thing against which he had made war crept back into Christendom. A certain spirit or element in the Christian religion, necessary and sometimes noble but always needing to be balanced by more gentle and generous elements in the Faith, began once more to strengthen as the framework of Scholasticism stiffened or split. The Fear of the Lord, that is the beginning of wisdom, and therefore belongs to the beginnings, and is felt in the first cold hours before the dawn of civilisation; the power that comes out of the wilderness and rides on the whirlwind and breaks the gods of stone; the power before which the Eastern nations are prostrate like a pavement; the power before which the primitive prophets run naked and shouting, at once proclaiming and escaping from their god; the fear that is rightly rooted in the beginnings of every religion, true or false: the fear of the Lord, that is the beginning of wisdom; but not the end.

It is often remarked, as showing the ironical indifference of rulers to revolutions, and especially the frivolity of those who are called the Pagan Popes of the Renaissance, in their attitude to the Reformation, that when the Pope first heard of the first movements of Protestantism, which had started in Germany, he only said in an offhand manner that it was 'some quarrel of monks.' Every Pope of course was accustomed to quarrels among the monastic orders; but it has always been noted as a strange and almost uncanny negligence, that he could see no more than this in the beginnings of the great sixteenth century schism. And yet, in a somewhat more recondite sense, there is something to be said for what he has been blamed for saying. In one sense, the schismatics had a sort of spiritual ancestry even in medi-æval times. It will be found earlier in this book; and it *was* a quarrel of monks. We have seen how the great name of Augustine, a name never mentioned by Aquinas without respect, but often mentioned without agree-ment, covered an Augustinian school of thought naturally lingering longest in the Augustinian Order. The difference, like every difference between Catholics, was only a difference of emphasis. The Augustinians stressed the idea of the impotence of man before God, the omniscience of God about the destiny of man, the need for holy fear and the humiliation of intellectual pride, more than the opposite and corresponding truths of free will or human dignity or good works. In this they did in a sense continue the distinctive note of St Augustine, who is even now regarded as relatively the determinist doctor of the Church. But there is emphasis and emphasis; and a time was coming when emphasising the one side was to mean flatly contra-dicting the other. Perhaps, after all, it did begin with a quarrel of monks; but the Pope was yet to learn how quarrelsome a monk could be. For there was one particular monk, in that Augustinian monastery in the German forests, who may be said to have had a single and special talent for emphasis; for emphasis and nothing except emphasis; for emphasis with the quality of an earthquake. He was the son of a slate cutter; a man with a great voice and a certain volume of personality; brooding, sincere, decidedly morbid; and his name was Martin Luther. Neither Augustine nor the Augustinians would have desired to see the day of that vindication of the Augustinian tradition; but in one sense, perhaps, the Augustinian tradition was avenged after all.

It came out of its cell again, in the day of storm and ruin, and cried out with a new and mighty voice for an elemental and emotional religion, and for the destruction of all philosophies. It had a peculiar horror and loathing of the great Greek philosophies, and of the Scholasticism that had been founded on those philosophies. It had one theory that was the destruction of all theories; in fact it had its own theology which was itself the death of theology. Man could say nothing to God, nothing from God, nothing about God, except an almost inarticulate cry for mercy and for the supernatural help of Christ; in a world where all natural things were useless. Reason was useless. Will was useless. Man could not move himself an inch any more than a stone. Man could not trust what was in his head any more than a turnip. Nothing remained in earth or heaven, but the name of Christ lifted in that lonely imprecation; awful as the cry of a beast in pain.

We must be just to those huge human figures, who are in fact the hinges of history. However strong, and rightly strong, be our own controversial conviction, it must never mislead us into thinking that something trivial has transformed the world. So it is with that great Augustinian monk, who avenged all the ascetic Augustinians of the Middle Ages; and whose broad and burly figure has been big enough to block out for four centuries the distant human mountain of Aquinas. It is not, as the moderns delight to say, a question of theology. The Protestant theology of Martin Luther was a thing that no modern Protestant would be seen dead in a field with; or if the phrase be too flippant, would be specially anxious to touch with a barge-pole. That Protestantism was pessimism; it was nothing but bare insistence on the hopelessness of all human virtue, as an attempt to escape hell. That Lutheranism is now quite unreal; more modern phases of Lutheranism are rather more unreal; but Luther was not unreal. He was one of those great elemental barbarians, to whom it is indeed given to change the world. To compare those two figures bulking so big in history, in any philosophical sense, would of course be futile and even unfair. On a great map like the mind of Aquinas, the mind of Luther would be almost invisible. But it is not altogether untrue to say, as so many journalists have said without caring whether it was true or untrue, that Luther opened an epoch; and began the modern world.

He was the first man who ever consciously used his consciousness; or what was later called his Personality. He had as a fact a rather strong personality. Aquinas had an even stronger personality; he had a massive and magnetic presence; he had an intellect that could act like a huge system of artillery spread over the whole world; he had that instantaneous presence of mind in debate, which alone really deserves the name of wit. But it never occurred to him to use anything except his wits, in defence of a truth distinct from himself. It never occurred to Aquinas to use Aquinas as a weapon. There is not a trace of his ever using his personal advantages, of birth or body or brain or breeding, in debate with anybody. In short, he belonged to an age of intellectual unconsciousness, to an age of intellectual innocence, which was very intellectual. Now Luther did begin the modern mood of depending on things not merely intellectual. It is not a question of praise or blame; it matters little whether we say that he was a strong personality, or that he was a bit of a big bully. When he quoted a Scripture text, inserting a word that is not in Scripture, he was content to shout back at all hecklers: 'Tell them that Dr Martin Luther will have it so!' That is what we now call Personality. A little later it was called Psychology. After that it was called Advertisement or Salesmanship. But we are not arguing about advantages or disadvantages. It is due to this great Augustinian pessimist to say, not only that he did triumph at last over the Angel of the Schools, but that he did in a very real sense make the modern world. He destroyed Reason; and substituted Suggestion.

It is said that the great Reformer publicly burned the *Summa Theologica* and the works of Aquinas; and with the bonfire of such books this book may well come to an end. They say it is very difficult to burn a book; and it must have been exceedingly difficult to burn such a mountain of books as the Dominican had contributed to the controversies of Christendom. Anyhow, there is something lurid and apocalyptic about the idea of such destruction, when we consider the compact complexity of all that encyclopædic survey of social and moral and theoretical things. All the close-packed definitions that excluded so many errors and extremes; all the broad and balanced judgments upon the clash of loyalties or the choice of evils; all the liberal speculations upon the limits of government of the proper conditions of justice; all the distinctions between the use and abuse of private property; all the rules and exceptions about the great evil of war; all the allowances for human weakness and all the provisions for human health: all this mass of mediæval humanism shrivelled and curled up in smoke before the eyes of its enemy; and that great passionate peasant rejoiced darkly; because the day of the Intellect was over. Sentence by sentence it burned, and syllogism by syllogism; and the golden maxims turned to golden flames in that last and dying glory of all that had once been the great wisdom of the Greeks. The great central Synthesis of history, that was to have linked the ancient with the modern world, went up in smoke and, for half the world, was forgotten like a vapour.

For a time it seemed that the destruction was final. It is still expressed in the amazing fact that (in the North) modern men can still write histories of philosophy, in which philosophy stops with the last little sophists of Greece and Rome; and is never heard of again until the appearance of such a third-rate philosopher as Francis Bacon. And yet this small book, which will probably do nothing else, or have very little other value, will be at least a testimony to the fact that the tide has turned once more. It is four hundred years after; and this book, I hope (and I am happy to say I believe), will probably be lost and forgotten in the flood of better books about St Thomas Aquinas, which are at this moment pouring from every printing-press in Europe, and even in England and America. Compared with such books, it is obviously a very slight and amateurish production. But it is not likely to be burned; and if it were, it would not leave even a noticeable gap in the pouring mass of new and magnificent work, which is now daily dedicated to the *philosophia perennis*; to the Everlasting Philosophy.

# The Erastian on the Establishment

Dean Inge is so obviously the most acute, the most cultivated and the most individual of the sceptical school which he represents, that there is sometimes inevitably an appearance of singling him out, when the singularity is only due to his own distinction. It is due, if we must put it more roughly, to there being so very few intellectuals of that school who are worth answering. I have often myself, perhaps, put it more roughly than I intended; but the double duty involved presents a problem not easily solved. The trouble is that he is really in such a false position that the true statement of it sounds itself like a taunt. Yet it may not be meant for a taunt, but only for a truth. His own position certainly does not seem as false to him as it does to us; but to excuse it requires a long explanation which is impossible in so short an expression. For instance, he wrote the other day a severe condemnation of those of the Anglican clergy who favour the Disestablishment of the Church of England. It may seem curt to retort, as I should be first inclined to do, that the Dean naturally hesitates to sever the one very slender strip of red tape that still connects him with Christianity. Yet it is quite true; and it is not necessarily merely hostile.

To understand the curious case of Dean Inge, in a spirit of Christian charity, we must leave for the moment all questions of creed and definition and call up another image before the mind. It is the image that was in the mind of Matthew Arnold when he openly said that, being almost an agnostic himself, he yet wished to preserve the institutions of religion, and especially the literature of religion; that he found these best preserved in the Church of England and advised nobody to leave it. We must call up the image of a historic hierarchy of priests who are also professors, and whose main business is scholarship and the study of letters; it was not for nothing that both Arnold and Inge had connections with Oxford. Most of such men would probably be Christian in hereditary sentiment and subject-matter; but their Christianity would not, so to speak, be the point. We can even imagine

*Universe*, April 1930. Collected in The Common Man, 1950

the institution better if we think of it as a Confucian rather than a Christian foundation. The idea of it is a classical culture that is undisturbed. But it has this further essential point; that if its traditions and rites must be undisturbed, so also must its doubts and negations be undisturbed. It must be so traditional that a sceptic is safe there.

Something like this may really have existed in Chinese and other pagan parallels. Something like it probably did exist among the last pagan priests of antiquity. A jolly old heathen Flamen or Pontifex Maximus did not want to be disturbed in explaining away the gods to his friends; and certainly did not want to make himself responsible for drawing the exact line between truth and fable in the metamorphoses of Ovid or the genealogies of Jupiter. And something of the same sort did exist in the Academic Anglicanism of the Erastian age in England, when scholarly Whigs and rather worldly bishops quoted indifferently Horace and Augustine and Gibbon over the nuts and wine. That is the Establishment which Dean Inge really likes to see established; that is the civilised institution which he does really and sincerely believe to be a good thing; a traditional home of learning and liberal education, though mainly for the few; a thing that to the outer world shall be as authoritative as the mediæval abbots, but in its inner life be as casual as the Greek philosophers; a thing that need not exclude the heretical, but does exclude the ignorant; a thing that can admit all questions so long as it is never questioned itself.

Now a cultural tradition of that kind can have many marks of dignity and national value; and a man may without absurdity or falsity wish to preserve it as a national thing. But there are a number of conditions to be remembered, which Dean Inge now seems continually to forget. For one thing, the nation must continue in the same mood of respect towards the college of professors, or whatever it is to be called. The modern mood is changing very rapidly; and I think it would be an exaggeration to say that all England is now filled with an affection and veneration for Dons. Another difficulty is that whatever this sort of Chinese synod can do, it cannot exist side by side with a real and passionate religion. It was defeated by the Christians at the end of the Roman era. It was defeated even by the Methodists at the end of the eighteenth century. It is often quoted of poor Charles II that he said that Puritanism was no religion for a gentleman. It is not so often added that he also said that Anglicanism was no religion for a Christian.

This, I fancy, is what the Dean really means; and it explains why he is at once such a conservative and such an iconoclast; such a sceptic and such a Tory. It is not, of course, in so many words what he says. When driven to defend his bunch of bigwigs, with their libraries and endowments, he characteristically takes an old book out of those dusty shelves, and quotes from Burke the thesis that the Church was only the State seen in one light and the State was only the Church seen in another light. Burke always struck me as, of all men, the man with the most imaginative and the most utterly unreal mind. Even as he uttered such a phrase, he must have known that the Church was packed with people who did not believe in it, and that the leaders of the State had almost ceased to pretend to do so. All the time, it is worth remarking, Burke was gravely discussing the admission to the Church of Dissenters whose whole enthusiasm was admittedly concerned with making their Calvinist God if possible more of a devil than he was before. He knew the world around him was crowded with such fanatics and with such blasphemers; and yet he could bring himself to imagine that the actual secular condition of all England was the Church of Christ, if one only slightly shifted one's point of view. But it was rather odd to maintain this even in Burke's time; it is perfectly crazy to maintain it in our time. Dean Inge admits, that two great calamities might really ruin his plan, and make the position of the Church of England impossible. But he thinks that neither is likely enough to be worth considering. One is—what would happen if a large body of England really abandoned Christianity? The other is—what would happen if England went over to Rome? The answer to both these impossibilities is very simple. It is that the second might happen any day, and the first has happened already.

Of course it is possible to play an endless game with the word 'Christian' and perpetually extend its epoch by perpetually diminishing its meaning. By the time that everybody has agreed that being a Christian only means thinking that Christ was a good man, it will indeed be true that few persons outside lunatic asylums can be denied the name of Christian. But it is really a mere alteration in the meaning of a word that prevents us saying frankly that a great mass, probably a majority, of our modern people are Pagans. Many of them make a mock of standards of family piety or public dignity that were generally accepted by the Pagans. But most of them, if they have any religion at all, have a religion of pantheism or pure ethics which most of the great Christian characters of history, Catholic or Protestant, would have instantly stamped as pagan. If you had asked Wesley, or Swedenborg, or Dr Johnson, or Baxter, or Luther, they would have called the modern mood heathen more promptly, if possible, than would Bossuet or Bellarmine. If it is true that the Church is simply the religion of the State, we have got precious near to saying that it is simply the irreligion of the State.

There was a bitter and cynical man (also, I am sure, an Oxford man) who said, 'The Church of England is our last bulwark against Christianity'. This is quite unjust as a description of the Church of England. But it is not altogether unjust as a description of Dean Inge. What is really at the back of his mind is this image of a great academic and cultural tradition, established as a national need but not specially as a spiritual need. It is to have religious texts—to criticise; religious ceremonial—to reform slightly and rather pompously from time to time; a sort of assumption on religion, in the sense that it could not tolerate the horrors of anything like the Russian denial of religion. But all through, it will be subject to one unmistakable test. It can coexist with Doubt; but it cannot coexist with Faith.

At the end of his article, Dean Inge tries to toss aside as impertinent the term Erastianism; the term is too obviously true not to irritate. But in any case he absurdly underrates its meaning at the moment. It is not a question of whether those who form a nation by being Englishmen could in the abstract form a religion by being Anglicans. It is a question of whether a Church which does at least exist, with some who belong to it and some who do not belong to it, should be ruled by those who do not belong to it. Erastianism exists today in the perfectly practical sense that any Jew, Holy Roller or Hyde Park atheist may dictate what that Christian Church shall do on any matter whatever, however intimate and sacred. Bradlaugh was a Member of Parliament; he might well have become a Cabinet Minister and appointed Bishops. Mr Saklatvala was a Socialist leader and might quite well be a Labour Minister, with a majority in the House and might by Act of Parliament make the Prayer Book anything he chose. That is State Establishment, as now universally understood; that is what Dean Inge desires and presumably defends; or must set about the delicate task of defending.

# Romantic Love

This morning I read an article in a very serious magazine, in which the writer quoted the remark of Byron that a certain sort of romantic love is woman's whole existence. The writer then said that the first people who ever challenged this view were the revolutionary Suffragettes at the end of the nineteenth century. The truth is that the first people who ever maintained this view were the revolutionary Romantics at the beginning of the nineteenth century. The habit of giving to romantic love this extravagant and exclusive importance in human life was itself an entirely modern and revolutionary thing, and dates from the romantic movement commonly traced to Rousseau; but I think much more truly to be traced to the influence of the German sentimentalists. Most people who curse Rousseau have never read Rousseau; or have only read the *Confessions* and not the *Contrat Social*. The critics read the *Confessions*, if only to condemn them; because the critics themselves are modern romantics and sentimentalists; men who like Confessions and dislike Contracts. The critics hate or avoid the *Contrat Social* not because it is sloppy and sentimental (for it is not) but because it his hard and clear and lucid and logical. Rousseau had his emotional weaknesses as an individual, like other individuals; but he was not an eighteenth-century philosopher for nothing. What the moderns dislike about him is not the silliness of his confessions, but the solidity of his convictions; and the fact that, like the old theologians, he could hold general ideas in a hard and fast fashion. When it comes to defining his fundamentals, Rousseau is as definite as Calvin. They were both ruthless theorists from Geneva; though one preached the theory of pessimism and the other the theory of optimism. I am not maintaining that I agree with either; but Rousseau would be as useful as Calvin in teaching some of his critics how to criticise.

But Rousseau is a parenthesis. Wherever the real Romantic Movement came from, whether from the German forests or the Geneva lake, it was a recent and revolutionary business, as compared with history as a whole. But

*Illustrated London News*, 1931. Collected in A Handful of Authors, 1953

it is obvious that the ordinary modern critic is entirely ignorant of history as a whole. He knows that his mother read Tennyson and his grandmother read Byron. Beyond that he can imagine nothing whatever; he supposes that his great-great-grandmothers and their great-great-great-grandmothers had gone on reading Byron from the beginning of the world. He imagines that Byron, who was a disinherited and disreputable rebel to the last, has been an established and conventional authority from the first. He therefore supposes that all women, in all ages, would have accepted the prehistoric Byronic commandment that the Byronic sort of romantic passion was the sole concern of their lives. Yet it is certain that women have had a great many other concerns and have been attached to a great many other convictions. They have been priestesses, prophetesses, empresses, queens, abbesses, mothers, great housewives, great letter-writers, lunatics founding sects, blue-stockings keeping salons, and all sorts of things. If you had said to Deborah the mother in Israel, or Hypatia the Platonist of Alexandria, or Catherine of Siena, or Joan of Arc, or Isabella of Spain, or Maria Theresa of Austria, or even to Hannah More or Joanna Southcott, that Byronic love was 'woman's whole existence', they would all have been very indignant and most of them flown into a towering passion. They would have asked in various ways whether there was no such thing as honour, no such thing as duty, no such thing as glory, no such thing as great studies or great enterprises, no such thing as normal functions and necessary labours; incidentally, we may add, no such thing as babies. They differed a great deal in their type of vocation and even in their theory of virtue; but they all had some theory of virtue that went a little further than that. Up to a particular moment in the eighteenth century, practically every thinking person would have accepted the colossal common sense expressed by a French poet of the seventeenth century: 'L'amour est un plaisir; l'honneur est un devoir'.

Then came the extreme emphasis on romance among the Victorians; for the Victorians were not notable for their emphasis on virtue, but for their emphasis on romance. Queen Victoria lived so long, and the Victorian Age was such an unconscionably long time dying, that by the time Mr Bernard Shaw and others began what they called a realistic revolt against romance, the sentimental German movement seemed to be not only as old as Victoria, but as old as Boadicea. It is highly typical, for instance, that Mr Bernard Shaw, in one of his earliest criticisms, complained of the convention according to which anybody was supposed to have 'penetrated into the Holy of Holies' so long as he was content to say that 'Love is Enough'. But, as a matter of fact, the very phrase 'Love is Enough' did not come to him from any conventional or classical authority; not even from any conventional or conservative Victorian. It came from a book by a Socialist and Revolutionist like himself; from a book by William Morris.

Of course the anti-romantic movement led by Shaw, like the romantic movement led by Byron, has gone forward blindly and blundered in every sort of way. The modern world seems to have no notion of preserving different things side by side, of allowing its proper and proportionate place to each, of saving the whole varied heritage of culture. It has no notion except that of simplifying something by destroying nearly everything; whether it be Rousseau breaking up kingdoms in the name of reason; or Byron breaking up families in the name of romance; or Shaw breaking up romances in the name of frankness and the formula of Ibsen. I myself value very highly the great nineteenth-century illumination of romantic love; just as I value the great eighteenth-century ideal of right reason and human dignity, or the seventeenth-century intensity, or the sixteenth-century expansion, or the divine logic and dedicated valour of the Middle Ages. I do not see why any of these cultural conquests should be lost or despised; or why it is necessary for every fashion to wash away all that is best in every other. It may be possible that one good custom would corrupt the world; but I never could see why the second good custom should deny that the first good custom was good. As it is, those who have no notion except that of breaking away from romance are being visibly punished by breaking away from reason. Every new realistic novel serves to show that realism, when entirely emptied of romance, becomes utterly unreal. For romance was only the name given to a love of life which was something much larger than a life of love, in the Byronic or sentimental sense. And anything from which it has passed is instantly corrupt and crawling with the worms of death.

# Index of Contents

*(Italics indicate verse)*